FIRST LADIES

A BIOGRAPHICAL DICTIONARY

Dorothy Schneider

Carl J. Schneider

Checkmark Books®

An imprint of Facts On File, Inc.

First Ladies: A Biographical Dictionary

Checkmark Books
An imprint of Facts On File, Inc.
132 West 31st Street
New York NY 10001

Library of Congress Cataloging-in-Publication Data

Schneider, Dorothy.
    First ladies : a biographical dictionary / Dorothy Schneider and Carl J. Schneider.
        p. cm.
    Includes bibliographical references and indexes.
    ISBN 0-8160-4195-4 (hc : alk.)—ISBN 0-8160-4196-2 (pbk. : alk.)
        1. Presidents' spouses—United States—Biography—Dictionaries. I. Schneider,
Carl J. II. Title.

E176.2.S36 2001
973'.099—dc21
[B]   00-068130

Checkmark Books are available at special discounts when purchased in bulk quantities for businesses, associations, institutions or sales promotions. Please call our Special Sales Department in New York at (212) 967-8800 or (800) 322-8755.

You can find Facts On File on the World Wide Web at http://www.factsonfile.com

Text design and layout by Rachel L. Berlin
Cover design (hardcover) by Cathy Rincon
Cover design (paperback) by Maxx Media

Printed in the United States of America

VB FOF   10 9 8 7 6 5 4 3 2 1
   (pbk)   10 9 8 7 6 5 4 3 2 1

This book is printed on acid-free paper.

CONTENTS

INTRODUCTION

Study of the first ladies—particularly first ladies of the nation's early years—is difficult. Primary sources about them are few and myths are many. Their admirers have buried them in praise, and their political enemies have vilified them. However, new scholarship on the position of first lady and the recent publication of several serious biographies are clarifying their history.

From the beginning, public expectations have influenced the conduct of presidential spouses, limiting their freedom and, to a greater or lesser extent, their privacy. In the early days of the republic, Americans worried lest European courts not recognize the dignity of the new nation as embodied in its president and his wife. A majority agreed that the Washingtons should not ape European court manners but at the same time must adopt a degree of formality to impress on Europeans the status of the new nation. The situation was complicated by the president's constitutional role as both head of state and head of government; thus, Martha Washington had to show herself as not only the wife of a chief executive but also the equal of a queen. In fact, the expectations of her were mostly ceremonial and social, like those of a royal consort. People worried about her title: Should she be called Lady Washington? Presidentress? The term *first lady* did not come into use until the days of Lucy Hayes, becoming widespread only in 1911, when Charles Nirdlinger's play *The First Lady in the Land* popularized it.

Ceremonial, social, and of course family duties were the major responsibilities of presidents' wives, and the measure of their success, for well over a century. Thus the enormous popularity of Dolley Madison, who reveled warmheartedly in the performance of these duties, and the criticism of Abigail Adams by her contemporaries, because she preferred "meddling" in politics.

Their social duties frightened some first ladies. Some simply withdrew into the shadows of the White House: Emily Apt Geer notes that "[O]f the eighteen presidents who preceded Hayes, only eight had wives willing and able to assume the responsibilities of a White House hostess for their husbands' full term." Some women with little social experience felt ill-prepared.

From 1841 to 1861, five first ladies hesitated to undertake these duties. Margaret Taylor and Jane Pierce prayed fervently that their husbands would lose the presidential election. Anna Harrison doubted her qualifications for the job. Letitia Tyler and Margaret Taylor were too ill and Jane Pierce too grief-stricken to do it.

Lack of psychological knowledge and medical ignorance darkened and shortened the lives of many 19th-century people, including wives of presidents. The beliefs of the day and mystification about women's reproductive systems encouraged the theory that women were more sickly than men, though during this period William Henry Harrison and Zachary Taylor died in office, and James Polk immediately afterward. The cultural restrictions that limited women to one role regardless of their temperaments and abilities inhibited some of them. Although religion consoled some, in the harsh form of Calvinism it depressed others.

Further, unlike Martha Washington, the Adams ladies, Dolley Madison, and Elizabeth Monroe, the first ladies of this period were not born or reared in ways that prepared them for the position. Some of them lacked the social status and experience of the world that helped the earliest first ladies mold the office of the wife of the U.S. president into one of prestige. The young democracy now brought to the White House women with no particular gift or training for the post, from families with no tradition of public service. Some of them shied away from the destiny allotted them. They thought of themselves not as women privileged to render an extraordinary service to the nation but as victims of politics.

During the years when the country was tearing itself apart over the issue of slavery, these women could not provide a symbol of unity, lacking as they did the necessary charisma, energy, or force of personality. Furthermore, they did not possess the sense of duty to the nation of a Martha Washington or an Abigail Adams that drove these women to serve at great personal sacrifice.

Most presidents' spouses have arrived in the White House when in their fifties. In the 18th and well into the 19th century, this was old age, and the women were often worn out by lifetimes of hardships, illnesses that the medicine of the time could not treat, and bearing children in an age when infant mortality was high. In the White House, the peaceful last years to which they had looked forward were denied them. They also dreaded the attacks of political enemies. From the days of George Washington, opponents have flung at presidents and their families any and all of the most dreadful accusations they could concoct: suicide, murder, infidelity, siring bastards, being of mixed blood, insanity, homosexuality, and a host of others.

First ladies feared for their husbands, for stress has aged and traumatized so many American presidents; four of the 42 have died in office of "natural causes," and Woodrow Wilson and Lyndon Johnson died soon after their terms ended. Perhaps worst of all, first ladies have to live with the possibility of assassination: Four presidents have been killed by assassins' bullets; additionally, Theodore Roosevelt and Ronald Reagan were wounded, Reagan gravely, and would-be assassins shot at but missed Franklin Roosevelt, Harry Truman, and Gerald Ford.

Over time, the social and ceremonial duties of the first lady have multiplied—even so activist a woman as Lady Bird Johnson estimated that she spent 75 percent of her time on formal obligations. Gradually, however, other responsibilities have been added, usually developing out of changes in the status of American women as they undertook more and more responsibility for the public weal. At first restricted to the duty of raising good citizens for the Republic, during the Civil War women took over "men's jobs" and undertook major responsibilities for medical care of the troops. During the mid- and late-19th century, they battled for their property rights and voting rights and left their homes to enter the workplace. During the Progressive Era (1890–1920), they undertook "public housekeeping" to bring about social and economic reforms. In 1919 they gained the vote. In the first half of the 20th century, they enabled the nation to win two world wars by taking jobs on the home front and joining the military. And in the latter half of the 20th century, they fought in the Congress and in the courts for equal rights. Such changes in the work and status of women over time have altered the demands of the office of first lady. Just as Hillary Clinton brought to the office vastly different experiences from those of Martha Washington, so the office demanded of her vastly different abilities and efforts.

Early in American history it became apparent that the popular wife of a president might help elect him, and James Madison's political opponents sometimes claimed that they had to run against both the Madisons. By the middle of the 19th century, politicians began to recognize that even a first lady with little interest in politics and policies could make enemies and win friends for her husband, and some first ladies, like Lucy Hayes, proved themselves skilled though retiring campaigners. In the latter years of that century, as women's reform efforts made it acceptable for women to participate openly in public affairs, as women's health, energy, and education improved, and as campaigns lengthened and "front-porch campaigns" became popular, the services of presidential nominees' wives were sought to win votes. They were expected to be on display as model wives and mothers, traveling with their husbands and gazing adoringly at them when they spoke. In 1888 Caroline Harrison complained, "If there is one thing above another I detest and have detested all my days it is being made a circus of, and that is what has come to me in my old age, as it were."

With the development of modern communications, the public called for even more information about these women, and their privacy ebbed further. In the first quarter of the 20th century, this trend continued, and Edith Roosevelt, Helen Taft, Ellen and Edith Wilson, Florence Harding, Grace Coolidge, and Lou Hoover became well accustomed to the spotlight. These women were, in fact, more prominently in the public eye than the vice presidents of their time.

Additionally, enabled by the changes in the status of women during the Progressive Era, first ladies were beginning to exercise new powers. In the late 19th century, Frances Cleveland had quietly assisted the causes of working women and women's education. Later, Ellen Wilson, Grace Coolidge, and Lou Hoover struck out on their own, more openly promoting their favorite projects—slum clearance, the education of the deaf, and the Girl Scouts, respectively—not so much as first ladies, but out of personal concern. At the same time, first ladies began to share presidential powers, acting as the president's surrogate not only on social and ceremonial occasions but also in political and executive affairs. Woodrow Wilson's incapacity following his stroke thrust executive power into Edith Wilson's hands, and she wielded it.

Beginning in 1932, Eleanor Roosevelt widened the scope and the potential of the first lady almost beyond recognition. Her husband's inability to walk necessitated that she become his eyes and ears, traveling widely, meeting all sorts of Americans, inspecting the programs he initiated, and reporting to him the state of the nation. However, she also initiated her own programs, publicly differed with her husband, and openly tried to influence pol-

icy and get women into important positions in government. She used the office of first lady as a bully pulpit, fully utilizing the power of the press and the new medium of radio to publicize the needs she identified and the causes she supported. During World War II she even experimented with holding a full-time governmental position, as assistant to Fiorello LaGuardia in the Office of Civil Defense, though that effort failed. In all this Franklin Roosevelt fully supported her. Supremely self-confident, he did not fear her strength or even her opposition. "She's my missus. What can I do?" he shrugged to the press. Privately, he encouraged her to pursue her own course—and send up trial balloons for his policies.

Her immediate successors could not match her energy, her political acumen, or her ambition. Bess Truman exercised a great deal of influence on affairs of state, but only in private. Mamie Eisenhower confined herself mainly to social and familial activities. But once any first lady has broadened her responsibilities—despite denunciations from the opposing political party—successors are legitimized in assuming them and sometimes even obliged to assume them.

Over the course of the 20th century—especially since the 1960s—the public came to expect the first lady to sponsor a specific cause. This expectation arose from the American habit of volunteering, from the idea that societal ills are "women's problems," and from the sense that the first lady should set an example. Thus, at the behest of presidential advisers and public relations experts, Pat Nixon championed volunteerism, Nancy Reagan campaigned against the use of drugs, and Barbara Bush sponsored family literacy. On the other hand, Lady Bird Johnson, Betty Ford, and Rosalynn Carter acted spontaneously. Johnson's work for the environment developed out of her childhood love of wildflowers. Ford coped with her own bouts with breast cancer and addiction by publicizing the prevention and cure of these diseases. Carter continued the efforts to improve mental health that she had been making ever since her husband served as governor of Georgia. The work of all these women on their personal projects has benefited the nation, which has by and large appreciated it—at least after the fact. Yet a first lady who wants to encounter as little opposition as possible is still well advised to choose a noncontroversial cause that the public regards as being within the "woman's sphere."

The duties and powers of the first lady have accrued in other ways as well. Edith Wilson, Florence Harding, Eleanor Roosevelt, Lady Bird Johnson, and Rosalynn Carter acted as partners with their husbands. Wilson was able to take over when her husband was incapacitated only because he had, almost from the time they met, made her privy to his problems and his ideas about how to handle them. Harding went as far as she dared to influence appointments and policy decisions. Roosevelt exercised broad influence in the president's administration—and tried for more. Johnson's husband relied on her political advice and consulted with her on such "women's issues" as education and the environment. Rosalynn Carter attended cabinet meetings and represented her husband at high-level policy meetings abroad—carrying a step further Presidents Nixon's and Kennedy's practice of sending their wives abroad on goodwill trips.

However, any activities that can be seen as invading official territory are controversial. As Bill and Hillary Clinton discovered when he put her in charge of reforming the health care system, both officials and the public fear interference in government by a person who is not elected and is responsible only to her husband.

A modern first lady is confronted by multitudinous duties, some old, some new:

1. She must look after the physical and psychological health of her family, under conditions that expose them to extreme stress and unwanted publicity.
2. She must entertain multitudes of strangers and attend a host of ceremonies. To prepare for this, she needs to inform herself about her guests and about the issues of the day. On all occasions her appearance will be under scrutiny.

3. She must respond to thousands of letters requesting favors and help or inviting her to make a speech or sponsor a good cause (especially cultural ones or those dedicated to historic preservation).
4. She must look to the appearance of the White House and its furnishings and create a home in the family quarters.
5. She must inform herself on what the government pays for, what expenses are charged to the president, what gifts she can legally and ethically accept, and what disposition may be made of the thousands of other gifts, so as not to hurt the donors' feelings.
6. She must meet the press and answer to reporters, who more and more consider themselves entitled to every scrap of information about her and her family, however personal. Yet she must always guard her tongue, for she will be perceived to reflect the president's opinions or to be speaking out of special knowledge.
7. Presidential advisers will ask her to choose a project, preferably one that will not arouse controversy, to publicize it, and probably to raise money for it.
8. Party politicians and presidential advisers will push her to campaign for her husband and other candidates and to represent him at ceremonies and perhaps also at conferences, traveling with or without him.
9. American business will hope that she advertise its products by wearing and using them.

This daunting job the first lady is expected to do cheerfully, pleasantly, without pay, and often under the fire of criticism. Fortunately, she will have good, though not unlimited, help. She can rely on the experienced staff of the White House and the protocol experts to run formal dinners and receptions. If she chooses, she can leave menu planning and household details to the housekeeper and kitchen personnel. She can enjoy the luxury of at-home services. Hairdressers will willingly come to her and stores will happily send merchandise for her inspection. She can delegate many tasks to her personal staff of 30 or so, including experts in social affairs, press relations, and public issues.

Nonetheless, she must budget her time to ensure that essential duties are not overlooked and that she can retain a few hours a day for what she considers her most important work. Unless she sets goals and priorities, she may lose an opportunity to make a difference to the nation and to promote those causes that, in the words of Lady Bird Johnson, "make her heart sing."

The office of first lady as it now exists has been created in part by the choices made by the 38 previous holders of that position. As historian Myra Gutin has noted, the position has also been affected by other factors beyond their control:

1. The first lady's age and training. Most first ladies reach the White House in their 50s, with their sense of values having been established much earlier in their lives.
2. Her husband's attitude toward her participation in his work. He may, like Harry Truman, seek her advice at every turn; he may, like Calvin Coolidge, shut her out altogether and even invade her territory by interfering with menus and her wardrobe; or he may, like Jimmy Carter, invite her to act publicly as his surrogate.
3. The social and historical environment of her time, particularly the status of women. A first lady can transgress the boundaries imposed by the mores of her day just so far. To go further would arouse such storms of criticism as to render her ineffective and possibly damage her husband's political future. Attitudes toward what is permissible for the first lady usually lag behind contemporary standards for women. In their own time, first ladies who concentrated on family and social duties were the most highly regarded. However, history has judged them quite differently, and more activist first ladies have risen in the public estimation over time. Eleanor Roosevelt, reviled in her own day, now tops every list of first ladies.

Clearly any first lady faces multiple problems common to all wives but accentuated by the prominence of her position. In her book *Political Wives* Susan Riley writes, "The key attitude is public deference to her husband, private loyalty and modest refusal to take any credit for his brilliant success. For the intelligent wife, this requires a daily display of diplomacy that borders on outright fraud. Let's not be coy: a lot of these women are smarter than their husbands. . . . She has to be innocuous without being inane, which as all modern examples prove, is impossible." These restrictions punish modern women. The increasing demands on the first lady now deny her both privacy and leisure. If her baby or her parent dies, the public expects her to curtail her grieving and carry on. The media expose her failings, her moods, her marital relationship, and even the pain caused by criticism of herself and those she loves. They allow her only the narrowest of margins for error.

The first lady is thus on the horns of a dilemma. At the beginning of the 21st century, with the nation still coming to terms with the increasing roles and choices for women, a good deal of the criticism of the first lady originates in disagreement among the populace over what a woman ought to be and do. The first lady has always been expected to personify the ideal woman, but what is the American ideal? Americans no longer agree on what a woman should be. An activist first lady risks being considered an aggressive threat by some, while a homebody invokes criticism as an irrelevant nonentity by others.

Given the attitudes of modern American women and the development of marriages as equal partnerships, first ladies may not go on accepting the obligations and limitations that custom thrusts upon them. If a woman whose husband has been elected president chooses to pursue her own career, nothing in the Constitution prevents her.

Whether the law permits a president to appoint his wife to office within his administration is debatable. As Carl David Wasserman has observed in his note "Firing the First Lady" in the *Vanderbilt Law Review* of May 1995 (48: 1215ff.), existing laws may affect the status of the first lady. For instance, the so-called Kennedy law, passed after President John F. Kennedy made his brother Robert the attorney general, forbids a public official to appoint or employ a relative, including his spouse, "in an agency in which he serves or over which he exercises control." However, the D.C. district court in the 1993 case of the *Associates of the American Physicians v. Hillary Rodham Clinton* held that the president may appoint a relative as a White House employee. Again, when Congress authorized White House office employees to provide services to the president's spouse (or, if the president is not married, a family member designated by the president as surrogate) "in connection with assistance provided by such spouse to the President in the discharge of the President's duties and responsibilities," it arguably implied that in those instances the first lady is serving as a federal officer. Furthermore, the services traditionally rendered by the first lady, all unpaid, may clash with the Antideficiency Act, which requires statutory authority for federal agencies to accept voluntary services.

Yet, as Wasserman comments, existing laws and judicial decisions leave many questions about the first lady unanswered. For instance:

1. Is the first lady a federal employee or officer? The Federal Advisory Committee Act (FACA) forbids closed meetings of certain governmental bodies if one of the members of a committee is not a federal employee or officer. If the first lady is not such a person, then Hillary Clinton may have performed an illegal act in closing the health care task force meetings. The district court held in the *Associates of the American Physicians* v. *Hillary Rodham Clinton* case that she is not a public official, but the D.C. circuit court to which the case was appealed held that she is, *de facto*, at least for the purposes of FACA. In this case the government lawyers termed her an "assistant to the president." One member of the circuit court held that she is not but found FACA unconstitutional as applied to presidential policymaking.

2. Would it be illegal for the first lady to accept a position as lobbyist after leaving the White House? Would it be illegal for her to accept a bribe to try to get corporate taxes reduced?

3. Can the president fire a first lady? Can he appoint someone else in her stead? In the past, when a first lady has not served because of her health or by choice, or when a president has had no wife, he has turned to another family member, a close friend, a past president's wife, or the vice-president's wife to perform social and ceremonial duties.

4. Does or should her position bar the first lady from earning money through outside sources? (While living in the White House, Eleanor Roosevelt often outearned her husband.) If a first lady has a career of her own, may she continue to advise the president on policies?

5. Is she limited by federal conflict-of-interest law prohibiting executive branch officers from "participating in government decisions that affect their financial interest" or those of their spouses? Can she claim executive privilege, as Hillary Clinton did?

6. What gifts may she legally accept? The law that limits the value of gifts that government officials may accept is ambiguous when it comes to the first lady.

7. Should the first lady be paid? First ladies who have spoken on the question have usually rejected the idea in favor of preserving their options about their duties.

8. Will the office be institutionalized further? Already the first lady has an office, a staff, and a number of prescribed duties. In all probability, public opinion and possibly the law will further restrict what she may and may not do. On the other hand, history, which shows that her influence has grown slowly but impressively, suggests that first ladies of the future may exercise even wider powers than in the past.

As conceptions and expectations of women change in the future, so will the office of first lady. That process will be dramatically hastened when the first woman is elected president. Even before that happens, however, events may force a more precise definition of the powers and duties of the president's spouse, particularly if first ladies choose to pursue their own careers while their husbands are in office. Hillary Rodham Clinton did so when she ran for a Senate seat from the State of New York in 1999 and 2000, and Lynne V. Cheney, wife of the vice president, did so when she announced in 2001 her plans to return to her position as resident scholar at the American Express Institute soon after her husband's swearing-in.

Note: For the presidents' wives who did not live to serve as first ladies, please see Appendix A.

PREFACE

Before the women's movement of the 1960s, few serious scholars considered first ladies at all. Biographers of presidents unabashedly admitted to knowing next to nothing about their subjects' wives. Even the feminists who have rescued women's history from oblivion in the past 40 years until very recently paid little attention to first ladies, looking askance at them as women made famous by their husbands, not in their own right.

The past two decades, however, have seen the publication of several outstanding books, some statistical, some biographical. Helped along by the much fuller primary materials available on recent first ladies, including some of their own authorship, scholars are now analyzing the institutional nature of the position, its requirements, and its restrictions. We are grateful particularly for the work of Carl Sferraza Anthony, Betty Boyd Caroli, Lewis Gould, Ann Grimes, Myra G. Gutin, James S. Rosebush, Gil Troy, and Robert P. Watson.

However, satisfactory modern biographies of many first ladies, including some of the most interesting, are still lacking. Sometimes, as in the case of Martha Washington, documents are sparse: almost none of her correspondence with her husband has been found, nor has anything she wrote before she was first widowed. The recent publication of such works as Anna Beiser Allen's *An Independent Woman: The Life of Lou Henry Hoover* (Westport, Conn.: Greenwood, 2000), Catherine Allgor's *Parlor Politics: In Which the Ladies of Washington Help Build a City and a Government* (Charlottesville: University Press of Virginia, 2000), and David Herbert Donald's *Lincoln at Home: Two Glimpses of Abraham Lincoln's Family Life* (New York: Simon & Schuster, 2000) gives hope of more to come.

We would remind readers who wonder that the Civil War affected the behavior and attitudes of first ladies and others many years after its close that this terrible war, which tore the country asunder and killed so many, still affects Americans even as this book goes to press. *The New York Times* of January 28, 2001 (Section 4, p. 4), reported that only in that month did the legislature of Georgia reduce to miniature—but still retain—the Confederate battle cross on its state flag.

We thank the librarians in the prints and photographs room of the Library of Congress for their assistance—although we deplore the Library's lack of pictures of recent first ladies in action. We call down blessings also on the heads of the public librarians in Essex, Connecticut, and Kennett Square, Pennsylvania, for their patience and efficiency in handling our innumerable requests for books on interlibrary loan. Professor Carl E. Schneider of the law school at the University of Michigan has guided us to information on the legal aspects of the office of first lady. We also thank our agent, Elizabeth Knappman, and our editor, Nicole Bowen, for their knowledge, ability, ideas, and warm support.

MARTHA DANDRIDGE CUSTIS WASHINGTON

(JUNE 2, 1731–MAY 22, 1802)
First Lady, April 30, 1789–March 4, 1797

MARTHA WASHINGTON
(Library of Congress)

On December 31, 1799, shortly after her husband's death, Martha Washington responded to the congressional request that he be buried in "Washington City," the new American capital. "I must consent to the request made by congress," she wrote, ". . . and in doing this I need not—I cannot say what a sacrifice of individual feeling I make to a sense of public duty." That principle governed her conduct throughout her 40-year marriage to George Washington. She was raised to be a southern belle and a plantation mistress. She delighted in domesticity, describing herself at Mt. Vernon as "fairly settled down to the pleasant duties of an old fashioned Virginia house-keeper, steady as a clock, busy as a bee, and as cheerful as a cricket." Yet in the public interest she repeatedly left the home she loved to share with her husband the hardships, discomforts, and dangers of his winter headquarters during the seven years that the American Revolution dragged on. After that war both the Washingtons hoped to spend the rest of their lives in the tranquillity of Mt. Vernon. But

George Washington bowed to the public will that he serve as the nation's first president and Martha Washington moved with him to New York and then to Philadelphia. Willingly and almost without complaint, she endured her separation from the relatives and friends she loved best to undertake the responsibilities of a "very dull life" in which she felt "more like a state prisoner than anything else."

—⁓—

Martha Dandridge was born at Chestnut Grove, a modest 500-acre plantation on the Pamunkey River in New Kent County, Virginia, on June 2, 1731. Her father, John Dandridge, came to North America from England when he was 15 years old with his older brother William. Starting out as merchants, they both rapidly acquired land and status. Her mother, Frances Jones, was the granddaughter of an Oxford-educated Anglican rector. Like most well-off girls of her time, Martha was probably taught domestic arts and household management by her mother and the three Rs by her parents and grandparents, an itinerant tutor, or an indentured servant. She learned to dance, perhaps to play an instrument a little, and to ride horseback expertly. She attended church regularly. Her social life and her affections centered in her relations with her seven siblings and the gentry of the countryside. She was slim and petite, just under five feet tall, with brown hair and hazel eyes.

When Martha was 17, she attracted the attention of Daniel Parke Custis, like her father a vestryman in her church. The 39-year-old Custis was a man eager to marry but still under the thumb of his wealthy, eccentric, and irascible father. The elder Custis did not allow Daniel to manage and eventually own one of his estates, White House, until he was far into his maturity. No young woman, the father seemed to think, was worthy of his only son—or, perhaps more important, of inheriting the considerable Custis fortune. Martha's marriage to Daniel was delayed until she was 19, when in a

sudden about-face Custis senior declared that he was "as much enamored with her character as you [Daniel] are with her person, and this is owing chiefly to a prudent speech of her own."

They were married at her home on May 15, 1750, and settled down at White House to raise a family. Custis indulged his young bride with fine clothes ordered from London. In the next seven years she bore four babies, two boys and two girls. But the infant deaths so commonplace in the 18th century soon claimed the first two. In 1757 her husband died suddenly, leaving her with her two small children: Martha Parke (Patsy) Custis, born in 1754; and John Parke (Jacky) Custis, born in 1755. He also left her perhaps the wealthiest widow in Virginia.

Since he died intestate, she inherited a third of his estate as her dower right, with the remainder divided between the two children, of whom she was the guardian. She thus had charge of a substantial amount of cash—more than $33,000—some 17,000 acres of widely separated estates, and several hundred slaves. She had to undertake responsibility for farming, buying supplies and selling produce, maintaining the property, paying debts, overseeing the well-being of hundreds of people, and fighting a troublesome lawsuit against the estate that had dragged on for years. She proved equal to these onerous tasks, turning for advice when necessary to male friends and relations and a reliable plantation overseer. Years later, drawing on this experience, she would urge her widowed niece Fanny Bassett Washington: "I very sincerely wish you would exert your self so as to keep all your matters in order your self without depending upon others as that is the only way to be happy to have all your business in your own hands without trusting to others that will promise and perhaps never think of doing it till they see you—I would rouse myself and not trouble any mortal. . . . I wish you to be as independent as your circumstances will admit and to be so, is to exert yourself in the management of your estate if you don't no one elce will—a dependence is I think a wrached state. . . ."

In those times of frequent early deaths of spouses and quick remarriages, the odds were high that the wealthy, competent, and agreeable 26-year-old widow Custis would soon attract suitors. Almost certainly she and George Washington were already acquainted and knew a fair amount about each other. In the Indian wars he had earned a reputation as a courageous and gifted officer. They met in the spring of 1758, perhaps at the home of a friend where Martha and her children were staying, and he soon followed up by visiting her at White House.

Washington, then 36, had been drawn to other young women. Sally Cary Fairfax, the wife of a close friend, may have been the romance of his life. In September 1758, when he was already engaged to Martha Custis, he wrote to Sally Fairfax:

How joyfully I catch the happy occasion of renewing a correspondence which I fear'd was disrelish'd on your part. . . . 'Tis true I profess myself a votary to love. I acknowledge that a lady is in the case, and, further, I confess that this lady is known to you. Yes, Madam, as well as she is to one who is too sensible of her charms to deny the power whose influence he feels and must ever submit to. I feel the force of her amiable beauties in recollection of a thousand passages that I would wish to obliterate till I am bid to revive them; but experience, alas, sadly reminds me how impossible this is. . . . You have drawn me, dear Madam, or rather I have drawn myself into an honest confession of a simple fact. Misconstrue not my meaning, 'tis obvious; doubt it not, nor expose it. The world has no business to know the object of my love declared in this manner to you when I want to conceal it. One thing above all things in this world I wish to know, and only one person of your acquaintance can solve me that or guess my meaning; but adieu to this till happier times, if I ever shall see them; the hours at present are melancholy dull. . . . I dare believe you are happy as you say. I wish I was happy too.

Years later, in 1798, Washington was to write that no one event of the years since he had seen her "nor all of them together, have been able to eradicate from my mind the recollections of those happy moments—*the happiest in my life*—which I have enjoyed in your company."

But Sally Fairfax was married, and Martha Custis was a desirable match. On January 6, 1759, George Washington and Martha Custis married, probably at White House. She wore a yellow brocade dress with its skirt open down the front over a white and silver petticoat, high-heeled lilac silk slippers embroidered in gold and silver, and pearls looped through her powdered hair. Soon after the honeymoon, she and her children joined her new husband in Williamsburg, where he was to serve as a representative in the assembly. A few months later they all traveled to Mount Vernon, which he had been renovating in anticipation of the marriage.

His wife's property now his, Washington used a part of her fortune for further improvements to Mount Vernon. By 1767 he had brought the plantation to profitability. There the couple settled into a happy domesticity: he was pleased to retire from public life, and she kept cheerfully busy running the large household and providing for the many family members and friends whom they constantly entertained. She was especially skilled in the hanging and curing of meat in the smokehouse. In her workroom, she knitted, received friends who called in the morning, and supervised the spinning, weaving, and making of clothes. Her household of slaves gave her the luxury of keeping for herself an hour after breakfast alone in her bedchamber, no interruptions allowed.

George Washington was fond of her children, and they of him. They called him "Pappa," but he could exercise little authority over them, for their mother indulged them. Her concern for them, no doubt aggravated by the deaths of her first two children and by Patsy's epilepsy, made her overcareful and unwilling to leave them. Had the Washingtons' hopes for more children been fulfilled, her anxieties might have lessened, but the months and years passed without her becoming pregnant. Patsy's health continued to deteriorate, however many remedies they tried or new doctors they consulted. Jacky, for all his charm, caused problems. The boarding school in which his mother had reluctantly agreed to place him at 14 reported him idle and troublesome. "I must confess to you," wrote his schoolmaster, "that I never in my Life know a Youth so exceedingly Indolent or so surprizingly voluptuous. . . ." The mere idea of Jacky's undergoing the risk of inoculation against smallpox, which at the time gave the patient a light case of the disease, so worried his mother that it was finally done without her knowledge.

When he was 18, he told his parents of his engagement to Nelly Calvert, whom they had met. His adoptive father advocated a delay, but his mother had pleasant visions of the young couple's living close by. In the midst of their uncertainty, Patsy died. To console his wife, Washington assented to Jacky's withdrawal from King's College, New York, and to the young people's marrying. But they disappointed Martha and George Washington by settling some distance from Mount Vernon.

In August 1774 the growing conflict with England further disrupted the Washingtons' domestic routine. Though she felt anxious, Martha Washington loyally supported the cause of the American patriots that her husband was making his own, telling the visiting Edmund Pendleton that she hoped he would stand firm; she knew that her husband would. In May 1775, after the battles of Lexington and Concord, Washington attended the Continental Congress in Philadelphia, where he accepted command of the army to be raised, agreeing to march them to Boston. His wife remained at home, where she supervised the building of new wings at Mount Vernon to give her and her husband more privacy from their many visitors. Consideration for her prompted Washington to write and send her his will and to suggest to Jacky and his wife Nelly that they pay an extended visit to her. She, however, thought the many worries expressed about her safety at Mount Vernon to be nonsense; she was not, she said, afraid of the royal governor.

Nonetheless, she packed up her valuables and went to stay with her brother-in-law's family.

When the general wrote asking his "Patsy," as he called his wife, to join him, she at once set out for his winter headquarters at Cambridge, Massachusetts, arriving in time for Christmas. She took Jacky, Nelly, and four slaves with her on the difficult three-week-long winter trip. An escort dispatched by her husband met her in Philadelphia, where she was entertained and where she learned of rumors that she had been living apart from her husband because she was a Tory. This cruel gossip, an early instance of the many attacks on General Washington during the American Revolution, was countered by the cheers that followed her on her way north.

At his Harvard headquarters, Martha Washington met her husband's immediate circle of officers, known as "The Family." The general worked out of the house where they lived and where she received visitors in her parlor. She formed a sewing and knitting circle to mend for bachelor soldiers and provide comforts and bandages for the hospital. She also helped the general's aides with the voluminous task of copying, though never anything secret. Some in her circle called her "Our Queen." Mercy Warren, wife of the president of the provincial congress, wrote, "I think the complacency of her manners speaks at once the benevolence of her heart, and her affability, candor, and gentleness qualify her to soften the hours of private life, or to sweeten the cares of the hero, and smooth the rugged paths of war."

Despite the brave front she presented, Martha Washington flinched at the gunfire she could hear coming from Boston and Bunker Hill. "To me that has never seen anything of war," she wrote, "the preparations are very terrible indeed, but I endeavor to keep my fears to myself as well as I can." She rejoiced with other Patriots when the British retreated to their ships and the Americans took over Boston. The Washingtons then moved to New York, and Jacky and his pregnant wife Nelly set out for their home. When the general traveled to Philadelphia to consult with the Continental Congress, his wife accompanied him in order to undergo a vaccination. She was still recuperating when he returned to New York but soon rejoined him on June 16, 1776. Two weeks later, the British fleet entered the New York harbor. Fearing that the British might capture the general's wife and hold her hostage, American officials sent her back to Philadelphia, where she could evacuate with the Continental Congress if necessary.

With the signing of the Declaration of Independence on July 4, 1776, Martha Washington had a new worry, for now her husband was exposed to the threat of the gallows or of the Tower of London. Her fears were exacerbated when reports reached her of his daring in battle, and when she learned that Benedict Arnold had plotted to surrender West Point and perhaps also General Washington himself to the British.

When the Americans were defeated in New York in October 1776, Martha began packing. Eventually she decided that she was of no use in Philadelphia, whereas at Mount Vernon she could oversee the work her husband wanted done there. Back home, hearing the constant bad news of his retreats, his worries about short enlistment periods, and the hopelessness of the militia system, she agonized about what to do if he were captured.

That winter set the pattern for those to follow in the agonizingly prolonged war. Every year Martha Washington joined her "Old Man," as she called him, in his winter headquarters where he rested and planned for the resumption of hostilities in the spring. Occasionally she found him ill, sometimes dangerously so. Often she found him tormented by the lack of adequate food, clothing, and comforts for his soldiers, as in the dreadful winter of 1778–79 at Valley Forge. The Continental Congress did not provide sufficient funding for the army. He worried constantly over desertions, the expiration of enlistments, and disloyalties and quarrels among his officers. Some officers jealously accused him of indecision or

inactivity. Others, like Alexander Hamilton, resigned their commissions.

His wife's presence cheered Washington and his soldiers. She encouraged him in withstanding the scurrilous attacks made on him: some accusing him of sexual peccadillos, particularly with slaves; some alleging that he had at first not favored independence. The officers' wives planned amusements to distract the men from their hardships and cares—horseback parties, singing, and telling riddles and stories. Martha seldom danced, but the general was an excellent dancer who could outlast many younger partners. Some of her reactions reflect the prejudices of her time, as when, in the spring of 1779, she wrote, "I saw the funniest, at the same time the most ridiculous review of the troops I ever heard of. Nearly all the troops were drawn up in order, and Mrs. Knox, Mrs. Greene, and myself saw the whole performance from a carriage. The General and Billy [his mulatto body servant], followed by a lot of mounted Indians, rode along the line. Some of the Indians were fairly fine-looking, but most of them appeared worse than Falstaff's gang. And such horses and trappings! The General says it was done to keep the Indians friendly toward us. They appeared like cutthroats all."

Martha never knew what kind of quarters she would occupy for the winter, nor what shelter could be found within the area where the Washingtons could be protected against capture. Sometimes she was loaned a comfortable and well-equipped house; sometimes she made do crowded into whatever was available. During the winter of 1779–80, the British were so close that soldiers came into their bedrooms at night to stand guard at the windows.

She dressed plainly, loyally shunning fashionable British clothes in favor of American products, many of them made by the Washingtons' own slaves. By example and in words, she suggested to others that they do more for American independence. In spring 1777 a Morristown matron reported, "I was never so ashamed in my life. [We] thought we would visit Lady Washington, and as she was said to be so grand a lady, we thought we must put on our best bibs and bands. So we dressed ourselves in our most elegant ruffles and silks, and were introduced to her ladyship. And don't you think we found her *knitting and with a specked* [checked] *apron on*. She received us very graciously, but after the compliments were over, she resumed her knitting. There we were without a stitch of work and sitting in state, but General Washington's lady with her own hands was knitting stockings for herself and husband. . . . she seems very wise in experience, kind-hearted and winning in all her ways. She talked much of the poor soldiers, especially the sick ones. Her heart seems to be full of compassion for them."

It was indeed. In one of her letters of 1783, she describes an incident in which more than 50 thinly clad soldiers whom the general had pardoned for various crimes came to thank him.

In the summers and falls Martha found surcease at Mount Vernon, renewing her body and spirit in the comfort and tranquillity of the home she loved, among family and friends. Her husband loved it too. He worried about it often, as when his steward was forced to entertain the British there, and they carried off a number of his slaves. Yet during the eight years of the war, he found the opportunity to visit his plantation just once, in 1781, for two days.

The Washingtons did not neglect family responsibilities over the course of the war. The general was a lynchpin for his birth family and continued to support them from a distance. Before the war was over, Jacky's death in 1781 imposed even more responsibility on his parents. The young man had been delighted when his stepfather had taken him to Yorktown, where he caught "camp fever," a form of typhoid. His mother's and wife's efforts to nurse him were in vain. He left behind four young children, and the Washingtons undertook to raise the younger two, George Washington Parke Custis and Eleanor Parke Custis.

Yorktown was the last major military operation of the Revolution. But it did not end the war, which by then had reached stalemate. In the spring of 1782 and again that November, Martha Washington joined her husband at Newburgh on the Hudson. In the spring and summer of 1783, American soldiers were leaving the army—some deserting, some discharged, some mutinying when they were discharged penniless. General Washington made an extended trip to northern posts, and in his absence his wife suffered from fever and colic. On his return, Congress required them to live in Rocky Hill, New Jersey, a furnished residence near Princeton, apparently until the conclusion of peace negotiations, begun in mid-August 1783. In November she returned to Mount Vernon. General Washington, finally relieved of his duties, joined her there on Christmas Eve.

At last the Washingtons were free, they believed, to take up the private life they had planned and always wanted. Martha's health was not what they would have wished, but they were surrounded by family and friends. In August 1784, the marquis de Lafayette visited them. That fall her favorite niece, Fanny Bassett, married her husband's favorite nephew, George Augustine Washington, and the young couple settled at Mount Vernon, he becoming an assistant to the general. Harriot Washington, another niece, also resided there, and the Washingtons hired a resident tutor for the grandchildren. The general cautiously invited his mother to live with them but warned her that she would not like it: "My house is at your service, and I would press you most sincerely to accept it, but I am sure, and candor requires me to say, that it will never answer your purpose in any shape whatever. For in truth it may be compared to a well-resorted tavern, as scarcely any strangers who are going from north to south or from south to north do not spend a day in it."

Economic depression and political differences within the young nation under the Articles of Confederation soon interrupted the Washingtons' little domestic peace. By 1786 friends were telling the general that he must intervene. In 1787 he attended the Constitutional Convention in Philadelphia, where he was made presiding officer. On September 22, the new constitution signed, he returned to Mount Vernon. Both the Washingtons were dismayed when he was unanimously elected to the nation's presidency in April 1789. Once more, Washington left his plantation for his public duty. And again, as in his generalship throughout the war, he would take no salary, but only his expenses, for which he received $25,000 a year.

Martha Washington resigned herself. As she later wrote to Mercy Warren,

> I little thought when the war was finished, that any circumstances could possibly have happened which would call the General into public life again. I had anticipated, that from this moment we should have been left to grow old in solitude and tranquility together: that was, my Dear madam, the first and dearest wish of my heart;—but in *that* I have been disapointed; I will not, however, contemplate with too much regret disapointments that were enevitable, though the generals feellings and my own were perfectly in unison with respect to our predilictions for privet life, yet I cannot blame him for having acted according to his ideas of duty in obaying the voice of his country. . . . with respect to myself, I sometimes think the arrangement is not quite as it ought to have been, that I, who had much rather be at home should occupy a place with which a great many younger and gayer women would be prodigiously pleased. . . . I do not say this because I feel dissatisfied with my present station—no, God forbid:—for everybody and everything conspire to make me as contented as possable in it; yet I have [seen] too much of the vanity of human affairs to expect felicity from the splendid scenes of public life.—I am still determined to be cheerful and to be happy in whatever situation I may be, for I have also learnt from experience that the greater part of our happiness or misary depends upon our dispositions, and not upon our circumstances.

A month after her husband's inauguration, Martha joined him in New York, the new capital city, where they lived in a three-story house at the junction of Queen and Cherry streets.

Their new household included the two grandchildren, two secretaries for the general, 14 white servants (some in the red-and-white Washington livery), several black slaves, and as steward the West Indian Samuel Fraunces, who had gained his expertise in wines and food as proprietor of his own New York tavern.

The Washingtons now faced the problem of how to present themselves to the nation and to the world. The president was both head of government and head of state, and his wife had to uphold both the democratic principles on which the United States was founded and the dignity of the new country in the eyes of the world. Their tasks were complicated by the tendency of European nations, particularly the defeated British and to a lesser extent the French, to sneer at Americans as ignorant backwoodsmen. This attitude affected the decisions not only of Martha Washington but also of the first ladies who came after her, as they strove to assert the position of the United States among the nations of the world.

As the first American president's wife, Martha Washington could draw on no precedents and no role models, nor could she pattern her dress and conduct on those of queens, for the United States had repudiated monarchy. Yet it seemed that some degree of formality and dignity should set apart the first citizens of the nation. The mere question of a title presented difficulties. Was she to be called "Madame Presidentress"? "Marquise"? "Lady Washington"? Some people so addressed her, but in the end she settled for "Mrs. Washington."

To control the mobs of visitors, the Washingtons set up a formal schedule. The president held levees on Tuesday afternoons for men only. His wife held a Friday evening "drawing room"—a kind of open house—which he attended as a guest, without hat or sword, to indicate informality. Nonetheless, these occasions were rather stiff. Martha Washington remained seated, often with Abigail Adams, wife of the vice president, by her side, and her guests bowed to her. The president, meanwhile, mingled among the guests. Tea, coffee, and cake were served, and sometimes ice cream and lemonade. According to some reports, to close the party the president's lady would stand and announce, "The General always retires at nine, and I usually precede him." She conscientiously returned calls on the third day. Around 1790, she wrote to her beloved niece Fanny Bassett Washington back at Mount Vernon, "I live a very dull life hear and know nothing that passes in the town—I never go to any publik place, indeed I think I am more like a state prisioner than anything else, there is certain bounds set for me which I must not depart from—and as I can not doe as I like I am obstinate and stay at home a great deal."

Despite the Washingtons' care, some of their critics denounced them for creating the trappings of an American royal court. Martha endured these attacks as something she could do nothing about. Abigail Adams reported on her quite differently: Mrs. Washington, she wrote, "received me with great ease and politness. She is plain in her dress, but that plainess is the best of every article. She is in mourning. Her Hair is white, her Teeth beautiful, her person rather short than otherways. . . . Her manners are modest and unassuming, dignified and femenine, not a tincture of ha'ture [hauteur] about her." On another occasion Adams wrote: "Mrs. Washington is one of those characters who create love and esteem. A most becoming pleasantness sits upon her countenance and an unaffected deportment which renders her the object of veneration and respect. . . . I found myself much more deeply impressed than I ever did before their Majesties of Britain."

The Washingtons accepted neither private invitations nor gifts. They went to assembly balls and visited museums and theaters. On Saturday afternoons Martha Washington gave children's parties. She always liked having young women around the house, perhaps in part as surrogates for her daughter Patsy, so she welcomed into her home Polly Lear, the wife of one of the president's secretaries. Polly and the Custis children were company for her when her husband went on tour. At Christmas 1789 the Washingtons moved to a larger house, on Broadway below Trinity Church. In 1790 it was decided that the nation's capital city would be built near Georgetown, but meanwhile the capital would move to Philadelphia. The president's wife was more at home there and enjoyed the city's nicer shops and livelier social scene. She also relished being close enough to visit Mount Vernon.

Nonetheless, she was appalled by talk of a second term for her husband. Originally both of them had hoped that he could resign before the end of the first term, for he had already been dangerously ill twice, and they were both getting older. Thus, although she seldom did so, she protested. But the nation faced sharp political divisions, and it was uncertain whether anyone other than George Washington could hold the country together during its growing pains and persuade the warring parties to work together. "Poor Patsy," he said to her; she apologized and said no more. In 1793 he was unanimously reelected.

Thomas Jefferson, Henry Knox, and Alexander Hamilton all resigned their cabinet positions to resume their private lives, but the Washingtons soldiered on. Inevitably, given the international tensions heightened by the French Revolution and the frailty of the United States, the president had to endure much criticism of his leadership. But in 1796 and 1797 a grateful nation held huge birthday celebrations for him. Finally, on March 4, 1797, he walked alone to stand beside John Adams in Congress Hall while Adams was inaugurated president. Neither wife attended the ceremony. The Adamses declined to purchase the contents of the presidential mansion, so the Washingtons sold some items and gave away others. Then they headed back to Mount Vernon, taking with them Lafayette's son (whose parents had sent him to the United States for safety during the French Revolution) and another young Frenchman.

George and Martha Washington relaxed into the private life they had craved for so long, setting their neglected home to rights with repairs and renovations. Even then, talk of the

general's again leading an army, this time against France, disturbed their peace. In just two years, on December 14, 1799, he died. "I shall soon follow him," said his wife. "I have no more trials to pass through." She moved to a small garret room, warmed only by charcoal heaters, where she knitted, sewed, and spent more time in bed. With the help of Tobias Lear, the general's secretary whom Martha's niece Fanny Bassett Washington had married after the death of her first husband, she responded to the letters of consolation and the announcements of honors bestowed upon her husband. He had left her the lifetime use of his property, but she assigned the management of her business affairs to others, especially to her granddaughter Eleanor (Nelly) and Nelly's husband Lawrence Lewis. She died on May 22, 1802, of a prolonged fever and was buried beside her husband in the tomb enclosure he had planned.

—⁓—

Martha Washington could be sharp-tongued about political opponents, whom she called "filthy democrats." Jefferson's casual lifestyle in the executive mansion displeased her, and she spoke sarcastically about it. She always saw to it that her husband received due respect. Even her beloved granddaughter, Nelly Custis, was called to account when she failed to dress for dinner at Mount Vernon. When at the end of the meal officers came to call, Nelly asked to be excused to tidy herself. "No," said her grandmother, "remain as you are. What is good enough for General Washington is good enough for any guest of his."

On the issue of slavery, Martha Washington was trapped within the conventions of her birth. All her life she had been served by slaves. Nothing in the record suggests that she ever questioned the morality of slavery, although she certainly heard reverberations of the debate about whether or not the Constitution of the United States should recognize that cruel institution. The founding fathers, many of whom she entertained, were well aware of the inconsistency of fighting for their own liberty while denying it to blacks. No doubt she was a kind mistress, insofar as slavery allowed kindness. A contemporary diary quoted one of her slaves as saying, "The General was only a man, but Mrs. Washington was 'perfect.'" In her letters, however, she expressed only the attitudes toward blacks common among slaveowners. She needed a housekeeper at Mount Vernon, she said, to look after "the women [slaves] that work[.] [T]hey always idle half their time away about their one [own] business and wash so bad that the cloths are not fitt to use." She also needed a steward, a "sober and attentive," careful, trustworthy man. These, she said, "are essential requisits in any large family, but more so among blacks—many of whom will impose when they can do it." She advised her niece Fanny Bassett Washington: "Charlot . . . is so indolent that she will doe nothing but what she is told. . . . if you suffer them to goe on so idele they will in a little time doe nothing but work for themselves." When her maid Oney, whom she had raised from the age of 10, ran away, Martha Washington was sure that some unscrupulous adventurer had lured her away. She was eager to take the runaway back and forgive her, but she never saw her again.

She enjoyed the company of children and young people and surrounded herself with them whenever she could. However, the frequent illnesses, short life expectancies, and medical ignorance of her time imposed much sorrow and many losses on her, beginning with the deaths in quick succession of two of her children and her first husband. She survived all four of her children. She was parted from her husband for long periods much more often than she liked. But her cheerful disposition and her determination to endure without complaint usually kept her from inflicting her disappointments, worries, and griefs on others. She put duty ahead of her own wishes but never pitied herself as a martyr.

The nation was fortunate that its first president's wife had no inflated image of herself but understood that she must maintain the prestige of his office and the status of the United States in the eyes of the world. Martha Washington led her life as a sensible woman, a devoted wife, and a loyal advocate of American independence.

CHRONOLOGY

1731 *June 2:* Martha Dandridge is born at Chestnut Grove plantation on the Pamunkey River in New Kent County, Virginia

1750 *May 15:* Martha marries Daniel Parke Custis

1751 *November:* Son Daniel is born

1753 *April 12:* Daughter Frances Parke Custis is born

1754 *February 19:* Son Daniel dies

Daughter Martha Parke Custis is born

1755 Son John Parke (Jacky) Custis is born

1757 *June:* Daughter Frances Parke Custis dies

July 8: Husband Daniel Custis dies

1758 *May:* George Washington and Martha Dandridge Custis become engaged

1759 *January 6:* Martha Dandridge Custis marries George Washington

February: The family moves to Williamsburg

April 7: The Washingtons move to Mount Vernon

1773 Daughter Martha (Patsy) dies

1774 Son Jacky leaves King's College to marry Eleanor Calvert of Maryland and settle at Abingdon, his estate up the river from Mount Vernon

1775 *May:* George Washington attends the Second Continental Congress in Philadelphia

June: George Washington accepts the command of the Continental Army

December: Martha Washington joins her husband at his headquarters in Cambridge, Massachusetts

1781 Son Jacky dies. The Washingtons take Martha Washington's grandchildren George Washington Parke Custis and Eleanor (Nelly) Custis, to raise

1783 *November–December:* As the Revolutionary War ends, the Washingtons return to Mount Vernon

1789 *April 30:* Martha Washington becomes first lady

May: Martha Washington joins her husband in New York, the nation's capital

1790 The nation's capital and the Washingtons move to Philadelphia

1797 The Washingtons return to Mount Vernon

1799 *December 14:* George Washington dies

1802 *May 22:* Martha Washington dies

FURTHER READING

Fields, Joseph E., comp. *"Worthy Partner": The Papers of Martha Washington*, introd. Ellen McCallister Clark. Westport, Conn.: Greenwood, 1994.

Lossing, Benson J. *Mary and Martha: The Mother and Wife of George Washington.* New York: Harper, 1886.

Thane, Elswyth. *Washington's Lady.* New York: Dodd, Mead, 1960.

Wharton, Anne Hollingsworth. *Martha Washington.* New York: Scribner's, 1897.

N.B.: No modern completely unfictionalized biography exists; primary materials are scanty.

ABIGAIL SMITH ADAMS
(NOVEMBER 11, 1744–OCTOBER 28, 1818)
First Lady, March 4, 1797–March 4, 1801

ABIGAIL ADAMS
(Library of Congress)

An ambitious woman, Abigail Adams wanted the ambitious husband she passionately loved to exercise his abilities to the fullest—and to give her the opportunity to exercise hers. She married a man who had no wish for her to hide her talents, though he could not fully share her vision of women's participation in public affairs. She insisted on the equal status of women and above all on their right to a good education. Because she lived in the 18th and 19th centuries, she defined her feminism in terms of husband and wife, lord and lady, each operating in a separate sphere. She read and admired the British feminist Mary Wollstonecraft. She hoped that U.S. law would allow a separate legal existence for married women, replacing British law, which regarded husband and wife as one, and the husband that one. Only such a legal change could enable a wife to sue an abusive husband. She wanted moreover to guarantee wives their share of the fruits of the married couple's mutual labors. She also wanted women to have a say in the choice of their daughters' husbands.

In her letters and domestic life, Abigail Adams set an example for the republican mother of her day, a woman fit to bear and raise sons as worthy citizens of the new United States of America. At the sacrifice of their company, she raised her sons for public service. Her eldest, John Quincy Adams, became the fifth president of the United States, making her the first woman to be both wife and mother of a president.

—⁓—

On November 11, 1744, in Weymouth, Massachusetts, Abigail Smith was born, the second child of Elizabeth Quincy and Reverend William Smith. Abigail's father, a Harvard graduate, came from a line of merchants, and her mother from a distinguished family of the Massachusetts theocracy. Her family never sent her to school, in part at least because of the weak health that was to plague her all her life. They educated her and her two sisters themselves— her father and grandfather with their ample libraries, her "merry and chatty" grandmother from her long experience, her mother by drawing on her expert housewifery and the skills with people she had acquired as a parson's wife, and all of them by wide-ranging, well-informed conversation. Her brother-in-law Richard Cranch, she later wrote, "put proper Bookes into my hands, . . . taught me to love the Poets and to distinguish their Merits." She read and memorized pages of poetry by Shakespeare, Milton, Pope, and James Thomson. Samuel Richardson's novel *Sir Charles Grandison* formed her ideal of manhood. She taught herself to read French. As a matter of course, she also learned the domestic arts, for although her parents kept servants (probably slaves), they honored honest toil by word and by example.

Her parents also instilled in Abigail a belief in religious sense that changed little from the time she publicly confessed her faith in 1759. She relied on it throughout her life for support and consolation, assuring herself in good times and bad that God's will ruled overall. Linked to it was a burning patriotism, which began in her childhood as she heard her pastor pray for the triumph of Great Britain in its war against France for the control of North America, and as her congregation celebrated days of prayer and fasting for the triumph of English Protestantism against French Roman Catholicism. During the American Revolution, Abigail Adams extended that belief in the righteousness of her country's cause to the newly formed United States of America. All her life she blamed foreigners for most of the troubles in America, even its internal quarrels.

The young lawyer John Adams had known Abigail Smith since she was 15 and he 24—at which time he thought her witty but lacking in candor. But when she was 17, he fell passionately in love with her, and she with him. From a worldly point of view, marrying her would help him since she brought with her a good family name, an ample dowry of household goods, and the prospect of a future inheritance of land. Reverend Smith, feeling that Adams was not quite good enough for a minister's daughter, preached on the text "For John came neither eating bread nor drinking wine, and ye say, He hath a devil." But there was no denying their love, and on October 25, 1764, Abigail and John Adams began their extraordinarily happy marriage.

When the Adamses married, they moved into a saltbox cottage he had inherited next door to his mother's house in Braintree, Massachusetts, with a couple of servants—not slaves—to help with the housework. As a matter of principle, John Adams refused to own slaves, and Abigail Adams denounced slavery as both immoral and destructive. Perhaps, she thought, it was a punishment visited upon the country for its sins.

Soon after their marriage, Abigail became pregnant. As she waited for her baby, she tried to perfect herself as a woman, shaping her ideal by reading James Fordyce's *Sermons to Young Women*. Fordyce advocated active man-

agement of the household; perfection in the domestic arts; frugality; modesty of dress—although splendor might be proper in some circumstances; extensive reading of history, biography, travel, and even novels that instilled virtue; and practicing a Christianity that stressed morality rather than theology. She also admired the Jesuit writer Batista Angeloni's denunciation of the inhuman tyranny that barred women from education.

From the beginning of the Adams's marriage most of the administration of the farm fell on Abigail, for although her husband enjoyed working on it, his law practice called him away for considerable lengths of time. She learned what to plant and how to sell their crops profitably. She ran a thrifty household and a productive farm, and before long she was able to invest her savings, often in land. This responsibility remained hers throughout their lives. More and more in her letters to her husband what she had started by calling "your" property became "ours," or even "mine."

The Adams household grew until by 1772 it included several servants and four children: daughter Nabby, the eldest; and sons John Quincy, Charles, and Thomas. (Another daughter had died at 13 months of age.) At that point the Adamses may have agreed to have no more children; later in life, Abigail said that she did not believe that a woman need have all the children that might come her way. The decision, if taken, was made easier by John's frequent absences, abstinence then being the most frequently used means of birth control. In any event, after 1777, when her third daughter was stillborn, she had no more children.

She thought a lot about child-rearing, feeling sympathy for her own mother as she faced its realities. She adopted Spartan standards, particularly with her sons, on whom she placed heavy demands. She was determined that they be educated for public service; she had in mind such a purpose when she led the seven-year-old John Quincy by the hand to a vantage point from which they watched the Battle of Bunker Hill. She also believed that after early childhood

boys should be taught by men, even if that meant placing her sons in another household to be tutored. If it meant sending them abroad to widen their knowledge and experience of the world, separating her from them for months or even years, she would make the sacrifice—and so would they. "I had much rather you should have found your Grave in the ocean you have crossd or any untimely death crop you in your Infant years," she wrote John Quincy in 1778, "rather than see you an immoral profligate or a Graceless child." Her vigilance for her children—and grandchildren—never ceased. When John Quincy was U.S. minister to Russia, she inferred from his and his wife's letters that the position was bankrupting him and wrote President Monroe suggesting that he be recalled. When he was in the Senate, she was still reproving him for his careless appearance and still instructing his wife to put a cracker in his pocket to keep his stomach from grumbling.

This system worked with John Quincy, who achieved all that she had dreamed for him and miraculously preserved his patience with his interfering mother. Both her younger sons, however, succumbed to alcoholism. Charles died of the disease, homeless, at 30—an enemy, his mother said, to no one but himself. "Weep with me," she wrote her sister, "over the grave of a poor unhappy child who cannot now add another pang to those which have pierced my heart for several years." Nabby, meanwhile, fell victim to her parents' discouragement of her suitor Royall Tyler, who later fared well as a playwright, in favor of Colonel William Shaw, John Adams's secretary. Shaw was certainly a promising young man but as a husband he was a disaster. His frequent job shifts reduced his wife and children to isolation and want.

As John Adams engaged in the political activity that led to the American Revolution, Abigail Adams was if anything even stronger than he in her views. In 1770 she already thought of England as a "cruel" mother country, believing that the colonies possessed much more genuine religion than hypocritical England. In 1773 she was writing of British statesmen,

"[T]hat Ambition which would establish itself by crimes and aggrandize its possessor by the ruin of the State and by the oppression of its Subjects, will most certainly defeat itself." In late 1774 she informed the celebrated British historian Catharine Sawbridge Macaulay, "The only alternative which every american thinks of is Liberty or Death." The ties of blood, like the Gordian knot, could not be undone, but the sword might cut them. "Is it not better," she asked, "to die the last of British freemen than live the first of British slaves?" By 1775 she had declared herself ready for independence, joining the Patriot cause to her religion: "Our Country is as it were a Secondary God, and the first and greatest parent. It is to be preferred to parents, to wives, children, Friends, and all things the Gods only excepted."

The Adamses talked over the dangers in which his speech and actions placed them and their children and decided—she with tears—that principle must overrule their concern for safety. Whether it was defending the British captain of the soldiers who fired into the mob at the Boston Massacre or committing what might be judged treason to England, he must do what they thought right.

Thus, when in August 1774 John Adams rode off to Philadelphia for the Congress convened to resist England's punishment of Massachusetts, his wife bade him godspeed, wrote him encouraging letters holding up the example of classical heroes, and proudly styled herself "Mrs. Delegate." From then on he was to be away from his family for ever longer periods. A week after the Battle of Lexington and Concord, he departed for the Second Continental Congress, leaving his family half an hour from the Boston battlefront and advising his wife to "fly to the Woods" with the children in case of danger. She was delighted when the American generals sent to Boston by Congress introduced themselves to her. Fired with the spirit of rebellion, she wished to put the principles of Thomas Paine's *Common Sense* into execution as soon as possible. Her letters to her husband therefore urged him to break with England at once.

I long to hear that you have declared an independency [she wrote on March 31, 1776], and by the way in the new Code of Laws which I suppose it will be necessary for you to make I desire you would Remember the Ladies, and be more generous and favourable to them than your ancestors. Do not put such unlimited power into the hands of the Husbands. Remember all Men would be tyrants if they could. If perticuliar care and attention is not paid to the Laidies we are determined to foment a Rebelion, and will not hold ourselves bound by any Laws in which we have no voice, or Representation. That your Sex are Naturally Tyrannical is a Truth so thoroughly established as to admit of no dispute, but such of you as wish to be happy willingly give up the harsh title of Master for the more tender and endearing one of Friend. Why then, not put it out of the power of the vicious and the Lawless to use us with cruelty and indignity with impunity. Men of Sense in all Ages abhor those customs which treat us only as the vassals of your Sex. Regard us then as Beings placed by providence under your protection and in immitation of the Supreem Being make use of that power only for our happiness.

However, when John responded jocularly, Abigail retreated, resorting to flirtatiousness: "I cannot say that I think you very generous to the Ladies, for whilst you are proclaiming peace and goodwill to men, Emancipating all Nations, you insist upon retaining an absolute power over Wives. But you must remember that Arbitrary power is like most other things which are very hard, very liable to be broken—and notwithstanding all your wise Laws and maxims we have it in our power not only to free ourselves but to subdue our Masters, and without violence throw both your natural and legal authority at our feet—'Charm by accepting, by submitting sway/Yet have our Humour most when we obey.'"

The British retreat from Boston relieved the Adams family's peril, but Abigail feared that Virginians could not withstand the enemy as well as New Englanders could. "I have sometimes been ready to think," she wrote her hus-

band at the end of March 1776, "that the passion for Liberty cannot be Eaquelly strong in the Breasts of those who have been accustomed to deprive their fellow Creatures of theirs [in the institution of slavery]. Of this I am certain that it is not founded upon that generous and christian principal of doing to others as we would that others should do unto us." On a visit to Boston to get the children and herself inoculated against smallpox, she heard the Declaration of Independence read from the state-house balcony.

With the autumn of 1776 came monetary inflation, and Abigail appealed to her husband to come home before all their property was lost and the family went hungry. He returned—and soon she became pregnant. She wondered whether she should induce him to stay home but finally decided that the disarray in colonial affairs made the need for him to be in Philadelphia more urgent than her own. He returned there in January 1777, and without him she endured a pregnancy in which she convulsed; the baby was stillborn. Despite the shortages of food and increasing inflation, she got by, managing without her black farmhand, who had left to join the Continental army, and scrimping so that she could invest in the colonial cause.

John Adams returned home in November 1777, intending to stay, but the Continental Congress appointed him commissioner to France. His wife accepted yet another separation, sacrificing herself once again to the public good. At first they thought the family would accompany him. However, he faced not only the dangers of a North Atlantic winter crossing but also the threat of capture by the British. Finally, they decided that he would take along only 10-year-old John Quincy. Abigail worried about her son's exposure to European temptations, but, she sternly reminded herself, "to exclude him from temptation would be to exclude him from the World in which he is to live." Her resolution was soon tested, for after they sailed she heard rumors—later proved false—that their ship had been lost or captured and that Benjamin Franklin, Adams's fellow commis-

sioner, had been assassinated in France. For the next six and one-half years, less one three-month period, the Adamses remained separated, as the Continental Congress kept Adams busy on one mission after another in France, England, and Holland.

Abigail heard from her husband infrequently, and she found his letters much too short. The hazards of sea and war had made the mail unreliable, and he feared to say too much about his activities lest his letters be captured. But to assuage her appetite for public affairs, he asked Congressional secretary John Thaxter, Jr., and perhaps also Massachusetts delegate to Congress James Lovell, to send her news. Lovell's correspondence both informed and entertained her, but it became a problem because of his suggestive tone.

On August 7, 1779, John Adams, now without portfolio, and John Quincy returned home—though not for long. On November 13 of that year, Adams sailed again, this time to negotiate for peace and to represent the United States at the British court. He took with him both John Quincy, by now adept at assisting his father, and Charles. Their mother thought that both of them needed their father's hand; that the experience would broaden their educations; and that heroes and statesmen are formed by facing challenges in a great period of history. They should be proud, she told them, of "a parent who has taken so large and active a share in this contest."

Once again Abigail turned to household and business management, collecting rent and her husband's legal fees. She bought more land, sometimes with his approval and sometimes without it. Learning that European goods provided the best hedge against inflation, she began with his help importing and reselling such goods as cloth, trimmings, dishes, gloves, fans, and tea. When John Adams sent Charles home from Holland—the homesick youngster had not flourished in the damp climate there—she sent him and Tommy to live with her sister, Betsy Shaw, and to be tutored by her brother-in-law. She participated in state politics, joining the campaign against John Hancock when he ran for governor of Massachusetts. His repeated elections to that office made her distrust democratic politics. When her husband differed with Benjamin Franklin on policy, Abigail Adams concluded that Franklin was an unprincipled "old Sorcerer." In her mind, her husband was right, those who disagreed with him were wrong, and that was that.

As she grew older, she became less hopeful and more traditional. She discarded her earlier belief that women were more capable of enlightenment than men, although she still insisted that they must be educated so that they could do their jobs as virtuous republican mothers. But her actions contradicted her declaration that she had no further ambition than reigning in her husband's heart. She wrote revealingly in 1781, "I never wondered at the philosopher who thanked the Gods that he was created a Man rather than a Woman."

By 1783 Adams, so long away from his own country, had grown homesick and discouraged by quarrels and setbacks in his work. He begged his wife to join him in Europe. After some hesitation—her health was poor, she feared a winter crossing of the Atlantic, she had no male protector to accompany her, and she would cut an "awkward figure" in diplomatic circles—she agreed to go. She took Nabby with her and left the two younger boys to continue their education with the Shaws. The journey began with nausea but ended in triumph. Embarking on June 24, 1784, Abigail Adams succumbed to seasickness. She was confined to a cabin where she could get air only by opening the door to quarters occupied by strange men; her servants and other women on the ship were too ill to care for her; and she had to depend on males for certain intimate services. But early in July she recovered and at once set about getting the ship scrubbed, instructing the cook, and even making some puddings herself. Arriving in London on July 21, she and Nabby bought European clothes while they waited for their menfolk to escort them to France.

On the four-day journey to Paris, she stared disapprovingly at dirty streets, smelly towns, and women working in the fields. As she furnished and staffed their large rented house in Auteuil, she found that the specialized French servants refused to work at anything but their own tasks. Her New England thrift was outraged by the necessity for eight servants—though the British ambassador had 50 and the Spanish ambassador 70. She soon learned enough kitchen French to give orders, but her lack of facility in the language made the required social calls difficult. She was shocked to learn that France had 52,000 registered prostitutes, and that the Sisters of Charity took in thousands of abandoned babies each year. She was also disgusted by Madame Helvetius, whom Franklin introduced as his ideal Frenchwoman—a blowzy widow in her 60s who publicly embraced Franklin and wiped up the puddle her little dog made with her gown.

But Abigail Adams was far too interested in life to let dirt and different standards of morality make her withdraw. After she met the friendly, plainly dressed, and unaffected Marquise de Lafayette, she came to admire the "ease and softness" of well-bred, educated Frenchwomen. She attended theaters and operas, even though the women in the ballets wore insufficient clothing for her taste. Nonetheless, she remained suspicious of a city where the business of life struck her as pleasure—the fault, she thought, of the Roman Catholic Church. Agreeing that this was no place for a young man, the Adamses shipped John Quincy back to Harvard. But Paris increased Abigail's self-confidence; widened her worldly knowledge; and gave sophistication to her dress, manners, and household furnishings. Above all, it increased her belief in the virtues of America, a country "uninfested with thousands of useless Virmin whom Luxery supports upon the Bread of Idleness, a Country where Virtue is still revered; and modesty still Cloaths itself in crimson."

In Adams's next post as American envoy to England, which he assumed in the spring of

1785, his wife helped him by bolstering his easily bruised ego, evaluating his associates, listening to his ideas, and energetically defending his reputation. She found a house for them at 9 Grosvenor Square, hired the inevitable eight servants, and resigned herself to even higher household expenses than in Paris. Her keen sense of obligation to uphold the standing of her country made her take pains with her appearance, her hospitality, and her attendance at court—the last a duty that she detested both for the expense it necessitated in elaborate clothing and for the boredom of standing for four hours waiting for, as she put it, a smile from the king. But she was relieved to find that he received her husband and her cordially, even though they represented the renegade American people. The British press was another matter. Inspired, she believed, by unrepentant Tories, it satirized both John Adams and the United States. She managed to hold her tongue when the English made false assumptions about America in her presence but she was sensitive about the courtesies she believed due her country.

For relief from her official duties Abigail attended chapel services, theaters, concerts, and lectures on natural science. She entertained American ships' captains at dinner, listening avidly to their news from home. She also corresponded with Thomas Jefferson, whom she had come to know well in Paris, and took care of his motherless and bewildered daughter Polly when she arrived from the States accompanied by the 14-year-old slave Sally Hemings—whom Abigail Adams promptly advised Jefferson to send back home. She and he differed politically; she cried at the news of Shays's Rebellion, which to her symbolized mob rule and disorder, while he admired it for its spirit of resistance to government.

In 1788 the family returned to the United States, where John Adams was given a hero's welcome. Living abroad had enlarged their ideas of the home they needed. Consequently, they bought a new house in Quincy. Although it was considerably bigger than the one where she had borne and raised her children, it looked to Abigail Adams like a "wren's house," in wretched disrepair, and the garden was a wilderness. They spent the summer putting it all in order.

Abigail shared her husband's delight at his election as vice president in 1788. She believed that George Washington and John Adams would form an executive branch strong enough to prevent a clash between aristocracy and democracy that might otherwise destroy free government. She also thought that Adams's sacrifices, and hers, had entitled him to the post. "I will take praise to myself, I feel that it is my due," she wrote, "for having sacrificed so large a portion of my peace and happiness to promote the welfare of my country which I hope for many years to come will reap the benifit, tho it is more than probable unmindfull of the hand that blessed them." Indeed, she believed that she had sacrificed more than any other woman in the country, ignoring the many women whose husbands, sons, fathers, and brothers had died in the American Revolution.

In Washington, as all through his life, John Adams depended on his wife's intelligence, wisdom, and insight into the motives of his friends and enemies. But her opinions derived largely from their mutual values and his political philosophy. She was often more precipitate and more extreme than he, but she rarely differed from him in substance. She strengthened and augmented rather than opposed his ideas.

This mutual agreement contributed not only to their marital happiness but also to a belief in the correctness of their own views that verged on arrogance—an attitude that did not diminish with age. Abigail's consistent agreement with her husband and her righteous anger at anyone who criticized him confirmed his faith in his own ideas, lessening his inclination to make the compromises that democracy requires. For all her fervent support of the new republic and her insistence on liberty, she did not trust the American people to govern themselves and feared mob rule. Rather, she thought the nation must be governed by an intellectual, principled, virtuous elite dedicated to duty and self-sacrifice—such as John Adams, and, by extension, his wife.

The Adamses often harshly criticized others in government. Even Thomas Jefferson, they thought, showed moral weakness in his accumulation of debts, his not remarrying, his slave-owning, and his religious skepticism. They saw every election as testing the new national experiment in democratic government. Could it survive, or must monarchy and aristocracy replace it to protect order? The French Revolution, which Jefferson saw as an effort to follow the American example, exacerbated the Adamses' fears. Abigail worried particularly about its attack on Christianity. "I am no friend of bigotry," she wrote, "yet I think the freedom of inquiry, and the general toleration of religious sentiment, have been, like all other good things, perverted, and, under that shelter, deism, and even atheism, have found refuge."

She brought cultivated talents to her new position. She was the most politically knowledgeable woman in the country, and her experience abroad had taught her how things were done in Europe among people of the highest rank. Her wide reading and acquaintance with the nation's most influential leaders made for brilliant conversation at the Adams table.

In June 1789 Abigail arrived in New York, then the capital city, where she spent a happy year in their rented Richmond Hill house. John Quincy was studying law in Massachusetts and Tommy was at Harvard, but Charles and Nabby and the grandchildren lived with them. She found it easy to make friends with the Washingtons, whom she admired, and was proud that the president always reserved a place for her at his wife's right. With her usual efficiency she ran a household of 18 and managed to entertain freely on the insufficient $5,000 a year that Congress awarded the vice president, sometimes by doing the cooking herself. Though the move of the national capital to Philadelphia disappointed her, she enjoyed the gayer social life there when her health allowed. But both Adamses worried about the emergence of and bitterness between political parties—to the point that she feared that another election might cause bloodshed.

Her always uncertain health deteriorated further over the next 12 years, keeping her from the full participation in public life that she so enjoyed. The Adamses always spent the summers at Quincy, but gradually Abigail had to remain there for longer and longer periods. In fall 1792 she was not well enough to return to Philadelphia. For the next five years, during all of her husband's second term as vice president, she had to remain in Quincy.

When President Washington refused a third term in 1796, John Adams doubted that he could himself be elected president, being perhaps too old at 61. His wife wrote, not altogether convincingly, that she took no "comfort or pleasure in the contemplation" of his presidency, wondering whether she could emulate Martha Washington's "patience, prudence, discretion." She feared that her outspokenness might hurt her husband and did not know whether she could be silent. He brushed this aside; any woman, he said, could be silent if she wanted to. But she knew herself better. When he was elected, she wrote: "I am my dearest Friend allways willing to be a fellow labourer with You in all those Relations and departments to which my abilities are competent, and I hope to acquire every requisite degree of Taciturnity which my Station call for, though . . . truly . . . it will be putting a force upon Nature." In fact, she spoke out when a Quincy townsman objected to her enrolling her two black servant boys in the local schools, she herself having taught them to read and write. Moreover, she told her husband, "I will never consent to have our Sex considered in an inferiour point of light. Let each planet shine in their own orbit, God and nature designed it so. . . . [I]f a woman does not hold the Reigns [sic] of Government, I see no reason for her not judging how they are conducted."

Business affairs kept Abigail in Quincy until the spring of 1797, two months after John Adams's inauguration. She arrived in Philadelphia on May 10 to claim her position as the president's wife and hostess. She was indignant to find that they were being charged twice the rent that the Washingtons had paid for the presidential mansion. He feared that being president would bankrupt him, but she managed so well that in four years they saved several thousand dollars from his $25,000 compensation to invest. This was in contrast to the Washingtons, who had had to supplement that money with private funds, and, later, the profligate Jefferson, who left the presidency deeply in debt.

By now Abigail Adams knew how to entertain elegantly, and conversation at her parties sparkled. She aspired to set fashions. Within her drawing room, she boasted, "is frequently to be seen as an assemblage of as much Beauty and elegance, as is to be met with in any foreign Court." Having experienced firsthand the European propensity to sneer at Americans, the Adamses were determined to maintain the dignity of the nation and its president. She particularly resented the many newspaper attacks on them and on the policies of her husband's administration. To answer them while still officially remaining silent, she privately arranged for articles favoring Adams to be planted in the press. The British ambassador's wife remarked that Abigail had "spirit enough to laugh at [Benjamin Franklin] Baches Abuse of her Husband, which poor Mrs. Washington could not."

Both Adamses were offended when Philadelphia staged a birthday celebration for Washington; the president's refusal of the invitation made for sparse attendance. The next year Philadelphia mended its ways and gave Adams a celebratory ball first—then one for Washington. Abigail enjoyed being cheered on the way to and from Quincy, and she was delighted when in 1799 a light infantry company from Massachusetts petitioned to be organized as "Lady Adams Rangers."

In the presidential mansion, Abigail Adams routinely rose at 5:00 A.M., breakfasted at 8:00, tended to family arrangements until 11:00, then dressed for the day. In the early afternoon she received callers, an average of 60 a day. After 3:00 she dined, then paid calls or drove out until

7:00 P.M. She regularly gave dinners for some 40 guests, most often for Vice President Jefferson, members of the cabinet, and senators. Her household tasks were eased by the British steward who hired and supervised the servants.

President Adams used his influence to appoint relatives and friends to government positions, a practice that the press and his political enemies condemned as nepotism. However, George Washington had himself conveyed to Adams his hope that kinship would not prevent his father from making use of John Quincy's talents within the government. Moreover, the Adamses told themselves, the president never appointed anyone who was not thoroughly qualified for the position—though Congress sometimes disagreed with them. Belief in the influence of the president's wife encouraged aspiring officeholders to besiege her with applications.

In fact, Abigail Adams was deeply involved with all the problems that her husband confronted as president. She inveighed against Thomas Pickering, his secretary of state; five months before the president dismissed him, she wrote, "He would not remain in office, if the President possesst such kind of resentments as I hear from various quarters, he permits himself to utter." She followed every turn of the threat of war with France and busily wrote letters to rally support for the conflict should it come. As usual, she was less cautious than her husband, much more willing to resort to arms, for she believed that the French were scheming to take over the United States, foment a slave rebellion, and sow atheism. She maintained her interest even when, in the summer of 1798, severe illness again laid her low and kept her from returning to Philadelphia with her husband in the fall. She finally recovered enough to reenter the political world in the summer of 1799 and that winter saw a busy social season in the executive mansion. President Adams prepared to stand for reelection, but she could see that he probably would not win.

In November she traveled to the new capital, Washington City, where she found the new president's house unfinished but rising from a sea of mud. She spent only three months there, deploring the lack of stairs and of bells for the servants, struggling to get along with only 13 servants though she estimated that the place really needed a staff of 30, and using a reception room to dry her clothes for lack of anywhere else. She kept her criticisms to herself, however, and instead put it about that she thought the house beautifully situated and that she enjoyed the views. While in Washington she entertained Thomas Jefferson, the president-elect (Abigail spoke of him as the "future Ruler"), and could not resist warning him against the men of his party and their plans for the nation. He laughed off her advice.

Regarding her husband's electoral defeat in December 1800, she wrote, "If I did not rise with dignity, I can at least fall with ease, which is the more difficult task." She only regretted that in the future her means of doing good would be much curtailed. She left the capital in early February 1801, traveling unescorted, remarking that she was "accustomed to get through many a trying scene and combat many difficulties alone." The president, after a final burst of political appointments, followed her at dawn on the day of Jefferson's inauguration.

In her last 17 years, Abigail Adams faced daunting trials. She was chronically and often acutely sick; her lifelong trouble with her eyes worsened. For a time she was too ill to speak, and she aged so much that old friends did not recognize her. She had to watch Nabby suffer and die at 48 of breast cancer. Her grandchildren often failed to live up to her standards. She thought the nation was forgetting her husband's accomplishments and glorifying Washington's. New England's opposition to the War of 1812 disgruntled her, but her natural energy and ebullience sustained her.

During this time, she enjoyed her husband's constant presence for the longest period in their marriage. Although he had no pension, they could still live comfortably on the money she had accumulated; if they did not live as elegantly as his high office justified, that was, in her opinion, the nation's disgrace, not theirs. Despite her chronic illnesses, she bustled about, rising at 5:00 A.M., rousing the servants and resuming her old duties of dairywoman. Eventually her brother's daughter Louisa and son Charles's daughter Susana came to live with them. So devoted was she to family, in fact, that eventually the household numbered 21. She advised son John Quincy in the performance of his duties and defended his political stances. "Forsake not the law of thy Mother," she wrote him. She carried on a correspondence with daughter-in-law Louisa's mother, Catherine Johnson, whom she thought a sensible, well-bred woman.

Her illness also did not prevent Abigail from entertaining many callers, and she enjoyed going to parties. She refused to engage in any conversation "which spends itself in railing at the times we live in . . . [which] are not made better by these complaints." Neither would she live in the past: "There is no occasion to invite more peevish companions for the last hours of Life than time and decrepitude will bring in their train." It is wiser to laugh than to snivel, she believed, for the person who enjoys is happier than he who suffers.

Despite her vow not to "molest or disturb the new administration," in 1801 Abigail wrote, "If we do not look down and pitty Things, we have equal reason to commisirate an infatuated deluded multitude who are hastning upon themselves more missery than they have enjoyed of tranquility & happiness for twelve years past." She felt strongly that the president of the United States should have a 12-year term to avoid the contentiousness of frequent campaigns. During the early years of the Monroe presidency, she was cheered by interparty peace, believing that it signaled the end of partisanship. Late in life, the Adamses reconciled with old friends with whom they had political differences, including Thomas Jefferson and Mercy Otis Warren.

As she reached the end of her life, she read Scott and Byron and Madame de Stael, though she continued to prefer the authors she had loved in her youth. She welcomed the liberalization of Christianity and saw hope in the Unitarian movement. Even as an old lady she displayed a lively, inquiring mind.

In October 1818 Abigail Adams contracted the typhus that killed her; she died on October 28. Her 83-year-old husband walked in her funeral procession.

—⁓—

Like Martha Washington, Abigail Adams sacrificed her private life to public duty throughout her life. Unlike her predecessor, however, she rejoiced in that duty. Her wide reading, her association with the prominent men and women of her day, her travels abroad as the wife of an important American official, and her observations of the Washingtons during Adams's vice presidency all prepared her to act as the president's wife with social and political sophistication. But that role could not contain her energies and enthusiasms, which, confined by the conventions of her era, now and then burst forth to overmaster her discretion, causing her critics to question her republican principles and accuse her of monarchism. Notwithstanding her wide experience of the world, Abigail Adams remained heart and soul a New Englander, with provincial pride of place. She was convinced that the kind of New Englanders she and John Adams represented—religious, intellectual, self-disciplined, and unfailingly dutiful—formed the elite most fit to govern the new republic.

CHRONOLOGY

1744   *November 11:* Abigail Smith is born

1763   *Fall:* Abigail Smith accompanies John Adams on a trip of several days, possibly to attend a court session

1764   *October 25:* Abigail marries John Adams

1765   *July 14:* Daughter Abigail (Nabby) is born—probably at Abigail Adams's parental home

1767   *July 11:* Son John Quincy is born

1768   Daughter Susanna is born; dies at 13 months

1770   *May:* Son Charles is born

1772   *September:* Son Thomas Boylston is born

1777   A daughter is stillborn

1778   *February 13:* John Adams and son John Quincy sail for France

1779   *August:* John returns home and frames the Massachusetts constitution, on which the U.S. constitution is later modeled in part

        November: John Adams sails as minister to England with sons John Quincy and Charles

1782   *January:* Charles returns to the United States

1784   *June 18:* Abigail and Nabby Adams sail for France

1785   *May:* John Adams is appointed minister plenipotentiary to England

1786   Nabby marries Colonel William Stephens Smith, American legation secretary

1788   *June 17:* The Adamses return to Massachusetts

1789   Abigail moves to New York as wife of the nation's first vice president

1790   *September:* The Adamses move to Philadelphia, the new U.S. capital

1796   John Adams is elected president

1797   Abigail becomes first lady

1800   *November:* The Adamses move to the president's house in Washington, D.C.

1801   The Adamses move to Quincy

1813   Daughter Nabby dies

1818   *October 28:* Abigail Adams dies

FURTHER READING

Adams, Abigail. *New Letters of Abigail Adams, 1788–1801,* ed. Stewart Mitchell. Boston: Little, Brown, 1947.

Akers, Charles W. *Abigail Adams: An American Woman,* ed. Oscar Handlin. Boston: Little, Brown, 1980.

Gelles, Edith B. *Portia: The World of Abigail Adams.* Bloomington: Indiana University Press, 1992.

Levin, Phyllis Lee. *Abigail Adams: A Biography.* New York: St. Martin's Press, 1985.

Withey, Lynne. *Dearest Friend.* New York: Free Press, 1981.

DOLLEY PAYNE TODD MADISON

(MAY 20, 1768–JULY 12, 1849)
First Lady, March 4, 1809–March 4, 1817

DOLLEY MADISON
(Library of Congress)

Dolley Madison was thoroughly at home in her time and in her country. Whatever her circumstances, she managed to enjoy her role and herself. Though in her Quaker youth she longed for pretty clothes, she delighted in her family and young friends. She rejoiced in the new pleasures that her first marriage allowed her, and in the political and social worlds to which her second marriage introduced her. As a widow she reveled in her position and influence. Her happy temperament overcame disappointment, pain, and poverty, enabling her to become, in the words of President Zachary Taylor, "our First Lady for a half-century," and the Mrs. Madison whom everybody loved.

Dolley Madison was born Dorothea Payne, the eldest daughter of nine children. Her Quaker parents, John and Mary Coles Payne, doted on her and gave her the nickname "Dolley." Soon after her birth on May 20, 1768, in North Carolina, they returned to their home in Virginia on Little Bird Creek farm. When she was seven, they moved to Scotchtown plantation, near Ashland, Virginia. They brought Dolley up as a Quaker, dressing her plainly and sending her to the school of the Cedar Creek Meeting, of which they were both clerks. They loved her blue eyes and black hair, protected her fine complexion with a linen mask and linen gloves, and gave her a secure and happy childhood. The family lived peacefully during the Revolutionary War, forbidden by their religion to participate in it.

When Dolley was 15, a grown woman by the standards of the day, her parents' consciences forced them to manumit their slaves. In 1783, now without hands to work their land, the Paynes sold their plantation and moved to Philadelphia, confident that they would find a solid Quaker community. The family settled in a rented house, the four girls in one bedroom, and the boys and their black nurse Mother Amy—who refused to leave the family—in the attic. John Payne invested in the starch-making business. In six years, at the age of 49, he went bankrupt. The Quaker community disowned him, apparently because he could not pay his debts. In another three years he died—but not before signing a petition to Congress urging emancipation of all slaves.

Dolley loved living in Philadelphia, known for the sophistication of its society and the elegance of its shops. She gracefully accepted the restrictions placed on her by the Quakers and enjoyed herself to the full within them. (Years later she advised her young niece: "Our sex are ever losers, when they stem the torrent of public opinion.") Her opportunities to socialize with other young people in the Quaker community and her many suitors brought her social self-confidence. She turned down one proposal after another, but at age 21, soon after her father's bankruptcy, she accepted a good Quaker man, as was expected of her. Attorney John Todd, a kind, patient, and intelligent man, had been courting her for several years. They were married on January 7, 1790, with the approval of the Quaker community.

As Todd was flourishing in his law practice, he was able to furnish their home luxuriously, outfit a carriage, and have his wife's portrait painted in miniature by the popular artist James Peale. Their first son, John Payne Todd, was born on February 29, 1792, just about the time that Dolley's father died. Dolley's mother carried on, supporting her family by running a boardinghouse, and aided by an inheritance from their former slave, Mother Amy, who had saved all her wages after her liberation and left them to her mistress. In the late summer of 1793, the Todds' second son, William Temple, was born.

Just then terror struck Philadelphia with the eruption of yellow fever. In the hysteria that accompanied it, John Todd behaved nobly, sending his wife and babies away to Gray's Ferry on the Schuylkill and remaining in the city. There he risked infection while he tried to comfort the sick by writing their wills and caring for his father and mother when they were stricken. He died in his wife's arms on October 24, 1793. Dolley then caught the fever, as did their newborn. She recovered; the baby did not. At 25 she was a widow, comfortably off, with one surviving child.

Her mother, Mary, who had nursed Dolley and her baby faithfully, was now 50 years old and no longer able to work. To her rescue came Dolley's sister Lucy, whom the Quakers had disowned for eloping with a non-Quaker, George Steptoe Washington, nephew and ward of the president. Lucy and George took Mary and one of her sons, Lucy's and Dolley's brother, to live with them, and Lucy and Dolley made themselves jointly responsible for their two younger sisters. One of them, Anna Payne, lived with Dolley until 1804, when Anna married Congressman Richard Cutts.

Dolley continued to live quietly and with propriety, cultivating a close friendship with fellow Quaker Eliza Collins. She went to Quaker meetings regularly and socialized mostly with Quakers. As always, she serenely accepted what fate brought. Her temperament, the comfortable circumstances in which her husband had left her, her relationships with her family and her many friends, and perhaps a new feeling of independence reconciled her to her situation. She grew even more attractive, so that, Elizabeth Collins said, "gentlemen would station themselves where they could see her pass," and cautioned her, "Really, Dolley, thou must hide thy face, there are so many staring at thee." Dolley enjoyed the advice and protection of Aaron Burr, her mother's former boarder and longtime friend, both in settling John Todd's estate and in writing her will, which named Burr the guardian of her son Payne. Indeed, for a time people speculated that Burr was courting her; the custom of the day allowed, and even anticipated, the quick remarriage of widows.

In May 1794 Congressman James Madison asked to be introduced to Dolley Todd, and Aaron Burr obliged. Almost 20 years older than Dolley, "the great little Madison" was a well-established lawyer and man of public affairs, the son of a wealthy Virginia family, and heir to the vast estate of Montpellier in the foothills of the Blue Ridge Mountains. Given their common backgrounds and Madison's readiness to marry, the couple's relationship evolved rapidly and rumors of their engagement began to fly. Martha Washington heard them, summoned Dolley to the presidential mansion, and told her, "If it is so, do not be ashamed to confess it; rather be proud; he will make thee a good husband, and all the better for being so much older. We both approve of it; the esteem and friendship existing between Mr. Madison and my husband is very great, and we would wish thee to be happy."

Dolley, hesitant, went off with her son and her sister for a long visit in Virginia. On her way home that August, she wrote accepting Madison's proposal. At the same time she wrote to her attorney, William W. Wilkins, seeking his approval and arranging for a settlement of her assets on her son. Wilkins approved, as did almost everyone else, except the relatives of her first husband and the Quakers, who did not want their members marrying outside their community. On September 15, 1794, the Madison marriage was celebrated at Harewood, Dolley's sister Lucy Washington's estate, with the bride in a white silk dress with a 23-inch waist. That day Dolley wrote to her friend Eliza Collins: "I give my hand to the man who of all others I most admire. . . . In this union I have every thing that is soothing and grateful in prospect—and my little Payne will have a generous and tender protector." Thus the Madisons began their extraordinarily happy marriage of 40 years. In time her love for him came to equal his for her. In defiance of the habit of that time, when spouses addressed one another as "my friend," they wrote to "my dearest," and "my beloved."

Competently and graciously, Dolley Madison entered on her new duties, overseeing both their Philadelphia three-story brick home and Montpellier, with its hundreds of slaves. Her husband had expanded the mansion there into a two-family dwelling, providing separate quarters for his aging parents. The Madisons entertained widely. James Madison detested narrow partisanship, and his wife chose to be nonpolitical, so they opened their homes to politicians of all factions and to distinguished foreign visitors, as well as to family and friends. In those days of difficult travel, people came to stay for weeks or even months. Dolley Madison set a generous table. Breakfast might include ham, salt fish, bread and butter, and tea; the afternoon dinner might present soup, several kinds of meat, thin slices of cabbage, pastries and puddings, claret, port, and madeira; and the early evening supper might be oysters and tea. All this was often supplemented with late-morning lunches and late-evening snacks sent to the guests' rooms.

The Quakers disowned Dolley for marrying outside their faith—leaving her free to wear the beautiful clothes she had long been eyeing, and a touch of rouge. She still spent her mornings supervising her household in the plain gown, white kerchief, and white apron of a Quaker housewife. But in the evenings she blossomed into silks and satins, topping them with the turbans she loved to wear that made her appear taller than her five feet six inches. Freed from Quaker restrictions, she reveled in assemblies and balls (though she never learned to dance), horse races, riding parties, musical frolics, receptions, and card games. She loved the theatre, music, art, and books. Sociable by nature, she made many friends for her more reclusive husband. She launched her young sisters into society, dressing them fashionably and arranging dance lessons for them.

When John Adams began his term as president, the Madisons chose to leave their public life in Philadelphia and spent most of their time at Montpellier. In 1800 Thomas Jefferson's election to the presidency changed their lives. Jefferson appointed Madison as his secretary of state. The Madisons entered Washington, the new seat of the U.S. government, as the president's guests. With their son Payne Todd and Dolley's young sister Anna, they stayed in the President's House for three weeks while they looked for a home of their own. Sensitive to jokes that the president was taking in boarders, they rented a small, inconveniently situated place for a couple of months, until Dolley retreated to Montpellier for the summer. She returned in the fall to a house that district commissioner Dr. William Thornton had found for them between the President's House and the congressional buildings.

Both Jefferson and Aaron Burr, his vice president, were widowers, so when Jefferson had women as guests he asked Dolley Madison—or her sister Anna—to preside as hostess—beginning, in effect, her reign as first lady. As her friend Eliza Collins (Lee) remarked, Dolley was well qualified for the position by her "hospitality and graciousness of deportment." Between them, Jefferson and she changed the atmosphere of the President's House and presidential enter-

taining. Intensely democratic, Jefferson opted for simplicity, trying to avoid the echoes of European court life introduced by Martha Washington and Abigail Adams in their desire to uphold the dignity of the new nation.

Dolley Madison brought to the presidential mansion and to her own home charm, good humor, sprightliness, affability, charity and tolerance, and agreeable manners. Genuinely interested in the people she met, she remembered their names and faces even after meeting them at a crowded levee. At her husband's request she presided at the head of their table to direct the conversation, while he took his seat on the side. Under her guidance conversation was spirited, not only at the table but also in the parlor to which the ladies retired after dinner for what she called "Dove Parties." She disliked and avoided contention. If anyone introduced a sensitive topic, she quickly changed the subject with a flow of diverting talk. As her friend Margaret Smith wrote, she was a "foe to dullness in every form, even when invested with the dignity which high ceremonial could bestow."

The residents of Washington delighted in her. Foreign diplomats in the city were not so sure, however—particularly the British, still unreconciled to the loss of their American colonies. The British ambassador took umbrage because Jefferson did away with diplomatic precedence, taking Dolley in to dinner rather than offering his arm to the ambassador's wife. His outrage prompted Madison to warn James Monroe, then representing the United States in England, that he might receive complaints on the matter from the British government. Monroe laughed; he and his wife had been treated similarly at the court of St. James. Dolley handled the British criticism with aplomb: When the ambassador's wife ridiculed her table as being "more like a harvest home supper than the entertainment of a Secretary of State," Dolley riposted, a witness said, that "she thought abundance was preferable to elegance; that circumstances formed customs, and customs formed taste; and as the profusion, so repugnant to foreign customs, arose from the happy circumstance of the superabundance and prosperity of our country, she did not hesitate to sacrifice the delicacy of European taste, for the less elegant, but more liberal fashion of Virginia."

Through it all she behaved discreetly. She was, she wrote in 1804, learning to hold her tongue well; interested though she was in people and their affairs, she forbore to gossip. During the trial of her friend Aaron Burr for treason, she refrained from comment, even to her sister. She ignored the many anonymous letters she received. Perhaps hardest of all, she abstained from answering the attacks on her husband that pained her even more than those on herself. She made it a policy to receive his enemies hospitably, now and then even converting them to friends. Through it all she preserved her independence of spirit, taking to heart her husband's warning words: "Be always on your guard that you become not the slave of the public nor the martyr to your friends."

Although she visited the congressional galleries and the Supreme Court and was eager to hear what was going on in the cabinet, Dolley expressed no political opinions. Believing that Madison, as she called her husband, would not want her to be an active partisan, she carefully avoided any appearance of influencing what she called "public business." Publicly she confined herself to such uncontroversial projects as raising money for the Lewis and Clark expedition.

She enjoyed shopping, whether it was for herself, for her sister, for Jefferson, for Jefferson's daughters, who lived in the country—for whoever asked. Her husband encouraged her, adding to her purchases his own gifts of jewels. Dolley also set fashions. One contemporary account describes her dressed for a state occasion, wearing "a turban of white satin, with three large white ostrich feathers hanging over her face. . . . Her dress, too, of white satin, made high in the neck, with long sleeves, and large capes trimmed with swan's down was rich and beautiful." She always carried a gold-and-enamel snuffbox, with its contents of fine, powdered tobacco to be sniffed. It made her sneeze, stained her fingers,

and necessitated her carrying both a bandana—for the rough work, she said—and a delicate lace handkerchief with which to finish off. It was an addiction that she shared with many another fine lady of the time. "In her hands," wrote a friend, "the snuff-box seems only a gracious implement with which to charm."

In the mornings and until the 4 P.M. dinner, she paid the obligatory calls that gradually multiplied to vex the wives of Washington officials until Eleanor Roosevelt's time. She reserved some mornings for visiting the poor. She frequented all sorts of social events. All this she accomplished despite the frequent illnesses and disabilities to which the lack of medical knowledge of the time condemned most people. She suffered from the bilious fever common in Washington those days, from whooping cough, from sudden deafness and toothache, and above all from a persistent eye ailment that at times caused her excruciating pain. Even when an infection of the knee kept her from walking for about three months, she drove out in her carriage to execute shopping commissions for President Jefferson, received guests with her knee in splints, and sat through the presidential celebration of the Fourth of July, since she could not stand.

On March 4, 1809, James Madison was inaugurated the fourth president of the United States. No other first lady entered on her husband's presidential term with as much experience as a presidential hostess. After the swearing-in ceremony, the Madisons received guests in their small house, she in a plain cambric dress with a long train and a bonnet of purple velvet and white satin, its white plumes almost brushing the chandeliers, "all dignity, grace and affability," wrote her friend Margaret Smith. That night they presided at the inauguration ball, at which Dolley Madison "looked a queen. She had on a pale buff-colored velvet, made plain, with a very long train, but not the least trimming, and beautiful pearl necklace, earrings, and bracelets. Her head dress was a turban of the same coloured velvet and white satin (from Paris) with two superb plumes, the bird of paradise feathers."

Her mode of entertaining more resembled Jefferson's informality than the stiffness of the Washingtons. Every week she gave a large dinner party for invited guests, with a servant standing behind each chair, but her Wednesday evening drawing rooms, where she served wine, punch, and cake, were open to all. For this president's wife, the President's House was the home into which she welcomed her guests. She chose not to receive their bows in state but to move about the rooms, greeting them warmly, concerning herself with their comfort and pleasure, and now and then dropping into a seat for a chat. Often she held a book in one hand so as, she said, "to have something not ungraceful to say, and, if need be, to supply a word of talk."

Numerous anecdotes describe her skill in putting her guests at ease. At one of her drawing rooms she greeted a backwoods youth standing by himself. Startled at being recognized by the great lady, he spilled his coffee, dropped the saucer, and tried to stuff the cup into his pocket. Nobody, his hostess told him, could avoid a mishap in such a crowded room. And how, she asked, was his excellent mother, whom she once had the honor of knowing and longed to hear about. As she dispelled his timidity, she motioned to a servant to bring him another cup of coffee. Quaker friends thought her the same unaffected person they had always known, and an elderly woman who asked, "P'rhaps you wouldn't mind if I jest kissed you, to tell my gals about," found herself warmly embraced.

One contemporary wrote that "the gladness which played in the countenances of those whom she approached was inspired by something more than respect. . . . We have not forgotten how admirably the air of authority was softened by the smile of gayety; and it is pleasing to recall a certain expression that must have been created by the happiest of all dispositions—a wish to please and a willingness to be pleased." People were not only honored but delighted to be invited to the President's House. The public loved her, sending her gifts and news of their hometowns, naming boats and dance songs after her, calling her "Lady Madison," "The Presidentress," or "Queen Dolley." To Henry Clay's remark "Everyone loves Mrs. Madison" she replied, "That's because Mrs. Madison loves everybody."

Defying the custom of the times, when men usually chose the furniture, James Madison turned over the redecoration of the President's House to his wife. With $6,000 in funds voted by Congress, she and architect Benjamin Latrobe undertook one of the perennial refurbishments of the presidential mansion that the constant flow of guests necessitate. They did the drawing room in Dolley Madison's favorite yellow, enhancing its grandeur with imported satin and damask, elaborate mantlepieces, and beautiful mirrors—all soon to be destroyed. They carefully chose furniture elaborate enough for Federalist tastes, impressive to foreigners, but simple enough to please Republicans.

This president's wife acted as his helpmate, not as a counselor or power behind the throne. Yet he believed in the mental equality of the sexes, and she had grown up accustomed to seeing her mother hold a position of trust among the Quakers and help to support the family. Letters show that Dolley assisted her husband with his correspondence, acting unofficially as his secretary for a time in 1813. She knew a great deal about what went on behind the scenes of government. The British author Harriet Martineau, no flatterer, wrote of her: "For a term of eight years she administered the hospitalities of the White House with such discretion, impartiality, and kindliness, that it is believed she gratified every one and offended nobody. She is a strong-minded woman, fully capable of entering into her husband's intellectual companionship, as well as to her ability in sustaining the outward dignity of his office." Just how Dolley responded to the hundreds of requests asking her to intervene in job appointments and other personal matters is uncertain, though during the War of 1812 she did secure clemency for the son of a Quaker friend jailed for his conscientious objection to fighting.

In 1811–12, the winter-long visit of her sister Lucy Washington, now a widow, and Phoebe Morris, the daughter of a friend, added to the gaiety. On March 29, 1812, Dolley arranged Lucy's wedding to Supreme Court justice Thomas Todd, the first to be held in the President's House.

Then the War of 1812 against England broke out. Despite her Quaker upbringing, Dolley Madison assured the fighting men of her support, saying, "I have always been an advocate for fighting when assailed." It was said that soldiers marching past the presidential mansion cheered her. Historians differ in their interpretation of an incident during the winter of 1812–13, when, at a ball to celebrate American naval victories, the son of the secretary of the navy, a young lieutenant, laid the flag of the captured ship *Macedonian* at her feet. She blushed—some think because she was touched, others because she was embarrassed.

The Federalists boycotted her parties, deeming them inappropriate in wartime. However, the president wanted them continued because they promoted goodwill and political tolerance. His second inaugural in 1813 was duly celebrated with a reception and ball. In the late spring and summer of that year, he fell seriously ill with malaria. His wife canceled her drawing rooms to nurse him.

By the winter of 1813–14, her husband well again, Dolley was back in the social swing. The next summer she presided over the Fourth of July celebrations, even as the British navy cruised near the mouth of the Potomac. The British threatened the president's life and the British admiral boasted in a note to Dolley Madison that he would soon make his bow in her drawing room. In late August the capital city was imperiled. The president was away inspecting the army. Determined to await his return and then flee with him if necessary, his wife packed up trunks of cabinet papers and ordered that the frame of the Gilbert Stuart portrait of George Washington be broken so that the painting could be taken from it. On August 23, 1814, with everything in readiness to go, she wrote to her sister Lucy: "French John [her steward] offers to spike the cannon at the gate and lay a train of powder which will blow up the British should they enter the house. To this proposition I positively object, without being able, however, to make him understand why all advantages in war may not be taken."

At the last desperate moment she obeyed a message from her husband to flee. In the confusion of the next few days, the Madisons sometimes met, only to part again, but they often missed each other. Dolley Madison found refuge where she could, staying the first night with a friend from whose house she could see Washington burning. When she stopped at a tavern that James Madison had designated as a meeting place, the hostess threw her out, shouting, "Your husband has got mine out fighting, and damn you, you shan't stay in my house." After a brief reunion with his wife at another inn, the president joined the troops preparing to retake the capital city. Dolley disguised herself for travel as a poor country woman. As soon as she heard of the British retreat from Washington, however, she turned back. Finding that the bridge had been burned, she revealed her identity to a ferryman to persuade him to take her across the Potomac. The president was already in the city by the time she reached it on August 28.

They returned to a scene of devastation. The British had paid special attention to the presidential mansion, damaging it to such an extent that the Madisons had to live in rented houses for more than two years, while renovations went forward. The mansion was painted white—the beginning of its designation as the White House. Dolley had saved nearly all the silver, the crimson velvet curtains from the Oval Room, the cabinet papers, a few books, and a small clock. "Everything else belonging to the publick," she wrote a friend, "our own valuable stores of every description, [and] a part of my clothers" had burned. "I confess that I was so unfeminine as to be free from fear, and willing to remain in the *Castle*. If I could have had a cannon through every window, but alas! those who should have placed them there, fled before me, and my whole heart mourned for my country!" Despite her own losses, she set about helping a group of women to establish an orphanage in Washington, not only acting as their directress and contributing money and a cow but also volunteering to cut out as many dresses as necessary and to oversee the seamstresses who made them up.

Clad in a series of new Parisian frocks, she resumed entertaining, first in a mansion known as the Octagon House and later in a smaller house. The brilliant social season of 1815–16 included her reception honoring Andrew Jackson's triumph at the Battle of New Orleans, which confirmed American independence and power. But she took equal care in planning the affair that welcomed the new British ambassador, to demonstrate that the United States still valued England's friendship. She made the best of the small house in which the Madisons were then living, decorating it from cellar to attic and brilliantly illuminating it by stationing at intervals black male servants holding flaming torches. She accompanied her husband, newly popular with the triumphant close of the war, to inspect a warship at Annapolis and attend a ball in Baltimore. At the end of his second term, the entire District of Columbia honored the president and his wife with a series of elaborate farewell parties that kept them in Washington for a few days after James Monroe's inauguration.

They left Washington for Montpellier, there to live quietly until the end of Madison's life. Their happiness together was marred by Payne Todd, whom his stepfather had always treated as his own son. As a youth, Payne's charm had covered his lack of character. He grew into a self-indulgent, dishonest, brutish sot. A misery and a public disgrace to his loving parents, too self-absorbed even to let them know his whereabouts except when he demanded their financial help. They tried everything—encouraging him to marry, giving him a government commission, withholding funds from him, bailing him out of debtors' prison, and setting him up in business. His stepfather estimated that in a depressed economy that threatened the Madisons' ownership of Montpellier, they had spent about $40,000 in efforts to help him.

Aside from the trouble with Payne, the Madisons were pleasantly busy, he with the management of the plantation, studying, and editing his papers; she with caring for her mother-in-law, helping her husband in his work, keeping house, gardening, reading the new novels by Sir Walter Scott and James Fenimore Cooper, and endlessly entertaining friends, family, American and foreign notables, and the many guests who descended on them uninvited. She wrote cheerfully, "Yesterday we had ninety persons to dine with us at one table, fixed on the lawn under a large arbor. The dinner was profuse and handsome, and the company very orderly. . . . We had no ladies except Mother Madison, Mrs. Macon, and Nellie Willis. . . . Half a dozen only staid all night." She challenged one small guest to a race on the veranda that ran the length of the house, telling the child, "Madison and I often run races here when the weather does not allow us to walk."

As he aged James Madison became an invalid prone to worries about money. As plantation agriculture declined in profitability, he had to sell off part of his estate and recognized that eventually all of it would have to go. With his wife's assistance, every day from 10:00 to 3:00 he worked on his papers, both as a public duty and in the hope that their sale might ensure her financial security. He advised his wife that they should fetch $100,000.

As his sight dimmed, he depended on her not only as secretary but also to read to him. She wrote to a cousin, "Not a mile can I go from home; . . . my husband is fixed here, and hates to have me leave him. This [1826] is the third winter in which he has been engaged in the arrangement of papers, and the business seems to accumulate as he proceeds, so that it might outlast my patience, and yet I cannot press him to forsake a duty so important, or find it in my heart to leave him during its fulfillment."

For 20 years she left Montpellier only rarely, once to accompany her husband to the

Virginia Constitutional Convention of 1829. Reporter Anne Royall described her there:

> She is a stout, tall, straight woman, muscular but not fat, and as active on her feet as a girl. Her face is large, fully, and oval, rather dark than fair; her eye is dark, large, and expressive; her face is not handsome. . . . It is diffused with a slight tinge of red, and rather wide in the middle—but her power to please, the irresistible grace of her every movement shed such a charm over all she says and does that it is impossible not to admire her.

After James Madison died on June 28, 1836, his wife mourned him deeply, but in her sorrow she practiced what she preached: "I considered it the positive duty of those who are afflicted to exert their religion and their reason in favor of resignation." Except for a five-week visit to White Sulphur Springs, Virginia, she stayed on at Montpellier for a year, managing the plantation with the aid of an overseer, answering letters of condolence with the help of her niece Anna Payne (who lived with her for the rest of Dolley's life), entertaining the visitors who continued to pour in, wrestling with business affairs, and trying to arrange the publication of her husband's papers. In 1837 Congress bought part of the papers for $30,000, including his invaluable account of the debates at the federal constitutional convention.

That October Dolley set out for Washington. She had long hoped to return, and residence there might speed publication of the rest of her husband's papers. She and Anna Payne lived in a house owned by James Madison, directly across from the White House, leaving Payne Todd as squire of Montpellier. Living again in Washington elated her. On her restricted income she had to wear outmoded clothes, but she enjoyed society as much as ever. Never did it occur to her to limit her guests or stint her hospitality. No longer the pattern of fashion, Dolley Madison became instead the arbiter of manners.

Again in her element, she paid more than 200 calls during her first winter. She entertained frequently and resumed her traditional parties on New Year's Day and the Fourth of July. Supremely nonjudgmental, she took people young and old as they were. She reclaimed her old friends and made new ones, especially among officialdom. She turned to men for masculine guidance on such matters as the reliability of phrenology and to women for their shared interests. She made matches, as well: Since President Martin Van Buren was a widower, she set about marrying off his son to give the White House a hostess. To a nephew in straitened circumstances who was wooing a penniless granddaughter of Thomas Jefferson, she blithely wrote: "It is my advice that you immediately secure for your life and even after, the lonely one who has promised you her hand—she who is I am persuaded a prize to any man. Why then should delay obstruct your happiness, when your father's house though small would be a pleasant abode for a few months, at the end of which you could take one more ample and suited to your mutual tastes." As a matter of course, she provided the wedding reception.

Only her own son defeated her. At 44, Payne Todd was drinking away his life and her money at Montpellier, from which he would disappear at intervals, taking the keys with him and leaving the overseer unable to feed the slaves or conduct agricultural operations. In 1839, at 71, Dolley Madison returned to the plantation for two years to run it herself. Only an experienced manager could have staved off its loss for a few more years. Try though she might, she knew little about farming. Never one to martyr herself, she kept open house and accepted most of the many invitations that came her way. She might speak of "the silly habit of exhausting health etc. to augment happiness," but she added, "This being the law, however, it does not become the individual to rebel."

In 1841, concluding that the only hope of financial security lay in James Madison's remaining papers, she returned to Washington. There she tried to salvage her affairs by peddling these documents and mortgaging her Washington house to William Astor—negotiations that necessitated her only trip to New

York City and her first train ride. Later she sold sizable pieces of Montpellier land to Henry W. Moncure of Richmond and rented the mansion to him for three years, in an effort to hold on to the remainder of the plantation to leave to her son. In 1844 a desperate letter from a slave signaled a crisis in her affairs. The slaves were being threatened with being auctioned off, perhaps because James Madison's brother William was suing for the execution of a promissory note that she had unwisely signed. Once informed of this, she sold Montpellier without delay, accepting a standing offer from Moncure. She retained the family burial place, some of the furniture, and "some few of the black people." The other slaves stayed on the plantation.

We know little of Dolley Madison's attitudes toward slavery. Her father had held firm to his antislavery principles, yet she was served by slaves most of her life. Harriet Martineau, quizzing James Madison, listened to him discourse on slavery's evils—he thought colonization the only viable solution—and comment on the burden it placed on conscientious mistresses of slaves like his wife. Obviously the Madison slaves turned to her in their troubles, and she herself owed much to James Madison's body servant Paul Jennings, who stayed on with her in her impoverished widowhood. She eventually sold him to Daniel Webster, who agreed to let him earn his freedom. Jennings later wrote of taking her groceries when she was living "in a state of absolute poverty" and giving her a little money from his own pocket.

Throughout her widowhood her financial situation went from bad to worse, as she borrowed when and where she could. The payments for Montpellier did not come through promptly, apparently because she never understood the need to clarify the title by specifying the exact number of acres sold. She had no head for business and no training in it. Her efforts to demonstrate her trust in her son by involving him in all her transactions only worsened her situation. She could not count on Payne to answer her letters, no matter how frantic her appeals, let alone volunteer information that might have helped her. Only when he needed money could she be sure of hearing from him. At 50, he had decided to go into silk manufacture, buying land in Virginia, beginning an elaborate building program, and importing French silk workers before he had planted mulberry trees. By 1844 he was asking his mother to request an appointment for him as consul at Liverpool; when she complied, President Tyler told her baldly that Payne was not fit for the office. She rarely reproached her son and seldom complained of the way he treated her. In 1845 she turned for consolation to St. John's Church, eventually joining the church that she and her husband had attended when he was president.

Always quiet about her heartbreaks and hardships, Dolley Madison continued to triumph in her busy social life. President Tyler's daughter-in-law and hostess made Dolley her mentor, invited her on all important occasions, and reserved a seat for her in the Tyler carriage. President Polk's wife Sarah, an intelligent, well-educated woman and the first first lady to serve officially as her husband's confidential secretary, sought Dolley's friendship. Secretary of State Daniel Webster's wife frequently sent small gifts and invited her and Anna Payne to dinner. Webster and some friends concocted a scheme to buy her an annuity, but she declined it. She was on board the *Princeton* when a gun exploded, killing several people. At the official celebration of the electric telegraph connecting Baltimore and Washington, immediately after the famous message "What hath God wrought?" came through from Baltimore, Samuel Morse asked Dolley Madison for a message; she sent her love to a friend.

In 1844 the House of Representatives unanimously passed a resolution "that a committee be appointed on the part of this House to wait on Mrs. Madison, and to assure her that, whenever it shall be her pleasure to visit the House, she be requested to take a seat within the Hall." In 1848 she joined Mrs. Hamilton and Louisa Adams in raising funds for the Washington monument and attended the lay-

ELIZABETH KORTRIGHT MONROE
(JUNE 30, 1768–DECEMBER 9, 1830)
First Lady, March 4, 1817–March 4, 1825

ELIZABETH MONROE
(Library of Congress)

Elizabeth Kortright Monroe was formed by the expectations of the New York mercantile society in which she grew up. As a privileged young woman of great beauty, she was expected to marry brilliantly. Many of her friends thought that in choosing James Monroe she had married beneath her. Her understanding of his character and prospects proved better than theirs: She not only enjoyed a devoted marriage with him but also became the first lady in the land. During his two-year term as U.S. minister to France she performed her one notable public deed in her visit to the imprisoned Madame de Lafayette, which resulted in the Frenchwoman's release. In France, too, both the Monroes developed a lasting appreciation of French manners, styles, and formality, on the basis of which they shaped their personal conduct and their social lives in the White House.

Born on June 30, 1768, to Laurence Kortright and his wife Hannah, the second of their five children, Elizabeth Kortright grew up in New York City. Her father was a wealthy Tory merchant of Flemish descent who remained in the United States after the American Revolution. When Elizabeth was nine, her mother died, and she was brought up by her paternal grandmother. As a remarkably beautiful young woman, dark-haired, just five feet tall, and known for the shapeliness of her arms and shoulders, she made her debut in the city's exclusive mercantile society. Though she reigned as a belle, her formal manners struck some people as cold and reserved. She evidently was not close to her family, for after her marriage they rarely wrote to her.

In 1785, when she was 16, Elizabeth Kortright met James Monroe, then a Virginia delegate to the Confederation Congress. They married on February 16, 1786, honeymooned briefly on Long Island, and lived with her father until the congressional session ended. They then went to Fredericksburg, where they settled into a comfortable two-story house. Monroe reluctantly turned to the practice of law to support his family, for though he owned considerable property, including slaves, he was short of cash. Nevertheless, he remained active in state and national politics, confounding those who had "twitted [Elizabeth] with the amiable reflection that she was expected to have done better."

In 1786 Elizabeth Monroe bore the couple's first child, Eliza. Devoted to each other, the Monroes disliked being apart; when he traveled on either business or politics, he took his wife and daughter with him. Summers they lived on their Albemarle farm, which Monroe bought in 1789, near the home of his close friend Thomas Jefferson. Winters they went where Monroe's career took him—whether to try cases before the Court of Appeals in Richmond or, as in 1791, to serve in the U.S. Senate in Philadelphia. In 1794 Elizabeth Monroe's ties to New York were cut when her father died, leaving almost no estate and his affairs in confusion.

That year, too, their lives abruptly changed with Monroe's appointment as U.S. minister to France. They seized the opportunity to master the language, learn elegant French manners and styles, and place their daughter in a French school. They adopted French customs so enthusiastically that they offended some visiting Americans, at least one of whom complained that Elizabeth Monroe had not called on her. James Monroe had to explain that his wife was following the French practice of expecting the visitor to call on her first.

Elizabeth's blue-eyed beauty dazzled the French, who called her *la belle Americaine*. They also came to admire her courage. The Monroes were troubled by Robespierre's imprisonment of and threats to execute Madame de Lafayette, wife of the French aristocrat who had come to America's aid during the American Revolution. Monroe's position constrained him from interfering in the internal affairs of their host country, but he later described his wife's visit:

> Mrs. Monroe drove directly to the prison in which Madame Lafayette was confined. As soon as it [her carriage] entered the street, the public attention was drawn to it, and at the prison gate the crowd gathered around it. Inquiry was made, whose carriage is it? The answer given was, that of the American Minister. Who is in it? His wife. What brought her here? To see Madame Lafayette. . . . On hearing that the wife of the American Minister had called with the most friendly motives to see her, she [Mme de Lafayette] became frantic, and in that state they met. The scene was most affecting. The report of the interview spread through Paris and had the happiest effect. . . . [T]he liberation of Madame LaFayette soon followed.

The Monroes returned to Charlottesville, Virginia, in the early summer of 1797. Out of financial necessity, he resumed his law practice, but he could not stay away from politics, working closely for the next two years with Thomas Jefferson and James Madison in managing the affairs of the Republican Party. In 1799 James Monroe was elected governor of Virginia. That May, Elizabeth Monroe gave birth to a son, who in 1800 fell victim to whooping cough. For a while he improved, and his father—who had to return from Albemarle to Richmond, where yellow fever was raging and a slave insurrection was threatening—sent the family to visit his sister in another county. The little boy died there, leaving his mother prostrate for many months. Their last child, daughter Maria Hester, was born in early 1803.

After three terms as governor, Monroe decided to return to private practice, but he could not resist President Jefferson's request that he accept appointment as envoy extraordinary to France to negotiate what would become known as the Louisiana Purchase. On March 8, 1803, James Monroe, his wife, and their two daughters sailed for France, where daughter Eliza returned to her former boarding school, while the rest of the family settled in Paris. When Monroe's mission was completed in July, they moved to London, where he was to assist in negotiating a treaty to settle British-American disputes over rights on the high seas. After Paris, London disappointed the family. Social relations with the British were tense; the damp, smoky air gave them constant colds; the high cost of living put them in debt; and London officials snubbed them. When Monroe left in late 1804 for yet another diplomatic mission, this time to Madrid to negotiate for Florida, his wife and children happily returned to France to visit friends. They apparently remained there while he went on diplomatic errands in various European capitals. The whole family finally returned to the United States in December 1807, exhausted and ill after a stormy winter Atlantic crossing.

For a couple of years the Monroes lived on his Virginia estate, where their daughter Eliza married George Hay, a distinguished lawyer and Virginia politician. Monroe stepped back into American politics. After an unsuccessful run for the presidency against Madison in 1808, he held successively a seat in the Virginia legislature, the governorship of Virginia, and the positions of secretary of state and secretary of war under President Madison.

In Washington the Monroes' finances necessitated their living plainly—at least by the standards of wealthy Europeans. The British minister commented that they entertained "very sparingly, which does not fail to be commented on in a place where good dinners produce as much effect as in any part of the world." However, the wife of the secretary of the navy found one of their dinners "the most stylish . . . I have been at. . . . The table wider than we have, and in the middle a larger, perhaps silver, waiter, with images . . . and vases filled with flowers, which made a very showy appearance as the candles were lighted when we went to table. The dishes were silver and set round this waiter. The plates were handsome china, the forks silver, and so heavy I could hardly lift them to my mouth, dessert knives silver, and spoons very heavy. . . . Mrs. Monroe is a very elegant woman. She was dressed in a very fine muslin worked in front and lined with pink, and a black velvet turban close and spangled." An editor's wife also commented on Elizabeth Monroe's appearance, remarking that she "paints [uses cosmetics] very much, and has besides an appearance of youth which would induce a stranger to suppose her age to be thirty: in lieu of which she introduces them . . . to her daughter Mrs. Hay of Richmond."

At intervals, the Monroes retreated to their modest home of Oak Hill on an estate that James Monroe had acquired from an uncle, only 30 miles away from Washington, with occasional visits also to their home near Albemarle. Then, in 1816, James Monroe was elected president of the United States. Despite their having "lived 7 years in W[ashington]," reported Margaret Bayard Smith, a resident of the capital city, "both Mr. and Mrs. Monroe are perfect strangers not only to me but all the citizens." However, she added cheerfully, "People seem to think we shall have great changes in social intercourse and customs. Mr. and Mrs. Monroe's manners will give a tone to all the rest." As expected, the Monroes with their French etiquette restored the formality of the Washingtons' times. Stiffness and correctness superseded Thomas Jefferson's republican simplicity and Dolley Madison's spontaneous warmth.

The change suited the diplomatic corps but not most Americans. The announcement that the president's wife would neither make nor return calls but instead would be at home mornings to receive visitors infuriated Washingtonians. Congress seethed. To make matters worse, she delegated the task of receiving most visitors to her daughter, Eliza Monroe Hay. Even in her happy days in Paris, Elizabeth Monroe had been criticized for not entertaining as much as was expected of a diplomat's wife. In the White House she failed to explain her reasons for cutting back: the incomplete renovation of the mansion and her own poor health. A leading newspaper of the day defended her decision. "[Mrs. Monroe's] retired domestic habits will be much annoyed by what is here called society, if she does not change the etiquette (if it may be called so) established by Mrs. Washington, Adams, and Madison. . . . To go through it, she must become a perfect slave to the sacrifice of her health."

As for her formality, she deemed it important to impress European diplomats, to show them that Americans could observe formal European conventions. In the effort to balance elegance with republican principles, she chose an etiquette uncomfortable for the many Americans who feared the trappings of monarchy. They accused her of snobbery and sometimes boycotted her parties. Insulted when she did not appear at White House dinners, officials' wives stopped coming. Louisa Adams, wife of Monroe's secretary of state, suffered much of the resulting acrimony. When the president's wife consulted her, explaining that she needed to conserve her strength, Louisa Adams sympathized, telling her that she must develop her own style. She understood the situation and

herself followed Elizabeth Monroe's practice, returning calls but not initiating them.

Senators, however, could not quite bear to absent themselves from the White House fortnightly drawing rooms. These were open to all who were suitably dressed—a rule that Elizabeth Monroe enforced so rigidly that she turned away one of her relatives whom she judged not properly arrayed. The first drawing room, held on New Year's Day 1818, began at 11:30 A.M. (though later drawing rooms began at 8:00 in the evening). Cabinet wives were ushered into the Oval Room, where President Monroe greeted them and presented them to his wife, who sat in state with a niece and her older daughter Eliza Hay. The Monroes then received the members of the diplomatic corps, in court dress, while their wives were admitted from another room. After an hour, the doors were opened to other guests, and a crowd surged in until 3:00. Servants circulated with wine, tea, and ices.

These receptions at least satisfied American curiosity about the White House and its furnishings. The Monroes used the furniture that they had brought and were still ordering from France: Louis XVI pieces with brass inlays, Empire gilt chairs covered in crimson satin and decorated with gold eagles, French mantelpieces with caryatids, and ormolu clocks. Guests also took stock of Elizabeth Monroe's Parisian clothes, some envying such outfits as a white figured silk dress trimmed with white point lace and topped by a hat with white plumes. Louisa Adams admired Elizabeth's poise, reserve, and skills as a hostess, which Louisa judged appropriate to the station, but she knew that most Washington ladies thought the president's wife haughty and cold. "Tastes differ," Mrs. Adams wrote, "and Dear Dolly was much more popular." In truth, Dolley Madison was an impossible act to follow.

White House dinners were usually for men, but either Elizabeth Monroe or her older daughter presided when ladies were invited. The guests, arriving at 4:00 or 5:00 P.M., were greeted by the president in the Oval Room. The president then took in to dinner the lady nearest him, and either the vice president or a cabinet member escorted the hostess. Servants handed around the food, which sometimes left guests hungry. Harrison Gray Otis, a gentleman of the old school, wrote to his wife: "I dined at the palace, and at the right hand of the Queen who was most exceedingly gracious and conversible, and I believe has no colour but what is natural, at least her colour very much increased during dinner time in the glow of occupation and attention to her guests. . . . A very superb dinner and much less funereal ceremony than common." Otherwise the Monroes stood apart from social life, usually accepting only invitations to ceremonial affairs, like the annual birthday balls for former president Washington.

Their older daughter Eliza Monroe Hay and her husband, one of President Monroe's advisers, lived in the White House, over which Eliza reigned supreme. Regrettably, her French schooling among aristocrats had turned her into a snob. She had no idea of how to conciliate people, nor did she want to. Instead, as virtual mistress of the White House she stirred up quarrels and inflamed hurt feelings, to the point that squabbles at local gatherings became matters for cabinet consideration. Some thought she deliberately fomented dissension to protect her own position. Early in her father's presidency, she caused trouble among the diplomatic corps—who regarded her as a private person with no official position—by insisting that the foreign ministers' wives pay the first call. When they did not, she refused invitations to their parties. Illogically, she insisted that she must not be given special treatment as the president's daughter, but she expected to receive it as the wife of her husband, a private citizen.

Louisa Adams described Eliza Hay as so "full of agreeables and disagreeables, so accomplished and ill bred, so proud and mean," with such a "love for scandal that no reputation is safe in her hands." Secretary of State John Quincy Adams reported one of her rude comments. When several callers in succession inquired after his wife, "Mrs. Hay after hearing me answer the same question four or five times . . . at last broke out 'Lord!' said she, 'how tiresome such questions are! Last winter one evening at the drawing room after Mr. Hay went to Richmond a hundred and fifty people came up to me one after the other asking when did you hear from Mr. Hay and how is Mr. Hay? At last I said to one of them—He's *dead!*—I have just got the news.—He's *dead!* And buried! And the subject is *so distressing* that I will thank my friends to say no more to me about him.'"

To a remarkable degree the Monroes lived in seclusion, although members of their extended families often visited for long periods. In 1820, when their younger daughter Maria Hester married her cousin Samuel L. Gouverneur at the White House, the family sent the secretary of state to explain to official Washington that they would limit the guest list for this first White House wedding to 42, as the bride wished. Eliza Hay, adding insult to injury, decided that wives of the diplomatic corps should not call on the newly married Gouverneurs, since they refused to call on her. Once again the president had to dispatch the secretary of state, this time to tell the ambassadors that the Gouverneurs would welcome their wives. To soothe hurt feelings, the Monroes planned a series of balls, the first of which, at the home of Commodore Stephen Decatur, succeeded brilliantly, but Decatur's death the next day in a duel necessitated the cancellation of the rest out of respect for this national hero.

Gradually, Washington society came to accept Elizabeth Monroe's social decisions. Her persistence succeeded, and her practices were emulated by her successors in the White House. Even at the end of the 20th century, the president and first lady rarely accept private invitations, and formal calls are a thing of the past. Louisa Adams's advice to Elizabeth Monroe to go her own way proved to be sound.

During her husband's second term, Elizabeth's health deteriorated, and her public appearances grew even more infrequent. In 1825, after the inauguration of President John Quincy Adams, she was too sick to move immediately, and it was some time before the Monroes left Washington for Oak Hill. The strain of the presidency had also told on Monroe. His years of public service had eroded his wealth, but he took up agriculture with some success. The Hay family had moved with the Monroes, and Eliza Hay assumed management of household affairs on the plantation. The younger daughter, Maria Gouverneur, who lived in New York, visited only rarely, possibly because she did not get on with her older sister. However, Elizabeth Monroe was able to make an extended visit to her younger daughter and the grandchildren on whom she doted in the fall of 1825.

At Oak Hill, the Monroes entertained such notable guests as Lafayette and President Adams, but they were spared the hordes of visitors who had inundated the Washingtons, Jefferson, and the Madisons in their retirement. Unfortunately their quiet life failed to restore Elizabeth's health, which continued to deteriorate. Despite a short rally, on September 23, 1830, she died. Eliza Hay, whose husband had died two days earlier, reached her mother's side just in time, but the summons to Maria Gouverneur went out too late. Elizabeth Monroe was buried at Oak Hill, but in 1903 her body was moved with that of her husband to Hollywood Cemetery in Richmond, Virginia, to lie beside that of her husband.

—⁓—

Elizabeth Monroe was a first lady little known and much misunderstood by her contemporaries. Today she is a first lady whom nobody knows. She ordered all her papers burned, and only one of her husband's letters to her survives. He occasionally mentioned her in his letters to other people, but, true to his times, he protected the privacy of their life together, and he gives no hint of whether they ever talked about the public business. The newspaper accounts of her in the Washington years tell mainly of her official appearances. People who saw her at dinner parties and drawing rooms left few impressions of her. Louisa Adams knew and liked her, but apparently was far from intimate with her. No account of her was left by either her imperious older daughter Eliza Hay or her shy younger daughter Maria Gouverneur. She was a first lady whom the public admired but did not love.

CHRONOLOGY

1768   *June 30:* Elizabeth Kortright is born in New York City

1786   *February 15:* Elizabeth marries Virginian lawyer-legislator James Monroe

1786   *December:* daughter Eliza Kortright is born

1790   James Monroe is elected to the U.S. Senate

1794   President John Adams sends Monroe to France

1796   President Adams recalls Monroe

1799   James Monroe becomes governor of Virginia

1799   *May:* Son James Spence is born

1800   Son James Spence dies at 16 months

1803   Daughter Maria Hester is born

President Jefferson sends James Monroe to France, London, and Madrid

1807   The Monroes return to the United States

1808   James Madison defeats James Monroe in the presidential election

1808   Daughter Eliza marries George Hay, lawyer and politician

1809   Daughter Eliza bears the Monroes' first grandchild, Hortensia Hay

1811   Monroe again becomes governor of Virginia but resigns in March to accept appointment as secretary of state

| 1816 | James Monroe is elected president | 1825 | The Monroes move to Oak Hill, Loudoun County, Virginia |
| 1817 | Elizabeth Kortright Monroe becomes first lady | 1830 | *September 23:* Elizabeth Monroe dies |

FURTHER READING

Ammon, Harry. *James Monroe: The Quest for National Identity.* Charlottesville: University of Virginia Press, 1971.

Logan, Mrs. John A. *Thirty Years in Washington, or Life and Scenes in Our National Capital.* Hartford: A. D. Worthington, 1901.

Minniegerode, Meade. *Some American Ladies: Seven Informal Biographies.* New York: Putnam, 1926.

Sandak, Cass R. *The Monroes.* New York: Crestwood, 1993.

Wooton, James E. *Elizabeth Kortright Monroe.* Charlottesville, Va.: Ash Lawn-Highland, 1987.

LOUISA CATHERINE JOHNSON ADAMS

(FEBRUARY 12, 1775–MAY 15, 1852)
First Lady, March 4, 1825–March 4, 1829

LOUISA ADAMS
(Library of Congress)

Daughter-in-law of the overwhelming Abigail Adams and wife of the formidable John Quincy Adams, Louisa Johnson Adams underrated her own courage, talents, and adaptability. The contemporary ideal of women, combined with her father's business failure, Abigail Adams's harsh criticism of her in the early years of her marriage, and her husband's refusal to discuss business with her fatally undermined her self-confidence and kept her from being all that she could have been. She titled the parts of her journal she chose to publish "Adventures of a Nobody." Nevertheless, she thought for herself. She was an accomplished translator of the classics, a creator of prose and poetry, and a perceptive critic of people and politics. A scholarly, intelligent woman, she struggled against and protested the restrictions imposed on the women of her day.

Louisa Catherine Johnson was born in London on February 12, 1775. Joshua Johnson, her American merchant father, and Catherine Nuth Johnson, her English mother, had seven daughters, of whom Louisa was the second, and one son. In 1778 the family moved to Nantes. There Louisa attended a convent school, where she acquired a thorough knowledge of French, a love of French literature, and a Roman Catholic outlook. In 1783 her father returned to London as American consul. In both France and England, the family lived in luxury and high style. Their excellent food, entertainment, and conversation—all offered in a beautiful setting—attracted many American guests.

Louisa's parents, recognizing her talents as superior to those of their other children, encouraged her to develop them, particularly in music and literature. She wrote prose and poetry, sang, and played the piano and the harp. She was presented at court. Her portrait at 18 shows her as petite, barely over five feet tall, with a fair complexion, hazel eyes, and curly red hair. Her father worried about her, fearful that she might develop unrealistic standards and expectations. Her insistence on excellence made her critical of others and hesitant to perform for fear that she might not measure up.

In 1795, 28-year-old John Quincy Adams, in London on a diplomatic errand, was introduced to the Johnson family. By February 1796 he was paying marked attention to Louisa, though he was so awkward with women that the family thought for a while that he was wooing her older sister. He impressed Louisa and her mother: He was, after all, the son of the vice president of the United States, a brilliant young man educated from childhood for high position. They did not yet recognize his insensitivity to the emotions and reactions of others.

The courtship was marked by quarrels and misunderstandings. Her father doubted that he was the man for her. His mother got wind of the courtship and did everything she could from faraway Massachusetts to deter him. John Quincy must not, Abigail Adams advised, let Louisa's beauty blind him to her inexperience, the difference in their temperaments, and her European upbringing. As her descendant Henry Adams remarked, Abigail Adams's judgment on this matter was sound, but "sound judgment is sometimes a source of weakness rather than of force and John Quincy already had reason to think that his mother held sound judgments on the subject of daughters-in-law which human nature, since the fall of Eve, made Adams helpless to realize."

Worse still, the young couple held different perceptions of marriage. Her parents' example had led her to believe that spouses were mutually attentive and considerate and that they encouraged and understood their children. His parents' example of marriage as a partnership had apparently taught him nothing. Neither his mother's views on female rights nor her accomplishments and abilities had instilled in him a genuine respect for women. Perhaps because he was eight years older than Louisa, he would insist on having his own way as her husband, regardless of whatever suffering it might cause her.

However, by May 1796 John Quincy had "coaxed [Louisa] into an affection for him" sufficient for her to consent to marry him. Then this prudent and ambitious man sailed to The Hague, postponing their marriage indefinitely on the grounds of insufficient money. Even her suggestion that she could continue to live with her family for a time after they married did not change his decision. Instead, he wrote her grumpy letters of admonition, instructing her to accept such "untoward Events" as their separation "as a test of character." At times she protested spiritedly against his "commanding" tone and repudiated his "boasted philosophy," but usually she wrote patiently and lovingly. Now and then she resorted to mockery and hints, as when she wrote to him of her dislike for Lord Chesterfield's condescension toward women. Even when her fiancé provoked her into losing her temper and telling him that their engagement had been one long lesson in restraint and philosophy, she still assured him that she admired his abilities and wanted to earn his esteem.

Finally, others forced a decision. President Washington's reassignment of John Quincy to Portugal, at a higher salary, undermined the young man's argument that he could not afford marriage, while his mother capitulated rather than have her 30-year-old son live in Portugal unmarried. Further, Louisa's father countered every reason not to marry that John Quincy set forth, even offering to supply a ship to carry the couple to Lisbon. (In the event, Adams was reassigned to Berlin and never served in Portugal.) Adams agreed to a wedding date of July 26, 1797, but on his return to London he created more unhappiness by waiting two days before he called on Louisa.

Nonetheless they honeymooned blissfully. John Quincy Adams confessed in his diary that "several circumstances occur to frustrate my intention of steady early rising." They rose about nine, breakfasted, and read and wrote until after noon. In the afternoon they walked and visited friends or bookshops. After their 5:00 P.M. dinner, they rested, read aloud until 10:00, ate a light supper about 11:00, and went to bed.

Soon, however, the newlyweds had to face disappointment and embarrassment. Joshua Johnson had failed in business and fled to the United States, leaving them to face his creditors. Louisa feared that people might think her father had deceived her husband into marrying a penniless daughter, and for years thereafter she suffered from depressions that resulted in physical illnesses.

In Berlin, Louisa attracted many friends with her beauty and social graces. Despite her poor health, devastating miscarriages, and inadequate housing, she liked court life, with its receptions, balls, operas, card parties, and military reviews. She enjoyed dancing with her new brother-in-law, Thomas Adams, as her escort. Even her dour husband on their first anniversary recorded in his diary that "from the loveliness of temper and excellence of character of my wife, I account it the happiest year of my life."

He was proud of her popularity, but he worried that she might say something to embarrass him. He refused to discuss the issues of the day with her as she would have liked, insisting that they were not fit subjects for women. They also quarreled occasionally over such issues as whether or not she might wear rouge.

On April 12, 1801, after five miscarriages, they exulted in the birth of a son, George Washington Adams. She endured a terrible delivery at the hands of a drunken midwife, which left her left leg paralyzed for five weeks. But she rejoiced that she had at last been able to give her husband the son he longed for. Three months later, the Adamses sailed for the United States.

Louisa Adams had yet to meet her new country and her husband's family. With his usual bluntness, her husband confessed to her on the voyage home his former love for another young woman, leaving her feeling inferior to his earlier sweetheart. On landing, they separated, he traveling to the Adams home in Quincy, Massachusetts, while she went to visit her family in Washington. She found them impoverished and humiliated, her father so broken in spirit and body that he did not even recognize her.

In late October 1801 John Quincy Adams finally came to fetch his wife and son. Together the couple dined at the White House and were warmly entertained at Mount Vernon by the widowed Martha Washington. They traveled from Washington to Quincy in bitter weather, she suffering from a cold and the baby from diarrhea. When she at last met her husband's family, they staggered her. "Had I step[p]ed into Noah's Ark, I do not think I would have been more utterly astonished. . . . Do what I would there was a conviction on the part of the others that I could not *suit*." Although they welcomed her, she felt they thought her "a maudlin, hysterical fine lady not fit to be John Quincy Adams' wife." Crucially, she was not Abigail Adams. As the young wife wrote, her mother-in-law "was in every point of view a superior Woman . . . the equal of every occasion in life," who "forms a most striking contrast to poor me." Only her father-in-law, she felt, truly liked her.

Instead of the aristocratic European circles in which she felt at home, Louisa Adams had to accommodate herself to American ways, "a forlorn stranger," she wrote, "in the land of my Fathers." In Quincy, for the first time in her life she was expected to spend her days feeding and caring for her husband and child. With relief she moved to Boston in late December 1801, visiting her in-laws as seldom as she dared. In her own home she had the solace of a sister's company. Here she could run her household with minimal interference from her mother-in-law. She began to build an independent life, attending legislative sessions and making new friends, such as the historian Hannah Adams; entertaining her husband's associates; and showing off her talents as hostess. In January 1803 she gave a party for 40 guests so brilliant that they stayed after midnight, and even her husband danced the whole evening. In July that year she bore a second son, John, named after her father-in-law.

Late that year John Quincy Adams's election to the Senate took his wife and sons to Washington. She loved living there with her mother and sisters in her brother-in-law's house. Even when all their menfolk were away and Cherokee Indians stopped at the remotely situated house, refusing to leave, she was not fazed: She delighted the invaders by playing the piano for them and giving them ribbons before sending them on their way, happy. She indulged in two of her favorite amusements, horseback riding and going to the race track. Her relations with Abigail Adams improved, as they corresponded about John Quincy's disregard for his health and dress; Abigail was delighted when Louisa bought her husband a horse to encourage him to exercise. Consequently, when he announced that he could no longer afford two households, assuming that his family must stay in Massachusetts year-round, his wife said that in that case she would remain in Washington. They quarreled, and he stamped off northward. He blinked first, admitting in a letter that "I never can be happy distant from you" and that he could neither sleep nor concentrate.

They clashed over their place of residence for years. When he rejoined her in October 1804, she reluctantly agreed that they would live in Quincy in the summer and Washington in the winter, but that their sons would be educated in Quincy throughout the year. Nonetheless, in summer 1806 she remained in Washington to have a baby while he taught rhetoric at Harvard. Her baby was stillborn—another disappointment to add to the series of miscarriages that she experienced throughout her childbearing years. (In her first 13 years of marriage, she was pregnant 11 times.) Soon pregnant again, she agreed to spend the coming winter in the Boston house that her husband had just bought, happy in the prospect of a reunion with her sons and John Quincy's talk of leaving the Senate.

On August 18, 1807, Louisa was delivered of another son, whom they named Charles Francis Adams. She and the baby returned to Washington that autumn, but in spring 1808 John Quincy Adams resigned from the Senate after he had outraged his Massachusetts supporters by voting for certain Jeffersonian policies. Now, he said, he would teach at Harvard, practice law, and write. His wife thought this far better than enduring more years in politics, where calumny followed principled action.

She was horrified when, in 1809, he told her that he had accepted the post of minister plenipotentiary to Russia, that she must accompany him, and that their two older sons must remain in Massachusetts. She never forgave him, for she believed that he had forced her to sin by abandoning her responsibilities as a parent. "To the end of time," she wrote bitterly, "life to me will be a succession of miseries only to cease with existence."

Not surprisingly, she hated Russia, speaking of the "sterile heartlessness of a Russian residence of icy coldness." For half the year the weather prevented her from even corresponding with her sons. During her six-year absence, her mother and older sister died, while another sister found herself disgraced by an out-of-wedlock pregnancy by a nephew of John Quincy

Adams. In his new post, the minister plenipotentiary withdrew into worry and study. The Adamses' relationship deteriorated, as he grew ever more critical and intolerant. Louisa struggled to run her household of "five indifferent chambers" and perform her duties as the wife of a diplomat on "the meanness of an American Ministers position at a European Court,"—that is, the inadequacy of his pay. Managing their 14 thieving servants tried her patience and her slender budget.

In 1810 John Quincy Adams described their exhausting schedule: "We rise seldom earlier than nine in the morning—often not before ten. Breakfast. Visits to receive, or visits to make, until three, soon after which the night comes on. At four we dine, and pass the evening either abroad until very late, or at our lodgings with company until ten or eleven o'clock. The night parties abroad seldom break up until four or five o'clock in the morning." They had to attend a multitude of ceremonial occasions: court balls, church festivals, launchings, civic fetes, and visits to schools, factories, and charitable institutions. Louisa Adams lived in Russia, she said, "as a stranger to all but the kind regards of the Imperial family," with whom the Adamses became good friends. As favorites of the czar they received his protection, and his friendship helped John Quincy Adams in his diplomatic mission.

In August 1811 Louisa bore another child. To her delight, the baby was a daughter, whom they named Louisa Catherine after her mother and maternal grandmother. In her joy at having a little girl, she was ready to be reconciled even to life in Russia. "Such a pair of eyes!!" she wrote. "I fear I love her too well." But the baby died in agony of dysentery at the age of 13 months. To spare her husband, Louisa bore up publicly, but privately she grieved to the point that she faltered in her religious faith and began to question her own sanity. Gradually she found distraction in reading, especially the memoirs of women, and in collecting recipes both for food and for home remedies.

In 1814 Adams was reassigned to London to negotiate the treaty ending the War of 1812. Since he expected to return in a year, he went alone. Just before his departure, he became more open with his wife, even deciding that she could handle practical matters and giving her a copy of his will, which named her as executrix for his European affairs. They corresponded frequently and fondly. Her letters show that she was evaluating their marriage. She told him that coping with a man past 40 was so uninspiring as to make a wife sink "into absolute silence or gaping for want of something better to do," yet she had to think up ways to keep him from falling asleep in his chair. How sad it was, she wrote, that they were happy only when apart, the only times when he treated her as an intelligent confidante. Had he taken a mistress, she teasingly asked, for after all "a woman of my age cannot be jealous." But she also told him how she longed for him.

In December 1814 she was astonished—and delighted—to receive a summons to meet him in Paris, whence they would soon move to London. She had to sell most of their possessions, ship their books, and prepare to cross difficult terrain and dangerous territory in the midst of winter. She left St. Petersburg in mid-February 1815 with seven-year-old Charles Francis, a maid, and two male servants, traveling in a Russian coach mounted on runners. Their food, which they had to carry with them, froze solid, even the wine, and had to be melted with candles. Once or twice the carriage sank so deep in the snow that it had to be dug out. At one stop she heard of a frightful murder on the road the night before and was warned that her manservant Baptiste was a notorious villain, but she had promised to take him to France and she decided—"from a proud and foolhardy spirit"—to go on. They lost their way, their horses were exhausted, the wheels that they eventually substituted for runners did not fit properly and broke, and the lodgings were unspeakable. They crossed the Vistula over ice so thin that men had to walk ahead of them with sounding poles to test its safety. Baptiste grew insolent and improved only slightly when she threatened to fire him, keeping, she said, "something in his look that did not please me, but I was afraid to notice it." She kept her moneybags hidden, hoping the servants would think she drew only enough at each town for the next stretch.

After a refreshing week with old friends in Berlin, she drove on through Prussia, then overrun by unemployed veterans of the Napoleonic wars. To escape insult and annoyance, she wore Charles Francis's toy soldier hat with a big plume and displayed his toy sword. She had to drive through fields covered with corpses. At Eisenach she heard that Napoleon had returned to France, and at Frankfurt her two male servants deserted her. She went on with only a Prussian lad of 14 as her courier. Even though she detoured to avoid the soldiers rallying to Napoleon, troop movements delayed her. Near Epernay, members of Napoleon's Imperial Guard accosted her, accusing her of being Russian. But by waving an American flag and crying *"Vive l'Empereur,"* she made her way through the undisciplined drunken rabble. She also invented a story that she was Napoleon's sister going to meet him. After an uneasy night during which stragglers pounded on the door of her inn, she learned that 40,000 troops had assembled around Paris, her destination, and a battle was impending. "This news," she wrote, "startled me very much, but on cool reflection I thought it best to persevere. I was traveling at great expense, a thing quite unsuited to the paltry salary of an American Minister, and I was sure that if there was any danger Mr. Adams would have come to meet me."

They arrived safely on March 23, 1815, and her nonchalant account of their six-week journey astounded her husband and the diplomatic corps. "I have really acquired the reputation of a heroine at a very cheap rate," she wrote. Two decades later she wrote a narrative of her adventure, to show "that energy and discretion follow the necessity of their exertion, to protect the fancied weakness of feminine imbecility." Women should use their abilities, she said. "Under all circumstances we must never desert ourselves."

After all her travails, Louisa relaxed in a Paris rejoicing at the return of Napoleon. With her husband she watched the emperor enter the city and saw him again at the theater. They visited Lafayette and enjoyed a round of dinners, balls, concerts, and art galleries. They then sailed for London, where John Quincy Adams served as American minister and where their two older sons rejoined them. For two happy years the reunited family enjoyed the city and each other's company.

In spring 1817 President Monroe appointed John Quincy Adams his secretary of state, thereby positioning him to run for president. The Adamses thus reentered the "Bull Bait" of political life that Louisa detested. She did her best to lighten their lives, trying to distract her husband from his strict regime and the despondency into which the political hurly-burly that he could not resist always cast him. Her ease in society balanced his dullness, while her experience and accomplishments strengthened his bid for the highest office in the land. She paid and received innumerable calls, making friends of the congressional wives whose husbands had the power to nominate the president. She entertained and was entertained. She played the piano and the harp and recited her own plays and poems. Refuting charges of snobbishness, she opened the Adams home on Tuesday evenings for parties so pleasurable that no one could stay away. She captivated even her husband, once luring him into an impromptu reel with her and their boys after their guests had left.

Her letters to her in-laws in Quincy included stories of these activities as well as her shrewd, satiric, and sometimes cynical political comments. By now her relations with her mother-in-law had improved a great deal. Abigail apologized for having misjudged her, and Louisa confessed to her diary that she should have listened to Abigail's efforts to instruct her and had failed to realize what "a kind and affectionate mother" Abigail could be.

Louisa Adams's January 1824 ball for General Andrew Jackson on the anniversary of his New Orleans victory was the talk of the town, helping her husband in his campaign for the presidency. But that campaign, in which Adams defeated Jackson, embittered both men. It dismayed Adams's wife, who thought her husband too intelligent for such a squalid affair. Supporters of the other three candidates charged that he had won the election unfairly and portrayed both Adamses as deceitful and gloating.

Although Louisa gave a grand reception on her husband's inaugural day in 1825, and both later attended a ball, the Adamses moved into the White House desponding. Her husband's depression over being elected by a minority of the popular vote clouded everything. To add to her troubles, menopause was affecting her health and making her morbid. The mansion itself did nothing to alleviate her unhappiness; she described it as a "half-finished barn" littered with rubbish. The only running water came from attic cisterns of rain, on which the two toilets depended, and no space was provided for bathing. Even 16 maids and several other servants could not keep the place clean and look after guests.

She did her best to brighten the atmosphere with music, poetry, and amateur theatrics, but it was uphill work. Her husband preferred reading alone to attending official social functions. Continuing charges of a stolen election and the frustration of his administration's programs depressed him, sometimes provoking him to take out his anger on her. She contrasted his treatment of her with the equal partnerships enjoyed by her mother and mother-in-law, fearing that the relationship between the sexes was decaying. Surely, she thought, the Almighty did not intend woman to endure "the undermining scorn of her companion." Their marriage lapsed into a three-year estrangement, during which she refused to join her husband on his Quincy vacations. Her psychological state made her vulnerable to one illness after another. The White House to her became a "dull and stately prison in which the sounds of mirth are seldom heard," where it was "impossible for me to feel at home or to fancy that I have a home anywhere."

All this destroyed her zest for entertaining, so that even though she arranged dinners for 30 or more guests, she often did not attend them. As first lady she resorted to a rather formal and rigid routine, in the pattern of Elizabeth Monroe, holding levees once a week and later reducing them to once a fortnight. She also gave large weekly dinners and occasionally invited in a smaller group for the evening. Otherwise she saw few visitors and seldom went out into society, living in "the dreadful tedium of an almost entire solitude." As time wore on and her health worsened, she retreated more and more into her own interests, reading and writing poetry, enjoying music, and breeding silkworms.

The Adamses acquired a reputation for hauteur and reserve that they could not dispel. In December 1828 one of their political enemies wrote, "Mr. and Mrs. Adams have gone a little too far in this *assumed* gaiety[;] at the last drawing room they laid aside the manners which until now they have always worn and came out in a brilliant masquerade dress of social, gay, frank, cordial manners. What a change from the silent, repulsive, haughty reserve by which they have hitherto been distinguished. The great audience chamber, never before opened, and now not finished was thrown open for *dancing,* a thing unheard of before at a drawing-room!" A quarter of the congressmen refused to pay even courtesy calls on them.

Family members were also going through private troubles. In 1817 John and Louisa Adams had taken in her sister's three orphaned children, who moved into the White House with them. Louisa found her two nephews playing amorous games with a "bold and cunning minx" of a chambermaid, but it was impossible to say whether they or she was the most "wheedled and dastardized." Her niece, Mary Catherine, a capricious young woman with "alluring ways which are apt to make every man forget himself," became engaged to the Adamses' son George. Finding that he apparently did not mean to wed for four to six years, Mary Catherine grew impatient and broke off her engagement in order to marry George's younger brother John, who had been expelled from Harvard in 1823. Louisa Adams subsequently wrote to her son Charles Francis: "I shall . . . only announce to you the fact that the wedding is over, that Madame is cool, easy, and indifferent as ever and that John looks already as if he had had all the cares of the world upon his shoulders and my heart tells me that there is much to fear." The young people honeymooned at the White House, where their child Mary Louisa Adams was born late in 1828.

Only when John Quincy Adams came to the bitter realization that he would not be reelected in 1828 did his wife rally. Once again he needed her support, and she prevented his allowing his ne'er-do-well brother Thomas and his wife to live with them. In spring 1829 their oldest son George, having neglected the family business interests in Boston for which he was responsible and impregnated a servant girl, either jumped or fell from a steamer and was drowned. Once again his mother stifled her own sorrow to comfort her husband, until in August she suffered an outburst of grief so strong that she could not even attend Charles Francis's wedding that fall.

Leaving the White House cured her despondency. By the summer of 1830, this strong woman was settling happily in the old Adams mansion in Quincy, helping her husband in his library and the garden, going fishing, and filling the evenings with music and conversation.

That fall she learned with dismay that her husband wanted to accept a proposal to run for Congress. For a short time she resisted, saying she would never return to Washington, that she could not face again the "mortification and agony" of politics. But in the end her recognition of the benefits his service would bring to the nation changed her mind. He ran, won, and launched a second career that lasted until his death, enduring calumny and the fury of his congressional colleagues in his struggle for the right of petition (redress of grievances) and against slavery. Eventually, under the influence of the great abolitionist and feminist Sarah

Grimké, Louisa also embraced abolitionism, coming to see that the oppression of blacks and of women sprang from the same motives.

Family matters brought both sorrow and joy to the Adamses. The financial responsibility for his alcoholic brother Thomas's family that his father's will had forced on John Quincy drained his resources. After Thomas's early death, Louisa watched over his demanding widow, finally nursing her through her tortured last illness. She efficiently managed the family households in Washington and Quincy, often crowded with needy relatives. She tried to help her sisters, who either died young or lived impoverished, difficult lives, and lovingly tended her hypochondriac brother Thomas. She worried over her alcoholic son John and the sufferings he inflicted on his wife. Her husband's insistence that she stay away from John's deathbed intensified her grief; it was the last occasion when she allowed her husband to override her own judgment.

On the other hand, her niece Mary Catherine, who had broken off her engagement to the Adamses' son George to marry his brother John, matured into a devoted woman who cared for her aunts in their old age and provided her aunt Louisa with delightful granddaughters. Louisa Adams found another happy relationship with Abby Brooks, the wife of Charles Francis. Spurning the example of her own mother-in-law, she welcomed her son's wife into the family. She helped Abby with her several children and warned Charles Francis of the hazards of too frequent pregnancies and the need of a young mother for a husband's tender care. She built up Abby's self-confidence, turning over the management of the Adams mansion in Quincy to her and advising her to ignore the suggestion of John Quincy Adams: "Accustomed to rule with sovereign sway," Louisa wrote of her husband, "he is not sufficiently considerate of female comfort which to him has always been a 'secondary consideration.'" Women, she told Abby, should throw off "the thraldom of the *mind,* which has been so long, and so unjustly shackled," and "preach the equality which God originally assigned to the Sexes as it regards intellectual capacity." Do not "deprecate your own talents," she advised.

She was teaching Abby the principles at which she had arrived after a lifetime of painful experience and serious thought. Although she considered the possibility of opening the worlds of business and politics to women, she rejected it as unworkable; it might inspire in women the same greed and selfishness that she believed characterized men, and the attraction between the sexes would disrupt public affairs. Instead, lovingly and compassionately, as respected wives and mothers, they should guide and educate their menfolk, restoring the kind of marriages of equal partnership that had existed, she thought, in the generation before hers—as in the marriages of her mother and mother-in-law.

Throughout the 18 years of his service in Congress, Louisa Adams watched her husband expend his energy and health, battling for the American people and their right of petition. As always when he was absorbed in public business, he often ignored her, so much that she wrote, "My situation is peculiar . . . never listened to." In time she developed a new independence and began to entertain a growing circle of friends. After the election of a new president of his own party restored John Quincy Adams to some of the dignity due his long service to his country and the high offices he had held, she revived her talent as a hostess, often entertaining more than 200 guests.

In Quincy, where they lived when the Congress was not in session, she worked side by side with her husband in a struggle to put in order his masses of papers and books. They still squabbled, she complaining that she was too old and feeble to keep up with his impatient demands that she find lost papers or move faster. Even in their 70s, she kept trying to change him. Vexed with his daily swims in the Potomac, she protested: "I have a reverence for age in its weakness, but no sympathy for that pretension which leads us to exploits unbefitting its dignity and beyond its strength." She never gave up, telling her son Charles, "He is

a man with whom you cannot temporise, and the didactic tone is the only one which can be operative. The little attentions which are mere commonplaces in the world are utterly lost upon a man who thinks it a great deal of offence to be asked to change his coat or to put on a clean shirt."

John Quincy Adams had been born and bred for public service. He collapsed on duty in the Capitol on February 21, 1848, and died two days later without recovering consciousness. His widow wrote to her sister:

> It has pleased the Almighty in his perfect wisdom to teach me this sad lesson for so long repining at our continued perseverance in Public life; which I began to think almost a calamity, in consequence of the creeping infirmities of age which were evidently unfitting us for the fatigues and anxieties attendant upon Public duties and the irregular habits which it necessarily produces. I lived in constant apprehensions of its ill effects, and alas my fears have been too fully realized. But the idea of quitting public life as long as he had the power of acting and the mind to sustain him was so fixed, it only worried him to suggest the wish, and he would constantly answer 'that he should die the moment he gave it up.' . . . but O can anything compensate for the agony of this last sad parting on Earth, after fifty years of union. . . . My senses almost gave way and it seemed as if I had become callous to suffering while my heart seemed breaking. . . . I fear I had indulged presumptuous hopes which blinded me to his real situation.

It had been an odd marriage. She had grown up in luxury; he had grown up in a household where frugality governed every expenditure. From the beginning he had placed his public duty above her happiness. From the beginning she had felt guilt, first because of her father's financial reverses, second because she could not conform to the Adamses' expectations of her, particularly those of her husband. With her British mother and European upbringing, she did not think herself suited to be an American. She and her husband squabbled over money, over how to raise their sons, over where they should live. For years she tried to break her husband's habit of censuring women for both their manner and their nature. Both husband and wife did what they perceived as their duty, but all too often their perceptions and their desires were at cross purposes. He led a fulfilling life; she did not.

Louisa Adams lived on in Washington, summering in Quincy until in 1849 a stroke reduced her to a state of "quiet and contended infirmity." In *The Education of Henry Adams* her grandson remembered her as "The Madam," who, he said,

> was a little more remote than the President [John Quincy Adams], but more decorative. She . . . seemed a fragile creature to a boy who sometimes brought her a note or a message, and took distinct pleasure in looking at her delicate face under what seemed to him very becoming caps. He liked her refined figure; her gentle voice and manner; her vague effect of not belonging there, but to Washington or to Europe, like her furniture, and writing-desk with little glass doors above and little eighteenth-century volumes in old binding, labelled "Peregrine Pickle" or "Tom Jones" or "Hannah More." Try as she might, the Madam could never be Bostonian, and it was her cross in life.

Louisa Adams had once thought that for life to be tolerable it must be an *"agrément"* sparkling with *"les folies brilliantes,* which give a playful varnish to the sombre colouring of real life." Time had taught her otherwise, though even after her hearing and memory faltered, she remained lively and witty. Her daughter-in-law Mary Catherine looked after her until her death on May 15, 1852. Congress adjourned to attend her funeral. She was buried temporarily in the Congressional Cemetery, but later that year her only surviving son, Charles Francis, moved her remains to the First Church of Quincy.

Louisa Adams's marriage forced her into public life, for which neither her temperament nor her health suited her. Her upbringing abroad left her feeling an outsider in the United States. Her critical intelligence found no outlet in the roles assigned her. She performed her duties as wife of the American representative to Prussia, Russia, and England and as first lady, sometimes brilliantly, sometimes indifferently. She brought to the position of first lady beauty, intellect, wit, and the graceful sophistication learned at the courts of Europe, but she did not shine in the White House. She set no new standards there but conformed to the patterns of her immediate predecessor, Elizabeth Monroe.

CHRONOLOGY

1775   *February 12:* Louisa Catherine Johnson is born in London

1795   Louisa Johnson meets John Quincy Adams

1796   Louisa Johnson accepts John Quincy's proposal

1797   Louisa marries John Quincy Adams at Church of All Hallows, Barking, England

1798   The Adamses arrive in Berlin, where John Quincy Adams is to negotiate a treaty with the king of Prussia

1801   *April 12:* Son George Washington is born; John Quincy Adams is recalled to the United States

1802   John Quincy Adams is elected to the Massachusetts Senate

1803   Son John is born; John Quincy Adams is elected to the U.S. Senate and the family moves to Washington

1806   A son is born but dies a few days later

1807   *August 18:* Son Charles Francis is born

1809   President Madison appoints John Quincy Adams minister plenipotentiary to Russia

1811   *August 12:* Daughter Louisa Catherine is born

1812	*September 15:* Daughter Louisa Catherine dies
1814	John Quincy Adams goes to Ghent on a diplomatic mission, but Louisa Adams remains in Russia
1815	Louisa Adams travels alone across Europe to Paris
	May 16: The Adamses depart for London, where John Quincy Adams is to be minister to England
1817	*April:* President Monroe appoints John Quincy Adams his secretary of state
1824	John Quincy Adams is elected president
1825	*March 4:* Louisa Adams becomes first lady
1829	Son George dies
	March 3: The Adamses leave the White House
1830	John Quincy Adams is elected to the House of Representatives, where for 18 years he champions abolitionism
1848	*February 23:* John Quincy Adams dies
1852	*May 15:* Louisa Adams dies at Quincy, Massachusetts

FURTHER READING

Allgor, Catherine. *Parlor Politics: In Which the Ladies of Washington Help Build a City and a Government.* Charlottesville: University Press of Virginia, 2000.

Corbett, Katherine, "Louisa Catherine Adams: The Anguished 'Adventures of a Nobody'," in *Women's Being, Women's Place: Female Identity and Vocation in American History,* ed. Mary Kelley. Boston: G. K. Hall, 1979.

Hecht, Marie. *John Quincy Adams: A Personal History of an Independent Man.* New York: American Political Biography, 1972.

Nagel, Paul C. *The Adams Women: Abigail and Louisa Adams, Their Sisters and Daughters.* New York: Oxford University Press, 1987.

———. *Descent from Glory: Four Generations of the Adams Family.* Cambridge, Mass.: Harvard University Press, 1999.

Shepherd, Jack. *Cannibals of the Heart: A Personal Biography of Louisa Catherine and John Quincy Adams.* New York: McGraw Hill, 1980.

ANNA TUTHILL SYMMES HARRISON

(JULY 25, 1775–FEBRUARY 25, 1864)
First Lady, March 4, 1841–April 4, 1841

ANNA SYMMES HARRISON
(Library of Congress)

A pioneer woman, a soldier's wife, Anna Symmes Harrison lived a life of toil, in which she knew hardship, danger, and the deaths of all but one of her 10 children. Throughout her days bearing family responsibilities alone, she endured the extended absences of her husband, in the military and in public office. She kept busy most of her life putting her hand to whatever came next to do. As far as is known, she never questioned her lot until her husband became president. Then, deprived of her hopes of a quiet retirement with him, she wept.

—⁓—

Anna Tuthill Symmes was born in a farmhouse named Solitude on the Flat-brook River, Sussex County, New Jersey, on July 25, 1775, the second child

53

of John Cleve Symmes and his wife Anna Tuthill Symmes. Her mother died the next year, and three years later Symmes took his younger daughter to live with her maternal grandparents, Henry and Phebe Tuthill of Southold, Long Island, while he fought as a colonel in the American Revolution. One tale tells that when the British were threatening Morristown, New Jersey, he dressed as a Redcoat, stuffed the four-year-old Anna into one saddlebag and turnips into the other, told British sentries that he was delivering the turnips to the supreme British commander, and transported her safely to the Tuthills' home.

Anna's grandparents brought her up as a Presbyterian, emphasizing the domestic arts and religion in her education. Her grandmother taught her to work with both her mind and her hands. She went to the best schools, including the Clinton Academy in East Hampton, and the fashionable New York boarding school of Isabella Marshall Graham. Graham, a Scotswoman, had chosen to live in the United States because she saw it as "the country where the Church of Christ would eventually flourish." These experiences inspired in Anna a lifelong love of learning and a serious outlook on the world.

In 1794, when she was a petite, "darkly beautiful" 19-year-old, with a full mouth and a cleft chin, her father took her to live with him and his third wife, Susanna, whom she grew to love. On his extensive holdings in the Northwest Territory, he had founded the town of North Bend, Indiana, about 16 miles west of Cincinnati. While he was building a new house for them there, the two ladies traveled to Lexington, Kentucky, where they spent part of the winter at the home of Anna's older sister Maria (Mrs. Peyton Short). There Anna met and fell in love with army officer William Henry Harrison. Although Harrison came from a distinguished family, Anna's father objected to the young soldier's choice of career: He had "understanding, prudence, education, & resource in conversation, about £3000 property, but what is to be lamented is, that he has no profession but that of arms." How did Harrison plan to support a

wife? asked Symmes. Harrison answered, "With my sword, sir, and my good right arm."

Symmes did not relent, but in late November 1795 the young people defied him by marrying while he was away. Some historians say that they were married in the log cabin of the presiding justice of the peace, Dr. Stephen Wood; others place the ceremony in Symmes's own house. Symmes resigned himself, writing a friend: "If I knew what to make of Captain Harrison, I could easily take proper arrangements for his family, but he can neither bleed, plead, nor preach, and if he could plow I should be satisfied. His best prospect is in the army, he has talents, and if he can dodge [harm] well a few years, it is probable he may become conspicuous." His judgment proved correct. Harrison did indeed gain fame, but he never made enough money to enable his family to live in comfort.

Nonetheless the couple lived happily together. Harrison's career prospered politically, as he served successively as secretary and then territorial delegate to the House of Representatives for the Northwest Territory, first governor of the Indiana Territory, commander of the Army of the Northwest in the War of 1812, state legislator, U.S. congressman, U.S. senator, and minister to Colombia. His achievements as a soldier, especially his victory leading a militia force against the Indian settlement at Tippecanoe, contributed to his reputation. Financially he was less successful, although he tried to supplement his income by farming, land speculation, and other abortive commercial enterprises.

The Harrisons started their life together while he was serving at Fort Washington, not far from her father's North Bend home. Beginning in 1796, Anna Symmes Harrison produced and devotedly tended one child after another: Betsey Bassett; John Cleves Symmes; Lucy Singleton; William Henry, Jr.; John Scott; Benjamin; Mary Symmes; Carter Bassett; Anna Tuthill; and James Findlay. She fell into the habit of addressing her husband as "Paw," while he called her "Nancy." The growing family moved with their parents to the log cabin Harrison built in North Bend; to Philadelphia for his stint in the House of Representatives; and to Grouselands, the 13-room, two-and-one-half-story brick Georgian mansion he built in Vincennes, Indiana. This building incorporated space for council meetings and entertainment as well as for family life. It had black-walnut wainscotings and elegantly carved mantels, sashes, and doors, but it was also designed to repel attacks, with heavy shutters on the windows inside and out, gunslits in the 18-inch-thick solid walls, and attic windows designed for sharpshooters.

The family lived in what was still pioneer country subject to Indian attack. Anna Harrison often had to rush the children indoors while a Methodist minister who lodged with them stood guard with a shotgun. She revealed just how isolated she sometimes felt on the frontier in an 1836 letter to a cousin. "I should like to know, wether your Father is still living, & how many brothers, & Sisters you have, indeed any thing, & every thing, that relates to any of my relations, friends, or acquaintance, will be truely gratefing to me, in this far off Country."

A busy wife and mother, she undertook the children's education herself, entrusting their spiritual welfare to the Methodist circuit rider. She managed her husband's landholdings—not very successfully—and carried out her official duties, whether as hostess of the Indiana Territory or the governor's lady. In her husband's absence during the War of 1812, she and the children lived with her father in a rented house in Cincinnati. After Harrison's resignation from the U.S. army in 1814, the couple took over the farm in North Bend that she had inherited on her father's death. They moved their old log cabin to it, naming it "The Bend" and gradually expanding it to 22 rooms.

In North Bend they sometimes entertained the entire church congregation for dinner after services held by itinerant preachers and received the many visitors who wanted to meet Harrison, the military hero. "Emigrants, tourists, travelers, and gentlemen from the east, many of whom came regularly consigned," gathered at their home.

Harrison was away serving in Congress from 1816 to 1819, in the Ohio Senate from 1819 until 1821, in the U.S. Senate from 1824 to 1828, and as minister to Colombia from 1828 to 1829. All this time, Anna stayed on at The Bend, in fragile health, raising their children alone and even founding a school for children in the area. As the children grew up, expenses mounted, with college tuition and weddings. As his mother warned her son William Henry, Jr., in 1824, "Money is very scarce and hard to be got." The Harrisons later had to bail out the younger William when his mounting debts forced him to abandon law for farming. After John Cleves died, his father had to mortgage most of his property to cover John Cleves's $12,000 indebtedness and the support of his widow and six children. William and Anna Harrison spent little on themselves, living humbly. Educator and abolitionist Horace Mann wrote, "The furniture of the parlor could not have drawn very largely upon any one's resources. The walls were ornamented with a few portraits, some in frames, some disembodied from a frame. The drawing-room was fitted up in more modern style; but the whole furniture and ornaments in these rooms might have cost $200 or $250."

Inevitably, in those days of early deaths, the Harrisons knew other griefs and disasters. The medical knowledge of the day could not save their children, one after another of whom died, the first in 1817, five more in the 1820s and 1830s, and three more in the 1840s. Anna Harrison's strong religious faith supported her in her mourning. As she wrote to her son William when his baby brother died, "I hope my dear, you will always bear upon your mind that you are born to die and we know not how soon death may overtake us, it will be of little consequence if we are rightly prepared for the event."

She strongly objected to her husband's decision to run for the presidency of the United States in 1836. Although she was unusually well educated for a woman of her day and accustomed to entertaining large numbers of guests, including persons of national reputation, she felt ill-equipped to function as first lady. Furthermore, both the Harrisons were in their sixties, and she worried about the stress to which the campaign would subject her husband. She did succeed in persuading him to refrain from electioneering on Sundays, but he campaigned the rest of the week. He lost in his first bid, in which she knew that he had never stood much of a chance.

The tumultuous campaign of 1840 found her even more reluctant. After another son's death in early June of that year, she fell seriously ill. She had little peace in which to recover because of the constant flow of visitors, one of whom described her as "one of the handsomest old ladies I ever saw . . . a perfect beauty and such a *good* person." When Harrison won the presidency, his wife wept openly. "I wish," she said, "that my husband's friends had left him where he is, happy and contented in retirement."

Because of illness, Anna did not attend her husband's inauguration. She asked their widowed daughter-in-law, Jane Irwin Harrison (Mrs. William Henry Harrison, Jr.), to act as his hostess until May, when Anna planned to travel to Washington in more clement weather. A month after the inauguration, as she was reluctantly packing to join her husband in the White House, word reached her of his death from pneumonia on April 4, 1841. Many attributed that death to the tensions of the campaign and the importunities of office seekers.

The administrators of President Harrison's estate had a thankless task, as an 1845 letter to his widow from her nephew John Cleves Short reveals: "The numerous creditors are howling in every direction for their money—while the admrs [administrators] are held up as miserable if not faithless, managers. I never go to town but what I am stopt in the street by these creditors, and the most formidable of them do not live in toun." Anna had to pay some of her husband's debts out of the pension voted her by Congress, a lump sum of $25,000, and she had to scrimp and borrow during her widowhood.

After her husband's death, Anna's religious devotion grew even more ardent. She followed public affairs closely, keeping herself informed on the policies of the Tyler and Polk administrations, with which she did not always agree. She opposed slavery and encouraged the grandsons who fought for the Union during the Civil War.

She stayed in her North Bend log cabin until it burned down in 1858. Thereafter, her health slowly declining, she lived with her only surviving child, John Scott Harrison. She loved telling stories of her girlhood to the neighborhood children and followed the Civil War exploits of John's son Benjamin, later to be president of the United States. She died on February 25, 1864, and was buried beside her husband on a promontory in North Bend overlooking the Ohio River.

—◊◊◊—

Anna Symmes Harrison was first lady only *in absentia,* during the single month that her husband, William Henry Harrison, survived his inauguration. She never lived in the White House. Her life was centered on her husband and their children. She remains the only woman who has been both wife and grandmother to an American president.

CHRONOLOGY

1775 *July 25:* Anna Symmes is born at Flatbrook, New Jersey

1776 Anna goes to live with her maternal grandparents on the death of her mother

1794 Anna goes to live with her father and his third wife in what is now southwestern Ohio

1795 ca. *November 22:* Anna Symmes marries William Henry Harrison

1796 *September 29:* Daughter Elizabeth (Betsey) Bassett is born

1798 *October 28:* Son John Cleves is born

William Henry Harrison resigns from the army to become secretary of the Northwest Territory

1799	William Henry Harrison is elected territorial delegate to the House of Representatives
1800	*September:* Daughter Lucy Singleton is born
	William Henry Harrison is appointed territorial governor of Indiana
1802	*September 6:* Son William Henry is born
1804	*October 4:* Son John Scott is born
1806	*Summer:* Son Benjamin is born
1809	Daughter Mary Symmes is born
1811	*October:* Son Carter Bassett is born
	William Henry Harrison leads a militia force against the Indian settlement of Tippecanoe
1812	William Henry Harrison rejoins the U.S. army
1813	*October 26:* Daughter Anna Tuthill is born
1814	Son James Findlay is born
	William Henry Harrison resigns from the U.S. army
1816	William Henry Harrison is elected to the U.S. House of Representatives
1817	Son James Findlay dies
1819	William Henry Harrison is elected to the Ohio Senate

1824	William Henry Harrison is elected to the U.S. Senate
1826	Daughter Lucy Singleton dies
1828	President John Quincy Adams appoints William Henry Harrison the first U.S. minister to Colombia
1829	President Andrew Jackson recalls Harrison
1830	Son John Cleves dies
1834	William Henry Harrison is appointed county recorder
1838	Son William Henry, Jr., dies
1839	Another son dies
1840	Another son dies
1841	March 4: Anna Symmes Harrison becomes first lady
	April 4: President William Henry Harrison dies; Anna Harrison continues to live in North Bend, Indiana
1858	Anna Harrison moves to the Indiana farm of her son John
1864	*February 25:* Anna Harrison dies

FURTHER READING

Holloway, Laura C. *Ladies of the White House.* Philadelphia: Bradley and Company, 1881.

Peterson, Norma Lois. *The Presidencies of William Henry Harrison and John Tyler.* Lawrence: University Press of Kansas, 1989.

Symmes, John Cleves. *The Intimate Letters of John Cleves Symmes and His Family Including Those of His Daughter, Mrs. William Henry Harrison Wife of the Ninth President of the United States,* ed. Beverly W. Bond, Jr. Cincinnati: Historical and Philosophical Society of Ohio, 1956.

Whitton, Mary Ormsbee. *First First Ladies: A Study of the Wives of the Early Presidents.* 1948. Reprint. Freeport, N.Y.: Books for Libraries Press, 1969.

LETITIA CHRISTIAN TYLER

(NOVEMBER 12, 1790–SEPTEMBER 10, 1842)
First Lady, April 6, 1841–September 10, 1842

LETITIA TYLER
(Library of Congress)

L etitia Tyler's daughter-in-law Priscilla wrote, "She was my beau ideal of a perfect gentlewoman." As far as is known, Letitia Tyler based her life on the image of the southern upper-class lady, unquestioningly accepting the politics, morality, and values of her southern father and husband. These included approval of the institution of slavery. Her horizons seemed to end with her family and their property. But no letter of hers survives, and no one knows what was really in her heart.

———※———

Letitia Christian was born at Cedar Grove plantation, about 20 miles from Richmond, Virginia, on November 12, 1790, to a socially and politically prominent family. She was the third daughter and seventh of the twelve children of

Robert, a wealthy planter, and his wife Mary Browne Christian. Little else is known of her girlhood, although presumably she received the minimal education commonly given to females of her place and class. Contemporary accounts describe her conventionally as a beautiful, refined, selfless, modest, gracious, religious woman who enjoyed knitting and gardening and was devoted to her family and friends.

In about 1808, Letitia met the highly eligible John Tyler, then a law student, from the nearby plantation Greenway and a similar Upper South background. He soon entered public life, and they carried on a placid, five-year courtship. He dared not kiss her hand until three weeks before their wedding, "so perfectly reserved and modest was she."

On March 29, 1813, they were married at Cedar Grove as tranquilly as they had courted. Almost immediately, the bridegroom left to serve briefly with the militia in the War of 1812, but his unit never encountered the enemy and he soon returned. The Tylers used an inheritance from her parents to build Mons-Sacer on a sizable section of Greenway lands that John Tyler had inherited; two years later they sold it and built another home, Woodburn, nearby. In 1821 they bought and moved to Greenway.

During these years, Letitia Tyler was bearing babies. Beginning in 1815, she had a baby about every two years; seven of the nine survived infancy. The Tylers apparently found their common ground in their children and their home. Although John went on to serve in both houses of Congress and in the legislature and governorship of Virginia, no evidence indicates that his wife took any interest in politics. On the one occasion she accompanied her husband to Washington, during the winter of 1828–29, people commented on her "beauty of person and eloquence of manner." Most of the time she stayed at home, tending her children and supervising plantation affairs.

Like most planters, the Tylers had much land but little money. They lived mostly on credit and were further straitened by his propensity for lending money to family and friends. Devoted to her children, Letitia was a hard-working and competent plantation mistress who bore the responsibility for the "welfare" of the slaves—as defined by their owners. It was up to her to see that they were fed; clothed in garments that were spun, woven, and sewn on the premises; and nursed when they were judged too ill to work. She centered her life on her duties as mother and slave mistress, maintaining a happy marriage and a close-knit family.

She did join her husband from 1825 to 1827 when he was governor of Virginia, ably conducting their social life. But the couple were plagued by lack of funds for entertaining. In desperation they invited members of the legislature to a meal where they served only Virginia ham, corn bread, and cheap whiskey, but the legislators did not respond as the Tylers had hoped with a larger appropriation for entertainment at the governor's mansion.

John Tyler was elected to the U.S. Senate in 1827 but resigned his seat in 1836 because of differences with his party. The next year he moved his family to Williamsburg.

Despite their mother's care and their father's sometimes heavy-handed letters adjuring his daughters to pattern their lives on hers and his sons to obey and treat her respectfully, not all the children married successfully. Son Robert, however, was fortunate in his marriage to the actress Priscilla Cooper. A strong bond developed between her and Letitia, of whom she wrote: "[She] must have been very beautiful in her youth, for she is still beautiful now in her declining years and wretched health. Her skin is as smooth and soft as a baby's; she has sweet, loving black eyes, and her features are delicately moulded; besides this, her feet and hands are perfect; and she is gentle and graceful in her movements, with a most peculiar air of native refinement about everything she says and does."

In 1839, shortly before Robert and Priscilla were married, Letitia Tyler suffered a stroke that partially paralyzed her. From then on she spent almost all her time in her bedroom, much of it in reading her Bible and prayer book. Nonetheless, she continued to supervise her household. Priscilla Cooper Tyler wrote, "Notwithstanding her very delicate health, Mother attends to and regulates all the household affairs, and all so quietly that you can't tell when she does it. All the clothes for the children, and for the servants, are cut out under her immediate eye, and all the sewing is personally superintended by her. All the cake, jellies, custards, and we indulge largely in them, emanate from her, yet you see no confusion, hear no bustle, but only meet the agreeable result."

When John Tyler was elected vice president of the United States in 1840, he planned to go on living in Williamsburg, where he thought his wife would be more comfortable. The unexpected death of President William Henry Harrison a month after his inauguration necessitated drastic changes. The family agreed that President Tyler would hasten to Washington. Son Robert and his family would soon follow and move into the White House with him, Priscilla to act as his official hostess. When Letitia Tyler later arrived, she took up residence in a second-floor bedroom. Since she spent her days in a wheelchair, she remained there, reportedly being carried down to the first floor only for her daughter Elizabeth's small private wedding in the East Room. Distinguished visitors such as Charles Dickens and Washington Irving went upstairs to meet her.

President Tyler, a supporter of states' rights, was often at odds with the nationalist leaders of his party. In fall 1841 he was burned in effigy and with a single exception his whole cabinet resigned. Congress meanly denied the Tylers an appropriation to redecorate and clean the White House and its furnishings, although the New York *Herald* described them as so dirty and dilapidated as to be a "contemptible disgrace" with "its beautiful pillars disgustingly besplattered with saliva of tobacco . . . the gorgeous East Room reflecting, from its monstrous mirrors, patched carpets, the penury of 'Uncle Samuel'—and the three inch stumps of wax lights in the sockets of magnificent chandeliers,

attesting to the rigid economy observed by its present possessors—the splendid drapery falling in tatters. . . ."

Throughout 1842, Letitia Tyler's health worsened, at last affecting her mind. After suffering a second stroke, she died on September 10, 1842, holding a rose in her hand. She was buried at Cedar Grove, her girlhood home.

— ⁓ —

Letitia Christian Tyler, first wife of President John Tyler, was the second in a series of presidents' wives who hardly functioned as first ladies. The public knew her only by repute as a gentle and loving wife and mother. Confined in her wheelchair to the upper floor of the White House, she experienced it as a place of physical and mental suffering, where she watched her husband's anguish as he battled Congress and his party and faced her own approaching death.

CHRONOLOGY

1790   *November 12:* Letitia Christian is born at Cedar Grove near Richmond, Virginia

1813   *March 29:* Letitia Christian marries John Tyler at Cedar Grove

1815   Daughter Mary is born

1816   Son Robert is born

        John Tyler is elected to the U.S. House of Representatives

1819   Son John Jr. is born

1821   Daughter Letitia is born

1823   Daughter Elizabeth ("Lizzie") is born

1825   Daughter Anne Contesse is born; she dies three months later

        John Tyler is elected governor of Virginia

1827   Daughter Alice is born

        John Tyler is elected to the U.S. Senate

1830	Son Tazewell is born	1840	John Tyler is elected vice president of the United States
1836	John Tyler resigns from the Senate and moves his family to Williamsburg	1841	Letitia Tyler becomes first lady
1839	Letitia Tyler suffers a stroke that leaves her partially paralyzed	1842	Letitia Tyler suffers a second stroke *September 10:* Letitia Tyler dies

Further Reading

Chitwood, Oliver Perry. *John Tyler, Champion of the Old South*. 1939. Reprint. New York: American Political Biography, 1990.

Coleman, Elizabeth Tyler. *Priscilla Cooper Tyler and the American Scene*. Birmingham: University of Alabama Press, 1955.

Klapthor, Margaret Brown. *The First Ladies*. Washington, D.C.: White House Historic Association, 1995.

Whitton, Mary Ormsbee. *First First Ladies: A Study of the Wives of the Early Presidents*. 1948. Reprint. Freeport, N.Y.: Books for Libraries Press, 1969.

JULIA GARDINER TYLER
(MAY 4, 1820–JULY 10, 1889)
First Lady, June 26, 1844–March 4, 1845

JULIA GARDINER TYLER
(Library of Congress)

In her youth Julia Gardiner Tyler was a prototype of the self-centered, some-what spoiled, wealthy young woman of her era. She occasionally rebelled against convention but seldom gave a thought to the status of women. Adversity showed her to be a woman capable of strength and independence, ready to do battle for her children and herself. Where money was concerned she insisted on her rights, whether to an inheritance from her mother or to a pension from the federal government—the very government to which she had been disloyal, as a supporter of the Confederacy.

—⁂—

Julia Gardiner was born to wealth and influence on May 4, 1820, on Gardiner's Island, New York. She was the first daughter and the third of four children of lawyer David Gardiner and heiress Juliana McLachlan Gardiner, who taught their children the values of social exclusiveness, advantageous marriage alliances, and money. Julia was schooled at Madame N. D. Chagaray's fashionable institute for young ladies in New York City, where she studied music, French literature, ancient history, arithmetic, and composition. As her parents wished, she grew up to become a beauty and a belle—five foot three, plump, dark-haired and dark-eyed, with an hourglass waist and a full bust. At 15 she thought it important to find as a husband "a very fine young man" with "considerable property" and "conversational powers."

Less to her parents' liking, she was also flirtatious, indiscreet, and daring. She particularly offended them by allowing her name and picture, captioned "the Rose of Long Island," to appear in an 1839 advertisement for a dry goods and clothing business—an unprecedented act for a young woman of her class. Soon afterward her family took her on a year-long European tour, during which she added to her string of suitors and was presented at the French court.

On visits to Washington in early 1841 and thereafter, she and her sister Margaret swept the field, with so many gentlemen callers that in 1843 her father had to rent an extra room to entertain them in the boardinghouse where the family was staying. The young ladies loved the informal dances for boarders at which Julia sometimes strummed the guitar and sang. They also promenaded on Pennsylvania Avenue and attended debates in both houses of Congress—more to be seen than to listen, for they often found the speeches dull and incomprehensible. They were entertained by the elite of the capital city. At a White House reception in 1842, Julia and her parents were introduced to President Tyler. Priscilla Cooper Tyler presided as hostess, while the president's invalid wife Letitia remained in her upstairs bedroom. The President greeted Julia with a "thousand compliments" as other guests "looked and listened in perfect amazement."

In her various visits to Washington from 1841 to 1844, Julia received several proposals, including two from congressmen, one from a Supreme Court justice, and one from President Tyler, whose wife had died in September 1842. That Christmas Eve, John Tyler invited the Gardiners to dine at the White House. By early February the families had grown so intimate that he felt free to tease Julia about her suitors, ask her to play cards with him, and invite the family to stay after the other guests had left. When they finally departed he kissed both girls good night, chasing Julia downstairs to catch her, and escorted them to their carriage. No one seemed particularly concerned that he was 30 years older than she and nine years older than her mother; Julia had had other beaux of his age. She admired the elegance of his conversation, "the incomparable grace of his bearing," and the "silvery sweetness" of his voice.

When he walked the Gardiner family home from church, rumors flew. By mid-February 1843, though still in mourning for Letitia Tyler and not going out publicly, the president had decided that he wanted to marry Julia. He proposed at the White House ball on Washington's birthday. "I had never thought of love," she later wrote, "so I said 'No, no, no,' and shook my head with each word, which flung the tassel of my Greek cap into his face with every move. It was undignified, but it amused me very much to see his expression as he tried to make love to me and the tassel brushed his face."

Despite her refusal, she kept on seeing Tyler and flirting with him. When in mid-March he repeated his proposal in the presence of her sister, Julia had to tell her parents, who were delighted. By the time the family returned to their East Hampton home, the president and Julia had reached a "definite understanding." Though her mother would not permit the fall wedding for which Tyler hoped, insisting that her young daughter needed more time, her parents raised no other objections. That summer Julia read Tyler's love letters aloud to her family and schemed with them to get a political appointment for her brother.

The Gardiners' return to Washington was delayed by their move to Manhattan, so they did not arrive in the capital city until late February 1844. Then accident and the matchmaking Dolley Madison took a hand. She arranged a cruise aboard the gunboat *Princeton* on February 28, 1844, with the president, Julia Gardiner, her sister, and her father among the guests. Julia was below decks listening to music, Tyler nearby, when they heard an explosion. She rushed to a ladder, heard that an explosion of one of the guns had killed her father and seven other men, and fainted into Tyler's arms. The president carried her off the boat and took her and her sister to spend the night at the White House. Not long afterward she told him that she was ready to set the date for their wedding. Years later she commented, "After I lost my father I felt differently toward the President. He seemed to fill the place and to be more agreeable in every way than any younger man ever was or could be."

After querying Tyler about his ability to furnish those "comforts and elegancies of life" to which Julia was accustomed, her mother consented to the marriage. All agreed to secrecy, concealing it even from the president's children. Only after the ceremony did he reveal to the nation and his children that he had married Julia Gardiner on June 26, 1844, at an Episcopal church in New York City. Dolley Madison preened herself: "I had some small part in elevating a girl in her twenties into the ranks of us old ladies who remember our own days as first lady." The newspapers chortled, because the White House had explained Tyler's absence from Washington by saying that he was resting from his arduous duties and seeking a few days' repose: "John don't know what's going on. We rather think that the President's 'arduous duties' are only beginning. 'Repose,' indeed!"

If Julia Gardiner Tyler had loved being a belle, she loved reigning as first lady even more. On her honeymoon she rhapsodized: "Wherever we stopped, wherever we went, crowds of people outstripping one another, came to gaze at the President's bride; *the secrecy of the affair* is on the tongue and admiration of everyone. *Everyone* says it was the best managed thing they ever heard of. The President says I am the best of diplomatists."

At 24, the youngest first lady in history and rich as well, she brought not only zest and gaiety but also opulence to the White House. At the Tylers' personal expense, she had the place cleaned, ordered new furniture, and put the White House coachmen and footmen into new livery. Still in mourning for her father, she dressed elegantly in either white satin or black lace, decked out with diamonds and pearls. She rode out in a four-horse carriage and promenaded with a greyhound given her by her husband.

Like White House hostesses before her, she turned to Dolley Madison for advice. But unlike her mentor, Julia Tyler emulated the grandiose manners and customs of European courts. Although "Hail to the Chief" had been played to honor the deceased George Washington at a birthday celebration, she began its official association with the U.S. president by having it played as her husband entered on state occasions. She gathered a "court" of four maids of honor—her sister, two cousins, and John Tyler's youngest daughter—to act as her ladies-in-waiting. For formal affairs she seated herself on a raised platform among this white-clad bevy, augmented by other young women of socially prominent families. "I determined upon," she wrote, "and I think I have been successful, in making my Court interesting in youth and beauty. Wherever I go they form my train." In January 1845 she broke with precedent by including this entourage in the receiving line headed by the president. As the guests left the line, her sister wrote, "they fell back facing us until we could see a crowd of admiring faces."

In the White House, Julia Tyler enthusiastically danced the polkas and waltzes that she introduced to presidential balls. At other people's parties, however, she refused to dance at all unless she had arrived early enough to open the ball. Her "court" always accompanied her, of course, with orders to stay grouped around her all evening.

She graciously accepted toasts to "Mrs. Presidentress," "the Lady Presidentress," and "Her Serene Loveliness." During the eight months of her tenure as first lady, she attracted much press attention; to make sure of it, she secretly employed a press agent, his job being, her sister said, "to sound Julia's praises far and near in Washington." When a New York music publisher put out "The Julia Waltzes," she could not wait to get copies. The dour John Quincy Adams wrote that Tyler and his new wife were the laughingstock of official Washington, but they made wonderful copy for reporters.

While Julia Tyler lived in the White House, all her family used the franking privilege to send mail without cost. She enjoyed acting as a conduit of requests for presidential favors and government appointments, and her family claimed their share of these political plums. No relative was too remote, no sinecure too minor, no maneuvers too shoddy; the family lobbied for them all, pressed by the brief time remaining in the president's term of office. In the White House Julia Tyler surrounded herself with her kinfolk.

Her stepchildren, three of them older than she, were another matter. John Tyler's older daughters were shocked and dismayed by their father's secret marriage so soon after their mother's death. Their reaction annoyed his new wife, who in any case was none too anxious to have them around during her White House reign. But she did include young Alice Tyler in her court, and she immediately charmed her stepsons. Eventually she was reconciled with all but one of her stepchildren, and some of the younger ones lived with her and their father when the Tylers left the White House. Letitia Tyler Semple never forgave her.

When she married, Julia Tyler told her brother, "I have turned my back upon New York and aim to become a thorough Virginian." She set about studying her husband's political views—and adopting them. With a confidence justified more by her youth than by expertise, she meddled energetically in politics. The president's earlier efforts to annex Texas had failed, but his new wife urged him to find a way around his opponents in the Senate and at her balls lobbied for the annexation. She flattered many senators with her flirtatious attentions in hopes of influencing votes and enlisting

support for the president's projects and appointments. When John Tyler signed the congressional joint resolution favoring annexation three days before he left office, he gave his wife the gold pen he used to sign it; thereafter she wore it on a chain on formal occasions.

"Nothing appears to delight the President more," Julia Tyler declared, "than . . . to hear people sing my praises." She certainly made him very happy. She might flirt with others, but the Tylers lived together on "dreams and kisses." She was not only an old man's darling but also an adoring wife, praising everything he did and defending him against all criticism.

For her last ball in the White House, on February 18, 1845, she entertained 3,000 people in four rooms lit with 600 candles. They consumed eight dozen bottles of champagne and other wines from open barrels. As the Marine band played, Julia Tyler opened the ball with the secretary of state, then danced a few steps with many other gentlemen. At midnight she and other ladies danced a cotillion with ambassadors from France, Russia, Prussia, and Austria. It was a grand success, even though President-elect Polk and his wife disappointed the Tylers by not appearing. Julia's brother Alexander, working from his sisters' notes, published an anonymous description in the New York *Plebeian*:

> As to [the president's] beautiful bride, whom I a stranger saw from time to time in foreign parts, I can scarcely trust my pen to write of her . . . tonight she looked like Juno and with her sister, cousins and Miss Alice Tyler constituted a galaxy of beauty, and I am told equal talent, which no Court of Europe could equal. . . . More diamonds sparkled than I have ever seen on any occasion in this country.

In a letter to her mother, Julia Tyler described the presidential couple's farewell to Washington:

> At five in the afternoon, a crowd of friends, ladies and gentlemen, assembled in the Blue Room to shake hands with us and escort us from the White House. As the President and

myself entered they divided into two lines, and when we had passed to the head of the room, surrounded and saluted us. General Van Ness requested them to stand back and himself stepped forward and delivered "on behalf, and at the request of many ladies and gentlemen citizens of Washington, a farewell address."

After leaving the White House, the Tylers moved to Sherwood Forest, a plantation on the James River near Richmond, Virginia, which John Tyler had bought and begun renovating shortly after the death of his first wife. Julia Tyler, now styling herself "Mrs. Ex-President Tyler," set about remaking and adding on to the place. God had blessed it, she said, but she could improve on it. She had her "Royal Barge," the *Pocahontas,* painted bright blue and lined its seats and thwarts with damask satin cushions trimmed in blue. The four black oarsmen wore "Bright blue and white check calico shirts— white linen pants—black patent leather belts— straw hats painted blue with Pocahontas upon them in white—and in one corner of the shirt collar (which is turned down) is worked with braid a bow and arrow (to signify the [Sherwood] Forest) and in the other corner the President's and my initials combined." She bought a new carriage and outfitted its coachmen in equal style. "'The full extent or nothing' is almost my motto now," she wrote to her mother.

Julia entertained extensively and lavishly. Like most southern planters, the Tylers socialized with their neighbors, and they enjoyed having casual visitors for meals and house guests who stayed for weeks or months. They regularly visited New York and other cities as well as such fashionable watering places as Saratoga and Newport. When in the late 1850s the family grew so large that they could not easily resort to these spas, Julia Tyler bought the Villa Margaret in Hampton, Virginia, as a refuge from the discomforts and dangers to the health of a summer at Sherwood Forest. She frequently traveled with her husband on his speaking engagements. He wanted his wife fashionably dressed for all occasions, and she was happy to oblige.

Between 1846 and 1860 she bore seven children in whom both parents delighted from the moment that the first, the "Little President," arrived on the scene. Both, but especially John Tyler, wanted more. He proved himself not only an experienced father but also a devoted nurse and baby sitter. She bore her babies with little difficulty and always had her mother or her sister to assist at the accouchement. Indeed, Julia Tyler was the first American first lady blessed with robust health, and her children inherited her sturdiness.

The Tylers had many people to support. In addition to their own brood, some of the children of his first marriage were still dependent, and some got into trouble. The Tylers employed two white women, and some 70 slaves toiled in the house and the plantation fields. Aging slaves and slave babies had to be fed and clothed—after a fashion—through the years in which they could not work. Plantation mistresses like Julia Tyler had to spend time and energy in supervising and caring for them.

Even with the backing of the Gardiner fortune, she spent beyond the Tylers' means. He increased the productivity of Sherwood Forest, but like almost all plantation owners he was cash poor. His propensity for lending money to poor risks added to the problems caused by his wife's spending, and this plus the large number of their dependents plunged them into financial difficulties. As early as the fall of 1845 he was borrowing money. He repeatedly borrowed from one bank to pay notes due at another. Speculation in timber and mining in hopes of making a fortune that would keep his family in luxury only deepened his troubles. Even though he sold off some of his land, he had to turn to the Gardiners for help.

Descended from slaveowners and wife of one whose political philosophy she adopted, Julia Tyler openly advocated states' rights and the perpetuation of slavery. In 1853 she published a letter in the *Southern Literary Messenger* rebutting the appeal of certain ladies of the British nobility for southern American white women to demand an end to slavery. She praised the plantation system as a civilizing force and repudiated Harriet Beecher Stowe's representation of slavery in *Uncle Tom's Cabin*. Using the arguments standard among southerners, she declared that slaves lived "sumptuously" compared to London laborers, that slave families were seldom separated, and that slaves were taught Christianity and encouraged to attend church. Despite its factual errors, her letter attracted favorable attention in the United States, particularly because it advised the British ladies to attend to the social evils in their own country.

Throughout the 1850s, John Tyler had endeavored to avoid a national confrontation over slavery. He was shocked when, in 1859, John Brown attacked Harpers Ferry and called for a slave insurrection. Briefly the Tylers hoped that they might return to the White House in 1861, believing that the nation could be kept whole and peaceful. The hope for a new presidency burned out as quickly as it had flared, but the Tylers continued to try to preserve the Union, even though they knew, as Julia wrote, that "the South is perfectly ripe for secession. . . . The South Carolina ladies say they would rather be widows of secessionists than wives of submissionists! And that they will never again attend a ball in the *United States*." In early 1861, even as one state after another seceded, the Tylers were in Washington, he as Virginia's special commissioner in a last desperate effort to keep the peace. Meanwhile his wife was reclaiming the city socially, gathering compliments and attending parties, receptions, dinners, and balls.

By the time they returned to Sherwood Forest at the end of February, John Tyler was urging secession. He had earlier conceived an impractical scheme for creating a new union of seceded and border states. "A number of the Northern States will come into the plan which he proposes," his wife optimistically wrote to her mother. When Virginia seceded, he served on a commission to negotiate a union with the Confederate States and was later elected to the Confederate Congress. Julia Tyler joined volunteer groups to support the Confederate war effort and encouraged her sons to enlist in its

Junior Guard—even her 13-year-old. She raged against her brother David, who with most of the Gardiners supported the Union: "I am utterly ashamed of the State in which I was born, and its people. All soul and magnanimity have departed from them—'patriotism' indeed! A community sold to the vilest politicians." The Yankee seizure of Villa Margaret in Hampton plunged her into new depths of fury. She believed and repeated even the most fantastic war rumors that buoyed up southern hopes, confidently expecting a southern triumph, for the South was "favored of heaven."

Although Julia did not accompany her husband to Richmond when the Confederate House of Representatives met in January 1862, a dream that he was dangerously ill sent her flying to his side. He seemed well, but just days later he lapsed into his last sickness; he died on January 18, 1862. At 41, she was left to rear seven children—the oldest just 15 and the youngest only two—to manage a plantation and slaves, and to confront her husband's debts, in a war zone. An epidemic of flu among the children multiplied her problems. Out of respect for her former position, the Union army placed a protective guard around Sherwood Forest, but soon her slaves began to leave.

In fall 1862 Julia decided to remove her six younger children to her mother's home on Staten Island, for which purpose she was granted a federal pass. She quarreled bitterly with her brother David, who with his family was already established there, and ordered him to leave. He refused, upon which she returned to Sherwood Forest, taking her two youngest with her—again under federal protection.

She made up her mind to sell the estate, but in Civil War Virginia, Sherwood Forest was unsaleable. She then put her eldest son in college in Lexington, hired a manager and two other white men to work the plantation, ordered her slaves sold south or hired out to the Confederate government if the Union army reappeared nearby, and prepared to go north. However, this time she could not get a federal pass without swearing allegiance to the Union.

Instead, she procured from southern authorities a pass permitting her and her two youngest children to sail on a blockade runner and take with her five bales of cotton to sell in Bermuda. She finally left without the cotton, which went separately; she profited handsomely by its sale. After enjoying Bermuda and the society of Confederates living there, she eventually reached Staten Island in late November 1862.

Even while using Yankee protection, Julia Tyler worked for the Confederacy, distributing peace pamphlets, gathering relief supplies, working for the exchange of prisoners-of-war, and campaigning for General McClellan to replace Lincoln as president. Her brother David was outraged. Their violent quarrels caused their mother to evict David and his family from the house and take her business affairs out of his hands. After her death in 1864, David Gardiner and Julia Gardiner Tyler disputed bitterly and at length in the courts over the division of the Gardiner fortune. In 1868 the court split it among several heirs; Julia received the house on Staten Island and three-eighths of the Gardiner estate in downtown New York City.

Toward the end of the war, having heard that Sherwood Forest had been vandalized, she wrote indignantly to the White House: "Will President Lincoln have the kindness to inform Mrs. (Ex-President) Tyler whether her home on the James River can be withdrawn from the hands of the negroes, who were placed in possession of it by Gen. Wild, and restored to the charges of her manager, Mr. J. C. Tyler . . . [even] though her estate has been subjected to wreck and devastation within doors and without." General Wild gave a different version, saying that the three former slaves and their families living on the plantation had cultivated some portion of it and merely wished to reap what they had sown. In fact, the house had not been much damaged, and its downstairs rooms were being used as a temporary school for blacks and whites. Julia Tyler had a more pressing worry: Her oldest son had been called to serve in the Confederate army, and before long her next oldest was clamoring to join him—

only to be rejected. Instead he was enrolled at college in Lexington, until Confederate desperation permitted his acceptance into the army.

After the war, pending the resolution of her suit against her brother, her means were straitened. By borrowing she managed to finance family living expenses and her children's education. Their Confederate sympathies subjected them to attacks, so she sent two of her sons to Germany to be educated and one of her daughters to Canada. She herself remained in the United States to fight for her property and her claims on her mother's estate. In the meantime, she tried to revive Sherwood Forest by using immigrant farmers on contract, in a sort of manorial system, an effort that reaped her another lawsuit. When that scheme failed, she resorted to a sharecropping system with former slaves. She also struggled to reclaim the Villa Margaret, which was being used to house teachers for the Freedmen's Bureau, in the process lecturing President Andrew Johnson on how to run the country. In 1869 she got the Villa back. Throughout the same postbellum period she was also involved in lawsuits with John Tyler's creditors.

In 1871 her daughter Julie died in childbirth, and she undertook to raise the baby, Julia Tyler Spencer. The next year she moved to Georgetown, where she was pleased by attention from the newspapers and old acquaintances. At this time she converted to Roman Catholicism and began proselytizing for that church. With the expenses of her dependents, her own fashionable lifestyle flitting from Washington to New York to Richmond and back, and the depression that followed the panic of 1873, she had to put on the market the Staten Island house, the Villa Margaret, and her property on Greenwich Street in New York. Even Sherwood Forest, to which she moved in 1874 to save money, was threatened, but between them she and her oldest son saved it, and it remains today in the hands of their descendants.

Julia lobbied intensively in Washington and Richmond to get jobs for two of her sons, with mixed results. In 1881 she finally won her campaign for a federal pension of $1,200 (later increased to $5,000) as a president's widow; she also claimed $8 per month as the widow of a veteran of the War of 1812. In 1882 she moved to Richmond, where she resumed her luxurious lifestyle, still enjoying being "the subject of great attention from the society people" on her occasional forays to Washington. There she died of a cerebral stroke at age 69 on July 10, 1889. She was buried next to her husband in Hollywood Cemetery in Richmond.

—⁓—

As first lady, John Tyler's second wife, Julia Gardiner Tyler, brightened her husband's life and the Washington social scene, both long clouded by the illness of his first wife. Most Washingtonians seemed to enjoy the bride's obvious pleasure in her position, and she received little press criticism, despite her exploitation of her position for her family's benefit and her sometimes reckless meddling in public affairs. She did not expand the role of first lady: The European courtly flourishes she added to social occasions she undertook more for the fun of it and for her own aggrandizement than out of concern for the dignity of the United States. In the White House she ardently promoted her husband's policies, and thereafter she adopted his loyalties to the institution of slavery and the cause of the Confederacy.

CHRONOLOGY

1820 *May 4:* Julia Gardiner is born on Gardiner's Island, N.Y.

1842 Julia Gardiner meets President John Tyler in Washington

1843 President Tyler proposes to Julia Gardiner

1844 *June 26:* Julia Gardiner marries President John Tyler and becomes first lady

1845 The Tylers move to his plantation, Sherwood Forest

1846 Son David Gardiner is born

1848 Son John Alexander is born

1849 Daughter Julia (Julie) Gardiner is born

1851 Son Lachlan is born

1853 Son Lyon Gardiner is born; Julia Tyler publishes a defense of slavery

1856 Son Robert Fitzwalter is born

1860 Daughter Pearl is born

1861 –65 Julia Tyler works for the Confederacy

1862 *January 18:* John Tyler dies

1871 Daughter Julie dies

1881 Congress awards Julia Gardiner Tyler a pension

1889 *July 10:* Julia Gardiner Tyler dies

FURTHER READING

Chitwood, Oliver Perry. *John Tyler: Champion of the Old South.* New York: American Political Biography, 1990.

Gardiner, John Lion. *The Gardiners of Gardiners Island.* East Hampton, N.Y.: Star Press, 1927.

Peterson, Norma Lois. *The Presidencies of William Henry Harrison and John Tyler.* Lawrence: University Press of Kansas, 1989.

Seagar, Robert. *And Tyler Too: A Biography of John and Julia Gardiner Tyler.* New York: McGraw-Hill, 1963.

SARAH CHILDRESS POLK
(SEPTEMBER 4, 1803–AUGUST 14, 1891)
First Lady, March 4, 1845–March 5, 1849

SARAH POLK
(Library of Congress)

Sarah Childress Polk was much praised in her day as a daughter to be proud of, a wife to be cherished, and a first lady to be admired. The ideal of *true womanhood* was in favor, suppressing feminine independence and individuality in favor of self-sacrifice. Women were taught to confine themselves to the domestic sphere and to find fulfillment in service to others. Conforming to these standards, Sarah Polk put her own ambitions, high intelligence, and political sophistication to the service of her husband and his career. When she left the domestic sphere to enter the world of politics, she did so quietly and privately, managing his campaign office at home while he electioneered in public. She confined her public appearances to the entertainments that formed a part of the domestic sphere. Even in the 42 years of her widowhood, she dedicated herself to her husband's service, preserving his memory.

Sarah Childress was born near Murfreesboro, Tennessee, on September 4, 1803, the younger of two daughters and third of six children of Joel Childress and his wife Elizabeth Whitsett Childress. Sarah's father had prospered as a planter, merchant, tavern keeper, land speculator, and militia major. He raised his children in luxury; Sarah was always dressed in beautifully colored silks and satins. From both parents she learned the value of high principles, while her family's entertaining of local and national politicians gave her experience of the political world.

After primary schooling at the Daniel Elam School in Murfreesboro, Sarah and her older sister, Susan, were tutored by the principal of Bradley Academy, where their brothers were enrolled and where James K. Polk was also studying. The sisters then went to board at the Abercrombie School in Nashville. There the students were entertained by the city's elite, including Andrew and Rachel Jackson. Two years later, in 1817, the Childress girls undertook a month-long, 500-mile horseback journey to the Moravian Female Academy at Salem, North Carolina, the best girls' school in the South. Their parents chose it not only for its academic training but also because it emphasized morality and piety. The girls studied grammar, syntax, history, geography, English, needlework, music, drawing, and the Bible. Though Sarah's studies were abruptly ended by her father's death in 1819, she had received an education available only to the most privileged young women of the time. All her life she read avidly, both to help her husband and for her own satisfaction.

Joel Childress had left a considerable estate, but it was soon dissipated by harsh economic conditions and mismanagement by the son who served as executor. Sarah, a striking, "Spanish-looking" young woman whose conversation bespoke her intelligence, lived the life of a Tennessee belle. At a reception for the governor she met her brothers' schoolmate James Polk, a promising, ambitious, and diligent young lawyer, politician, and clerk of the Ten-

nessee court. He courted her for four years. Legend has it that Andrew Jackson advised him to marry Sarah, "who will never give you trouble. Her wealthy family, education, health, and appearance are all superior." Legend further says that she accepted his proposal only on the condition that he run for the legislature.

By 1823 the two young people were planning their wedding—he newly elected to the state legislature, she to become a paradigm of the political wife, combining the domestic virtues of the time: high principles, a good mind, and a degree of political sophistication unusual in a young lady of her day. They were married from her home on January 1, 1824, in an elaborate ceremony with eight attendants followed by a seven-course wedding supper. According to custom, the couple were feted by both her relatives in Murfreesboro and his in Columbia. In Columbia they rented a cottage for a year, and then settled across the street from his parents in a house with an unfinished second floor and a separate kitchen and smokehouse. They attended the Presbyterian Church, the faith in which the bride had been raised. Because of his father's religious doubts, Polk had not been baptized as a child. As he lay dying, he spoke of his desire for baptism, to the delight of his staunchly Presbyterian wife and equally staunchly Presbyterian mother, each of whom brought her own minister to perform the ceremony. Polk, however, insisted on being baptized a Methodist.

In 1825 James Polk was elected to the U.S. House of Representatives. Sarah Childress Polk stayed in Columbia for the first year of his term, at her husband's insistence, because he did not want her to suffer the dangers and hardships of the trip to Washington. Moreover, accommodations in the nation's capital left much to be desired. As he wrote, "The few inns and hotels are crowded and the prices are exorbitant. I am staying at Captain Benjamin Burch's boardinghouse on Capitol Hill, where I have a sleeping room and an office. I share meals with other congressmen. . . . However, this will be the last time I will be a Washington bachelor." They had no children to consider, nor ever would, probably because an early illness had rendered him sterile.

When James returned to Washington in 1826, his wife accompanied him, traveling with two slaves. With one exception, she was with him thereafter throughout his life, serving as his observer, reporter, nurse, secretary, adviser, and emotional center. He wanted and needed her with him. Once, the story goes, when she suggested that she stay in Columbia to look after the house, he said, "Why? If the house burns down, we can live without it."

In 1826 the Polks "messed" in a boarding-house with congressmen from other states. This arrangement, common at the time, left her free from household responsibilities as they entered Washington's political, social, and religious life. She read religious tracts, permitted nothing to interfere with their attendance at the Presbyterian Church, and always obeyed her denomination's ban on horse racing and the theater. Despite her scruples about such popular recreations and her conspicuous piety, her social grace and gift for repartee made her welcome in official Washington. Whether or not she was as politically ambitious for her husband as tradition has it, her social success certainly forwarded his career. They mingled in select government circles, where Sarah was a favorite, particularly among the men, who complimented her and wrote poetry to her.

She took to life in Washington, increasing the knowledge of politics she had absorbed in her parents' home and in her acquaintance with Andrew Jackson and other Tennessee politicians. She frequented the House of Representatives, always attending when her husband spoke, read the papers, and heard the political gossip circulating in the capital. While she and her husband agreed on most issues, occasionally she dissented, even before other people. On his position against paper money, for instance: "Mr. Polk," a contemporary reported her as saying, "you and your friends certainly are mistaken. . . . Why if we must use gold and silver all the time, a lady can scarcely carry enough money with her."

Her stands on principle sometimes presented a political danger for her husband, as in the Peggy Eaton affair. Peggy O'Neale had grown up in her father's tavern and boarding-house, but he gave her a fashionable education. A headlong, flirtatious beauty, she married John Bowie Timberlake, an alcoholic who failed in business. One of her father's boarders, Senator John Henry Eaton of Tennessee, helped the Timberlakes, squiring Peggy to social events while her husband was away working at a job that Eaton had gotten for him. People gossiped. After Timberlake's death in 1828, Eaton followed the advice of Andrew Jackson to "Marry Peg forthwith." When in 1829 Jackson became president of the United States, he appointed Eaton his secretary of war. Other cabinet wives vowed never to associate with this "loose woman" and repeated the ugly rumors circulating about her. Jackson defended her, and a cabinet crisis erupted, resulting in the resignations of several cabinet members.

Sarah Polk sided with the cabinet wives who defended convention by condemning Peggy Eaton, though unlike most of them she continued to greet the outcast. James Polk was embarrassed, since Jackson expected unqualified support from him. Moreover, Sarah's stance gave rise to talk that he was henpecked. In all her public life, the only criticism of her was that she dominated her husband. Vice President George Dallas phrased it: "She is certainly mistress of herself and I suspect of somebody else also." Her admirers spoke of her instead as her husband's "guardian." So vital was she to his career that a Nashville newspaper called her a "membress of the Congress-elect."

To resolve the Eaton dilemma, in the fall of 1830 Sarah was told to stay in Columbia while James returned to Washington alone. She joked to friends that she was saving "money to make a display on next winter," and sent her husband off with a shopping list of clothes for her.

Sarah returned to Washington in 1831, thereafter always accompanying her husband to the capital. Annually the Polks traveled between their Columbia home and Washington, enduring the discomforts and hazards incident to mid-19th-century journeys. Once, as they were fording a stream, water flooded into the carriage. Since neither of the Polks could swim, they had to be rescued by a quick-witted fellow passenger who saved them from anything worse than a "genteel wetting." "Mrs. Polk," wrote her husband, "seems to consider it the greatest adventure of her life, but would not I judge be willing to try the experiment again."

Although the Polks had no children, they cared for several relatives. After his father's death in 1827, James's mother and younger brothers and sisters depended on his support, an onerous task because of family quarrels over their father's estate. The death of the son who had mismanaged the Childress estate left James that burden as well. Throughout the years the Polks looked after nephews, nieces, and James's younger brothers, sometimes taking them into their home, caring for them in their illnesses, and standing by them in their times of trouble, which ranged from unhappy marriages to a duel. On his deathbed one of these brothers thanked Sarah Polk for her kindness, "more," he said, "the kindness of a Mother than a Sister." During the Polk presidency the first lady filled the White House with young relatives.

Despite some stress in the early years of their marriage, the Polks handled their own finances well and James bought land in western Tennessee and in Mississippi. Thanks in part to their close relationship with President Jackson, their fellow Tennessean, Polk's political career flourished. In December 1835 he was elected Speaker of the House. In keeping with his new position and their increased duties in hospitality, the Polks moved to a suite of rooms on Pennsylvania Avenue, as, said he, "awkward positions might ensue when the affairs and measures of Congress are discussed at meals" in a boardinghouse. "As would inevitably happen," Sarah responded, "and if you were there they couldn't openly criticize the Speaker, could they?" She took pride in her husband's new status: "The Speaker, if the proper person and with the correct idea of his position, has even more power and influence upon legislation, and directing the policy of parties than the President or any other public officer." As an old lady, she remembered that in 1837 Andrew Jackson had prophesied her husband's presidency, saying, "The sceptre shall come back to Tennessee before very long, and your own fair self shall be the queen."

In 1838, in the service of his party, Polk chose not to run for his safe congressional seat but instead to campaign for the governorship of Tennessee. His wife did not travel with him lest she violate the standards of proper womanly behavior. However, she worked behind the scenes, not only sending him needed documents but also helping organize the campaign, scheduling his speeches, mailing out campaign literature, and handling his correspondence. In his absences on campaigns, she kept him abreast of political gossip and newspaper reports. The Democrats won, and James K. Polk served as governor for two years. During his term Sarah assisted him with his paperwork and settled comfortably into the social life of Nashville. The indefatigable governor frequently refused invitations on the grounds that he could not spare the time, but with his encouragement his wife accepted them and made many warm friends.

It looked, however, as if James would pay a high price for leaving Congress. Despite his wife's expert support and reassurances, his hopes for running for the vice presidency of the United States in 1841 evaporated, and he lost the campaigns for governor in both 1841 and 1843. Moreover, Sarah worried about her husband's health; from boyhood he had not been strong, and the arduous, unsuccessful Tennessee campaigns weakened him still more. As he turned to his private law practice in Columbia, to strengthening his party ties, and to looking after the family business affairs, she urged him to work less compulsively and to enjoy more leisure time—advice almost impossible for him to take. "I must confess that I feel sad & melancholy at the prospect before me, or I should say before you," she wrote him. "The fatigue, exposure and absence for four months cannot present to me a bright prospect. I have not the assurance that the body and constitution can keep up under such labours as you have to go through, and it is only the *hope* that you can live through it, that gives me a prospect of enjoyment."

At the end of the 1843 campaign, James pinned his hopes on another attempt at the vice presidency. Instead, at the 1844 Democratic convention he was nominated for president—a dark horse, but still the nominee. Sarah worked early and late on the campaign from its headquarters in their home in Columbia, handling correspondence with campaign workers and releases to the papers. The unanimous endorsement as a potential first lady that she won built up support for her husband. Supreme Court Justice John Catron urged Polk to break with the tradition that presidential candidates did not campaign by attending a party rally in Nashville and taking his wife with him. She, Catron urged, would win "the women, the young men," and "the vain old ones." Polk refused. Andrew Jackson told Sarah, "I will put you in the White House you can so adorn if it costs me my life!" Although she was pessimistic about the outcome of the election, her husband triumphed.

On the way from Nashville to Washington for the inauguration, the pious Sarah asked James to refuse to receive visitors on Sundays. She also requested that a band greeting them not break the Sabbath peace. Nevertheless, after a victory celebration in Nashville, they made a grand progress to the nation's capital by steamboat, carriage, and train, with torchlight parades, cannon salutes, and fireworks.

On March 4, 1845, the retiring and incoming presidents rode together in an open carriage to the Senate chamber, where Congress welcomed Polk while his wife, friends, and other relatives watched from the gallery. Sarah wore a striped satin gown in dark red and gray, a mantle of beige wool lined with quilted rose-colored taffeta, and a dark red velvet bonnet. The swearing-in of the president and the inaugural address took place on the eastern steps of the Capitol; the Bible upon which he took the oath was given to his wife. For the inaugural ball that night she wore a marine blue velvet dress with a fringed cape. She carried a fan that her husband had given her, with medallions of the eleven presidents from George Washington to Polk, interspersed by the U.S. shield and the goddess of liberty; the reverse side of the fan pictured the signing of the Declaration of Independence.

The new first lady stood in strong contrast to her immediate predecessor, Julia Gardiner Tyler, who had entered the White House at 24; Sarah Polk was 41. Julia Tyler had reigned regally, while Sarah supported Jacksonian democracy. Julia Tyler begged Congress for money to refurbish the White House, and when she was refused she lavished her own money on it and spent extravagantly on entertainment. Sarah Polk, on the other hand, saved half the public funds appropriated for White House renovation and entertainment. Julia Tyler introduced new dances at White House balls. Sarah Polk, refusing the pleas of young girls to let them dance at the White House, said: "How indecorous it would seem for dancing to be going on in one apartment while in another we were conversing with dignitaries of the republics or ministers of the gospel." Julia Tyler dressed in dramatic blacks and whites, extravagantly ornamented with laces, diamonds, and plumes. Sarah Polk's dress was described as "rich but chaste"— somber velvets and satins. She accepted unsmilingly the compliment of a congressman who said, "This is a very genteel affair," answering, "I have never seen it otherwise." Nonetheless, Sarah Polk continued Julia Tyler's custom of having "Hail to the Chief" played when the president entered the room. Some said that Polk was so slight in physique that he might otherwise be overlooked.

In 1845 the nation seemed ready for what Sarah Polk had to offer: principle, piety, dignity, and self-command. The press enthused and predicted success and popularity for her, and she did not fail them. She knew how to make a point tactfully. When her niece heatedly defended her against the charge that Mrs. Clay, wife of the defeated candidate, made better butter, she replied, "Now, Ophelia, you should go back to your friend tomorrow and tell her that you are sorry for the sharp replies you made. Also tell her that I said if I should be fortunate enough to reach the White House, I expected to live on $25,000 per year, and I will neither keep house nor make butter. This answer will not offend her, and neither will I be offended."

The new first lady opened the presidential mansion to visitors, graciously welcoming Democrats and Whigs alike. To the 19-year-old Varina Davis she appeared stern, austere in her tastes, and disapproving of anything frivolous, but withal "very decorous and civil in her manner to all." The Polks neither gossiped nor criticized, speaking pleasantly even of their political enemies. They willingly accepted overtures for reconciliation—though on occasion Sarah Polk could be vindictive, particularly when anyone criticized her husband.

She also showed tact in developing her role as adviser to the president, preferring real power to its display—disguising it with conventional ladylike manners. She won praise for never discussing "a subject in relation to which her sex was expected to be ignorant." Publicly, whenever she spoke on political issues, she always added, "Mr. Polk thinks so." Privately she freely expressed her opinions, which her husband sought on political problems and on the decisions of the cabinet, whether or not he accepted them. She acted as his private secretary, taking full charge of all White House papers, and they worked on his speeches together. Because his health, duties, and interests restricted his social life, he relied on her to make friends for them both. She reported to him what she had learned in her weekly meetings with members of Congress. She won the respect of politicians of all stripes, many of whom confided in her.

Sarah Polk identified completely with her husband, deriving her power from his and exerting her influence for the causes he endorsed. She particularly encouraged his schemes for national expansion, approving them on the grounds that God intended the United States to occupy the continent. In support of the Mex-ican War, she is reported as stating that "whatever sustained the honor and advanced the interests of the country, whether regarded as democratic or not, she admired and applauded."

As far as is known, Sarah had no causes of her own. Women were then beginning to enter undergraduate colleges and medical schools; Elizabeth Cady Stanton, Susan B. Anthony, and Lucretia Mott were founding the woman suffrage movement; and married women were fighting for the right to their own wages, but Sarah Polk took little interest in these developments. Her tact failed to conceal her preference for the company of men rather than women. Aside from her relatives, Dolley Madison, and one or two of the cabinet wives, Sarah had few close woman friends, and most of her correspondence was with men.

The Polks had the reputation of being kind to their slaves, by contemporary standards. They dismissed overseers who treated slaves too harshly, sold slaves only for disobedience, and tried to keep slave families together, though the records indicate a higher than usual infant death rate among their slaves. James opposed every effort to change the institution of slavery but provided in his will that his slaves be freed after both he and his wife had died. A reported remark of Sarah's suggests that she reconciled the institution of slavery with her Christianity by attributing it to the predestination in which many Presbyterians believed: "Mr. President, the writers of the Declaration of Independence were mistaken when they affirmed that all men are created equal. . . . There are those men toiling in the heat of the sun while you are writing, and I am sitting here fanning myself, in this house as airy and delightful as a palace, surrounded with every comfort. Those men did not choose such a lot in life, neither did we ask for ours; we are created for these places."

Before the inauguration, concern for costs had prompted Sarah to consider renting living quarters and using the White House only as an office. She did move in, however, reducing the staff to 15 servants and replacing a number with slaves, some from her husband's plantation, some newly purchased. Her formal attire was supposedly Parisian, but at least some of her clothes were made by her free black maid. She had a sizable collection of jewelry, though customarily she wore a cameo bearing her husband's profile. In July 1845 the Washington *Union* described her renovation of the White House as "in a republican style, . . . neat, and sufficiently rich, without any indication of extravagance."

Twice a week Sarah opened the White House to all comers for evening receptions, at which the presidential couple shook hands with everyone. On Wednesday evenings in summer, the Marine Band played on the lawn. Even though she banned cards, dancing, and hard liquor from the White House, earning herself the nickname of "Sahara Sarah," people still accepted her hospitality—though some allegedly adjourned afterward across the street to the oasis of Dolley Madison's house.

In entertaining Sarah depended on conversational exchange rather than spectacle. She paid little attention to the menus, hour, or details of her dinners, not even noticing whether her guests had napkins. At a White House dinner party, Whig Henry Clay praised her housewifery, though, he gruffy added, he could not say as much for her husband. She answered, "I am glad to hear that my administration is popular. And in return for your compliment, I will say that if the country should elect a Whig next fall, I know of no one whose elevation would please me more than that of Henry Clay. And I will assure you of one thing. If you do have occasion to occupy the White House on the fourth of March next, it shall be surrendered to you in perfect order from garret to cellar." On another occasion when someone asked what she was reading, Sarah replied, "I have many books presented to me by their writers, and I try to read them all; at present this is not possible; but this evening the author of this book dines with the President, and I could not be so unkind as to appear wholly ignorant and unmindful of his gift."

Sarah Polk devoted much of her time and energies as first lady to protecting the health of the president, which had been frail since boyhood. When he could not attend social events because of the pressures of work, she reported to him afterward on the state of mind of their guests, especially cabinet members. To save him time, she screened newspaper reports for him, marking those of special interest. For the sake of his health, the Polks rarely left the White House. On the few trips James did allow himself, she usually traveled with him and did her best to persuade him to take breaks from his compulsive labors.

Despite his success in office, capped by the treaty that brought an end to the Mexican War, James Polk kept to his announced intention to serve only one term. In the last months of his presidency, crowds flocked to the White House to bid farewell. Praise for the first lady came from all sides. She was even applauded for having forbidden dancing in the mansion. Although this ruling had initially made many people unhappy, now she was complimented for dignifying the office by avoiding worldly amusements. On the Polks' progress back to Tennessee, thousands more echoed these sentiments, and they were met everywhere with parades, bands, and dinners in their honor.

In Tennessee they hoped for a restful retirement at Polk (formerly Grundy) Place, a mansion they had bought and were refurbishing in Nashville. But the exhausting journey after the arduous labors of the presidency took its toll, and James fell ill. He recovered for a time, but in June he was stricken again, this time fatally. He died in Nashville on June 15, 1849, at the age of 53. His will spoke of his wife's devotion, acknowledging that she "constantly identified with me in all her sympathies and affections, through all the vicissitudes of both my private and public life."

Despite her success as first lady, in which she had exercised unprecedented influence, Sarah Childress Polk undertook nothing and achieved nothing in the second half of her life, although she continued to be honored. Prominent visitors to Nashville and state officials called on her regularly and participants in parades uncovered their heads as they passed her house. Yet she did no charitable work and developed no new interests—to the disappointment of some of her contemporaries. Early biographer Laura Carter Holloway remarked: "Had she chosen any art or mode of mediating the conditions of those around her [during Reconstruction] or of adorning and rendering attractive the social life in her home circle in the numberless ways which to one in her situation were easy and practical, the good she could have done would have been incalculable, but her morbid exclusiveness rendered her unsociable and her Christian virtues, too much inclined to austerity, closed her house to every form of gaiety." To console her, her mother sent Sarah Polk Jetton, a grandniece, to live with her. "Sallie" faithfully performed her duties as companion, even after she married and had a child.

In many respects her life—public and private—ended with her husband's. "Life," she said, "was then a blank." From the age of 46—wealthy, still physically attractive, intelligent, and experienced—she lived on as a recluse for 42 years, seldom leaving home except to go to church. She indignantly repudiated rumors linking her romantically with James Buchanan, stating that she had too much respect for her beloved husband to change her name. She turned her home into a shrine to James Polk, where she preserved his papers and memorabilia of his career, some of which she donated to the Tennessee Historical Society. She responded to requests from office seekers to use her influence in their favor.

Until 1860, when she sold it, she managed from afar the Mississippi plantation her husband had left her. During the Civil War she proclaimed herself neutral and received both Union and Confederate officers. She refused to take an oath of allegiance to the United States, on the grounds that as the widow of a man who had been president of the entire United States, she could not support one "party" over the other. She suffered relatively little from the war being waged around her, though she did incur financial loss.

Still much revered, Sarah Childress Polk died on August 14, 1891, and was buried at Polk Place beside her husband. In 1893 both bodies were reburied on the capitol grounds in Nashville.

Sarah Polk (left) with her grandniece Sarah Polk Jetton *(Library of Congress)*

In many ways Sarah Polk was the first *real* first lady since the election of Andrew Jackson. The wives of Jackson, Martin Van Buren, and William Henry Harrison never reached the White House. Letitia Tyler, John Tyler's first wife, was an invalid who seldom left her bedroom; Julia Gardiner Tyler, his second wife, spent only a few months there. Sarah Childress Polk was a reassuringly solid presence, dignified and conforming to the public's stereotype of what a first lady ought to be.

She had perfect qualifications. In addition to her personal gifts and virtues, her good education, and her high principles, she was interested in politics and experienced as a political wife. Washingtonians liked and respected her. Without children to distract her, she devoted all her attention and energies to the job. And indeed she performed impeccably. She was all that her contemporaries asked of a first lady, and more besides. In the White House she exercised unprecedented power over the national agenda, yet managed to preserve her image as a model of propriety.

CHRONOLOGY

1803 *September 4:* Sarah Childress is born in Tennessee

1815 Sarah Childress enters the Abercrombie School in Nashville, Tennessee

1817 Sarah Childress enters the Moravian Female Academy in Salem, N.C.

1819 Sarah Childress's education ends with the illness and death of her father

1824 *January 1:* Sarah Childress marries James K. Polk

1825– 39 James Polk serves in the U.S. Congress

1839– 41 James Polk serves as governor of Tennessee

1844 James Polk is elected president

1845 *March 4:* Sarah Childress Polk becomes first lady

President Polk sends troops to Texas

1846 War with Mexico is declared

1849 *March 4:* The Polks leave the White House

June 15: James Polk dies; Sarah Polk lives on in Nashville, Tennessee

1891 *August 14:* Sarah Polk dies

FURTHER READING

Bumgarner, John Reed. *Sarah Childress Polk: A Biography of the Remarkable First Lady.* New York: McFarland, 1997.

Claxton, Jimmie Lou Sparkman. *88 Years with Sarah Polk.* New York: Vantage, 1972.

Means, Marianne. *The Woman in the White House.* New York: Random House, 1963.

Nelson, Anson and Fanny. *Sarah Childress Polk: Wife of the 11th President of the United States.* 1892. Reprint. Newton, Conn.: American Political Biography, 1994.

Sellars, Charles. *James K. Polk: Jacksonian, 1795–1843.* Princeton, N.J.: Princeton University Press, 1957.

———. *James K. Polk: Continentalist, 1843–1846.* Princeton, N.J.: Princeton University Press, 1963.

MARGARET MACKALL SMITH TAYLOR

(SEPTEMBER 21, 1788–AUGUST 14, 1852)

First Lady, March 5, 1849–July 9, 1850

Margaret Taylor was, in the words of a visitor to her home, "a most kind and thorough-bred Southern lady." Accurate as that description was, it did not take into account the strength that carried her through almost 40 years of the hardships of frontier life. She was an army wife, and these years defined her: Her husband wrote of her, "I am confident the feminine virtues never did concentrate in a higher degree in the bosom of any woman than hers."

———ɷɷɷ———

Margaret Mackall Smith was born on September 21, 1788, in Calvert County, Maryland, to Walter Smith, a wealthy planter, and his wife, Ann Mackall Smith. The Smiths were a distinguished family; Walter Smith had fought as an officer in the American Revolution. When Margaret was 21 she met Zachary Taylor, then an army lieutenant, at her older sister's home in Kentucky. She married Taylor, by then a captain, on June 21, 1810. The bridegroom's father gave his son a wedding present of 324 acres at the mouth of Beargrass Creek in Kentucky.

For most of her married life, Margaret Taylor lived on frontier army posts, far from the gentle country and life she had known in her girlhood. Although her husband was the son of a prosperous Kentucky planter who had served in the constitutional convention of 1792, Zachary had not attended West Point and exercised little influence over his assignments. He had to make his career on his own, moving frequently from one hardship post to another. Like most military couples, the Taylors had to endure long separations when circumstances precluded her accompanying him.

In their early life, that sometimes entailed her taking the children to live with a relative, probably her sister.

Most of the time, however, Margaret moved with Zachary, sharing the dangers and deprivations of a harsh and lonely existence, since few wives ventured into these sparsely settled regions. As her husband, then commanding Fort Knox, wrote to his brother in December 1813, "Peggy . . . says she is very lonesome and is in hopes that you will be as good as your word in paying the visit you promised."

In these primitive conditions and far from the support of her friends and relatives, Margaret gave birth to her five daughters and only son. She had to raise them in quarters never meant for families, sometimes spending winters in a cabin and summers in a tent. She had to wait and worry while her husband engaged in fierce battles with Indians. She also had to cope with the illnesses indigenous to the areas where he was posted: In 1820, "a violent bilious fever" attacked both her and her babies at Bayou Sara, Louisiana. Three-year-old Octavia and 15-month-old Margaret died that year. Later, their mother had to endure separation from her surviving children, whom she sent east to be educated.

Spring 1828 found Zachary Taylor in command at Fort Snelling, in what is now Minnesota. For a little more than a year, the family lived at this isolated outpost in relative comfort in a house with four rooms on the main floor and kitchen and pantry in the basement. Another happy period came from 1832 to 1836, when Colonel Taylor commanded Fort Crawford in the Michigan Territory, now Wisconsin. There Margaret and her two youngest children, Mary Elizabeth (Betty) and Richard, lived in a two-story frame house, 30' x 26', with a tiny wing on the south side and a kitchen and wine cellar in the basement. To help her run it, she brought two slaves from Louisville, but she skimmed the milk and fed the chickens herself. The Indian commissioner at Fort Crawford wrote sympathetically of her situation, speaking of "delicate females, belonging to some of the best families in the nation, reared in tenderness, amidst all the luxuries and refinements of polished society, now living in a fort. . . ."

The Taylors wanted an easier life for their children, and they made financial sacrifices for their education. Despite this the children chose the military life they were accustomed to. All three surviving daughters married military men, and their only son, Richard, become a lieutenant-general in the Confederate army. When daughter Ann in 1829 married Robert Crooke Wood, then an assistant surgeon at Fort Crawford, her father allegedly swore, "I will be damned if another daughter of mine shall marry into the Army. I scarcely know my own children or they me." Yet in June 1835, in the face of their disapproval and her father's personal dislike for the groom, Sarah Knox Taylor married Lieutenant Jefferson Davis. They had courted, sometimes clandestinely, for three years, and Knox, as she was called, had reached the age of consent. Acceding to what they could not prevent, her parents gave the bride a generous wedding gift of money and corresponded with her thereafter. In a letter to her mother on August 11, 1835, Knox wrote: "I have just received your affectionate letter forwarded to me from Louisville; you may readily imagine the pleasure it afforded me to hear from you. . . . How often, my dear Mother, I wish I could look in upon you. I imagine so often I can see you about attending to your domestic concerns—down in the cellar skimming milk or going to feed the chickens." She reassured her mother that she was living in healthy country. But a little more than a month later, she was dead of malarial fever.

In 1837 Zachary Taylor requested a prolonged leave to attend to his private affairs— among them, he said, "visiting my Children who are at school in Philadelphia and Kentucky, and who have been absent from us for . . . several years." Instead he was ordered to Florida to fight the Seminole, and his wife accompanied him. There, according to memoirist Mrs. John A. Logan, "she superintended the cooking of his food; she ministered to the sick and wounded; she upheld the *morale* of the little army by the steadfastness of her own self-possession and hope. . . ." The Taylors finally got their leave in the spring of 1840, upon which they plucked daughter Betty from her Philadelphia boarding school and vacationed in upstate New York and with Kentucky relatives.

On their 1840 assignment to Baton Rouge, Margaret furnished a room in the garrison as a chapel and found an Episcopalian priest to conduct occasional services there. She chose to live in a four-room cottage on the Mississippi that had originally been built for the Spanish commandant and that she restored with the help of soldiers and her two slaves. At last she had a home she loved for her husband, daughter Betty, sometimes her son Richard, and herself. In her "Spanish cottage" with its verandas enclosing the dwelling on every side, she rejoiced in Betty's presence and in visits from daughter Ann's four children. For a time she could revel in cosy domesticity, but in 1845 her husband was off again to fight in Mexico, leaving her in "a dreadful state of mind." Legend says she vowed that if he came home safely she would never go out in society again.

Nevertheless, on his return the Taylors often entertained friends and relatives in their cottage, small as it was. By then a general, Taylor had developed a political as well as a military circle of friends, which included William Henry Harrison and Winfield Scott. In a Florida campaign of the late 1830s, Taylor had won repute and the nickname "Old Rough and Ready." Now his conduct and success in the Mexican War in 1846 made him a national hero, and his wife and daughters joined him for the celebration of his triumph in New Orleans. Margaret was described in the period as of medium height, slender, erect, gray-haired, and stately, with an agreeable voice.

The Taylors subsequently returned to the Spanish cottage, she in hopes of a quiet retirement shared with her husband. At age 59 she was in "feeble health," had moved more times than she liked to think of, and was ready for a peaceful life. But the Whigs had already begun to consider Taylor as a presidential candidate for 1848. His wife reportedly thought of the idea as a plot to deprive her of his company and shorten his life. For months, he said, she prayed every night for the election of his opponent, Henry Clay. Nonetheless, Taylor was elected. A contemporary newspaper reported that a fellow boat passenger, not recognizing him, asked him if he was a Taylor supporter, to which the president-elect replied, "Not much of a one—that is, he did not vote for him—partly because of family reasons, and partly because his wife was . . . opposed to sending 'Old Zack' . . . to Washington, where she would be obliged to go with him!"

Margaret did move to the White House, but she could not bring herself to act as first lady, delegating those duties to her 24-year-old daughter Betty. Even during the week before the inauguration, Margaret declined the Polks' invitation to dinner, sending her daughter in her stead while she remained at the Willard Hotel. Once installed in the White House, she went to church every day at St. John's on Lafayette Square and entertained friends and relatives in the family's quarters upstairs. The rest she left to pretty and vivacious Betty, who married her father's aide Colonel William W. S. Bliss in December 1848.

During the Taylors' time in the White House, their staff consisted of white servants augmented by 15 of President Taylor's house slaves. By this time the issue of slavery had so divided the nation that the president preferred to keep these slaves out of sight, assigning them to the family quarters upstairs.

Margaret Taylor lived in the White House just as she would have lived anywhere else. She decorated her room like the one she had left in Baton Rouge, spent a lot of time knitting, and enjoyed the conversation at family dinners with a few friends as guests. She had frequent houseguests for lengthy visits. Daughter Ann Wood often brought her daughters from Baltimore, while a young niece, Becky, made her home in the White House when she was on vacation from boarding school. Varina Davis, who had succeeded the Taylors' daughter Knox as wife to Jefferson Davis, called regularly. "I always found the most pleasant part of my visit to the White House to be passed in Mrs. Taylor's bright pretty room," she wrote, "where the invalid, full of interest in the passing show in which she had not the strength to take her part, talked most agreeably and kindly to the many friends admitted to her presence." Later, in May 1850, Davis wrote, "I found the old lady sitting with her feet in the fender shivering, and she seemed so charmed to see me, said she felt so wretchedly lonesome, and chilly." Davis's descriptions of Margaret Taylor as a slender, gentle, refined woman completely contradict the rumors inspired by that lady's avoidance of the public eye—for example, one story held that she smoked a corncob pipe, whereas her grandson later testified that tobacco smoke made her "actively ill."

The family worried about *her* health, not their father's. But on July 4, 1850, after attending a two-hour outdoor ceremony in the Washington heat, he returned home and consumed cherries and iced milk. That night he fell ill of "cholera morbus." He died on July 9, urging his wife not to grieve, but she collapsed. Varina Davis reported, "The tearing Mrs. Taylor away from the body nearly killed me—she would listen to his heart, and feel his pulse, and insist he did not die without speaking to her."

Taylor's state funeral was a nightmare for his widow; Varina Davis reported that she "trembled silently from head to foot as one band after another blared the funeral march of the different organizations, and the heavy guns boomed in quick succession to announce the final parting." Nevertheless, the widow pulled herself together to move out of the White House that very evening. Her efforts to bury her husband as she wished, refusing to embalm his body and taking it to Louisville for a private ceremony, gave rise to still uglier rumors that she had poisoned him—rumors so persistent that they were silenced only 140 years later by the exhumation of his body. She never spoke of the White House again except in relation to her husband's death.

A week later, Margaret left Washington, staying for a time in Baltimore with the Woods before traveling with her two remaining daughters to meet her son in New Orleans. For the rest of her life she lived with her daughter Betty Bliss and her family in a little waterfront cottage at East Pascagoula, Mississippi. Her husband had left her his income-producing Louisville warehouses, a small lot there, 105 shares of Bank of Louisville stock, five slaves, and $1,716 from the sale of furniture.

Margaret Taylor's death on August 14, 1852, was of so little moment that the *New York Times* confined its obituary to one line: "Mrs. General Taylor, relict of the late President, died at East Pascagoula, on Saturday night." She lies buried beside her husband on Taylor family property in Louisville, now the Zachary Taylor National Cemetery.

—m—

Like Anna Symmes Harrison and Letitia Tyler, Margaret Taylor was first lady of the land in name only. It was a role she never sought and that she refused to undertake. For most Americans she is nameless and faceless; not even a portrait of her survives.

FURTHER READING

Bauer, K. Jack. *Zachary Taylor: Soldier, Planter, Statesman of the Old Southwest.* Newton, Conn.: American Political Biography, 1993.

Dyer, Brainerd. *Zachary Taylor.* New York: Barnes and Noble, 1967 (1946).

Hamilton, Holman. *Zachary Taylor: Soldier of the Republic.* Hamden, Conn.: Archon, 1966 (1941).

———. *Zachary Taylor: Soldier in the White House.* Hamden, Conn.: Archon, 1966 (1951).

Klapthor, Margaret Brown. *Maryland's Presidential First Ladies: Mrs. Zachary Taylor and Mrs. John Quincy Adams.* Calvert County, Md.: Calvert County Historical Society, 1966.

ABIGAIL FILLMORE
(Library of Congress)

In many ways Abigail Fillmore embodied an American democratic ideal. She was a self-made woman who married a self-made man. Both of them trusted in the power of education, struggled to achieve it for themselves, and worked to make it available to others. Both of them genuinely loved learning for its own sake. But try as they might they never attained the easy self-confidence of those born in more comfortable circumstances. Yet Abigail Fillmore made a lasting cultural contribution to the White House and the nation.

———ᘺᘺ———

Abigail Powers was born in Stillwater, New York, on March 17, 1798, the second daughter and youngest of the seven children of Baptist clergyman Lemuel Powers and his wife, Abigail Newland Powers. When she was two, her father died and her mother took the children to the frontier town of Sempronius, New York, in the Finger Lakes region, where a group of relatives were settling. Abigail grew up there, taught by her mother and reading her way through the library her father had left. At 16 she began to teach, learning as she taught.

Three years later she met Millard Fillmore at the New Hope Academy in Sempronius, where she was then employed. Only two years younger than she, for a brief time he was her student. He was the son of a dirt farmer, well below her father on the social ladder, but they found kindred spirits in each other. They shared a passion for education and self-improvement, and both eagerly continued to study, he concentrating on the law, as they supported themselves by teaching.

Millard and Abigail fell in love and became engaged in 1819, but his poverty and her family's objections to her marrying someone socially inferior postponed their wedding and kept them apart over much of the next seven years; for three years they did not even see each other. Finally, on February 5, 1826, they were married by an Episcopalian priest in Abigail's brother's home. The bride was tall and slender, with an oval face and high forehead; a prominent nose; a straight, wide mouth; and auburn-brown hair worn in curls. The couple settled in East Aurora, New York, at first on the Fillmore family farm, and then in a small house of their own near Millard's office, where he practiced law even as he studied it. Abigail taught for another two years, until her first baby was born on April 25, 1828. They named the little boy Millard Powers Fillmore and called him by his middle name.

The couple had much to rejoice over that year, for Millard was elected to the state legislature. He went off to board in Albany during the legislative session, leaving her at home to worry lest he meet and prefer "fairer and more accomplished females." In her loneliness, she wrote him in January 1830, "I have just got my work done and sit down, have been putting on the baby's red shoes, his others are worn out. I wish you were here to see him maneu-

vre. He laughs and stamps, and plays with his shoes. I wish you could read to me as you frequently have done after I sit down to sewing. . . . I am happy and proud in the thought that your heart is firm, and that no fascinating female can induce you to forget her whose whole heart is devoted."

In 1830 they moved to Buffalo, then a flourishing town of 8,000, where Fillmore opened a law practice with a friend. With more money coming in, the couple bought a six-room frame house two blocks from the main street, a simple Federal two-story building with a center hall. They began to establish themselves in the friendly community, attending formal dinners for the first time in their lives, as well as chamber recitals, lectures by celebrities, dances, and plays. They joined the Unitarian Church and the Lyceum, and as good citizens they helped start a lending library and improve public education. With relief from money worries and a little leisure, Abigail studied French and the piano and tended flowers in their conservatory and garden. Above all, she read, and their shared passion led them to accumulate a library that in time amounted to more than 4,000 books. Friends remarked on the gallant attentions Millard paid his wife—courtesies, it was said, that most men paid only to guests.

In 1832 the Fillmores had another birth and another election to celebrate. Abigail bore a little girl, whom they named Mary Abigail and called Abby, while Millard was elected to the U.S. Congress on the Anti-Masonic ticket. The family stayed in Buffalo while he served his two-year term, after which he returned to his law practice. On his reelection in 1836, however—this time as a Whig—he took his wife with him to Washington.

At that time the nation's capital was not an ideal place to bring up children, particularly for parents of limited means. The Fillmores would have to stay in one of the boardinghouses frequented by most congressmen. Because the Washington climate was notoriously unpleasant and unhealthy, and in the Fillmores' judgment the schools were inferior to those in Buffalo, they left the children with relatives in Upstate New York. During the legislative sessions from 1836 to 1842, except for a time in 1840–41 when they took Abby with them to Washington, the parents forwent the pleasure of their children's company.

In Washington, when she was not writing instructive and loving letters to the children, sewing, or shopping, Abigail devoted herself to the duties of a congressman's wife and to self-improvement. She followed the tedious Washington protocol for paying calls; kept herself informed on political affairs so that she could advise her husband, who often consulted her; listened to congressional debates; and read newspaper reports and editorials. Occasionally she attended ceremonial affairs, although she disliked attracting attention to herself, and performed her social duties conscientiously, if without much zest. She took advantage of the capital's cultural life, visiting galleries, going to concerts, attending lectures, and reading whenever she could find the time. She went to church regularly and occasionally indulged in some lighter amusement, like the race track.

In 1842 Abigail suffered an accident in Buffalo in which she hurt her foot; she never recovered from it. She spent most of that fall in bed, but, although she sought treatment in New York City and at Saratoga Springs, she could never again walk or stand for long periods without pain.

That same year, Millard decided to abandon his congressional career to seek other political office. Having failed to secure either the governorship of New York or his party's vice presidential nomination, he returned to private law practice for five years. Meanwhile, their children were growing up. At 16, Powers was old enough to enter his father's law office as a clerk, and Abby, in adolescence, was progressing with her music. In 1847 Millard was elected state comptroller. Abigail accompanied him to Albany, where they again stayed in a boardinghouse, this time because, he wrote, "my wife's health is too poor to think of troubling her with the cares of housekeeping for the present." The

children were in Massachusetts, Powers at Harvard, and Abby at a Lenox finishing school.

In Albany, Abigail enjoyed talking with intellectuals and attending lectures. She was well received in state government circles, where she found more social life there than she wanted. Vacationing in Newport, Rhode Island, she found the society there amusing, "But," she wrote, "it does not interest me." Even at their boardinghouse she kept to herself.

As her husband's career prospered, Abigail's health deteriorated. In 1848 Millard ran on the Whig ticket as the party's nominee for the vice presidency. By that time she was suffering from headaches, a cough, and back and hip problems. When her husband was elected vice president of the United States and moved to Washington in early 1849, Abigail stayed in Buffalo, unable to face packing and moving, although they missed each other. Ill, alone, and depressed, she experienced morbid presentiments of an early death. Nonetheless, she made calls, received visitors, and kept up with the national political situation through the newspapers, so that she could continue to counsel her husband. She occasionally forwarded to him requests from the numerous office seekers who besieged her, and at least once she and Abby visited him in Washington.

Then President Zachary Taylor died suddenly and unexpectedly on July 9, 1850, and Millard Fillmore became president the next day. Abigail Fillmore moved into the White House with little enthusiasm and little self-confidence. She worried that the sophisticates of Washington might find her dull—even though within small gatherings people found her well-informed conversation interesting. Reluctantly, she made ready to do her duty. While she delegated some of her social responsibilities to Abby, she usually attended the White House Tuesday morning receptions, as well as the Friday evening levees, the Thursday evening dinners for a large number of guests, and the more intimate Saturday dinners for about 20. Large receptions were particularly trying for her, because she found it so painful to stand. Some historians interpret her poor health as an excuse she could hide behind, while others believe she did the most she could.

The first lady was shocked to find no books in the White House. She prompted the president to ask Congress for an appropriation and the members came through with $2,000, which she used to purchase several hundred of her favorite books, and to refurbish a second floor oval parlor as a library. There she at the piano and her daughter at the harp played for their friends, and she spent pleasant hours reading in solitude.

Abigail learned that living in the White House had its compensations: The family were at last all living together, Powers as his father's private secretary and Abby as part-time hostess. The competent household staff took care of the domestic work. With the new library, a better heating system, a kitchen range to replace the open fire for cooking, and the redecoration of some of the rooms, the family was comfortable. She did not have to pay calls or accept invitations, and as first lady she could entertain authors she admired, such as Washington Irving and William Makepeace Thackeray, and invite artists, such as singer Jenny Lind, to visit her.

Despite her husband's principled stand against nepotism, Abigail secured a political appointment for one of her brothers. She also responded to requests for favors and help from other individuals—relatives, acquaintances, and even strangers—and from some churches and charities. In affairs of state she continued to advise her husband—most importantly, it is said, by urging him, vainly, to veto the notorious Fugitive Slave Bill of 1850.

At the end of President Fillmore's term, the family looked forward to resettling in Buffalo, finding a house suitable to the family of an ex-president, and touring the South before returning home. However, at President Pierce's inauguration Abigail caught a cold. That turned into pneumonia, perhaps complicated by the doctor's treatment of cupping and blistering. Three weeks later, having borne "all of her sufferings with uncomplaining fortitude," she died in the Willard Hotel in Washington on March 30, 1853. Her grieving family took her body back to the Forest Lawn Cemetery in Buffalo for burial. The nation mourned her as a dignified, genteel, pious, humble, and high-principled woman.

———— ✺ ————

The little known about Abigail Fillmore reveals a woman who felt herself ill-prepared for the position of first lady. Those of her predecessors whom everybody admired and talked about had been women born to wealth or at least comfort, like Martha Washington and Dolley Madison, or women of prominent families with wide experience of the world, like Abigail and Louisa Adams. For a woman raised in poverty on the frontier and largely self-educated, the prospect was daunting. Moreover, the world in which she might have found her calling as a scholar was closed to her by the absence of higher education for women. Although she conformed satisfactorily to the standards of her day and was generally well-received by Americans as first lady, she lacked the self-confidence to shine in that role, or to change it. Nonetheless, she left her mark by establishing the White House library and by improving cultural life there.

CHRONOLOGY

1798   *March 17:* Abigail Powers is born in Stillwater, New York

1800   The Powers family moves to Sempronius, New York

1818   Abigail Powers meets Millard Fillmore at an academy in New Hope, New York

1819   Abigail Powers becomes engaged to Millard Fillmore

1826   *February 5:* Abigail Powers marries Millard Fillmore

1828   Millard Fillmore is elected to the state legislature

April 25: Son Millard Powers is born

1832   Millard Fillmore is elected to Congress

March 27: Daughter Mary Abigail is born

1844   Millard Fillmore runs for the New York governorship

1848   Millard Fillmore is elected vice president of the United States

1850   *July 10:* Millard Fillmore succeeds as president; Abigail Fillmore becomes first lady

1853   *March 30:* Abigail Fillmore dies

FURTHER READING

Grayson, Benson Lee. *The Unknown President: The Administration of Millard Fillmore.* Washington, D.C.: University Press of America, 1981.

Holloway, Laura C. *The Ladies of the White House.* Philadelphia: Bradley and Company, 1881.

Raybach, Robert J. *Millard Fillmore: Biography of a President.* Newton, Conn.: American Political Biography, 1992.

Scarry, Robert J. *Millard Fillmore.* New York: McFarland, 2000.

Seale, William. *The President's House,* Vol. I. New York: Harry N. Abrams, 1992.

Snyder, Charles M. *The Lady and the President: The Letters of Dorothea Dix and Millard Fillmore.* Louisville: University Press of Kentucky, 1975.

Whitton, Mary Ormsbee. *First First Ladies, 1789–1865: A Study of the Wives of the Early Presidents.* 1948. Reprint. Freeport, N.Y.: Books for Libraries Press, 1969.

JANE MEANS APPLETON PIERCE
(MARCH 12, 1806–DECEMBER 2, 1863)
First Lady, March 4, 1853–March 4, 1857

JANE PIERCE
(Library of Congress)

Jane Pierce grew up expecting to become a happy wife and mother—at least insofar as her rather fragile health would permit. This hope was crushed by the deaths of her three sons, from which she never recovered. For all her propriety and for all her defiance of her family in marrying Franklin Pierce, there is little evidence that she ever matured enough or achieved enough independence from her family to function as a good wife. She gave her husband little reassurance or support, personal or political, in the manifold problems of his presidency and made little effort to lighten his burdens or his spirits. He seems to have catered to her preferences throughout their life together—with the outstanding exception of his accepting and indeed probably seeking the presidency. What dimly emerges is a portrait of a rather spoiled woman beset by bad health and ill fortune. Certainly as far as her husband's professional life was concerned, Jane Pierce was a handicap rather than an asset.

Jane Means Appleton was born at Hampton, New Hampshire, on March 12, 1806, the third daughter and third of six children of Congregational minister Jesse Appleton and his wife Elizabeth Means Appleton. The next year her father assumed the presidency of Bowdoin College, so she spent her early years in Brunswick, Maine. When her father died in 1819, her mother moved the family to her own mother's mansion in Amherst, New Hampshire.

Jane may have contracted tuberculosis from her father; in any event, she was frail and nervous as a girl. She apparently enjoyed her studies, particularly literature, and took seriously the stern Calvinist religion in which she was raised and the strict sense of propriety of her New England background.

Sensitive and lacking in self-confidence, with almost no stamina, Jane was far from an ideal choice as a wife for a man in public life. Too sickly to assume household responsibilities, she was never an easy woman to live with; her "nerves" made her demanding. She scolded more than she praised, and she could not express affection easily.

Nevertheless, when she and the budding lawyer and politician 22-year-old Franklin Pierce met in 1826, they fell in love. He was a graduate of Bowdoin and a former student of Jane's brother-in-law. Her mother disapproved of him, objecting to his manners, considering him socially inferior, and worrying about his drinking. As a northerner, Elizabeth Appleton disliked Franklin's stand on slavery: He opposed it in theory but regarded it as constitutionally protected; he stood with the South on states' rights. Other members of the Federalist Appleton family objected to him on the grounds of his affiliation with the Democratic Party. Certainly the couple differed in temperament and background: Franklin Pierce gregarious and vain, a son of the frontier; Jane Appleton retiring and proper, a daughter of the aristocratic New England theocracy.

During their eight-year courtship, Franklin was elected successively to the New Hampshire House of Representatives and to the U.S. Congress. Jane dreaded the duties that would become hers as the wife of a congressman. She thought politics a dirty and uninteresting business and blamed Franklin's involvement in it for tempting him to drink more. Nonetheless, she refused her mother's advice and married him in Amherst on November 19, 1834, in a quiet ceremony attended only by members of the bride's family and the groom's father. Her brother Robert escorted her, and one of her brothers-in-law performed the ceremony.

The bride wore a traveling dress, and the young couple left immediately for Washington, where they settled into a quiet boardinghouse. For a time Jane Pierce tried to adapt to her new life. In her first few months in Washington, she described herself as "not very unhappy" in a letter to her new father-in-law:

> We still continue to be pleased with our accommodation here and are in fact as comfortably situated as we could be. . . . I find Washington very much as I expected both in appearance and climate—as to the former, my expectations were not very highly raised, and the latter has realized the favorable impression I had of it. Today however is so excessively windy that I am disappointed in my wish of going to church which is a deprivation to which I hope I shall not often be subjected— these high winds are common here, and exceedingly disagreeable. . . . We have an invitation to dinner to Gov Cass' on Wednesday which is accepted notwithstanding my predilections for a quiet dinner at home. The gentlemen and ladies of our [boardinghouse] family are quite social and pleasant and we are on a very easy footing as we should be to live so long together.

Jane approved of the White House and its current occupant, President Andrew Jackson. Despite her preference for dinners at the boardinghouse, the Pierces attended several large evening parties, though her health troubled her.

At the end of the session, the Pierces settled in Hillsborough, New Hampshire, where Franklin had bought a house and hired a couple to run it for his wife. When he returned to Washington after a summer's law practice, she did not accompany him but instead went home to her mother. Her husband wrote to her every day, worried about her health, and she seemed to miss him. In February 1836 she bore a son, Franklin Jr., who lived for only three days; afterward, her health deteriorated further.

That fall she rallied enough to accompany her husband to Washington, though she continued to deplore his involvement in politics and urged him to pursue another career. But he was rising fast, and soon after they had settled into their comfortable, rather elegant boardinghouse, he received news of his election as senator for the term beginning March 4, 1837. She was unimpressed by his success; one of their fellow boarders wrote that she seemed "in very delicate health and wanting in cheerfulness."

In spring 1837 she stayed with relatives in New England and did not return to Washington until December. That winter and the following spring, the Pierces' lives were darkened by deaths and hard times in their extended families and poor prospects for him in the Senate. They toyed with the idea of moving west to a region of greater opportunity. "Oh, how I wish he was out of political life!" she wrote. "How much better it would be for him on every account." In 1838, in the heat of a Washington June, she retreated to her invalid's bed.

In August they moved to Concord, New Hampshire, where they maintained their home for the rest of their married life. Jane had never liked Hillsborough, and her husband hoped that his law practice would do better in the larger town, though he continued to commute to Washington for the congressional sessions. She was miserable living with her husband in the capital she hated, and equally miserable when she stayed in New England, because they were apart. The birth of sons Frank Robert in September 1839 and Benjamin in April 1841 gave her new ammunition for her campaign to get her husband out of politics: The family must have, she said, a healthier environment than Washington in which to raise their children, an argument that won him over.

On February 16, 1842, near the end of his senatorial term, Franklin Pierce resigned his seat and took his family back to Concord, where he resumed his law practice. Despite his wife's efforts, he could not completely resist the lure of politics; turning his attention to local affairs, he made political speeches, chaired the New Hampshire Democratic Party, and served as a federal district attorney. For several years, however, he refused repeated invitations to resume a national political career, even turning down President Polk's offer to appoint him attorney general of the United States.

Her husband had given Jane her wish. In Concord they lived quietly out of the public eye, and she liked attending the South Congregational Church there. But his attempts to make her happy were frustrated in 1843 with the death of their son Frank Robert from typhus. She had to watch her four-year-old suffer and die in agonizing pain, and her own health, which had briefly improved, worsened. Her husband struggled to resign himself to his son's death: "The chastisement is a fearful one but . . . it was doubtless needed. We are commanded to set up no idol in our hearts and I am conscious that within the last two years particularly my prevailing feeling has been that we were living for our children. . . . We should have lived for God and left the dear ones to the care of Him who is alone able to take care of them and us."

With the outbreak of the Mexican War in 1846, Franklin felt it his duty to fight and accepted a commission as brigadier general. Before he left, he carefully arranged for the welfare of his anxious, disapproving wife and their remaining son Bennie, hiring live-in help for her. He wrote his "Dearest Jeanie" faithfully all during his service, signing himself "Yr own affectionate Frank."

Franklin came home safely. Their house had been sold during his time in Mexico, and for several months after his return Jane and Bennie stayed with Lowell relatives. For a while all three Pierces lived in a boardinghouse before finally settling into a satisfactory living arrangement with Mr. and Mrs. Willard Williams in a cottage in Concord. Mrs. Williams cooked and ran the household, and with no domestic responsibilities and the family together, Jane grew healthier. She concentrated her energies and emotions on her young son, focusing especially on his religious training in the same strict evangelicalism in which she had been raised. They had family worship in the morning, and she listened to Bennie's prayers in the evening. Sundays were days of cold meals, listening to Bible stories, and learning hymns, with church attendance in both the morning and the afternoon. Her husband's law practice was prospering, and the Pierces were living as she had always hoped.

But it was not to last. By 1852 Jane must have been aware that the prize that few politicians can resist was being dangled before her husband: the presidency of the United States, for on a trip to Boston with Franklin in May that year, a gentleman addressed her as the "future Presidentress." Nonetheless, when she learned that her husband had been nominated as the Democratic candidate for president, she fainted, and her husband had to take her away. They went off to visit Cambridge and Newport and Providence, but the excitement followed them everywhere. Son Bennie, indoctrinated by his doting mama, wrote to her that "I hope he won't be elected, for I should not like to be at Washington and I know you would not either."

During the campaign it was no secret that Jane Pierce besought God fervently for her husband's defeat. The candidate, grasping for an honor he had never expected, received nothing but discouragement from his immediate family. Yet even his wife's relatives enthused about the great honor that might be coming to her husband, and gradually, at least in her spells of relatively good health, she learned to contemplate the future "with less despondency" than at

other times, when "the expectation seems too heavy to be borne." After his election she prepared to move to the White House only with the greatest reluctance.

Then tragedy befell the Pierces again. They had been visiting with friends and supporters in Boston, and Jane and Bennie went from there to Andover for Christmas. On January 6, 1853, all three took the train back from Boston to Concord; it derailed, and Bennie was killed before their eyes. Both parents interpreted the accident as an act of God. He thought it a punishment for his weaknesses. In the wildness of her grief, she told her husband that "God decided to take our precious little boy, so that you will have no distractions as you set out to effect reconciliation between sections of our nation." Implicitly she was accusing him of sacrificing their son to his ambition, and this crushed him.

Jane stayed away from the inauguration. According to a friend, Bennie's death had "paralyzed her energy." It was arranged that she would be escorted from Boston to Baltimore, where she would stay until the excitement of the inauguration died down. Franklin, who had hoped to celebrate the day with his wife and their adored son, set forth alone, leaving orders for flowers and a bracelet to be delivered to her that day. Her family, including those who had once opposed her marriage, urged her now to take her place in the White House at her husband's side. She yielded after a fortnight, but she still felt anger toward him for having concealed his eagerness to be president. She anticipated no happiness in Washington, and consequently she found none.

Abby Kent Means, Jane's aunt by marriage, moved into the White House with her, serving as hostess for the few social occasions scheduled, which allowed Jane to avoid this aspect of her duties as first lady. With the benefit of a generous appropriation by Congress, the White House was refurbished, but under the supervision of an army captain. Jane did bestir herself to put away the elaborate presidential china left by her predecessors, substituting for it a plain blue-and-white American-made set that she said was "good enough." The supervision of the household was entrusted to a New Hampshire couple experienced in operating a hotel. On rare occasions she appeared at White House dinner parties, but she cut a melancholy figure, preferring quiet dinners with New Hampshire relatives and friends—or solitude. The convivial president told his guests, "You need no introduction to this house, it is your house and I am but the tenant for a time." But his wife did not frequent the evening receptions he instituted on Fridays from 8:00 until 10:00, leaving him to receive with Mrs. Means.

The first lady spent much time alone, reading the Bible, brooding on her grief, and writing notes to her dead son in which she repented her inability to express her love for him more openly. She left the White House mainly to go to church and gently urged White House employees to do likewise. The president read prayers to his wife and servants each day, and between them the Pierces imbued their home with an austere piety. Federal Commissioner of Patents Charles Mason wrote, "Everything in that mansion seems cold and cheerless. I have seen hundreds of log cabins which seemed to contain more happiness."

The president had always been a sociable man who throughout his marriage had been left to construct a social life on his own. In the White House he fell into the habit of going about alone, paying calls on friends in the evenings and enjoying the gay society of the capital, leaving the dismal mansion to visit the theater and concerts.

Varina Davis, second wife of Jefferson Davis, did what she could to help the first lady. Her husband was Pierce's secretary of war and close personal friend. She had already supported more than one president's wife, having comforted Margaret Taylor in the shock of her husband's death. Jane enjoyed the Davises' baby son and frequently asked Varina to ride in her carriage with her. Varina sympathized with her, writing that she "was a broken-hearted woman in weak health, and not a person who found it easy to become acquainted with strangers." Jane, Varina continued,

> was brought to Washington, more dead than alive. Certainly there was little in the new life she led there to comfort or cheer her, and her depression was rendered still greater by being a constant sufferer from an obscure ailment. She was very small, and never could have been pretty, but was very well read, intelligent, and gentle, and was a person of strong will and clear perceptions; her husband's society was the one thing necessary to her, and he was too overworked to give her much of his time. . . . She had a keen sense of the ridiculous, but was too ceremonious to indulge it often. She lived much within herself. With her sorrow pressed close to her stricken heart she bore her position with patience and gentle dignity.

Varina gradually encouraged the first lady into more activity. Jane Pierce would not accompany her husband to concerts or lectures, but she did consent now and then to sail with him on the Potomac and to vacation with him. Two years into his term she appeared at the traditional New Year's reception, an affair jammed with guests of all classes. Thereafter she began to attend the Friday evening receptions, where, said a contemporary, "traces of bereavement" were "legibly written on a countenance too ingenuous for concealment" despite her welcoming smiles. In 1856 the Pierces scheduled a round of official dinners.

On March 3, 1857, on the eve of President-elect Buchanan's inauguration, Jane left her husband in the White House to make his official farewells, while she went to stay with friends. He joined her the next day, and they lingered in Washington's warm spring weather for another month. They went on to Philadelphia and thence to New England, where they spent the summer at various places—a summer darkened by news of the death of Jane's intimate companion, Abby Means.

In November Franklin took Jane abroad for two years, hoping to improve her health. Throughout the journey she carried with her

Bennie's Bible and a small box that Abby Means had given her, in which she kept locks of hair of her dead—her sons, her mother, and her sister. In their travels the Pierces bought souvenirs and paintings, including 16 obscure "old masters." Returning to Concord in the summer of 1859, they purchased 60 acres on the edge of town on which they planned to build a house, then went to the West Indies to avoid the New Hampshire winter. Many of his supporters hoped that Pierce would again run for president in the 1860 campaign, but he firmly rejected their pleas, especially as his wife was sicker than ever.

From then on they often stayed with their former caretaking couple, the Williamses, who had bought a larger house in Concord. But Jane found it difficult to live in a town that had so many memories of Bennie and spent much of her time with relatives in Massachusetts. She died on December 2, 1863 (the cause of death was listed as "consumption"), and was buried in Concord beside her children. Her husband mourned her as a woman whose "natural endowments were of a high order. . . . She inherited a judgment singularly clear and correct, and a taste almost unerring."

—⁂—

Remote, otherworldly, and reclusive, "the very picture of melancholy," Jane Pierce barely cast a shadow in the White House, but it was the shadow of gloom. Her husband's best friend, Nathaniel Hawthorne, remembered her as never seeming to have anything to do with "things present." She reluctantly moved into the White House soon after her adored third and only living son was killed in a train wreck.

Anguished and broken in spirit, she had no heart for her duties as first lady.

With her frail health, her Calvinistic upbringing, and the loss of all three of her children, Jane Pierce may have been doomed to unhappiness no matter what her husband's job or where they lived. But she interpreted her third son's death as the judgment of God on her husband's worldly ambition and saw her suffering as the direct result of her husband's presidency. Her heartaches so dominated her that only rarely could she act as first lady.

CHRONOLOGY

1806   *March 12:* Jane Means Appleton is born

1834   *November 19:* Jane Appleton marries U.S. congressman Franklin Pierce

1836   *February:* Son Franklin Jr. is born; he dies soon after birth

1839   *September:* Son Frank Robert is born

1841   *April:* Son Benjamin is born

1842   Jane Pierce persuades her husband to retire from the U.S. Senate

1843   Son Frank dies

1846   Franklin Pierce volunteers for service in the Mexican War

1852   Franklin Pierce is elected to the presidency

1853   *January 6:* Son Benjamin is killed

        March 4: Jane Pierce becomes first lady

1857   *March 4:* The Pierces retire to Concord, Massachusetts

1863   *December 2:* Jane Pierce dies

FURTHER READING

Boas, Norman F. *Jane M. Pierce. (The Pierce-Aiken Papers)*. Stonington, Conn.: Seaport Autographs, 1983.

———. *Jane M. Pierce. (The Pierce-Aiken Papers). Supplement*. Stonington, Conn.: Seaport Autographs, 1989.

Colman, Edna M. *White House Gossip: From Andrew Jackson to Calvin Coolidge*. Garden City, N.Y.: Doubleday, Page, 1927.

Davis, Varina Howell. *Jefferson Davis: A Memoir by His Wife*. Vol. I. New York: Belford, 1890.

Gara, Larry. *The Presidency of Franklin Pierce*. Lawrence: University Press of Kansas, 1991.

McClure, Alexander K. *Recollections of Half a Century*. Salem, Mass.: Salem Press, 1902.

Nichols, Roy. *Franklin Pierce: Young Hickory of the Granite Hills*. 1958. Reprint. Newton, Conn.: American Political Biography, 1993.

MARY ANN TODD LINCOLN
(DECEMBER 13, 1818–JULY 16, 1882)
First Lady, March 4, 1861–April 14, 1865

MARY TODD LINCOLN
(Library of Congress)

Mary Todd Lincoln was an ambitious woman born in a time when women could gain high position and fortune only through men. Self-centered and largely unprincipled, she eventually achieved her aspiration to become first lady of the United States, but it brought her less happiness than misery. She saw her husband and three of her sons die. She affronted society even as she sought to lead it. In the end, the fame she had sought turned to ignominy as the nation judged her either villainous or mad.

—⁓—

Mary Ann Todd was born in Lexington, Kentucky, on December 13, 1818, the third daughter and fourth of seven children of businessman Robert Smith Todd and Eliza Parker Todd. Her happy childhood in a well-to-do family was

95

disrupted by the death of her mother when she was six and the introduction of an unsympathetic stepmother when she was seven; she remembered the period as "desolate." Her schooling was extensive: six years at the Shelby Female Academy of Episcopalian priest Dr. John Ward, four years boarding at Madame Charlotte Mentelle's select school for young ladies near Lexington (run by refugees from the French Revolution), and another year at Ward's academy. Mary excelled at school, loving her lessons and developing a passion for reading. She studied reading, writing, grammar, arithmetic, history, geography, natural science, French—in which she became fluent—cooking, and religion. She also learned dancing and acting and developed her talent for mimicry. Her mentors directed her education toward making her a future republican mother, fit to raise children for the new nation.

Mary emerged a polished, attractive young woman whom her sister Elizabeth Edwards described as possessing "clear blue eyes, long lashes, light brown hair with a glint of bronze," a lovely complexion, and a beautiful figure. Her brother-in-law thought her an engaging conversationalist who "could make a bishop forget his prayers." Yet though she was warmhearted, her sharp tongue and her habit of mimicking others gave people pause. In a society where, Mary said, men treated "their wives and females generally . . . as if they had no right to possess mind or understanding," she did not confine herself to the "womanly" concerns considered proper. As a child she had exhibited an interest in politics when she joined the Whigs, her father's party. As a young woman she expressed her opinions rather than asking questions and listening raptly to the men's answers. Nevertheless as a Todd she was invited to parties and cotillions in Lexington as a matter of course, though she later remembered her adolescence as a time "when friends were few." Like most well-off Lexington women, she apparently filled her time with amusements, paying calls, and going to church, though she probably read more than most. But she undertook no good

works and embraced no causes, despite her affection for the slaves who served her and her horror of the institution that chained them.

After she left school in 1836, Mary escaped from the "circumstances that rendered unpleasant . . . our father's home"—that is, her stepmother—to visit her older sister Elizabeth, now Mrs. Ninian Edwards, in Springfield, Illinois. She was exhilarated by the activities of this new state capital and the discussions of whether her brother-in-law should run for Congress. When the visit ended in the fall, desperate to avoid the company of her stepmother, she helped in Ward's academy as an apprentice teacher.

In 1839 Mary returned to Elizabeth Edwards's home in Springfield living as she had in Lexington, largely in a woman's world. She became an intimate friend of Mercy Levering, with whom she exchanged affectionate letters, assuring Mercy, in the manner of female correspondents of the day, that "Your mate misses you too much from her nest." Both of them expected to marry, and Mary dearly hoped that Baltimorean Mercy would wed a Springfield man.

She usually saw eligible men at organized social affairs such as weddings, dances, and picnics. Convention forbade a single man to call at her home except on the invitation of a male of the household, but the hospitable Edwardses provided many opportunities. Though Mary never considered herself popular, she had several suitors, among whom she preferred the lawyer and legislator Abraham Lincoln, nine years older than she, whom she met in 1839.

Mary had a high opinion of herself, and she meant to marry a future president of the United States. Her sister Elizabeth called her the most ambitious woman she had ever known, one who "loved glitter, show, pomp, and power." Despite Abe's awkward manners, his skimpy coats, his shabby trousers, and his mismatched socks, she saw possibilities in him that caused her to reject others, including Stephen Douglas, whom she told, "I can't consent to be your wife. I shall become Mrs. President, or I am the victim of false prophets, but it will not be as Mrs. Douglas." Furthermore, she had discovered in Lincoln one of those rare men who believed in justice and equality even for married women. She needed such a husband, for she was a woman who defied convention and tradition. She showed no interest in the struggle for women's rights that had begun in 1848. Instead, she wanted the reputation for being a sacrificing, ladylike "True Woman" devoted to hearth and home as well as the freedom to do exactly as she pleased.

Abraham Lincoln was a diffident suitor who questioned whether he could make her happy, worried about his ability to support her, and may have feared that he had a venereal disease. Nor was Mary Todd in any hurry. She was enjoying her relatively independent life in Springfield and knew that she would lose her civil and legal rights when she married. The Edwardses vigorously opposed the match, believing Mary and Abe "so different that they could not live happily as man and wife."

They were indeed an unlikely pair. He was tall and lanky; she was short and plump. He came from a poor family of undistinguished descent, she from a prosperous and respected background. He had educated himself; she had received an education reserved only for the most fortunate young women of her day. He had been raised in the backwoods, she in one of the most sophisticated cities west of the Alleghenies. He had grown up in a log cabin, she in a house where 10 slaves did the housework, cooked, washed, ironed, sewed, and tended the children. But the two shared insecurities that afflicted them all their lives. His probably originated in his backwoods upbringing and his poverty, hers in the early loss of her mother and separation from her family. His insecurities expressed themselves in melancholia, hers in hot-tempered, hysterical outbursts in which she attacked others. He got along with people, whereas she made many enemies.

In 1840 Abe and Mary reached an understanding, though they did not enter into a formal engagement. On January 1, 1841, he was late in picking her up for a party, so she went without him, and when he arrived he found her flirting with another suitor. The argument and parting that ensued threw Abe into a depression so severe that it frightened his friends. He wrote to his law partner that he was now the most miserable man alive, and feared that he would never be happy. "To remain as I am is impossible; I must die or be better, it appears to me." Mary too suffered regrets and wanted him back. When a mutual friend brought them together in 1842, begging them to be friends, both agreed.

Some historians have tried to account for the couple's troubled courtship by postulating Abraham Lincoln's romantic love for someone else. Others have cast Mary Todd in the role of seductress, one psychohistorian accusing her of having trapped him into sleeping with her and then insisting that he marry her on the grounds that she might be pregnant. What is certain is that after almost two years of secret meetings and his assumption of blame for the authorship of satirical newspaper skits that she had written, Mary told her sister on November 4, 1842, that they were going to marry at once. The Edwardses, defeated, arranged for the ceremony in their home. The bride wore her sister Frances's white satin dress and a pearl necklace.

For a year they boarded in a modest room at the Globe Tavern in Springfield, where Mary Lincoln was sometimes left alone for a month at a time while her husband rode the circuit on his law practice. On August 1, 1843, she was delivered of the first of their four sons, whom she named Robert Todd after her father. That fall the couple set up housekeeping in a four-room frame cottage in Springfield. The next spring, with help from Mary's father, they bought a five-room cottage with a loft and some outbuildings on an eighth of an acre of land, where their other three sons were eventually born and four-year-old Eddie died of turberculosis in 1850. In 1856, with money from the sale of property given her by her father, they finished the upper story by installing four new bedrooms, turning their cottage into a Greek-Revival upper-class house.

With her husband away on the circuit for about half of each year, Mary Lincoln was immersed in a world of babies and housekeeping. In those days, when pregnancies prevented women from appearing in public, the arrival of four babies at three- or four-year intervals long restricted her activities to the domestic front. Frequent migraine headaches and an injury during the birth of her youngest son made parenthood even more stressful for her.

She bought ready-made clothing for her menfolk, but she made pillows, sheets, and curtains herself and did the mending and darning. With a careless husband and four boys tramping dirt in from the unpaved streets on which animals roamed freely, she struggled to keep the unscreened house clean.

To make matters worse, she performed more of the household work than economy necessitated or her husband wanted, apparently because she had a hard time keeping servants. She scrimped on their wages, and her neighbors heard her shouting at her hired help, though one black woman who laundered for her for years described her as "taking no sassy talk but if you are good to her, she is good to you and a friend to you."

Overwork does not improve the temper, and her family suffered accordingly. Historians disagree on the relationship between husband and wife. Certainly she indulged in hysterical outbursts, and some say she physically abused her husband, driving him out of the house. Records show that she threw books at him, and once she threw a log, but he did not retaliate. He once commented about her bad behavior, "If you knew how little harm it does me and how much good it does her, you wouldn't wonder that I am meek." Yet Mary later spoke of those years as the happiest of her life.

When in public she dressed in style, in gowns made by a seamstress and store-bought bonnets and hats. She entertained more modestly than women with live-in help, counting on her charm as a hostess and her conversational abilities to compensate for a lack of elaborate menus. Even in her husband's absence she might invite a bachelor for an evening of political talk. As Lincoln's prominence and income grew in the 1850s, she gave receptions for as many as 500 people, midwestern versions of the levees of the east, where she served food buffet style. In 1860, when the Republican National Committee came to Springfield to notify Lincoln of his nomination for the presidency, she provided a table set with glasses, decanters, cakes, and sandwiches and hired a butler to announce the guests. Some of the committeemen criticized her for serving alcohol, but they still described her as "amiable and accomplished, gracious, and a sparkling talker."

Both the Lincolns adored and indulged their children, to a degree that scandalized their friends. Their father always wanted them to be happy, and to that end he would take them and the neighborhood boys fishing and join in their mischief rather than checking it. On the other hand, he was not always a reliable caretaker. The story goes that on one occasion he put his boys into a wagon and pulled it along as he walked and read—too absorbed to notice when the baby fell out. Their mother sometimes gave way to her temper and whipped the boys, especially if they frightened her by running away, though she preferred to describe herself as one who corrected with a gentle word—as she said, "a happy, loving, laughing Mama." Most of the time she thought of them as darlings and permitted them to make noise and keep pets to their hearts' content. She played with them and organized parties, like a "children's gala for fifty or sixty boys and girls." When company came, the boys were trotted out, said Lincoln's law partner William Herndon, "to monkey around, talk, dance, speak, quote poetry, etc." Their father was in no hurry about their education, saying "Let them run. He [Tad, their youngest son] has time enough to get pokey." Both parents wanted the best for their children, and they sent Robert, their eldest, to Philips Exeter and Harvard, though the separation from him went to his mother's heart.

Like many a wife, Mary Lincoln tried to change the man she had chosen to marry. She nagged Abe unendingly but often without result about his clothes and his table manners.

He must, for instance, stop rubbing his hands down the front of his trousers. Let the servant answer the door, she told him when he went himself, in his shirtsleeves, and told the caller that his wife was upstairs putting on her "trottin' harness."

Whatever their quarrels, Mary believed in her husband and told him so, always insisting that he would become president. She put all her knowledge of politics and the woman's intuition on which she prided herself into her ambitions for him. She would be his chief adviser, providing him with the human insights necessary to political success. She was delighted when he was elected to Congress in 1846. Even though congressional wives with children almost never accompanied their husbands, in 1847 she and their sons went with him to Washington, where they boarded just across from the Capitol. Not all their fellow boarders welcomed the presence of the Lincolns' lively sons, but Mary loved the city, with its theaters, concerts, receptions, balls, and smart shops.

In the spring, she gave up the effort of living in one room with two youngsters, one of them ailing, and went on a visit to Lexington. But the Lincolns missed each other, and in the summer of 1848 they vacationed together at Niagara Falls before returning to Springfield. He finished the rest of his term in Washington alone and then sought a patronage post as commissioner of the Land Office, with the eager and active assistance of his wife, who wrote numerous letters for him—but without the desired result. Some of his colleagues attributed his refusal of the governorship of Oregon, which he was offered, to her opposition.

As things turned out, Abe was better off politically and economically in Illinois. For the next six years his political career stalled. Mary was bitterly disappointed by the failure of the Illinois legislature to appoint him U.S. senator in 1855, and she ended her friendship with the wife of the man to whom Abraham Lincoln had thrown his votes—by no means the only friend whom she sacrificed to politics, for she measured friendship by compliance with her wishes.

Though she herself could not bear criticism she never ignored a provocation, however minor, but harbored grudges and retaliated harshly. Political enemies she called "dirty dogs" and "connivers."

Mary never allowed her husband's political energies to flag, however often he might sink into depression and however much he might joke about his career and her ambitions. Herndon called her "like a toothache, keeping her husband awake to politics day and night." Others thought her a staunch supporter who refueled the energies that his depressions drained. If Abe said, "Nobody knows me," she replied, "They soon will." He was, she insisted, not to be content with any office but the highest in the land. His neglect of his law practice in favor of politics worried her not at all, regardless of the loss of income. From 1854 he politicked energetically, gaining fame for his speeches, particularly in the Lincoln-Douglas debates of 1858.

When her husband was nominated and then elected president of the United States, Mary Lincoln campaigned vigorously by means of letters in which she presumed to clarify her husband's positions. She exulted when he came home calling out, "Mary, Mary, *we* are elected." In victory she preened, postured, and demanded favors. In an era when ladies still worried about traveling without an escort, she went off alone to New York to buy a wardrobe. She had never governed her tongue, and despite the convention that a lady should be mentioned in the press only when she was born, married, and died, she talked freely to reporters about politics and patronage, earning herself the title of Lincoln's "kitchen cabinet." She reveled in the train trip from Springfield to Washington, despite the threats on her husband's life addressed to her and even to their sons, and enjoyed the crowds along the way who clamored to see her and the children. Yet so dangerous was the state of the nation that Abraham Lincoln had to leave his family behind to secretly take another train from Harrisburg and be smuggled through Baltimore for fear of assassination.

Whether she realized it or not, the relationship between Mary and her husband was inevitably changing. As the chief executive of the nation, he operated in a realm that she could not enter. Her desire to wield power behind the throne was more and more frustrated as he wrestled with the problems of the presidency. Shrewd as she might be politically, Mary lacked the vision and the judgment to understand what was happening to the nation.

She entered a Washington divided over slavery and states' rights, where southern ladies refused to attend her teas. Nevertheless, she enjoyed the inauguration ceremonies. At the first inaugural ball she wore a watered blue silk gown with pearls, gold bracelets, and diamonds, and she remained to dance and talk long after Lincoln had retired at midnight.

Mary immediately set about refurbishing the shabby White House with a $20,000 congressional appropriation. The Civil War interrupted her, breaking out on April 12, 1865, only five weeks after the inauguration. Rumors that the Confederates intended to occupy the White House and kidnap the Lincoln family made the Union military authorities urge her to take the children back to Springfield. She refused and, instead, in mid-May set out on the first of the 11 shopping expeditions to Philadelphia and New York she made from the White House—bypassing and angering Washington merchants.

She and William Wood, commissioner of public buildings, spent some two weeks buying curtains, rugs, and wallpaper for the White House, and in less than a year she had exceeded her four-year congressional allowance. The papers took note, and an embarrassed president told her, "It would stink in the nostrils of the American people to have it said that the President of the United States had approved a bill overrunning an appropriation of $20,000 for *flub dubs,* for this damned old house, while the soldiers cannot have blankets." He threatened to pay the bills from his salary, to which his wife responded, "We can not afford that." To appease him she tried to sell secondhand White House furniture and manure from the stables and reduced the staff, taking on the responsibilities of steward herself. She even took kickbacks from the gardener, who was padding his expense accounts.

Reckless as she was with government funds, Mary managed the Lincoln finances so well that they lived on nearly the same budget as they had in Springfield, saving $70,000 from the $100,000 in salary her husband received during his presidency. The feat is all the more remarkable because she spent so lavishly on her own clothes that she was dubbed "The Illinois Reine." Adopting the style set by Napoleon's empress Eugenie, which sometimes called for 25 yards of material for a single dress, Mary employed Elizabeth Keckley, a former slave who had earned her own freedom with her needle, to fashion her gowns. When she could, Mary looked for gifts from merchants and haggled over their bills, postponed paying them, or failed to pay them altogether. She even asked friends for items of clothing they were wearing. Her clothes earned her as much criticism as admiration. To many her predilection for youthful styles and bright colors, her tight lacing to reshape her short, plump figure, and her elaborately flowered headdresses made her ridiculous. Her husband saw her differently, touchingly remarking that "my wife is as handsome as when she was a girl and I a poor nobody then, fell in love with her and once more, have never fallen out."

The war dictated some of the first lady's activities, as she reviewed troops and visited hospitals, where she brought flowers and liquor, read books and wrote letters for the soldiers, and raised money for and helped to serve special meals.

She entertained competently and enthusiastically, charming some of her women guests with her "simple and motherly manners" and entrancing some of the men with her animation and intelligence. She never neglected her social duties. Even when her migraine headaches raged or she was suffering from a fever, she made her public appearances at the twice-a-week winter and spring receptions where as many as 4,000 guests attended, at the levees on New Year's and other holidays, and at special entertainments for American officials and foreign guests. Her efforts were all the greater since she herself chose the menus, supervised the cooking, and arranged the flowers. Presidential bodyguard William Crook said that the White House was "more entirely given over to the public in Lincoln's administration than in any other." In early 1862 she invited almost 500 guests to a soirée on which she spent $1,000 of the Lincolns' own money, evoking from the *Washington Star* the accolade that it was "the most superb affair of its kind ever seen here." But some citizens questioned whether such extravaganzas were appropriate in wartime.

Being a native of Kentucky caused Mary problems. She was loyal to the Union and opposed the institution of slavery; feminist editor Jane Swisshelm, her close friend, reported that Mary opposed slavery more vigorously than her husband and urged him toward emancipation. But her southern upbringing and accent roused suspicions about her loyalty to the Union. Three of her half-brothers were fighting for the Confederacy, and a full brother was serving as a surgeon in its army. When the husband of her half-sister Emilie Todd Helm died in the southern cause, Mary tactlessly had the White House draped in black for him. Nonetheless, Emilie Helm denounced the Union even while she accepted the protection and hospitality of its president. Another half-sister, Martha Todd White, tried to exploit her relationship to the Lincolns for profit so blatantly that Mary refused to see her. Mistrust of the first lady mounted to charges of treason.

In truth she deserved much of the hostility she roused. The White House staff responded to her hot temper, jealousies, and tactlessness by calling her "the Hell-Cat." Mary thought "Honest Abe" "almost a monomaniac on the subject of honesty" and refused to govern her conduct by his standards. She accepted expensive gifts, even diamonds and a black barouche with four black horses, in exchange for using her influence in patronage appointments. She urged her husband to appoint members of her family and enlisted the aid of others to persuade him to decide things her way—pressing so hard that he teased that if she had her way, she would remove his entire cabinet. She lobbied officials at her receptions and made requests of them in such a way as to suggest that she was expressing the president's feelings. Her comments on McClellan ("a humbug") and Grant ("a butcher") finally provoked Abe to say, "Well, mother, supposing that we give you command of the army. No doubt you would do much better than any general that has been tried."

Tragedy darkened Mary's time as first lady. The years that she had hoped to enjoy as the triumphant climax of her life cost her her reputation, her favorite son, and the husband on whose career she had staked all her hopes. In February 1862 both Willie and Tad fell ill of a fever—perhaps a "bilious" fever or malaria, but probably typhoid contracted from the filth of the Potomac River, which provided the White House drinking water. Tad eventually recovered, but Willie, already weakened by an earlier case of scarlet fever, died in agony from cramps, diarrhea, and intestinal spasms. His prostrate mother, who in the eyes of her detractors could do nothing right, was criticized, especially by the mothers of men killed in the Civil War, for mourning too long and too much and for not accepting the consolations of religion. Even her sister reproached her for "a long indulgence of such gloom," while according to her seamstress and intimate, Elizabeth Keckley, the president (who himself could not sleep and was suffering from nightmares) told her, "Try and control your grief or it will drive you mad."

She did not—perhaps could not. Instead, she took to her bed, refused to enter the rooms where Willie had died and been laid out, destroyed all reminders of him, and for a time avoided the company of little Tad. She decided that God was punishing her for extravagant parties—a judgment that many of her enemies endorsed—and she came to believe that every Lincoln triumph would be followed by tragedy.

When she finally emerged from her seclusion, Mary wore deep mourning for a year, six months longer than customary—and then bought another expensive, half-mourning wardrobe of lavenders, grays, and purples. In the summer and fall she visited New York and Boston, where, along with many other mourners of the period, she sought out spiritualists to reunite her with her dead—a practice that she continued the rest of her life. She took them so seriously that she tried to persuade her husband to use them as guides in the conduct of the war.

Mary Lincoln traveled often, sometimes without a chaperone. Occasionally she represented the president, reviewing troops and inspecting ships, but she frequently traveled for her own ends, such as vacations and shopping expeditions. For support and company she turned more and more to friends, many of them male, organizing a salon to discuss books, politics, and people with them. Among them were men of ill repute, some womanizers, who interested her with their intelligence and knowledge. Like the rest of her acquaintances, members of the "Blue Room set" were subject to Mary's patronage campaigns and to her appeals to help the "contrabands"—former slaves who had escaped to Union military camps and thence migrated to Washington. She also turned to some of this set for help in renegotiating her delinquent bills.

Although the Lincolns saw far more of each other in the White House than in the years when his law practice had taken him from home for months at a time, they no longer shared an agenda. Excluded from the circles of power by circumstances and by her own self-centered interpretation of events, Mary looked to other people to promote her ends. If she could not persuade the president to her own point of view, she tried to influence him through others. In the midst of a civil war that threatened the existence of the Union, she saw the president's campaign for a second term in terms of her own problems, writing to Elizabeth Keckley, "If he is reelected I can keep him in ignorance of my affairs; but if he is defeated, the bills will be sent in and he will know all."

The president's first term had been so anguished that his reelection brought him forebodings of death, which Mary Lincoln shared. She nevertheless promenaded at the inaugural ball of 1865 in white silk with a bertha of point lace, a lace shawl over her shoulders, jasmine and violets in her hair, and carrying an ermine fan with silver spangles—all the while fretting because tradition did not permit her, the "Presidentress," to lead the procession on the arm of her husband.

With the end of the Civil War in sight, the Lincolns enjoyed one triumphant moment reviewing the victorious Union troops in Virginia—marred by a nasty outburst of jealous temper from the first lady when she arrived in a coach to find General Ord's wife on horseback alongside the president. Then, on April 14, 1865, bullets fired by assassin John Wilkes Booth ended all happiness for Mary Todd Lincoln. "Oh, my God," she screamed, "and have I given my husband to die?"

She sat through the death watch in uncontrolled agony, collapsing moments before the president died. She blamed herself for his death, writing to a friend, "My own life has been so chequered; naturally so gay and hopeful—my prominent desires, all granted me—my noble husband, who was my 'light and life,' and my highest ambition gratified—and that was, the great weakness of my life. My husband—became distinguished above all. And yet owing to that fact, I firmly believe he lost his life. . . ." She took to her bed in an hysterical state for more than a month and embraced her mourning for the rest of her days.

Mary had long detested the new president, Andrew Johnson, whom she suspected to be a conspirator in the assassination, but she could not resist seeking patronage from him. An ugly dispute with the Springfield authorities about Abraham Lincoln's burial place roused her to activity, but she did not make the White House available to the Johnsons until May 23. She did not know where to go, saying that Springfield would drive her mad with its memories. Finally, with sons Robert and Tad, she resorted to a series of Chicago hotels, doing almost nothing, seeing almost no one, self-dramatizing, and transforming Abraham Lincoln in memory into a saint.

The need for a permanent home drove Mary to examine her financial situation. The administrator of her husband's considerable but still unsettled estate of $85,000 allowed each of his heirs—his wife and sons—$1,500 a year to live on, but her creditors for the debts that she had accumulated in the White House were pressing hard. In desperation she returned jewelry she had bought, offered clothing for sale, tried to sell mining stock, and refinanced her debts at a high rate of interest—though she was still compulsively buying china. She asked wealthy acquaintances for contributions to the subscription fund for her benefit started by Horace Greeley, handing out her dead husband's canes to encourage them, suggesting that they might buy her a house, and signing her letters to them with a fictitious name. She raised about $10,000, an amount that she considered too small, using it to pay her debts. She begged Congress for a pension, arguing that she should receive the salary her husband would have earned in his second term as president had he lived. Instead, they voted her the remainder of his salary for a year—$22,025.

In spring 1866, still on shaky financial footing, she bought and furnished a house in Chicago but had to rent it out in less than a year. Never again would she live in her own home. She decided to sell the clothes she no longer needed with the help of Elizabeth Keckley and a commission agent who promised her sales of $100,000. She and Keckley canvassed their friends in the white and black communities, and crowds flocked to "Mrs. Lincoln's Second-hand Clothing Sale," but almost no one bought.

In summer 1867 Mary began to travel in search of relief from her physical ills—back trouble, eye problems, headaches, cystitis, and possibly urinary tract infections, many brought on by her nervous afflictions. To add to her misery,

William Herndon, Lincoln's former law partner and her enemy, was circulating the story that her husband had loved only Ann Rutledge and that his marriage had been "a domestic hell."

Finally, in November she inherited $36,000 from the settlement of her husband's estate, making her a wealthy woman. However, she interpreted the settlement as an attempt to interfere with the sale of her clothing and blamed her son Robert for it. Quarrels over money resulted in Elizabeth Keckley's publication of a "novel" about Mary Lincoln and ended their friendship. The mounting notoriety brought more press accusations of her having taken bribes, having diverted funds to pay for her parties, and having sold her husband's speeches and linen shirts, and she retaliated with public attacks on several politicians. Her behavior caused speculation about her sanity.

The next fall, Mary Lincoln sought refuge in Europe. For two years she lived in Frankfurt, Germany, where she put Tad in school. She liked German and expatriate British society and the relative anonymity it afforded her. She made friends, women with whom she discussed her aches and pains and men with whom she conversed and flirted. She read, wrote letters, saw the sights, shopped, and practiced spiritualism. In the winter she traveled south to Italy, and in the spring she went north to Scotland.

In July 1870 Mary was awarded the annual pension for which she had persistently campaigned—though she had hoped for a larger sum than the $3,000 voted by the Congress. Her friends and the Republican Party's sense of what it owed the widow of Abraham Lincoln overcame dislike for a woman who had often trampled on convention. For a time she continued to wander—to Leamington, England, for its water cure; to London; back to Italy. Finally, in May 1871, at Tad's urgent pleading, they came back to the States, where they settled in a Chicago hotel.

Mary Lincoln's relationship with her oldest son, Robert, had deteriorated in the years since he left for college, particularly after his father's death. As a grown man he clearly showed his preference for living independently of her. She approved of his choice of wife, and painful though it was for her to return to Washington, she attended his wedding there in September 1868. Throughout her European stay she wrote to his bride, Mary Harlan Lincoln, frequently and fondly and sent presents to her and later to her baby. However, this happy relationship did not survive a brief visit with the Robert Lincolns on her return to the States, though she continued showering her son and granddaughter with gifts.

When 18-year-old Tad died in misery on July 15, 1871, after a protracted illness, Mary was devastatingly alone. A sad, purposeless woman, she abandoned herself to mourning, seeking cures for her many ailments, and spiritualism. In her own eyes the victim of unmatched suffering, she again took to her bed. She dosed herself with chloral hydrate for her insomnia. She observed the 14th of every month as the anniversary of the death of her husband, the 15th as the anniversary of Tad's death. Herndon continued his attacks on her and even on her dead husband, to which she responded passionately but ineffectually.

Not surprisingly, her way of life increased her eccentricity. On May 19, 1875, she opened the door of her hotel room to a lawyer who told her that she was charged with lunacy and insisted on her going immediately to court to defend herself before a jury, with only the help of a lawyer chosen by Robert Lincoln. She did not know that her son had sworn out a warrant against her, that he had hired men to follow her, and that he had organized a case against her, paying $50 apiece to six doctors to certify her as of unsound mind, mostly on the basis of what they had been told about her. Robert's agents brought 17 witnesses against her, including the doctors, employees of the hotel where she was living, salesclerks who had waited on her, and Robert himself. Her lawyer called no witnesses, not even the accused herself. An all-male jury found her insane.

Today the law would offer protection denied her in 1875, a time when many doctors thought of women as given to hysteria and madness because of their biology and resorted to diagnoses of mental illness to explain physical symptoms that the medical knowledge of the period could not account for. They failed to distinguish between eccentricity and insanity—to the extent that between 1860 and 1880 the population of Illinois insane asylums increased six-fold. Many a doctor—and certainly many a man—interpreted a woman's defiance of convention and failure to observe the standards of behavior proper to the ideal "True Woman" of the period as lunacy. The press accusations of madness against Mary Lincoln—accusations provoked by political enmity and pique from a male-dominated world—counted against her at the trial, as did her practice of spiritualism, which some alienists (the 19th-century version of psychiatrists) labeled "theomania."

None of the evidence suggests that Mary Lincoln was a danger to herself or to others. Undoubtedly her behavior inconvenienced, hurt, and angered other people; to some degree it always had, for she was incapable of looking at the world and her own actions through anyone else's eyes and judged other people in terms of whether they forwarded or impeded her own ends.

Robert, never her favorite son, had endured much from her as a mother, and suffered more when Tad's death left him the only survivor of her immediate family. In bringing her to court, it is possible he was motivated by money. Certainly she had been generous to his daughter and to him; by then she had given him almost $25,000, loaned him other significant amounts, and sold him her Chicago house at half price. But he had known her extravagance throughout his life, and with her pension and her inheritances from her husband and son Tad, a considerable sum was at stake. It must have been easy for Robert to persuade himself that at least in financial matters she was irresponsible. And, against all expectations of the day, she did not surrender to male control.

The all-male jury took only 10 minutes to find Mary insane. She lost control of her property and was committed to a private asylum in Batavia, Illinois. The doctors in charge of such institutions, knowing as little of what to do for their patients as what ailed them, resorted to rest, quiet, and an assortment of drugs that included opium, morphine, and whiskey-laced eggnogs, as well as chloral hydrate in large doses. Above all, believing that lunacy corrupted the moral sense, they spent hours instructing their patients in right conduct. They interpreted deviations from the code they preached as further proof of madness.

Mary accomplished the difficult feat of getting released from the asylum in a little less than four weeks. She managed to smuggle a letter to a Washington friend, the remarkable Myra Bradwell, the first woman lawyer to gain permission to practice before the U.S. Supreme Court. With the aid of her attorney husband, Bradwell secured Mary's release to live in the Springfield home of her sister Elizabeth Edwards. For the next year Mary struggled to wrest control of her property back from Robert and eventually succeeded. On June 15, 1876, another Illinois jury found her sane and capable of managing her own affairs. Determined to get her revenge, she charged her only remaining son with robbery, demanded the return of everything she had ever given him, and sent back his relatively few gifts to her.

Fearful that Robert might renew his charge of insanity, and embarrassed before her Springfield friends and neighbors, Mary fled again to Europe, settling in the spa town of Pau for the next four years and concentrating on her financial affairs. In 1880 failing health drove her back to the States, where she boarded in the long-suffering Elizabeth Edwards' home. Nearly blind, Mary spent her days exploring the possessions she had accumulated in her 64 trunks and sitting alone in the dark. Encouraged by Robert, by then President Garfield's secretary of war, the newspapers wrote of her hysterical condition. She spent the winter of 1881 in a New York medical hotel, complaining that "I feel like I am being hacked to pieces." She passed the weary hours in lobbying to have her pension increased to $5,000 a year, the amount awarded Lucretia Garfield, offering friends fees on a contingency basis to help her. The Congress complied, even awarding her $15,000 in back payments.

Her last success came too late for her to enjoy. She died on July 16, 1882, and was buried in Springfield's Oak Ridge Cemetery. Since she died intestate, Robert Lincoln inherited her fortune of $84,000.

———— ⁓ ————

No first lady desired the position more than Mary Todd Lincoln, and no first lady entered the White House in more troubled times. She brought to the role political shrewdness, energy, personal charm, and intelligence—all limited by her selfishness and lack of self-control. The abuse of her enemies, unprecedented in its viciousness, exacerbated her worst qualities. She had always seen being first lady as a prize to be won rather than as an opportunity for service, and when she reached the position she exploited it. Ignoring the tragedy of a nation in a civil war to concentrate on her own suffering, she failed to achieve the honor that might have been hers.

CHRONOLOGY

1818   *December 13:* Mary Ann Todd is born in Lexington, Kentucky

1826   Mary Todd attends the Shelby Female Academy

1832   Mary Todd attends Madame Charlotte Mentelle's school for young ladies near Lexington

1836   *Spring:* Mary Todd visits a married sister in Springfield, Illinois

        Fall: She helps as an apprentice teacher in Ward's academy

1839   Mary Todd moves to Springfield, Illinois, to live with her sister

        Fall: Mary meets Abraham Lincoln

1840	Mary Todd promises to marry Abraham Lincoln
1841	*January 1:* Mary Todd and Abraham Lincoln break off their courtship
1842	*November 4:* Mary Todd marries Abraham Lincoln
1843	*August 1:* Son Robert Todd is born
1846	*March 10:* Son Edward (Eddie) Baker is born
1850	*February 1:* Son Eddie dies
	December 21: Son William (Willie) Wallace is born
1853	*April 4:* Son Thomas (Tad) is born
1860	Abraham Lincoln is elected president
1861	*March 4:* Mary Todd Lincoln becomes first lady
1862	*February 20:* Son Willie dies
1865	*April 14:* Abraham Lincoln is assassinated
1867	Mary Lincoln tries to sell her clothes and jewels
1868	Mary Lincoln travels abroad with Tad
1870	Congress grants Mary Lincoln an annual pension of $3,000, later increased to $5,000
1871	*May:* Mary Lincoln returns to Chicago
	July 15: Tad dies
1875	*May 19:* A court judges Mary Lincoln insane
1876	Another court finds Mary Lincoln sane; she travels abroad
1880	Mary Lincoln returns to Springfield, Illinois, where she lives with her sister
1882	Mary Lincoln dies and is buried in Oak Ridge Cemetery beside Abraham Lincoln

---

FURTHER READING

Baker, Jean H. *Mary Todd Lincoln: A Biography.* New York: Norton, 1987.

Crook, William Henry. *Through Five Administrations,* ed. Margarita Spalding Gerry. New York: Harper, 1910.

Donald, David Herbert. *Lincoln at Home: Two Glimpses of Abraham Lincoln's Family Life,* New York: Simon and Schuster, 2000.

Helm, Katherine. *The True Story of Mary, Wife of Lincoln.* New York: Harper, 1928.

McMurtry, R. Gerald, and Mark E. Nealy Jr. *The Insanity File: The Case of Mary Todd Lincoln.* Carbondale: Southern Illinois University Press, 1993.

Ross, Ishbel. *The President's Wife: Mary Todd Lincoln: A Biography.* New York: Putnam's, 1973.

Sandburg, Carl, and Paul M. Angle. *Mary Lincoln Wife and Widow.* 2 pts. New York: Harcourt, Brace, 1932.

Strakes, George. *Mary Todd Lincoln and the Illuminati.* Bloomington, Ind.: First Books Library, 2000.

Turner, Justin G., and Linda Levitt Turner. *Mary Todd Lincoln: Her Life and Letters.* New York: Knopf, 1972.

ELIZA MCCARDLE JOHNSON
(OCTOBER 4, 1810–JANUARY 25, 1876)
First Lady, April 15, 1865–March 4, 1869

ELIZA JOHNSON
(Library of Congress)

Eliza McCardle Johnson was molded by her time and her environment. A southern woman born and raised in modest circumstances, she devoted her entire self to the welfare of her husband and their five children. In her lifetime she suffered the deaths of her two older sons, both alcoholics, one by accident and one by his own hand. She endured treatment as an enemy in Confederate territory during the Civil War, threats on her husband's life, and his trial after his impeachment. Whether in small-town eastern Tennessee or in the White House, she instilled her values into her family, believing that as long as they did what they thought right, all would turn out for the good. Her daughter wrote, "She was the stepping stone to all the honor and fame my father attained."

Eliza McCardle was born October 4, 1810, in Greeneville, Tennessee, the only child of John McCardle and his wife Sara Phillips. Her father, who may have been a shoemaker, was an innkeeper in nearby Warrensburg in 1824. After he died in 1826, Sara McCardle supported her daughter by weaving, while Eliza helped by making crazy quilts and hand-weaving sandals. She gained what education she had from her mother, the private libraries of friends, and some attendance at the local Rhea Academy.

When Andrew Johnson came to Warrensburg in 1826, he was taken with Eliza's brown curls and blue eyes. She was equally taken with him—although she probably did not remark on their first meeting, as legend has it, "I might marry him someday." Another story says that soon after that first meeting Johnson told his mother that some day he would marry Eliza. In any event, a local justice of the peace married them on May 17, 1827, when she was 16 and he 18. By that time Johnson had his own tailoring business, which he carried on in the front room of their home while they lived in the back room. He had only a rudimentary grasp of reading and writing, but he was determined to improve himself, and she to help him. She is reported as saying, modestly, "I taught him to form the letters, but he was an apt scholar and acquired all the rest of it himself." He was ambitious, and she was ambitious for him. Trusting to hard work and education to achieve success, she or someone he hired read aloud to him while he stitched. At her suggestion, he joined a debating society to learn public speaking, and in 1828 he began his career in local politics, as alderman and then as mayor.

Already they were establishing the cooperative pattern of their lives—he working to support his family and develop his political career, she ably managing the accounts and the household. They prospered, and between 1828 and 1852 Eliza Johnson bore five children, all of whom reached adulthood. The couple bought a farm and a few slaves, eventually acquiring as many as eight or nine. Some historians say that Andrew Johnson bought his first slave at an auction when a slave named Dolly asked him to buy her—an indication that she thought that he would make a kind master. Certainly slave ownership symbolized status and a degree of affluence in their area. By 1851 the Johnsons were able to buy a large brick home in Greeneville, which housed them and Andrew's widowed mother.

Andrew's election to the state legislature in 1835 and to the U.S. House of Representatives in 1842 changed his wife's life little. Eliza stayed at home, supervising the family businesses, tending the children, and giving them their basic education. When her husband was elected governor of Tennessee in 1853, she had already contracted tuberculosis, which weakened her for the rest of her life. Given her debilitating illness, a year-old baby to tend, and two older sons who may already have been showing signs of the alcoholism that afflicted them throughout their adult lives, she did not move to Nashville with her husband. Nor did she accompany him to Washington when he was elected to the U.S. Senate in 1857. Only in 1860 did she finally join him there, briefly, until the Civil War broke out in the spring of 1861 and the Johnsons returned to Greeneville.

The Civil War, Andrew Johnson's opposition to secession, and his denunciation of secessionists as traitors jeopardized his life and made the lives of his family uncomfortable, if not actually endangered. Their peril did not decrease when in March 1862, President Lincoln appointed Johnson military governor of Tennessee. His constituents in the eastern part of that state supported his pro-Union stand, but their territory was overrun by the Confederate army, which confiscated the Johnson home, scattered his papers, and appropriated his holdings. Nashville and the rest of western Tennessee supported the Confederacy, but by the time of Johnson's appointment to the military governorship, Union forces controlled the area, and accordingly he had to live there, among people who hated him for what they regarded as his disloyalty to the South.

Eliza Johnson, living with her daughter Mary Johnson Stover in the east, was enjoined from disposing of their possessions. In April 1862 the Confederate commanding general ordered her to leave the area he controlled within 36 hours, but she told him that she could not, since illness confined her to her bed. By mid-September she had recovered enough to make the difficult and dangerous month-long journey with sons Charles and Frank and the Stover family through Confederate territory to Nashville. The Confederate authorities challenged them every few miles and sometimes ordered them to retrace their steps. Regarded as enemy aliens, they had trouble finding shelter, and at least once were forced to camp alongside some railroad tracks, suffering from the cold. Finally they reached Nashville on October 12.

Soon afterward Eliza again set out with her daughter Mary. Partly she hoped to set her son Robert straight, for he was then in trouble with his military unit in Cincinnati because of his drinking. Partly she sought healing from the waters in Vevay, Illinois. She returned to Nashville in May 1863. That year her son Charles was killed when he was thrown from a horse; the next year son-in-law Daniel Stover died of tuberculosis. In August 1864 Eliza and her two remaining sons went to Massachusetts, perhaps in search of treatment there for Robert's alcoholism. (Robert committed suicide in 1869.)

March 1865 found them back in Nashville. Not even Andrew Johnson's inauguration as vice president of the United States, a post he had earned by his loyal services in Tennessee, altered the Johnsons' established pattern—he living wherever his career and duty to his country called him, she tending to family responsibilities at home. But Andrew Johnson's ascent to the presidency after the assassination of President Lincoln on April 14 finally reunited the family. The news horrified Eliza Johnson, who, daughter Martha Johnson Patterson wrote to her father, "is almost deranged fearing that you will be assassinated." The prospect of being first lady also repelled her.

Eliza resolved the dilemma by rejecting the position, insofar as she was able, and choosing to live in the White House exactly as she would have lived anywhere else. The Johnsons moved their whole family into the White House: sons Robert and Frank; daughter Martha, her husband, Tennessee senator David Patterson, and their two children; and widowed daughter Mary Stover and her three. Happy in having them all close to her, Eliza Johnson established herself in the private quarters upstairs and occupied herself with her family. She seldom breakfasted with the others but had lunch and dinner with them regularly. Her grandchildren visited her every day after their lessons. In the mornings Eliza left the small bedroom she had chosen for herself to look through the living quarters, sometimes calling on her husband in his office. She watched over the health and happiness of the staff, always sending messages, flowers, and delicacies when they were sick or in trouble. Much of the time she spent in her room, rocking while she sewed and read. But she never learned to love the White House, telling a staff member, "It's all very well for those who like it—but I do not like this public life at all. I often wish the time would come when we could return to where I feel we best belong." She told a member of the staff that she had been far more content when her husband had earned the family living as an industrious young tailor than she was in the White House.

Eliza seldom appeared in public, though her successor, Julia Dent Grant, wrote that "she always came into the drawing room after the long state dinners to take coffee and receive the greetings of her husband's guests . . . dressed elegantly and appropriately." When she did attend a reception, she had to sit down for most of the evening, explaining, "My dears, I am an invalid." However, when Queen Emma of the Sandwich Isles visited, Eliza stood at her husband's side to receive the queen but then sat down to receive their other guests. One Easter morning she sat in the portico downstairs to watch the egg-rolling. Her most famous public appearance was at Andrew Johnson's 60th birthday celebration, when 400 children of people involved in public life entertained the presidential couple by dancing the highland fling, a sailors' hornpipe, and various other dances, ending with a Virginia Reel. For the most part, however, Eliza Johnson was a mystery to the public, almost a myth. Her pleas of bad health protected her from criticism—although in 1867 she was well enough to travel to Boston, New York, Philadelphia, Pittsburgh, and Louisville.

Eliza wisely turned over the responsibilities of first lady to her daughter Martha. Educated at a Washington convent and in vigorous good health, Martha disarmed critics early on by allegedly saying, "We are plain people from the mountains of Tennessee, brought here through a national calamity. We trust too much will not be expected of us." She made no pretensions but handled her duties competently whether she was running the household, redecorating the White House, handling the correspondence addressed to her mother, or acting as hostess by her father's side. "The White House has been kept in order, elegance, and liberal hospitality," wrote a Washington journalist. "No old friends cut, no new ones toasted [snubbed]; but an even tenor of sociability has made all feel welcome." Like her mother, Martha enjoyed Andrew's confidence. Her sister Mary Stover on occasion helped her, and her brother Robert acted as his father's aide.

Although she had absented herself from her social duties as first lady, Eliza kept in close touch with what was going on in her husband's life. She told Martha what he ought to eat and how he liked his food. She also read widely, preferring serious books to fiction, and each day clipped the papers and magazines for Andrew. According to legend, she sorted the clippings into two piles: the good news to show him in the evening and the bad news to save for the next morning after breakfast, when he regularly visited her room. She could always control his anger, it was said, by placing a hand on his shoulder and saying, "Now, Andy." She always believed that he would try to do the right thing, even though he occasionally erred, and she

firmly supported his determination to stand by his principles, despite political pressures. After Johnson was impeached in 1868, Eliza shared both his anguish during the trial and his relief when he was acquitted, telling the staff member who brought her the news, "I knew he'd be acquitted; I knew it."

When the Johnsons left the White House in March 1869, a Washington newspaper praised their conduct in the White House: "They have received no expensive presents, no carriages, no costly plate. They will be remembered in Washington as high-minded and honorable people." They returned to their renovated home in Greeneville, cheered by crowds along the way; but the former president could not content himself with the simple life that Eliza loved. In 1875 he was once again elected to the U.S. Senate, only to die on July 31 that year. Eliza was too weakened to attend his funeral, and six months later, on January 15, 1876, she died at the home of her daughter Mary. She was buried alongside her husband at the Andrew Johnson National Cemetery in Greeneville.

—⁘—

Perhaps foremost among a first lady's duties is to look after her husband and keep him as fit as she can for his demanding, stressful job. Eliza Johnson had dedicated her life to just such an end, and in it she found her success and happiness. She assumed the major responsibility for their family, managed their finances to relieve him of that worry, and consoled and heartened him by her faith that he would always do what he thought right. When after his presidency Andrew Johnson was vindicated by being returned to the Senate, Eliza received a telegram reading, "Permit a stranger to you, but a friend of his, to tender to you his earnest congratulations for this 'crowning victory' in his career. In the first speech I ever heard him make, he attributed to your influence his success in life."

CHRONOLOGY

1810 *October 4:* Eliza McCardle is born in Greeneville, Tennessee

1827 *May 17:* Eliza McCardle marries tailor Andrew Johnson

1828 Johnson begins his political career as alderman

1828 *October 5:* Daughter Martha is born

1830 *February 19:* Son Charles is born

1832 *May 8:* Daughter Mary is born

1834 *February 22:* Son Robert is born

1835 Andrew Johnson is elected to the state legislature

1842 Andrew Johnson is elected to the U.S. House of Representatives

1852 *August 5:* Son Andrew, Jr. (Frank), is born

1853 Andrew Johnson is elected governor of Tennessee

1854 Mary Johnson marries Daniel Stover

1855 Martha Johnson marries David T. Patterson

1857 Andrew Johnson is elected to the U.S. Senate

1860 Eliza Johnson first travels to Washington

1861 With the outbreak of war, the Johnsons return to Tennessee

1862 Abraham Lincoln names Andrew Johnson military governor of Tennessee

October: Eliza Johnson travels to Nashville to join her husband

1863 Son Charles is killed after being thrown from a horse

1864 *August:* Eliza Johnson travels to New England with sons Robert and Frank

1865 *March 4:* Andrew Johnson is sworn in as vice president, but Eliza remains in Nashville

April 15: With the assassination of Abraham Lincoln, Eliza Johnson becomes first lady

August 6: Eliza Johnson goes to Washington with her sons and daughters and their families

1869 *March:* The Johnsons return to Greeneville, Tennessee

April: Son Robert commits suicide

1875 Andrew Johnson is elected to the U.S. Senate

July 31: Andrew Johnson dies in Washington

1876 *January 15:* Eliza Johnson dies at Mary Johnson Stover Brown's farm near Greeneville

---

FURTHER READING

Benedict, Michael Les. *The Impeachment and Trial of Andrew Johnson.* New York: Norton, 1999.

Colman, Edna M. *White House Gossip: From Andrew Jackson to Calvin Coolidge.* Garden City, N.Y.: Doubleday, Page, 1927.

Crook, William Henry. *Memories of the White House: The Home Life of Our Presidents from Lincoln to Roosevelt,* comp. and ed. Henry Rood. Boston: Little, Brown, 1911.

———. *Through Five Administrations,* ed. Margarita Spalding Gerry. New York: Harper, 1910.

Thomas, Lately. *The First President Johnson: The Three Lives of the Seventeenth President of the United States.* New York: Morrow, 1968.

Trefousse, Hans Louis. *Andrew Johnson: A Biography.* New York: Norton, 1997.

JULIA DENT GRANT

(JANUARY 26, 1826–DECEMBER 14, 1902)

First Lady, March 4, 1869–March 4, 1877

JULIA GRANT
(Library of Congress)

Julia Grant led a more independent, daring, and self-reliant life than other women of her time—in large part because she was a soldier's wife. The lives of such American women have historically been more influenced by the demands of their husbands' profession than by the expectations of women in their own day. They endured hardship, danger, and long separations. Moreover, the Civil War moved women into more public roles, and Julia Grant experienced its full impact. She found her happiness in her husband and in the family they created together, but that process required of her both courage and independence of judgment.

Julia Dent was born on January 26, 1826, at White Haven plantation, near St. Louis, Missouri, the first daughter and fifth of eight children of prosperous, slave-owning farmer Frederick Dent and his wife Ellen Bray Dent. Her mother was descended from a preacher who had helped to carry Methodism west of the Ohio River. Julia grew up a tomboy, with a love for the outdoors and little interest in her studies. She was educated at a log school near her father's homestead until, in 1837, at age 11, she was enrolled in the private school of Phillip Mauro in St. Louis, where she studied for the next six years. Her mother saw to her training in the domestic arts and gardening.

At 18, just out of school, Julia was not as pretty as her sisters, but petite with dark, glossy hair that she wore in a chignon, a nice complexion, and bright coloring. Her lightheartedness, pleasant manners, and good disposition made her popular. She excelled in dancing and horseback riding, and she sang charmingly. Her paternal aunt, Mrs. John J. O'Fallon, introduced her to St. Louis society and impressed Julia with her philanthropy.

Soldiers were stationed near White Haven, and the hospitable Dents invited them to visit. Among them was a former classmate of Julia's brother Frederick at West Point, Ulysses S. Grant—"Ulys"—who, after meeting Julia in 1844, came three or four times a week, sometimes staying overnight. Four years older than she, he admired her warmth and vivacity, her lively conversation, and even her slightly crossed eyes. They rode together through the countryside, stopping now and then for Julia to botanize or for him to read Sir Walter Scott aloud to her. They went walking and fishing, and he told her about his travels to New York and Philadelphia. With the Dent family, Ulys attended picnics, dances, hayrides, cornhuskings, and camp meetings. Even though he did not dance, he escorted Julia to balls.

Julia and her mother thought Ulys was destined for great things. However, her father thought the young soldier unworthy of his favorite daughter, and they differed on the burning issue of slavery and on the Mexican War—a conflict that Grant described as "one of the most unjust ever waged by a stronger against a weaker nation." The prospect of that war helped Grant decide to propose before he went off to battle. As an old lady Julia Grant loved to tell the story—how she had once worried about crossing a swollen river and told him that if anything happened she would cling to him, and how he used her "threat" as a theme in his proposal. Her father thought her too young and ill-suited for army life and only reluctantly consented to the match in 1845, with the proviso that the marriage be postponed.

Julia was left at home to wait and worry for three years while her soldier went off to war. During that time, as she accumulated a trousseau and household linens, she joined in the social life of St. Louis, going with groups of girls to church teas and bazaars, to concerts, theaters, races, circuses, and the horticultural gardens. At White Haven she skated, camped, and canoed. She heard talk of phrenology, animal magnetism and hypnotism and dabbled in mind reading and "second sight." Ulys wrote to her regularly, describing his experiences, and longed for her rare letters to him. At last, in the summer of 1848, he returned.

They were married on August 22, 1848. The bride walked down the staircase of her father's St. Louis house wearing a Parisian frock of watered silk with cascades of lace, caught with her favorite flower, cape jessamine. She was attended by three bridesmaids in white, the bridegroom by three fellow officers who would later fight for the Confederacy. Ulys gave Julia a daguerrotype of himself, which she wore on a ribbon around her wrist, the picture enclosed in a chased gold locket. She treasured it all her life.

The next morning they set off on their honeymoon as the guests threw bouquets after them. They took a boat down the Mississippi, an adventure that delighted Julia, then went to Ohio to visit Ulys's parents. Upset by their son's marriage into a slaveholding family, Jesse and Hannah Grant had stayed away from the wedding, but her husband's siblings received the sweet-natured young bride warmly. Julia Grant's experiences with her own testy and dogmatic father taught her how to handle her father-in-law, while their Methodism made a common bond between the bride and her mother-in-law.

The Grants spent the winter after their marriage at a lonely barracks at Sackett's Harbor on Lake Ontario, giving Julia her first chance to show her mettle. Despite the isolation and cold, she worked to turn the bare quarters into a home and went to the quilting bees and other home-centered activities in the area. Her husband escorted her to dances, though he never danced a step. At her suggestion, he gave her an allowance to run the house, and she learned to keep accounts, after a fashion. When water froze in the jugs and snow covered part of the windows, she piled on the featherbeds and he built up the wood fires. When she nagged him about his carelessness in dress or threw out his smelly pipe, he would tease her or simply keep silent for a long time. They learned how to handle each other and set the pattern of happiness in their marriage.

In spring 1849 they moved to Detroit, where they lived for a year in a small house in a working-class neighborhood. Again Julia quickly made friends within the garrison. In May 1850 she went back to St. Louis to give birth to a baby, named Frederick Dent—the first of four children in a famously happy family life. Busy as she was, Julia kept up a social life. She was an ideal army wife, adaptable and ready for anything, sunny in disposition and equable in the face of change and hardship. Only separations necessitated by her husband's postings troubled her; in his absences she moved from place to place. She was living with her in-laws in Ohio when Ulysses Jr. (Buck) was born in 1852, and later returned with the children to White Haven. Her husband so depended on her and missed her that in 1853 he confided to a friend, "I have the dearest little wife in the world, and I want to resign from the Army and live with my family."

He did just that in 1854. Unconfirmed rumor had it that a charge of intemperance would have been brought against him had he not resigned. Such stories still mar his reputation, and the truth of them may never be known. Some historians have observed that because Grant was a small man, a little alcohol would have affected him more than most. Early in their marriage he had joined the Sons of Temperance, with his wife's approval. Julia herself reported that even when he was prostrated by one of the migraine headaches from which he suffered, he refused the medicinal alcoholic draft that his doctor prescribed. "If General Grant was ever a victim of the liquor habit," wrote his sister-in-law, "it was a condition which he happily concealed from those nearest his heart, closest in their association with him, and who loved him best." A contemporary journalist, Sylvanus Cadwallader, wrote that General John "Rawlins' ablest coadjutor in restraining Gen. Grant from drinking was the latter's excellent wife. . . . Everything seemed absolutely safe when she was present." Other colleagues attested that he "was never under [alcohol's] sway to the direct or indirect detriment of the service for a single moment."

After Ulysses's resignation from the army, he needed civilian work. His father, bitterly disappointed that Ulysses had left the army and disapproving of Julia's ownership of the slaves bestowed on her at birth by her father, offered his son a job in his tannery, but only if the couple would live apart. They refused, deciding instead that Ulysses would farm the 60 uncleared acres that Julia's father had given her as a wedding present. His father thereupon promised him $1,000 to stock it, and her father provided four slaves. Daughter Ellen (Nellie) was born on the farm in 1855.

Ulysses S. Grant, as his wife once observed, "was made for great things, not for little things," and both his father and his father-in-law were disappointed in a young man who at 32 seemed to be going nowhere, and who had a growing family to support. Julia Grant, however, never wavered in her faith in him. Talk-

When General Grant conquered Vicksburg in the summer of 1863, a St. Louis crowd serenaded his wife—a moment that she always recalled as one of her proudest. As she took the children to join him at Vicksburg, the steamboat they were on was shelled, but they were unharmed. Julia was there to nurse her husband when his horse fell and rolled over him, and the children kept him amused during his two-month convalescence. She began to call him "Victor" when they were alone, glorying in his triumph. By early 1864, he was being mentioned as a presidential candidate, although he staunchly insisted that he wanted only to win the war. Because her husband was becoming such a great man, Julia thought of having an operation to correct her crossed eyes, but he told her, "Did I not see you and fall in love with you with these same eyes? I like them just as they are, and now, remember, you are not to interfere with them."

When Ulysses S. Grant was appointed supreme commander of the Union forces, his wife moved to Washington, D.C. Having gained self-assurance through practice in St. Louis society and the machinations of garrison life, Julia conducted herself with dignity as she was plunged into the political and social maelstrom that surrounded the Lincoln White House. With the general or without him, she now attracted attention wherever she traveled. She did war work, visiting hospitals and patronizing the Sanitary Commission fairs that supported the care of sick and wounded soldiers and helped their families.

In fall 1864 Julia took a house in Burlington, New Jersey, where the neighbors found her "a sensible, plain, good woman." When the general joined her there in November, he said to two men on the railroad platform, "They say I live here, but I don't know where." When he could not go to his family, they went to his camp on the James River in Virginia. That Christmas, Fred, who had been hunting, was arrested as a rebel spy, upon which he announced, "I am Frederick Dent Grant, sir, son of General Ulysses S. Grant, Commander-in-Chief, who will be very angry if I am killed." His father was amused at his adventure, and his mother unconcerned.

After Christmas, Julia sent the older children back to school in Burlington, while she and Jesse stayed on in Virginia. According to Julia's sister, when Mary Todd Lincoln visited the camp that spring, she infuriated the usually even-tempered Julia by expecting her to back out of the room, as if in the presence of royalty. However, Julia herself denied that there had been any unpleasantness. She did witness embarrassing displays of Mary Lincoln's wifely jealousy, and she wrote of her pique when Mary Lincoln ignored the Grants after the capture of Richmond.

Julia and Ulysses received an invitation, purportedly from Mary Lincoln, to sit in the presidential box at the Ford Theater on April 14, 1865, for a performance of *Our American Cousin*. The messenger who brought it told Julia that the general had accepted, but she refused, on the grounds that she had to return to Burlington to tend to her children. She later came to think that the invitation had come not from the Lincolns but from the conspirators in the assassination plot. Both Julia and her family believed in her psychic powers, and family legend says that she had dreamed of disaster that night. She had also been nervously aware of a man who had eavesdropped on a conversation between Jesse and her in a hotel dining room, and of a man on horseback—she thought the same one—who had peered into the Grants' carriage and again stared at them at the depot. In any event, chance and her disquiet combined to save her husband's life, for the group around John Wilkes Booth that plotted Lincoln's death had indeed also targeted Grant.

For the next few years after the war, Grant held an ill-defined but powerful and remunerative office as the nation's "general-in-chief," a position created for him. The family traveled together through the North, which honored the general at every opportunity. Then, while her husband toured the South, Julia and the children settled into their new home in

Washington, where her father soon joined them. President Andrew Johnson valued General Grant, and his daughters made friends with Julia. She herself compiled a distinguished guest list as she began entertaining—a process complicated by the people who crashed her first reception to see her famous husband. Thereafter, the Grants announced in the newspapers that the general would be happy to see his friends at his home. They were themselves invited everywhere. Meanwhile, Julia attended theaters, lectures, concerts, and, true to her Methodist upbringing, sermons.

When her husband was nominated for the presidency in 1868, Julia invited close friends to their home to celebrate. Later, in the Galena, Illinois, house given them by friends and admirers, Ulysses gave Julia the news, "I am afraid I am elected." With the Grant presidency began the Gilded Age. In the 30 years from his March 4, 1869, inauguration until the end of the century, property became more concentrated in the hands of the rich. The Grants' association with the wealthy dazzled them, all the more so after their Hardscrabble days, and they basked in their new way of life.

The inaugural ball, held in the newly altered Treasury Building, was mismanaged; in the crush, some of the guests fainted from the dust in the air, some went supperless, and some had to leave without their wraps and walk through slush for want of carriages. However, the Grants smiled throughout the celebration, she in white satin and point lace, with pearls and diamonds. She devoted that spring to planning White House renovations, and in the summer they traveled in the Northeast. Toward summer's end, Wall Street capitalists tried to corner the gold market, with the assistance of Ulysses' brother-in-law, Abel R. Corbin. With her husband dictating, Julia wrote a strong letter to Grant's sister, telling her, "The General says, if you have any influence with your husband, tell him to have nothing whatever to do with [Jay Gould and James Fisk, Jr.]. If he does, he will be ruined, for come what may, [your brother] will do his duty to the country and the

trusts in his keeping." Scandal hovered, but the presidential couple were exonerated.

In fall 1869 Julia Grant undertook her duties as White House hostess, under the guidance of Mrs. Hamilton Fish, wife of Grant's secretary of state. The first lady needed the help, for as her army friend Mrs. John A. Logan wrote, "She often failed to remember that Mr. and Mrs. So-and-So had been twice married, were or were not temperance leaders, Protestants, or Catholics, and of such personal tastes or opinions as to make it dangerous to express oneself too frankly. The President at such times would lead her on to her own undoing, and then chuckle over her embarrassment." Her bad eyesight made it difficult for her to recognize people, so she surrounded herself at receptions with cabinet and Senate wives who could whisper their identities.

Julia reveled in entertaining and trying to win goodwill for her husband. The Grants mingled simplicity and ostentation curiously. In some matters they chose more informality than their predecessors, ignoring strict adherence to the rules of precedence and accepting invitations and paying calls as they wished. One day a week, Julia held a reception, her husband often dropping in at the end. They welcomed all; according to social commentator Ben Perley Poore, at their parties "There were . . . ladies as lovely as Eve, and others as naughty as Mary Magdalene; . . . chambermaids elbowed countesses, and all enjoyed themselves."

On the other hand, Julia required female guests to wear hats and forbade males to smoke or carry weapons. She entertained more elaborately than her predecessors, serving dinners of 20 or even 30 courses on French china featuring a gold eagle and shield, with hand-painted flowers native to the United States in the center. Six wineglasses and a bouquet of flowers stood by each place. She replaced the quartermaster whom her husband had put in charge of the kitchen with an Italian steward who made the White House cuisine famous, both at the small parties the president preferred and at state dinners. Despite the richness of her hospitality, the pace of which quickened throughout the Grants' White House years—even during an economic recession—the public generally liked Julia Grant. Most Americans perceived her as the *New York Tribune* described her: ". . . a sunny, sweet woman; too unassuming to be a mark of criticism, too simple and kindly to make the mistakes which invite it."

Julia was no paragon of domesticity, confessing in her memoirs to her ineptness in knitting and sewing. Even as an army wife she had relied on servants to cook and keep house, and her slave maid often traveled with her during the Civil War. In the White House the Grants installed their own housekeeper, the capable Mrs. Muller, but the first lady regularly made the rounds and stopped to chat with the servants about their family affairs. Shrewdly observing that Washington was poised for growth, she advised them to buy homes for themselves while prices stayed low. When one of them chose to ignore her advice, she took matters into her own hands: "Harris, if you do not buy a home at once, and commence paying for it while houses are cheap, your opportunity will soon be gone. . . . If you do not go out and select a home and commence to pay for it, I will buy one for you myself; and I will take out of your wages each month enough to pay for the installments."

Julia liked to show off her husband. To get him talking, she would deliberately tell a story wrong, prompting him to take it over—a strategy she confided to some of his friends, hoping that they would adopt it. Filled with self-importance, she saw herself as adviser to the great man that she had always known her husband to be. For the most part, observed his White House secretary, she simply told him "to do what he thought right, and perhaps induced him to do it." Sometimes, however, she warned him about people she distrusted and strongly expressed her opinions on national policy, just as she had advised him on battle tactics during the Civil War. His secretary, Adam Badeau, felt that the president benefited by his wife's insight into other women, describing her as a needed

mentor "to caution and urge and stimulate and advise." Sometimes Ulysses took her advice; more often he brushed her off, telling her, "Do not trouble yourself about me, my dear little wife. I can take care of myself." Sometimes he chided her good-naturedly: "Mrs. Grant, I think you are a—what shall I call you—mischief!" Or, "It is lucky you are not the President. I am afraid you would give trouble." Nevertheless, people suspected that she influenced him more than he acknowledged, even when it came to cabinet appointments, and she suggested as much in her memoirs. Certainly she, his father, other relatives, and friends assailed him with requests for favors, rendering him vulnerable to charges of nepotism.

The Grants' family life continued to be idyllic in the White House. The president and his wife always went to breakfast arm-in-arm. The whole family worshiped regularly at the Metropolitan Methodist Church, where Julia worked diligently and Ulysses was a trustee. They gave children's parties nearly every Saturday and closed the gates to the White House, so that the children could play in private. Family meals were merry, with Ulysses pelting the children with little balls made of bread and then getting up to kiss whomever he hit. For recreation they rode, though the president's occasional mad dashes on horseback made his wife so nervous that she preferred to drive alone in her landau. The whole family loved to hear Ulysses read aloud, Julia particularly because her weak eyesight made reading painful. For the summers the Grants went to their home near the ocean in Long Branch, New Jersey.

With Fred at West Point and Buck at Harvard, the Grants sent Nellie to Miss Porter's in Farmington, Connecticut, but with her mother's assurance that if she had to study too hard she need not stay. Predictably, she soon returned to the White House, where she spent her days in driving and her nights in dancing. Jesse, their youngest, pleaded that he be allowed to return to Washington from his school near Philadelphia, and his father yielded at once. Soon after Fred graduated from West

Point, he went to Europe as an aide to General Sheridan—a position offered him at his mother's request. Nellie, too, went to Europe with friends of her parents, and both young people were received like royalty there.

In the White House Ulysses and Julia often wrote notes to each other. On May 22, 1875, she wrote, "Dear Ulys: How many years ago to day is [it] that we were engaged: Just such a day as this too was it not? Julia." He wrote back, "Thirty-one years ago. I was so frightened however that I do not remember whether it was warm or snowing." He liked to tease her, as he once did with the conundrum, "Why is victory like a kiss?"—the answer being, "It's easy to Grant." He had learned it, he told her, from a young woman from whom he had collected two kisses. His wife wailed, "Why, Ulys, how could you? I really think some girls very bold—dreadful."

Julia looked forward with pleasant anticipation to a second term. Criticism of the president and his family on many scores, including nepotism and association with what the New York *World* identified as the "clique of money-changers," narrowed Grant's margin of victory over his seven challengers. At the second inaugural ball, this time held in a building erected for the purpose, guests shivered in the elaborately decorated but unheated rooms, and one woman died of the cold. Julia endured the evening in a white and silver brocade gown of material given her by the emperor of China.

In spring 1873 the Grants reluctantly announced 18-year-old Nellie's engagement to Algernon Charles Frederic Sartoris, an Englishman whose own parents doubted his reliability. Nonetheless, the presidential couple gave her an elaborate White House wedding on May 21, 1874, at which the groom carried a bouquet with a silver banner bearing the word *LOVE*. As wedding gifts Ulysses and Julia presented their only daughter with a diamond necklace and earrings, a point-lace fan, a lace handkerchief, and a check for $10,000. After the ceremony they traveled sadly to New York to see the young couple off to England. That fall Fred Grant, by then a lieutenant colonel on General Sheridan's staff, delighted his parents by marrying Ida Marie Honore, the sister of the wealthy Mrs. Potter Palmer of Chicago. With Fred stationed in Washington and Nellie and her husband returned from England, Julia Grant now had both a daughter and daughter-in-law to assist her in entertaining.

Her happiness, however, was dampened by new troubles. She had never developed an understanding of the ethics of public service or an accurate judgment of other people's integrity. Impulsive and absentminded, she was as trusting as her husband—sometimes foolishly so. She made mistakes, such as deciding that she would receive Washington officials at the New Year's Day reception of 1874 despite the recent death of her father. Criticism of her husband made her feel, as she phrased it, "hard and revengeful," and she judged others on the basis of their loyalty to him. She held grudges against those she thought were his enemies, as when she publicly snubbed Mrs. George H. Williams, the wife of the attorney general, who she believed was responsible for blackmailing letters. On the other hand, she remained uncritically devoted to those she regarded as friendly, as when she begged the cabinet not to censure the secretary of war, who had been impeached for graft, and thereafter received his wife in the White House.

Despite these difficulties, Julia hoped for a third term. Ulysses did not, and without telling her, he personally mailed a letter to the Republican State Convention in Pennsylvania announcing that he would not run and gave copies to the press. To her protests when she discovered the fait accompli, he replied, "I know you too well. It would never have gone if [you] had read it." Despite her disappointment, the first lady graciously stocked the larder for her successor, and Grant ordered wines for them—not anticipating that Rutherford B. Hayes would run a dry White House. The Grants welcomed the Hayeses at a state dinner and at a friendly luncheon on inaugural day.

Julia cried when they left the White House, telling her husband, "Oh, Ulys, I feel like a waif, like a waif on the world's wide common." Waifs, however, can hardly embark, as the Grants did in May 1877, on a trip around the world. They had a grand time and were honored and feted wherever they went. All their life together she was ready to have fun with him. When they were cruising off the island of Calypso, an officer advised her to stuff her own Ulysses' ears with cotton to avoid the fate of Homer's Ulysses; she told him that she did not need to—she had learned from Penelope never to stay at home when her husband traveled. Nonetheless, she kept a close watch. "Mrs. Grant," wrote Badeau, "always awed even Princesses if they paid too much attention to her great husband."

After two and a half years abroad, she rejected his proposal to go to Australia; thoroughly tired of travel, she wanted to go home. To her delight, when they returned in the fall of 1879 they found that Republicans were considering Ulysses Grant's nomination for a third term. He, too, wanted the nomination, but no matter how much she pled he would not go to the convention to push for it. "Julia," he said, "I am amazed at you." Disappointed as they were that the nomination went to James Garfield, they supported him in his campaign.

The Grants settled in New York and, with the aid of funds contributed by friends, adopted a luxurious mode of life. The delight they had always felt in their children increased with the birth and company of grandchildren, and Julia flourished in her role as matriarch. Then, in May 1884, the collapse of the brokerage firm with which Ulysses was affiliated and a colleague's absconding with its funds left them impoverished. The Grants honorably turned over everything they had, though their creditors tried to refuse them, insisting that she keep personal mementos and gifts received in the White House years and on their travels; these, however, she promptly gave to the Smithsonian Institution.

To earn money, General Grant turned to writing articles on the Civil War, then to working on his memoirs, for which Mark Twain had persuaded a publisher to offer him a generous contract. Despite the diagnosis of inoperable cancer of the throat, he labored at his writing early and late, determined to ensure the security of his family after his death. He died on July 23, 1885, his work done, leaving his wife a loving letter instructing her to "Look after our dear children and direct them in the paths of rectitude." The memoirs made her a wealthy woman.

Through her own memoirs and other reports, Julia Grant left a record of her conflicted feelings on the issue of women's rights and responsibilities that had been agitating the 19th century since 1848, when Elizabeth Cady Stanton and Susan B. Anthony organized the first convention on the subject. In 1891 Julia, then in her mid-60s, visited the Woman's Building of the Chicago World's Fair, where she met the 22-year-old sculptor Enid Yandell and told her that she didn't approve of women sculptors as a rule: "I think every woman is better off at home taking care of husband and children. The battle with the world hardens a woman and makes her unwomanly." She added that a woman without a husband should either get one or stay at home to take care of her father and brothers. Yandell deferentially inquired whether there are no circumstances under which a woman might take a job. Julia replied that she might be old-fashioned, that she did not like "this modern movement," but she did not think so—though, she conceded, women made good teachers, governesses, and nannies. Yandell posited the case of a brother who cannot get ahead because he must support his sisters, capable of earning their own livings yet idled by their gender, and also that of a father who must struggle to support a large family of girls. "You may be right," Julia conceded. "In that case, they ought to go to work."

Her attitude toward blacks originated in her heritage as the daughter of a slaveowner who had given her slaves of her own. When the Grants moved to the free state of Illinois, she hired out these slaves, and they belonged to her up until the Emancipation Proclamation. She wrote in her memoirs of the "comforts of slavery," yet when a White House usher asked her whether blacks were to be admitted to her open receptions, she said, "Admit all who call." However, as she noted in her memoirs, no blacks came either that day or any other, "thus showing themselves modest and not aggressive, and I am sure they, as a race, loved [Ulysses Grant] and fully appreciated all that he had done for them."

After Ulysses died, Julia lived for years in New York and later Washington, often traveling to visit her children and grandchildren. Much venerated, she attended many tributes to her husband, including the dedication of his tomb in New York's Riverside Park in 1897. She engaged in good works—in the Spanish-American War she headed the Women's National War Relief Association—and wrote her own memoirs. She died on December 14,1902, and was buried beside her husband.

—◆—

Like Mary Todd Lincoln, Julia Dent Grant always believed in her husband and predicted great things for him. But unlike her predecessor, she lacked interest in and knowledge of politics and other worldly affairs. Not until her husband's generalship in the Civil War transformed him into a national hero did she begin to mingle with the rich and powerful. They awed her, and she was quick to embrace their style. Fortunately, when she reached the White House the realization of how little she knew prompted her to rely on the advice of others; nevertheless, her naiveté and lack of judgment about people often imperiled her. Some of those whom she trusted betrayed her, but her basic simplicity and sincerity carried her through the problems of her husband's administration. In the final analysis, it can be said that Julia Grant thoroughly enjoyed life as a traditional first lady.

CHRONOLOGY

1826   *January 26:* Julia Dent is born at White Haven near St. Louis, Missouri

1837   Julia Dent enters the private school of Phillip Mauro in St. Louis

1843   Julia Dent leaves school

1844   Julia Dent meets Ulysses S. Grant

1848   *August 22:* Julia Dent marries Ulysses S. Grant

1850   *May 30:* Son Frederick Dent is born

1852   *July 22:* Son Ulysses is born

1854   Ulysses S. Grant leaves the army and takes up farming

1855   *July 4:* Daughter Ellen (Nellie) is born

1858   *February 6:* Son Jesse Root is born

1860   The Grants move to Galena, Illinois

1861   Ulysses S. Grant returns to the army and is commissioned a brigadier general

1864   Ulysses S. Grant is appointed supreme commander of the Union forces

Julia Grant moves to Washington, D.C., then to Burlington, N.J.

1868   Ulysses S. Grant is elected president of the United States

1869   *March 4:* Julia Grant becomes first lady

1874   *May 21:* Daughter Nellie marries from the White House

1877   *March 4:* The Grants leave the White House and subsequently tour the world for two years

1884   The Grants are plunged into poverty; Ulysses Grant begins work on his memoirs

1885   *July 23:* Ulysses S. Grant dies

1902   *December 14:* Julia Dent Grant dies

FURTHER READING

Colman, Edna M. *White House Gossip: From Andrew Jackson to Calvin Coolidge.* Garden City, N.Y.: Doubleday, Page, 1927.

Crook, William Henry. *Through Five Administrations,* ed. Margarita Spalding Gerry. New York: Harper, 1910.

Grant, Julia Dent. *The Personal Memoirs of Julia Dent Grant,* ed. John Y. Simon. Carbondale: Southern Illinois University Press, 1975.

Grant, Ulysses S. *Personal Memoirs of U.S. Grant.* 2 vol. New York: Charles L. Webster, 1885.

Porter, Horace. *Campaigning with Grant.* New York: Bison, 2000.

Ross, Ishbel. *The General's Wife: The Life of Mrs. Ulysses S. Grant.* New York: Dodd, Mead, 1959.

LUCY WARE WEBB HAYES

(AUGUST 28, 1831–JUNE 25, 1889)
First Lady, March 4, 1877–March 4, 1881

LUCY HAYES
(Library of Congress)

Lucy Webb Hayes earned a college degree in 1850, only nine years after Oberlin College gave the first baccalaureate degree to a woman. Her education evidently confirmed the values her family had instilled, especially temperance and opposition to slavery. She presented herself as a traditional woman, responding personally, not politically. Despite the hopes of the women's rights movement, the temperance movement, and church groups, she chose to engage in private charities rather than to support causes publicly. Although she wept over the conditions of the American Indians when Paiute leader Sarah Winnemucca described them to her, she responded only by providing a scholarship for one Indian girl to study at the traditionally black Hampton Institute in Virginia. When Washington slum dwellers appealed to her, she sent notes, wagon loads of supplies, and gifts of money. In the early years of their marriage, she urged her husband to defend fugitive slaves in court, and after the Civil War she employed the former slaves of her father's family and en-

124

couraged them to get an education. Ultimately she was a principled woman, content to remain in the mainstream of her times.

———∿∿∿———

Lucy Ware Webb was born in Chillicothe, Ohio, on August 28, 1831, the youngest of three children and the only daughter of physician James Webb and his wife Maria Cook. This prosperous, well-regarded couple were strong temperance advocates. Dr. Webb died of cholera in 1833, leaving his family amply provided for. Lucy attended several local schools. She adored her maternal grandfather, Isaac Cook, a judge, a member of the state legislature, and a strong advocate for temperance as well as for a state-supported system of elementary education. Early on she learned to deplore slavery; at the time of his death her father was engaged in freeing some slaves he had inherited.

In 1844 the Webbs moved to Delaware, Ohio, where Lucy attended prep school and some college classes at Ohio Wesleyan, a Methodist institution. She was a 15-year-old student in Ohio Wesleyan's preparatory course when 24-year-old budding lawyer Rutherford B. Hayes first glimpsed her. He had already heard much about her from his mother, who had decided that Lucy would make a good wife for him and strengthen his wavering Christian faith. His older sister, Fanny Platt, praised Lucy as having a fine disposition and being "tolerably good-looking," except for her freckles. She was also "remarkably intelligent," and "so frank, so joyous, her spirit sheds sunlight all about her."

In fall 1847 Lucy, a petite 16-year-old with hazel eyes and dark hair that she wore in a braid around her head, enrolled in another Methodist institution, Cincinnati Wesleyan Female College. She did well in her classes, which probably included rhetoric, geometry, geology, astronomy, and mental and moral science. Every two weeks she had to write an essay or discuss a "ponderous question," such as

"Which Requires the Greater Sacrifices of Its Votaries, Religion or Vice?" Thus she absorbed Methodism's emphasis on morality throughout her youth. Somewhere along the line the feminist ferment of the time gained her attention, for in one essay she commented on the growth of women's education, because "it is acknowledged by most persons that [woman's] mind is as strong as man's. . . . Instead of being considered the slave of man, she is considered his equal in all things, and his superior in some."

Before Lucy graduated in 1850, Rutherford Hayes had renewed his acquaintance with her and was wondering about rumors of her engagement to someone else. However, by spring 1851 Lucy and Rutherford were courting, and in June she accepted his proposal, saying, "I thought I was too light and trifling for you." A bit pompously, he cherished hopes that she would further cultivate her "good" but "untrained" mind and resolved to "school her a trifle in this thing of letter writing." During their engagement, she devoted herself to helping the impoverished. They were married on December 30, 1852, in her home, with a Wesleyan professor performing the afternoon ceremony. The bride wore a white-figured satin dress with a fitted bodice and full skirt, her floor-length veil covered with orange blossoms. That evening the newlyweds took the train for Columbus, where they spent a joyous month-long honeymoon with Rutherford's family, going to concerts, "dinner parties, tea drinking and evening fandangos with unremitted zeal." When they returned to Cincinnati, they moved in with Lucy's mother.

So began a happy marriage—one in which the couple remained closely involved with both their extended families, whose members frequently visited back and forth, helped each other, cared for their aged kin, and assumed responsibilities for one another's children. Until the outbreak of the Civil War, Lucy Hayes was wrapped up in domestic life. In November 1853 she gave birth to the first of their eight children, five of whom survived infancy: Birchard Austin, Webb Cook, Rutherford Platt, Fanny, and Scott

Russell. While her husband built up his law practice with his partner, John Herron, and attended club and political meetings, Lucy was occupied with the children and the supportive families of Webbs and Hayeses. She socialized and visited back and forth with her own and her husband's relatives. Her husband's favorite sister, Fanny Platt, pushed her toward an active interest in the women's rights movement, taking her to a lecture by Lucy Stone.

In September 1854 the Hayeses settled into their first home of their own, which her mother and brother shared with them. Rutherford's sister, Fanny Platt, died in childbirth in 1856, depriving Lucy of intimacy with a strong woman interested in public affairs. On the other hand, the new Republican Party with its antislavery principles stimulated her interest in politics, which in turn encouraged her husband to begin his political career—a career that she would come to regard as *theirs*. Most of the time, however, she was parenting her children, supervising her household and its servants, and carrying on a busy social life, attending concerts, lectures, and church services.

The Civil War changed this pleasant mode of life. The Hayeses had not anticipated the conflict, believing that differences between North and South could be settled peaceably, or at worst without general warfare. When war began, however, Lucy wrote, "The Northern heart is truly fired—the enthusiasm that prevails in our city is perfectly irresistible." That enthusiasm moved Rutherford to volunteer his services as major of the 23rd Ohio Volunteer Infantry, and his wife to support his decision in the name of the "holy and just cause." During the next four years he saw active duty and was wounded several times.

Like hundreds of thousands of other soldiers' wives, Lucy Hayes waited, worried, and coped with family problems. When her husband rode off, he left her pregnant, a condition that increased the severity of the headaches she frequently suffered. She and her husband had both welcomed Abraham Lincoln's presidency, but she did not understand Lincoln's difficulties

with keeping the border states loyal to the Union and his hesitation in emancipating the slaves; consequently, she thought him too weak a leader. Her interest in the conduct and strategy of the war pleased her husband. She bore her fourth baby at the end of 1861, with no hope in sight for the early end to the war that both the Hayeses had anticipated.

In September 1862 Rutherford was seriously wounded in his left arm and telegraphed his wife to come to him. She set out at once, leaving the older children with relatives and entrusting to her mother the task of finding a wet nurse for the baby, whom she was breastfeeding. After a prolonged search, only a chance encounter with soldiers of his unit enabled Lucy to find her husband, in Middletown, Maryland, rather than in Washington, D.C., as she had expected. For two weeks she nursed him and visited other wounded in nearby homes and makeshift hospitals. Then she shepherded a group of wounded soldiers back to Ohio, commandeering Pullman seats for them when they found no room in the coaches. The "society folk" who occupied the rest of the Pullman resented their presence, until they discovered Colonel Hayes's identity—but Lucy indignantly refused their subsequent offers of delicacies.

When Colonel Hayes recovered, he was posted to the Kanawha River in West Virginia. There his wife and two older sons joined him, traveling by boat and then riding the last 28 miles over rough roads in an army ambulance. In one of those curiously peaceful lulls that winters sometimes gave soldiers, the family frolicked and went on expeditions, though on one occasion they strayed too far and had to rush back to camp pursued by Confederate soldiers. The family's second visit to Rutherford, in June 1863, was marked by sorrow when their baby died. Lucy stoically sent his body back to Ohio for burial and stayed with her husband. That winter the Hayes family rented out their Cincinnati house and again went to join the colonel. Lucy had her sewing machine sent from Ohio and made soldiers' uniforms for her sons. The enlisted men, who liked her, played a joke on one of their mates by telling him that a woman in the colonel's tent sewed for the regiment. He naively put in a request to the colonel, who passed it along, and the colonel's lady mended the private's blouse. Lucy mothered the young officers and enlisted men, including the 20-year-old Lieutenant William McKinley. When the 23rd broke camp in the spring of 1864, she and several other wives chartered a boat and for a time kept parallel with the marching soldiers.

The months that followed were particularly hard for Lucy as she awaited the birth of her fifth child while her husband fought. Horrified by stories of Southern brutality, she criticized President Lincoln's gentle treatment of Confederate prisoners, but Rutherford reproached her, reminding her that some Confederate soldiers were humane, and some Union soldiers brutal. That summer Colonel Hayes's Cincinnati supporters nominated him for Congress, and although he refused to leave his military duties to campaign, he was elected in October 1864.

After her baby was born in September 1864, Lucy suffered a severe attack of the rheumatism that had plagued her since girlhood, keeping her away from Lincoln's second inauguration. The plunge from joy at the Union victory to grief over the assassination of Lincoln caused her to write bitterly, "I am sick of the endless talk of Forgiveness—taking them back like brothers. . . . Justice and Mercy should go together. Now dont [sic] say to me Ruddy that I ought not to write so." Rutherford Hayes left the army as a brigadier general, and he and his wife stood together in Washington for the Grand Review that celebrated the Union triumph.

Following the custom of the day, his family did not accompany Rutherford when he went to Washington to undertake his duties as congressman, but Lucy's visit there in January and February of 1866 absorbed her in the issues of the day. She was particularly interested in congressional efforts to extend the life of the Freedman's Bureau, which helped freed slaves, and to change President Andrew Johnson's lenient policy toward the South. After she re-

turned to Cincinnati, she found she missed talking politics with her husband.

In April, however, the death of their baby George from scarlet fever focused the Hayeses on family affairs. Lucy felt that her mother's poor health and other family responsibilities necessitated her continued presence in Cincinnati, and Rutherford began to feel that "There is nothing in the small ambition of Congressional life . . . to compensate for separation from you." That fall both their mothers died. When she could, Lucy joined her husband in Washington, and during the congressional recess that winter they traveled with a group of congressmen to New Orleans. Despite her "Radical Republican" views on slavery and reconstruction, Lucy made friends wherever she went. In summer 1867, with his wife's encouragement, Rutherford ran successfully for the governorship of Ohio. That fall Lucy bore their only daughter, Fanny.

By this time Lucy had developed a full-fledged interest in and considerable knowledge of public affairs and politics, and she involved herself in her husband's career. Despite the responsibilities of a growing family, as governor's lady she influenced legislation behind the scenes, particularly backing Rutherford's efforts to reform state prisons and welfare institutions. She worked actively to raise private money to found a home for soldiers' orphans and successfully lobbied for its transformation into a state institution. As the governor wrote a relative, "Lucy employs herself about the soldiers' orphans . . . about the decoration of soldiers' graves and about the deaf and dumb pupils at the Reform Farm for boys."

Despite pressure from relatives to embrace the cause of woman suffrage, she did not dispute her husband's stand that "the proper discharge of the functions of maternity is inconsistent with the like discharge of (the political duties of) Citizenship." Indeed, Lucy gave little evidence of believing that women needed or deserved any rights that they did not already have. Despite the pleas of relatives, friends, and other suffragists, and despite her friendship with such women as her classmate Dr. Rachel

Bodley, dean of the Woman's Medical College of Pennsylvania, she would not speak out on either professional education for women or encouraging business enterprise among them. When hopeful people praised her publicly for her interest in higher education for women, she made no reply; on such occasions she was given to picking up and kissing a nearby child.

After Rutherford's second term as governor, the Hayeses frequently discussed their resolve to live as private citizens, but neither of them could keep away from politics. They attended political conventions, she supported his unsuccessful run for the Senate in 1872, and they fumed over President Ulysses S. Grant's offer to appoint him to a post they considered below his merits. In spring 1873 they retreated—Lucy with considerable reluctance—to Fremont in northwestern Ohio, to a home built for them earlier by Rutherford's uncle Sardis Birchard, who had for long periods of time looked after the Hayeses older sons there. (A sizable inheritance from him later resolved the Hayes's economic difficulties.) In Fremont, Lucy gave birth to her last child, another son, who almost died during his birth (and did die a year later). Both husband and wife talked much of their happiness on their country estate, but in 1875 Rutherford began to campaign for a third term as governor. To keep from harming his chances, Lucy refused to join other Fremont women militantly crusading for temperance. His win put Rutherford into a position to run for the U.S. presidency in 1876. He wrote that his wife "enjoys our return to public life more than I do."

Both of them rejoiced when Rutherford received the Republican nomination for president. A reporter describing the Hayeses' notification of the event wrote, "[W]atching the action with kindling eye and sympathetic face, sat Mrs. Hayes, a tall sweet-faced brunette, with an indescribably charming mingling of high bred reserve and old fashioned heartiness of both voice, manner and bearing. . . . [S]he preserves the comeliness of mature youthfulness." The election was so close that its result remained in doubt for months; the last electoral votes had still not been counted on March 1, 1877. Demonstrating their strength of character, the Hayeses were openly serene during this difficult period, despite receiving threats through the mail. In Harrisburg, Pennsylvania, as they were on their way to Washington, they learned that Congress had finally declared Hayes president. Given the tradition of never holding the inaugural ceremony on a Sunday, President Grant arranged for his successor to be sworn in secretly at a White House dinner on Saturday, March 3, to prevent the absence of a president for a 24-hour period from March 4 to March 5. Hayes took the oath again on March 5, this time publicly, stating in his inaugural address that he would serve only one term.

Lucy Hayes entered the White House at a time when the roles of American women were changing, particularly as they entered the world of work outside the home. She was the first wife of an American president to hold a college degree and was known for her interest in human welfare. Some enthusiasts called her a representative of the "New Woman Era." Such was her popularity, however, that conservatives could think of her as a traditional wife and mother, one who centered her hopes and ambitions in her children and in her husband's career. Her appearance supported this impression: at age 45, standing four and one-half feet, she kept her hair dressed simply, usually wearing a comb or flowers in her hair instead of a hat, and her décolletage was always filled in by lace or a scarf. Overcome by admiration for her modesty and Madonna-like appearance, journalist Mary Clemmer Ames applied to Lucy Hayes the term "first lady," a term not then in popular usage. She embodied middle-class propriety and Christian morality. In an administration marked by constant attacks from her husband's political enemies, this reputation protected her from the severe personal assaults suffered by other first ladies.

The Hayeses celebrated his inauguration with a reception at the Willard Hotel followed by a torchlight parade, the uncertainty about the election having precluded preparations for an inaugural ball. With no provisions for a staff of her own, and daughter Fanny only nine, Lucy invited young cousins and daughters of friends to help her with social and secretarial duties. Some of these, like her cousin Emma Foote and her husband's niece Emily Platt, stayed at the White House so long that they were regarded as members of the family. Lucy also took with her several servants who had previously worked for her. Thus supported, she immediately began to entertain, holding her first reception on March 15, 1877.

Rutherford protected his wife against the favor-seekers who had besieged so many presidents' ladies by announcing that no applications made to members of the presidential family would be considered, and that he would appoint no relatives—a move that caused some hard feelings within the Hayeses' close-knit families. Nevertheless, Lucy received requests from people who thought she could help them with their problems or did not know where else to turn, and occasionally she bent her husband's rule by asking for a government job for someone in desperate straits.

Rutherford could not, however, protect his wife against criticism for refusing to serve liquor, even though she did not advocate prohibition; she simply thought that people should set practices within their own homes. When a Washington minister's wife asked her to forbid the use of wine in the White House, she replied: "Madame, it is my husband, not myself, who is President. I think that a man who is capable of filling so important a position, as I believe my husband to be, is quite competent to establish such rules as will obtain in his house without calling on members of other households. I would not offend you, and I would not offend Mr. Hayes, who knows what is due to his position, his family, and himself, without any interference of others, directly or through his wife." Indeed, early in his administration the president himself made the decision to continue the family's practice of serving no liquor in their home, a decision that ensured the political sup-

port of the temperance movement. Nevertheless, in the eyes of the public, it was his wife who imposed the ban, and as a result she remains "Lemonade Lucy."

The ban on alcohol in the White House was instituted only after their first state dinner, given for two Russian grand dukes, at which the Hayeses did serve wine, though neither of them drank any. On that occasion Lucy surprised Washington by the elegance of her cream and gold dress, decorated with pearl embroidery and ribbon rosettes. Later, however, she was criticized for her "economical dressing," even though she actually dressed expensively, but with a preference for flowers over jewelry.

She took criticism stoically, writing to her son that "without intending to be *public*[,] I find myself for a quiet[,] mind-her-own-business woman rather notorious." On another occasion she described herself as a "sham" who "can conceal a good deal." Emily Apt Geer, her biographer, implies that Lucy paid for her apparent serenity with her headaches, rheumatism, and vaguely defined bouts of ill health. As Lucy wrote to her husband when she took a short vacation, "Some times I feel a little worried as I think of you all alone and this press and annoyance going on but I keep myself outwardly very quiet and calm—but inwardly (some times) there is a burning venom and wrath—all under a smiling and pleasant exterior—am I not a whited sepulchre."

A happy-hearted woman who entertained extensively, Lucy replied to a question of whether she did not tire of hostessing by saying, "Why, I never get tired of having a good time." She and the president banned dancing and cards on principle. They also abandoned the evening receptions open to all that for years had inflicted severe damage on the White House. Nonetheless, they tried to make the official social life represent the country at large rather than restricting it to the privileged—for example, providing opportunities for tourists to meet the president in the afternoons. They introduced receptions honoring the diplomatic corps, to which they also invited other senior government officials. William Henry Crook, who served in the White House through five administrations, testified that "[N]one of the official receptions before or since Mr. Cleveland's time have ever equalled the diplomatic receptions given by the Hayes." Lucy gave many women's luncheons and received many delegations of women seeking her support for their causes. At Thanksgiving the president and his wife entertained what Rutherford called "my office family," following an early dinner with games for the children and hymn singing for which Lucy played the piano. At Christmas they had gifts for all the White House employees, which the Hayes children distributed while their parents read out the recipients' names.

Lucy Hayes made relatively few changes in the presidential mansion. Denied a congressional appropriation to renovate it, she scrounged in the attics and cellars for usable furniture. Her pride in White House history motivated her to lobby members of Congress, successfully, to purchase a portrait of Martha Washington. She had a plant room built in place of the billiard room, opening up the state dining room so that guests could look out on the conservatories. Some of her guests found it off-putting to eat from the 1,000-piece dinner service she bought, with different American flora and fauna reproduced on each piece. Journalist Emily Edson Briggs asked, "When one swallows an oyster who wants to be reminded of the huge, ugly shell, a faint suggestion of a coffin?" and others were repelled by depictions of wolves circling their prey. The Hayeses used Abigail Fillmore's circular library as their living room and the site of their family prayers. They installed running water in the White House bathrooms and put in its first telephone. They also had a croquet ground laid out on a White House lawn and made the premises the site of an annual Easter egg-rolling party.

Much of Lucy's time and energy went to supporting good works. She worked for the completion of the Washington monument and visited historical sites and educational institutions around Washington, including the na-

tional Deaf Mute College and Hampton College, which educated black women and men. She decorated the graves of Civil War soldiers and frequently sent flowers from the White House conservatories to hospitals and other institutions. Lucy traveled with the president on his numerous tours, undertaken in the hope that personal interaction with the citizens would unify the nation, making friends for him wherever they went. Southern as well as northern newspapers praised her, the *Richmond Dispatch* writing, "Mrs. Hayes has won the admiration of people wherever she has been." Like her husband, she hoped that conciliation rather than coercion would bring harmony between North and South—vainly, for the removal of federal troops from the South resulted instead in Democratic administrations there and denial of rights to black citizens.

The Hayeses celebrated their silver wedding anniversary by renewing their vows in the Blue Room of the White House before the minister who had performed the original ceremony. Lucy wore her wedding gown, with the seams let out. The next day, with the White House lavishly decorated with flowers and, for the first time, the conservatories lit by gas jets, the Hayeses descended the stairs while the Marine band played Mendelssohn's wedding march. Lucy always cherished the silver plaque given her on that occasion by the veterans of her husband's Civil War regiment, inscribed "To The Mother of Ours."

During the White House years, Lucy Hayes allowed herself occasional vacations of two or three weeks, sometimes visiting relatives and friends, sometimes staying at resorts. On one trip she maintained her reputation as a good fisherwoman by catching a 15-pound trout at Saranac Lake. The Hayes family usually spent their summers in a house on the grounds of the National Soldiers' Home earlier purchased for that purpose by the government. Their attachment to Rutherford's Civil War regiment made this arrangement particularly attractive to them.

As the Hayeses prepared to leave the White House, praise for them mounted. Laura Holloway described Lucy Hayes as "the most widely known and popular President's wife the country has known," one who "represents the new woman era. . . ." By then the Women's Christian Temperance Union had commissioned a portrait of her to be hung in the White House, in tribute for her association with temperance, though their money-raising strategy, which appealed to people to give what they could, even a dime, made Lucy feel insulted— "only worth ten cents."

On March 5, 1881, the Hayeses traveled from Washington back to their estate, Spiegel Grove, in Fremont, Ohio. Although the former president promised that he and his wife would do their part to promote the welfare and happiness of their family, town, state, and country, Lucy Hayes was ready for a rest. Her health, never sturdy, had deteriorated in the White House. Against her wishes, however, public duties intruded. Temperance organizations insisted on presenting her with testimonials of their appreciation, among them six autograph books of tributes. Most of these praised her extravagantly, but Mark Twain wrote, "Total abstinence is so excellent a thing that it cannot be carried to too great an extreme. In my passion for it I even carry it so far as to totally abstain from Total Abstinence itself." True to her moderate principles and policies, in her retirement Lucy did not participate publicly in the activities of the temperance organizations.

She did continue to serve as president of the Methodist Episcopal Woman's Home Missionary Society, interesting herself particularly in the small industrial homes that the society ran in the South and in problems of immigration, which prompted her to announce that "Home Missions seek to protect our land from imported heathenism." She instructed the society's officers not to introduce resolutions to approve activities of the woman suffragists. In her last years Lucy also joined in local activities, particularly those of the church. As she always had, she extended charity to those in distress. She rejoiced in having most of her children living with their parents or nearby, and in

the arrival of grandchildren. She remodeled the Hayes home and enjoyed the animals they kept and the gardens she oversaw.

Lucy Hayes died of a stroke on June 25, 1889. The nation mourned with her family and friends. She was buried in Oakwood Cemetery in Fremont, Ohio, but in 1915 the Hayeses' remains were moved to their estate, Spiegel Grove, when it became a memorial park.

———~~~———

When Lucy Webb Hayes entered the White House, the public in general and reformers in particular expected her to be a more active first lady than her predecessors. After all, she was the first wife of a president to hold a college degree, and as the wife of the governor of Ohio for three terms she had established a record as a woman interested in and knowledgeable about politics and public affairs, one who worked actively for the reform of state institutions and state support of orphanages. She spoke of her husband's career as "ours." In the White House, however, she presented herself not as a representative of the "New Woman" but as a traditional woman, praised on all sides as a model of domesticity, a charming hostess, and a supportive wife. If any advance in the role of first lady were made during her tenure, it came from the expectations placed on her as a college graduate and the greater freedom to travel and make public appearances that her generation allowed women, rather than from any actions of her own.

CHRONOLOGY

1831 *August 28:* Lucy Ware Webb is born in Chillicothe, Ohio

1833 Lucy's father dies

1844 The Webbs move to Delaware, Ohio, where Lucy attends classes at Ohio Wesleyan

1847 Lucy meets Rutherford B. Hayes

1850	Lucy graduates from Cincinnati Wesleyan Female College
1851	Lucy becomes engaged to Rutherford B. Hayes
1852	*December 30:* Lucy Webb marries Rutherford Hayes
1853	*November 4:* Son Birchard Austin is born
1856	*March 20:* Son Webb Cook is born
1858	*June 23:* Son Rutherford Platt is born
1861	*December 21:* Son Joseph is born
1863	*June 24:* Son Joseph dies
1864	*September 29:* Son George Crook is born
1865– 67	Rutherford Hayes serves in the U.S. Congress
1866	May 24: Son George dies
1867	*September 2:* Daughter Fanny is born
1868– 72	Rutherford Hayes serves as governor of Ohio
1869	Lucy Hayes helps to found the Ohio Soldiers' and Sailors' Orphans' Home
1871	*February 8:* Son Scott Russell is born
1873	*August 1:* Son Manning Force is born
1874	*August 28:* Son Manning Force dies
1876– 77	Rutherford Hayes serves as governor of Ohio
1876	Rutherford Hayes is elected president of the United States
1877	*March 3:* Lucy Hayes becomes first lady
1880	Lucy Hayes becomes the first president of the Woman's Home Missionary Society of the Methodist Episcopal Church
1881	*March 4:* The Hayeses leave the White House
1889	*June 25:* Lucy Hayes dies at her home in Fremont, Ohio

FURTHER READING

Colman, Edna M. *White House Gossip: From Andrew Jackson to Calvin Coolidge.* Garden City, N.Y.: Doubleday, Page, 1927.

Crook, William Henry. *Memories of the White House: The Home Life of Our Presidents from Lincoln to Roosevelt,* comp. and ed. Henry Rood. Boston: Little, Brown, 1911.

———. *Through Five Administrations,* ed. Margarita Spalding Gerry. New York: Harper, 1910.

Geer, Emily Apt. *First Lady: The Life of Lucy Webb Hayes.* Kent, Ohio: Kent State University Press, 1984.

Grant, Julia Dent. *The Personal Memoirs of Julia Dent Grant,* ed. John Y. Simon. Carbondale: Southern Illinois University Press, 1975.

Hoogenboom, Ari. *Rutherford B. Hayes: Warrior and President.* Lawrence: University Press of Kansas, 1995.

Williams, T. Harry, ed. *Hayes: The Diary of a President, 1876–1881.* New York: David McKay, 1964.

LUCRETIA RUDOLPH GARFIELD
(APRIL 19, 1832–MARCH 13, 1918)
First Lady, March 4, 1881–September 19, 1881

LUCRETIA GARFIELD
(Library of Congress)

Like the Fillmores, the Garfields were people of modest origins who respected education, had a strong work ethic, and held to the pietistic, middle-class values of their time. Lucretia Garfield's religion taught her to live a moral life, and her times taught her that as a woman she was the moral lynchpin of her family, responsible for their good conduct. Thus she struggled to accept the death of a child as God's will and the infidelity of a husband as an occasion for saintly forgiveness. She centered her life on domesticity because she believed that was proper conduct for a woman. Her husband wanted a large family; she dreaded pregnancies, writing him, "If your jewels [children] cost you what they do me, you would not sigh for more, I am sure." However, adherence to her values brought her the rewards she desired. She turned a shaky love affair into a happy marriage, and she saw the man she adored elected president of the United States. She carefully preserved their correspondence, despite its humiliating evidence of her suffering over his conduct during their engagement and the early years of their marriage—and she triumphed before the people who had pitied her for his treatment of her.

— ⚬ᴍᴍᴍ ⚬ —

Lucretia Rudolph was born April 19, 1832, in Garrettsville, Ohio, the first of four children of farmer and carpenter Zebulon Rudolph and his wife Arabella Mason Rudolph. A sickly childhood deepened the little girl's interest in reading. She attended Geauga Seminary in Chester, Ohio, and in 1850 entered the Western Reserve Eclectic Institute (later Hiram College), newly founded by her father and other members of the Disciples of Christ. After graduating, she taught in various Ohio towns.

She had known James A. Garfield, son of a poor farmer, as a fellow student at Geauga Seminary and as a student and teacher at the Eclectic Institute. They began to correspond in November 1853 and continued while she taught in various Northern Ohio communities and through the years that he attended Williams College and returned, in 1856, to teach at Hiram. They courted through their correspondence, gradually revealing themselves and confiding in each other. Their letters reflect the ways in which the beliefs of their time affected women's education, activity, and health. James, a teacher, educational administrator, and occasional preacher who believed wholeheartedly in the advantages of education, nonetheless warned "Crete" against studying and working too hard. Every time she caught cold he (and her mother) blamed the infection on overstudy and overwork.

Early in 1854, Crete and James agreed on an engagement, albeit rather uneasily. She loved him deeply and passionately, but, having been reared in a reserved family, she could not easily express her love; he wondered whether she had the "warmth of feeling" to make him happy. For years their courtship was an up-and-down, on-and-off process. Sometimes their meetings in person disturbed the intimacy that they had constructed on paper. During 1856–57, their relationship faltered.

Nevertheless, on November 11, 1858, they were wedded at her home. During their engagement James, a victim of what his biographer Margaret Leech calls "his artlessly polygamous impulses," entered into relationships with other women, a practice he continued throughout the earliest years of their marriage. At first, perhaps to reassure himself that he was behaving honorably, he insisted upon friendship between Crete and these women, adding to her heartbreak when she suspected the physical consummation of the affairs. During the winter of 1857, things had come to such a pass between them that she took a job teaching in Cleveland rather than be humiliated at Hiram by the failure of their relationship. The next spring he decided that he must marry her because that was what everyone expected; otherwise he could not feel himself "an honorable, generous man." She understood his feelings. "My heart is not yet schooled to an entire submission to that destiny which will make me the wife of one who marries me because an inexorable fate demands it . . . ," she wrote that summer. "There are hours when my heart almost breaks with the cruel thought that our marriage is based upon the cold stern word *duty* . . . I hope time may teach me to be satisfied with the love you will teach your heart to give."

In their first five years of married life, because of James's preaching obligations, his duties in the Ohio legislature, and his service as an officer in the Civil War, the Garfields lived together only 20 weeks. In his absences Crete read widely and maintained a social life, attending the theater and traveling now and then. Like their courtship, their marriage wavered during its early years. Crete did not find it easy to be as demonstrative as her husband would have liked, and he was often indifferent and neglectful. She persisted in hoping for change; in 1860, pregnant with their first child, she wrote, "It seems to me sometimes that you do not care very much whether we are ever any nearer and dearer to each other; but I do not believe this.

I know that you desire to become the true husband and to see me the wife who can fill up the whole measure of your happiness." But he set a lower goal: "I hope we may be able to get along as pleasantly and happily as is possible [given] the chances and changes of life." Worse still, he told her that he "felt that it was probably a great mistake that [they] had ever tried married life." Their first daughter, Eliza, was born on July 3, 1860. In 1859 James had been elected to the Ohio Senate, but the eruption of the Civil War interrupted his incipient political career. Despite their pacifist leanings, the Garfields so strongly opposed slavery that in the summer of 1861 James recruited soldiers for the Union. Appointed as an officer, he trained his recruits by poring over an army manual, then took them off to Kentucky and fought in several battles. He was a quick study who became an excellent officer and eventually rose to the rank of major-general of volunteers. In summer 1862 illness forced him to return to Ohio to recuperate. This proved to be a turning point in the Garfields' marriage. Joined by his wife and toddler, James spent his convalescence in Howland Springs, Ohio, where relations between the couple gradually improved, albeit with occasional flare-ups of their old problems. All during their marriage they had lived in boarding or rooming houses, and during the war Lucretia had been living with her parents. Now they arranged to rent a house; they would later own a home in Ohio. They were drawn closer together by their daughter Eliza's death from diphtheria in December 1863, only two months after the birth of their second child, Harry Augustus, on October 11.

In 1863 James Garfield was elected to the U.S. House of Representatives. He was subsequently reelected to several successive terms, rising high in the Republican leadership. Following the custom of the day, Crete did not accompany her husband when he first entered Congress. In spring 1864 she got her first taste of the nation's capital when she visited him and attended some congressional debates. At that time, however, James was depressed and restless and talked of going back into the army or

settling in the West. In June he confessed that he had fallen in love with Lucia Gilbert Calhoun, a widowed 20-year-old writer of domestic and social issues for the *New York Tribune*. As usual, his wife forgave and sympathized with him, and he promised to break off the affair— a promise he had trouble keeping. As he wrote to her, "I still believe that I am worthy to be loved after all the books are balanced. Still, I do not know what I shall be after I have fathomed the deep waters of the gulf through which I shall try as bravely as I can to wade. . . . I ought to have a great deal more head, or a great deal less heart."

That winter Lucretia and baby Harry lived with James in Washington for several months, and on October 17, 1865, she was delivered of their third child, James Rudolph. For several congressional sessions thereafter the Garfields boarded or rented in Washington. During these years, their daughter Mary (Molly) was born on January 16, 1867. That July, Lucretia was still worried about her husband's womanizing: "I almost wish you would not see Mrs. Calhoun. Somehow I cannot but feel that to her at least you would compromise our love were you to go into her presence. . . . But whatever you do, I shall ever love you, and I hope you love me too well to ever be untrue to our love or do aught to give anyone occasion to say that you are." Both of them were relieved when James retrieved his letters from Mrs. Calhoun. Immediately thereafter the Garfields sailed together for a four-month trip to Europe.

They built a house in Washington in 1869, shortly before the birth of their son Irvin on August 3, 1870. At last they could live together permanently, in Washington and in Ohio, even though James was frequently away during the 1870s, campaigning or on congressional missions. Lucretia also traveled occasionally, journeying back to Ohio to look after her aged parents; getting her sons settled in prep schools; or vacationing at Lawnfield, the Mentor, Ohio, farm the Garfields bought in 1876. Despite their separations, their letters grew rapturous as they reassured each other that they had put their dark days behind them and attained marital love and bliss. She supported him wholeheartedly when he was accused of questionable financial practices in the Credit Mobilier scandal in 1872. On November 21 of that year another son, Abram, was born, and yet another, Edward, on Christmas Day, 1874. Edward died on October 25, 1876. By 1875 Crete was telling James that she believed him worthy of the presidency, given his "true manliness and statesmanship."

Despite her growing family, Lucretia kept her mind well occupied during her time in Washington. Journalist Mary Clemmer Ames wrote of her:

> I know her and know that she is her husband's equal not only, but in more than one respect his superior. She has 'the philosophic mind' . . . ; she has a self-poise, a strength of unswerving, absolute rectitude her husband has not and never will have, though her temperament does not give her the capacity for the seasons of moral enthusiasm which are possible to him. Much of the time that other women give to distributing visiting cards, in the frantic effort to make themselves 'leaders of society,' Mrs. Garfield spends in the alcoves of the Congressional library, searching out books to carry home to study while she nurses her children.

Indomitably middle-class, Lucretia at once embraced and resented her domestic duties. On the one hand, she wrote before she was married, "[W]oman's province is her home, and if she is not fitted to make it a place around which warmest affections cluster, and on whose hearthstone attractions center, she is not prepared to act her part in life." But on the other hand, after she wed she wrote: "It is horrible to be a man but the grinding misery of being a woman between the upper and nether millstone of household cares and training children is almost as bad. To be half civilized with some aspirations for enlightenment, and obliged to spend the largest part of the time the victim of young barbarians keeps one in a perpetual ferment!" Her tasks were sometimes eased and sometimes compli-

cated by the presence of numerous relatives who occasionally came to stay with her.

To a certain extent, Lucretia was sympathetic to the feminist upheavals of her day. She struggled with the dilemma of the educated woman confined by society to housekeeping and child-rearing duties and resented the denial of women's right to education, saying of one critic: "I judge he thinks all we are made for is work, and as for accomplishments, it is a sin even to think of them What an idea of life! Bake bread, wash dishes, scrub, iron and mend. . . . True, these things must all be attended to, . . . but to make their thorough performances the end and aim of life, and the only object to receive any attention is most intolerable." She also wrote that "it has become almost a proverb that when a lady is married, she may as well lay aside her books, still I do not believe it contains very much wisdom after all." Yet she concluded that women ought to learn to take pleasure in performing domestic duties supremely well: "The wrongly educated woman thinks her duties a disgrace and either frets under them or shirks them if she can. She sees man triumphantly pursuing his vocations, and thinks it is the kind of work he does which makes him so grand and regnant, whereas it is not the kind of work at all, but the way in which, and the spirit with which he does it."

She did not support woman suffrage, on the grounds that it would disturb domestic peace, and she railed against suffragists: "The cry has been by the women asking suffrage. You men are so influenced by bad women that we virtuous women must have the power to make laws to put down all these bad influences. They have been defeated in the courts; now with lofty heroism they go to these [fallen] women and promise them *justice* and protection 'legally financially socially & morally' if they will but give them aid in bringing to woman the law[-]making privilege. If this does not *out Tammany Tammany* itself [demonstrate political corruption], then what can?" To a woman whom she suspected of spreading gossip about her husband, she wrote, "[But how you] could have given credence and currency to such a report

. . . , I am utterly unable to explain . . . unless in your infatuation over the Rights of Woman you allowed spite to triumph over reason."

After his many years in Congress, Lucretia welcomed her husband's candidacy for the presidency. In the last part of the 19th century, candidates relied mostly on "front porch campaigns," receiving large numbers of visitors at their homes. As a result, their wives played a larger and more public role in campaigns than hitherto. Thus, James's election as president in November 1880 was due in no small part to his wife's assistance.

On March 4, 1881, Lucretia undertook the duties of first lady, and for a few months she executed them tactfully and with dignity. At the inaugural ball, held in the new National Museum, the president's slender, brunette wife wore light lavender satin trimmed with point lace, a cluster of pansies at her neck, but no jewelry. She conducted a press interview with aplomb and developed a sense of importance about her position, feeling that she must guard its dignity. She took her place at the president's side, not only in reception lines but accompanying him when he toured the Navy Yard workshops. She understood her husband's election as bringing "a terrible responsibility . . . to him and to me." He solicited her advice, and she began by informing him of her insights into the character of candidates for political appointments. She then took sides in partisan sparring and urged him to action: "You will never have anything from these men ['Stalwarts,' opponents within the Republican Party] but their assured contempt, until you fight them *dead*. You can put every one of them in his political grave if you are a mind to & that is the only place where they can be kept peaceable."

As a congressman's wife, Lucretia had entertained only modestly and had most enjoyed membership in the Washington Literary Society. Her new social responsibilities worried her, so she turned for advice to Mrs. James B. Blaine, wife of the secretary of state. She began a file of artists and authors whom she planned to invite and hesitantly decided to offer alcoholic beverages at the White House. However, as she had done throughout her married life, she concentrated most on caring for her husband and family and making a home for them in the White House, to which end she lobbied Congress for money to refurbish it. She studied its history: "These little scraps of reminiscence [of previous first ladies] that I gather up now and then lend this old place a weird charm. . . ."

In May Lucretia came down with malaria. Her distraught husband nursed her through its monthlong course. Then while she was recuperating in New Jersey, Charles Guiteau, a disappointed office-seeker, shot the 49-year-old president on July 2, 1881. The wounded man's first thought was of his wife: "Tell her I am seriously hurt, how seriously I cannot yet say. I am myself, and hope she will come to me soon. I send my love to her." Lucretia returned at once to the White House to nurse her helpless husband through 80 days of suffering, doing her best to raise his spirits and showing much courage and self-control. According to White House memoirist William Crook, Lucretia's own physician, Mrs. Susan Edson, acted as both doctor and nurse. To make the president a little more comfortable in the heat of a Washington summer, they set up a primitive air-conditioning system, filling the White House cellar with crates of ice, with a pipe leading to the president's room to carry the cooler air. Yet despite all efforts to save him, James Garfield died on September 19, 1881.

Fortunately, Lucretia had the means to raise her children in her widowhood, thanks to a fund of $360,000 raised by public subscription, a grant from Congress of $50,000, and a congressional pension of $5,000 annually. In the last 18 years of her life, she divided her time between South Pasadena, California, and Lawnfield in Ohio, living happily as matriarch of a clan of loving children and grandchildren. Understanding the importance of the historical record, she had her husband's papers arranged and indexed and gave the scholar Theodore Clarke Smith not only access to them but also the benefit of her own recollections. She spent much of her time in reading, translating Victor Hugo, and addressing women's groups on literature. During World War I she volunteered for the Red Cross.

On March 13, 1918, Lucretia Garfield died of pneumonia in South Pasadena. She was buried in Cleveland, Ohio, in the Garfield Memorial in Lake View Cemetery.

—— ···· ——

In 1865 her husband wrote of Lucretia Garfield, "It is very gratifying to me to know that my so precious wife has won the honest admiration of so many good people." Again: "I have been wonderfully blessed in the discretion of my wife. She is one of the coolest and best-balanced women I ever saw. She is unstampedable. There has not been one solitary instance of my public career when I suffered in the smallest degree for any remark she ever made." During the Garfields' short residence in the White House, the president turned to the first lady for counsel, and she remained for him the staunch supporter she had always been in their private and public lives.

Chronology

1832   *April 19:* Lucretia Rudolph is born in Garrettsville, Ohio

1850   Lucretia Rudolph enters Western Reserve Eclectic Institute (later Hiram College)

1854   Lucretia Rudolph becomes a teacher

1858   *November 11:* Lucretia Rudolph marries James A. Garfield

1859   James Garfield is elected to the Ohio senate

1860   *July 3:* Daughter Eliza Arabella is born

1863   James Garfield enters Congress

October 11: Son Harry Augustus is born

December 3: Daughter Eliza dies

1865   *October 17:* Son James Rudolph is born

1867   *January 16:* Daughter Mary (Molly) is born

Fall: The Garfields take a European trip

1870   *August 3:* Son Irvin is born

1872   *November 21:* Son Abram is born

1874   *December 25:* Son Edward is born

1876   *October 25:* Son Edward dies

The Garfields buy an Ohio farm, later known as Lawnfield

1879   James Garfield is elected to the U.S. Senate

1880   James Garfield is elected president of the United States

1881   *March 4:* Lucretia Garfield becomes first lady

July 2: James Garfield is shot

September 19: James Garfield dies

1918   *March 13:* Lucretia Garfield dies

Further Reading

Leech, Margaret, and Harry J. Brown. *The Garfield Orbit.* New York: Harper and Row, 1978.

Logan, Mrs. John A. *Thirty Years in Washington, or Life and Scenes in Our National Capital.* Hartford, Conn.: A. D. Worthington, 1901.

Peskin, Allen. *Garfield.* Kent, Ohio: Kent State University Press, 1998.

Shaw, John, ed., *Crete and James: Personal Letters of Lucretia and James Garfield.* East Lansing: Michigan State University Press, 1994.

FRANCES (FRANK) FOLSOM CLEVELAND
(JULY 21, 1864–OCTOBER 29, 1947)
First Lady, June 2, 1886–March 4, 1889;
March 4, 1893–March 4, 1897

FRANCES CLEVELAND
(Library of Congress)

Born late enough to benefit from the new opportunities opened by the 19th-century American women's movement, Frances Folsom Cleveland used her college education as many of the women's colleges of the time intended—to become a more polished and literate wife and mother. She met her husband's standard of a good wife, "a woman who loves her husband and her country with no desire to run either." Yet she financially supported the Women's Christian Temperance Union, which enthusiastically endorsed woman suffrage, even though her husband distrusted women's organizations—those that involved women in politics most of all—on the grounds that they encouraged women to neglect their children. Frances Cleveland was neither a New Woman nor a member of the burgeoning Progressive Era. Nonetheless, she was affected by some

139

of the more advanced ideas she had learned in college, for she served for 50 years on her alma mater's board, made a point of opening the White House to working women, and in modest ways tried to improve the lot of blacks.

—⁂—

Frances Folsom, known within her family as "Frank," was born in Buffalo, New York, on July 21, 1864, to lawyer Oscar Folsom and his wife Emma Harmon Folsom. When her father died in a buggy accident in 1875, his close friend and law partner Grover Cleveland became administrator of the estate and the little girl's unofficial guardian—a good one, to whom she was devoted. He planned carefully for her welfare and happiness. She was well educated, attending a French kindergarten, Miss Bissell's School for Young Ladies, the Medina (New York) Academy for Boys and Girls, and a Buffalo public high school before she entered Wells College in 1882.

Until the 1830s, no American college had opened its doors to women. In less than half a century, despite physicians' warnings about the dire effects of too much study on women— damaging the female constitution and impairing the ability to have children—education for women had become widely available in private women's colleges and public coeducational universities. As the daughter of a prosperous family, Frances Folsom could take the opportunity for granted. She was to be the third first lady in succession to benefit from higher education.

Frances loved both the educational and the social life of Wells College. She was popular with her women classmates and with young men. She was briefly engaged twice, and she turned down another proposal, writing her mother, "When I marry it must be someone more than a year older than I am, someone I can look up to and respect." Meanwhile, her "Uncle Cleve," as she called her guardian, kept up a correspondence with her, sending her flowers from the governor's mansion in Albany and, after 1884, from the White House. Final exams kept her from accepting his invitation to his inaugural, but during spring break she and her mother visited the White House, where the president's teacher-writer sister, Rose Elizabeth Cleveland, acted as his White House hostess. Frances enjoyed the company of young people whom the president and his sister had invited to meet and escort her; among them was Harriet Lane, who had served ably as hostess for President James Buchanan. However, Frances enjoyed even more the walks, rides, and long conversations she shared with the president.

Rose Cleveland thought Frances "a woman capable of great development; a much stronger character than appears on the surface." She was delighted as she watched her bachelor brother, then in his late 40s, court and then, in August 1885, propose to his young ward, who accepted him with her mother's approval. The engagement was kept secret, while Frances and her mother, at the president's insistence, toured Europe for several months, picking up a Parisian trousseau along the way. Meanwhile, the rumor mill was grinding, though for some time many believed Frank's mother to be the object of the president's affection. Reporters pursued the Folsoms wherever they went.

While on the European trip, Frances read as much as she could about her fiancé's career in an effort to prepare herself for the White House. When she saw a cartoon implying that he had fathered an illegitimate child, her mother explained that when he was 22, he and several other male friends, including Frank's father, regularly visited a woman named Maria Halpin. She had a child, presumably by one of them, but no one knew whom. Cleveland, the only bachelor among Maria's intimates, took the responsibility. Frank decided not to worry about something that had happened before she was born, and she serenely ignored reporters who asked whether she knew that as a sheriff Cleveland had presided over hangings, and that he had hired a substitute to fight in the Civil War.

However, the newspapers stopped asking such questions to report the romance of the engagement and wedding. Here was a middle-aged bachelor who had known his ward from her infancy and watched over her throughout her adolescence and young womanhood, patiently waiting for her to grow up. Now that their engagement was announced, Frances and her mother were spirited off the homebound ocean liner to the Gilsey House in New York, where the president visited her while in the city for the Memorial Day parade. From a window she watched him march, while the bands played the rollicking Gilbert and Sullivan tune "He's Going to Marry Yum-Yum." On June 1, 1886, Frank and her mother took the overnight train to Washington; Rose Cleveland met them at the station the next day and escorted them to the White House for the wedding ceremony.

The president had sent invitations to only 31 people—cabinet members, relatives, and close personal friends. He would have preferred, he said, to be married in a quiet private ceremony in New York, but he believed that every young woman was entitled to a beautiful wedding. So for this first and only wedding of a serving president in the White House, the mansion was elaborately decorated with flowers and candles. Frances had planned for her grandfather to give her away, but he had died while she was sailing home from Europe, so at 6:30 in the evening of June 2 while the Marine Band played Mendelssohn's "Wedding March," President Cleveland escorted his tall, slender, blue-eyed, chestnut-haired bride down the grand staircase, along the hall, and into the Blue Parlor. He wore black evening clothes with a white lawn necktie and a white rose in his lapel. Her short-sleeved wedding gown, by the great Parisian couturier Worth, was of corded ivory satin trimmed with India silk, edged with orange blossoms, with a four-yard train; a coronet of bridal flowers held her five-yard silk tulle veil in place. A Presbyterian minister and the bridegroom's clergyman brother performed the ceremony, which the president had rewritten to omit the word *obey* from the bride's vows. For the champagne supper in the East Room, the main table held a full-rigged ship made of roses,

pansies, and pinks, flying the national colors on the mainmast and small white flags with the initials *CF* in gold on the other masts; it was set on a mirrored sea. Each guest received a slice of wedding cake in a white satin box with a card autographed by the bride and groom. About 9:00, the bride changed to a going-away dress of gray silk with a large gray hat lined with velvet and crowned with ostrich feathers; the couple left the mansion by a rear door and drove to the station where a special train waited.

Despite the president's outrage at their "colossal impertinence," reporters and sightseers tracked down the honeymooners at the resort of Deer Park, Maryland. A week later, despairing of finding privacy, the couple returned to the White House. Soon thereafter they gave two receptions, one for the diplomatic corps and one for the general public. On both occasions Frances Cleveland wore her wedding gown, the sapphire-and-diamond engagement ring the president had given her, and his wedding gift of a diamond necklace.

"At this time," wrote Lucy C. Lillie, in *Lippincott's Magazine* for July 1887, "the first impression [Frances Cleveland] created was of a girlish figure, tall and willowy, with a well-shaped and well-poised head, soft brown hair, brilliant eyes under finely-marked brows, and a mouth and chin absolutely faultless. The character of the face, if girlish, was intelligent and thoughtful. Although the dimples came readily, the smile was exceedingly sweet, and seemed a fitting accompaniment to her well-modulated voice." Columnist Frank Carpenter praised the first lady extravagantly as having "the good nature and tact of Dolly Madison, the culture of Abigail Adams, the style and vivacity of Harriet Lane, and a beauty greater than that of any of the ladies of the White House still remembered by the old stagers of Washington."

Breaking from the habit of earlier presidential families, the Clevelands made their home away from the White House, at least in part to escape the crowds that gathered wherever the first lady appeared—so many people as to be physically threatening. Except for the official season with all its social obligations, they worked in the mansion and lived in their own home, Oak View—or Red Top, as the press called it—a small farmhouse on the outskirts of the capital, which the president had bought shortly before their wedding. Neither of them had ever owned a home before, and they enjoyed enlarging and decorating it, adding a second floor and building verandas on both floors. Summers they vacationed at Buzzard's Bay in Massachusetts, where they made lifelong friends.

Frances was fortunate in being able to turn to the experienced Harriet Lane as her guide to society, protocol, and operating the White House. She had a housekeeper and employed a classmate, Minnie Alexander, as her secretary—the first time a presidential spouse had had anyone but a family member to assist with her mail. During her husband's second term, the first lady herself typed some of her letters; later a federal clerk was assigned to help her with social planning. Frances filled the White House with flowers and songbirds—so many canaries and mockingbirds that she lost track of their numbers, although she knew each one by name.

"Frankie," as they called her, became the darling of the press, public, and tradesmen. Manufacturers of patent medicines, perfumes, candy, and underwear often used her picture, without her consent. She felt powerless to stop them; things had changed a great deal from the days when Julia Gardiner (Tyler) had shocked society by posing for an advertisement. The papers buzzed about Frances Cleveland's ability to play the piano, take photographs, speak French and German, and read Latin. The White House staff also adored her. White House memoirist William Crook wrote that he had never seen any other woman who possessed the same kind of "downright loveliness." She was, he wrote, "in the full bloom of youth, her beauty and grace and carriage enhanced and made almost luminous by an atmosphere of spirituality that enveloped her as truly as she lived and breathed." White House usher Ike Hoover described her as the most "brilliant and affable"

of all the first ladies he knew: "Here we had a lady who took real pleasure in seeing people."

Even aside from her youthful appeal and the romantic circumstances of her marriage, Frances Cleveland seemed foreordained to popularity as first lady. Contented with her life, position, and place as a woman, she did not challenge tradition. She was at a stage of life when she was preoccupied with establishing her marriage. A beautiful woman, she set fashions: Her hairstyle was widely imitated, and when she stopped wearing bustles, other women followed suit. Socially she delighted everyone—particularly her husband. Legend has it that one day her mother called the president to watch his wife receive without him; as the two of them stood beaming, he chuckled, "She'll do! She'll do!"

The first lady was healthy, active, and ready to enjoy life. She traveled everywhere with her husband; in 1887 he took her along when he was to speak at the centennial of Clinton, New York, and eagerly showed her his boyhood haunts. Minor mishaps plagued the trip—a head cold for him, an insect bite for her. "Half the people came to hear the president speak," she quipped, "but he had laryngitis; the other half came to admire my beauty and I had a black eye." On their extended trip through the South and West in the fall of 1887, thousands of Americans flocked to meet the presidential couple, eager to shake their hands—so many that Frances's arm had to be packed in ice every night. She was credited with transforming the president, turning him from a recluse almost into a gallant. "Her husband," wrote Frank Carpenter, "now dresses faultlessly under her watchful eye. He has become gentler and more polite and even seems to enjoy the pleasantries of social intercourse."

Frances Cleveland adopted an impeccable charity, the Needlework Guild, which made clothes for poor people. She was reputed to have an interest in women's issues, but she refused to lend her name to the controversial cause of woman suffrage. A teetotaler, she sent money privately to the Women's Christian Temperance Union but ignored the organization's request that she stop wearing low-cut gowns. She failed in an attempt to organize a charity to help orphaned and poor black children but joined the Colored Christmas Club, which donated money for needy blacks during the holidays, personally distributing gifts to the children and attending a Punch-and-Judy show for them. She worked with a black woman who founded the Washington Home for Friendless Colored Girls.

When Frances departed at all from the well-established practices of earlier first ladies, she did so quietly but firmly. She scheduled Saturday-afternoon receptions to enable working women to attend. When an official complained that they were crowded with "a great rabble of shop girls," she gave orders that nothing was to be scheduled to conflict with her receptions, "so long as there were any store clerks, or other self-supporting women and girls who wished to come to the White House." The first lady was on the outskirts rather than in the center of the movement to protect working women against exploitation, best exemplified by the Consumers' League, founded in 1890. Nonetheless, her influence as first lady made even her indirect support important.

Reputedly Frances believed in education for women as a means of achieving equality. In 1887 she participated in the graduation ceremonies at Wells and accepted a seat on the board of the college—a position she was to hold for more than 50 years. In later life she would go several steps beyond her predecessor Lucy Hayes in promoting college and professional education for women by helping to found the University Women's Club and urging the state of New Jersey to "open up educational opportunities for girls, like young men."

Despite his wife's popularity, Grover Cleveland was not reelected in 1888, mainly because of his opposition to a protective tariff. To defeat a nasty whispering campaign that alleged, without foundation, that he beat his wife, Frances wrote an open letter to Mrs. Maggie Nicodemus, who had brought this allegation to her attention: "I can only say in answer to

your letter that every statement made by the Rev. C. H. Pendleton in the interview which you send me is basely false, and I pity the man of his calling who has been made the tool to give circulation to such wicked heartless lies. I can wish the women of our country no greater blessing than that their lives may be as happy and their husbands as kind, attentive, considerate and affectionate as mine."

After they left the White House in 1889, the Clevelands sold Oak View at a $100,000 profit and moved to a house on Madison Avenue in New York City. Frances, at least, cherished hopes of a return to the White House, for she told a servant there, "Now, Jerry, I want you to take good care of all the furniture and ornaments in the house, for I want to find everything just as it is now when we come back

Frances Cleveland *(Library of Congress)*

again. We are coming back just four years from today." She told a *New York Times* reporter, however, that leaving the White House was easy for her because she was young and still had her life ahead of her. As a private citizen, she said, she looked forward to "the real life and the real home."

In New York the Clevelands lived quietly and modestly, buying a summer home, Gray Gables, on Buzzards Bay in 1891. On October 3, 1891, Frances gave birth to their first child, Ruth—after whom the Baby Ruth candy bar was named. The next year Grover Cleveland was reelected to the presidency, after a campaign in which his wife's image was used on buttons, cards, and souvenir plates—sometimes above his own picture—without his permission. On March 4, 1893, he rode alone to the inaugural ceremony, which was held outdoors. After the traditional White House luncheon, he stood on an open reviewing stand for three hours, while Frances watched from the window of a drugstore. That evening the Clevelands arrived at the inaugural ball in the Pension Building. They toured the ballroom, the first lady in a dress of heavy white satin with an empire front and a train trimmed with point lace and crystal beads; stiff satin bows adorned the shoulders, and the huge puffed sleeves were also beaded.

The White House years of 1893–97, however, differed from Frances's honeymoon experience during her husband's first term. No longer the carefree bride, now she was a mother of a toddler and pregnant with her second child. The frightening experience of seeing little Ruth being passed from tourist to tourist necessitated the Clevelands' closing off the White House grounds to the public, a much-criticized action that gave rise to rumors that the child was somehow deficient. Again the family resorted to living as much as duty permitted in a private house, Woodley, on the Potomac beyond Georgetown.

That summer the president discovered that he had a cancer in his mouth that must be removed. To avoid a political crisis, the operation was secretly performed on a friend's yacht, while the first lady took Ruth to Gray Gables,

where they usually summered. Frances called in reporters and asked them not to print stories that might upset the public; the president, she assured them, would soon arrive.

Family life preoccupied her, and she stayed with her children as much as she could. The Clevelands' second child, Esther, was born on September 9, 1893. Their third daughter, Marion, was born in July 1895. Frances encouraged her husband to relax and take more time away from the office. Most afternoons they went for a drive. One afternoon when she was late, he canceled their plans, determined to teach her punctuality. However, when she called to say she was ready, "What do you suppose I did?" he told a friend. "Why, I got up, put on my coat and gloves again, and went driving." He enjoyed her "managing" him with such traditional wifely ploys as slipping furniture that he had rejected into the White House.

Despite the demands of a growing family, Frances saw to her duties as hostess. Shortly after the beginning of the second term, she honored two visiting women heads of state. First she extended "various courtesies, formal and informal," to Princess Kaulani of Hawaii and publicly sympathized with the princess's "effort to accede to the Hawaiian throne from which the Hawaiian people had deposed her aunt, Liliuokalani." Then, in May 1893, she broke with tradition by calling on the queen regent of Spain, Princess Infanta Eulalie, in her Washington hotel. The first lady later gave an elaborate 10-course state dinner in the Infanta's honor, with boutonnieres of yellow orchids for the men and red roses for the ladies in tribute to Spain's red and yellow flag. As the end of the second term neared, she gave an elegant lunch for 48 honoring her sister-in-law Rose Cleveland. Her receptions often turned into "crushes." A contemporary, Helen Nicolay, described her last one:

A little before three o'clock Mrs. Cleveland entered . . . , and took her place in the improvised passageway, near the northern door leading from the Red into the Blue Room. . . . Then the doors were opened and the real reception began, when for two hours people of high and low degree, white and black passed through the room at the rate of twenty-five a minute. Mrs. Cleveland had a smile and a hearty handshake for each one, and her quick wit and gracious tact were exercised to the utmost in kindly deeds. The little woman, for instance, who was so absorbed in gazing at her hostess's beautiful face that she missed the outstretched hand was given another chance, after she had quite passed on; and the children were greeted with special kindness. There were touchingly many children . . . who had been brought because it was Mrs. Cleveland's last reception and in after years they would be proud to have seen and touched the hand of this most popular mistress of the White House.

When President Cleveland's second term ended, the first lady wept as she bade farewell to the White House staff. The Clevelands subsequently bought a house, Westlands, in Princeton, New Jersey, where they could enjoy both the peace of the countryside and stimulating company. There on October 31, 1897, their son Richard Folsom was born, and on July 18, 1903, their last child, Francis Grover. To their great grief, their daughter Ruth died of diphtheria in 1903. After that Frances could never bear to return to Gray Gables, so they bought another summer place near Tamworth, New Hampshire; two years later, they remodeled it to 27 rooms with 13 bedrooms and named it Intermont.

Grover Cleveland died on June 24, 1908, his eldest surviving child 14 and the youngest four. He left an estate of a quarter of a million dollars; his wife never accepted the annual pension of $5,000 due her as a presidential widow.

Five years later, in 1913, Frances Cleveland married Thomas Jex Preston, Jr. Changing careers in midlife, Preston had left business and enrolled as Princeton's first adult student, earning his bachelor's, master's, and doctoral degrees in archaeology. At least in part through Frances's influence he was hired to teach art and archaeology at Wells College. Soon after their marriage he joined the Princeton faculty.

Always busy, Frances Cleveland Preston was active in the Women's University Club and in raising money for Wells College while continuing her other charitable work. During World War I, she headed the speakers' bureau of the National Security League and herself gave speeches to promote the war effort. In 1928 she ventured far enough into politics to sit with the wife of the Democratic candidate for president, Alfred E. Smith, at public meetings. She also saw much of her children, who gathered at Tamworth every summer. When her son Francis organized a summer theater group there, she sold tickets.

As Frances grew older, blindness threatened. She learned Braille and with a Braille typewriter made transcripts for blind students, an activity she continued after her cataracts were successfully removed. Margaret Truman writes that as a very old lady Frances once lunched at the Truman White House. When Margaret introduced General Eisenhower to "Mrs. Preston," he asked, "And where did you live in Washington, ma'am?" To his embarrassment she answered, "In the White House."

Frances Cleveland Preston died in her sleep on October 29, 1947, at the home of her older son, Richard. She was buried beside Grover Cleveland in Princeton.

———

Frances Folsom Cleveland was a woman of uncommon good sense. Married at 22 in a blaze of publicity—the only woman married in the White House to a governing president—she kept her head. In the main she took her husband's advice on being a first lady: "You will find that you get along better in this job if you don't try anything new." She was a gracious, charming, and elegant first lady, who delighted the heart of her much older husband and his supporters. What influence she had over the president was in the domestic sphere, where, said White House usher Ike Hoover, she "would watch over him as though he were one of the children." Yet in quiet ways she was an advocate for women's education, foreshadowing the practice of subsequent first ladies of adopting causes of their own.

CHRONOLOGY

1864 *July 21:* Frances Folsom is born in Buffalo, New York

1875 Frances's father dies; Grover Cleveland becomes her unofficial guardian

1882 Frances Folsom enters Wells College

1884 Grover Cleveland is elected president of the United States

1885 With her mother, Frances Folsom spends 10 days at the White House, ostensibly to visit Rose Cleveland.

Fall: Frances Folsom accepts Groveer Cleveland's proposal of marriage and tours Europe with her mother

1886 *June 2:* Frances Folsom marries Grover Cleveland in the White House and becomes first lady

1889 The Clevelands move to New York, where Grover Cleveland practices law

1891 *October 3:* Daughter Ruth is born

1892 Grover Cleveland is reelected president

1893 *March 4:* The Clevelands return to the White House

September 9: Daughter Esther is born

1895 *July:* Daughter Marion is born

1897 *March 4:* The Clevelands retire to Princeton, New Jersey

October 31: Son Richard Folsom is born.

1903 *July 18:* Son Francis is born

1904 ca. *January:* Daughter Ruth dies of diphtheria

1908 *June:* Grover Cleveland dies

1913 *February 10:* Frances marries archaeology professor Thomas Jex Preston, Jr.

1947 *October 29:* Frances Cleveland Preston dies in her sleep

FURTHER READING

Brodsky, Alyn. *Grover Cleveland: A Study in Character.* New York: St. Martin's, 2000.

Carp, Frank. *Carp's Washington.* New York: McGraw-Hill, 1960.

Hoover, Irwin H. *Forty-Two Years in the White House.* Boston, Mass.: Houghton Mifflin, 1934.

Jeffers, H. Paul. *An Honest President: The Life and Presidencies of Grover Cleveland.* New York: Avon, 2000.

Nevins, Allan. *Grover Cleveland: A Study in Courage.* New York: Dodd, Mead, 1934.

———, ed. *Letters of Grover Cleveland.* Boston: Houghton Mifflin, 1933.

Severn, Sue. "Frances (Clara) Folsom Cleveland," in *American First Ladies,* ed. Lewis Gould. New York: Garland, 1996.

CAROLINE (CARRIE) LAVINIA SCOTT HARRISON

(OCTOBER 1, 1832–OCTOBER 25, 1892)

First Lady, March 4, 1889–October 25, 1892

CAROLINE HARRISON
(Library of Congress)

Caroline Scott Harrison profited from an extraordinarily good education for a woman of her day. A mistress of domestic skills, she was also an advanced woman, a lifelong participant in the clubs that were just beginning to move women out of their homes into church and civic work, and an advocate for women's education and opportunities for women in the professions. She persuaded her husband to appoint the first woman to serve on a presidential staff. All during her adult life and particularly in her White House years she reflected and contributed to the changing lifestyles of American women. She represented not the radical section of the women's movement but the liberal forefront of the middle-class women throughout the nation without whose involvement suffrage could not have been won. Her work—and that of women like her—for women's education and political participation was as necessary

147

to the success of the first American women's movement as that of Susan B. Anthony and Alice Paul.

—ᴍ—

Caroline Lavinia Scott was born on October 1, 1832, in Oxford, Ohio. She was the third daughter and third of five children of Presbyterian minister and Miami University professor Dr. John Witherspoon Scott and his wife Mary Potts Neal Scott. Her cultivated family valued the life of the mind and taught "Carrie" to love literature and the arts. She was educated first at a girls' school in Cincinnati founded by her father and then at the Oxford Female Institute, which he had also established and where he served as principal. In 1851–52, her senior year there, Carrie taught piano and sewing; the year after she graduated she taught music in a girls' school in Carrollton, Kentucky. She was a petite and slightly plump young woman, with heavy brown hair and brown eyes—warmhearted, sympathetic, vivacious, and playful.

In her college years, Carrie had met Benjamin Harrison, grandson of President William H. Harrison, son of a congressman, and a student of her father's. They courted under difficult circumstances, for Dr. Scott locked the gates of his Institute early in the evening and only reluctantly allowed the women students to receive gentlemen callers. As usual, love found a way for young couples to meet, and Carrie and her beau enjoyed buggy and sleigh rides and races. Later in life when she was complimented on her dancing, she used to say, "[Dancing] was considered a great sin at Oxford, but we managed to have just as much fun without it." In fact she defied the rules, persuading Ben to take her to dancing parties, where he gravely watched while she danced. They kept their engagement a secret on their campuses.

After Ben graduated from Miami University in 1852, he went to Cincinnati to read law in an attorney's office, where he fretted at the infrequency of Carrie's letters and worried that she was damaging her health by working too hard. He persuaded himself that delaying their marriage was dangerous for her health: "The anxiety of an engagement of already two years standing, and still promising a very distant confirmation have told with fearful effect upon her constitution," he wrote a friend. "The question then, John, is narrowed down to this: Shall I marry Carrie now and thus relieve her of those harassing doubts and fears which wear away her life, or shall I agree to stand aside and let her hasten to an early grave?" Or, the 20-year-old Ben wrote later, he himself might die, quoting his father as saying that "if Carrie and I were not married now, this fall, we would never be. The reason he assigned, was that I would never live another year."

They were married on October 20, 1853, her father presiding at the ceremony, which took place at dawn. The bride wore a simple gray traveling dress, and the newlyweds caught the 5:00 bus—the only public transportation available that day.

The Harrisons started out on a shoestring. Benjamin had $800 that he had borrowed on land left him by a relative. He and Carrie lived at first on the Harrison family homestead, The Point, at the mouth of the Big Miami River. After he was admitted to the bar in 1854, they moved to Indianapolis, shipping all their possessions in one large box. For a while Ben supplemented the pittance he was earning from his law practice by securing an appointment as crier of the federal court for $2.50 a day. They shared a two-story frame house with another young couple, but even this was beyond their means, particularly after Carrie's pregnancy necessitated a hired girl and medical expenditures. She went back to Oxford, where she stayed for some time after the birth of their son Russell on August 12, 1854. When she returned to Indianapolis in October, the Harrisons rented a three-room house, where Carrie did the housework and Ben helped with the outside chores. When Carrie fell ill and the baby failed to flourish, Ben scraped together enough money to send them for a rest cure at both their families' homes.

An invitation to enter into a law partnership with Will Wallace helped the Harrisons turn the economic corner and introduced Ben to politics. He eventually associated himself with the Republican Party and its struggle against slavery. Both the Harrisons were active in the First Presbyterian Church, where he served in various lay positions (he had once seriously considered the ministry as a profession), and she worked with the choir, socialized in the ladies' sewing society, worked on fairs and oyster suppers to raise money, and taught Sunday school. Their daughter Mary Scott was born on April 3, 1858, and that year they were able to afford a larger house and hired help. In 1860 Ben's fortunes profited still more when he was elected reporter of the state supreme court. Another daughter, born in June 1861, died at birth.

By the outbreak of the Civil War in 1861, the Harrisons were well established, residing in their own comfortable two-story house. Caroline Scott Harrison exhibited the skills proper to a lady of her time, playing the piano, doing expert needlework, and painting china and watercolors in a studio in their home, complete with a kiln. The younger women to whom she taught these skills liked her because of her ready laughter and her intellect. Besides her church work, she was among the public-spirited women then showing an interest in civic affairs, and she served from 1860 to the end of her life on the board of managers of the Indianapolis Orphans' Asylum. Moreover, her husband, rising in prominence within his party, had formed the habit early in his political career of consulting his wife, whose opinions he valued. Still the high-spirited woman she had been from her girlhood, she cajoled her serious, workaholic husband to balance his life with such frivolities as novel-reading and socializing.

In 1862 Benjamin Harrison helped raise the 70th Indiana Infantry, became its colonel, and began transforming himself into a seasoned commander. In 1864 his unit was attached to Sherman's army and engaged in the Atlanta campaign, and in 1865 he was given the brevet rank of brigadier general. Carrie, meanwhile, engaged in the volunteer effort that financed most of the care for wounded Union soldiers, becoming a leader in the Ladies Patriotic Association and the Ladies Sanitary Committee, even as she worried about her soldier husband. On occasion she visited him at camps in Kentucky and Tennessee, where she worked mending uniforms and doing chores. At home in Indianapolis, she also tended hospitalized soldiers.

When he was furloughed in February 1865, Benjamin took his wife and children with him from Indianapolis to Honesdale, Pennsylvania, where Carrie's sister lived. There all four Harrisons were stricken with scarlet fever, but they soon recovered, and before long General Harrison insisted on rejoining his troops. With them he marched in the grand review of Sherman's army in Washington, whence he wrote to his wife, "I know you love me, Carrie, with more devotion than most women are capable of, and I, so far as my heart or person are worth your acceptance, have given them all to you." He promised her a little keepsake in token of his resolution that "no object of ambition or gain could ever lead me away from the side of my dear wife and children" and of his hope "that by mutual help and by God's help, we may live the residue of our lives without having our hearts' sunshine clouded by a single shade of mistrust or anger." Finally, on June 8, 1865, the 32-year-old veteran was discharged and free to rejoin his wife, who shared his triumph at several victory rallies.

Back in civilian life and in his position as supreme court reporter, Benjamin rose rapidly in his profession and in the ranks of the Republican Party. His income from his practice rose to $10,000 annually, enabling him in 1874–75 to build a spacious house of 16 rooms. Just as she had done earlier on, Carrie balanced her domestic work with activities outside the home. At church she was a leader in the missionary society. She took a literature class once a week and art lessons twice a week, regularly exhibiting her hand-painted china and watercolors and donating them to Indianapolis institutions. She participated actively in the club movement that was taking women out of their homes into public activities and helped to found the Impromptu Club, where women and men read, discussed, and dramatized literature. The family became prominent in Indianapolis social, church, and charitable circles.

Although her husband's long absence during the Civil War had made Carrie loath to see him build a political career that might again take him away from home, she gradually developed expertise as a politician's wife. In 1877 the Harrisons called on President and Mrs. Rutherford B. Hayes at the White House, and in 1879 they entertained the Hayeses at a lawn party in Indianapolis. While her husband was campaigning successfully for the Senate in 1880, Carrie sent one of his speeches defending James Garfield to that presidential candidate; when Garfield won the presidential election, he invited the Harrisons to his Ohio farm. A severe fall on ice prevented her going; some scholars date her deteriorating health from that incident. The next year she and her children went to Washington to see Benjamin Harrison sworn in as a U.S. senator. The Harrisons and their daughter took rooms in a boardinghouse, and Caroline Harrison began her Washington years as a political wife.

Health problems haunted her. In 1883 she underwent surgery that hospitalized her for a long period, and in 1886 she was seriously ill again. Partly because of these troubles and partly because of other interests, she limited her entertaining to simple receptions and dinners, both in the boardinghouse and in the apartment to which they later moved. She was also active as a member of the board of lady managers of the Garfield Hospital.

By this time Carrie had developed a sophisticated political sense, and when politicians began speaking of her husband as a contender for the Republican presidential nomination, she recognized that her husband's chances depended mainly on his winning over the supporters of James G. Blaine. In 1888 the Republican convention nominated Harrison as a dark-horse candidate. As was common for that time, he conducted a "front-porch campaign," a form of politicking that tried the patience of candidates' wives, subjecting them to endless streams of visitors and their homes and possessions to theft and damages. Carrie entertained hosts of overnight guests and laid out refreshments for innumerable Republicans, watching her furniture break and her carpets wear thin; even the Harrisons' fence was lost. Stoically she remarked, "Well, it's the White House or the poor house with us now." To counter the Democratic propaganda publicizing popular first lady Frances Cleveland, the Republicans used images of their candidate's wife on schoolchildren's tablet (writing pad) covers and other propaganda.

Public interest in Carrie soared still higher after her husband won the presidency. A thousand guests attended her last reception in Indianapolis, and when she and her daughter went to New York to shop, reporters followed them everywhere. She quipped that the newspapers knew more about her family than they knew about themselves. After the election she told a reporter, "All last fall I sat in my sewing room and watched the procession of feet pass across the parlour floor wearing their path into the nap [of the carpet], and disappear like the trail of a caravan into the General's room beyond. Day by day, I watched the path grow wider and deeper, and at last the caravan spread out and engulfed us all. But I don't propose to be made a circus of forever! If there's any privacy to be found in the White House, I propose to find it and preserve it."

Nonetheless, a great deal of publicity centered on the family. Even before the inauguration the incoming first lady was swamped with requests for her opinions on everything from fashions to morals, with pleas for official appointments, and with solicitations for recipes and bits of her dresses to use in quilts. "You might as well shake a red rag at a bull," she told a reporter, "as say *crazy quilt* to me." Washington columnist Frank Carpenter advised against giving "these women the idea that their every request will be granted. Already they are asking for locks of Mrs. Harrison's pretty brown hair. If such requests multiply and are granted, our First Lady will be shorn like that Woman's Rights crank, Dr. Mary Walker [recipient of the Congressional Medal of Honor for Meritorious Services in the Civil War]."

After Benjamin Harrison was sworn in as president on March 4, 1889, the Harrisons enjoyed the traditional lunch at the White House, hosted by the Clevelands. The review followed in the afternoon, and the inaugural ball was held in the Pension Office that evening. For the ball Carrie wore a pearl brocade gown with elaborate gold embroidery and a long train, the opening at the throat filled with lace. Most of the time, however, she dressed so quietly and behaved so modestly that shopkeepers failed to recognize her when she visited their shops.

She immediately faced the task of organizing her household, which included her 90-year-old father; her son Russell and his wife Mary ("May") and daughter; and her daughter Mary ("Mamie"), son-in-law James Robert McKee, and the "Baby McKees": the McKees' two-year-old son, Benjamin Harrison, and infant daughter, Mary Dodge. Both her daughter and daughter-in-law helped Carrie with her social duties. Later she invited her niece Mrs. Mary ("May") Lord Dimmick to live in the White House and act as her secretary. Carrie's social obligations caused her no problems, for she and her husband were accustomed to the "best" society, both in Indianapolis and in Washington. Nevertheless, she limited her entertaining and did not opt for brilliance in it, preferring to devote her time and energy to charities, particularly the Garfield Hospital and the Washington City Orphan Asylum, and to her china-painting. To the press's approval, she did away with the practice of handshaking in receiving lines and made dancing again a regular part of public receptions. She also helped decorate the first Christmas tree ever set up in the White House.

The first lady was horrified at the condition of the White House and the inadequacy of its private quarters. She undertook her own campaign to remedy matters, inviting members of Congress to examine the mansion, which she believed was on the verge of collapse. She built public support by conducting tours for reporters and solicited the help of influential people, such as President Buchanan's White House hostess Harriet Lane. She then enlisted architect Fred D. Owen to draw three plans—one for a completely new building on 16th Street; one for changes to the present building; and (her own favorite) one for the preservation of the building with two new wings, the west wing to be devoted to offices and the east wing to an art gallery, with an enlarged botanical conservatory connecting the two wings and a large garden within the rectangle thus created.

Carrie came close to getting what she wanted, but in the end the bill failed in Congress, and she, her daughter, and her daughter-in-law were reduced to overhauling the existing building as best they could with relatively modest funds. They had rooms repainted and replaced drapes, carpets, and upholstery. To rid the basement of rats, they had concrete floors poured, the walls tiled shoulder-high, and the kitchen gutted and rebuilt with modern equipment. They put in bathrooms and installed electric lights—which terrified the whole family so much that if the White House usher failed to turn off the lights when he left, they remained on all night.

Carrie interested herself in the history of the mansion and personally gave tours of it. She persuaded Benjamin to order an inventory of the furniture at the executive mansion, complete with a history of each piece; began and displayed a collection of the china of former presidents' ladies; and designed the Harrison White House china, made by Haviland, with the country's arms in the center and a cornstalk-and-flower border to symbolize abundance and natural beauty. The china that she herself painted, always with at least one four-leaf clover, was much sought after for souvenirs, and she gave many pieces to church bazaars. For her grandson Benjamin she decorated a porcelain bathtub with pink magnolia blossoms.

By the time she reached the White House, Caroline Harrison had engaged in a lifetime of social, philanthropic, and patriotic service. As first lady she followed the mode of life she had established early in her marriage, that of a politically well-informed woman who chose to emphasize her domestic duties but also recognized charitable and civic responsibilities. She traveled widely with her husband, notably to an 1889 celebration of the centennial and re-creation of George Washington's inauguration in New York, and on an 1891 cross-country tour to California. Warmly greeted everywhere, Carrie was undeniably a political asset to her husband. However, in the summer of 1889 she provoked a storm of criticism when she accepted a 20-room seaside cottage at Cape May Point, New Jersey, from Postmaster General John Wanamaker and his friends. The public outrage was so great that the president eventually paid $10,000 for the house. Little wonder that Carrie wrote to a friend, "I have about come to the conclusion that political life is not the happiest— you are [so] *battered* around it in that life seems hardly worth living." On the other hand, senator's wife Julia Foraker wrote that Caroline Harrison "was a lovely woman, well bred, above all too kind of heart ever to neglect the amenities. Her tact and good manners saved many an occasion when her husband's dourness was freezing people stiff with discomfort and offense."

Carrie impressed some people, particularly in Washington society, as a homebody; the *Cleveland Leader*'s reporter Frank G. Carpenter commented that she was "the best housekeeper [the] Pennsylvania Avenue mansion has yet known." Yet some in the press criticized her for what Mrs. John A. Logan, wife of a U.S. senator, called her "excessive domestic proclivities." Julia Foraker wrote, "The Harrisons gathered . . . women who could give all their time to social perfections undistracted by suffrage, divorce, interior decoration or other extraneities." Evidently deceived by appearances, Foraker and others like her ignored or knew nothing of the stands taken by Caroline Harrison, placing her far in advance of her immediate predecessors, particularly on woman's issues like suffrage and professional education. She had spent her years in Indianapolis in the grassroots of the move-ments that had carried women as volunteer workers into public life. Now a mature, experienced woman, she was not impeded by the inhibitions of a Lucy Hayes or a Frances Cleveland about lending her name to worthwhile causes.

In 1890 Carrie helped to found and then became the first president-general of the Daughters of the American Revolution (DAR), an organization that in its early years supported woman's rights. She not only lent the DAR the prestige of White House backing but also supported its "every move that had political implications," seeing in it "great political potential" for a network of government workers to form a "powerful political force for women." Her first speech to the DAR, emphasizing the contributions of early American women to the founding of the country, was also the first speech composed by a first lady and delivered publicly: "It has been said 'that the men to make a country are made by self-denial,' and is it not true, that the society to live and grow and become what we desire it to be, must be composed of self-denying women? Since this society has been organized and so much thought and reading directed to the early struggles of this country, it has been made plain that much of its success was due to . . . women of that era. The unselfish part they acted constantly commends itself to our admiration and example."

In 1890 Carrie also helped to raise money for the Johns Hopkins University medical school, on the condition that it admit women. She encouraged her husband to hire Alice Sanger, a family friend, as the first woman stenographer on the president's staff. She may have struck many society women as "small and fat" and "too much given . . . to making everybody comfortable," but she dared to act on her beliefs, and they were advanced beliefs for her day.

Her critics also underestimated Carrie's political influence. Not only did she advise her husband on major issues, but at a time when many "respectable" people regarded labor unions as the cutting edge of anarchy, she stood at the president's side to review parades of organized workers that included Irish immigrants and blacks. She publicized her husband's principles by sending copies of a speech of his to Republican leaders.

Caroline Harrison's White House years were marred by frequent illnesses, especially respiratory disease. Poor health also rendered her more vulnerable to emotional trauma, like the shock she suffered when the wife, daughter, and maid of Navy secretary Benjamin F. Tracy were all burned to death in a fire in their home. Much affected, she had their bodies laid out in the White House, and she arranged the flowers herself. In 1891 she nursed her family through the grippe and then contracted it herself, leaving her with lung trouble, which the doctors diagnosed as tuberculosis. Benjamin took her to recuperate at Loon Lake in the Adirondacks. The year 1892 was an election year, but out of concern and respect for Carrie, neither Benjamin nor his opponent Grover Cleveland actively campaigned for the presidency. In September she asked to return to the White House, where she died on October 25, just two weeks before the president lost the election. Her body was taken by slow train to Indianapolis, where she was buried in Crown Hill Cemetery.

———〜〜———

As first lady, Caroline Harrison looked and acted like the grandmother that she was. Her devotion to her family and her efforts to remodel and enlarge the White House made her appear to some merely a model of domesticity. Like many another upper-middle-class woman of her day, however, she was accustomed to a life in which she played many roles, among them those of political wife, artist, clubwoman, and volunteer. In the White House, although she was a practiced hostess, she played down her social duties in favor of those roles she found more important and more interesting. She also showed herself to be a good lobbyist, a political asset and influence, and a courageous woman who publicly supported organized labor.

CHRONOLOGY

1832 *October 1:* Caroline Lavinia Scott is born in Oxford, Ohio

1849 Caroline Scott enrolls in Oxford Female Institute

1851–52 Caroline Scott is "Assistant in Piano Music" of Oxford Female Institute

1852 Caroline Scott teaches music in a Carrollton, Kentucky, school for girls and becomes engaged to Benjamin Harrison

1853 *October 20:* Caroline Scott marries Benjamin Harrison

1854 *August 12:* Son Russell is born

1858 *April 3:* Daughter Mary Scott is born

1860 Caroline Scott Harrison begins service of more than 30 years on board of managers of the Indianapolis Orphans' Asylum

1861 *June:* A daughter is born but dies at birth

1861–65 Caroline Harrison becomes a leader in the Ladies Patriotic Association, the Ladies Sanitary Committee, and other local groups concerned with the care of wounded soldiers

1880 Benjamin Harrison is elected to the U.S. Senate

1888 Benjamin Harrison is elected president of the United States

1889 *March 4:* Caroline Harrison becomes first lady

1890 Caroline Harrison becomes first president-general of the Daughters of the American Revolution and joins a movement to raise funds for the Johns Hopkins University medical school on condition that it admit women

1891 Caroline Harrison contracts a cold that develops into tuberculosis and nervous prostration

1892 *October 25:* Caroline Harrison dies

FURTHER READING

Carpenter, Frank. *Carp's Washington*. New York: McGraw-Hill, 1960.

Colman, Edna M. *White House Gossip: From Andrew Jackson to Calvin Coolidge*. Garden City, N.Y.: Doubleday, Page, 1927.

Crook, W. H. *Memories of the White House: The Home Life of Our Presidents from Lincoln to Roosevelt,* comp. and ed. Henry Rood. Boston: Little, Brown, 1911.

Hoover, Irwin Hood. *Forty-Two Years in the White House*. Boston: Houghton Mifflin, 1934.

Seale, William. *The President's House: A History*. New York: Harry N. Abrams, 1992.

Sievers, Harry Joseph. *Benjamin Harrison*. 3 vols. Indianapolis, Ind.: Bobbs-Merrill, 1968.

IDA SAXTON MCKINLEY
(JUNE 8, 1847–MAY 26, 1907)
First Lady, March 4, 1897–September 14, 1901

IDA MCKINLEY
(Library of Congress)

Born to prosperity and happy expectations, Ida Saxton McKinley as a young woman was attractive, intelligent, popular—and stubborn. Her family educated her conventionally but showed themselves advanced for their time in also training her in business. However, the illness that plagued her for years— variously diagnosed as stroke, epilepsy, phlebitis, and psychological breakdown— rendered that advantage largely useless. She was one of many women of her time and class to suffer such mysterious afflictions—among them Alice James, Charlotte Gilman, and for a time Jane Addams. Physicians of that era theorized that women's physiology made them hysterical, a belief that prolonged or even caused the invalidism and/or depression of many a middle- or upper-class woman. Instead of fresh air, sunshine, exercise, a sensible diet, and a healthy degree of activity, doctors prescribed bedrest, confinement, and drugs. Conscientious and loving husbands confronted with such advice became overprotective. Carl Sferrazza Anthony, biographer of first ladies, suggests that doctors may

155

have used sedatives to control Ida McKinley's unpredictable and sometimes embarrassing or even rude behavior, thus diminishing her ability to act as first lady.

———ɯɯ———

Ida Saxton was born in Canton, Ohio, on June 8, 1847, one of the three indulged children of businessman James Asbury Saxton and Kate Dewalt Saxton. Her parents gave her the education usual for fortunate young women of her time and area. She attended first the local public schools and then private schools in Delhi, New York, and Cleveland. Finally, with her younger sister, Mary, she was "finished" at Brooke Hall Seminary in Media, Pennsylvania.

Back home in 1868, Ida—petite, pretty, auburn-haired, blue-eyed, and lively—took her place in Canton society. Among her many activities, she taught Sunday school in the Presbyterian Church of which her parents were pillars, won a popularity prize when she appeared in a church entertainment, and masqueraded as the Queen of Hearts. At a church picnic she met William McKinley, a handsome, up-and-coming, and ambitious young lawyer who had recently set up practice in town.

In 1869, however, Ida and Mary left Canton to tour Europe. James Saxton paid the expenses for Canton schoolteacher Jeanette Alexander to chaperone a group of young women through Ireland, Scotland, England, Holland, Belgium, France, Germany, Austria, and Switzerland during the summer and fall of that year. Ida's letters home talk about visiting castles and museums, bargain-hunting, and arguing with their chaperone over plans. Occasionally they mention her correspondence with a young man, John Wright, of Canton, of whom she "thought considerable"; his plans to meet her in New York after the trip; and her shock at his death while she was away. Ida's letters also mention chronic headaches that sound like migraine but may have signaled the onset

of the nervous affliction from which she suffered for much of her adult life.

The Civil War had made it clear that women could not always rely on a husband for support, that they were sometimes left on their own. With the men away fighting, women gradually began moving out of their homes into the workplace, most often as government workers or teachers, a movement that accelerated after the Civil War, which had widowed so many women and deprived others of the men they might have married. This shift made it acceptable, if a bit advanced, for a daughter of a prosperous family like the Saxtons to work for a few years between school and marriage. On her return from Europe in early 1870, Ida's father put her to work in his bank for three years, until his death. She apparently started as a clerk, was promoted to cashier, and managed the bank for short periods in her father's absence.

As Ida resumed her social life in the small city of Canton, it was almost inevitable that she would again meet William McKinley. One story says that they often met on their way to church—she to Presbyterian services and he to Methodist—and he soon suggested that they walk to the same church. They were both eminently eligible, she as the accomplished daughter of a locally prominent family, he as a Civil War veteran and the newly elected county prosecuting attorney. He proposed and was accepted on a moonlit buggy ride, and her father consented to the marriage.

They were married before a thousand guests on January 25, 1871, in her church, with both her Presbyterian and his Methodist ministers officiating. The couple honeymooned in New York, then started their married life in Canton's St. Cloud Hotel while they waited for the completion of the small house given them by Ida's father. In that house Katherine, their first child, was born on their first Christmas together. Ida centered her life around her little blonde daughter, and for over a year she and William prospered and were happy.

The year 1873 shattered that happiness and metamorphosed Ida McKinley, turning her from a normal if perhaps overly protective young wife and mother into a fear-filled shadow of herself. Early that year, her mother died; then, a month later, she gave birth to another daughter, a sickly baby whom the family named Ida. The delivery was difficult and left the elder Ida depressed and ill. Less than five months later, on August 22, 1873, the baby died. The grieving young mother suffered severe headaches, convulsions, seizures, and blackouts. There was talk of epilepsy, and the doctors diagnosed phlebitis, an inflammation of the veins that frequently kept Ida in bed.

The harsh theology that told parents that the suffering, deformity, and death of their children were God's punishment for parental offenses against Him still lingered. Wondering how she had offended, Ida asked whether He would also take little Katie from her. Sad, irritable, and morose, she guarded her toddler so fiercely that she infected the child with her fears. According to biographer Thomas Beer, Katie refused her uncle's invitation to go for a walk with him: "No, I mustn't go out of the yard, or God'll punish Mama some more." All these fears were to be cruelly justified when on June 25, 1875, Katie died of typhoid fever.

Thereafter, Ida McKinley became a semi-invalid. Her condition manifested itself in seizures; headaches; crippling, irregular menstrual cycles; digestive problems; long-lasting colds; depression; and premature aging. The doctors could do little to help but sedate her. The formerly proud, willful Canton belle turned into a weak, dependent woman, constantly demanding care from the husband she adored and who adored her, jealous of his time and attention, frightened for his safety—and often drugged into a passivity that apparently made it difficult for her to relate to other people. She was thus reduced to a sort of half-life. Ida clung to her husband, making so many demands on him as sometimes to call him away from his duties as an elected official. Her need for his presence was so great that she had his portrait painted and hung where she could see it from her bed.

William responded by devoting himself to her. They were seldom apart; even with the heavy responsibilities he bore as successively a member of the House of Representatives, governor of Ohio, and president of the United States, he was always at her beck and call. His colleagues said of him that he could always be found at his office or with his wife. He gave up his long walks and horseback rides to fetch and carry for her. She had only to mention a wish to send him running to fulfill it. When she had a seizure in public, he placed a handkerchief or a napkin over her face to protect her from stares and carried on the conversation until she recovered. If he stayed away longer than anticipated, he could expect to find her on his return "sobbing like a child." William's constancy to his wife and her needs evoked the envy of other women and inspired his political supporters to praise him as a knightly model of compassion.

For her part, Ida recognized the burden she was placing on William and struggled to recover, traveling from doctor to doctor and taking the prescriptions they gave her. Sometimes she managed to perform her duties as housewife and as her husband's hostess, after a fashion, particularly while he was in the Ohio governor's mansion. Despite the hovering danger of seizures, she continued to appear publicly. Unlike Jane Pierce, she encouraged her husband's political ambitions and did not protest when politics took him away from her to speak or attend conventions. She traveled with him whenever she could, preferring never to be apart from him. She also studied political issues and formed sensible opinions so that she could discuss them with him. His involvement in the temperance movement in 1874 resulted from her interest in it. Often, however, Ida could only go through the motions of living; her condition had altered everything.

In 1876 William McKinley was elected to the first of his several terms in the House of Representatives, and the couple sold their Canton home and moved into Washington's Ebbitt House. A nurse looked after Ida while William worked in the Capitol or in a rented office across the hall from their suite. He catered to her in every way, forestalling her anxiety at his absence with notes telling her of his plans, enduring the stuffy atmosphere that she found most comfortable, and forgoing his cigars in her presence. She spent her days rocking, embroidering, and crocheting, but sometimes rallied enough to attend social functions. The couple enjoyed the friendship of President Rutherford B. Hayes and his wife Lucy. They lunched at the presidential mansion several times, and for one two-week period Ida McKinley filled in as White House hostess for Lucy Hayes in her absence. The McKinleys also knew and admired General William Booth, the founder of the Salvation Army. Occasionally they entertained constituents and congressional colleagues—they particularly welcomed children. Twice during the congressional years Ida accompanied her "Major" [his final Civil War rank] to California, and she sometimes returned to Canton without him.

Defeated for another term in the House in 1890, William McKinley was elected governor of Ohio in 1891. In their four years in Columbus, the McKinleys lived in hotels, and Ida's health seemed to improve. She became more active socially and they entertained more, even hosting a formal party with dancing. In reception lines she stood as long as she could, holding a bouquet so that she need not shake hands, then seated herself next to her husband. They attended operas in Cleveland, sitting in a box rented for them by the governor's friend and supporter Mark Hanna, a financier and politician. They went to concerts and plays, especially Shakespearean drama, and met theatrical stars. At home they played cribbage together—although the governor always let his wife win. Privately and publicly he continued to look after her, reassuring her by waving to her at arranged times from the street or from his office. In 1893, when he was in financial difficulties to the tune of $100,000 as cosigner of a loan with a bankrupt merchant, she offered him all her own money, including the real estate that she had inherited from her father, telling her protesting lawyers, "My husband has done everything for me all my life. Do you mean to deny me the privilege of doing as I please with my own property to help him now?" Nevertheless, McKinley's political supporters paid the debt.

In 1896, when William McKinley ran for president, his campaign organized a Women's McKinley Club in Canton and produced campaign buttons with Ida McKinley's picture. The campaign was often brutal; she was accused of being an English spy, a mulatto, a Roman Catholic, and a lunatic, and her husband was labeled as a drunk, the pope's agent, a swindler, and a wife-beater. In response, Republicans produced a romanticized biography of Ida McKinley. A thousand people greeted the candidate and his wife on their return to Canton, but few of the many supporters who flocked to their Canton home during the "front-porch" campaign customary at that period glimpsed her. However, she was on view and in command of herself when 500 guests attended the McKinleys' lavish celebration of their 25th wedding anniversary. When her husband was elected, she was frightened—not unreasonably, for in her lifetime two presidents had been assassinated, James Garfield only 15 years previously. "Oh, Major, they will kill you, they will kill you," she said, to which he responded, "This little woman is always afraid someone is going to harm her husband."

Arriving in Washington, Ida McKinley was too ill to accept the Grover Clevelands' invitation to dinner at the White House on March 3, 1897. At the inauguration the next day, however, observers thought she looked pale but happy. After the swearing-in ceremony, the McKinleys lunched at the Capitol, then went to the White House, where they received a few intimate friends and dined informally. For the ball that evening the first lady wore a silk brocade with a train, high neck, and long sleeves, diamonds in her hair and at her breast, but she could not complete the traditional grand march through the ballroom, and the president had to take her home early. At this stage of her life contemporaries described her as frail in appearance, with graying hair. "Her voice was gentle and refined," wrote Senate wife Ellen Maury Slayden, "and her face almost childishly sweet."

Independently wealthy, Ida McKinley took with her into the White House her German maid and a $10,000 wardrobe that included eight formal gowns. She often wore an aigrette, a cluster of egret feathers worn on a hat or in her hair, evoking a protest from the Audubon society. Incapable of injecting merriment or gaiety into the entertainment, the first lady moved drearily through receptions and state dinners, though sometimes she rallied, as when she arranged a series of musicales in early 1898. Contrary to custom, she was always seated by her husband's side, where he could help her if illness struck. "Everybody was under a certain strain when the McKinleys were hosts," wrote Senate wife Julia Foraker. "Mrs. McKinley, so physically unequal to the thing she bravely was attempting to do, and the President, masking his tender concern about his wife under a deferential solicitude for his guests that went to our hearts." The president continued to wait on his wife and care for her as if she were a child. Sometimes when he left a long night session in his office he would find her still awake at 2:00 A.M. and would sit on the bed holding her until she fell asleep. Jennie Hobart, wife of the vice president, tactfully rendered her assistance, visiting Ida almost every day, standing close by to assist on formal occasions, and always responding to appeals to substitute for her or to give her companionship.

In the White House the first lady punctiliously attended to her household duties, but she had no enthusiasm for renovation and remodeling. Even in 1900, when the White House centennial raised hopes for the execution of one of Caroline Harrison's plans to expand the mansion's facilities, Ida McKinley announced that she would put up with "no hammering." Nonetheless, she insisted on having her surroundings her way; when she first saw her own apartments, they had been freshly painted yellow, but she would not enter them until they had been done over in blue.

Ida received intimate friends and official visitors mornings and afternoons in her own reception room. She and the president usually had guests for their 1:00 luncheon, and she held a reunion in the White House for her classmates at Brooke Hall. Still, she went out less than her predecessors. She spent much of her time alone, reading and knitting or crocheting literally thousands of pairs of house slippers with leather soles—blue for Union sympathizers, gray for Confederate loyalists, and red for orphans and widows. Often she contributed slippers like these to charities to be auctioned off. Every Sunday she sent to the Metropolitan Church flowers from the White House greenhouses that she had personally picked for the altar, asking that after the service they be sent to an invalid. Hospitals also received flowers as well as delicacies from the White House kitchen.

Ellen Maury Slayden's account of a call on Ida McKinley stresses her remoteness:

> [She] sat propped with pillows in a high armchair with her back to the light. Her color was ghastly, and it was wicked to have dressed her in bright blue velvet with a front of hard white satin spangled with gold. Her poor relaxed hands, holding some pitiful knitting, rested on her lap as if too weak to lift their weight of diamond rings, and her pretty gray hair is cut short as if she had had typhoid fever. She shook hands with us lightly, but didn't speak until the words 'Mrs. Maxey of Texas' seemed to strike her and she then said in a faraway tone, as if talking to herself, 'That's a long way off.' Mrs. Maxey murmured some commonplace about her kindness in receiving us, and she went on, saying 'I've had a great deal of experience. . . , my husband was in Congress a long time, and then he was governor of the state.' . . . We all shrank from being there with a poor, suffering woman who ought to have been hidden from the gaze of the curious.

Possibly the first lady was heavily drugged at this juncture. Yet friends who had long known her thought that her health was better in the White House than previously, and on some occasions she could be charming and witty. When provoked, however, she treated her guests rudely, subjecting political opponents to partisan diatribes. She once accused the wife of the secretary of war of wanting to be "in my place." She embarrassed a young English girl who had confessed that though she enjoyed Washington she loved her own country best. "Do you mean to say," asked the first lady, "that you would prefer England to a country ruled over by *my husband*?" Even Republicans were not spared; she told a prominent senator of her own party: "I think it's about time you men did something. My husband has carried the Republican Party for twenty years. Now I'd like to see somebody else do something." She was petulant, jealous, and spitful toward those she perceived as rivals for her husband's attention.

Some thought her a good judge of people, and because she had influence over her husband in political appointments, her dislike could harm her enemies and help her friends. Given the closeness of the marital relationship, it was natural for President McKinley to discuss with her such important issues as the tariff and the chances of a bill's passage. Scholars have long speculated, inconclusively, on how much Ida's interest in sending missionaries to the Philippines swayed his decision to annex those islands after the Spanish-American War. She did not reserve her opinions for his ears alone but tried to involve the Presbyterian board of foreign missions. Julia Foraker wrote,

I went to call on her one day during the Philippine agitation and found her full of plans for saving the Igorots, particularly the children. I had my little son Arthur with me that day; she always liked me to bring him, and I remember her offering him a rose and Arthur, a little shy, hesitating to take it, and Mrs. McKinley being hurt by this and showing it, tears coming into her eyes. . . . Her love for children and the tragedy of her own loss made her so sensitive. . . . People today have forgotten about little Katie and baby Ida . . . , ghosts in long-ago moonlight, yet playing a strangely real part in the national career of the man who became our twenty-fifth President.

In 1900 William McKinley won reelection to a second term as president, this time with Theodore Roosevelt as his vice president. The first lady's health worsened, and she canceled the social season. In 1901 she recovered enough to accompany her husband on a cross-country tour, but it had to be cut short in San Francisco when she developed an infection in a finger that spread to her heart. She returned to Canton to recuperate, and that summer she had to resort to a wheelchair. On September 5 William and Ida were visiting friends in Buffalo, where she was resting when anarchist Leon F. Czolgosz shot the president at the Pan-American Exposition. Even as he fell, William beseeched that the news be broken to his wife gently. Everyone feared its effect on Ida's health, but she rallied to the emergency and supported her husband's spirits during the days that he lay dying; he died on September 14. She rode the train carrying his body back to Washington and soon thereafter returned to Canton, where she lived with her sister. "No one could have said," wrote Julia Foraker, "that she could have lived with so much courage through the lonely years that followed. She who had been shielded from every sort of responsibility and weariness now recognized reality, even took an interest in certain of her business affairs."

Ida Saxton McKinley died from apoplexy on May 26, 1907. She was buried temporarily until the completion of the McKinley mausoleum in Canton.

—⁓—

Ida McKinley's record as first lady has raised questions about whether she could have done more and whether her illness and dependence were unavoidable or simply her means of holding on to her husband's love and attention. In 1881 she suffered a seizure after he mentioned seeing an attractive woman at President Garfield's funeral. Yet she could also display great strength. Although William was not there in Canton to support her when her father died in 1887, she took that loss well, and when in 1899 her renegade brother George was murdered by a discarded mistress, the first lady carried on with her duties, refusing even to wear mourning. When her husband lay dying, she retained remarkable self-control. It was said that after his death, she never again had a seizure. No one then or now—certainly not Ida McKinley herself—could or can say to what extent her condition was physical, to what extent psychological, or to what extent induced by her medications. All that aside, nothing in the record suggests that she ever considered changing or developing the role of presidential spouse. Although she did exert her influence with her husband in aid of the temperance and missionary movements, her efforts to fulfill her duties as first lady were directed mostly toward hostessing. Despite her training in business, she left no evidence of having any ambition for a career, no trace of concern for changing the status of women, and no indication of interest in the rapidly growing suffrage movement. She remains a first lady without substance, of limited vision, half-alive—in the words of Julia Foraker, "a pathetically spoiled. . . woman."

Chronology

1847   *June 8:* Ida Saxton is born in Canton, Ohio

1869   Ida Saxton tours Europe with her sister Mary

1870   Ida Saxton begins clerking then cashiering in her father's bank and teaching Sunday School

1871   *January 25:* Ida Saxton marries attorney William McKinley

1871   *December 25:* Daughter Katherine is born

1873   ca. *December:* Ida McKinley's mother Kate Saxton dies.

ca. *March:* daughter Ida is born

August 22: Daughter Ida dies; Ida Saxton McKinley develops phlebitis and a complex nervous illness, becomes a semi-invalid

1875   *June 25:* Daughter Katherine dies

1876   William McKinley is elected to Congress

1891   William McKinley is elected governor of Ohio

1896   William McKinley is elected president of the United States

1897   *March 4:* Ida McKinley becomes first lady

1898   Ida McKinley's brother George is murdered

1901   Ida McKinley accompanies William McKinley on a cross-country tour, develops blood poisoning, and spends the summer in their Canton, Ohio, home

September 5: William McKinley is shot

September 14: William McKinley dies

1907   *May 26:* Ida McKinley dies of apoplexy

Further Reading

Armstrong, William H. *Major McKinley: William McKinley and the Civil War.* Kent, Ohio: Kent State University Press, 2000.

Belden, Henry S., comp. and ed. *Grand Tour of Ida Saxton McKinley and Sister Mary Saxton Barber, 1869.* Canton, Ohio: Reserve Printing, 1985.

Foraker, Julia. *I Would Live It Again: Memories of a Vivid Life.* New York: Harper, 1932.

Hartzell, Josiah. *Sketch of the Life of Mrs. William McKinley.* Washington, D.C.: Home Magazine Press, 1896.

Leech, Margaret. *In the Days of McKinley.* New York: Harper and Row, 1959.

Logan, Mrs. John A. *Thirty Years in Washington.* Hartford, Conn.: A. D. Worthington, 1901.

Slayden, Ellen Maury. *Washington Wife: Journal of Ellen Maury Slayden from 1897–1919.* New York: Harper and Row, 1962.

EDITH KERMIT CAROW ROOSEVELT

(AUGUST 6, 1861–SEPTEMBER 30, 1948)

First Lady, September 14, 1901–March 4, 1909

EDITH ROOSEVELT
(Library of Congress)

Edith Carow Roosevelt was a woman of the 19th century who lived to feel at home in the 20th. She saw herself first as a wife and mother, who famously "managed" her ebullient husband, but she also enjoyed the public life that his various official posts brought. She formed her own independent opinions, particularly in political affairs, which she sometimes understood more objectively and accurately than he. After Theodore Roosevelt's death her capacity to grow and change led her to active participation in politics. In 1920, in the first election in which American women could vote, she campaigned for the Republican Party, and again in 1942, when her nephew-in-law Franklin Roosevelt was the Democratic candidate, she campaigned against him.

Edith Kermit Carow was born to fortune and position on August 6, 1861, in Norwich, Connecticut, the elder of two daughters of businessman Charles Carow and his wife Gertrude Elizabeth Tyler Carow. Edith claimed descent from several prominent Americans, notably the Puritan minister Jonathan Edwards. She had a privileged childhood in New York City, although the family peace was troubled by her father's alcoholism and business failure and her mother's hypochondria.

"Edie" was a neat, self-possessed child, with an air of remoteness. She and Theodore Roosevelt knew each other from childhood. His sister Corinne was her closest friend, and Edie studied McGuffey's readers and learned to write along with the Roosevelt children in the Roosevelt brownstone. When she was four and "Teedie" was six, they watched together as Abraham Lincoln's funeral procession passed through New York City.

From the time Edie was six, her father's business difficulties made family life unstable; often her mother had to turn to relatives for help or shelter. Edie's lessons with the Roosevelt children continued, however, and their governess/aunt taught her needlework, at which she excelled. Their father produced plays in which she acted and took her along to study nature on the Hudson River and to sail in Central Park. All the children attended classes in dancing and deportment together. Only the Roosevelts' extended trips abroad separated them, and even then they corresponded faithfully.

At the age of 10, Edie was enrolled in the fashionable Comstock school, which emphasized religion and high moral standards. The curriculum omitted sciences and higher mathematics, deeming them inappropriate for girls, but cultivated her appreciation of music and stressed literature, which she loved—especially Shakespeare—and languages, which she found difficult, though she acquired fluency in French. In her teens she summered either on the New Jersey seashore or with the Roosevelts at Oyster Bay, Long Island. In 1877 Harvard freshman Theodore rated her "when she dresses well and do'n't frizzle her hair" as "a very pretty girl." She visited him with his family in Cambridge, and he often singled her out during vacations.

Edith Carow and Theodore Roosevelt may have been engaged before his first marriage; he later intimated as much, and Edith reminisced that he had proposed to her repeatedly in 1877 and 1878, but they quarreled in August 1878. That fall he met Alice Lee and resolved to marry her, though he continued to think Edith "the most cultivated, best-read girl I know," and they saw each other often. In February 1880 he told her of his engagement to Alice before anyone else outside his family. Despite her shock and pain at the news, Edith attended their October wedding, where she "danced the soles off her shoes," and she saw the newlyweds frequently at social events.

She passed her days as she had been raised to—reading and going to art exhibits, concerts, Bible readings, and parties. She danced at Corinne Roosevelt's debut and was a bridesmaid at her friend's wedding. Family tradition says that Edith toyed with and rejected the possibility of marrying for money to recoup her family's finances. In fall 1881 she gave a party to celebrate Theodore Roosevelt's election to the New York assembly. She mourned her father's death in the spring of 1883, for she had been close to him; in her old age she described him as "an angel."

Theodore Roosevelt's young wife Alice died in childbirth of Bright's disease on February 14, 1884—the same day as his mother. The stunned young widower had the baby baptized Alice and handed her over to his older sister Anna (Bamie) Roosevelt. He returned to Albany for the rest of the legislative session and then went west to work out his grief in hard physical labor. He avoided Edith, believing second marriages a betrayal, and asked his sisters not to invite her when he was with them. Inevitably, though, they met—by accident, in September 1885, at Bamie's home. He began to call on her, invited her to a ball in his house, and saw her socially elsewhere. He found her more self-assured, tolerant, and sympathetic than before, and on

November 17 that same year, he proposed. They agreed on a secret engagement, for Theodore had still not decided on a choice of career, and he reproached himself for what he perceived as his "inconstancy" to his dead wife.

In spring 1886 Edith sailed with her mother and sister to help them establish a home in Italy, where living was less expensive. Theodore went west at the same time, but by fall he was back east, determined to enter public service. After losing a race for the mayoralty of New York, he embarked for London, where he and Edith were to marry. When his cousin James West Roosevelt learned of the engagement he wrote to Theodore: "Now that you are to marry a girl who has been one of my best friends, a girl whose main characteristic is truth, I am very much delighted. . . . You are marrying a woman who can enter into your plans and who can appreciate your aims. . . . You are marrying one also who will love you—that is best of all."

On December 2, 1886, Edith and Theodore were married at the fashionable St. George's Church, Hanover Square, in London. They honeymooned that winter in France and Italy, spending several weeks in the company of her mother and sister and then idyllically on their own. Back in England they met historian George Otto Trevelyan and poet Robert Browning and they stayed in the country house of Lord North.

In Edith, Theodore gained a healthy, intelligent wife well qualified socially for the positions in which his career would place her. She was also tactful, adept in conversation, and her own woman—self-controlled and reserved to the point of seeming aloof. Fortunately for both bride and groom, their concepts of woman's vocation as wife and mother coincided, though he was more enthusiastic than she about women's rights to education and suffrage. Both of them thoroughly enjoyed domesticity and deplored a double standard of morality for men and women.

Edith was taking on a daunting task in marrying Theodore, a man who demanded the utmost from himself and everyone around him.

An activist in work and play, he was endlessly restless and ambitious but also zestful, energetic, and ready to enjoy life—especially the family life that began almost immediately: When the newlyweds returned to New York in late March 1887, the bride was pregnant. She also insisted that Theodore's three-year-old daughter Alice live with them, though he had been willing to fall in with his sister Bamie's hopes of raising the child. Edith demanded that Alice call her "Mother," creating a confusing situation for the little girl, who had been taught to pray for her mother in heaven. Apparently made to feel like an outsider in her father's new family, Alice came to prefer living with Bamie. (According to report, years later, immediately after her brilliant White House wedding, Alice turned to her stepmother to thank her, but Edith replied, "I want you to know that I'm glad to see you go. You've never been anything but trouble.") Edith's opinion of her husband's first wife did not help the situation. If Alice Lee had lived, she asserted, she would have bored Theodore to death.

In May, taking Alice with them, the Roosevelts moved to Sagamore Hill, the 22-room house that Theodore had built in Oyster Bay for his first wife. There they set the pattern of giving over mornings to work—she supervising the household, sewing, and answering letters, he writing—and afternoons to walking and rowing. Winters they spent in New York City in Bamie's house.

On September 13, 1887, Edith gave birth to her first child, a boy who was named Theodore. The new father and mother were still adapting to married life, a process in which his preferences usually won out. She enjoyed a quiet family life that left room for reading and time alone with him; he liked activity and company. To please him, she entertained and took up tennis, and after a time, she began to travel with him on political jaunts. Theodore, too, found ways to adapt, as he later wrote to a son: "[I]f Mother had been a mere unhealthy Patient Griselda I might have grown set in selfish and inconsiderate ways. Mother . . . when necessary, pointed out where I was thoughtless, instead of submitting to it."

In spring 1889 the Roosevelts' lives changed when President Benjamin Harrison appointed Theodore Civil Service Commissioner. Edith, pregnant again and doubtless worried because a previous pregnancy had resulted in a miscarriage, was left at Sagamore Hill to manage the Roosevelt farm and finances as well as the children, while her husband lived in Washington and spent his annual vacation in the west. Their baby, another son, whom they named Kermit, arrived prematurely but safely on October 10.

In December Edith left the children at Sagamore Hill with Bamie and went to Washington to arrange the small house her husband had rented there, as well as to explore the city, enjoy its social life, and be received as a guest at the White House for the first time. She was welcomed, making friends and winning the admiration of men such as historian Henry Adams, who was amused at the way that Theodore "stands in such abject terror of Edith. . . . What is man that he should have tusks and grin!" At the end of the social season she went back to Sagamore Hill. That fall for the first time she visited Theodore's Dakota ranch and, wearing long skirts and many petticoats to protect her against the cold, camped with him in Yellowstone Park.

To the delight of both parents, a daughter, Ethel—a "jolly, naughty, whacky baby"—was born at Sagamore Hill on August 13, 1891. As had become their habit, the family spent the winter in Washington, though Edith, who handled the accounts, worried over expenses and contemplated the "dire resort" of renting Sagamore Hill. (Her efforts to economize, it should be noted, always assumed servants aplenty and a mansion to live in.) Theodore laughed at his own profligacy: "Every morning Edie puts twenty dollars in my pocket, and to save my life I never can tell her afterward what I did with it." Nevertheless, as a national economic depression persisted, he too became anxious. Moreover, his alcoholic brother Elliott,

father of Eleanor Roosevelt, was a constant problem. Until Elliott's death in 1894, Edith feared that one of the scandals in which he was repeatedly involved would damage her husband's reputation.

Theodore also fretted about what he considered his own lack of success. His wife learned to cheer him by involving him with the children—an activity he enjoyed so much that she began to call him her "oldest and rather worst child." He taught his sons and daughter to swim by forcing them to jump off the dock and demanded that on walks they go "Under or over but never around." Edith reenforced these rather Draconian methods of child rearing by her casual attitude toward the bruises and cuts such adventures brought—for instance, adjuring a bleeding son Teddy to drip into the bathroom basin, not on the rug.

In 1894 Edith reflected the changing times by participating in the Washington social season despite her pregnancy; their son Archibald was born on April 9. That fall she advised Theodore not to run again for the mayoralty of New York City, citing the financial insecurity of elective office—advice that bitterly disappointed him and that she later regretted so much that she vowed never again to give her opinion. Few could keep such a promise—and certainly not Edith Roosevelt.

The year 1895 took the Roosevelts back to New York City, where Theodore had been appointed police commissioner. Now, during the summers, he could commute to Sagamore Hill—at least when his vigorous and sometimes controversial execution of his duties allowed. However, Bamie's New York house was no longer available to relatives on demand. Her engagement to a divorced man had precipitated a crisis; the state of New York did not recognize his divorce, and if they lived there he might be prosecuted for bigamy and she for property confiscation. They settled the matter by living elsewhere. So for the winter of 1896, Theodore and Edith rented Bamie's house.

Spring 1897, however, sent them back to Washington, where Theodore Roosevelt was to be assistant secretary of the navy. There, on November 9, their fifth and last child, Quentin, was born. Afflicted with an abdominal tumor, Edith did not recover for months. Alice was sent to live with Bamie; when she complained that this arrangement was "worse than boarding school," her stepmother told the girl that that was why she had been sent there. Alice eventually adjusted.

Despite his worry about his wife, Theodore went off to fight with the Rough Riders in the Spanish-American War. "Come back safe darling 'pigeon,'" she wrote to him. "[I]t is quite right you should be where you are." She visited him for a few days in Florida just before his regiment sailed. Her sadness and worry during their separation, she said, led her to sympathize with the Civil War women who had endured four years of such misery. As soon as the regiment returned she rushed to his camp to see him.

Oyster Bay gave Roosevelt a hero's welcome, and he began planning to run for governor of New York. After he launched his campaign in Carnegie Hall in October 1898, Edith had her first taste of life as a politician's wife, as she worried that anarchists might attack him. His election sent her to Albany to inspect the executive mansion, fortunately large enough to house the new governor's family. For the inaugural reception she armed herself with two bouquets, holding one in each hand, so that she could not be expected to shake hands with the more than 5,000 guests—a practice she followed throughout her public life. She looked young for her age, but her position and experience were making her a somewhat formidable woman who awed children and adults alike, though some of her friends attributed this reaction to her "necessary queenliness" as the governor's wife.

She renovated the Albany mansion to accommodate the houseful of boisterous, happy children, whose father joined in their pranks. An aide helped her with the entertaining, taking charge of the food, seating, and music, while she saw to the flowers. The governorship allowed Edith to see more of Theodore than

previously and to appear with him publicly. Moreover, the money he earned by writing was easing their financial situation. She could take time to join a discussion group of intellectual women, go on long rambles, and take a train to Washington or New York City to see friends and attend opera and theater. Her husband adored her.

Reluctant to change this life she liked so well, and forgetting her vow to withhold her opinions, she discouraged Theodore's talk of being a running mate for William McKinley in the 1900 presidential election. Theodore and she drafted a statement putting him out of the running for the vice presidency. From her box at the Republican convention, however, she watched as enthusiasm for the hero of San Juan Hill carried him to the nomination. Edith accepted defeat graciously. While her husband campaigned, she looked after his mail and their family, but under the stress she noticeably lost weight.

As it happened, Theodore's tenure as vice president was brief. Only six months after McKinley's inauguration on March 4, 1901, the president was assassinated. Theodore Roosevelt began his presidency on September 14; at 42, he was the youngest man ever to assume that responsibility. When Edith remarked to former President Cleveland at McKinley's funeral, "Oh, Mr. Cleveland, my husband is so young!" he reassured her: "Don't worry. He is all right." Still, it was a sad time: "I suppose in a short time I shall adjust myself to this," she wrote, "but the horror of it hangs over me, and I am never without fear for Theodore." She consoled herself with the thought that their money worries were over, and she would not have to make calls.

She found the family living quarters in the White House cramped and stuffy, "like living over the store," she told her husband. Edith chose the oval library with its connecting door to the president's office as her sitting room, and the children quickly took over all of the White House and its grounds for their play. She hired no housekeeper, taking on those responsibilities herself. Every morning the Roosevelts breakfasted *en famille;* then the first lady answered her mail, read several newspapers and glanced through the clippings gathered for her husband. She arranged her day in consultation with the servants and with her social secretary, Isabelle Hagner, whom she relied on to deal with the press. Once a week in the late morning she discussed current events and social obligations with the wives of cabinet members; other mornings at 11:00 she studied French, drove, or shopped. After lunch, for which the president always brought guests, she received callers. About 4:00 P.M. she and Theodore went horseback riding. She had time before dinner to talk with the children and read to them, and their father often dropped in to roughhouse. The mischievous Roosevelt children kept the press well supplied with stories of their antics and the miniature zoo they kept in the White House.

The nation welcomed their energetic first lady, whose vitality was appealing, particularly after the sickly Ida McKinley. Like all other presidential couples, the Roosevelts had their share of criticism, but Edith took in good stead the relatively small amount that fell to her. When Mrs. Stuyvesant Fish, famous for her conspicuous consumption, criticized the first lady for spending too little on clothes, Edith regarded it as a compliment and pasted the news report in her scrapbook. Her husband was proud of her: "Edith is too sweet and pretty and dignified and wise as mistress of the White House," he wrote, "and is very happy with it." She was indeed happy. She had no financial worries, and she could live in a style to which she gladly became accustomed. She entertained indefatigably, instituting musicales and on formal occasions ordering dinners of many courses; when necessary she supplemented the White House kitchen staff with a caterer. She adeptly managed the conversation, "keeping table talk off the rocks," as Senate wife Julia Foraker said, and giving guests opportunities to speak, despite the president's volubility. Guests were taken aback by their informal style but liked her unaffected kindness and his earnestness and dignity.

Edith was unruffled by the mixed demands of her official duties and her boisterous family. Despite her children's pranks—whether smuggling a pony upstairs on the elevator, stiltwalking through the mansion, or crawling under the table during formal dinners to beg people they knew for food—she longed for another baby. This wish was not to be realized; she suffered two miscarriages while in the White House. However, she remained in firm control over her children as well as her stepdaughter. When the time came to plan Alice's debut, Edith insisted that it be kept to a level of expense that the Roosevelts could afford, overriding the debutante's desire to use the money that her mother's parents had lavished on her.

Edith was also economical when it came to housekeeping in the executive mansion. If the president's last-minute invitees to lunch left the table hungry because the food she had ordered would not stretch, the first lady remained serenely unconcerned. She conceived of her role in the White House as an extension of that she had enjoyed since her marriage: wife, mother, hostess, and great lady.

Regarding the White House as a museum of American history and the presidency, the Roosevelts commissioned the architectural firm of McKim, Mead and White to draw up blueprints to enlarge and restore it to its 18th-century style. The architects' drawings, which included plans for a new wing of offices on the west side of the building, persuaded Congress to appropriate half a million dollars for the restoration. The Roosevelts moved out of the White House for six months in 1902, and renovations began. The first lady supervised the work from Sagamore Hill, rejecting changes that did not appeal to her. In hopes of keeping down the president's weight, she had a tennis court installed. When they returned to Washington, Edith resumed her formal dinners, buying 120 place settings of new china—white Wedgwood with a motif that incorporated the Great Seal of the United States. She added significantly to Caroline Harrison's collection of White House china, which she put on permanent display.

Theodore Roosevelt's election in 1904 delighted the whole family. His first term had begun in grief over McKinley's assassination; now the Roosevelt clan and the nation could celebrate wholeheartedly. After the swearing-in ceremony, the lunch at the White House for 200 guests, the parade, and the small family dinner, the president and his wife marched in procession before some 7,000 people at the inaugural ball. She wore a square-necked, short-sleeved gown of robin's egg blue silk brocade with raised gold embroidery woven in Paterson, New Jersey (the design for which was destroyed). Even after the ball, the energetic Roosevelts could hardly bear to end the day, chatting with their houseguests and having nightcaps until very late.

With another four years ensured, the first lady again plunged into action. During the crisis of the Russo-Japanese War, Edith acted as an unofficial conduit to the president from a trusted British adviser. She accompanied the president on a speaking tour of the South; he thought her "the feature of the occasion everywhere" and "great fun" to have along. She invited to the White House such gifted Americans as historian Henry Adams, stained-glass artist John La Farge, sculptor Augustus St. Gaudens, and novelist Henry James, whom she especially enjoyed. She arranged to add a drawing room to Sagamore Hill and bought a shack in the Blue Ridge Mountains for a country retreat, which she called Pine Knot.

Late in the fall of 1905 the president and first lady sailed south to inspect the construction of the Panama Canal. When in the following year he won the Nobel Peace Prize for his mediation in the Russo-Japanese War, he and Edith agreed that he could not accept the $40,000 prize money, which he contributed to establish an Industrial Peace Committee—although, he told Kermit, "I very much wisht for the extra money to leave all you children."

The assassination of earlier presidents, especially that of William McKinley, had roused apprehensions in both Theodore and Edith. She at once depended on the Secret Service and detested its necessity. Complaining about being watched as she napped on the porch at Sagamore Hill, she said that she felt as if she were hatching anarchists. At Pine Knot she instructed Secret Service men to hide in the bushes to protect the president without being conspicuous. In the last months of his presidency, Theodore ordered his new military aide, Archibald Willingham Butt, to accompany the first lady whenever she went out alone, to ensure her safety. Butt became her confidant—or, as he put it, her "knight." He rambled with her on her long walks and "snooped"—went looking for antiques—with her.

In the triumph of his 1904 election, Theodore had blurted to the press that he would not accept another nomination for president—to the distress of his wife, who knew he could never content himself out of office. In 1908 he kept to his promise, deeply as he regretted it, and Edith worried about him: "I want him to be the simplest American alive," she wrote, "and . . . he wants to be also . . . but the trouble is he has really forgotten how to be." He proposed that when he left office he would go on a safari that would take him out of the country, to give William Howard Taft, his chosen successor, a free hand. Missing him, his wife decided, would be a cheap price for an adventure that would keep him occupied after almost eight years of running the country.

The Roosevelts' last presidential social season included a White House debut for their daughter Ethel. At Hampton Roads they welcomed the Great White Fleet that had sailed around the world to display America's might: "That is the answer to my critics," the president said. "I could not ask a finer concluding scene to my administrations." They left the White House in a glow of popularity; Edith was overcome by a gift of a necklace of solitaires from a group of Washington society women. She and her husband had pleased the nation by setting an example of ideal family life, full of fun, and the president, always staunchly supported and sometimes governed by his wife, had enjoyed success in foreign mediation and domestic trust-busting. Theodore wrote to his son Kermit: "I should have liked to stay in as President. . . Mother and I are in the curious and very pleasant position of having enjoyed the White House more than any other President and his wife whom I recall."

Edith had not anticipated the shock of her own transition: from first lady surrounded by family to private citizen and empty nester, with only a grown daughter at home. Theodore had departed on his safari, so after a couple of months of virtual solitude at Sagamore Hill, his wife took Ethel, Archie, and Quentin to Europe for five months. They returned home in November, and then she was off again with Ethel in March 1910 to meet Theodore at Khartoum. From there, sightseeing all the way, they headed for Europe, where welcomes awaited them at courts and from the general populace.

They returned to an enthusiastic reception in the United States in June. In response, the former president professed himself "ready and eager" to help solve the country's problems—an encouraging statement to the many who longed to restore him to the White House. For the present he resumed his writing career, becoming an editor of *Outlook* and negotiating the publication of his book *African Game Trails*. Meanwhile, he kept himself in the public eye with a speaking tour of 19 states and by campaigning for progressive Republican candidates. "Politics are seething abominably," Edith wrote, and she hoped that the coming of winter would see her husband "safely caged at Sagamore." Nothing, however, could suppress his passion for politics; he continued energetically to pursue the presidential ambition that he hardly acknowledged to himself, and his wife could not curb him, although she saw "no possible result which could give me aught but deep regret." She tried to moderate his speeches, but she could not turn him from his goal. The race eventually cost him such old friends as President Taft, split the Republican Party, and occasioned an assassination attempt that broke one of Theodore's ribs and left a bullet lodged a quarter of an inch from his heart. The nation sympathized and admired his grit but elected Woodrow Wilson president. "I have lived, most reluctantly, through one party split," wrote Edith, "and no good comes of it."

Thereafter, Sagamore Hill saw a quieter time, particularly once Ethel had married and moved from home. Edith missed the excitement of public life and the exuberance of family activity. Her husband continued to write and to vacation in the west, and he organized an expedition to Brazil. She went with him for the first part of the South American trip, but her return voyage was saddened by the death of the young woman accompanying her, and she was left to worry about the dangers Theodore was confronting. Ill health prevented Edith from going with him to Kermit's wedding in Europe in June 1914. The next year she underwent a "necessary operation," possibly a hysterectomy.

Edith's physical problems and the deaths of friends and relatives weakened her, so that when Theodore again filled Sagamore Hill with political and military men favoring the entry of the United States into World War I, she felt herself unable to "keep up with the pace." At his request, however, she organized a "battalion" of women to march in a military preparedness parade. After the United States finally declared war, the "vile and hypocritical" President Wilson refused to let the former president take a regiment to France, but the four Roosevelt sons signed up to fight, while their father traveled the country recruiting. Edith Roosevelt was as Spartan as her husband in encouraging her sons' patriotic eagerness for military service. Nonetheless, she grew depressed, writing to Kermit that "my life is over, and I am tired of my old body anyway, and I shall be glad to get rid of it." She tried to make her husband "feel a responsibility for me that will perhaps cut his flights by tying him to my apron strings"—but no apron strings could restrain him, and she ended by traveling with him. Then word came that their son Quentin had been killed. Together the parents bore their grief, each concerned for the other, remembering that she had always said, "You cannot bring up boys as eagles and expect them to turn out sparrows."

On the day of the armistice, November 11, 1918, an ailing Theodore entered the hospital. Every day his wife sat by him, reading Shakespeare; she slept in an adjoining room. He returned to Sagamore Hill for Christmas, but he died on January 6, 1919, from an embolism—still planning political activities, perhaps even a run for the presidency. Abiding by custom, Edith stayed at home during the funeral, reading the service. In February she sailed for Europe to be reunited with two of her sons and to visit Quentin's grave. After spending several weeks with her sister, she returned to Sagamore Hill in May.

She kept busy, campaigning for the Republican ticket in fall 1920 and taking note that for the first time American women would be voting for a president. Although, she said, "I have salt water around my heart," she traveled abroad extensively, often departing from the beaten tracks of tourism. Turning to writing, she contributed a chapter to a book of travel and compiled her mother's schoolgirl letters—though she destroyed most of Theodore's letters to her and hers to him. She forced herself to go to social and cultural events, became a patron of the arts, and donated even more generously to private charities. In 1927 she bought an ancestral home in Brooklyn, Connecticut, furnishing it with antiques and with the products of a local cabinetmaker. Edith willingly talked with biographers of her husband, even though she sometimes detested the books that resulted. She took pride in the careers of her remaining sons and in the activities of her grandchildren.

The 1932 nomination of Franklin Delano Roosevelt, Theodore's nephew by marriage, as the Democratic candidate for president distressed Edith, a lifelong Republican; ironically, hundreds of people congratulated her in the belief that she was the candidate's mother. Thereafter, she campaigned for his opponent, Herbert Hoover, defying criticism for opposing a relative. Still, she thought Franklin Roosevelt "a shrewd statesman," even though she denied that his New Deal in any way resembled the liberalism of Theodore Roosevelt's Bull Moose movement, and after FDR was elected Edith corresponded happily with the new first lady about the White House. In September 1935 she spoke to the National Conference of Republican Women, calling upon them in the crisis of the Great Depression "never to fall back in our purpose to leave to our children, and to our children's children, the freedom of life and thought which has been ours."

Later that fall Edith broke a hip, an accident that hospitalized her for months. During World War II she lost her son Kermit to alcoholism and suicide and her soldier son Ted to a heart attack; her son Archie was wounded but recovered. Her powers, physical and mental, were diminishing, and by the end of the war she was longing "for restful death." Nevertheless, on occasion she roused herself to talk with visitors, for, she believed, *La gaité, c'est une politesse* (gaiety is a form of politeness). She was bedridden for the last year and a half of her life and died on September 30, 1948, leaving instructions for her funeral and burial next to Theodore Roosevelt in Youngs' Cemetery in Oyster Bay.

———— ⋙ ————

Edith Kermit Roosevelt, wrote Franklin Delano Roosevelt, "managed TR very cleverly without his being conscious of it—no slight achievement as anyone will concede." It was indeed an accomplishment—for as his daughter Alice quipped, "At a funeral father always wants to be the corpse, and at a wedding he always wants to be the bride." The wisdom almost universally attributed to Edith Roosevelt seems to have been a benign common sense that she applied to affairs great and small and enforced with decision and firmness. She realized her ideal of what she wanted to be—in her husband's words, "the best of wives and mothers, the wisest manager of the household, and at the same time the ideal great lady and mistress of the White House." She exercised considerable influence over her husband's career and his decisions. Her daughter Ethel commented, "We all knew that the person who had the long head in politics was Mother," and

President Theodore Roosevelt said that whenever he went against her advice he paid for it: "She is not only cultured but scholarly."

CHRONOLOGY

1861 *August 6:* Edith Kermit Carow is born in Norwich, Connecticut

1883 Edith Carow's father, Charles Carow, dies

1886 *December 2:* Edith Carow marries Theodore Roosevelt

1887 *September 13:* Son Theodore is born

1889 Theodore Roosevelt is appointed Civil Service Commissioner in Washington, D.C.

      October 10: Son Kermit is born

1891 *August 13:* Daughter Ethel is born

1894 *April 9:* Son Archibald is born

      Theodore Roosevelt becomes president of the New York City board of police commissioners

1897 Theodore Roosevelt becomes assistant secretary of the navy

      November 9: Son Quentin is born

1898 Theodore Roosevelt organizes the volunteer cavalry regiment, the Rough Riders, to serve in the Spanish-American War

      Fall: Theodore Roosevelt is elected governor of the state of New York

1900 Theodore Roosevelt is elected vice president of the United States

1901 *September 14:* Edith Roosevelt becomes first lady when President McKinley is assassinated and her husband assumes the presidency; she establishes an office with a staff in the east wing of the White House.

1902 The White House is restored using plans commissioned by the Roosevelts

1909 *March:* The Roosevelts leave the White House and Theodore goes on safari

1918 *July 14:* Son Quentin is killed in World War I

1919 *January 6:* Theodore Roosevelt dies

1943 *June 3:* Son Kermit dies in World War II

1944 *July:* Son Theodore dies, a Major-General and Medal of Honor Winner in World War II

1948 *September 30:* Edith Carow Roosevelt dies at Sagamore Hill at Oyster Bay, New York

FURTHER READING

Caroli, Betty Boyd. *The Roosevelt Women.* New York: Basic Books, 1999.

Colman, Edna M. *White House Gossip: From Andrew Jackson to Calvin Coolidge.* Garden City, N.Y.: Doubleday, Page, 1927.

Cook, Blanche Wiesen. *Eleanor Roosevelt.* Vol. 1, 1884–1933. New York: Viking, 1992.

Crook, W. H. *Memories of the White House: The Home Life of Our Presidents from Lincoln to Roosevelt,* comp. and ed. Henry Rood. Boston: Little, Brown, 1911.

McCullough, David. *Mornings on Horseback.* New York: Simon and Schuster, 1982.

Morris, Edmund. *The Rise of Theodore Roosevelt.* New York: Ballantine, 1988.

Morris, Sylvia Jukes. *Edith Kermit Roosevelt: Portrait of a First Lady.* New York: Coward, McCann, 1980.

HELEN (NELLIE) HERRON TAFT
(JUNE 2, 1861–MAY 22, 1943)
First Lady, March 4, 1909–March 4, 1913

HELEN TAFT
(Library of Congress)

Helen Herron Taft exemplifies the kind of woman born to have a career of her own. Possessed of high intelligence, energy, zest, and ambition, she could make plans and put them into action. Given the opportunity to run things, she excelled. Denied that opportunity, her frustrated talents found expression only by interfering in the life of her husband, a man of great abilities and attractive personality whom she chivied into a job he did not want and for which he was not suited. She lent some support to the women's movement of her own time, but for herself decided that the rewards available in those careers easily open to her would not bring her as much satisfaction as she could get from reflected glory.

———

Helen (Nellie) Herron was born in Cincinnati, Ohio, on June 2, 1861, the fourth of 11 children of John Williamson Herron and Harriet Collins Herron.

Her father was an influential Republican lawyer, a classmate of Benjamin Harrison, and a one-time partner of Rutherford B. Hayes. Nellie began her education at Miss Nourse's private school, which emphasized languages, literature, and music. An excellent student, she attended classes at Miami University in Oxford, Ohio. She continued her education all her life, reading widely and studying languages, history, art, and music.

When she was 16 or 17, a family visit of several weeks to the White House instilled dreams of being first lady. Like Mary Lincoln, Nellie resolved to marry a man who could take her there. Unlike Mary, however, she might have chosen other ways to satisfy her craving for achievement and position, for she was born into a family that educated her in a time and place more open to opportunities for women. Cincinnati had long been a city of cultural and intellectual excitement. When the Beechers and the Stowes lived there, they had been hotly involved in the great political debate of their time over slavery. In Nellie Herron's day the struggle for women's suffrage, begun in 1848, was well under way; the man she was to marry openly espoused it, as did his mother and aunt. In addition, some advanced women were filtering into the higher professions.

As a young woman Nellie struck people as serious, unsmiling, even cold and stubborn, with strong opinions that she offered and defended aggressively. High-strung, nervous, and emotional, she sometimes seemed bossy. On the other hand, she was quick-witted, well-informed, and attractive—small, slim, and energetic.

Theoretically she disliked the restrictions on women that kept them from doing as much as men. She dreaded her debut but found the season that followed it more enjoyable than she had anticipated. Around that same time she worked in her father's law office, reading, studying, and helping him. She vacillated between the exercise of her abilities at work and the pleasures of the social world, which she professed to regard as "frivolities." She wanted to cultivate her musical talent but accepted her parents' refusal of music lessons. She talked of writing a book but did not begin. She entertained hopes of entering a profession or writing criticism of art or music.

Equally, she wavered between marriage and a career. For two years, from 1881 to 1883, she taught at a private school in Walnut Hills, Ohio, and even thought of starting her own school. She did not greatly enjoy the experience: "It takes a little gulp," she wrote, "to swallow the idea of always teaching. . . . Of course a woman is happier who marries exactly right—but how many do? Otherwise I do think that she is much happier single and doing some congenial work." Mixed in with this dilemma was her fear of a sexual relationship. She was uncomfortable with young suitors, preferring married men older than she, and wondered why men and women could not just continue as friends rather than talk of love.

Ambitious and able as she was, and eager as she was for independence, she never achieved the adventurous fortitude to break with convention. Even when she tried to flout convention, she did it conventionally—indulging in "fast behavior" by visiting a saloon, where she smoked and drank beer. This rebellion was no more than her youthful way of kicking up her heels, for in the end she decided to marry. Perhaps the very height of her ambition contributed to her decision, for while she might have had a career, the idea of a woman president was still inconceivable. Furthermore, she had found just the man she wanted—a man onto whom she could project her own ambitions, a man with potential for achievement, who would always assure her that she was brainy and audacious and give her a free hand to do as she liked.

William Howard Taft's family and hers had long known each other. As young adults, when Nellie Herron was a debutante and Will Taft a law student and law reporter, they began to socialize with a group of friends who went in for amateur theatricals, vaudeville shows, and charade parties. In 1883 she and some friends organized a salon to discuss "topics intellectual and economic," to which they invited Will and his brother. According to his psychobiographer Judith Icke Anderson, this amiable, gentle, sweet-natured young man had striven all his life to please his parents and fulfill their hopes for him. He found in Nellie Herron a woman just as ambitious for him as his mother had been. He fell in love, began to court her seriously in 1884, and proposed on May 1, 1885. She kept him waiting for almost a month before she accepted and even then stipulated that the engagement be kept secret.

Their yearlong engagement was not always a happy time for him; his sister wrote that the overweight Will was often a "mountain of misery" because of his fiancée's frigidly maintained distance. But if Nellie felt little physical attraction toward him, she was drawn to him for other reasons. First, he flattered her with his belief in her powers: perhaps, he suggested, in the future she might "feel like writing editorials. I believe you would soon learn to write articles which in their incisiveness, force, and relevancy would astonish yourself. . . . Your thought and speech are marked especially by direction, force, and clearness. When I grow blind or imbecile, you can support me by editing a newspaper." Moreover, she approved of the "very satisfactory progress" that he was making in his career. He was honest, engaging, cooperative, ready to work, and loyal; and, she wrote her mother shortly before her marriage, "a lot of people think a great deal of Will. Some people even say that he may obtain some very important position in Washington." So plans proceeded for the house the couple were building overlooking the Ohio River.

They married on June 19, 1886, and went abroad for their three-month honeymoon. Though she thought of herself as frugal, in fact all her life Nellie lived in comfortable circumstances and had servants to wait on her and eventually to care for her children. The year 1887 saw the newlyweds ensconced in their new house, and William Howard Taft appointed as a judge of the superior court of Ohio. The opportunity delighted him, setting him on the

right track for the very career he wanted, but Nellie did not like it, fearing "the narrowing effects of the Bench." For years he strove for a judicial career, while she tried to maneuver him toward the presidency.

Nellie rejoiced and persuaded her reluctant husband to accept when President Benjamin Harrison appointed him solicitor general of the United States in February 1890. Joyfully she and their six-month-old first-born, Robert, moved to Washington with Will. For the next two years, the gregarious Tafts enjoyed the social life of the city, even though after the birth of their daughter Helen in 1891 Nellie had two babies to care for. She also found time to coach her husband; he disliked pleading cases, as his new position required, and she was determined to make him a graceful, colorful orator. She instructed him not to overprepare, to avoid citing too many precedents, and not to talk too long.

She was disappointed when President Harrison sent her husband back to Cincinnati in 1892 to serve on the Federal Circuit Bench, where, she wrote, "I saw him as a colleague of men almost twice his age and, I feared, fixed in a groove for the rest of his life." He himself found it a groove he liked; nothing except a seat on the Supreme Court of the United States would have suited him better.

In Will's frequent absences from home, traveling the circuit, Nellie plunged into "a number of civic movements," including the kindergarten movement. Most importantly, she took over "the organisation and management of the Cincinnati Orchestra Association," in which she found at last "a practical method for expressing and making use of" her love of music. She did a top-notch job, having a vent for the executive abilities that, suppressed, made her prod and poke her husband. In her spare time she bore her last child, Charles, in 1897.

Three years later another American president changed the Tafts' lives. In January 1900 President William McKinley asked William Howard Taft to head a commission to the Philippine Islands to establish a new government. Nellie was immediately ready to pack: "I wasn't sure what it meant," she wrote, "but I knew instantly that I didn't want to miss a big and novel experience. I have never shrunk before any obstacles when I had an opportunity to see a new country and I must say I have never regretted any adventure." The appointee demurred; he had opposed the annexation of the Philippines, and he had no experience in executive work. McKinley and Nellie prevailed. With her sister Maria accompanying them, the Tafts entrained for the west coast and sailed from San Francisco. Nellie had no qualms about taking along their children—ten-year-old Robert, eight-year-old Helen, and two-year-old Charlie—anticipating "smooth sailing" throughout their adventure. She was either very daring or very unimaginative, for in addition to all the problems of traveling and living in foreign cultures, they were to encounter epidemics of bubonic plague and cholera.

Nonetheless, she thoroughly enjoyed the whole experience. She found the other members of the commission and their families good company. The trip to the Philippines was so interesting that she hated to see it end, and she loitered for months along the way. Hawaii enchanted her, and she toured it enthusiastically, even riding the surf in a canoe. With Maria and the children she lingered for the summer in Japan, where Nellie loved being received by the empress and being entertained by the foreign community. She had been reading Japanese history, and the country charmed her. She was not even particularly upset when Robert contracted diphtheria and she and Maria were quarantined with him, while the other two children were sent to the Grand Hotel to be cared for.

Finally, Will's accounts of the interesting events in Manila persuaded Nellie to leave Japan for the Philippines, a country in the midst of a guerrilla war. On arrival she was taken aback, though undaunted, to find their home heavily guarded. She immediately set to work developing the "great possibilities" of the rather run-down house Taft had found for them and taking in hand the servants he had hired. In the process she began to learn the ways of the East

and to teach the East some of her own. "Over none of the servants did I exercise the control I thought to be necessary, but this was due to the fact that for three months they had been obeying the master; the master had paid them their wages, and to the master they looked for all orders. It took me some time to discover this, but when I did I began to handle household accounts without assistance."

Her status gave her profound satisfaction: "Of course," she wrote to her sister-in-law, "the position gives us a great deal of attention which I for one would never have otherwise and of course we feel we might as well make the best of it while we have the opportunity. We are really so grand now that it will be hard to descend to common doings. We have five carriages and two smaller vehicles, and fourteen ponies, a steam launch and dear knows how many servants." She shopped, played cards, entertained, and was entertained—all so avidly that she had little time for reading or volunteer work, though she took an hour-long Spanish lesson every day. She traveled into remote areas with and without her husband, priding herself on going "where no white woman had ever been." When a trip demanded weeks on horseback, she learned to ride.

She returned from one of these journeys to find that in her absence preparations had been made for William Howard Taft's induction as governor of the Philippine Islands. The prospect delighted both her and the Filipinos, who loved the big, affable man with his ready smile. After the swearing-in ceremony in the Cathedral Plaza on July 4, 1901, the Tafts put on a lawn party for the 2,000 guests her husband had invited. Rain descended in torrents, but the guests crowded into the house and onto its verandas. General Arthur MacArthur, the former military governor, went back to the United States, and the Tafts moved into the spacious Malacanan Palace.

Although today the Tafts' attitudes toward the Filipinos seem condescending, the governor was replacing a military government with a civil one, and he planned to develop self-government. The governor's lady urged the women of the Philippines to accept medical attention and adopt proper diets for their babies, and she helped found a "Drop of Milk" organization to distribute sterilized milk. Both the Tafts tried to learn the customs of the country, to understand the political and religious forces at work there, and to meet its people—on terms of equality, they said. Nellie Taft learned native dances, donned islander costume, and invited Filipinos to her parties. "The situation in the Philippines while I lived there was most interesting," she later observed, "and I became familiar with every phase of it. It meant more than politics. The questions involved real statesmanship. Mr. Taft always held his conferences at our home, and, naturally, I heard these matters discussed more freely than one would in Washington. It was politics 'over the tea cups.'"

Rumors of the possibility that William Howard Taft might become president of the United States reached even the Philippines. The prospective candidate thought them ridiculous, but both his mother and his wife took them seriously. His mother, who knew her son, warned him to keep out of politics; his wife, set on what she wanted, thought the prospect did "not seem at all unreasonable." When McKinley was assassinated, William's close friend Theodore Roosevelt succeeded to the presidency. Shortly thereafter, William's serious illness necessitated a return home; Nellie too was ailing, worn out by her duties in a tropical climate and close to a breakdown. On December 24, 1901, the family sailed for home, where they recovered their health.

Soon President Roosevelt began to call on William for diplomatic errands, beginning in 1902 with a trip to the Vatican to negotiate for lands in the Philippines owned by the Roman Catholic Church. As usual, Nellie could hardly wait, but her departure was delayed when her son Robert became ill with scarlet fever. William's 74-year-old mother sailed with him in Nellie's stead, but as soon as Robert improved Nellie sailed with the children to join her diplomat husband. Along the way, two of the chil-

dren developed whooping cough, but they had recovered by the time the Tafts were reunited in Rome. Nellie enjoyed Italy: As her mother-in-law observed, "Nellie is not at all timid and as she speaks French we can go anywhere." Nellie and her mother-in-law were both pleased because the Tafts were received as important personages, and they met "many renowned and interesting people, both Roman and foreign." The Pope granted an audience to Nellie, her two older children, and her mother-in-law. To escape the heat of a Roman summer, she took the children to a mountain retreat, where they remained for a few weeks after William departed. On September 3 she and the children left Italy at last to rejoin him in the Philippines.

William was in Manila when in 1903 he received a telegram from President Roosevelt offering him an appointment to the Supreme Court—the ambition of his life. "I had always been opposed to a judicial career for him," Nellie wrote in her memoirs, "but at this point I shall have to admit I weakened just a little. I remembered the year of illness and anxiety we had just been through; and sometimes I yearned to be safe in Washington even though it did mean our settlement in the 'fixed groove' that I had talked against for so long." Governor Taft selflessly refused the twice-offered appointment, believing that duty to the islanders held him to his post. Six months later, however, Roosevelt asked him to be secretary of war. "This was much more pleasing to me than the offer of the Supreme Court appointment," wrote Nellie, "because it was in line with the kind of work I wanted my husband to do, the kind of career I wanted for him and expected him to have, so I was glad there were few excuses for refusing to accept it open to him"—particularly as the appointment was not to take effect for a year.

Nellie began to enjoy her new status as cabinet wife on the way back home in 1904, for the Japanese received the Tafts with "ceremony and official dignity." Once in Washington, however, she discovered that her new position "would not be at all like entering upon the duties and privileges of the wife of the Governor of the Philippine Islands. I thought what a curious and peculiarly American sort of promotion it was which carried with it such diminished advantages."

She rented a pleasant house, spacious enough for the family, and ran it with her usual efficiency, although, she said, "I did sometimes sigh for the luxurious simplicity and the entire freedom from petty household details that I had left behind me in Manila." Nevertheless, Nellie relished Washington's social life, and the Tafts dined out or entertained almost every evening. She patiently embarked on the burdensome task of paying official calls, making some good friends in the process, and took her turn every Wednesday afternoon at being "at home" to many callers, including inquisitive strangers. She often accompanied her husband on the many diplomatic errands on which the president sent him, enjoying every new or familiar place they visited, loving both the "rush" of their lives and William's increasing importance in the government. Summers at their house in Murray Bay, Canada, were often interrupted by his responsibilities.

To Nellie's annoyance, the subject of her husband's appointment to the Supreme Court kept cropping up, whereas she had become focused on his being the Republican nominee for the presidency in 1908. She urged William "to display a little more enthusiasm on his own account" for that office, but he responded by writing to the president that he would not be in the least disappointed were Roosevelt to support someone else. Nevertheless, a Taft boom got under way, encouraged by Roosevelt—whom Nellie distrusted for not having acted more promptly. The summer of 1907 allowed William only a few weeks at Murray Bay between a whirlwind speech-making tour and the family's departure for the Philippines. There William was to open the first Philippine legislature and then the family would embark on a trip around the world via the Trans-Siberian Railway. On the way, while still in the States, Nellie lost track of the day of the week and allowed her husband and herself to be seen publicly playing cards on

Sunday—a faux pas that she believed might fatally harm his chances for the presidency. "Playing cards was bad enough," she wrote years later, "but to have forgotten Sunday altogether was a great deal worse. . . . Up to the day Mr. Taft was elected I looked for the story to rise up and smite us." That trip gave her a taste of real campaigning, and she was amazed at the stamina it required.

On their return, Nellie was distressed to see the lead other candidates for the presidency had taken in the race—particularly William Jennings Bryan. She did not accompany her husband on his long campaign tour, choosing to remain in Cincinnati with their families, but, she wrote, "[I]n a way I think I was under as great a nervous strain as my husband was, without the steadying help of the hardest kind of work." Moreover, she wanted the presidency and he did not, craving as he always had a judicial post. He yielded to her urgings and those of his brothers and the president. He was elected by a wide margin.

The incoming president was pleased to accept Teddy Roosevelt's invitation to the Tafts to spend the night of March 3, 1909, in the White House, but relations between Nellie Taft and Edith Roosevelt were less than cordial: "My impression," wrote the new first lady, "is that neither Mrs. Roosevelt nor I would have suggested such an arrangement for this particular evening, but, it having been made for us, we naturally acquiesced." Not even the blinding snowstorm that raged on March 4 could diminish Nellie's pleasure in the inauguration. President Roosevelt had announced that he would not ride back to the White House with his successor after the swearing-in. Nellie, wearing a purple satin suit, proudly took the former president's place beside her newly inaugurated husband. "No President's wife had ever done it before," she wrote, "but as long as precedents were being disregarded I thought it might not be too great a risk for me to disregard this one. Of course, there was objection . . . , but I had my way."

Entering the White House as its mistress made her shed tears of joy. Despite weather that made her lunch guests so late that the luncheon after the inaugural ran into the new president's tea for his Yale classmates, everyone mingled and enjoyed the party. Nellie took some time out from the festivities to roam the house and assign rooms to the family members who were arriving later. That evening she was off to the inaugural ball in the Pension Building in her heavy white satin gown embroidered with goldenrod. Arm in arm, the Tafts led the procession around the hall; she worried only that her long train might be stepped on.

The next morning Nellie began making changes. For the first time ever, she introduced twin beds into the White House. In place of the former "gentlemen ushers," she stationed liveried footmen at the door to receive visitors and instruct sightseers—in defiance of "democratic simplicity." She substituted a housekeeper for a steward, to relieve her "of the supervision of such details as no man, expert steward though he might be, would ever recognise." The Swedish cook she hired was often sorely tried, since Nellie never had any idea how many people her husband would invite for lunch until 30 minutes before lunchtime—and at that the president might arrive an hour late with even more guests. The first lady also installed a silver-cleaning machine and built a vault for the presidential silver, with special receptacles for each important article and velvet-lined trays in drawers for the flat silver. Paying the servants was no problem, for the nation had recently taken over that expense, and the president was given a hefty raise to $75,000 a year. Nonetheless, Nellie Taft ran an economical White House, keeping close tabs on the housekeeping, buying food in wholesale lots, and installing a cow on the White House lawns.

The Tafts plunged into entertaining, both formal and informal, aiming to make Washington the social center of the country. They were good hosts who wanted to make things pleasant for their guests, and usually succeeded. Nellie found ways to alter customs to increase the comfort of guests at state occasions, moving their reception from one entrance to another to avert their standing in drafty corridors, decreasing the time they had to wait, or with her husband joining their guests for tea instead of retiring after the formal presentations. Nellie also introduced dancing at formal receptions; even state functions, she found, could "by the exercise of a little art" be made "most enjoyable affairs."

Her experience in Manila inspired Nellie to "convert Potomac Park into a glorified Luneta [the national park and favorite promenade in the Philippines] where all Washington could meet, either on foot or in vehicles, at five o'clock on certain evenings, listen to band concerts and enjoy such recreation as no other spot in Washington could possibly afford." She had a bandstand erected and arranged for band concerts twice a week. She also arranged to have 100 cherry trees planted in the park. When he heard of her efforts, the mayor of Tokyo sent thousands of young trees; although many of them were diseased, others survived to transform Washington every spring.

Just 10 weeks after the inauguration, Nellie suffered a stroke, keeping her from the full enjoyment of the position of first lady to which she had looked forward for so long. It incapacitated her for almost a year and limited her thereafter. Her sisters helped by taking her place as White House hostess when necessary, and her husband spent much time with her during her recovery, reading to her, trying to make her laugh, and tenderly helping her regain the ability to speak. Though embarrassment about a lingering facial paralysis made her shy about public appearances, she resumed her duties as soon as she could, both in the White House and in the Tafts' new summer home in Beverly Farms, Massachusetts.

Thereafter, Nellie wrote of her early days in the White House, "[M]y own problems became to me paramount and I began to give them my almost undivided attention and to neglect the political affairs which had for many years interested me so intensely. Perhaps with my husband safely elected I considered all important affairs satisfactorily settled. At any rate I found little time or inclination at the moment to worry about who should have the high offices in the new President's gift, or what policies should be pursued during his administration."

Her interest in his work revived after she set her house in order. As first lady she did sometimes prevent the appointment of officials against whom she bore a grudge, and she never hesitated on social occasions to break in on her husband's discussions of policy with his advisers. She rebuked him publicly and walked into his private conferences unannounced; she was said to sit outside the door at cabinet meetings; and she often supplied her husband with forgotten names or numbers. She tried to keep him awake in public—no easy task—and to get him to his appointments on time; before going out he always stopped by to see her so that she could check his attire. "As the wife of Mr. Taft, as President," she said, "I would interest myself in anything that vitally affected him, or in which he was absorbed. I do not believe in a woman meddling in politics or in asserting herself along those lines, but I think any woman can discuss with her husband topics of national interest and, in many instances, she might give her opinion of questions with which, through study and contact, she has become familiar."

Nellie's parties, like the one in which she introduced her daughter Helen to society, were long remembered. Of particular note was the lawn party that she gave on the occasion of the Tafts' silver wedding anniversary. Close to 5,000 people attended, and the couple was inundated with silver gifts—so many that in later years she had the monograms taken off the smaller pieces and used them as wedding gifts. Forty generals' wives joined together to give her a platinum watch adorned with diamonds. The party attracted some 15,000 onlookers beyond the fences.

William Howard Taft was miserable in the presidency, which he thought of as an "awful agony." Nonetheless, in 1912 he accepted the Republican nomination, after a fight so bitter that Theodore Roosevelt and his supporters bolted to found the Bull Moose Party. Nellie passionately wanted her husband to be reelected, but she did not expect it, and he was in fact defeated by Woodrow Wilson. She left the White House with the greatest reluctance, so sad that the servants hesitated even to say goodbye.

Happy days still lay ahead for the Tafts, however. Nellie enjoyed the people she came to know in New Haven, Connecticut, where her husband held a chair at Yale University from 1913 to 1921. Then William achieved his lifetime's ambition when President Warren Harding appointed him Chief Justice of the United States Supreme Court. He died in 1930, but his widow lived on for another 13 years, happy in her family, and proud of them too. Her son Robert became the most prominent Republican senator of his day and a presidential candidate, while Charlie grew up to be a highly successful lawyer. Helen achieved a distinguished career in academia, earning a Ph.D in history from Yale and a law degree from George Washington University; she also served as professor of history, department chair, dean, and acting president of Bryn Mawr.

Living alone with her housekeeper in a roomy red brick Washington mansion set among magnolias, Nellie Taft attended musicales, teas, luncheons, and bridge parties. She traveled abroad when she wished, and every spring she visited Charleston to see the azalea gardens. Late summers she visited her country home in Canada.

Nellie held views just advanced enough to make her feel progressive, but not far enough ahead of popular opinion to shock or offend. On women's education, for instance, she took a stance similar to that of many women's colleges of the day: She thought education important for women, "not to make them competitors with men, but to round out their femininity." She stated:

> My idea about higher culture for women is that it makes them great in intellect and soul, develops the lofty conception of womanhood;

not that it makes them a poor imitation of a man. I am old-fashioned enough to believe that woman is the complement of man, and that what is most feminine about her is most attractive to man and therefore of the greatest utility to the world. No fundamental superiority or inferiority between the two appears plain to me. The only superiority lies in the way in which the responsibilities of life are discharged. Viewed in this light, some wives are superior to their husbands, some husbands to their wives, some girls to their brothers, and women to men in varying circumstances. . . . [F]or the aggregate woman the highest mission is the ability to preside over a home and to fulfil [sic] the highest obligations of a home with grace, dignity, and an exalted sense of duty.

She believed that the world of public affairs belonged to men—though she kept herself well-informed about it. A somewhat desultory suffragist, she wrote, "I favour bestowing upon women every civic right, but I should like to put in a prohibitory clause debarring them from running for office. If women should indulge in a scramble for office, I think that the natural scheme would become disjointed and the aim of the home destroyed. I can see nothing unfeminine in women casting the ballot." She also felt that women should not have business careers.

Nellie found the conversation of many women dull, but she enjoyed traveling and social activities with women relatives and companions, and she had close women friends, including the distinguished Mabel Boardman, for many years president of the American Red Cross.

Helen Herron Taft died at her Washington home on May 22, 1943. She is buried in Arlington National Cemetery, with her husband.

—⁂—

The position of first lady, to which she had aspired from girlhood, brought Nellie Taft both satisfaction and disappointment. She delighted in its prestige, to the degree that her health permitted. Yet it frustrated her because, despite her intelligence, energy, and knowledgeability, it shut her out from the man's world of affairs. Ironically, she scored her triumphs as first lady in the traditional role of hostess. As with most presidential spouses, no one knows exactly how much Nellie Taft as first lady influenced her husband's decisions as president. "I am not trying. . . ," she wrote, "to pose as a woman endowed with an especial comprehension of such problems of state as men alone have been trained to deal with. I confess only to a lively interest in my husband's work which I experienced from the beginning of our association and which nothing in our long life together, neither monotony, nor illness, nor misfortune, has served to lessen."

CHRONOLOGY

1861	*June 2:* Helen (Nellie) Herron is born in Cincinnati, Ohio
1878	Nellie Herron spends several weeks in the White House as the guest of Lucy Webb Hayes
1881–83	Nellie Herron teaches school
1886	*June 19:* Nellie Herron marries William Howard Taft
1889	*September 8:* Son Robert is born
1890	William Howard Taft is appointed solicitor general of the United States
1891	*August 1:* Daughter Helen is born
1892	William Howard Taft is appointed a federal circuit judge
1897	*September 20:* Son Charles is born
1900	William Howard Taft is appointed head of the Philippine Commission
1901	William Howard Taft becomes governor of the Philippines
1903	William Howard Taft is appointed President Theodore Roosevelt's secretary of war
1908	William Howard Taft is elected president
1909	*March 4:* Nellie Taft becomes first lady

May: Nellie Taft suffers a stroke that leaves her impaired in speech

1913   *March 4:* The Tafts move to New Haven, where William Taft teaches constitutional law at Yale

1921   William Howard Taft is appointed Chief Justice of the United States Supreme Court

1930   *March 8:* William Howard Taft dies

1943   *May 22:* Nellie Taft dies in Washington from a circulatory disorder

---

FURTHER READING

Anderson, Judith Icke. *William Howard Taft: An Intimate History.* New York: Norton, 1981.

Colman, Edna M. *White House Gossip: From Andrew Jackson to Calvin Coolidge.* Garden City, N.Y.: Doubleday, Page, 1927.

Morris, Sylvia Jukes. *Edith Kermit Roosevelt: Portrait of a First Lady.* New York: Coward, McCann, 1980. (For the relationship between Edith Roosevelt and Helen Taft.)

Taft, Helen Herron. *Recollections of Full Years.* New York: Dodd, Mead, 1914.

Willets, Gilson. *Inside History of the White House.* New York: Christian Herald, 1908.

ELLEN LOUISE AXSON WILSON

(MAY 15, 1860–AUGUST 6, 1914)

First Lady, March 4, 1913–August 6, 1914

ELLEN AXSON WILSON
(Library of Congress)

Ellen Wilson's brief life spanned the Progressive Era. Throughout that period, American women struggled toward the goal they had set in 1848—to obtain votes for women. Ellen came to believe in this cause, though concern for her husband kept her publicly silent on it and she did not live to see the suffragists' success. During those same years, American women also undertook "public housekeeping," in an effort to fashion a better society in which to raise their children. They achieved a myriad of reforms and improvements, such as juvenile courts, public libraries, public parks, child labor laws, and better conditions for women workers. For her part, Ellen Wilson lobbied through Congress her bill for improved housing in Washington.

She guided her life on principle. "I wonder," she wrote, "how anyone who reaches middle age can bear it if she cannot feel, on looking back, that whatever mistakes she has made, she has on the whole lived for others and not for herself." Her decision to marry came at the sacrifice of the full development of her sizable artistic talent. She also believed, however, that no one could "rest on the laurels of another person. [Each] must grow to the limits of . . . [her] own spirit, mind and ability." Accordingly, she took what time remained from her responsibilities to others to cultivate her intellect and her art.

—⁓—

Ellen Louise Axson was born on May 15, 1860, in Savannah, Georgia, the eldest of four children of the Rev. Samuel Edward Axson and his wife, the beautiful and brilliant Margaret Jane Hoyt Axson. Ellen came from a highly educated family that included several clergymen, so she grew up in parsonages in North Carolina and Georgia. During the Civil War her father served for a time as chaplain of a Confederate regiment, while his wife and child stayed with relatives in Athens and Savannah, Georgia. In 1865 the Axsons settled in Rome, Georgia, which Ellen always thereafter thought of as her home. Her mother tutored her until she was 11, when she enrolled in the local "female college"—probably a sort of glorified high school—from which she graduated in 1876. She was still hungry for education, but her father could not afford to send her to Nashville University, as she had hoped. Instead, she read omnivorously, took courses in German, French, and art as a postgraduate at her alma mater, and began to support herself by drawing crayon portraits.

At 19 Ellen Axson was a lighthearted, spunky, petite young woman who loved rowing and shooting. Standing 5'3" tall and weighing 115 pounds, with copper hair and dark brown, deep-set eyes, she did not use cosmetics, but she did crush red rose petals and rub them on her cheeks with a rabbit's foot. She spoke in a soft southern voice, with a slow drawl. She did not take her many suitors seriously, but she enjoyed the deep, sentimental friendships with other girls common during the period. She and her close friend Beth Adams planned to set up a hall for unmarried women, which Beth would manage and Ellen support with her art. At this stage Ellen believed that although ideally marriage should be for mutual self-improvement, in fact it usually brought "the common woman's fate—to give much and receive little—after perhaps a few weeks . . . of blind, unreasonable, infatuation."

On November 4, 1881, Ellen's life changed when her mother died of childbed fever after giving birth to her fourth child. Relatives on both sides came to the aid of the shattered family, one of Ellen's aunts taking the baby to raise, her paternal grandfather substituting at his work for her grieving father, and an uncle arranging for Ellen to go on a trip to New England and New York the next summer. In April 1883, Woodrow Wilson, a young lawyer, came to hear Ellen's father preach. He and Ellen had first met in Georgia when he was six years old and she was two. This time he was instantly smitten with Ellen's "splendid, mischievous, laughing eyes." Both intelligent, well-read, and gifted, the two fell deeply in love, and she accepted his proposal that September.

Ellen wondered whether she would make Woodrow the kind of wife he needed, given her "badly regulated energy and concentration," which kept her doing one thing all day long, sewing or painting. He marveled that besides her "feminine" qualities she could afford him intellectual companionship: "I hope," he wrote her, "you don't know much about the Constitution of the United States, for I know marvelously little about art and if you know *both* subjects how am I to be head of the house?" In fact he had interested her from the start because of his intellect.

They could not marry at once, for he had little money, and she had responsibilities to her family. Her father had had a nervous breakdown and eventually was committed. Consequently, Ellen and her young brothers lived with their paternal grandparents in Savannah. Edward Axson died on May 28, 1884—probably a suicide. Deeply upset, Ellen tried to break her engagement, but Woodrow overrode her scruples.

With the money she inherited, Ellen could fulfill her dream of going to New York to study art. On the way she stopped in Wilmington, North Carolina, to meet the Wilson family. Her fiancé then accompanied her to New York to help her get settled in a boardinghouse. She delighted in the Art Students' League and in the cultural life of the city. In her busy life she found time on Sunday afternoons to teach African-American children in a city mission. She and Woodrow corresponded regularly. Already she was counseling him, building his hopes, and nurturing him. He wrote that since his early dreams of public service had been defeated for lack of funds, he now aspired to guide public policy through his writing. She reminded him that, while she herself thought the highest rank of workers were writers of noble books, he could go into public life later. They promised each other never to withhold confidences. Now, she told him, she was glad to be a woman, looking forward to a "*service* of love" in which she would take care of him and he of her. Yet, she warned, she clung to her "right of private judgment."

Her ambitions were now for him. Yes, she acknowledged, she had talent, more than the average art student, and with hard work she might eventually place high among American artists. But giving it up was "a pitiable price to pay for such a love" as his. "My darling, it would not be a sacrifice to *die* for you. How can it then be one to live for you?"

When Woodrow received an offer from the brilliant Dr. Carey Thomas to teach history at the college for women that she was building at Bryn Mawr, the young couple were able to marry. His fiancée promised to work so that he could devote more of his salary to professional expenses; although he felt a duty to support her, he promised her the freedom to make her own decision. They were married on June 24, 1885, in his parents' home, the bride wearing a white dress of her own design and the ceremony performed by her grandfather and his father. They honeymooned for six weeks in Arden, North Carolina, where they studied German and the young husband prepared his lectures for the fall.

Once in Bryn Mawr, they rented rooms in one of the cottages that provided faculty housing on campus. Before long Ellen was pregnant and suffering severe nausea. To protect Woodrow she planned to have her baby at the home of one of her relatives, since her husband was struggling through his first year of teaching as well as preparing for his doctoral examinations—and besides, she joked, she couldn't have the baby born a Yankee. Margaret Woodrow Wilson was therefore born in Gainesville, Georgia, on April 16, 1886. In June the new father—and newly minted Ph.D.—came to pick up his family, and they spent the summer visiting relatives and friends.

Back in Bryn Mawr, helped by a part-time nurse for the baby, Ellen studied German and read history, political economy, and political philosophy so that she could translate and digest German monographs for her husband. She suggested that they spend the remainder of her inheritance for a trip abroad the next year, so that he could study in Berlin. The acute nausea of another pregnancy put an end to that plan; they used the money instead to buy furniture for an 11-room house they leased. During the prolonged convalescence then accorded new mothers, Ellen became concerned about her 10-year-old brother Eddie, who was stammering; she therefore planned for him to live with her and Woodrow. She also extended an invitation to her brilliant young cousin, Mary Hoyt, to stay in their home while she attended the college. Her daughter Eleanor remembered that during most of the time she was growing up the Wilson family had relatives living with them. For their third year at Bryn Mawr, they had a household of six: Ellen and Woodrow, Ellen's brother Eddie, Mary Hoyt, and the Wilsons' two babies—16-month-old Margaret and Jessie, born in Gainesville on August 28, 1887.

Woodrow had never wanted to teach women, and in his third year at Bryn Mawr he despaired of his situation; only his wife could assuage his "ugly moods." In 1888, he joyfully accepted an offer to teach at Wesleyan University, then a men's institution. They leased another large house in Middletown, Connecticut, and Ellen plunged happily into the Wesleyan campus life. Soon, however, she was again prostrated by pregnancy. Her husband resolved that they should have no more children, particularly as she was showing the symptoms of a developing kidney disease. Despite these problems, the Wilsons offered Ellen's brother Stockton a home with them so that he could prepare for college teaching, and in the summer of 1889 Ellen tutored him in German. On October 16 that year she gave birth to her third little girl, whom they named Eleanor Randolph. The birth was attended by Dr. Florence Taft, whom an anxious Woodrow had accepted only after his brother-in-law physician had assured him that aside from their nervousness during menstruation, women could serve as competent physicians as well as men.

In fall 1890 the Wilsons moved again, this time to Princeton University, where Professor Wilson joined the faculty. They rented another large house, but this time, with Stockton Axson studying at Johns Hopkins, Eddie Axson at the Bingham School in North Carolina, and Mary Hoyt at Bryn Mawr, Ellen and Woodrow lived there alone with their three daughters. Their dreams of a house of their own moved toward realization when Woodrow's father suggested that they buy or build a home together.

Before they committed themselves completely, however, they conferred on Woodrow's professional future. Ellen gave him shrewd advice on how to handle an offer from the University of Illinois for its presidency. Think carefully, she suggested, about the choice between scholarly and administrative work, and if you choose scholarship use the Illinois offer to raise your Princeton salary. That was neither the first nor the last time that she helped him manage his career, for she had a way of quietly seeing to it that he met helpful people and finding—almost creating—a lectureship for him. She listened critically to the articles and reviews that her husband read aloud to her before he submitted them. As a faculty wife interacting with students, she also instigated the introduction of an honor system at the college.

No matter how hectic Woodrow's schedule of lecturing, writing, and attending meetings might be; no matter how many visitors came and went; and no matter what the children's activities, Ellen maintained the Wilson home as a serene refuge for her husband, where family and friends could relax and play together. He was, she wrote a friend, "almost terribly dependent on me to keep up his spirits and to 'rest' him. . . . If I am just a little sky-blue he immediately becomes blue-black!" She made few demands on him, taking most domestic cares on herself. When in his extended absence thieves began breaking into Princeton homes, she equipped herself with a pistol to fend them off.

She home-schooled her daughters, taught them their catechism and religious lessons rather than sending them to Sunday School, and made their clothes. She acted as a loving daughter to her father-in-law and as a surrogate mother to her brothers and the other young relatives who lived with the Wilsons while attending school. Their three-story, half-timbered home, Library Place—built in 1895–96 and designed, decorated, and landscaped by Ellen Wilson—was usually crammed to the attics with relatives; their household averaged 10 persons, including the two servants. She donated time to local charities and took part in the social life of the Princeton faculty. While her husband toured England and Scotland in the summer of 1896, she found time to resume her neglected painting, all the while reading art and travel books about the places he was visiting.

In 1902 Woodrow Wilson was elected president of Princeton—a popular choice, and one that made his wife proud, even as she dreaded the new duties confronting her. The Wilsons sold their beloved Library Place, and Ellen Wilson did over the president's mansion to her own taste, delighting in creating beauty and order, her goal to "emphasize the loveliness of life." She bought antiques for the main rooms, installed central heating and another bath or two, and redesigned the gardens. As part of the inaugural ceremonies, the Wilsons received the great black educator Booker T. Washington—an action that scandalized some of their southern relations. The extensive entertaining incumbent upon the president's wife sometimes bored her, but she took it in stride and tried not to complain. Fortunately, the Wilsons could now afford for her to go abroad, on occasion with her husband, another time with a daughter, and she reveled in the opportunities to visit European museums. She was astonished to see numbers of women traveling alone: "This is certainly the woman's century," she wrote. "They have taken possession of the *earth*!"

When her brother Eddie and his wife and baby drowned in 1905, Ellen suffered intensely. Characteristically, she tried to handle her grief by concentrating on her duties and on the welfare of others. "I used to think," she wrote on another trying occasion, "that it didn't matter if you gave way if no one knew. Now I know that every time you let yourself go weakens you. I have not dared to give way a minute." A relative said of her that "She has a tragic capacity for suffering and being still about it." Her family needed her, and she tried to be strong for them, but it was hard—all the harder for the religious doubts that were now plaguing her, in response to which she began to read philosophy.

In spring 1906 a burst blood vessel in Woodrow's eye signaled blood pressure so high that his doctors forbade him to work. A summer in the lake district of England set him to rights and allowed him to resume his duties, provided that he follow a more relaxed schedule, which his wife undertook to ensure. Ellen now had multiple responsibilities to her husband, her daughters, and her extended family; volunteer work; and duties to fulfill as the wife of Princeton's president. Consequently, she had to scrounge for time to devote to her own interests—especially her painting and her elaborate landscape gardening. Nevertheless, she somehow managed to design a stained glass window for the presidential mansion. Donated by two trustees, the window portrayed Aristotle and was inscribed "The human good is the activity of the soul in accordance with virtue."

Woodrow's struggle to democratize the Princeton social system exhausted him and worried her. Ellen unquestioningly, even fiercely, supported her husband's stiff-necked positions in campus politics. As he was later to prove in the struggle over the League of Nations, Woodrow Wilson would rather die than compromise.

Some scholars believe that Woodrow's friendship with popular Bermuda hostess Mary Allen Hulbert Peck may have troubled the Wilson marriage. On July 20, 1908, he wrote from England to his wife, who was summering in the artists' colony in Old Lyme, Connecticut, "You have only to believe and trust me, darling, and *all* will come right,—what you do not understand included. I know my heart now if I ever did, *and it belongs to you.*" Nonetheless, his friendship with Mary Peck, then embroiled in divorcing her husband, grew increasingly intimate; he signed his letters to her "with infinite tenderness." Later on he himself deemed the episode "a contemptible error" and "a passage of folly and gross impertinence," admitting that a jealous wife would have been tortured by "the catholicity of his admiration for women." Ellen exhibited not a whit of jealousy, her daughter Eleanor wrote, feeling that since she did not consider herself merry-hearted, her husband ought to have friends who were. As for him, he liked "charming and conversable" women—and found beautiful women more conversable than plain women.

Throughout their marriage, however, Ellen and Woodrow relished each other's minds. They thought independently and enjoyed their differences with good humor. Sometimes for amusement they talked to each other in proofreading style, inserting punctuation. In both their minds *his* career, *his* needs, and *his* interests came first. He lived surrounded by adoring women—wife, daughters, and even some distant relatives.

In the summer of 1910, Woodrow and Ellen Wilson decided on a dramatic change in the direction of their lives, moving from the academic to the political world. That fall he accepted the

Democratic nomination to run for governor of New Jersey; he was elected on November 8. Ellen found her new role unexpectedly relaxing, for New Jersey furnished no governor's mansion and imposed little official entertaining on her. Their daughter Margaret was in New York City; the rest of the family lived at the Princeton Inn. Ellen devoted most of her time to helping her husband, talking with his friends and supporters, reading newspapers, and handling correspondence. When William Jennings Bryan visited Princeton in March 1911, she arranged an intimate dinner for him. She also toured state institutions with the governor—experiencing for the first time extensive travel by automobile. Woodrow was reveling in popularity and legislative achievements, and by early summer 1912 his gubernatorial record and the support of William Jennings Bryan had won him the Democratic nomination for president.

Although she was concerned about her husband's physical stamina, Ellen believed that he was destined for great things. As she wrote to her brother, "Maybe these husbands ought not always to be encouraged to get the things to which their ambitions lead them, but how can wives who love them do anything except help them?" Thus she serenely assumed her role as candidate's wife, a calm center within the political hurly-burly. Some of Woodrow's associates thought her a better politician than her husband. At the gubernatorial summer home, Sea Girt, she entertained the people who flocked around the nominee and protected time for her husband to craft his speeches. She accompanied him on a campaign tour through Georgia and corrected false reports—she had spent $140.84, not $2,000, on clothes; she did not approve of women's smoking. Ellen chatted easily with reporters and disarmed the candidate's political enemies by her frank disclosure of the truth, but she knew when to refrain from speaking. Their two older daughters were already trying to persuade their parents to support suffrage for women, the national campaign for which was then rising to a climax. They converted their mother, but she would not speak publicly about

it, fearing to embarrass the temperamentally patriarchal candidate. He remained intransigent on the issue for years.

When Woodrow Wilson was elected president, his wife wrote a cousin: "I must make believe very hard now that I am a different kind of woman,—in *some* respects,—not *all,* thank Heaven." The Wilsons had to negotiate a bank loan of $5,000 to pay for the Wilson ladies' "Washington trousseaux," and Woodrow gave his wife her first piece of jewelry, a diamond pendant. For the first time, she employed a personal secretary, her husband's cousin Helen Bones.

Ellen was easily fatigued, and her daughters worried about her health. They protected time for her to rest at the Shoreham Hotel before the inaugural, but even so she had to compose herself after a fit of weeping. Friendly support and advice from William and Helen Taft helped her. Dressed in a brown suit with black trim and a large black hat with brown ostrich plumes, Ellen listened to the inaugural address that the family had already heard the president rehearse at home, moving from her reserved seat to stand directly below him while he delivered it. "There," wrote her daughter Eleanor, "utterly oblivious of the thousands watching her, she gazed up at him, like a small child, a look of rapture on her face." Later, the inaugural ball canceled by the president on the grounds of unnecessary expense, the Wilsons dined *en famille* in the state dining room and then watched the fireworks display from the White House.

The next day Ellen plunged into official entertaining, during the next three months hostessing 41 receptions with an average attendance of more than 600, as well as entertaining at teas, musicales, and dinners; there were also numerous overnight and weekend guests. Her three daughters and two staff members (Helen Bones and Isabelle Hagner, the social secretary who had served Edith Roosevelt and Helen Taft) all helped her. She redecorated the family quarters and planned an addition of five bedrooms and three baths on the third floor of the White House. She took time to be with her husband on almost daily drives, and the family often attended the theater. As he always had, the president discussed "every important move" with his wife, and she worked on his speeches. He listened to her suggestions on political appointments and her opinions on people and issues.

Most remarkable, however, was the rapidity with which Ellen began to exercise her influence as first lady to achieve important reforms, undertaking the most significant project of her tenure almost immediately. On March 22, 1913, she listened to the chair of the women's department of the National Civic Federation tell her about the living conditions of black citizens in Washington. Three days later the two women drove through the alley slums and toured model houses. The first lady immediately invested in the Sanitary Housing Company that built them and soon accepted the honorary chair of the woman's department of the National Civic Federation. In this position she worked on the Committee of 50 to draft the Alley Dwelling Bill and lobbied members of Congress and their wives for its passage. Black newspapers praised her even as they denounced the president for his indifference to Jim Crow segregation.

Ellen learned enough about the working conditions of women government employees to recommend to her husband's chief adviser, Colonel Edward M. House, such improvements as the installation of decent rest rooms, lunchrooms, and sanitary drinking cups in government buildings. She also interested herself in the enforcement of school attendance laws, the regulation of child labor, and legislation to promote the use of school buildings as social recreation centers.

She had a happy summer in Cornish, New Hampshire, where the Wilsons announced their daughter Jessie's forthcoming marriage to Francis Bowes Sayre, a young lawyer in the New York district attorney's office. The first lady joined the local artists' club and a discussion group; painted and sold some of her work, giving the proceeds to charity; and most of all looked forward to her husband's visits—visits that were for him times "of contentment, renewal, and delight." "Oh, how ineffably lovable and splendid you are," she wrote to him. "I love you till it *hurts*." From Cornish she followed his actions closely through newspaper accounts.

The Wilson ladies returned to Washington in mid-October 1913, and the first lady began at once to entertain and to make final arrangements for Jessie's wedding. The ceremony was celebrated on November 25 in the East Room of the White House, with 500 guests in attendance. That winter Ellen drew elaborate plans for redoing the White House gardens, including a "rose walk" for the president from the residence to his office. She counseled her daughter Nell through a tumultuous season, Nell having broken an earlier engagement because she had fallen passionately in love with Secretary of the Treasury William G. McAdoo, 26 years her senior, and he with her.

Late in March 1914 the first lady suffered an "ugly fall," from which she recovered very slowly, and went through minor surgery. The fall revealed she had tuberculosis of the kidneys and Bright's disease. She did as much as her health allowed to plan for Nell a quiet family wedding with fewer than 100 guests; the marriage took place on May 7. She tried to tell herself that her difficulties sprang from nervous exhaustion, but her health worsened. The doctors knew that she would soon die of Bright's disease, and that summer she herself realized that she would not live to see the gardens she had planned in full bloom. She wrote her last letter to Jessie, whose pregnancy had elated her.

At Ellen's request, Woodrow asked the Congress to act promptly on the Alley Dwelling Bill; it passed the Senate just in time for her to learn of its success. In her last conscious moment, she spoke to the doctor, saying, "If I go away, promise me that you will take good care of my husband." Ellen Wilson died on August 6, 1914. Her family buried her in Myrtle Hill Cemetery in Rome, Georgia, with her parents.

The White House staff called Ellen Axson Wilson "The Lady," meaning, wrote black White House seamstress Lillian Parks, "The Great and Good Lady." Brief though her tenure was, she was the first wife of a president to exercise the power of her position for projects of her own. In the reform spirit of the Progressive Era (1890–1920), she took thought for women government employees and for the education of children and the regulation of their labor. Most importantly of all, this southern-born woman concerned herself with the miserable living conditions of black residents of Washington, D.C., helping to draft and lobbying for the Alley Dwelling Bill of 1914.

CHRONOLOGY

1860   *May 15:* Ellen Louise Axson is born in Savannah, Georgia

1865   After sojourns in Beech Island, South Carolina; McPhersonville, South Carolina; and Madison, Georgia, the Axson family moves to Rome, Georgia

1876   Ellen Axson graduates from the Rome Female College

1883   *April 8:* Ellen Axson meets Woodrow Wilson

   September: Ellen Axson and Woodrow become engaged

1884– Ellen Axson studies at the Art Students'
85   League in New York City

1885   *June 24:* Ellen Axson marries Woodrow Wilson

September: The Wilsons move to Bryn Mawr, Pennsylvania, where Woodrow Wilson teaches at Bryn Mawr College

1886   *April 16:* Daughter Margaret is born

1887   *August 28:* Daughter Jessie Woodrow is born

1888   The Wilsons move to Middletown, Connecticut, where Woodrow Wilson teaches at Wesleyan University

1889   *October 16:* Daughter Eleanor Randolph is born

1890   The Wilsons move to Princeton, New Jersey, where Woodrow Wilson serves successively as professor and president of Princeton University; Ellen Wilson works in a volunteer women's employment society

1895– The Wilsons build a house based on her
96   plans, and Ellen Wilson resumes painting

1910   Woodrow Wilson is elected governor of New Jersey

1911   *March:* Ellen Wilson arranges for her husband to meet William Jennings Bryan

1912   Woodrow Wilson is elected president of the United States

1913   *March 4:* Ellen Wilson becomes first lady

   November 25: Daughter Jessie weds Francis Bowes Sayre

1914   *March 1:* A fall in her room reveals that Ellen Wilson is suffering from tuberculosis of the kidneys and Bright's disease

   May 7: Daughter Eleanor weds Secretary of the Treasury William Gibbs McAdoo

   August 6: Ellen Wilson dies

FURTHER READING

McAdoo, Eleanor Wilson. *The Priceless Gift—The Love Letters of Woodrow Wilson and Ellen Axson Wilson*. New York: McGraw-Hill, 1962.
———, with Margaret Y. Gaffey. *The Woodrow Wilsons*. New York: Macmillan, 1937.

Saunders, Frances Wright. *First Lady Between Two Worlds: Ellen Axson Wilson*. Chapel Hill: University of North Carolina Press, 1985.
Slayden, Ellen Maury. *Washington Wife: Journal of Ellen Maury Slayden from 1897–1919*. New York: Harper and Row, 1962.

EDITH BOLLING GALT WILSON

(OCTOBER 15, 1872–DECEMBER 28, 1961)
First Lady, December 18, 1915–March 4, 1921

EDITH WILSON
(Library of Congress)

Edith Bolling adopted many of the values of the grandmothers and father who raised her. She grew up expecting to marry and be supported. She paid little attention to public affairs until she met Woodrow Wilson, and even less to the gradual entry of women into the ranks of schoolteachers, clerks, and typists that had begun after the Civil War and accelerated during the Progressive Era of her young womanhood. Nonetheless after the death of her first husband she showed herself an astute businesswoman. She regarded the woman suffragists who picketed President Wilson as guilty of harassment and unfeminine behavior. Yet despite her apparent indifference to the advancement of women, she herself became, for a brief period, the most powerful woman in the United States.

Edith Bolling was born in Whytheville, Virginia, on October 15, 1872, the fourth daughter and seventh of 11 children of William Holcombe Bolling and his wife, Sallie White Bolling. William Bolling belonged to an old and wealthy Episcopalian Virginia family; among his ancestors was Pocohontas. Forced off the family plantation by its devastation during the Civil War, he turned to the practice of law, later winning a circuit court judgeship.

Her invalid paternal grandmother taught Edith the three Rs, the Bible, and her own Anglicized version of French, as well as dressmaking and crocheting. She demanded that Edith look after her 27 canaries, wash and iron her caps, and help her turn over during the night. She trained the child to report on household affairs, instilling in her the art of careful observation. She also passed along her tendency to strong instantaneous likes and dislikes and her philosophy that "Anyone can do anything they try to." Edith's maternal grandmother sang ballads and filled her head with romantic visions of love and marriage. Her father read the classics aloud in the evenings and occasionally hired a tutor or governess for his children. The girl's formal schooling was restricted to two years: a miserable one at 15 when she suffered cold and inadequate food at Martha Washington College, a finishing school in Abingdon, Virginia; and a happy one at 17 at the fashionable Powell girls' school in Richmond.

She grew up a 19th-century southern belle, the product of an already passing way of life, and so she remained until the end of her days. She particularly attracted men considerably older than she, beginning at 15 with a 38-year-old beau of her sister's. She centered her life on men: first the father she idolized; then the first husband, nine years her senior, who supported her and several members of her family in a style to which she happily accustomed herself; and finally the second husband, 16 years older than she, who brought her fun, romance, power, and prestige.

At 19, while visiting a married sister in Washington, D.C., she met Norman Galt, her brother-in-law's cousin. A member of a family who owned the city's major jewelry store, he courted her for four years. Apparently she then decided to accept a marriage of convenience, wedding him on April 30, 1896. At first they lived with his father, but as family illnesses and deaths left Norman sole owner of the family business, they moved into a small house of their own, and then, on his father's death, into his mansion. In the seventh year of the marriage, the birth of a son, who died after three days, left Edith unable to bear children. Thereafter she led the life of a wealthy woman, developing a reputation for her fine clothes, jewelry, and orchids; driving around Washington in her electric brougham; attending Episcopalian church events; going to theater and opera; and touring the luxury hotels of Europe. She did not, however, move within the social circles of official Washington—the so-called Cliff Dwellers—for they looked down on people "in trade." Devoted to family, she cared for several ailing relatives and her widowed mother.

Twelve years after the marriage, in 1908, Norman died, leaving the store to his wife. With the guidance of longtime employees, Edith oversaw the business herself, participating in all conferences and making final decisions but leaving day-to-day management to them. Later, when troubles erupted in the store's management, she sold it to the employees. Otherwise she hardly altered her style of life. She not only supported and looked after members of her birth family but also played surrogate mother to several younger women. In 1911 she took as a protégée Alice Gertrude (Altrude) Gordon, the orphaned young daughter of a close friend, traveling with her abroad and enthusiastically encouraging her love affair with Admiral Cary Grayson. Grayson had served as physician to Presidents Theodore Roosevelt and William Howard Taft, and he became naval aide to President Woodrow Wilson.

Edith Galt had never taken an interest in politics, any more than she had in causes. She was not a public-spirited woman, nor was she well-informed. In 1913, however, a sister-in-law who had campaigned for President Wilson talked about him so much that Edith bestirred herself to read his speeches, attend his first big reception, and even go to hear him speak before Congress, though she thought his ideas impractical and utopian. From Grayson she heard of how stricken the president was at the 1914 death of his wife Ellen.

In many ways the Galt-Wilson relationship was an affair waiting to happen. In her mid-40s, she was buxomly attractive, high-spirited, and physically active, a woman who had never experienced the romance she had dreamed of as a girl. He was a highly sexed man of 59 who liked female company and conversation and who all his life had been surrounded by adoring women. In September 1914, about a month after the death of Ellen Axson Wilson, congressional wife Ellen Maury Slayden wrote in her diary:

> I said casually, 'When the President marries again'—and Mrs. Lansing exclaimed, 'Oh, Mrs. Slayden, how can you speak of such a thing!' I asked, 'Why not? He is a youngish man, and we have reason to believe rather leans to the ladies.' 'But,' Mrs. L. went on, horrified, 'he wouldn't *dare* to marry again while he is in the White House; public opinion would not permit it.' I reminded her that the public was having to reconcile itself to some worse things about him than marriage, and we . . . ended by betting five pounds of Huyler's [chocolates].

At any rate, when the pair did meet, their passionate natures erupted. Grayson had told Edith Galt of the miasma of depression in the White House after Ellen Wilson's death and asked her to meet the president's cousin, Helen Bones, who lived there. She did, and subsequently she took Helen for drives and walks. In March 1915, clad in a designer suit spattered with mud from a walk and allegedly believing the president absent, she stepped out of the White House elevator with Helen and came face to face with the president and Grayson. In a lively conversation at tea that day, Edith Galt and Woodrow Wilson discovered that they had much in common—particularly the South. Thereafter he courted her ardently, proposing on May 3—for, he said, "I would be less than

a gentleman if I continued to make opportunities to see you without telling you what I have told my daughters and Helen [Bones]: that I want you to be my wife." True to her training as a lady, she postponed her response—though, if she had to answer instantly, she said, she would have to refuse. Encouraged, he pressed on, aided and abetted by his three daughters, Helen, and Grayson, all of whom rejoiced at the president's recovered ebullience.

In May Edith sailed with the president to New York to review the fleet. That summer she visited him at his vacation home in Cornish, New Hampshire. He exercised the appeal of his power by confiding his problems, stressing his need for her to help him bear his great responsibilities. "Much as I enjoy your delicious love letters," she responded, ". . . I believe I enjoy even more the ones in which you tell me . . . of what you are working on, . . . for then I feel I am sharing your work and being taken into partnership, as it were." She later wrote:

> In this way I followed day by day every phase of the mosaic which he was shaping into a pattern of statecraft, and we continued this partnership of thought and comradeship unbroken to the last day of his life. . . . [E]xcept for formal interviews with officials, I always 'sat in' when one or two people we knew came to discuss policies. In that way I was never a stranger to any subject, and often able in small ways to be of help.

In late June she accepted his renewed proposal, but with the condition that she would marry him only after he left the White House. He protested: With war raging in Europe, how was he to soldier on without the constant presence and support of the woman he loved? Soon she "volunteered" to "enlist" as his aide. When they were apart, he sent her daily the most important state papers with his own annotations. In mid-September they told the rejoicing Wilson family of their engagement.

The president's political advisors, concerned that the announcement of his engagement so soon after his first wife's death might damage his chances for reelection, did not share in the joy. However, rumors of the courtship were already circulating and revived scandalous whispers of his relationship with a divorcée, Mary Hulbert Peck, during his first marriage: She allegedly had accepted a bribe not to publish his witty, affectionate letters to her, and Woodrow admitted that he had not had "the moral right to offer [Mary Peck] the ardent affection which they express." He offered to release Edith from the engagement. She may have hesitated briefly while she brooded about the revelation, but in the end she opted in his favor, always thereafter insisting that Wilson and Peck had never been anything more than friends, and that he had tried to help Peck's invalid son. Edith blamed the revival of the scandal on three of Wilson's advisers, whom she never forgave.

These troubles roused fears within the president's family and among his advisers that he would fall sick unless he could have his way. "If he does not marry, and marry quickly," said Colonel Edward House, the president's powerful confidant, "I believe he will go into a decline." The president announced the engagement on October 6, 1915; at last he and his fiancée could freely appear together in public.

White House usher Ike Hoover decorated Edith Galt's home for the wedding, which was held on December 18, 1915. He constructed a lane of American Beauty roses on the staircase and a canopy of greens lined with heather in the drawing room. The bride wore black velvet, a black velvet hat trimmed with pigeon feathers, and orchids. The president escorted her down the staircase, and they took their vows under the canopy before some 50 guests—mostly family, cabinet members, and White House staff. Her mother gave her away, and an Episcopal priest and a Presbyterian minister conducted the service jointly. The newlyweds ducked the press by driving to Alexandria, where the president's private railroad car waited to take them to their honeymoon at The Homestead in Hot Springs, Virginia. After the wedding night, a jubilant Woodrow jigged and sang the words to a popular song, "Oh, you beautiful doll, You great

big beautiful doll"—not inappropriately, for Edith was a tall, buxom beauty. Throughout their marriage he addressed her as "little girl."

Edith settled easily into the White House. She made few changes in either décor or personnel. Accustomed to servants, she got along well with them and they liked her, although she reprimanded them if they interrupted the president's work or did not stand in his presence. She inherited several senior staff: her social secretary, Edith Benham, daughter of an admiral; housekeeper Elizabeth Jaffray; and usher Ike Hoover, a man of long experience who had the White House well in hand. Edith had always been perfectly groomed, and she already possessed an extensive wardrobe and beautiful jewelry. From her home she brought a few belongings, including her sewing machine, for she was an expert needlewoman. As first lady, she concentrated on taking care of her husband, managing his personal finances as well as the budget for their White House household expenses. The war in Europe complicated entertaining, for representatives of warring nations could not be invited together. However, it also curtailed the dinners and receptions, leaving the newlyweds more time to enjoy each other.

After nights spent together in the enormous Lincoln bed, the couple rose early, initially at 6:00 A.M. and later at 5:00, to play a round of golf, breakfast, and then study papers together until his secretary arrived at 9:00. Sometimes the first lady took notes as the president thought through his problems. They walked together to his office, where she occasionally lingered until about 10:30, after which she usually returned alone to work on her mail and guest lists. Most days they lunched together, and in the afternoons she received guests such as the wives of ambassadors at half-hour intervals, giving them tea before a fire. At 5:30 P.M. the president and first lady often went for a drive, sometimes in her electric car, or rode horseback together. In hilarious sessions in the White House basement, during which both the president and the Secret Service tried to hold her up, she tried to learn to ride a bicycle but failed. In the evenings,

Edith Wilson with husband at the first airmail ceremony *(Library of Congress)*

unless they had official duties, they dined together, sometimes motoring into the countryside for dinner at an inn. Then they might work on state affairs, read, or play pool. Her influence on him grew as she acted as his personal assistant, protecting him against the nuisances of unwanted visitors and letters.

The presidential couple attended the theater and vaudeville shows regularly. Saturdays they reserved for themselves, often taking weekend cruises. They resolved their differences in religion by attending both Episcopalian and Presbyterian churches.

In January 1916, an election year, the new first lady accompanied the president on a speaking tour of the Middle West. After the Democ-

ratic convention in St. Louis renominated him as a matter of course, Edith stumped effectively along with her husband. Republican and socialist campaigns slandered them both viciously, and she doubted that he could be reelected. Although his professed commitment to peace gained him many votes, he won the election by the barest of margins.

Back in the White House, the Wilsons continued to work closely together, discussing the decisions he had to make. She coded and decoded the messages with which he communicated with officials abroad, and sometimes she read his notes to him as he typed. Under the pressure of events the president grew irritable, and she planned ceaselessly to divert him, introducing games they could play together in the evenings. She was infuriated by the appearances of woman suffragists wherever he went, calling them "unladylike" and "disgusting." Their cause meant less than nothing to her, whereas his peace of mind was everything.

When the United States entered World War I on April 6, 1917, Edith knew at once that taking care of the president was her most important war work. She tried to avoid interruptions to their daily routine, seeing to it that he slept enough, exercised enough, and played enough. If she did not go around the golf course with him, she waited in the car, working on her mail, reading the papers, or knitting. She installed a billiard table in the White House. Their numerous leisure activities evoked criticism: "The casualty lists are three and four columns long every day," wrote Congressional wife Ellen Maury Slayden, "but just as regularly the first item of the society news is . . . that President and Mrs. Wilson occupied their box at Keith's or Poli's last night."

When she could, the first lady donned a Red Cross uniform to serve sandwiches to the soldiers and sailors passing through Union Station. She sewed for the Red Cross, named and christened ships, and sold Liberty Loan bonds. With the cabinet wives she pledged to economize, taking the bus to conserve gas and selling the wool from sheep grazing on the White House lawn for the benefit of the Red Cross and the Salvation Army. With the chairwoman of the Women's Committee of the Council of National Defense, she wrote an open letter to women of Allied countries, begging them to protect the chastity of American soldiers, who were beset by temptation, "removed from homes and families," and "living the unnatural life of the camp."

Still, Edith spent most of her time with her husband. On most subjects she formed her opinions on his, but not on judgments of people, where she clung to her instant likes and dislikes. Like the president's other advisers, official and would-be, she found it difficult to change her husband's mind once he had made it up,

since Wilson was convinced of his own ability to discern what was right. For instance, she could not dissuade him from pleading with the public for a Democratic majority in Congress, even though he agreed with her intellectually: He had promised party leaders to do so and could not break his word.

The first lady followed the armistice negotiations step by step, often bearing the sole responsibility for decoding the president's messages. After the armistice on November 11, 1918, she helped appoint the commissioners who were to accompany the president and her to Europe for the peace conference. Against the advice of his other counselors, the president was determined to attend the conference and looked forward confidently to incorporating what he called his 14 points into a treaty that would bring lasting peace to the world through a league of nations. They sailed on December 4, 1918, but once in Europe they waited weeks for the conference to begin. Meanwhile they visited soldiers in hospitals or wherever they were billeted, reviewed troops in muddy fields, and shared Christmas dinner with them.

While they waited for the start of the peace talks, the Wilsons were greeted enthusiastically, almost worshipfully, wherever they went and entertained lavishly. The British were still not at ease with American power and still obsessed enough with protocol for Buckingham Palace to fret over whether men should wear military uniforms and women tiaras during the Wilsons' visit. In the event the king did not wear a uniform because the president did not, and women wore their tiaras because although the first lady did not own one, she assured everyone that she would enjoy seeing others wear theirs. The Italian court pondered another weighty matter when the president refused to attend an opera on Sunday. The Italians resolved the dilemma by presenting *Aida* with religious solos interjected and calling it a "sacred concert."

When the conference finally began in Versailles in mid-January 1919, observers noted how much influence the first lady had with the president. She sat in on some of his meetings with his advisers and was a conduit for gossip that he did not otherwise hear, particularly about the quarrels among jealous American commissioners. As at home she tried to distract him from his worries and his horror at the destruction that the war had inflicted. She helped relieve the fatigue that afflicted him from two sets of meetings—one to negotiate a peace treaty and the other to draft the Covenant of the League of Nations. With the help of Premier Clemenceau of France, Edith hid in an antechamber from which she could hear her husband's presentation of the Covenant for a vote.

When it passed, they sailed home triumphantly, only to find stiff opposition to the League in Congress. The president was appalled, and the first lady raged, privately denouncing the Covenant's most visible foe, Senator Henry Cabot Lodge, as a traitor. Back in Europe in March to complete work on the Treaty of Versailles, they confronted new problems and disagreements among both the Americans and representatives of the other allies. The presidential couple and their friends, Grayson and Edith's former protégée Altrude, now Grayson's wife, held "indignation meetings often over things that are said and done by the very people we would have a right to expect support from," Altrude later reported, "and we blow off steam and feel better afterwards." Meanwhile, the first lady increasingly objected to Colonel Edward House, the president's longtime close adviser, whom she saw as usurping her husband's power and taking credit for his achievements. She began a deliberate campaign to get rid of him, and eventually Wilson broke with House, whom, he believed, had "given away everything I had won before we left Paris"—that is, Wilson thought that the House had made compromises with other nations that Wilson had not authorized.

On April 3, 1919, the president fell violently ill; the first lady believed that House's actions had literally sickened him. While some of his associates suspected a stroke, modern authorities speculate that he had encephalitis. The public was told only that he had suffered a bout of influenza, but thereafter his advisers found him changed, and the president's health and political fortunes went downhill. After exhausting months of negotiations he returned home in early summer with a treaty that he believed essential to peace, but many congressmen thought it would dangerously entangle the United States in European quarrels. The president refused to consider any modifications, even though he was warned that only acceptance of the Senate's amendments would ensure its passage.

Wilson took his case for ratification of the treaty and acceptance of the Covenant of the League of Nations to the people on a speaking tour that Edith later described as "one long nightmare." The Wilsons started out by train in early September. The exhausted and ailing president refused to rest and could hardly eat; he did not care if he died, he said, as long as the treaty was ratified. The trip, with 37 formal speeches and frequent appearances on the back platform of the train in 22 days, would have enervated even a healthy man. "Never a moment to relax and rest," wrote the first lady. "From one city to the next a small local committee would accompany us, which meant constant entertaining even on the train." Crowds of people turned out to hear the president speak from the train—his wife's hand against his back to help him balance—and filled auditoriums to listen to him describe the advantages of the treaty. As the train headed back east, Woodrow was enduring terrible headaches but insisted on continuing his efforts. When in Colorado he could no longer bear the pain, his wife and the doctor together managed to persuade the president that the public must not see him in his condition, with his speech distorted and one side of his face fallen. The train steamed back to Washington at full speed, while Edith sat with him, chatting, knitting, and studying papers.

Back at the White House, the headaches continued, and the president could not see from one eye. The first lady and the doctors embarked on the reckless course of keeping the truth from everyone—the vice president, the cabinet, Congress, and the public. Edith had the press to tea, joked with them, and told them that the president regretted that he could not meet with them. A few days later he suffered a (or another) stroke, which paralyzed his left side and disturbed his mental processes. The first lady took over, keeping out American officials and foreign diplomats, *even the vice president,* delivering to the president only such messages as she saw fit. "The only decision that was mine," she later wrote defensively, "was what was important and what was not, and the *very* important decision of when to present matters to my husband." Nonetheless, accusing her of "petticoat government," many people called her the *Presidentress, Lady President, First Woman President, Iron Queen,* and *Regent.* While the suffragists she detested fought for the vote, this unschooled woman, who had said that in the 1912 election she had not even known the names of the presidential candidates, took upon herself the power of influencing the course of international affairs and presiding over a United States torn with the violence of race riots, strikes, strikebreaking, and the fears of communism that these events evoked.

To Edith Wilson, Woodrow was her husband first and president second. The doctors had assured her that staying in office was essential to his survival. He himself wanted to remain in office—even hoped for a third term—and she believed that being forced to resign before the ratification of the peace treaty would kill him. She also believed that the nation and even the world's welfare depended on that ratification, which needed his leadership— even if that leadership was only ostensible. Moreover, she was convinced that the president could fully recover his powers. Some scholars believe that she did not fully realize the import of what she was doing. Almost from the time she had met the president he had shared state secrets and talked over his problems with her, and what political ideas she had came from him. Consequently, she felt competent to convey his thoughts and wishes accurately, and she always denied that she made a single decision on her own.

No one knows how much information the first lady actually relayed to her husband, which newspaper stories she read him, and how much she suppressed lest he be upset. Within her limitations Edith Wilson probably followed the path the president would have pursued fairly closely. He had, after all, been giving her a crash course in domestic and especially foreign affairs of state ever since they met, and he taught expertly. Except for judgments of people, where her own strong likes and dislikes prevailed, she accepted his dicta as gospel truth and, like him, assumed that God's purposes and his were identical. However, no longer did leadership and inspiration issue from the White House. The president's powers of concentration and foresight were lost, his emotional state was volatile, and his wife and he simply dealt with problems as they arose, to the best of their limited capacities. However, on the advice of the president's physicians, the Wilsons spent most of their free time on such diversions as movies and motoring.

The president's health improved gradually, but not without setbacks. At one point he was threatened with toxemia from obstruction of the prostate, and his wife had to decide whether or not to operate when the doctors differed. She chose not to—correctly, as it proved. In a matter of weeks he could sign bills, if she guided his pen. When government officials sent messages to the president through her, more often than not she replied that the president would consider the problem. Even when she came back with direct answers, officials often could not understand them. She consulted Bernard Baruch and some cabinet members, but, she said, "I did not see much of [Secretary of State] Lansing, for I never liked him."

Why top officials did not act more forcefully remains an unanswerable question. The Wilsons were both formidable characters, both utterly convinced of his rightness and righteousness, and both jealous of his powers. In fact as soon as the president recovered to a degree, he forced Secretary of State Robert Lansing to resign, for daring to call cabinet meetings while Wilson was *hors de combat.* Moreover, when Lansing questioned the president's ability to govern, Wilson's secretary Joseph Tumulty threatened that if Lansing proceeded he and Dr. Grayson would deny that Wilson was incapacitated.

The president's illness had not changed his position on the treaty, nor had it softened his stubborn refusal to accept any amendment to it. When at the behest of some of his advisers the first lady questioned whether some compromise might not be worthwhile to secure Senate ratification, he reproached her. He could not bear, he said, for her to question his stance; to compromise would be to break faith with the leaders of other nations who had also signed the treaty. Thus chastened, she warned officials that she would never again ask her husband to do anything he considered dishonorable. Six weeks after his breakdown, however, even he recognized that the cause was lost. Both of the Wilsons believed that Senator Lodge had wrecked all hope for the United States's joining the League of Nations out of personal spite. "A snake in the open," the first lady called him. In 1939 she laid the blame for World War II on him, for she believed that a strong League would have prevented it.

Not until early December 1919 did the President see two senators; even then, at his insistence the first lady stayed in the room and took notes. In January 1920 officials submitted a draft State of the Union message, which was returned with penciled notes in Edith's hand—changes that she said the president wanted, though many officials were skeptical. She continued to screen visitors until April 1920. By then Wilson was reportedly contemplating the possibility of retiring—though only if he was convinced that his illness was harming the nation. At the same time, he began presiding over cabinet meetings that he called himself. He even spoke of running for a third term, although those close to him recognized the impossibility of such a dream.

The Wilsons did not rejoice in Warren Harding's election to the presidency in 1920. The first lady took the Harding slogan of a return to normalcy as a personal insult, since, she felt, she had kept things as normal as possible in the months past. She took one of her immediate dislikes to Florence Harding: The incoming first lady wore too much rouge, she talked too much, and she did not shake hands with the White House housekeeper. Quick to suspect shabby treatment, Edith took offense when, after the two presidents rode to the Capitol together, the elated Hardings ran up the Capitol steps, while Wilson had to be taken to an elevator in the back. He was too weak to attend the swearing-in ceremony.

The Wilsons remained in Washington, living in a comfortable three-story brick house with five bedrooms and five baths on S Street. With the help of friends—especially Bernard Baruch, who bought the adjoining lot to ensure their privacy—Edith had the house ready for the move from the White House, right down to the placement of her husband's 8,000 books on the shelves of his study. She had an elevator installed and the large Lincoln bed copied for him. When he missed a White House timepiece, she had a grandfather clock made for him. A secretary helped him with his correspondence; a male night nurse tended him; and a black couple looked after them both.

For a while the former president tried to practice law, but he soon found that impracticable because of his scruples about accepting cases that "touched in some way the Government structure." The Wilsons thereafter settled into a relaxed routine, enjoying the visits of many celebrities and the many honors that were bestowed upon the former president. Friends gave him a Rolls Royce with two interchangeable bodies, one as a limousine and the other as a touring car, painted in Princetonian orange-and-black. His devoted wife not only arranged everything for his convenience but also provided him with gaiety and amusement. When he became disturbed about changes in the American way of life, she helped him write a booklet as a guide to Americans. The work went slowly; often he summoned her from sleep to add or change a few phrases. Late in 1923, with great effort, he spoke on the radio on behalf of an organization working to support the League of Nations.

Woodrow Wilson died on February 3, 1924, leaving his widow the executor of his $250,000 estate. She continued to live in the S Street house, passing the days of this second widowhood much as she had those of the first: traveling, playing games, seeing friends, and going to the theater. In some respects, though, her second marriage had changed her. As Altrude Grayson put it, "Mrs. Wilson never went in for causes, except her great Cause. She always hesitated to use the name she bore for anything like raising money. She devoted a great deal of time to correspondence and contacts concerning the President." Edith Wilson welcomed new honors in her husband's memory and worked actively to make his birthplace a national shrine, as well as to establish the Woodrow Wilson Foundation and the Woodrow Wilson School of Public and International Affairs at Princeton.

Now she knew the names of the presidential candidates, and she even campaigned for Franklin Delano Roosevelt. After his election she frequently visited the White House. Even her discovery that Roosevelt had taken a desk from the *George Washington* that had been a personal gift to her husband did not disturb their friendship, although she told him: "You're nothing but a common thief."

Characteristically, she wrote *My Memoir* because the appearance of a book by her old enemy, Colonel House, had irritated her. She had never intended to publish her book, she said, but Bernard Baruch insisted. The book was published in 1939, after Pulitzer Prize–winning author Marquis James had persuaded her to delete some of her nasty personal remarks about House and others on her list of dislikes.

She lived on in good health, able to dine out and go to a concert on the eve of John F. Kennedy's inauguration and to attend the inauguration itself, afterward lunching at the Capitol. Late that year, on December 28, 1961, her heart failed, and she died.

Ironically, Edith Wilson, who despised woman suffragists, who until she met Woodrow Wilson knew and cared nothing about politics, and who always placed the health and happiness of her husband above the welfare of the nation, wielded more power during her "regency" than any other president's wife before or since. She took counsel with few except the man she loved, severely impaired by a stroke, and his doctors. She did not consult the cabinet, nor did she seek advice from any senator or representative. Instead, she prevented officials from seeing the president and kept the truth of his condition from them, thereby rendering impossible the proper execution of their duties. For a time she was the most powerful first lady in history.

CHRONOLOGY

1872   *October 15:* Edith Bolling is born in Whytheville, Virginia

1896   *April 30:* Edith marries jeweler Norman Galt

1903   A son is born but dies within days, leaving Edith Bolling Galt incapable of bearing more children

1908   Norman Galt dies

1915   *mid-March:* Edith Galt meets Woodrow Wilson

        June 29: Edith and Woodrow become engaged

        October 6: The engagement is announced

        December 18: Edith Galt marries Woodrow Wilson and becomes first lady

1916   Woodrow Wilson is reelected president

1917   *April:* The United States enters World War I

1919   The Wilsons attend the Paris Peace Conference

        April 3: Woodrow Wilson suffers a stroke or a bout of encephalitis

        October 2: Wilson suffers a stroke

1921   *March 4:* The Wilsons retire to a Washington house on S Street

1924   *February 3:* Woodrow Wilson dies, and Edith dedicates herself to perpetuating his memory

1939   Edith publishes her autobiography, *My Memoir*

1961   *December 28:* Edith Wilson dies

FURTHER READING

Anthony, Carl Sferrazza. "Wytheville's First Woman President," *Roanoker Magazine* (October 1990).

Hatch, Alden. *Edith Bolling Wilson, First Lady Extraordinary.* New York: Dodd, Mead, 1961.

Ross, Ishbel. *Power with Grace: The Life Story of Mrs. Woodrow Wilson.* New York: G.P. Putnam's Sons, 1975.

Schachtman, Tom. *Edith and Woodrow: A Presidential Romance.* New York: G.P. Putnam's Sons, 1981.

Weaver, Judith L. "Edith Bolling Wilson as First Lady: A Study in the Power of Personality, 1919–1920," *Presidential Studies Quarterly* (Winter 1985).

Wilson, Edith. *My Memoir.* Indianapolis: Bobbs-Merrill, 1939.

FLORENCE MABEL KLING HARDING
(AUGUST 15, 1860–NOVEMBER 21, 1924)
First Lady, March 4, 1921–August 2, 1923

FLORENCE HARDING
(Library of Congress)

In many respects Florence Harding was a model of the "New Woman" of the Progressive Era: determined, competent, and independent, with a firm belief in spousal equality and woman suffrage. Like many another New Woman, she retained her sense of responsibility for a woman's traditional duties while simultaneously adopting new ambitions. She loved business and hated cooking, but she felt that running her home efficiently was as important as managing a business efficiently. Some thought her cold and tightfisted, bossy and abrasive, intense and strident. Others admired her business skills, her organizing abilities, her forthrightness, and her political acumen. For a time Warren Harding called his wife "Boss," later replacing this with "Duchess," a name that many of their friends and associates adopted. Her ambitions for her husband had much to do with his becoming a candidate for the presidency and with his victory in 1920 at the polls. Despite his womanizing, the couple created a working partnership that endured throughout his political career.

Florence Mabel Kling was born in Marion, Ohio, on August 15, 1860, the first of three children and the only daughter of Amos and Louisa Kling. Her father, born of German stock, was one of the wealthiest men in town and a tyrant who dominated his family. He expected his beautiful, refined wife, who came from a more aristocratic family of French and English heritage, to be quiet and obedient, a model for their children. From Florence he required submission and respect; when she displeased him, he whipped her with a cherry switch. Yet he also saw to it that she learned about business and finance from his own enterprises, and he tolerated her interest in animals, especially horses and dogs. She became an excellent horsewoman, boldly riding astride rather than sidesaddle.

Florence's father fostered her talent for music and sent her to the Cincinnati Conservatory of Music to finish off her musical education. As obstinate as he, she returned from Cincinnati in a defiant mood, going to the local skating rink with boys he did not approve of, staying out too late, and acting a "mite wild," as one neighbor put it. Her father retaliated by locking her out when she did not meet his curfew, leaving her to seek shelter with a girlfriend.

In 1880, in an ultimate act of rebellion, and to the dismay of both their families, Florence eloped with Henry De Wolfe, a neighborhood friend who already showed promise as an alcoholic wastrel. Years later she spoke of that unhappy relationship as a "great mistake . . . I did all that was possible to correct it and obliterate it." Six months after the elopement, Florence gave birth to a baby boy, whom she named Marshall. Henry De Wolfe soon abandoned her and the baby, and her father denied her refuge at home. She supported herself by giving piano lessons. In 1884 she filed for separation from her husband and in 1886 obtained a divorce, ending their common-law marriage.

Once the separation took effect, Amos Kling offered to take Marshall as his own child—in effect, adopting him—relieving Florence of all financial responsibility for the boy but accepting no responsibility for her welfare. Cruel as the choice was, Florence accepted the offer. Without the child she could make a new life for herself, unencumbered by the obligations of motherhood, but she did see him on occasion and kept a room in the Harding house for him. He never thrived, and he died in 1916 at the age of 35, a failure like his father. He left two children, and Florence showed an interest in them and in his widow.

The rough treatment she had received at the hands of her father and her first husband scarred her. Always temperamentally independent, she now perforce became self-reliant but also inwardly insecure, suspicious, and distrustful of the fidelity and even the abilities of others—to the point that she saw snubs and insults where none were intended. She felt that she had to do everything herself and she knew that she could.

Florence Kling met Warren Harding, publisher of the *Marion Star,* when she was giving his sister a piano lesson. Again her father disapproved of the man to whom she was attracted, thinking little of his prospects. Again she defied her father. Speculation about the match began as soon as the engagement was announced. What, people asked, did Warren see in her? Florence was several years older than he, lacking in beauty and charm, and saddled with an unconventional past. Perhaps, they conjectured, her financial prospects as the only daughter of a wealthy man attracted him. The truth was that Florence had pursued Warren with such determination that he could not resist her. His own father had reportedly commented that it was a good thing Warren was not a girl, since he could never say no and would always be pregnant.

Amos Kling did his bullheaded best to prevent the wedding, barring the couple from holding the ceremony at the Epworth Methodist Church, where he was a trustee. They married instead in the Harding home. Many guests attended at the risk of being refused loans from Kling's banks. In a rare act of defiance, Florence's mother quietly slipped in by the back door to witness her daughter's marriage. The ceremony itself began precisely at 8:00 P.M. on July 8, 1891, and ended breathlessly at 8:30, the timing dictated by Florence's superstitious belief that no important event should occur when the minute hand was on the rise between 6 and 12. At the reception Florence Harding said—perhaps in jest, perhaps not—that she would make her husband president. Considering her iron will, it was a prophecy not to be taken lightly.

It took years for the Hardings to reconcile Amos Kling to their marriage. Louisa Kling had responded to their overtures shortly before her death in 1893, but even at his wife's funeral Amos ignored his daughter. Warren persisted, unperturbed by his father-in-law's rejection, and Florence was at least willing to visit her father and invite him into their home. Amos finally capitulated in 1905.

After the wedding, people continued to gossip about the Harding marriage. It was clear that she was pushing her amiable, easygoing, not very strong husband to meet her high expectations. Her demands eventually drove Warren to the verge of a nervous breakdown, prompting him to seek relief in a prolonged rest at the Kellogg Battle Creek Sanitarium in Michigan. Indulging his love of travel, he attended Ohio Republican meetings, where his resonant voice and handsome features attracted attention. His enemies said he was escaping an overbearing wife whom he humored and who awed him, but in fact he valued her advice and respected her judgment. He also understood that he needed her.

During Warren's stay at Battle Creek, the *Marion Star*'s circulation manager resigned. In her husband's absence, Florence went down to the office to help out, thinking to stay for only a few days. Instead she took over and remained for 14 years, during which she transformed the newspaper into an up-to-date enterprise, financially successful and with expanded news coverage. Under her management new presses were installed, a wire press service was subscribed to, customer accounts were collected when due, and a woman reporter was hired—perhaps the first in all Ohio. Whereas her husband had simply sold papers over the counter in his business office, Florence hired newsboys to deliver them. The socialist leader Norman Thomas, once one of her delivery boys, remembered how she ran the business side of the newspaper: "She was a woman of very narrow mentality and range of interest or understanding, but of strong will and, within a certain aura, of genuine kindliness. She got along well with newsboys of all sorts and kinds, in whom she took a genuine interest. It was her energy and business sense which made the *Star*." Some believed that she used the newspaper as a launching pad for her husband's political career.

In 1899, after a conference with his wife, Warren Harding announced his candidacy for the state senate. Florence Harding enthusiastically entered political life with him, becoming her husband's campaign manager, arranging his public appearances, controlling the finances, and working with the politicians supporting her husband. She used her experience in the newspaper business to establish cordial relations with the press. After his election she accompanied the new state senator to Columbus to keep him in sight as well as attend to the social and political contacts necessary for his career. Warren Harding, gregarious and handsome, was widely popular and as his political career flourished and he was elected state senator and then lieutenant governor of Ohio, a watchful Florence remained at his side to advise, encourage, warn, manage, and—not always successfully—keep Warren from making a fool of himself with the many women he attracted. She worried also, and with reason, about the shady politicians with whom he was associating.

Florence herself was not universally liked. Journalist Mark Sullivan's portrait of her in her Columbus days is revealing:

> Daytimes she bustled, sparrow-like, in and out of Harding's office with pert chatter to him and his friends. Evenings at home she sat in at the games of bridge and poker, or, if she were

unneeded as a player, kept the glasses filled, always brightly jabbering. In appearance she was a little too mechanically marcelled, too shinily rouged and lipsticked, too trimly tailored. Towards her, Harding was always gravely deferential, and his men friends learned to be the same.

Nevertheless, even Warren had his breaking point; on at least one occasion after Florence had nagged him about his cigar, posture, and suit, he stormed, "Goddammit, shut up!"

Despite her indomitable energy, Florence's health was fragile. In February 1905 she endured her first major illness when one kidney stopped functioning and had to be removed. The experience caused her to think of death and aged her, making her meticulous about her appearance and loath to be photographed. She was warned that worry and stress might aggravate her condition, yet with the husband she had, she could not help but worry. Her hospitalization of five months' duration left him free to begin a torrid affair with her best friend, Carrie Phillips, wife of neighbor and friend Jim Phillips, who was away being treated for a nervous collapse. The affair continued after their respective spouses returned home and flamed fitfully for years.

Warren Harding's genial inability to restrain his libido was probably unmatched among American presidents until the exploits of John F. Kennedy and Bill Clinton. It is impossible to tell how much his wife knew, as distinguished from suspected, about his constant infidelity throughout their marriage, but she could not avoid learning about the Carrie Phillips affair when, in the summer of 1911, she intercepted a letter from Carrie to Warren—a letter that she was probably meant to see.

At this juncture Florence considered divorcing Warren, but neither of them really wanted to separate. He did not want to marry his lusty mistress, as she was pressing him to, since divorce would stain his reputation and jeopardize the public acclaim he relished. Florence could be domineering, but she protected,

improved, and promoted his business and political aspirations and personal well-being—all without the selfish absorption exhibited by Carrie Phillips. If Florence divorced Warren, she had no other home to go to (her father had remarried in 1906) and no other career to build. Besides, she had long since recognized Warren's potential, especially the speaking ability so vital to a political career. They therefore reached a tacit agreement to preserve their partnership. Inevitably, however, the experience, which had robbed her of her confidante and best friend, heightened her anxieties, aggravated her distrust of others, and increased her rigidity, withdrawal, and severity. His romantic adventures continued, and when she knew about them, they continued to infuriate her.

In 1914 Warren Harding was elected a U.S. senator, and he and his wife moved to Washington. There he began an extended affair with young Nan Britton, by whom he may have had a daughter, while at the same time he continued to write erotic verse to Carrie Phillips. It was Florence, however, on whom he relied for guidance. She faithfully attended Senate debates on suffrage for women, the League of Nations, and immigration. When he dictated correspondence, she listened and suggested changes. She consulted with politicians from Ohio, seeing to it that constituents were served and received favors and governmental appointments. She also learned which contacts could best serve her purpose and the ways in which Washington functioned. Socially, however, her position as the middle-aged, dowdy wife of an undistinguished senator, hampered by her bad health, left her lonely and frustrated. She did not know how to disguise her avid and shrewd pursuit of her ambitions, which alienated other political wives. One event brightened her days: her growing friendship with the politically experienced socialite Evalyn Walsh McLean, possessor of the notorious Hope diamond, who helped her find her way through the maze of Washington society and politics.

By 1916 Warren Harding's name was being mentioned as a possible presidential candidate;

Flo Harding with husband Warren in their "Front Porch Campaign" *(Library of Congress)*

by 1920 the pressures for his candidacy were more serious. Florence was importuned by Republican political leaders who knew that Warren would not run unless she asked him to do so. Unexpectedly, she refused: In an interview with a Kansas City reporter she said: "*I do not intend to permit him to run*. Because of the condition of his health it would bring a tragedy to us both." The spectacle of President Woodrow Wilson, "harried and beaten by the cares of office," she said, gave her pause.

Nonetheless, the superstitious Florence Harding listened to an astrologer named Madame Marcia. Madame's advice, combined with the persuasive powers of Harding's managers and supporters, who dangled before her the prospect of becoming first lady, changed her mind. To ensure her husband's nomination, she accompanied him to Chicago in June 1920 for the Republican convention, working more

actively than had any candidate's wife before. She courted the press, delighting reporters with her colorful remarks, and cajoled delegates to support the nomination of her husband if the convention became deadlocked. She lobbied unashamedly, the only woman among approximately 500 men doing the same thing. She disarmed the men she was lobbying by declaring that she wanted her husband to succeed because he wanted it, and by never saying anything sharp or offensive about anyone else.

Equally, the Duchess stayed close to the candidate during the first part of the campaign, conducted mainly from the Harding front porch. She set up photo opportunities, arranging visiting groups carrying slogans and banners on the stone steps of the porch. She even posed herself, smiling gamefully as she tried to hide her swollen ankles and wrinkles: "Come on, boys. I always take a frightful picture and I hate this. But I know you've got to do it." She visited her husband's headquarters almost daily, freely expressing her opinions to her husband's campaign managers, who in turn sought her daily assessment of the previous day's accomplishments, welcoming her as an equal participant. She maintained an easygoing relationship with them, clapping her friend Fred Upham on the shoulder and cracking, "If it had not been for you and me they would have given up the headquarters and quit the fight."

Florence's prominence in the campaign invited attacks on her from the Hardings' political enemies. When opponents dug up the scandal of her relationship with Henry De-Wolfe, she foolishly denied having had a child. Lurid tales made the rounds while the Harding spokesmen struggled to accommodate Florence's various stories. Eventually the issue remained a standoff, neutralized by the Republicans' discovery that the Democratic candidate, James Cox, had also been divorced. Anti-Semitic rumors circulated about Florence's birth family, and prejudice against Roman Catholics prevented her appointment of Kathleen Lawler as her social secretary and caused her to conceal Catholic relatives. The nastiness of the accusations against her provoked her to develop an illusory collection of ancestors and to prattle about her putative maternal French Protestant ancestry. To one reporter the Duchess snapped, "I am 100 percent American. Always remember that."

In fall 1920 the Hardings took their campaign on the road, in a whistle-stop train tour that covered wide segments of the country. Warmly received, Florence sat at the window of the railroad car while Warren was resting, ready to wave to people gathered at stations and road crossings. She studied the reactions of the crowds to Warren's speeches and introduced film stars as campaigners. Throughout the campaign she stressed the importance of the women newly enfranchised by the 19th Amendment, ratified only that year.

Warren won the election, and Florence embraced her new opportunities. Whatever qualms she had about the challenges she faced, the Duchess overcame them, telling a friend, "[Y]ou and I both know if Warren had been defeated I would have been the most miserable woman in the world this morning instead of being the happiest. I am a regular fraud to say that I am scared out of my happiness by the responsibility, even as great as that responsibility is, for I am not. . . ." Everyone expected her to be a powerful influence in the Harding administration. William McNutt of the United News Service editorialized: "Anyone who tries to figure the Harding of the next four years without counting the influence of Mrs. Harding will get a wrong result. They have been, are and will continue to be full partners. . . . With suffrage [for women] a fact in the United States, the first lady of the land, whose husband has been elected by suffrage, will wield an influence second to that of no woman who has ever occupied her position."

Even before the inauguration, the president-elect sought his wife's help in reviewing applicants for public office, relying, as he typically did, on her "keen judgment" of people. In the first flush of the triumph of women's suffrage, the public accepted such a role for the first lady as never before. One newspaper editor argued: "When the people elect a President they at the same time elect a Presidentess and it is shocking to assert that she shall not exercise the natural prerogatives of a Presidentess. . . . [W]e are quite willing to make use of the intuition of the President's wife." Unfortunately, as her biographer Carl Anthony remarks, Florence Harding "was also a bad judge of bad character," as her approval of the men who were soon to involve her husband in scandal would attest.

As expected, Florence Harding was an activist in the White House. Despite her shaky health, she backed many causes, some of them controversial. Foremost among her passions were the veterans of World War I, whose plight was brought to her attention by her friend Evalyn Walsh McLean. The first lady arranged for 20 veterans to ride in the inaugural parade; she visited them in hospitals, sent them cards on their birthdays, and assisted them in financial emergencies. If she saw a man in uniform walking on the street, she gave him a ride, and every year she held a garden party for wounded servicemen from all the hospitals in the area. She also used her considerable influence with the bureaucracy in charge of veterans' affairs: Hundreds of individual veterans' problems were investigated because of her intercession. Florence demanded that "her boys" receive the best care. Largely at her insistence, the president issued an executive order on October 14, 1921, awarding veterans advantages in applying for positions as postmasters.

In addition, the first lady embraced the cause of animal rights, aligning herself with the controversial National Society for the Humane Regulation of Vivisection as well as the more conventional Animal Rescue League and the Society for the Prevention of Cruelty to Animals. She had always loved animals; besides, she argued, "Cruelty begets cruelty; hardness toward animals is certain to breed hardness toward our fellow men. . . . That is why I am always willing to give every encouragement to humane causes." She ordered the removal from the state dining room of all the animal heads that Theodore Roosevelt had shot and hung as trophies, and she refused to attend Wild West shows, rodeos, and other exhibitions that she saw as inflicting pain on animals. She initiated measures to protect the wildlife on the White House grounds and was quite capable of stopping to berate a drayman or cabbie for abusing his horse.

The first lady's own experiences as a single mother and in business had made her a feminist, well aware of the new problems faced by the many women moving into the workplace and confronting the changed world wrought by World War I and its aftermath. "I have such great faith in the women of America," she told Pontiac, Illinois, reporter Irma Skinner, "that I think it is through them that order will come about after the chaotic condition into which our country was thrust as a result of the war." At their request, she advocated for hundreds of individual women—some seeking public jobs, some facing immigration problems, some struggling for pension rights. She even intervened in a New York state case, asking Governor Nathan Miller to commute the death sentence of a woman who had killed her husband in self-defense.

Florence Harding also worked with and for groups of women. She invited women's organizations—including those of African-American and Roman Catholic women—to the White House to encourage them, give them recognition, and, she said, "help the women of the country to understand their government and their duty to government." She raised funds for a free clinic for pregnant women; sat on the board of Sunshine House, which helped "unfortunate and needy" working women—the only Republican among the board members; lobbied for the first federal reformatory exclusively for women prisoners; encouraged women to participate in sports, setting up a White House championship women's tennis match; and demonstrated her faith in women aviators by accepting an offer to fly in a hydroplane piloted by a woman, thereby becoming the first first lady to fly. She was also the first to hold informal press conferences for women reporters. Liberal supporters of birth control criticized her for inviting Roman Catholics to the White House, while its enemies criticized her for not condemning birth control advocate Margaret Sanger.

Florence Harding also urged women's participation in politics. "The time has passed for discussion about the desirability of having the women actively participate in politics," she said. "They *are* in politics, and it is their duty to make their participation effective, and of real service to their country. This necessarily means that much and aggressive effort is needed to maintain their interest, and to inform them concerning issues and public problems." If you are politically ambitious, she told women, work within the party system. "Of course, you must bear in mind that the entrance of women in the political world was so sudden when it finally did come, we must be willing to bide our time a little." The first lady's support of women in politics extended to the aggressive National Woman's Party led by Alice Paul, which, with women's suffrage a reality, had begun working for the passage of an equal rights amendment. Florence accepted an invitation to open and dedicate the party headquarters, thereby enraging Republican National Committee women who believed that the National Woman's Party threatened the two-party system.

The first lady participated in every aspect of her husband's administration. She engaged in frank political discussions with government officials, holding her own with men of such stature as Senator Henry Cabot Lodge. She considered herself a colleague of cabinet members, and the feeling was mutual. Her husband gave her wide latitude, frequently saying, "I'll have to check with the Duchess." She was particularly successful in dealing with the press, talking with them openly, creating photo opportunities for them as no first lady before her had done, and entertaining them privately at the White House.

Less inhibited than her predecessors, the down-to-earth Florence Harding reflected her times. She introduced into the White House such new fads as jazz, mah-jongg, and the radio. She reopened the gates of the "people's house," shut since the United States entered World War I, welcoming tourists into its grounds and guiding tours of the mansion herself. When a maid pulled the curtains to protect her against the gazes of sightseers, the first lady cried, "Let 'em look in if they want. It's their White House!"

Nonetheless, Florence Harding was not universally loved. In the eyes of some of her critics the new first lady lacked "good breeding." For instance, she pronounced her husband's first name *Wurn* or *Wurrun,* and she didn't know how to dress. Her Ohio heartiness, her dowdiness, and her glittering pince-nez did not accord with the standards of Washington society. Alice Roosevelt Longworth sniffed at her "small town goucheries," faulting her as a "nervous, rather excitable woman whose voice easily became a little high-pitched, strident." More substantial criticism attacked her extravagant White House entertaining, her blindness to the corruption of men she recommended for government jobs, and her occasional lapses of judgment—such as sending a check to feed an old horse at a time when striking railroad workers and miners were going hungry. Moreover, Florence could be acrimonious, frequently toward the husband who betrayed her sexually and on occasion toward other people, including those on the "enemies list" she compiled in a little red book, begun back in her days as a Senate wife.

By spring 1923 it was gradually becoming clear that between them the Hardings did not have the ability to govern a nation, nor had they succeeded in finding trustworthy officials. Instead, they had surrounded themselves with looters and extortionists, who among them were bleeding the country. Scandal hovered and would later break about the Teapot Dome and other oil leases; about the "Ohio gang" who were blackmailing violators of laws, especially the prohibition law; and about looting by the Alien Property Custodian and the director of the Veterans' Bureau. The worried presidential couple undertook a grueling transcontinental tour, in the course of which the president contracted pneumonia. He died on August 2.

In a way the Hardings were fortunate. They had been widely popular, and he died before scandal erupted, revealing the treachery and corruption that pervaded his administration. Florence Harding accepted her loss stoically, believing that his death in office was in the stars. Newspapers praised the heroic way she bore her grief, and the *Boston Transcript* editorialized that "If the Constitution permitted . . . she could take the chair vacated by her adored husband and life pal, and pick up the reins where they fell from his lifeless hands and administer the affairs of this great nation with ability, wisdom, justice and in a statesmanlike manner."

The night the president's body lay in the White House, his widow spent part of the night talking to him. Evalyn Walsh McLean heard her say, "No one can hurt you now, Warren." She devoted the short remainder of her life to trying to ensure that that was so. Lurid stories, aggravated by the lack of an autopsy, began to circulate about the president's death. Among them was the allegation that the first lady had administered poison to protect her husband—whose personal repute was as yet untainted—from becoming tarred by the scandals then on the verge of becoming public knowledge. In her widowhood she occupied herself principally with gathering up and destroying all her husband's correspondence, in an effort to protect his reputation and to save him from disgrace.

Although Congress did not grant her the usual presidential widow's pension, the estates of her father and husband had made her wealthy, and she earned an annual salary of $13,300 as a contributing editor of the company that published the *Marion Star*.

For the short time remaining to her after her husband's death, she shifted restlessly between Marion, Ohio, and Washinton, returning to Marion for the last time in July 1924. That year she made her only official appearances as a former first lady, at a congressional tribute to Warren Harding, the funeral of Woodrow Wilson, and the dedication of a Connecticut high school. She died of myocarditis and nephritis on November 21, 1924. That day she had written a check to provide a good Thanksgiving dinner for "her boys" who guarded the Harding vault. There she was buried, beside her husband.

———※———

Many surveys rank Florence Harding near the bottom of all first ladies. Margaret Truman has called her the country's worst first lady, one who was mean-spirited, vengeful, without redeeming qualities of mind or spirit, and consumed by ambition. Indeed, Florence made a crashing mistake in picking as her candidate for president of the United States a man who could win the office but could not perform its duties, and she has shared in the debacle of his reputation. She was also quick to take offense and unforgiving, but she was too complex a woman

to be so abruptly dismissed by her critics. Harding biographer Samuel Hopkins Adams wrote:

> Some part of the growing acrimony which Mrs. Harding exhibited toward her husband, and sometimes toward others, may be attributed to her semi-invalidism. Against this she struggled valiantly.

Her friend Evalyn McLean summed her up as "one of the most vigorous-minded women who ever presided over the household of a president."

This activist first lady, of whom her husband said that she wanted "to be the drum-major in every band that passes," received relatively little criticism during her White House days. In the afterglow of the passage of the 19th amendment, which recognized women as citizens, the country briefly, and for the only time in its history, managed to welcome a first lady with a mind of her own—one willing to use the powers of her position to support her principles.

CHRONOLOGY

1860   *August 15:* Florence Kling is born in Marion, Ohio

1880   *March:* Florence Kling elopes with Henry A. De Wolfe

1880   *September 22:* Florence's son Marshall is born

1882   *December 22:* Henry De Wolfe disappears, leaving no money or explanation

1883   Florence begins to support herself and her son by giving piano lessons

1884   *September:* Florence Kling files for separation from Henry De Wolfe

1885   Florence Kling gives up her son to her father

1886   Florence Kling divorces Henry De Wolfe

1891   *July 8:* Florence Kling marries newspaper editor Warren G. Harding; later that year she takes a full-time position at the *Marion Star* after her husband's nervous breakdown

1899–	Warren Harding serves in the state senate		Warren Harding begins his affair with Nan Britton
1903			
1904–	Warren Harding serves as lieutenant governor	1916	*January 1:* Son Marshall De Wolfe dies
05			
1906	Florence Harding's son Marshall marries Esther Naomi Neely	1920	Warren Harding is elected president of the United States; his wife votes for her husband for president, the first future first lady to be able to do so
1910	Warren Harding loses the race for governor of Ohio	1921	*March 4:* Florence Kling Harding becomes first lady
1911	Florence Harding learns of her husband's affair with Carrie Phillips	1923	*August 2:* Warren Harding dies in office
1914	Warren Harding is elected to the U.S. Senate	1924	*November 21:* Florence Harding dies

---

FURTHER READING

Adams, Samuel Hopkins. *The Incredible Era: The Life and Times of Warren G. Harding.* Boston: Houghton, Mifflin, 1939.

Anthony, Carl Sferrazza. *Florence Harding: The First Lady, the Jazz Age, and the Death of America's Most Scandalous President.* New York: Morrow, 1998.

Daugherty, Harry M. *The Inside Story of the Harding Tragedy.* New York: Churchill, 1932.

Gutin, Myra G. *The President's Partner: The First Lady in the Twentieth Century.* New York: Greenwood, 1989.

McLean, Evalyn Walsh. *Father Struck It Rich.* Boston: Little, Brown, 1935.

GRACE ANNA GOODHUE COOLIDGE
(JANUARY 3, 1879–JULY 8, 1957)
First Lady, August 2, 1923–March 4, 1929

GRACE COOLIDGE
(Library of Congress)

As a middle-class young woman of the Progressive Era (1890–1920), Grace Goodhue Coolidge went to college and then got a job, taking advantage of the opportunities opened up by the 19th-century woman's movement. Moreover, she found a cause—working for the deaf—about which she cared, and which she supported all her adult life. Yet she was no New Woman to strike out on her own. Rather, she unquestioningly obeyed her husband's dictates for her conduct, to an extent that attracted comment and criticism.

———✲———

Grace Anna Goodhue was born on January 3, 1879, in Burlington, Vermont, the only child of Andrew Issachar Goodhue and Lemira Barrett Goodhue. She inherited the happy, gregarious temperament of her father, an engineer

211

and steamboat inspector. Her parents imbued her with the middle-class values of the Puritan ethic, centering their social life on church activities. Her mother made her clothes and taught her the household arts. Despite a spinal curvature that kept her out of school for a year, Grace grew up a lively extrovert who could whistle and throw a ball as straight as a boy. She found schoolwork easy but often neglected it for a church social or a box supper. At some sacrifice her parents gave her "advantages"— piano lessons, voice lessons, elocution lessons. In high school, preferring a Congregational minister, she persuaded her parents to transfer their membership from the Methodist to the Congregational Church. She grew into an attractive young woman, 5'4", with dark hair, gray-green eyes, and a generous mouth.

In 1897, when she was 18, Grace enrolled in the University of Vermont, but problems with her eyes forced her to withdraw at Thanksgiving, to return the next year. Meanwhile, her father was building a new, larger house, finishing off the third floor for the use of Grace and her friends. A classmate, Ivah Gale, came to live with the Goodhues, sharing Grace's bedroom and study. They and other young women founded a chapter of the "fraternity"—as they called it— Pi Beta Phi, an organization in which Grace eventually became regional president and with whose members she kept up a correspondence and a friendship throughout her life. She learned to dance, though she was not permitted to attend dances, skated, tobogganed, sleighed, sang in the glee club, participated in dramatics, wrote poetry, had her share of beaux, and studied enough to graduate. On Sundays she attended the morning church service, stayed for Bible class afterward, and in the evening went to the Christian Endeavor meeting.

After graduation, to her mother's distress, Grace—following in the footsteps of a neighboring young woman whom she admired—left home to train as a teacher of the deaf at the Clarke School in Northampton, Massachusetts. According to report, she was a gifted, empathetic teacher, working first with the primary children and then with those in the intermediate grades. All her life she worked to improve opportunities for the deaf and deepen public understanding of them.

In her second year at Northampton, Grace met Calvin Coolidge, a young lawyer with political ambitions. She caught her first glimpse of him through a window when he was shaving, clad in long johns and a hat which, he later explained, held his hair where he wanted it. Her hilarity at this spectacle caught his attention, and he began to court her. Although—or because—they were of opposite temperaments, they were attracted to each other almost at once. She was merry-hearted and gregarious; he was quiet and uncomfortable in company, but ambitious and determined.

They shared a common ethic and agreed in their ideals. She later wrote:

> Marriage is the most intricate institution set up by the human race. If it is to be a going concern it must have a head. That head should be the member of the firm who assumes the greater responsibility for its continuance. In general this is the husband. His partner should consider well the policies which he advises before taking issue with them. There are adjustments to be made from time to time, and each should make those which contribute to efficiency and permanency. In my humble opinion the woman is by nature the more adaptable of the two and she should rejoice in this and realize that in the exercise of this ability she will obtain not only a spiritual blessing but her own family will rise up and call her blessed. . . . I have such faith in Mr. Coolidge's judgment that if he told me I would die tomorrow morning at ten o'clock, I would believe him.

His proposal, the bare announcement "I'm going to be married to you," set the pattern for their relationship.

Grace's mother disliked Calvin, but her father approved of him. The couple were married on October 4, 1905, in a quiet ceremony at the bride's home. She wore a pearl-gray silk dress with a train for the wedding, and for their immediate departure thereafter a navy-blue broadcloth suit with a silk blouse, a hat tipped over her pompadour with flowers heaped at the back below the brim, and the groom's wedding gift of a gold rope chain with a double locket engraved with her new initials. They honeymooned briefly in Montreal and then hurried back to Northampton, where he was campaigning for election to the school board. They lodged for a time at the Hotel Norwood, and then in a house they rented from a professor on leave, but soon they found a permanent home in half of a double house, for which Calvin chose the furniture.

On September 7, 1906, the Coolidges' first son, John, was born. A few months later, as a new member of the state legislature, Calvin Coolidge began the first of many extended sojourns away from home, as one political office succeeded another: state representative, state senator, president of the state senate, lieutenant governor, and governor. Except for the two years 1910–11, when he was mayor of Northampton, the family stayed at home while Calvin commuted back and forth to Boston. They spent their summers at his father's farm in Plymouth, Vermont.

Another son, Calvin, was born on April 13, 1908. Grace brought up her sons for the most part single-handedly. She put up a tent for them in the backyard and helped them build a playhouse; taught them to play baseball, in the process developing a lifelong passion for the sport; and helped them construct "cars" out of wooden boxes and roller-skate wheels. So completely were they her charge that when their father stayed alone with them such a minor accident as a boy's falling out of bed would cause him to summon her home.

The Coolidges seldom entertained. Although she was never a clubwoman, Grace took part in some of the activities of other young Northampton matrons in the community and particularly at church. During World War I she joined the other ladies in Red Cross work and bond drives. She did not play cards, but friends invited her to their card parties and she took her sewing. She scrimped and saved, sewed the babies' layettes and her own clothes, and darned her husband's socks. He brought her 52 pairs to darn when they were first married and warned her that there were more to come. When she asked him if he married her to get his socks darned, he replied, "No, but I find it mighty handy."

When Calvin was elected governor of Massachusetts in 1918, the family still remained in Northampton. Social obligations necessitated that the governor's lady visit Boston more frequently than in the past, often accompanied by her sons during school vacations. The pattern of living apart was broken, however, only by Calvin's election to the vice presidency of the United States in 1921. At that point the Coolidges entered their sons in boarding school, and Grace joined her husband in Washington, D.C.

Inexperienced in formal social events, either as a hostess or as a guest, she was fortunate to be mentored by Lois Kimsey Marshall, wife of the outgoing vice president, and by Emily Clark Stearns, the wife of one of Calvin's wealthy backers, Frank Waterman Stearns. With their guidance plus her own sunny disposition, wit, and genuine enjoyment of people, Grace became popular almost at once, despite the limitations imposed by her husband's decision to reject Frank Stearns's offer to buy them a Washington house and instead to live in the Willard Hotel. She was good with names and faces and completely unaffected; when reporters asked how much she would entertain, she replied, "We haven't entertained much. We never could afford it, but I'm sure I shall enjoy it." The world leaders she met impressed her as "just folks with the rest of us." As Stearns commented, "One of [Calvin Coolidge's] greatest assets is Mrs. Coolidge. She will make friends wherever she goes, and she will not meddle with the conduct of his office." While the Harding administration was embroiled in blatant corruption, the Coolidges had the good sense not to gossip and to tend to their own affairs.

On August 2, 1923, the death of President Warren G. Harding catapulted Calvin Coolidge into the presidency. Both the Coolidges were very much aware of the dignity of the office, which they did everything to protect—even, at the president's insistence, eating their meals in the state dining room and requiring that the family dress for dinner every night. In the midst of the raucous Jazz Age that followed World War I, the Coolidges ran a staid White House. Grace wrote of her entry into it: "This was the wife of the President of the United States and she took precedence over me; my personal likes and dislikes must be subordinated to the consideration of those things which were required of her. It therefore became quite natural to refer to him as 'the president' and to address him as 'Mr. President' in the presence of others." Her husband told her nothing about his working life. When she asked for his schedule, he responded, "Grace, we don't give that out promiscuously." She was driven to postpone decisions about her own schedule until she made sure that he did not need her; often she dressed for an occasion and waited with her hat on, not knowing whether or not she was to accompany him. On the other hand, he sometimes made appointments for her without consulting her. "I am rather proud," she wrote, "of the fact that after nearly a quarter of a century of marriage, my husband feels free to make his decisions and act upon them without consulting me or giving me advance information concerning them."

All their married life Calvin Coolidge made almost all decisions, great or small, from menus and guest lists to where and how they lived. She went where he allowed and returned home at the hour he set. He had only to say "Better not" to dissuade her from a course of action. He forbade her to dance in public, to drive a car, to have her hair bobbed, to wear culottes, to ride horseback, and to fly. His permission was required for her to visit her parents. For the most part she accepted his rule unquestioningly, covering up any embarrassment she may have felt. Once, however, from the White

House she wrote a friend to explain that she could not accept an invitation to the Army-Navy game: "Of course, if I went I should have to go with 'bells on' and there's no fun in that. Couldn't get permission, anyhow. I guess nobody but you has a real idea of how shut in and hemmed about I feel. Well, I'm not complaining. I'm only telling you." Once she rather wistfully speculated that he had a low opinion of her education. "Sometimes," she said, "I wonder if Mr. Coolidge would have talked with me more freely if I had been of a more serious turn of mind." He preferred to talk to her about family matters, to joke and tease, and to reminisce about his boyhood.

Part of their relationship can be explained by the period in which they lived, when women's accomplishments and appearance were fair game for critical male comment. Over and over he told jokes at her expense that a woman at the end of the 20th century would find humiliating, and another woman even of her time might have found boorish. He talked, for instance, of selling her piecrust to the road commissioner to pave the roads, and he dropped her biscuits on the floor, stamping his foot to create a thud when they hit. He ignored most birthdays and anniversaries, seldom giving her anything, even on Christmas. He never kissed her when they met or parted, whereas she warmly hugged her friends. On the rare occasions when she openly disagreed with him, he punished her with silence.

Yet beyond question Calvin Coolidge loved his wife. She could and did tease him as no one else dared. He was extremely dependent on her; in one of his frequent bouts of dyspepsia—brought on, some said, by his constant nibbling on raw peanuts—she confided to a friend that he "would hardly let me out of the room in which he was sitting for three days." White House seamstress Lillian Parks thought that President Coolidge made a surrogate mother out of his wife, calling her "Mama" (she also calling him "Poppa"), bragging to her, and seeking her approval. He took pride in her beauty; chose hats and shoes for her; and in the

White House, stringent as he was in his economies, encouraged her to buy expensive dresses, and lots of them. He never wanted her to wear the same gown twice. In his autobiography he wrote, "We thought we were made for each other. For almost a quarter of a century she has borne with my infirmities, and I have rejoiced in her graces."

Calvin Coolidge is generally acknowledged to have been a passive president, doing little to resolve problems and nothing to arouse controversy. Grace Coolidge behaved similarly. She gave no speeches; once, when women reporters pressed her to speak, she gave a five-minute talk with the hand signals of the deaf. She endorsed no causes, pled no one's case, and exerted no influence. She followed her husband's advice: "I think you will find that you will get along at this job fully as well if you do not try anything new." Within her limited orbit, however, she charmed everyone who met her and achieved a popularity greater than that of most first ladies. Even Alice Roosevelt Longworth, often a sharp critic of first ladies, applauded her.

Grace was a model of domesticity, yet she did not censure the many women then entering the workplace and speaking up on politics. "Everyone talks of the restlessness of women since the war," she said. "Soon there will not be an intelligent woman who is content to do nothing but live a social life." Nonetheless, both the Coolidges disapproved of the tactics of Alice Paul, whose radical maneuvers had helped secure the passage of the women's suffrage amendment. Now, in the 1920s, Paul was fighting against protective legislation for women workers and for women's rights to choose to work at night and to work overtime, a position with which the president strongly disagreed.

Calvin's propensity for checking his wife's mail, guest lists, seating charts, and menus and for prowling the White House kitchens and pantry to ensure that nothing was wasted presumably lightened the first lady's duties. In the mornings she arranged flowers for her own room and the west sitting room and did her mail, answering many letters in her own hand

or later on a typewriter and leaving others to her secretary. Then she went for a brisk walk of several miles and sometimes shopped. In the afternoons she received delegations, groups, and individuals and posed for photo opportunities. Twice a week during the social season, at tea, she received groups of 25 or 30 people who had requested invitations through friends, going around the circle to speak with each guest. During Lent she enjoyed giving musicales, with tea afterward in the state dining room. Thus, the Coolidges entertained extensively—some say more so than any preceding presidential couple. The first lady often invited stars of the theatre to the White House and attended symphonies and plays, breaking precedent by sitting in the orchestra rather than in a box. She loved movies and read popular books.

Grace Coolidge kept a small menagerie in the White House, including many birds, an assortment of dogs, and a pet raccoon, some of which terrorized servants and visitors. She enjoyed these animals, especially the dogs, to the point of fatuity. She had a calling card engraved for one dog and left it with her own when she called on intimate friends. She also sent friends' pets greetings from her dogs.

While the president cultivated a reputation for eccentricity, his wife grew expert at covering up his gaffes. She treated his long silences as jokes, recounting such times as when a hostess told him that she had bet that she could get more than two words out of him, and he replied, "You lose." When at a White House dinner he stood up to leave before the last course was served, the first lady committed what she herself described as a grave social error when she reminded him that his guests had not finished. "I have," said he, and stumped off. She laughed and teased the ladies who had been seated on his right and left because they had failed to rein him in.

His eccentricity showed in the economies he advocated and practiced, both in his official and his personal life. On March 4, 1925, for instance, he staged a minimalist inauguration and vetoed the traditional White House

Grace Coolidge with pet raccoon *(Library of Congress)*

luncheon after the swearing-in ceremony. Instead the Coolidges and the vice-presidential couple lunched on sandwiches and coffee, leaving the cabinet members and their wives waiting downstairs, unfed—a dilemma from which they were rescued only by the unauthorized intervention of the president's military aide. The Coolidges received the governors in the late afternoon and that night held a small dinner for family and intimate friends, but no inaugural ball. On that occasion, however, Grace was, as always, beautifully dressed. She was known for her wardrobe; although even in the White House she made some of her dresses herself, her closets held many expensive gowns. Slim, graceful, and easy to fit, she wore her clothes well, favoring soft feminine styles, with trains, rich materials, fans, and picture hats. Following her

husband's preferences, she chose skirts mid-calf or to the floor, seldom wore black, and used little makeup.

Though warned that the White House was so dilapidated as to pose a danger to its inhabitants, the Coolidges did little about it until after the 1924 election, when they installed a new vacuum cleaner, electric refrigerators, water softeners, and an incinerator, and replaced the elevator. In spring 1927 they removed to 15 Dupont Circle so that the basic framework of the mansion could be repaired. Unfortunately, they were badly advised, and the renovations they undertook added extra weight that eventually threatened the building with collapse. Nevertheless, the first lady greatly enjoyed the new sunroom built over the south portico, which she called her "sky parlor." Disappointed by the lack of original furniture in the White House, Grace went so far as to get Congress to pass a resolution authorizing the acceptance of period furniture, particularly colonial furniture, as gifts, but the public did not respond—perhaps because the president and first lady did not personally plead the case to them. She crocheted a bedspread for the Lincoln bed, hoping that successive first ladies would emulate her in leaving some such memento in the White House.

Weekends the Coolidges frequently entertained on the presidential yacht, sailing on Saturday afternoon and returning Monday morning. The president wished to get in touch with the people, and to this end they spent their summers in different parts of the country: Vermont, Massachusetts, Wisconsin, and the Black Hills of South Dakota. On these vacations Grace, clad in a long bathing suit and black stockings, learned after a fashion to do the Australian crawl, paddle a canoe, and row a boat. Perhaps her deepest embarrassment as first lady came when she got lost on a forest walk and was late for lunch. Her husband thereupon transferred the Secret Service man who had accompanied her, because, the president said, the man ought to have known enough to prevent their becoming lost. Nevertheless the action roused suspicions of jealousy. Even about such a popular first lady, wild rumors circulated: She was pregnant, or, alternatively, she planned to divorce her husband when they left the White House.

The great tragedy of the Coolidges' White House years was the death of their 16-year-old son Calvin from blood poisoning in 1924. They did not grasp the seriousness of an infection on his foot until too late, and in those days before antibiotics the doctors could do nothing to save him. He died in agony, pleading with his father to help him. His parents buried him in Plymouth, Vermont, the home of his paternal ancestors, and in his memory they planted a tree from Plymouth on the White House grounds, where they could easily see it. Both the Coolidge boys were good sons: In a letter that came to light after his death, young Calvin had modestly

reminded his correspondent that he could not claim the title of "first boy"; his father, not he, was the president, and "the first boy of the land would be some boy who had distinguished himself through his own actions." Grace came to think of her dead son as among the saints. As she wrote in a poem that she published to help other grieving parents, she believed that he would guide her own way into heaven.

The president did not forewarn his wife of his famous announcement "I do not choose to run" that prevented his nomination in 1928, nor did he inform her of it after the fact. She learned about it more or less by chance several days after it had become public. After they left the White House on March 4, 1929, the Coolidges returned to the nine-room house and the life they had known in Northampton. The former president wrote a newspaper column and magazine articles for sizable amounts of cash. The former first lady wrote about her Washington experiences and published poems in popular magazines, but she also resumed her former activities in the local church and the community. She did her own shopping, sewed, knitted socks, and did jigsaw puzzles and doublecrostics. She employed the same household helper she had had for years, and a neighbor woman helped with the cleaning.

Their peaceful days were studded with pleasant events. Grace received an honorary doctorate from Smith College acknowledging her as an outstanding wife and mother. She quipped that it should have been a D.D.—doctor of domesticity. On September 24, 1929, John Coolidge married Florence Trumbull, daughter of the governor of Connecticut. Calvin and Grace Coolidge made an extensive tour of the American South and West, including a weeklong stay at William Randolph Hearst's fabled San Simeon.

Only when they found that their longtime home gave them no privacy did the Coolidges leave it. The former president could not even sit on his front porch without sightseers' clogging the road. They found the privacy they craved in The Beeches, a larger house situated on a seven-acre estate overlooking the Connecticut River, still close enough to Northampton that Grace could walk downtown.

When Calvin Coolidge died suddenly on January 5, 1933, leaving her some $700,000, his widow described herself as "just a lost soul. Nobody is going to believe how I miss being told what to do. My father always told me what I had to do. Then Calvin told me what I had to do." Nonetheless, she undertook some of his responsibilities, taking his place as trustee of Mercersburg Academy, the Clarke School for the Deaf, and a local educational and recreational facility. From 1935 to 1952 she presided over the Clarke School board and helped to raise large sums of money for the institution. She followed closely the experiments with electronic aids for the deaf, encouraged the broadening of training for teachers of the deaf, and advocated lip-reading, believing that signing limited the world of the deaf. However, she still preferred to work quietly behind the scenes, avoiding what she called the "exploitation" of her name.

As a distinguished citizen of Northampton, Grace handed out Eagle Scout badges and launched local Christmas seal campaigns. She enjoyed her son's family and treated herself to baseball games and a European tour of 10 countries. Rumor had it that she would remarry, and she did briefly consider a proposal from a prominent Republican before deciding to refuse him. Although she had worked for Herbert Hoover's reelection in 1932, she liked Eleanor Roosevelt and spent a night in the Roosevelt White House, but for the most part she remained uninterested in politics. In 1936 she sold The Beeches and built another house in Northampton with no basement, a small reception room and several service rooms on the ground floor, her living quarters on the second floor, and the servants' quarters on the third.

For years Grace Coolidge had advocated world peace, but she spoke out early for American intervention in World War II and worked hard as a private citizen to do her bit for the war effort. She walked to the stores to save gas, vol-

unteered at the local Red Cross, supported war bond drives, entertained soldiers, and raised funds to bring child refugees from Germany to the United States. She also acted as honorary chair of the Queen Wilhelmina fund for Dutch victims of the Nazis, and of the Hampshire County Fight for Freedom Committee. Most of all, she acted as hostess for the personnel of the navy's Women in Voluntary Service to America (WAVES), whose officers' candidate school was stationed at Smith College, and even lent her house rent-free to the commanding officer.

After the war, Grace had more time for recreation—movies, the theater, reading the bestsellers of the day, and listening to comedy shows on the radio. Her heart had troubled her for several years, and in 1954 her health began to fail. In her last years she lived at Road Forks with her girlhood friend Ivah Gale, a young girl to help them, and her chauffeur. She died on July 8, 1957.

———— ⁓ ————

Grace Goodhue Coolidge was a first lady who was all the public and her husband asked: gracious, charming, beautiful, elegantly dressed, devoted to her family and to her animals, apolitical, passive, and utterly noncontroversial—a round peg in a round hole. She supported her favorite cause only quietly and privately. She did nothing to expand the office of first lady and nothing to disturb anyone. A foreign diplomat gracefully remarked, "To look at her is gladness enough." More prosaically, popular entertainer Will Rogers dubbed her "Public Female Favorite No. 1."

CHRONOLOGY

1879   *January 3:* Grace Anna Goodhue is born in Burlington, Vermont

1902   Grace Goodhue graduates from the University of Vermont with a Ph.B. (bachelor of philosophy)

1905	*October 4:* Grace Goodhue marries Calvin Coolidge; they settle in Northampton, Massachusetts
1906	Calvin Coolidge is elected to the Massachusetts House of Representatives
	September 7: Son John is born
1907	*January 1:* Calvin Coolidge enters the state legislature
1908	Calvin Coolidge is elected to the General Court
	April 13: Son Calvin is born
1910, 1911	Calvin Coolidge is elected mayor of Northampton, Massachusetts
1911	Calvin Coolidge is elected to the Massachusetts senate
1913	Calvin Coolidge is elected president of the Massachusetts senate
1915	Grace becomes eastern regional president of Pi Beta Phi
1915, 1916, 1917	Calvin Coolidge is elected lieutenant governor of Massachusetts

1918	Calvin Coolidge is elected governor of Massachusetts
1921	The Coolidges move to Washington, D.C., when Calvin Coolidge is elected vice president of the United States
1923	*August 2:* Grace Coolidge becomes first lady when, after President Harding's death, Calvin Coolidge takes the oath of office in his father's Vermont house
1924	*July 7:* Son Calvin dies
	Calvin Coolidge is elected for a second term as president
1929	*March 4:* The Coolidges return to Northampton, Massachusetts
	September 24: Son John marries Florence Trumbull, daughter of the governor of Connecticut
1932	Grace Coolidge works in the Republican campaign for the reelection of Herbert Hoover
1933	*January 5:* Calvin Coolidge dies
1935	Grace Coolidge becomes president of the board of the Clarke School for the Deaf
1957	*July 8:* Grace Coolidge dies of heart disease

FURTHER READING

Burns, Paul A. "Profile of the First Lady," *New Yorker* (May 15, 1926): 17–18.

Coolidge, Grace Goodhue. *Grace Coolidge: An Autobiography,* ed. Lawrence E. Wikander and Robert H. Ferrell. Worland, Wyoming: High Plains, 1992.

Gutin, Myra G. *The President's Partner: The First Lady in the Twentieth Century.* New York: Greenwood, 1989.

Ross, Ishbel. *Grace Coolidge and Her Era: The Story of a President's Wife.* New York: Dodd, Mead, 1962.

White, William Allen. *A Puritan in Babylon.* New York: Macmillan, 1938.

LOU HENRY HOOVER

(MARCH 29, 1874–JANUARY 7, 1944)
First Lady, March 4, 1929–March 4, 1933

LOU HOOVER
(Library of Congress)

Lou Henry Hoover was a child of the Progressive Era (1890–1920) in which she matured. In her late teens she trained as a teacher, a practice by then fairly common for the daughter of advanced middle-class parents who wanted to ensure that she could earn her own living. Thereafter, however, she took a degree in geology, a field then all but closed to women. Although she centered her life on Herbert Hoover and their sons, she supported and supplemented her husband's work with her own, both in the mining industry and in relief work. Together they published a scholarly translation of an important 16th-century mining text. Born gifted and to a prosperous family, she used her talents to the benefit of humanity but never tested their limits.

Lou Henry was born on March 29, 1874, in Waterloo, Iowa, the older of the two children of banker Charles Delano Henry and Florence Weed Henry. When Lou was 10 years old, the family moved to California, where they lived for several years in Whittier and then in Monterey. She adored her father, who taught her to share his enjoyment of outdoor life—camping, riding horseback, hunting, fishing, and studying rocks, trees, and flowers. As she got older, he explained the banking business to her, invited her to stop at the bank after school, and showed her how to keep books. Her mother taught her cooking and sewing and encouraged her to help care for her sister Jean, eight years her junior. Lou liked to read and presided over a literary club. Her nominally Episcopalian family did not object when she went to Quaker meetings with her friends.

After graduating from high school, she studied teaching, first in Los Angeles and then in San Jose, where she graduated at 19. That summer a lecture by geologist John Casper Banner of Stanford University determined her to enroll in his department. At Stanford Lou also studied Latin, participated in sports, and made friends among both faculty and students—among them Herbert Hoover, then a senior and an assistant to Dr. Banner. The only woman in her classes, Lou was well-accepted: She was bright, she worked hard, she could outwalk many of the men, and the students voted her "all right" with them. She fended off the question of whether she would marry by saying that she wanted a man who loved mountains, rocks, and oceans—a man like her father.

Bert Hoover was particularly attracted to the tall, lithe young woman, and she to him. They saw a great deal of each other throughout their common year at Stanford, and by the time he graduated they knew that one day they would marry. Meanwhile, he went off to work as a mining engineer, and Lou continued her studies. When she graduated in 1898, she announced to her family her intentions of marrying Bert. She taught briefly in Monterey, until he was offered a job—with a raise—in China.

He arrived in Monterey on January 31, 1899, and 10 days later they were married. Lou had decided to join the Society of Friends (the Quakers), to which Bert belonged, but the young couple could find no Quaker meeting nearby. (She never fulfilled her resolution to become a Quaker.) In the event a young Roman Catholic Spanish priest, a friend of the Henry family, presided over the wedding, held at noon in the Henry home. The bride wore a double-breasted brown travel suit with a white blouse, and her sister played the violin. That afternoon the newlyweds took the train for San Francisco, cheered on in Palo Alto by her college friends. Their families traveled to San Francisco to see them off as they sailed for China, carrying books on the Chinese language and culture. During the long sea journey, Lou Hoover, with her facility for language, began to learn spoken and written Chinese.

Thus began a notably happy marriage, in which the pair shared work and play. In China they settled in Tientsin (present-day Tianjin), near Bert's work. They lived in the large foreign colony, and Lou explored the territory until she found a brick Western-style house with a veranda and tile roof, where she enjoyed establishing the first of their many homes. As she put it, she never saw a room that she did not want to do something to. Unfazed by the complexities of setting up housekeeping in a foreign culture, she quickly decided to "board with the cook," giving him a sum of money from which he was to feed them and take his pay—the "squeeze." She also employed house servants, rickshaw men, and a gardener, arranged to have furniture built, and bought household goods from the local shops, where she admired the Ming dynasty porcelain that she later collected. Then as throughout their lives the Hoovers chose their friends for their interest, not their rank, and they loved having guests. Constrained though she was by the hierarchies of the foreign colony, Lou kept her entertaining as simple and informal as she could.

Evenings the pair studied mining laws. Lou helped her husband collect, translate, and summarize Chinese mining works, and they cataloged the mining laws of the world. Sometimes she accompanied him on trips, riding mules, protected by guards against bandits, and staying in primitive local quarters. She took lessons in Chinese, soon learning enough to facilitate their travels and gaining an insight into the Chinese character that her husband never did acquire. Together they spent weekends exploring Peking (present-day Beijing) and took a boat trip on the Yellow River. When the Boxer Rebellion broke out, endangering all foreigners, she resisted her husband's efforts to send her to a place of safety. During the month that they were besieged, she armed herself with a revolver and rode her bicycle to take hot tea to the home-guard defenders, gathered bed linens for bandages for the wounded, and took her turn on fire watches. She had to sweep spent bullets off their front porch, their house was shelled, and a bullet punctured her bicycle tire while she was riding it. They survived unharmed, despite the publication of her obituary in the Monterey paper, and later Lou said that she would not have missed the experience.

Driven from China, the Hoovers decided on London as a base of operations. The center of the developing mining industry, it was the right place for them to be at the time. They kept up on the American news and dreamed of a return to a California home someday. Bert's work took him all around the world, and as often as she could, his wife followed, always returning to a London apartment near Hyde Park Gate. When he briefly went back to China, Lou and her sister Jean lived in Yokohama, Japan, where they donned kimonos, learned the tea ceremony, and marveled at Japan's rapid modernization. More trips ensued—to Burma (present-day Myanmar) and to Australia by way of California. Wherever they went, the Hoovers collected artifacts, studied cultures, and studied the political situation.

Even the birth of Herbert Clark Hoover, Jr., on August 4, 1903, did not deter his mother. With improvised equipment and a nurse willing to accompany them, she took the baby along, beginning when he was five weeks old. In the first year of his life, young Herbert circumnavigated the world twice. By the time Allan Henry Hoover was born on July 17, 1907, Lou had the expertise and the equipment to continue their travels unfazed. When faced with a year in Mandalay, with its surrounding jungles, she consulted a child specialist, asking him every question she could think of about the children's development and what food, clothing, and medicines they might require; recorded his answers; stocked up on supplies; and off they went. Once there, she helped her husband develop decent housing and sanitation for the mine workers and their families.

The Hoovers had to deal with the moral dilemmas that confronted them as his rapid advance in management increased Bert's wealth and responsibilities. Lou took pride in his efforts to stabilize the mining industry, to ensure the participation in management of local talent, and to improve workers' conditions, saying, "You are a good human engineer, too." When the financial manager of the company absconded with $700,000 in company funds, she agreed with her husband and the other officers of the company that the loss must be covered, even at the risk of their own fortunes; moreover, she personally gave an allowance to the criminal's family. When the Hoovers later put together a book of his lectures, they included a chapter on the moral obligations of mining engineers.

The similarity of their training and interests enabled Lou to do research for her husband. While working in the British Museum, she found a copy of the standard 16th-century mining manual, George Bauer's *Agricola de re Metallica*, until then lost to the profession because of the difficulty of the language and Bauer's propensity for inventing new Latin words for new processes; even the woodcuts had lost meaning for modern readers. The Hoovers undertook to translate the work, she concentrating on the language and he on laboratory experiments to test Bauer's findings. This five-year project, which took them to Germany, resulted in the 1912 publication at their own expense of a scholarly translation that reproduced the vellum and woodcuts of the original. They gave away about half of the 3,000 copies to mining students and experts.

In 1908 Bert started his own consulting company, and the Hoovers rented the Red House, a large dwelling near Kensington Gardens that could hold their boys' menagerie of pets and their own many books. The family could return to this London home after their trips to Ceylon, the Malay Peninsula, the United States, Japan, Siberia, and throughout Europe. To enable the boys to get an American education, the Hoovers also rented a cottage on the Stanford campus in California and bought property nearby on San Juan Hill, where eventually they would build their own home. Lou included in her sons' training the kind of outdoor experiences that she had so enjoyed with her father in her girlhood, and Bert engaged them in such engineering feats as building tree houses and digging tunnels.

The family was back in London when the guns of August 1914 signaled the beginning of World War I. Despite all her travels, Lou had made a place for the family in the London community through both frequent entertaining and community activities; she had, for example, served as president of the American Women's Club there. The Hoovers now immediately began helping as many as possible of the 70,000 Americans stranded in Europe by the war's outbreak, many of them short of funds in an economy that rejected anything but the local currency. Combining his own cash and what he could gather from friends, Bert began lending them money, arranging for them to obtain cash on their credits and helping them book transportation home, while Lou rallied "half a dozen women whom [sic] I knew would keep their heads and could work" to help women and children unaccompanied by men. They found boarding places and collected clothes for the Americans, helped them locate relatives, and even arranged tours to amuse them while they waited for a ship. Miraculously, 40,000 U.S. citizens were sent home in three weeks. The

Hoovers themselves, who had earlier booked passage on two ships, had no time to think of their own situation.

Finally, Lou and the boys sailed on October 3, while Bert stayed behind to head up Belgian relief, some of which he financed himself, taking no salary for his work. Concerned for their sons' safety and determined to have them rooted in America, but wishing for a united family, the Hoovers kept them now in Palo Alto, now in London. During the war, Lou crisscrossed the dangerous North Atlantic several times. In her London stays she acted as accountant for American Women's War Relief funds, chaired a committee to establish free canteens for soldiers in London railroad stations, and worked to maintain an American Women's Hospital, operate a fleet of motor ambulances, and set up economic relief (for example, a knitting factory) for unemployed British women. She also made several trips to the Continent to be with her husband. In the United States she divided her time between caring for her sons and fund-raising for war relief—though, she said, public speaking scared her to death. Nonetheless, she persuaded her audiences to contribute shiploads of supplies and the Rockefeller Foundation to pay the freight.

America's entrance into the war in spring 1917 brought Lou and her sons back to the States. Shortly thereafter, the family moved to Washington when President Woodrow Wilson appointed Herbert Hoover food administrator for the nation, even while Bert continued to conduct Belgian relief. Bert assigned his wife the task of encouraging American women to plant gardens, preserve food, and cut down consumption. She secured the help of housewives, restaurants, and food merchants to eliminate waste; her own household, of course, set the example.

At this time Lou Hoover also volunteered to lead a troop of Girl Scouts—her introduction to the work to which she later dedicated so much of her life. The movement, she believed, built the character of young girls and developed their initiative: "It teaches play, individual helpfulness, and citizenship." She hiked with her own and other troops, folk-danced with them, visited them in summer camps, planted war gardens with them, and attended regional conferences.

The plight of ill-housed women workers in wartime Washington evoked Lou's sympathy. Finding a Progressive Era solution in the cooperative arrangements for working women called "Jane [Addams] Clubs," she organized women government employees into "girls' clubs" and rented inexpensive quarters for them. When she put a cafeteria into the food administration building, so many other government workers ate there that it made a profit, which she used for other facilities for women war workers. During the flu epidemic of 1918, she set up medical care for the women in their clubs, and after the war she helped some of them find new jobs.

At war's end in November 1918, Lou Hoover saw her husband off to another stint of war relief work in Europe. Then she headed for California, put the boys in school there, and set about sketching plans for the family's dream house. "Our house must be an elastic thing," she told them, "never entirely finished, always growing with the needs of our family and be adaptable to our changing needs." She built an eclectic, fireproof house with flat roofs and terraces, on one of which she placed a fireplace, on another a tennis court, and on yet another a swimming pool. She planned multipurpose rooms; for example, the dining room, a step up from the living room, could also be used as a stage.

Meanwhile, Lou had to set up another home, in a New York apartment in the Waldorf Tower, to accommodate her husband's new work with the European Children's Relief program. Commuting between the two coasts, she helped Bert with fund-raising. In New York she devised banquets with an invisible guest, symbolized by an empty high chair. The kind of food being offered undernourished European children was served on tin dishes at rough board tables, for which the diners paid $1,000 a plate.

In spring 1921 the Hoovers faced yet another move when President Warren G. Harding appointed Herbert Hoover secretary of commerce. In the pattern that he had been following since the outbreak of World War I, Bert again chose public service rather than the enormous salary and opulent lifestyle that could have been his in private industry. The Hoovers made this decision, even though during the war years they had diminished their fortune by their charities.

Lou set about filling their spacious new house at 2300 S Street with flowers and vines and installing Japanese goldfish in the garden pond. Her sons brought along their numerous pets, though their mother finally drew the line on discovering alligators in her bathtub. Among their guests the Hoovers now numbered members of Congress, the cabinet, and even the president and the first lady, as well as friends from Europe and Asia. "I never entertain," said the hostess. "I just ask people to come in to see us and we enjoy each other." Never fazed, she often improvised last-minute menu changes to feed the unexpected guests about whom her husband had forgotten to tell her.

Lou encouraged amateur athletics for girls and women, ultimately becoming the only woman officer of the National Amateur Athletic Federation. In 1923 she formed its women's division into the National Woman's Athletic Association, working to promote physical training, though she opposed competitive professional athletics for women. She urged women to enter politics, famously remarking that "Bad men are elected by good women who stay away from the polls." A good political party, she believed, needs "as many feminine as masculine minds." On the other hand, she had never been a radical suffragist: "I just thought that when a majority of us really believed that we should have the vote we could sit down and talk it over with our fathers, our husbands, and our brothers. I never thought that women were downtrodden by the men before they had the vote. The main reason I wanted it was because I do think it is a good thing for laws affecting the community and the nation to be discussed over the dining table and in the library of the home."

Lou was a gentle, moderate feminist. As she put it, "I never can feel I can play the 'Progress of Women' against the 'Abstract Right for Humanity.'" Women should have professions, she said, though never at the cost of neglecting their families. She described the woman without a career as "lazy. The modern home is so small there is little work to do. The baby? It isn't a baby for long. There is no reason why a girl should get rusty in her profession during the five or six years she is caring for a small child." She herself never held a paid job (except for brief months of teaching), never ran a household without servants, and never cared for a small child without the help of a nurse.

She concentrated on training women rather than on expanding opportunities for them. For three decades she employed her abilities in the service of the Girl Scouts, seeing in it a way "to develop wise and resourceful citizens." The organization became for a time the most effective group motivating young girls to learn a variety of skills, enjoy outdoor life, and develop initiative.

In summer 1923, at the Hardings' invitation, the Hoovers accompanied them on a cross-country trip, during which the president died. Lou comforted Florence Harding, traveling with her from the west coast back across the country and then to the Harding home in Marion, Ohio. After she returned to Washington, Lou broadened her public activities to include work for international peace. The scandals of the Harding administration prompted her to urge women to work for law enforcement, particularly through the General Federation of Women's Clubs. Many organizations sought her services as a speaker. She pled with delegates to the National Congress of Mothers and Parent-Teachers Associations to help improve the public schools in the District of Columbia. In fall 1924 she took on the task of fund-raising for the Visiting Nurse Society.

After President Calvin Coolidge announced that he did not choose to run for reelection in 1928, Herbert Hoover entered the presidential race, with the wholehearted support of his wife and sons. She toured the country with and without him, jesting that "I enjoy campaigning because my husband makes the speeches and I receive the roses." He won in a landslide, and his wife proudly rejoiced. The rain that fell on the Hoover inaugural on March 4, 1929, did not darken the spirits of those who attended the reception immediately after the parade—among them 700 friends who had worked with the Hoovers on war relief—or of those who danced at the inaugural ball. The Hoovers themselves had every reason to anticipate the same successes and happiness that they had known throughout their married lives. The nation was enjoying an economic boom, and it had elected as its leader a defender of free enterprise.

Lou Hoover was the most cosmopolitan first lady ever to step into the White House. She had traveled and lived all over the world, in all sorts of places, and had studied their cultures. Most recently, as the wife of the president-elect, she had toured South America for six weeks with her husband. She had met and entertained hundreds of influential people, both formally and casually, on planned occasions and on the spur of the moment. She had some facility in several modern languages. All her married life she had run households with staff. She had experienced life in Washington as the wife of an important official, whose work she had followed closely and assisted. She had built an impressive record as a volunteer, with decorations and honorary degrees in recognition of her accomplishments. The *Washington Post* described her as "a very handsome woman who looks younger than her years except for prematurely gray hair, which she wears coronet fashion around her head, and holds her slender body in an attitude of erect alertness . . . [with] the unconscious grace of movement of an athlete and out-of-doors woman." She dressed expensively, preferring simple, well-made clothes but leaning toward somber colors.

With practiced ease Lou set about establishing yet another family home in the private quarters of the White House. She gave them a touch of California, with flowers, birdcages, vines, and summer furniture. On the other hand, her sense of history prompted her to have pieces of the Monroe French furniture copied for the Rose Drawing Room (paying the bills from her own funds), and to surround the Lincoln bed with mid-19th-century bureaus and chairs. For her husband, who chose Lincoln's study to use as his own, she recreated the decor exactly as it had been in Lincoln's time, ransacking the storerooms for four of the original chairs and negotiating the transfer of Lincoln's work table from Hartford, Connecticut, back to the White House.

Three young secretaries assisted the first lady with her duties. She kept on all the White House staff and tried to make their quarters more comfortable. Nevertheless, and despite her kindness to them when they were ill or troubled, many of them found her difficult to work for. She approached household management and formal entertainments in the same scientific spirit that she brought to her studies, working out an elaborate system of hand signals to give the servants instructions, and she set up reviews of formal events. Because the Hoovers liked their privacy, the servants whispered over their meals and hid in closets at the approach of the president or first lady. Some felt repressed, not trusted to exercise their own judgment, while others felt overburdened by sudden influxes of unexpected guests, for, just as in all their other homes, the Hoovers filled the White House with openhanded hospitality. Reportedly they dined alone only on their wedding anniversaries. Sometimes they invited so many dinner guests that the president hosted one table in the state dining room and the first lady another in the family dining room.

After the Great Depression of 1929 struck the nation, the president worked obsessively. His wife suggested a retreat where they could enjoy the casual, outdoor life they both loved. They found one about five hours away by car,

in the Blue Ridge Mountains. She designed and had constructed a main building surrounded by several log cabins, all at the Hoovers' expense; the camp was later given to the nation to become part of Shenandoah National Park. It was one of many of their gifts to the nation. Herbert Hoover took no salary as president, and from their own resources the Hoovers supplemented the government allowances for the operation and furnishing of the White House. They also built and staffed a school for the children of the impoverished area that surrounded the camp.

The first lady's busy schedule caused her no problems. She dealt respectfully with traditions but kept her entertaining as informal as possible within their limits. She also drove her own car and traveled with picnic lunches. However, the increasing criticism directed at the president worried her. As unemployment rose to a frightening level, drought dried up farm income, and people went hungry and homeless, the nation blamed him. The family's refusal to publicize their many charities worsened their already bad press. The first lady was no more forthcoming with reporters than her husband, instituting a no-interview, no-quotation policy. Having always thought of themselves as people who tried, even at personal sacrifice, to improve conditions for workers and relieve suffering, the Hoovers were confused and hurt. In World War I to *hooverize*—conserve food—had been an honorific, patriotic term. Now people talked of Hoovervilles—clusters of shanties or cardboard boxes in which the homeless slept. In the past the Hoovers had been loved and lauded for their good works; now they were condemned and vilified. When in 1930 the first lady included among her guests a black woman, the wife of a congressman, critics (especially southern legislatures) lashed out at her, with accusations that she had "defiled the White House"; the president responded by inviting the black president of Tuskegee to the White House for lunch.

Like her husband, Lou tried hard to prevent a loss of confidence throughout the nation. She wrote personally to people seeking

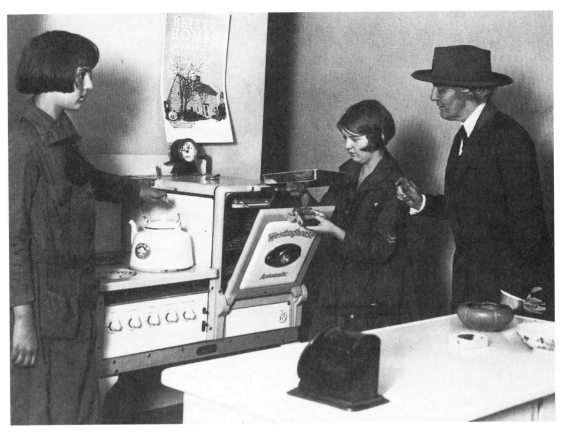
Lou Hoover in leader's uniform with Girl Scouts *(Library of Congress)*

help, explaining what her husband was doing to better the economic state of the nation, but her letters could not begin to stem the ebbing tide of confidence in capitalism itself. She urged people who were not in financial trouble to keep on spending: "If we stop buying things we need, employment will drop tremendously." She tried to promote American products, and on some evenings appearing in cotton gowns; she suggested that women help needy local people, undertake cooperative ventures, and barter within their own communities; and she urged the National Congress of Parents and Teachers to supply clothing and books so that children could stay in school.

Nevertheless, by spring 1932 Americans were marching in protests and rioting in the streets. The president's popularity reached a new low when General Douglas MacArthur, allegedly exceeding the president's orders, burned the huts erected just outside Washington by desperate World War I veterans pleading for bonuses. Despite all this, the Republican Party and the president himself still had hopes of his reelection, and the first lady campaigned actively with her husband.

Voters swept Franklin D. Roosevelt into office. The Hoovers did not hold the usual preinaugural dinner for the Roosevelts on March 3, 1932, and Hoover sat stiffly silent, ignoring the cheers of the crowds, as he and Roosevelt rode to the inaugural. The Hoovers left the "perilous pitiless pinnacle" of the White House in anguish and bitterness, convinced that President Roosevelt would move in disastrous directions.

Their Palo Alto home was a refuge. Lou actively involved herself in campus and community life, as usual filling the house with young people. On campus she pushed for programs to involve women students in sports and in professional physical education courses for teachers. Her husband, as well as she, now had time to give their grandchildren the outdoor adventures that they loved. She refused Eleanor Roosevelt's request to serve as vice-chair of the Women's Committee on Mobilization for Human Needs in favor of continuing her Girl Scout work; in 1935 she was elected president of the National Girl Scouts Council. Most mornings she spent on her still voluminous mail. Both the Hoovers, however, foresaw a disastrous national future, filled with demagoguery and threats of communism and fascism.

With the approach of World War II, the Hoovers moved to New York, where Bert had already set up an office in anticipation of war relief work. In 1940 a request for him to head National Finnish Relief took them back to a suite in the Waldorf Towers and to a pattern of commuting between the east and the west coasts. Lou helped her husband set up Dutch and Norwegian relief committees and assisted with fundraising while still carrying on her Girl Scout work. She also accepted the chair of the Western Women's Committee to support the Salvation Army appeal to clothe a million European refugees. Wartime demands sapped her energy.

On January 7, 1944, Lou returned from a concert to rest before dinner, but in the early evening a heart attack ended her life. A thousand people, among them 200 Girl Scouts, attended the service conducted in New York by an Episcopalian priest and Rufus Jones of the American Friends Service Committee. Another memorial service was held in Palo Alto, where she was buried. After her husband's death in 1964, her body was interred with his at West Branch, Iowa. As she had wished, the Palo Alto house was deeded to Stanford University as the home of its president.

In the letter that constituted her will, Lou Hoover wrote to her sons: "You have been lucky boys to have had such a father and I am a lucky woman to have had my life's trail alongside the path of three such men and boys." She left in her papers thousands of dollars' worth of uncashed checks sent to her in repayment of "loans"; even her husband did not know many of the recipients. In the Girl Scouts' magazine journalist Will Irwin paid tribute to her scholarship, her tolerance, and the help she had given thousands: "She died the youngest woman of her years I have ever known."

———

For Lou Hoover, the demands of being first lady limited rather than broadened her life. She had loved her years as the wife of a mining engineer and wealthy businessman roaming the world. She reveled in discovering new places and cultures, embarking on new intellectual adventures, and socializing with interesting people. In a happy marriage based on Quaker ideals of gender equality, she shared with her husband the raising of their family, his interest in mining, and his work in relieving suffering. Her husband's disastrous experience as president increasingly reduced her public image to the conventionalities of tea and sympathy—being his hostess and his moral support. The nation knew little of the woman who exercised multiple private charities, restored to the White House discarded furniture of previous administrations, eliminated a few outworn customs, and gently advocated opportunities for women and girls. Her tenure at the White House was an interlude rather than a defining experience.

CHRONOLOGY

1874 *March 29:* Lou Henry is born in Waterloo, Iowa

1884 Lou Henry and her family move to California

1891 Lou Henry enters State Normal School in Los Angeles

1892	Lou Henry transfers to San Jose Normal School
1894	Lou Henry graduates from San Jose Normal School and enrolls at Stanford as a geology major
1895	Lou Henry and (Bert) Hoover agree privately to marry in the future
1898	Lou Henry graduates from Stanford
1899	*February 10:* Lou Henry marries Herbert Hoover and goes to China
1903	*August 4:* Son Herbert Clark is born
1907	*July 17:* Son Allan Henry is born
1914	Lou Hoover sets up a Women's Committee to care for unaccompanied women and children trapped in Europe by World War I.
1915	Lou Hoover helps Belgians organize marketing system to sell lace in the United States and England and helps organize and operate an American Women's Hospital
1917	In the United States. Lou Hoover advocates for voluntary food conservation, sets up girls' clubs in Washington to help young women workers find housing, and becomes leader of a Girl Scout troop
1921	Henry Hoover is appointed secretary of commerce; Lou Hoover organizes conference on law enforcement
1922	Lou Hoover becomes national president of the Girl Scouts
1923	Lou Hoover is elected vice president of the National Amateur Athletic Federation
1928	Herbert Hoover is elected president
1929	*March 4:* Lou Hoover becomes first lady
1933	*March 4:* The Hoovers leave the White House but continue to work actively as volunteers
1940	Lou Hoover becomes honorary chair of the American Women's Division of the Commission for Relief in Belgium
1944	*January 7:* Lou Hoover dies of a heart attack.

FURTHER READING

Allen, Anne Beiser. *An Independent Woman: The Life of Lou Henry Hoover.* Westport, Conn.: Greenwood, 2000.

Burner, David. *Herbert Hoover: A Public Life.* New York: Knopf, 1979.

Furman, Bess. *Washington By-line.* New York: Knopf, 1949.

Gutin, Myra G. *The President's Partner: The First Lady in the Twentieth Century.* New York: Greenwood, 1989.

Parks, Lillian Rogers (with Frances Spatz Leighton). *My Thirty Years Backstairs at the White House.* New York: Fleet, 1961.

Pryor, Helen B. *Lou Henry Hoover: Gallant First Lady.* New York: Dodd, Mead, 1969.

ANNA ELEANOR ROOSEVELT ROOSEVELT

(OCTOBER 11, 1884–NOVEMBER 7, 1962)

First Lady, March 4, 1933–April 12, 1945

ELEANOR ROOSEVELT
(Library of Congress)

A liberated woman with a strong sense of both public and private duty, Eleanor Roosevelt constructed careers of her own in teaching, writing, and international diplomacy. She was born into a family and class that asked of her only that she marry well, raise a family, and shine in society. Her husband's polio and the influence of several remarkable women, including experienced social workers and reformers who began their careers in the Progressive Era (1890–1920), turned the course of her life in other directions—toward the future rather than the past; toward public life. As a private citizen and as first lady, she used her intelligence, charm, and strength in the service of the people of the United States and of the world.

In New York City on October 11, 1884, Eleanor Roosevelt was born, the first child of Elliott and Anna Hall Roosevelt. The family was marked for tragedy, and Eleanor suffered recurrent bouts of depression throughout her life. Her wealthy parents had no work: Anna was first and foremost a society beauty, and Elliott a charming alcoholic ne'er-do-well. Anna, rejecting her daughter as plain and old-fashioned in favor of her two younger sons, addressed Eleanor as "Granny." Elliott affectionately called her his "own Little Nell," giving her the love she craved but sometimes abandoning her to wait outside the door of his club while he drank himself into a stupor.

Eleanor adored her father. His standards for the ideal woman—noble, studious, religious, loving, good—set the goals for which she strove throughout her life. However, when she was only seven years old, his brother Theodore sent Elliott away to a Virginia sanitarium. The next year, in his absence, her mother died, and eight-year-old Eleanor and her two brothers were sent to the care of their austere maternal grandmother. Within months Eleanor was again trying to comfort her father, by letters and on his longed-for visits, for the death of her four-year-old brother Ellie from diphtheria. When she was 10, Elliott died in delirium tremens. Desolate without the father on whom she had centered her life, she turned for consolation to daydreaming of him and to secretly reading Dickens and Scott.

Eleanor took her first steps toward liberation in the years she spent at Allenwood, a feminist, progressive, French-speaking London boarding school, from 1899 to 1902—years that she always described as the happiest of her life. There the perceptive Mademoiselle Marie Souvestre recognized and cultivated her talents, offered her appreciation and affection, taught her how to dress, encouraged her strong impulses to compete, expected her to challenge her teachers and to argue for her own point of view, and interested her in politics. Making Eleanor her favorite, she took the girl traveling during school holidays. To her own surprise

Eleanor, who had spent her childhood subjected to disapproval and belittlement, found herself the most popular girl in the school among both faculty and students, one who excelled in her studies, especially in languages and literature, and in sports, especially field hockey. Her new independence and self-confidence gave her the strength to survive the revelation in 1901 of the ugly circumstances of her father's death, which her aunt, Edith (Pussie) Hall, blurted out, adding that Eleanor would probably never have the beaux that the other women in her family attracted, because she was the "ugly duckling."

When Eleanor returned to New York in 1902 to make her debut, she did not enjoy the social activities demanded by her position and her family. She did not think herself a belle, yet as her cousin Alice Roosevelt observed, "She was always making herself out to be an ugly duckling but she was really rather attractive. Tall, rather coltish-looking, with masses of pale, gold hair rippling to below her waist, and really lovely blue eyes. It's true that her chin went in a bit, which wouldn't have been so noticeable if only her hateful grandmother had fixed her teeth." Several eligible young men courted Eleanor, including Nicholas Biddle, Lyman Delano, and Harvard undergraduate Howard Cary.

Meanwhile, she was following Mademoiselle Souvestre's advice to "Give some of your energy, but not all, to worldly pleasures. . . . And even when success comes, as I am sure it will, bear in mind that there are more quiet and enviable joys than to be among the most sought-after women at a ball." After her debut, therefore, Eleanor devoted herself to the service of others, taking over the running of her Grandmother Hall's house. She assumed the major responsibility for her younger brother Hall, getting him settled at Groton, his boarding school, writing to him every day, and visiting him frequently—a responsibility she faithfully fulfilled for the next 40 years, until he died from alcoholism in 1941. She took classes in sociology and political economy; volunteered at a settlement house; and joined the

Consumers' League, where she witnessed the working conditions of department store clerks and garment workers.

Socially she developed a reputation for her interesting, sophisticated conversation; people found her a person of substance, worth listening to. An older family friend, Robert Munro Ferguson, introduced her to Greenwich Village artists and writers, such as Ellen Emmet, and her Aunt Bye (Anna Roosevelt Cowles, Theodore Roosevelt's sister) acquainted Eleanor with the political world at her home in Washington, D.C., known during the presidency of Theodore Roosevelt as "the little White House."

By Christmas 1902 Eleanor was attracting the persistent attentions of her distant cousin (and her father's godson), the highly eligible Franklin Delano Roosevelt, then a Harvard undergraduate. By Christmas 1903 he had proposed and she had accepted him. His widowed mother, Sara, reacted to the news by doing her best to postpone if not prevent their marriage; she was not prepared to give up her only child to another woman, even though that woman longed for her love and did her best to please her. From others Franklin was overwhelmed with congratulations on his great good fortune.

Eleanor determined to be a model wife and daughter-in-law, placing her own interests and ambitions secondary to those of Franklin and his mother. The young couple were married on March 17, 1905, and took up residence in New York, where Franklin was studying law at Columbia. That summer they returned home from a three-month honeymoon in Europe to find that Sara had rented a house for them three blocks from her own, furnished it, and engaged their servants. Eleanor, already pregnant, settled into the conditions that patterned the next half-decade of her life: bearing and caring for four babies (Anna in 1906, James in 1907, the first Franklin, Jr., in 1909, and Elliott in 1910), one of whom (Franklin, Jr.) died in infancy; struggling to be an ideal traditional homebody, against her own nature; and allowing her domineering mother-in-law to decide where and how they lived and how they raised their children. (Sara repeatedly told her grandchildren, "I was your real mother, Eleanor merely bore you.") Whenever Eleanor ventured to learn something new, like driving a car or playing golf, a discouraging word from Sara or Franklin soon put a stop to it. She did revel in her first home of her own, a summer place on Campobello Island in New Brunswick, Canada, but most of the year she was required to live either at Sara's Hyde Park home or in the New York six-story townhouse that Sara had had built next to her own, and into which Sara walked without notice at any time. Under this tyrannical regime, Eleanor frequently withdrew into depression, staying at home while her high-spirited husband socialized.

She rejoiced, however, when in 1910, bored with his duties in a New York law firm, Franklin Delano Roosevelt (often referred to as FDR) accepted the invitation of New York Democrats to run for the state senate. His win opened Eleanor's prison doors, and she happily walked through to a new life in Albany—one that she took to as her natural element, for which her study abroad had prepared her. She chose her own home, developed a new lifestyle, and let her social conscience, her innate vitality, and her intelligence begin to transform her into a woman of public affairs. Efficiently setting up her new household and taking over the maternal duties that Sara had stolen from her, she began entertaining and attending political and social events. She charmed FDR's political colleagues and their wives, earning the friendship and respect of both his allies and his political enemies. She lobbied for causes and seized on every new opportunity to educate herself about the political process and social issues, turning for help to everyone from roughneck Tammany politicians to women reformers.

The Roosevelt marriage was rejuvenated. The couple reached a compromise on social activities: He could attend as many as he liked and stay as long as he liked, and she did not have to sit through frivolities (often alcoholic) that bored her. Franklin Roosevelt began listening to his astute wife, valuing the expertise she had picked up from her Aunt Bye and Uncle Theodore, her understanding of his colleagues and his constituents, and her coaching on his style of speaking. In 1911 FDR came out for suffrage for women, leaving Eleanor "somewhat shocked, as I had never given the question serious thought." However, she added, "I realized that if my husband were a suffragist I probably must be, too." In June 1912 the Roosevelts attended their first national Democratic convention together, supporting the nomination of Woodrow Wilson for president. This support paid off with FDR's appointment as assistant secretary of the Navy, and in March 1913 the Roosevelts moved to Washington, D.C.

Eleanor had come into her own. Her marriage was happy, and she had learned to handle her difficult mother-in-law—though with occasional quarrels and confrontations. During this period many people, even Sara, spoke of her physical attractiveness: The Gibson girl styles of the day suited the tall (six-foot), thin woman with beautiful hair and eyes. She bore two more children (the second Franklin, Jr., in 1914, and John, in 1916), without much interruption in her busy schedule. She had begun to recognize her own abilities and to pride herself on her efficiency in performing her duties as wife and mother; reliable prop to the many troubled members of her extended family; Washington hostess with many social engagements; and thinking, public-spirited citizen. Her linguistic accomplishments stood out at diplomatic dinners, where she sometimes translated for all the guests. Somehow she found time to read history and economics. Her energy, skills, and devotion to duty made her a model for other political wives—despite the migraine headaches that plagued her. "I could never say in the morning 'I have a headache and cannot do thus and so,'" she later wrote. "I could not be a burden and add any care to a man who had plenty of official things to do."

Franklin's position, the Roosevelt name, and the couple's great charm and obvious abilities opened doors to them. They knew many people, and almost every afternoon Eleanor dutifully called on cabinet wives, Supreme Court wives, and congressional wives—10 to 30 of them a day, for a visit of no more than six minutes. Almost every evening she and Franklin entertained or were entertained at a dinner and perhaps a dance. They particularly enjoyed the two evenings a month they kept for "The Club," a group of brilliant conversationalists—friends and political allies—who for the sake of the company resignedly ate salad and the scrambled eggs that Eleanor prepared at the table in a chafing dish.

For Eleanor the entry of the United States into World War I in 1917 meant the end of such social activities and the beginning of new duties: knitting, learning to drive, raising funds for a recreational center for wounded men who needed physical therapy, entertaining troops as they moved through Washington's Union Station, organizing the Red Cross canteen, and helping Addie Bagley Daniels, FDR's boss's wife, to organize the Navy Red Cross. She worked at these tasks every day from 9:00 in the morning until past midnight. For Franklin the partying continued—complete with flirtations. The divergence of their interests, her heavy obligations to their children, with whom she spent long summers at Campobello, and the pressures of his work caused them to spend more and more time away from each other. Sometimes his actions distressed her, as when, in the name of patriotism, he and her cousin Alice Roosevelt Longworth spied on a romance between Bernard Baruch and one of their friends.

In 1918, as she was nursing her husband and the children through the deadly flu of that season, Eleanor discovered incontrovertible evidence of what much of Washington already knew and her cousin Alice had already hinted to her: For some time, Franklin had been conducting an affair publicly with Eleanor's social secretary, Lucy Mercer. After finding Lucy's love letters Eleanor immediately offered him a divorce. FDR realized that he had much to lose besides a wife whom many other politicians envied him; he would also be losing the political career that both of them had been arduously building. His trusted political adviser Louis Howe told him that he needed his wife, and his mother told him flatly that she would cut him off without a cent, thus depriving him of the funds that he needed to support a political career and his comfortable lifestyle. He therefore capitulated, falsely telling Lucy that Eleanor would not give him a divorce. Crushed, publicly humiliated, heartbroken, and deprived of her hard-found self-confidence, Eleanor nonetheless behaved generously. She did not want to duplicate her mother's coldness toward her erring father, rejecting him so completely that Anna had even refused to see Elliott when she lay dying. Eleanor did not want to deprive Franklin of his career, nor their children of a father. She set terms for the continuation of their marriage to which he agreed, making promises that he did not keep—in particular, his avowal never to see Lucy again.

Out of this maelstrom of emotion and betrayal, the Roosevelts somehow rescued the strength and courage to fashion a remarkable partnership—a marriage of true minds. No one knows whether they ever resumed physical relations, though certainly they had no more children. But they parented their children; presented a united front to the world; protected and defended one another; respected each other; tolerated one another's different temperaments and opinions; and above all worked together to create not merely a successful political career but, in time, an oustanding presidency.

They both tried—Eleanor to join in his social pleasures, Franklin to spend more time with the family and to please her. She labored to communicate her feelings better, speaking up when she was hurt or irritated. When she wanted to leave a party or if he started to flirt, she asked Franklin to leave with her. She tried to modify her own tendencies to Spartanism and Puritanism. Above all, she changed focus, aiming to be more than just a helpmeet. Her Grandmother Hall, she believed, had wasted her life by concentrating only on her family: "I wondered then and I wonder now whether, if her

life had been less centered in her family group, that family group might not have been a great deal better off. If she had some kind of life of her own, what would have been the result? . . . I determined that I would never be dependent on my children by allowing all my interests to center in them." Nor would she award "love and unquestioned loyalty" unless the behavior of the recipient had earned it. "The life you live is your own," she decided. "Life is meant to be lived." Accordingly, Eleanor resolved to create an independent life, with friends and work of her own. She and Franklin could follow parallel but separate courses.

She had assigned herself no easy task. She continued to suffer from the old troubles: Franklin's neglect, his attentions to other women, and his refusal to leave his mother's homes, as well as Sara's repeated attempts to alienate the children's affections and her spoiling of them. Eleanor's emotional upsets added to her pain from migraine headaches, loss of appetite, and trouble with her teeth and gums.

Eleanor changed her life privately and publicly. Privately, she defied both her mother-in-law and the racism rampant in Woodrow Wilson's Washington by hiring a complete new staff of black servants. Publicly, she defied and denounced the Red Scare that followed World War I, which Attorney General A. Mitchell Palmer had fomented to the point of destruction of personal liberties. She also denounced the extreme actions of the organizations that supported such scare tactics, including the Daughters of the American Revolution, which had shifted from a progressive to a conservative organization. She participated actively in several groups that Palmer disapproved of, including the newly formed League of Women Voters, the Women's Trade Union League (which encouraged union activities among working women), and the Foreign Policy Association. The answer to communism, she believed, was not a witch hunt but progressive change in American society.

Her new friends included women of varied backgrounds and interests, many of whom she met when she volunteered as an interpreter for the International Congress of Working Women in October 1919. Her new acquaintances included labor organizer Rosa Schneiderman and reformers such as the Republican feminist Margaret Dreier Robins, who devoted her fortune to the causes of peace, full employment, union protection, and economic security for all. Under the influence of these and other women, Eleanor committed herself to the campaign to promote the entrance of the United States into the League of Nations and the World Court. In addition, as she closed down her war work, she made a final effort "to get restrooms for the girls in the [Navy Department] with a woman doctor in charge!"

In 1920 the Democrats nominated FDR for the vice presidency. While Eleanor had little respect for the politicians of the day, she nevertheless agreed to play the role of admiring wife on her husband's campaign train and to keep a diary at his request. On this trip shrewd Louis Howe, FDR's political strategist and aide, rescued her from boredom by consulting her on speech drafts and press conferences, with FDR's advance man Stephen Early joining in. Howe taught her how to treat political reporters, and she soon made friends with them. Perhaps most importantly, Howe helped her to develop new patterns of behavior with FDR that made it possible for her to resign herself to his womanizing and even treat affectionately and protectively his new assistant, Missy Le-Hand, who became his intimate associate.

With the campaign lost, Eleanor enthusiastically began a new life in New York City. While Franklin turned to making money by practicing law and speculating, she took lessons in shorthand, typing, and cooking. She joined the Women's City Club, an organization of professional women dedicated to social reform and municipal affairs, and agreed to direct the League of Women Voters' national legislation committee. In these activities she met and was inspired by such women as suffragist leader Carrie Chapman Catt; journalist and publicist Esther Lape, who became her close friend and mentor on social reform; and Elizabeth Read, who became her personal attorney. They introduced her to social feminists Marion Dickerman and Nancy Cook. Under the tutelage of these women Eleanor became a "New Woman"—an independent, politically engaged activist. In her League work she turned for advice to Louis Howe and FDR, who taught her political maneuvers. However, it was on her own initiative that she introduced a resolution in the League to condemn Calvin Coolidge's attack on women's colleges as hotbeds of radicalism and wrote editorials against slavish adherence to political parties.

In summer 1921 Franklin contracted polio, which required Eleanor to devote every ounce of her energy and all of her time to nursing him, keeping him interested and ambitious in public life, and protecting his political career. With her strong support, he faced the crisis optimistically, rejecting his mother's insistence that he retreat to Hyde Park and live the life of a pampered invalid. Louis Howe conspired with them to keep from the press the extent of the damage to his body. It was a dreadful year for Eleanor, for on top of Franklin's illness, she had to contend with Sara, who was fighting her at every step and manipulating Anna's adolescent rebellions. In April 1922, for the only time in her life Eleanor broke down, sobbing inconsolably for hours—after which she pulled herself together and resolved never to allow such weakness again.

The incident had given Anna some insight into what her mother was enduring, and Eleanor began hesitantly to confide in her only daughter. Franklin's disability also changed his wife's relationship with her sons, for now she had to take his place in playing with them—swimming, hiking, camping, mountain climbing, riding, and sailing.

As Franklin recovered, he spent most of his time on a boat fishing off the coast of Florida, with Missy LeHand as his primary companion and hostess. His wife sometimes visited, usually taking along a friend of her own. His and her lives and interests diverged further without disturbing their genuine devotion. They shielded each other from prying eyes, even Sara's. Although he was responsible for the family expenses, Eleanor began to make herself financially independent, adding her earnings from lectures, magazine articles, and guest appearances on radio shows to the income from her trust fund. These activities fitted well with Louis Howe's urging that Eleanor enter mainstream Democratic Party politics as a surrogate for her disabled husband.

With FDR's encouragement and on his property, Eleanor built a home for herself with political organizer Nancy Cook and educator Marion Dickerman at Val-Kill, near Hyde Park. Beginning in 1925, the three women engaged in multiple joint activities, operating the *Women's Democratic News,* with Eleanor Roosevelt as editor; the Todhunter School in New York City, with Marion as principal and Eleanor as teacher; and the Val-Kill furniture factory, which Nancy ran, with Eleanor as salesperson. Together and with the Roosevelt boys, the three spent halcyon days throughout the 1920s. However, Cook and Dickerman divided their loyalties between Eleanor Roosevelt and Franklin, and in the early 1930s the friendship cooled.

The 1920s saw also Eleanor's rapid development as a woman of importance in politics. Given the idealism among newly enfranchised American women, especially those who had fought so hard for suffrage, she believed that although men entered politics to build careers, women entered to change society. She also believed in women's grassroots activities and their sharing information. Working through the League of Women Voters, the Women's Trade Union League, the Women's City Club, and especially the Women's Division of the New York State Democratic Committee, she raised funds; edited newsletters; moderated panels; debated; and toured the state on behalf of numerous causes—public housing, improved sanitation, public transit, parks and playgrounds, school lunches and school nurses, unemployment insurance, workers' compensation, occupational safety, the eight-hour day, protective laws for women workers, mandatory education, child-labor legislation, pure food, and women's right to serve on juries. She frequently represented New York at national conventions of political women.

Louis Howe backed Eleanor in most of her efforts, though he thought others politically unwise. He took particular pains to tutor her in public speaking, instructing her to "Have something to say, say it, and sit down." She took voice lessons to lower her pitch and register. Most importantly, she learned to let her concern for people show in her use of eye contact.

She told her husband—and maybe herself—that she was doing it all for him. Certainly she was keeping the Roosevelt name prominent in Democratic circles as Franklin recuperated and struggled to regain some control over his legs. "You need not be proud of me dear," she wrote him. "I'm only being active till you can be again. It isn't such a great desire on my part to serve the world and I'll fall back into habits of sloth quite easily!" Encouraging the belief that she was politically naive, she strove to conceal her developing political skills and her joy in the process.

Eleanor opted to concentrate on women's issues, particularly the inclusion of women on the committees of the Democratic Party and their right to choose their own delegates. As she noted, "The whole point in women's suffrage is that the Government needs the point of view of all its citizens and the women have a point of view which is of value to the Government." Of course, "women's issues" covered international peace and almost all social reform, to which she brought the support of women's organizations across the country, despite which in 1924 the Resolutions Committee of the Democratic Party refused even to hear the women's proposals for its platform. Nonetheless the Roosevelt name was increasing in importance in Democratic circles. Al Smith recognized Eleanor's growing political expertise when he asked her to run his campaign for reelection as governor of New York against her cousin Theodore Roosevelt, Jr., whom she publicly described as a "young man whose public service record shows him willing to do the bidding of his friends." To publicize his involvement in the Teapot Dome scandal of the Harding administration, she designed and drove around the state in a vehicle with a steam-spouting teapot—a ploy that she herself called a "rough stunt."

As advanced as her views were, when in the 1920s feminists split over the Equal Rights Amendment (ERA), Eleanor Roosevelt sided with those who came out against it, on the grounds that it would invalidate the hard-won laws that protected working women against exploitation. Not until the 1940s, when the Fair Labor Standards Act protected both working women and working men, would she withdraw her opposition to the ERA. Meanwhile, she fought for the 48-hour workweek for women, the Child Labor amendment, and state funds for maternity and pediatric clinics. She also got herself arrested for picketing in support of striking paper box makers.

By 1928, Eleanor was prominent in national Democratic circles. Under her leadership in the New York Democratic Party, women had finally won equal representation—if not equal power. She urged them on—to organize, study, work, and learn to play the game of politics as men do. She created a controversy when she spoke out on the divisive prohibition issue, remarking that it was just as important to enforce the constitutional amendments that guaranteed the vote to black Americans as to enforce the 18th amendment forbidding the sale of alcoholic beverages.

His wife's activities never perturbed Franklin Roosevelt, who was running for governor of New York. Indeed, as far as is known, he interfered with her plans only once, when he asked her not to take flying lessons. Otherwise he shrugged off the criticism directed at her, blandly telling reporters, "She's my missus. What can I do?" She had been instrumental in his nomination. On the advice of Louis Howe, he had avoided phone calls beseeching him to accept it, thinking that he needed more

time to strengthen his legs, but he did take Eleanor's call—and she handed the phone to Al Smith. FDR campaigned to triumph, while Smith lost the presidency in a landslide. Eleanor was crushed by Smith's defeat, remarking on her husband's victory, "If the rest of the ticket didn't get in, what does it matter?"

She was now faced with the problem of what to do next. What she wanted out of life, she had already written, was "the opportunity for doing something useful." Half the week, she decided, was enough to devote to being New York's first lady. In the time remaining she would carry on with her own work, particularly teaching at the Todhunter School, which, she said, she liked "better than anything else I do." She resigned as editor of the *Women's Democratic News,* rejected several lecture offers, and refused invitations to speak on politics, but she continued to operate behind the scenes. Her extended experience with New York state politicians made her advice invaluable to the governor as he set up his new staff—such as her suggestion that he appoint Frances Perkins labor commissioner.

With the help of Malvina Thompson, her new secretary, Eleanor Roosevelt conducted her multifarious activities with her usual aplomb and efficiency. She spent the first three days of the week in New York at Todhunter, but she was on hand late every Wednesday afternoon to pick up her work in Albany. She filled the nine guest rooms of the executive mansion every weekend, entertaining frequently at dinners, strategizing with Democratic women, speaking, promoting business enterprises for women, dividing the supervision of FDR's 1930 campaign for reelection with Louis Howe, and working with the Junior League to protect women's rights to work in the unemployment crisis although society then held that women should not "take jobs away from men." She was the governor's lady, but she publicly supported strikes, and she pushed FDR to take more liberal positions, often against the advice of his staff. Because he could not easily travel, she inspected state hospitals, prisons, and public projects, and reported

Eleanor Roosevelt campaigning *(Library of Congress)*

to him. He taught her to observe carefully: She must always look for herself rather than take the word of officials; not just read the menus but actually lift the lids of the pots on the kitchen stove; look at the clothes on the line. "One time," she told a reporter, "he [FDR] asked me to go and look at the state's tree shelter-belt plantings. I noticed there were five rows of graduated size. . . . When I came back and described it, Franklin said: 'Tell me exactly what was in the first five rows. What did they plant first?' and he was so desperately disappointed when I couldn't tell him, that I put my best efforts after that into missing nothing and remembering everything." To the facts that he required Eleanor learned to add her own perceptions of people, observing their attitudes and facial ex-

pressions. All in all, she was, in her own words, "in the front line trenches of life."

As she had all her adult life, from the Allenswood years on, Eleanor continued to make new friends. Among them was her bodyguard, Earl Miller, whom Franklin had insisted on when she claimed the right to drive her own car. With Miller she developed a kind of Queen Victoria/John Brown relationship. Twelve years younger than she, he called her "the Lady," but he teased her and frolicked with her, gave her riding lessons and a horse, coached her in tennis, taught her to shoot and to dive, played the piano and sang for her children, monitored household expenses for her, championed her, and watched over her happiness as well as her safety. She cooked special meals for him, gave parties for him, and acted as godmother to his children.

Despite her success in preserving her independence while FDR was governor of New York, Eleanor abhorred the prospect of becoming first lady of the nation. In a panic she saw herself doomed to a perpetual round of teas and reception lines, so imprisoned by her position that she could do no work of her own. Later she wrote, "I did not want my husband to be president. . . . It was pure selfishness on my part, and I never mentioned my feelings on the subject to him." Nonetheless, during the 1932 campaign she spoke, traveled with the campaign party when asked, and coordinated the Women's Division of the Democratic National Committee, on which the party depended for organizing much of its grassroots work. Her success foreshadowed her importance in the campaigns of the future. Although she followed tradition in not speaking directly for her husband's election, and despite the scurrilous attacks on her, she won many votes for FDR. In 1936 the decision to have her ride the campaign train but not appear at stops was immediately altered when the crowds called for her. In 1940 her speech at the Democratic Party convention transformed its ugly mood into a decision to give FDR the running mate he wanted. That year it was her persuasion that led her husband to turn his attention from international affairs long enough for a few campaign speeches.

Her integrity and achievements and her value to the 1932 campaign much impressed an Associated Press (AP) political reporter, Lorena Hickok. Noticing that she was the only woman in the press corps, Eleanor gave her special access, and when FDR's election became probable the AP assigned Hickok to cover Eleanor regularly. The more Hickok saw, the more she admired and liked the woman she followed everywhere—taking public transportation, buying apples from an unemployed man on a street corner, eating lunch at a drugstore counter. Gradually Eleanor began to confide in "Hick," and they began an intimate friendship—an intense and often stormy one at first—that Eleanor's biographer Blanche Wiesen Cook speculates developed into an affair. Eleanor's numer-ous obligations prevented her from giving Hick all the time and attention she demanded, and in 1942, even while she was living in the White House, Hick became involved with another woman. However, her professional advice helped the first lady: Among other things, Hick taught her to trust the good faith of reporters when talking to them off the record, hold press conferences for women reporters (to encourage the employment of women), and publish "My Day" (Eleanor's newspaper column reporting her own activities). Hick sacrificed her job to the relationship, realizing that she could not objectively report on her friend; instead she went to work for Harry Hopkins in the relief administration.

Just as when she became governor's lady in Albany in 1932, on the eve of becoming first lady Eleanor Roosevelt decided to curtail her activities "somewhat." She would give up teaching and radio programs that required her to endorse products, and she returned several writing contracts. However, she would continue to write and make a "few speeches." She set a new style when she walked to her preinaugural appointment to go through the White House with Mrs. Hoover. Once she had moved in, one tradition after another fell as Eleanor brushed aside the Secret Service, ran the elevator herself, pushed furniture around, and greeted her guests at the door instead of waiting to descend after they were all assembled. More importantly, she began a crusade to urge women to political activism for economic change, writing a book entitled *It's Up to the Women!*, publishing articles, giving interviews and radio talks, and speaking all over the country. She advised her audiences to serve simple, nutritious, frugal meals, support trade unions, and patronize merchants who provide decent working conditions. She herself wrote to a fashionable shop, "I feel sure that you will understand that I will have to wait before coming to you again until you have some agreement with your people which is satisfactory to both sides." She gave a civics course to the New York Junior League, emphasizing the need for reform. She toured the slums of Washington,

D.C., reported on them to the press, and suggested that Congress should act.

Eleanor Roosevelt also did her duty as a traditional first lady, not only at the many diplomatic dinners but at teas and receptions for thousands of American guests. One afternoon she shook the hands of 3,100 Daughters of the American Revolution in an hour and a half. "I was a symbol which tied the people who came by me in the long ever-recurring receiving lines to their government," she said. Numerous accounts testify that somehow she managed to personalize these impersonal encounters, and the Roosevelt warmth and personal touch transformed even official visits from heads of state and heads of government. Famously, the first lady served hot dogs to the king and queen of England at Hyde Park. She added two formal entertainments to the traditional list: a White House Gridiron Widows party to take place on the night of the Gridiron dinner, which barred all women; and a garden party for women executives in the government.

In her desperation at seeing herself limited to the traditional role of the first lady, Eleanor Roosevelt asked her husband whether she could take over some of his mail. However, she made herself far more useful to him by acting as a "listening post" for FDR when he repeatedly sent her to tour the country. During his first two terms she and her secretary Malvina Thompson (Tommy) traveled more than 280,000 miles around the United States, inspecting everything from relief projects to coal mines. "My God!" said a miner to his mate in a famous cartoon, "Here comes Mrs. Roosevelt." When unemployed veterans had marched on Washington during Herbert Hoover's term, he sent soldiers to smash the huts they had built. When they came back in Roosevelt's term, he sent his "missus," and she listened sympathetically. Not only did she report to her husband, but she pled their cause to him: "Franklin, surely you will not . . ." Furthermore, she spoke out for the poor and defenseless through radio, lectures, and her column informing American citizens of the plight of the 25 percent of the population

Eleanor Roosevelt with the British royal family (Library of Congress)

who were unemployed in the throes of the Great Depression. At last they had an advocate—someone who cared, someone who would respond when they asked for help. They wrote to her in the thousands (300,000 pieces of mail in the first year), and she brought their needs to the attention of officials who might help. She personally answered as many letters as she could—perhaps 50 a day—people knew she cared. On one trip to the migrant-labor camps in the San Joaquin Valley, "Mrs. Roosevelt spotted a cluster of makeshift shacks constructed of old boards, tarpaper and tin cans pounded flat, one of the ditch bank communities that were commonplace in California then," remembered Senator Helen Gahagan Douglas. Mrs. Roosevelt stopped the car and walked across the field. "One of the bent figures straightened to see who was approaching and recognized her at once. 'Oh, Mrs. Roosevelt, you've come to see us,' he said. He seemed to accept as a natural event of American life that the wife of the President of the United States should be standing in a mucky field chatting with him."

Into "the Eleanor basket" that she kept at her husband's bedside she not only deposited reports she thought he should read but plans of action—including recommendations for the appointment of women to government jobs. She telephoned the administrator of the Agricultural Adjustment Act to ask why the government was dumping pigs into the Mississippi while people went hungry—and government policy changed. She championed Appalachian miners blacklisted for striking, and out of that championship came Arthurdale in West Virginia, an experimental planned community where their families could homestead—to which Eleanor donated her lecture fees and for which she raised money from private sources. She invited to the White House people whom she thought it important that her husband hear, such as southern textile workers and northern garment workers. Except on state occasions, she decided who sat next to him at dinner.

If Eleanor Roosevelt served her husband as listening post, she also launched trial balloons for his policies—and for policies she herself was advocating. "Sometimes I say things," she told the women at one press conference, "which I thoroughly understand are likely to cause unfavorable comment in some quarters, and perhaps you newspaper women think I should keep them off the record. What you don't understand is that perhaps I am making these statements on purpose to arouse controversy and thereby get the topics talked about and so get people to thinking about them."

Her compassion and understanding embraced all kinds of people outside the mainstream. Although she had been brought up and lived for much of her adult life among people infected by racism, she resigned from the Daughters of the American Revolution when that organization refused its hall to the black singer Marian Anderson; Eleanor arranged for her to sing from the Lincoln Memorial instead. When a hotel insisted that the black educator Mary McLeod Bethune use the freight elevator, the first lady used it too. She gave a garden party for the District of Columbia's Training School for Delinquent Girls, three-fourths of them black. When Birmingham's segregation laws divided the blacks and whites at the Southern Conference on Human Welfare, the first lady placed her chair so that it straddled the dividing aisle. She joined the National Association for the Advancement of Colored People (NAACP), worked with its executive secretary Walter White for an antilynching bill, and attended and acted as a patron of an art show depicting lynching. During World War II, she argued against racial discrimination in the armed forces, in industry, and in public housing.

Worried about young people in the economic crisis, when hundreds of them were riding the rails, and thousands—perhaps a third of the nation's unemployed—could see no hope for employment, Eleanor pushed for a governmental youth program to put them to work for the service of the public, either in government jobs or for nonprofit organizations—an idea eventually realized in the National Youth Administration. She involved herself with the left-leaning American Student Union and the American Youth Congress. They must be heard, she said, even when they took advantage of her hospitality to heckle FDR, and even when they supported the Soviet Union during the period of its nonaggression pact with Germany from August 23, 1939, to June 22, 1941. "I have never said anywhere that I would rather see young people sympathetic with communism," she wrote. "But I have said I would rather see the young people actively at work, even if I considered they were doing things that were a mistake."

Eleanor Roosevelt's independent, fearless conduct and her liberal views often brought down on her vicious political attacks. For the most part she handled such attacks equably and patiently, especially when they were directed solely at herself. Those that targeted her children and suggested that her husband's polio had affected his mind unsettled her most. However, as she once advised Franklin, "It has always seemed to me that the chance of just such attacks as this was a risk one had to take with our form of government and if one felt clear oneself, the rest did not really matter." Somehow she managed to rise above the hatred, commenting, "I think I am more hardened to criticism than the President is, and it makes very little dent upon me, unless I think there is some real justification and something should be done."

Although she had no official position, elected or appointed, Eleanor Roosevelt established a widespread influence throughout the government during FDR's first two terms. It derived partly, of course, from the fact that no official ever knew what she did on her own and what she did with FDR's knowledge or at his request. Even when she wrote an official that "the President thinks it would be a very good thing if . . . ," the original idea might have been hers. She once began a speech, "I was talking with a man the other day, and he said . . ." A listener asked, "Who was that man?" "Franklin," she answered. Beyond question FDR held the presidential power firmly, and he often denied his wife's requests and refused to adopt the policies she advocated. However, he respected her and listened to her, and this enhanced her influence.

Of all her duties, Eleanor interested herself least in running the White House kitchen. She cared little about the quality of food, and she told herself and others that her husband shared this indifference. As housekeeper she hired a Hyde Park housewife, Mrs. Nesbitt, a thrifty manager but one who was devoted to "plain foods, plainly prepared," with menus of notoriously unappetizing fare repeated week after week. FDR eventually joked that he wanted to be elected for a fourth term so that he could fire her, but close associates were dismayed that he

put up with it. The Roosevelt guests almost always enjoyed themselves—but not what they ate.

Since the end of World War I, Eleanor had worked hard to promote world peace. Although she saw in the approach of World War II the destruction of her hopes, she did not retreat into isolationism as so many Americans did before the Japanese bombing of Pearl Harbor in late 1941. As she observed the actions of Hitler and Mussolini, she had to accept that the use of force was necessary to overcome evil, and her pacifism gradually gave way to interventionism. She had hoped for another form of national service for the youth of both genders, but when FDR made clear the need to draft young men into the military, she backed him. Her support, her determination to "accept my responsibility and do my particular job whatever it might be to the extent of my ability," and her expressed hope that "that will be the answer of every individual citizen of the U.S.A." helped lead the nation out of its isolationism and into patriotic support for the war effort.

Remembering the superpatriotism inspired by World War I and the Red Scare of its aftermath, Eleanor Roosevelt immediately moved to protect the democratic values threatened by World War II. If the United States had to fight fascists, it also had to defend itself against those who would sacrifice its citizens' basic rights and privileges to that end. She was determined that the social and economic reforms of the previous eight years not be lost in the need for more productivity to rearm the nation and help the Allies. Unions should retain the right to bargain and to strike, and industries should not refuse to hire German Americans and Italian Americans because of their descent. In the midst of hysterical fears of Japanese spies after Pearl Harbor, she stressed the loyalty of Japanese Americans. Despite bombing scares she refused to close the doors of the White House to the American public. On a lecture tour in late 1940, Eleanor called attention to the continuing need to improve housing, and the rejection for physical reasons of almost 40 percent of the young men drafted prompted her to speak of the need for a comprehensive health program. She urged industry to hire women in jobs always before done by men. She talked constantly about how the world would look after the war, and in time her ideas were incorporated into Franklin Roosevelt's call for four freedoms: freedom of speech and worship and freedom from want and fear.

As the United States moved toward war, FDR was not consulting her about the international affairs that engrossed him, so she looked for tasks on her own. Her plan to go to Europe with the Red Cross to help organize the relief effort for refugees was turned down, for fear that in a Hitlerian triumph the president's wife might be captured and held hostage. By June 1940 she was seeking asylum for British children. Thousands of Americans were ready to welcome them into their homes; to get around the immigration laws, Eleanor advocated giving them visitors' visas. They were transported across the Atlantic in unarmed ships under a safe conduct from all belligerents, to remain in the United States for the duration of the war.

Jews, however, were another matter, although Eleanor tried. As a young adult she had echoed the anti-Semitic slurs voiced by her family and friends; now she wrote articles for *Liberty* magazine that deplored anti-Semitism. In vain she worked with Jews for a bill that would admit 20,000 children in excess of the German quota. She finally succeeded in getting a few hundred Jewish refugees admitted to the United States when the State Department was turning away thousands. At the end of her life, she still spoke of her regret at her inability to achieve more.

When in the fall of 1941 Fiorello La Guardia invited her to assist him in directing the Office of Civilian Defense (OCD), Eleanor thought that her opportunity for a "real job" of war work had finally come. She accepted, promising to offer volunteers meaningful jobs to benefit nursery schools, housing projects, and homes for the aged, and to train them to meet emergency calls. But the position did not work out. The strong-willed La Guardia wanted to emphasize defense; the strong-willed first lady wanted to emphasize social services. Her unwise appointments of close friends at high salaries evoked denunciations from Congress. La Guardia resigned, and so did she in February 1942, when she came to realize that she was endangering the continuance of the OCD. She concluded that a president's wife could not have an official government job.

In late 1942 FDR proposed to his wife that they try once again to live as husband and wife, that she stay home and act as his hostess more frequently. Unable to forget the past, she countered by asking again for a war-related assignment, such as visiting American troops in England. He assented, and she departed on October 21 on a trip disappointing to her husband's hopes for a renewal of their marriage but immensely beneficial to the troops and indeed to British-American relationships. As usual, she recognized needs—like that of the soldiers for warmer socks—and moved to fill them. As usual, too, she made every visit a series of warm personal encounters, memorable not only to the soldiers and sailors but to the hundreds of their families to whom she wrote after she had seen them. She talked with British women in every line of work and visited the day nurseries set up for their children. She visited troops, black and white, in army camps, Red Cross clubs, and B-17s. The trip was a major success, and her proud husband beamed with pleasure when he personally met her at the airport on her return.

The first lady carried on with her customary heavy schedule, lecturing at Cooper Union; touring the headquarters of the Women's Army Auxiliary Corps; visiting the first unit of black combat pilots; talking with women in shipyards; and speaking of the need for a support system of day nurseries, community laundries, and family restaurants to help women work long hours in industry and maintain their homes, often with their husbands overseas. At FDR's request she went to an Arizona camp that housed interned Japanese Americans, where she marveled at the way they had built a community in the desert, complete with schools. Nevertheless, she urged that they be allowed to return to their homes, a plea that led to the issuance of exit permits to those among them who had work to do and a place to go.

In August 1943 the president sent the first lady to the South Pacific. She went alone, even leaving Tommy (her secretary) at home on the grounds that the 20,000-mile trip would be too strenuous for her. Eleanor found her experiences depressing and feared that she was giving more trouble than she was doing good, but the soldiers found it "good to hear a kind lady saying nice things." Her manner with them was inimitable. When she talked with them in groups, she loved to tell the story of the marine who complained to his sergeant that he hadn't seen any Japanese. "Just go out there and shout 'To hell with Hirohito,'" he was advised. Pretty soon he came back, despondent. Hadn't his shouts evoked a response? Oh yes, but they had shouted back, "To hell with Roosevelt." And how, he asked, could he shoot a fellow Republican?

Eleanor energetically went everywhere she was allowed, always preserving her aplomb. When she unexpectedly entered a Red Cross club, two privates who were not wearing their pants gasped, but she chatted away with them unabashedly. She evoked the admiration even of the top brass, who had originally thought her trip a nuisance. Admiral "Bull" Halsey marveled: "She went into every ward, stopped at every bed, and spoke to every patient. . . . 'Was there anything he needed? Could she take a message home for him?' . . . I was ashamed of my original surliness." When she returned to the United States, phones rang in soldiers' homes all over the country with the message, "The White House is calling."

Eleanor's sadness at the terrible sights she had seen overseas was alleviated by FDR's plans for what would happen at the war's end, especially the G.I. Bill that would help veterans to get an education and a job and to buy a home. Her concern for her husband's well-being during her travels was relieved by her daughter's move into the White House and FDR's increasing reliance on Anna. As D-Day approached in the spring of 1944, Anna understood far better than Eleanor that FDR's health was failing. In her long-established pattern, Eleanor continued to push him to move on matters with which she was concerned, while Anna did all she could to provide him with rest and pleasant society—including, without her mother's knowledge, that of FDR's former mistress, the now widowed Lucy Mercer Rutherford.

Eleanor and Franklin did have time to relax together on the slow train trip to the 1944 Democratic convention in San Diego to accept his nomination for a fourth term. Christmas that year brought the family together at Hyde Park, rejoicing at the prospect of war's end. Franklin told their son Elliott that Eleanor was "the most extraordinarily interesting woman" he had ever known. When Elliott relayed these words to his mother, he learned that she shared Franklin's hope that "the day would soon come when their intimidating workloads could be rearranged to give them more time together." However, it was Anna, not Eleanor, who accompanied him to Yalta. Then, in April 1945, FDR died at Warm Springs, Georgia—in the company of Lucy Mercer Rutherford.

As always, Eleanor Roosevelt did her duty. She rode the train that bore his body back to Washington along tracks lined with mourners. She saw the new president, Harry Truman, sworn in, and asked him, "Is there anything we can do for you?" She then moved out of the White House, telling reporters, "The story is over."

As she dealt with her husband's death, Eleanor realized how much she had relied on him, how he had provided the center for her life and work. "He might have been happier with a wife who was completely uncritical," she wrote. "That I was never able to be, and he had to find it in other people. Nevertheless, I think I sometimes acted as a spur, even though the spurring was not always wanted or welcome. I was one of those who served his purposes."

She mourned for her husband, but her story was not over; it was only entering on a new and important chapter. She still called matters of concern to the attention of the White

House—particularly after President Truman wrote her an eight-page letter in longhand on affairs of state. She sent him comments on civil rights, fair employment practices, the needs of other nations, and means to world peace. He responded by nominating her in late 1945 as the country's delegate to the United Nations (UN). She protested her lack of expertise in parliamentary procedure and of experience in foreign affairs, but he assured her that her aides would supply the information she needed. In this position, which she held throughout Truman's presidency, she used the international respect that she had earned, the political know-how taught her by FDR and Louis Howe, and her extraordinary personal skills and warm sympathy to shape and get adopted the Universal Declaration of Human Rights.

It was not an easy task, for she had to get past the hurdles put in her way by other members of the American delegation, particularly the Republicans John Foster Dulles and Senator Arthur Vandenberg. She had to reconcile the religious scruples of some delegates and the special interests of others, all the while avoiding collisions with the communists. For two years she toiled with endless patience, so exhausting her colleagues that one begged her not to forget their own human rights. "Now, of course, I'm a woman and don't understand these things," she would begin soothingly. "Never," a State Department adviser remarked, "have I seen naiveté and cunning so gracefully blended." In 1948 Eleanor earned a standing ovation from the General Assembly on the passage of this Magna Charta for humankind; years later, the first United Nations Human Rights prize was awarded to her posthumously.

The experience refocused Eleanor's energies on world peace and efforts to help victims of the war. Furthermore, another president now found in this influential woman the strong support on which FDR had relied. Her work to form the Americans for Democratic Action bolstered Harry Truman's foreign policy in the cold war with the Soviet Union, even as she kept him informed of her reservations about it. She de-

plored the enmity between the communist bloc and the United States, but she felt strongly that the United States must stick with its convictions.

Moved by concern for the plight of the survivors of the Holocaust, many of whom were still lingering in camps in Europe or desperately trying to reach Palestine, Eleanor Roosevelt entered the postwar controversy over the creation of a Jewish state in Palestine. She had for a long time opposed a Jewish state because Arab resistance would, she feared, be intractable and bloody; she was also horrified by the Zionist extremists responsible for the bombing of the King David Hotel in Jerusalem on July 22, 1946. But when the United Nations, with U.S. support, adopted a plan for the partition of Palestine in November 1947, she approved. Means to implement the partition plan, however, could not be agreed upon within the Truman administration and Eleanor became increasingly unhappy with what she saw as efforts to retreat from partition. She protested to the secretary of state, among other powerful individuals, and in a letter of March 22, 1948, she wrote President Truman a letter she described as "frank and unpleasant" in which she said "I realize that I am an entirely unimportant cog in the wheel of our work with the UN, but I have offered my resignation to the Secretary since I can quite understand the difficulty of having some one so far down the line openly criticize the Administration policies." President Truman refused to accept her resignation.

Eleanor commented on national and international affairs in her column "My Day," which she resumed writing the Monday after her husband was buried. In 1948 she began radio and television work, which continued intermittently thereafter. In 1949 she started a question-and-answer column in *McCall's* magazine, and that year she published *This I Remember,* the second book of her three-volume autobiography. (The third volume, *On My Own,* appeared in 1958.) She also publicly disputed Francis, Cardinal Spellman on the issue of federal aid to parochial schools, keeping calm even when he accused her of being "an unworthy American mother" and

Eleanor Roosevelt with Presidents Kennedy and Johnson *(Library of Congress)*

coolly reminding him that "The final judgment, my dear Cardinal Spellman, of the worthiness of all human beings is in the hands of God."

Eleanor exercised her strength within the Democratic Party to try to bring young people into its leadership and to put liberal planks into its platform. She also advised President Truman to pay more attention to women, city dwellers, and liberals. Despite her fear that he was growing more conservative, at the last minute she endorsed him in the 1948 campaign. More enthusiastically, she advised Adlai Stevenson to run for governor of Illinois, and she backed him strongly in his runs for the presidency in 1952 and 1956. In 1960 she finally accepted that even with her backing Stevenson could not be nominated again; therefore, with some reluctance, she came out for John F. Kennedy. During his

presidency, she accepted a place on the advisory council of the Peace Corps and sent him a list of possible women appointees. She helped to reform the Democratic Party in New York by her vigorous opposition to the "boss rule" of Carmine G. DeSapio, Tammany Hall leader.

In the 1950s, Senator Joseph McCarthy made unsupported accusations of communists within the government and elsewhere in the United States. He paralyzed many Americans with fear, but Eleanor Roosevelt spoke out against him. She carried out work for the United Jewish Appeal, the NAACP, Brandeis University, and the Citizens Committee for Children. Even after she had left the United Nations, she volunteered for the American Association for the United Nations, traveling around the country to organize chapters.

How well she understood her own feelings about power remains an open question. Her biographer, Blanche Wiesen Cook, has observed that she was highly competitive. In the 1930s, Louis Howe, assuming that FDR's presidency would end with his second term in 1940, asked her, "Eleanor, if you want to be President in 1940, tell me now so I can start getting things ready." She lightly brushed aside the question, saying that one politician in the family was enough. After FDR's death she refused proposals that she run for the Senate, and, later, for vice president. She peremptorily halted a 1952 movement to draft her as the Democratic presidential candidate. "No woman," she said, "has, as yet, been able to build up and hold sufficient leadership to carry through a program." Besides, "If I do not run for office, I am not beholden to my Party. . . . I am too old [at 62] to want to be curtailed in any way in the expression of my own thinking."

In 1952 she traveled around the world as its first lady, serene and gracious at all receptions, welcoming or not. "Don't worry about it," she told a horrified Madame Pandit when left-wing students cross-examined her. "I have been booed for 15 minutes at a time." She told the Japanese "that it is the causes of war which bring about such things as Hiroshima, and that . . . if there is another Pearl Harbor, there will be undoubtedly another Hiroshima." In Karachi, Pakistan, people knelt in the streets when she passed. Her comment: "I hadn't realized how much they cared about Franklin."

Eleanor Roosevelt never deserted her principles or the causes to which she had devoted so much service. In the last two years of her life, she sponsored hearings in which young civil rights workers testified to southern judicial and police harassment of black protestors; chaired President Kennedy's Commission on the Status of Women; and testified for equal pay for equal work before a congressional hearing. She died of a rare form of tuberculosis on November 7, 1962, and was buried beside her husband at Hyde Park, New York. The world mourned.

———〜〜〜———

Among first ladies, Eleanor Roosevelt stands out for her courage. She long since had conquered the terrors of her girlhood and young womanhood, her shyness and dependence on her husband and mother-in-law. When she entered the White House she fearlessly wielded her influence as first lady, upholding and defending her principles, translating them into action. In the 12 years that she lived in the White House, she converted her influence into power.

Her energy, her self-discipline—sometimes to the point of self-denial—and her devotion to duty were accompanied by high intelligence and a lively curiosity. Perhaps her most remarkable characteristic, however, was her capacity for friendship. This expressed itself in everything she did, whether giving a speech, shaking hands in a reception line, visiting an army hospital, or descending into a mine pit. She always saw individual people rather than an audience or a crowd. She liked them, she assumed the best about them, and she reached out to them.

No other first lady has touched so many lives. Eleanor Roosevelt brought to all whom she met in the United States and around the world what she said she was taking to the United Nations: "A sincere desire to understand the problems of the rest of the world and our relationship to them, a real goodwill for people throughout the world, a hope that I shall be able to build a sense of personal trust and friendship with my co-workers."

CHRONOLOGY

1884 *October 11:* Anna Eleanor Roosevelt is born

1892 Eleanor Roosevelt's mother dies

1894 Eleanor Roosevelt's father dies

1899– Eleanor Roosevelt attends Allenwood in
1902 London

1903 Eleanor Roosevelt accepts Franklin Delano Roosevelt's proposal of marriage

1905 *March 17:* Eleanor Roosevelt and Franklin Delano Roosevelt are married

1906 *May 3:* Daughter Anna Eleanor is born

1907 *December 23:* Son James is born

1909 *March 18:* Son Franklin, Jr., is born

November 1: Son Franklin dies

1910 *September 23:* Son Elliott is born

Franklin Roosevelt is elected to the New York state senate

1913 Franklin Roosevelt is appointed assistant secretary of the U.S. Navy

1914 *August 17:* Son, the second Franklin, Jr., is born

1916 *March 13:* Son John is born

1918 Eleanor Roosevelt discovers her husband's affair with Lucy Mercer and resolves to build a life of her own

1920 Franklin Roosevelt is nominated vice president but loses the election; the family moves to New York City

1921 Franklin Roosevelt contracts polio

1925 Eleanor Roosevelt, Nancy Cook, and Marion Dickerman form the Val-Kill partnership, which eventually establishes the *Women's Democratic News,* the Todhunter School, and the Val-Kill furniture company

1926 Eleanor Roosevelt begins to teach in the Todhunter School

1928 Franklin Roosevelt is elected governor of New York

1932 Franklin Roosevelt is elected president of the United States, a position in which he serves until his death

1933 *March 4:* Eleanor Roosevelt becomes first lady

1937 Eleanor Roosevelt begins a series of 13 radio broadcasts of "My Day" for Ponds Cosmetics

1941 *September:* Eleanor Roosevelt accepts a position in the office of Civil Defense, which she resigns in February 1942

1942 *September 17:* The Roosevelts begin a two-week inspection tour of factories, army camps, and navy yards

October 21: Eleanor Roosevelt begins a trip to England

1943 *August:* Eleanor Roosevelt goes to the South Pacific

1945 *April 12:* Franklin Delano Roosevelt dies, and Eleanor moves to Hyde Park

President Truman appoints Eleanor Roosevelt delegate to the United Nations

1948 *December 10:* The Universal Declaration of Human Rights is passed by the United Nations

1950 Eleanor Roosevelt travels to England, Scandinavia, and France

1952 Eleanor Roosevelt acts as roving ambassador to India, Pakistan, the Middle East, Indonesia, and Japan

Eleanor Roosevelt heads the U.S. delegation to the inauguration of President Carlos Ibanez in Chile

1957 Eleanor Roosevelt visits the USSR as correspondent for *Look* magazine and has an interview with Khrushchev

1962 *November 7:* Eleanor Roosevelt dies

FURTHER READING

Beasley, Maurine H., Holly C. Shulman, and Henry R. Beasley, eds. *The Eleanor Roosevelt Encyclopedia*. Westport, Conn.: Greenwood, 2000.

Cook, Blanche Wiesen. *Eleanor Roosevelt*. Vol. 1, 1884–1933. New York: Viking, 1992.

———. *Eleanor Roosevelt*. Vol. 2, 1933–1938. New York: Viking, 1999.

Glendon, Mary Ann. *A World Made New: Eleanor Roosevelt and the Universal Declaration of Human Rights*. New York: Random House, 2001.

Goodwin, Doris Kearns. *No Ordinary Time: Franklin and Eleanor Roosevelt, The Home Front in World War II*. New York: Simon and Schuster, 1995.

Lash, Joseph P. *Eleanor and Franklin*. New York: Norton, 1971.

———. *Eleanor: The Years Alone*. New York: Norton, 1972.

———. *Love, Eleanor: Eleanor Roosevelt and Her Friends*. Garden City, N.Y.: Doubleday, 1982.

Roosevelt, Eleanor. *On My Own*. New York: Harper, 1958.

———. *This I Remember*. New York: Harper, 1949.

———. *This Is My Story*. New York: Harper, 1937.

Elizabeth (Bess) Virginia Wallace Truman
(February 13, 1885–October 18, 1982)
First Lady, April 12, 1945–January 20, 1953

Bess Truman
(Library of Congress)

In one sense, Bess Truman never left home. Delighting in being called "the independent lady from Independence," she clung to the values of her Missouri birthplace all her life. Through the many years she lived in the nation's capital as the wife of a senator, the vice president, and the president of the United States, her birthplace remained her home. Her sense of herself and her social position, her self-sacrificing loyalty to her maternal family, her values, her devotion to duty, her integrity, and her dignified but unpretentious bearing all derived from her midwestern homeland.

———— ෴ ————

Elizabeth (Bess) Virginia Wallace was born in Independence, Missouri, on February 13, 1885, the oldest child and only daughter of David Willock Wallace and Margaret (Madge) Gates Wallace. Three sons followed: Frank, George, and Fred. Their handsome, gregarious, and alcoholic father had a checkered career in politics. At the time of his death in 1903 he held the post of deputy surveyor in the Kansas City office of the United States Bureau of Customs, a job more significant in the title than in the substance. Unable to support his family and deeply in debt, he committed suicide in 1903.

Bess's mother was the daughter of George Porterfield Gates, cofounder of the successful Waggoner-Gates Milling Company and one of the wealthiest men in Independence. Madge Wallace was "a lady," said Margaret Truman, "from the top of her well-coifed head to the tips of her elegant fingers." On the other hand, Jeney Childs, a retired schoolteacher in Independence, saw her as a "very, very difficult person . . . [T]here wasn't anybody in town she didn't look down on." Bess grew up in an atmosphere of gentility, instructed in the social graces appropriate to her maternal family's position. She was also a tomboy, the "champion slugger" on her brothers' sandlot baseball team. By the time she graduated from high school, she was a formidable opponent on the tennis court, a "demon ice skater," an expert horseback rider—and she could whistle through her teeth.

As a young woman she suffered the results of her father's suicide. Overwhelmed by the "shame" of it, her mother never recovered from the shock and became a virtual recluse, reliant on Bess, who as the oldest child, was saddled with responsibility for the household and family. Bess asked herself what had gone wrong with her parents' marriage, concluding that her mother's tender but passive love had left David Wallace psychologically unsupported. If she ever found a man she could trust, Bess resolved, she would share her husband's whole life—his failures as well as his successes.

Financially, the Wallaces' dependence on Grandfather Gates continued, and Bess gave up all thought of going to college. Instead, at 20 she went to the Barstow School in Kansas City, an academically respectable prep school for girls who were headed for college and a finishing school for those who were not. There she earned excellent grades, made new friends, played as the star forward on the basketball team, and won the shot put in the spring track meet. After a year she returned home to resume her position as a social leader in the younger set and her responsibilities as head of the Wallace family and companion to her mother. Popular as always, she organized a bridge club, played tennis, went horseback riding, enjoyed picnics, and supported charities such as the Needlework Guild, which collected clothing for the needy. In 1910 Harry Truman, her long-time schoolmate, reentered her life.

Harry had known Bess since 1890, when the Truman family had moved to Independence from the farm of Harry's maternal grandparents, about 16 miles south. He first saw her at the Sunday School of the First Presbyterian Church—and was smitten. As Harry told the story, he knew at that moment that she was the girl for him. "I've never had but one golden-haired, blue-eyed sweetheart," he wrote her when they had been married 16 years, "and just as perfect and as beautiful as I dreamed of when I was ten and twelve and sixteen." For years he yearned for her in vain. She was a popular social leader; he was a poor farmer's son who had to work even while in high school. After graduation in 1901, Harry went back to the family farm for nine years, during which she never gave him a thought.

Then in the summer of 1910 he showed up at the Wallace home, and Bess, curious about the change in his appearance and demeanor, invited him in. During their long courtship she turned him down more than once, but by November 1913 she was deeply in love. She told him that she had begun to think that if she married anyone, he would be the one. He just sat and stared, until Bess said, "Harry Truman, you're an enigma." Another three and a half years passed, during which they were unofficially engaged, waiting to marry until Harry's prospects improved. By March 1917 they were planning their wedding, only to have their plans thwarted by World War I. Duty-bound, Harry had already joined the Missouri National Guard and expected to be sent overseas when the United States entered the war. He postponed their marriage, unwilling to risk saddling her with a crippled or blinded husband. Bess protested—she had waited so long and would be 33 in a few months—but he was adamant. Consequently, she spent the war years selling war bonds, serving on a local committee that entertained soldiers, managing the household and her imperious mother, and waiting for Harry.

Harry returned safely, and they were married on June 28, 1919, in the Trinity Episcopal Church in Independence. After a brief honeymoon, they moved in with Bess's mother—temporarily, they thought, but in fact for many years. Madge Wallace's own marriage had made her morbidly fearful lest Bess marry someone who could not support her, and Harry Truman's precarious finances frightened her. Although she demanded much of her daughter's time and attention, the Trumans managed to work out a happy and productive relationship. Despite frequent misgivings and major financial worries, Bess achieved her desire to share her husband's whole life. When he owed money, she scrimped and saved and took a paying job in his office. She accepted his decisions and contributed to his accomplishments, both socially and politically.

Throughout their life together, Bess tried with little success to change Harry's speech and conduct to conform to the genteel standards to which she had been raised. Occasionally he would yield for the moment, but he seldom changed his ways permanently; for example, if she told his valet not to pack his red pants when they went off on a trip together, he would be sporting them the next week. One of her Independence friends confided to Bess with embarrassment that she had long been trying to get her husband to say "fertilizer," not "manure." Not to worry, said Bess; for years she had been trying to get Harry to say "manure." Toward the end of their lives, she finally won the battle to get him to use a power rather than a hand

mower—only to be horrified when he started it up at 10:30 on Sunday morning, as their friends passed on their way to church.

When they married, Harry's prospects were shaky. Just weeks before their wedding he and Eddie Jacobson, a friend from the army, had opened a men's clothing store in Kansas City. In 1922, a short three years later, it failed, a victim of the first postwar recession. Refusing to file for bankruptcy, Harry spent the next 20 years paying off the store's creditors. As if this were not hard enough on a wife, he entered politics.

In 1921 the Pendergast machine in Kansas City asked him to run for the post of eastern judge of Jackson County, an administrative job roughly the equivalent of county commissioner in other states. As judge Harry would control county funds, the awarding of county contracts, and the hiring of county employees; he would also oversee the condition of county roads. Although his wife thought the judgeship a bad idea and endured many sleepless nights about it, she suppressed her objections.

Bess's role as the wife of a successful politician evolved over time, not without stress and strain. She set limits on what she would do to help her husband publicly: "A woman's place in public is to sit beside her husband, be silent, and be sure her hat is on straight," she once remarked. In private he consulted her, both for her advice and for the reassurance of knowing that she was there; he especially valued her observations about the possible reactions of voters. He talked out the alternatives, and if she disagreed with his conclusions or his plans, she voiced her opinions, which might or might not change his mind. Now and then she was overheard saying to him under her breath, "You didn't have to say that."

At home in Independence, although the town was hard hit by the recession, Truman's life as the wife of the eastern judge of Jackson County followed much the same quiet domestic course set during her young womanhood. The society pages of the *Examiner* regularly recorded that she had played bridge with her club and was serving as secretary of the Needlework Guild. But the couple was living in her mother's house, where her mother set the rules and met political talk with a chilly silence. Madge Wallace's extravagance conflicted with Bess's penny-pinching. Bess found some relief from this tense domestic situation in visiting her mother-in-law and in her own behind-the-scenes political activities.

Her nerves were further strained by the frustration of her hopes of bearing a child. She suffered a miscarriage the first year of her marriage, when she was 35, and a still more discouraging one a couple of years later. The next time she became pregnant, she superstitiously refused to buy baby clothes or supplies. The baby girl arrived on February 17, 1924, in the midst of a blizzard, at the Wallace home. The new mother cried, certain that her husband had wanted a boy, but his obvious delight soon soothed her. The family had to scramble for something to wrap the baby in, and an open bureau drawer served as a bassinet until the next morning, when Harry could plow through the drifts with a shopping list of baby things. The little girl had to wait much longer for a name. Her mother wanted to name her Margaret Wallace after her maternal grandmother, but her father insisted on equal representation for the Trumans. Not until four years later did they settle on Mary (after Harry Truman's sister) Margaret. Bess, who called her daughter Marg, turned into the disciplinarian of the family, while Harry spoiled his Margie.

Meanwhile, the family was facing new problems. The year Margaret was born, Harry Truman lost reelection to his judgeship. For a while he sold automobile club memberships and stock in a bank that he was organizing with friends. Despite his success in these endeavors, the Trumans soon decided jointly that he should accept the Pendergast offer to back him for presiding judge of the county court. The position came with a modest salary but prospects for building Harry's political reputation. His victory in that election and again in the election of 1930 prefigured his future as a politician rather than a businessman. He trav-eled frequently—his wife seldom agreed to accompany him—and constructed a broader political base, eyeing the governorship or perhaps a national post.

When he was out of town, on reserve duty with the army or attending to his duties as judge, Bess wrote to him frequently and fondly, keeping him in touch with the local political situation, sending clippings from local newspapers, and providing her own comments and reports. She frequently dropped in at his office and checked up on his staff. She dealt with phone calls urging the judge to attend funerals or see job seekers and protected him against dangerous political alliances. Even when he was around, she sometimes acted for him.

Harry's 1934 decision to run for the U.S. Senate was hard for his wife to accept. As always when confronted with significant change, Bess was reluctant. She would have preferred that he stay in Missouri as county collector. Furthermore, there were problems at home: Her mother would feel abandoned if left behind, and her brother Fred, who also lived in the Wallace home, seemed unable to earn a living independently. She dreaded the unfamiliarity of Washington and worried about how Margaret would adjust to the change. In the midst of the Great Depression, it seemed to Bess foolhardy to refuse the relative security of the collector's job. Nevertheless, even though to her displeasure her husband was beginning to call her "The Boss," she recognized his right to make his own decision and put her doubts aside. She stood beside him when he announced his candidacy, and she sat on platforms next to him as he conducted his difficult campaign, learning to swallow her fury when his opponents attacked him. When he was elected, she told a reporter, "Of course I'm thrilled to be going to Washington. But I have spent all my life here on Delaware Street and it will be a change."

It certainly was a change, and to her surprise Bess came to like it, although all her life she remained ambivalent. In her old age she said that ideally she would live half the year in Washington and half in Independence. Once in

Washington, she competently set about getting settled, finding an apartment and putting Margaret into a private school. She found the city friendly and familiar in its southern warmth, her fellow Missourians in government circles welcoming, and other newcomers to the city eager to meet the Trumans. She had a natural base in the Congressional Club, where she could talk with women who were similarly situated, and she learned the formalities of making duty calls and holding the Thursday "at homes" mandatory for senators' wives. She met and enjoyed spending time with the cabinet wives, as well as Secretary of Labor Frances Perkins and First Lady Eleanor Roosevelt, whom she especially admired. Just as she had in Independence, Bess frequented her husband's office, taking an interest in the staff's personal lives, reading and signing letters, and handling routine correspondence. She listened to Senate debates from the gallery and kept close tabs on the legislative process. As she and 10-year-old Margaret saw the sights together, they discovered each other as friends.

Bess never neglected to write home, spending at least an hour daily at the task, making sure that her mother had a letter from her every day, even Sunday. When summer came she headed back to Independence with Margaret. Senator Truman drove them home, but in a week he returned to work and loneliness in the Washington heat. The separation strained their marriage. Alone in a hotel room, he missed the company of his wife and daughter, and he missed the discussions of legislative struggles that he often shared with Bess. He worried over money, thinking himself a financial failure, while his wife worried over reports that he was invited to parties almost every night. Nevertheless, he wrote her loving letters and kept her up to date, sending her the *Congressional Record,* telling her what was going on in the back rooms of the Capitol and on the floor of the Senate, letting off steam, and saying what he could not say publicly. Her questions in response forced him to think out his positions more clearly. From Independence she cheered him on, praising his achievements.

Thus they established a pattern that held for years, with Bess and Margaret Truman spending long intervals in Independence between their sojourns in Washington—and Madge Wallace urging them to spend even more time in Missouri. Bess still felt responsible for her mother, her brothers, and her brothers' families. She justified remaining in Missouri by citing the constant shortage of cash and Margaret's tendency to catch one cold after another. Not even invitations to the White House or her husband's appeals that he needed her as a hostess budged her, though she wrote him in the fall of 1937, "It's a h_ _ _ of a way to live—the way we do."

Over time, life in Washington appealed to her more. As the wife of a senator with an increasing reputation, she felt more sure of herself and became more active socially and in the Congressional Club. She grew increasingly eager to help her husband play the game of politics. Whether in Independence or Washington, she had a ringside seat at the dramatic events that unfolded as the United States struggled to define its role in the events leading to World War II. She kept in touch with every detail of Harry Truman's career and kept him in touch with his Missouri political base. During his 1940 reelection campaign, all three Trumans commuted frequently between Missouri and Washington. In the primary and in the election, Bess not only labored behind the scenes but also appeared with the candidate, working the crowd, shaking hands, and greeting the voters.

She was delighted with his victory. Back in Washington, she reveled in the pace of events as the government geared up for war. Senator Truman was attracting attention by his clashes with wartime administrators and fellow senators, while she egged him on, commenting on his speeches, and suggesting that he study public speaking. In July 1941 Harry put Bess on his payroll at a salary of $2,400, more than anyone else in his office was making; he claimed that she earned every penny of it, but some on the staff disagreed. After Pearl Harbor, she ran the office for him while he traveled in the investigations of defense expenditures that made the Truman name a household word. Every Wednesday she spent five or six hours volunteering at the United Service Organization, which provided aid and entertainment to soldiers and sailors.

Bess was dismayed when her husband was offered the Democratic nomination for the vice presidency in 1944. The state of President Roosevelt's health suggested that he would not survive a fourth term and that Harry Truman would therefore have to assume the burdens of a wartime presidency. Bess objected in part because of her lifelong dislike of change, but she had other sound reasons. She did not want to leave the reasonably serene and comfortable life of a senator's wife, which she had worked so hard to master, for the hurly-burly of the White House. For 10 years she had observed the vicious attacks launched at the Roosevelt family, and she fully understood the demands on both the president and the first lady. She detested the inevitable glare of publicity and the invasion of her family's privacy. She and her husband agreed that the White House was no place for their daughter, and Margaret did not want to live there. Furthermore, Harry was 60, and Bess feared what the presidency might do to his health.

All her life Bess had been making sacrifices, putting herself and her concerns second to her mother's peace of mind, her brothers' welfare, her fears that Margaret might be kidnapped, and her husband's career. Now she let Harry know that she was against his accepting the nomination—but she went just so far in exerting her influence. He loved her dearly, she knew, and might well have yielded if she had told him the whole truth: that the prospect was close to intolerable for her. Aware of his sense of duty to his country, she refused to blackmail him emotionally.

Harry Truman finally yielded to the heavy pressures and appeals to party loyalty put on him by Democratic leaders, foremost among them President Roosevelt. He was elected vice president in 1944. As she settled into her new position as second lady, Bess dared to hope that with the war going well, pressures on President Roosevelt would ease and he might yet survive his fourth term. When he died on April 12, 1945, she burst into tears. Then, pulling herself together, she changed her dress, arranged to have a friend sit with her visiting mother, and took Margaret with her to the White House, where, in her first official act as first lady, she paid a condolence call on Eleanor Roosevelt. Subsequently, she went down to the cabinet room to see her husband sworn in as president of the United States.

On the train bearing Franklin Roosevelt's body to Hyde Park for burial, Bess Truman stayed up to help her husband with the speech he was soon to give to Congress. Back in Washington, having urged Mrs. Roosevelt to take all the time she needed to move, they found that they could no longer remain in their apartment, which the Secret Service found impossible to guard. On April 16 they moved to Blair House, and on April 19 the first lady and her daughter inspected the now-vacated White House.

The mansion was a mess—infested with rats, the furniture worn and dingy, the private rooms shabby and in need of paint. Bess had to redecorate before the family could move in on May 7—the day Germany surrendered. At the same time she was hastily assembling her staff. In those first weeks she wrote a friend, "We are not any of us happy to be where we are but there's nothing to be done about it except to do our best—and forget about the sacrifices and many unpleasant things that bob up."

She had no intention of following in Eleanor Roosevelt's globe-trotting footsteps or of emulating her predecessor's lifestyle. Neither would she give speeches, allow private interviews, or hold regular press conferences, though she would attend women reporters' luncheons and teas, and she would answer their written questions with written replies. "If you had been given a choice would you have gone into the White House?"—No. "Do you think we will ever have a woman as president?"—No. "What would you and President Truman like to do when his term of office expires?"—Return to Independence. Too frequently to suit reporters, she simply answered, "No comment." She rebuffed attempts to pry into matters she considered none of their "damn business," like what she was going to wear to a tea. "You do not need to know me," she told one protesting reporter. "I am not the chief executive, and I have nothing to say to the public." Only rarely did she relax this attitude, as when in 1952 she gave women reporters a tour of the extensively restored White House. Hunting for newsworthy items, the press was reduced to reporting on her frequent visits to Independence.

The Trumans gave a formal reception for the prince regent of Iraq on May 28, 1945, and soon thereafter Bess retreated, with Margaret, to the house in Independence, to oversee its renovation as the summer White House. She was fleeing what she called "the Great White Jail," resorting to the absentee pattern of the early Senate years by seeking refuge in Independence with the Wallace family. Meanwhile, her husband's new responsibilities had disrupted their established mode of working together. He could not, for example, confide in his wife such state secrets as the decision to use the atomic bomb. She felt left out, though his letters clearly show that he wanted to discuss with her the new problems he faced as the most powerful leader in a war-torn world. Just as they had when he first went to Washington, the Trumans had to evolve fresh ways of living and working together.

In time they did, and though few in the public suspected it, Bess Truman eventually became an important political force. White House usher J. B. West bore witness to this in his book *Upstairs at the White House:*

> At nine o'clock, Mr. Truman picked up his briefcase, took Mrs. Truman by the arm, went into his study, and closed the door. They worked together until eleven o'clock almost every night, editing his speeches, discussing his policies, designing his politics. In public,

Mrs. Truman never said a word. She stayed as far in the background as Mrs. Roosevelt had projected her own personality into the foreground. . . . Although it went unsuspected by nearly everybody in government, Bess Truman entered into nearly every decision the President made.

The first lady was more than a sounding board or an editor. It was her idea to send theatrical companies abroad, such as the one that presented *Porgy and Bess,* to show the best of American culture to other countries, and it was her idea to make the National Institutes of Health a center for a massive effort to conquer diseases. A good reader of character, she cautioned the president against people mainly interested in self-aggrandizement and recommended people who would give their loyalty to the country and to him. Her political shrewdness helped him maneuver through Congress such important measures as the Marshall Plan. She always supported him emotionally, particularly after the death of his mother.

Bess Truman managed the presidential household competently and thriftily. Tactfully, she dismissed Eleanor Roosevelt's housekeeper, Mrs. Nesbitt, whose cuisine had been the despair of Franklin Delano Roosevelt and his guests. A good housekeeper herself, the first lady watched carefully for dust and cobwebs and continued the economy she had practiced for years, for the president's salary barely covered expenses, and the Trumans had no private fortune.

The White House staff liked her and her manner toward them, "correct but not formal." She gave herself no airs and would brook no nonsense. She could not abide "fakers, shirkers or flatterers," said Alonzo Fields, head butler, but toward those who did their jobs she was understanding and kind. Another staff member, Lillian Parks, remembered that she would laugh so hard that her whole body would shake, and usher J. B. West commented on her wit: "dry, laconic, incisive and very funny. It's difficult to capture in words because it was so often silent. She was at her funniest with a straight face, perfectly deadpan. If you weren't looking for one raised eyebrow, one downturned corner of her mouth, you might miss the joke entirely." Once when a butler stumbled and dropped a plate of cake, Mrs. Truman laughed and asked, "Well, as food for thought, what *was* the dessert?"

During the final months of World War II and for a time thereafter, Bess curtailed the social season, deeming elaborate entertainment inappropriate when so many were hungry and homeless. As the world began to recover from the war's catastrophes, to the surprise of Washingtonians the small-town, midwestern Bess Truman restored an elegance and brilliance to formal presidential entertaining that it had not known since before the Great Depression—even though by 1948 she was having to cancel events for fear the White House would collapse on the heads of the guests. She herself did not much enjoy such affairs. The limelight shriveled her soul; in its glare she stiffened, looking bored, pained, even disapproving. Senatorial wife (and later Senator) Lindy Boggs commented on what delightful company the first lady had been when arranging things for a reception, and how the minute the doors opened she froze. "Instead of being the outgoing, warm and lovely woman that she had been previously, the huge crowds simply made her sort of pull up into herself."

Bess dressed classically—in simple dresses, in tailored clothes, and for evenings in long gowns cut with straight lines, usually with a strand of pearls. In an evening gown, her daughter reported, Bess Truman looked regal. Often she chose black, because "You can't go wrong with it." Her husband always thought that "She looks exactly as a woman of her age should look."

In his 1948 campaign Bess worked long hours for Harry's reelection, though she doubted the outcome. She stepped up her entertaining to the point that reporters commented on her heavy schedule. Even though her mother was seriously ill, without a word of protest the first lady and Margaret accompa-

nied the president on the famous whistle-stop tour of the country that won him the election. They smiled and waved from the back platform of the train to the throngs that cheered them at every stop, even though to Bess's disgust her husband insisted on introducing them as "The Boss" and "the one who bosses the Boss." Bess even made a speech in Texas—"Good morning, and thank you for this wonderful greeting"—and she allowed reporters to invade their Independence home and take pictures of the president as he addressed the nation by radio. On election night, while Harry Truman slept serenely in a hotel, his wife and daughter stayed up to listen to the returns, retiring only when his victory was assured. Recalling that the tart-tongued playwright Clare Booth Luce had called her "an ersatz first lady," Bess pondered aloud, "I wonder if she will think I'm real now."

Her tasks in both household management and entertaining were complicated by the necessity of moving into Blair House for most of her husband's second term, from 1949 to 1952. After the leg of Margaret's piano fell through the floor, an investigation of the White House's structure revealed problems so radical that engineers considered razing the whole building. The Trumans insisted that as much as possible of the mansion be saved, at least its walls. They moved some of the furniture from the White House into Blair House, but the first lady had to find alternative locations for larger functions. She therefore arranged to hold the 1949 inaugural ball in the National Gallery of Art—much amused to have $80,000 to spend, because the Republican Congress, anticipating the election of a Republican president, had voted enough money for a lavish celebration.

Blair House had other drawbacks—security among them. In 1950, Puerto Rican nationalists tried to shoot their way into Blair House, killing one guard and wounding another. Once her husband's safety was ensured, Bess wept in private, then pulled herself together to reassure Margaret by telephone and to keep an appointment for a ceremony at Arlington cemetery. The first lady kept her pleasures private, too.

She went to the movies with Margaret, read mystery stories, and attended every baseball game she could fit into her schedule. She kept in touch with old friends, especially Senate wives; when she entertained her Independence bridge club at the White House, her old friends found her unchanged and unpretentious. Above all she enjoyed her family, all of them so close that the staff called them "The Three Musketeers." They did everything together— reading, eating informally, listening to the radio, playing the piano, and just talking.

Throughout their marriage the Trumans had had Madge Wallace with them almost constantly, eventually moving her to live with them in Washington and, as long as her health would permit, shuttling her back and forth for frequent visits to Independence. She never fully approved of her son-in-law, and even in the White House she intimated to some of the servants that the president was not quite good enough for her daughter. Yet when she died at the White House in 1952, he wrote in his diary, "She was a grand lady. When I hear these mother-in-law jokes I don't laugh. They are not funny to me, because I've had a good one. . . . My mother was a good mother-in-law. . . . It gives me a pain in the neck to read the awful jokes that the so-called humorists crack about mother-in-laws."

That year President Truman declined to run for a third term, and with Dwight Eisenhower's inauguration in 1953 he and Bess returned to the old Wallace home and the quiet life they loved in Independence. Reporters and politicians gave them a rousing send-off from Washington's Union Station.

In those days former presidents received no pension and were provided with no guards or staff. Harry eased their financial situation by publishing his memoirs, but what saved the day was the farm that he inherited from his mother, most of which he sold to developers in the mid-1950s for enough money to guarantee his family's financial security.

On his 71st birthday in 1955, after he had turned the first spade of dirt on the future site of the Truman Library, the Trumans broke new ground in another way by opening their home to 150 people for a buffet dinner. Margaret was amazed; never had she thought to see her mother standing at the door of her "sanctuary" to welcome so many guests. The Trumans subsequently vacationed in Hawaii on a friend's estate, where they saw the sights and Bess fished. Later they drove to Washington to see old friends and catch up on the political gossip. In 1956, despite having to cope with reporters and crowds, they so enjoyed six weeks in Europe that they returned the next year. On April 21, 1956, Margaret married *New York Times* editor Clifton Daniel and in 1957 the Trumans rejoiced in the birth of their first grandchild. As she grew older, Bess suffered increasingly from the arthritis that had plagued her for years and underwent a mastectomy.

The assassination of John F. Kennedy in 1963 grieved both the Trumans, reminding them of the narrow escape Harry Truman had had 13 years earlier during the attack on Blair House. At that time Congress appropriated funds to guard the nation's former presidents and their families. Nevertheless, it took all of President Lyndon Johnson's famous powers to persuade Bess Truman to accept the Secret Service, though she still refused to allow them into the house or onto the property.

Despite her joy in Margaret's four boys and other family pleasures, the former first lady found that she missed Washington. To a reporter who met her on the street in Independence and whom she invited up on the veranda of her house to chat, she confessed how much she had liked some aspects of living in the White House, especially the fresh flowers and not having to worry about getting someone to mow the lawn. She also missed the cultural life of the city, her long-standing friends there, and being in the political mainstream.

When Harry Truman died in late 1972, his widow and his daughter were touched by the nationwide mourning. Bess Truman especially valued the expressions of loss and sympathy from average citizens, such as the thousands of

Missourians who waited outside the Truman Library to pay their last respects. At her request, the ceremonies were held in Independence; the guest list for the funeral was limited to 250. As usual, she kept herself under iron self-control, tears coming to her eyes only when her husband's old artillery outfit fired a 21-gun salute.

Refusing her daughter's suggestion that she move to New York, Bess stayed on in Independence, rereading almost every day the 38th wedding anniversary letter that her husband had written her in 1957. She reached out to old friends, near and far, and chatted with Margaret three or four times a week on the telephone. Even when she was in a wheelchair, she kept up on political events, deploring the capitulation of the Democratic Party to its left wing. In 1974 she surprised everyone by accepting the position of honorary chair in Missouri senator Tom Eagleton's bid for reelection; she enjoyed that race particularly because she got to discuss baseball with major-league star Stan Musial, her co-chair. Two years later, at 91, she did the same thing for Missouri Congressman Jim Symington in his run for the Senate, feistily analyzing the flaws of his opponents; she also endorsed Missouri State Senator Ike Skelton.

Bess reveled in the renewed respect for Harry Truman, a stalwart exemplar of integrity, in the wake of the Watergate scandal. She was delighted when former members of the Truman administration created the Truman Scholarship Program to train young people for government service. She remained indifferent to her own popularity; responding to the news that she had been listed in a Gallup poll as one of the 20 most admired women in the United States, she remarked, "I don't know why." She was still the woman who had, over her husband's protests, burned most of her letters to him. "Think of history," he had begged her. "I have," she said, casting another letter onto the fire.

Bess Truman died at 97, on October 18, 1982. Her body lies in the courtyard of the Truman Library next to her husband's, for, he had said, "We're going to be buried out here. I like the idea because I may just want to get up some day and stroll into my office. And I can hear you saying, 'Harry—you oughtn't.'"

—⁓—

Bess Truman clung to her Missouri heritage, but she also became a naturalized citizen of the nation's capital. Her years as the wife of a senator of national reputation earned her many friends there; her work in her husband's office and their close, confiding relationship made her knowledgeable about national affairs. Yet throughout his career her sense of obligation to her birth family made her return often to Independence, leaving him lonely and without a hostess, even in the White House. As first lady she opted for privacy, refusing to emulate Eleanor Roosevelt but continuing to consult and advise with her husband in his presidency, exercising an important influence on his decisions. Just as she photographed badly, so Bess Truman publicly presented a stiff and rather dull image that kept strangers from guessing at the forthright, competent, and well-informed woman with the rollicking sense of humor and enchanting laugh whom her friends knew. Yet she restored the White House social season to an éclat lost during the years of the Great Depression and World War II.

CHRONOLOGY

1885 *February 13:* Elizabeth (Bess) Margaret Wallace is born in Independence, Missouri

1890 Harry S. Truman meets Bess Wallace

1901 Bess Wallace graduates from high school

1903 Bess Wallace's father commits suicide

1905 Bess enrolls in the Barstow School, Kansas City, Missouri

1911 *June:* Bess Wallace refuses Harry Truman's proposal

1913 *November:* Bess Wallace and Harry Truman become engaged

1919   *June 28:* Bess Wallace marries Harry Truman, who has just opened a men's clothing store in Kansas City

1922   Harry Truman is elected eastern judge of county court

1924   *February 17:* Daughter Margaret is born

1926   Harry Truman is elected presiding judge in Jackson County

1934   Harry Truman is elected to the U.S. Senate

1940   Harry Truman is reelected to the Senate

1941   *July:* Bess Truman is put on Harry Truman's Senate office payroll

1944   Harry Truman is elected vice president

Madge Wallace moves in with the Trumans

1945   *April 12:* Franklin Roosevelt dies and Harry Truman becomes president; Bess Truman becomes first lady

1952   *December 5:* Madge Gates Wallace, Bess Truman's mother, dies at the White House at age 90

1953   *January 20:* The Trumans return to their old house at 219 Delaware, Independence, Missouri

1962   *November:* Bess Truman undergoes a mastectomy

1972   *December 26:* Harry Truman dies in Kansas City and is buried in the courtyard of the Truman Library in Independence

1982   *October 18:* Bess Truman dies at 219 Delaware; she is buried next to Harry in the courtyard of the Truman Library in Independence

---

FURTHER READING

Ferrell, Robert H., ed. *Dear Bess: The Letters from Harry to Bess Truman, 1910–1959.* Columbia: University of Missouri Press, 1983.

Hay, Peter. *All the Presidents' Ladies: Anecdotes of the Women Behind the Men in the White House.* New York: Viking, 1988.

McCullough, David. *Truman.* New York: Simon and Schuster, 1992.

Truman, Margaret. *Bess W. Truman.* New York: Macmillan, 1986.

———. *First Ladies: An Intimate Group Portrait of White House Wives.* New York: Fawcett Columbine, 1995.

MAMIE GENEVA DOUD EISENHOWER
(NOVEMBER 14, 1896–NOVEMBER 1, 1979)
First Lady, January 20, 1953–January 20, 1961

MAMIE EISENHOWER
(Library of Congress)

Mamie Geneva Doud Eisenhower, the last first lady to be born in the 19th century, grew up in comfort in a loving family, the pampered daughter of a well-to-do father, with servants to attend to the household chores, a personal maid, and beaux from the best families of Denver escorting her to parties and outings. Her marriage to an impecunious lieutenant fresh out of West Point thrust her into a way of life for which she was ill prepared, and her difficulties in adjusting to it caused problems in the marriage. She learned, however, to be the kind of wife her husband wanted and to develop her marked talents as hostess, a role that she enjoyed and that served her husband well in both military and civilian life. She remained what she was trained to be, a woman who enjoyed what she regarded as woman's proper sphere—clothes, appearance, family, and social life.

261

Mamie Geneva Doud was born in Boone, Iowa, on November 14, 1896, the second of four daughters of businessman John Sheldon Doud and his wife Elvira Mathilde Carlson Doud. Her father was descended from a family that had helped found Guilford, Connecticut, and later moved to the Midwest and started a meatpacking business. Her mother's family, which had emigrated from Sweden in 1868, adhered to the strict doctrines of the Swedish Evangelical Church, even in Mamie's lifetime. When she was nine months old, the Douds moved to Cedar Rapids. When she was eight years of age, her father retired and moved his family to Denver, Colorado, where she grew up; they wintered regularly in San Antonio.

All her life Mamie had to combat debilitating bouts with sickness. An indulged child, at the age of eight she developed rheumatic fever and was taken out of school for the greater part of a year. Her father, who valued "ladylike" accomplishments more than book learning, did not set much store on education for girls and did not hesitate to interrupt her schooling for treats and travel. She did attend Miss Wolcott's finishing school "for ladies of refinement" for the school year 1914–15. She took lessons in ballroom dancing, the piano, and voice. At home she learned to run a house with servants, manage domestic financial accounts, embroider and sew, and stock a hope chest. In time she became one of Denver's most captivating belles.

Mamie made her debut at the Doud winter home in San Antonio in 1915. She captivated Dwight David (Ike) Eisenhower, a brand-new second lieutenant fresh out of West Point and stationed at nearby Fort Sam Houston, who began a courtship that soon eliminated all competition. Mamie was delighted with his gift of an engraved silver jewel case and wheedled her parents into allowing her to keep it. When Ike proposed right after Christmas 1915, Mamie's father warned her of the financial hardships that lay ahead and raised such objections to Ike's announcement that he was

transferring to the army air force that he abandoned that ambition.

Rumors of war with Mexico and Germany hastened the young couple's wedding. On July 1, 1916—the same day that Ike was promoted to first lieutenant—they were married in a ceremony at the Doud home in Denver. Ike was always fond of his in-laws, calling them *Mother* and *Dad* and signing his letters to them as *son*. Mamie's parents were equally devoted to him, despite John Doud's initial reservations.

After a short honeymoon during which they visited Ike's parents in Abilene, Kansas, the young Eisenhowers moved into Infantry Row at Fort Sam Houston, the first of the 37 homes Mamie moved in and out of during the 45 years of her husband's public service. She was not prepared for life as an army wife. There was not much money; housing could be miserable; social life was rigidly prescribed; and Ike's duty came first, often interrupting married life. For the first time Mamie had to make her own bed, scrub floors, and prepare food. Her mother's formula had been: "If you don't learn how to cook, no one will ask you to do it." Determined to show her parents that she could succeed in her new world and helped by their generous present of money, she did what she could to make the cramped two-room quarters at Fort Sam livable: She made curtains, rented a piano, and laid down a red Khiva rug from her hope chest. From Ike she learned basic cooking so that they would not have to spend $40 a month to eat at the officers' mess every day.

Ike's duties often required his absence from home, sometimes for long periods. Accustomed to being the center of attention, Mamie was stunned when she was left alone. When she cried or complained, Ike comforted her, but he told her: "Mamie, there's one thing you must understand. My country comes first and always will. You come second." That she and the marriage survived can be credited to his patience and to her resilience and determination—as well as the pride that sustained her. She did not discuss her hurt and loneliness with her parents, nor would she admit that her family's warnings about financial hardships had been well founded; often at the end of the month, Ike and Mamie were down to a quarter. She herself kept the family checkbook and carefully avoided getting into debt. She loved Ike, and she knew, as she put it later, that she had made her own bed. "Nothing came before his duty," she once said. "I was forced to match his spirit of personal sacrifice as best I could. Being his wife meant I must leave him free from personal worries to conduct his career as he saw fit."

The Eisenhowers were a popular couple. Their quarters became known as the "Club Eisenhower," where friends gathered for cards, music, games, and spur-of-the-minute barbecues. Mamie understood that their parties were important not only in furthering Ike's career but in giving him opportunities to relax among friends and colleagues. As his career skyrocketed, she became accustomed to entertaining people of rank and position.

When the United States entered World War I in April 1917, Ike hoped for overseas duty, but to his disgust he was assigned mostly to training missions within the United States. Sometimes Mamie could accompany him, other times not. Camp Stanley, near San Antonio, provided no quarters for wives, so Mamie stayed at Fort Sam and Ike visited when he could. Desperately lonely, on one occasion Mamie, who had never driven before, drove their car out to surprise Ike—provoking his wrath. Their first child, Doud Dwight (Icky) was born on September 24, 1917, in the army hospital at Fort Sam while Ike was away. Rank held, even within the hospital: As the wife of a lowly first lieutenant, Mamie felt abandoned and neglected while the doctors and nurses pampered the wives of higher-ranking officers.

With Ike far away at Camp Oglethorpe in Georgia, Mamie so exhausted herself caring for the baby that she sickened and fell into a coma. Her husband rushed to her side on emergency leave. She recovered, but they were warned that her childhood bout with rheumatic fever had left her with a weakened heart. All her life she tired easily. Temperament, physique, and the haunting memory of her older sister Eleanor's death at 16 from a heart condition combined to produce the many psychological and physical problems that beset her: claustrophobia, fear of flying, fear of insects, overreactions to heat and cold, inability to walk far, gallbladder trouble, asthma, and the Ménière's syndrome that disturbed her balance and led to allegations of alcoholism.

She was well enough to join Ike at Camp Colt, near Gettysburg, Pennsylvania, where he commanded the newly constituted Tank Corps. For her the outstanding experience of World War I was a ride in a tank, from which she emerged drenching wet with perspiration, with ringing ears and stinging eyes. The death of Mamie's younger sister Edna Mae ("Buster") in the 1918 flu epidemic saddened them; now Mamie had only one sister left, Mabel Frances, whom they called Mike. At Camp Colt Mamie had to keep house and care for Icky in a tiny apartment in a damp house without gas or electricity, heated only by a potbellied stove. Still, the Eisenhowers enjoyed life on the base, learning to play bridge and having card parties.

After the war they lived an up-and-down existence. When they could be together, as at Camp Campbell, Kentucky, they always made many army friends. On the other hand, the separations occasioned by Ike's military assignments strained the Eisenhower marriage. Sometimes dismal housing—seedy furniture, grimy rugs, torn curtains, 12-hour-long power shutdowns, and frigid dampness—sent Mamie back to San Antonio for a time. Then on January 2, 1921, their son Icky, the joy of their lives, died of scarlet fever. Devastated as he was, Ike could at least bury himself in his work. Mamie, just 24, having already experienced the deaths of all four of her grandparents and two of her sisters, could only resort to a desperately gay frivolity. She teetered, Ike feared, on the ragged edge of a breakdown.

That fall Ike was sent to Panama as executive officer to the commandant, General Fox Conner—a posting that proved to be a turning point in the Eisenhower marriage. Mamie dreaded the move. She was pregnant again, and Panama was a hardship post, riddled with malaria and yellow fever. Nevertheless, she refused Ike's offer to try to change his orders and accompanied him to Panama. The voyage was a misery; bumped from their spacious cabin by a general, they were cramped in a small cubicle with a double-decker bunk. Mamie suffered from morning sickness, seasickness, and claustrophobia. They sweated in the hot, steamy air and swatted at the insatiable insects.

At Camp Gaillard, perched on the edge of mudslide-plagued Culebra Cut, they found a "stilted ark" of a house—unoccupied for a decade, damp, mildewed, overgrown with vines, and infested with lizards, spiders, cockroaches, snakes, bats, bedbugs, and mosquitoes. Household help was untrained, with shaky English and strange convictions. Sharing all these afflictions with the friendly folk on post made them bearable, and Mamie adapted. Having the baby under such conditions, though, was too much. At her parents' insistence she went back to Denver, where on August 3, 1922, she gave birth to the son whom she and Ike named John Sheldon Doud Eisenhower in honor of her father. Two months later mother and son returned to Panama, accompanied by a nurse, Katherine Herrick, who stayed with the family for four years.

Back in Panama, Mamie found Ike absorbed in reading and study assigned by General Conner in preparation for the next war. Feeling excluded, she tried to put a brave face on her distress in her letters home: "Ike got away yesterday a.m. and I got up at 5:30 and went down to where they bid him farewell—it may be five weeks but probably only two. We are not afraid and have loads of parties to go to as the ladies are having 'hen parties.' Am having a 'Tea' Sunday afternoon from 4:30 to 5:30 for 60 ladies—quite a mob but will pass an awfully lonesome time of day." She took out her emotions in digestive problems and obsessive fears for the baby. General Conner's wife, Virginia, thought she saw Ike and Mamie "drifting apart."

Sometime in 1923, despite Ike's pleas, Mamie gave up and went home. "I was down to skin and bones and hollow-eyed," she later recorded, "so ill I'd have to walk all night long. The porch was screened on three sides and I would walk all night long, listening to mosquitoes buzz. I could hear the monkeys scream in the jungle and I felt like screaming too." Home, though, proved no panacea; she had outgrown it. She faced the fact that to stay married to Ike she had to accommodate to the demands of his career. Her health restored, she once again sailed for Panama, determined to commit to army life, support her husband, and join in his recreations. She developed a close friendship with Virginia Conner and plunged into fundraising for a base hospital, whipping up enthusiasm with games and parties.

In the interim between the two world wars, Ike, with Mamie's support, stayed on the fast track. Assignment to the General Staff school at Fort Leavenworth, Kansas, made him eligible for the highest ranks. She provided the tranquil environment he needed in which to study, despite the presence of their rambunctious toddler, and the Eisenhowers were happy together. At her suggestion, in 1928 he turned down an appointment to the General Staff at the War Department in favor of an assignment in Paris to prepare a book on the battlefields of World War I. The volume attracted the praise of that war's hero, General John Pershing, and prepared Ike for his command in the European Theater of Operations in World War II. In Paris the Eisenhowers made important friends among American diplomats as well as within the military community. Mamie's talents as a hostess drew people to the Eisenhower apartment, where they joined in songfests around the piano and ate Ike's cooking. The three Eisenhowers also traveled, driving around France and into Belgium, Germany, and Italy.

Back in Washington in 1929, Ike became aide to chief-of-staff General Douglas MacArthur. Mamie kept busy changing the decor of their apartment as the seasons demanded in that un-airconditioned era, and making her mark as a Washington hostess. Club Eisenhower reassembled, and the Eisenhowers mingled with some of the most powerful people in the capital. Although Mamie could not offer elaborate food, her guests sat down to a beautiful table with carefully planned flower arrangements. Sparkling with wit and charm, she made parties gay with her laughter, and she and Ike both played cards well. They were entertained by higher-ranking officers, a tribute to Ike's professional success and to Mamie's popularity.

During the Great Depression (1929–39) army salaries were cut. Despite regular checks from Mamie's father, the Eisenhowers were pinched for money, though they held on to their cook. In an era where hunger sometimes dropped Americans on the street, what Mamie saw around her introduced her to poverty— which repelled her. She wrote to her parents: "Yesterday I spent the morning and $1.50 in phone calls calling people for the Parent-Teacher's card party on Fri. Such a job, and this AM I was out at nine, calling in person on the families who didn't have phones. Believe me this is the last time I'll let myself in for anything like that again. . . . Such queer dirty apts as I saw this AM—felt like I should have been disinfected when I got home."

In 1932, for the first time Mamie took an interest in the presidential election, though professional soldiers traditionally neither voted nor expressed political opinions. Still, she stayed oddly detached from the historic events going on around her. Ike strongly disagreed with MacArthur's decision to disperse the desperate World War I veterans who marched on Washington asking for a bonus and burn the pathetic shacks they had erected for shelter. Ike's 10-year-old son recognized his father's distaste for having to participate in this brutal rejection of men who had served their country in the trenches, but Mamie rejoiced that MacArthur praised her husband for carrying out his orders.

The year 1935 presented the Eisenhowers with a choice. Should Ike remain in the army, where several high-ranking officers were maneuvering to get him on their staffs, or should

he accept one of the tempting civilian job offers that paid more and would enable the family to stay in Washington? Despite that agreeable prospect, Mamie told Ike that she did not think he belonged in civilian life, and Ike went to the Philippines on MacArthur's command. Mamie, frightened at the dangers to her health of life in the tropics, lingered in Washington—a decision that stunned and hurt her husband. John, in his last year in school, stayed with her. She tried to convince herself that Ike would not like the Philippines, but after a year she had to face the knowledge that he was not coming back, lonely though he was without his family. She pulled herself together and joined him in October 1936.

The reunion was not an easy one. During their year apart Ike had created a social life of his own, in his leisure doing what he pleased when he pleased with his bridge group and his golf partners and welcomed by hostesses as an extra man. Although in his absence Mamie had been escorted around Washington by several male friends, she was jealous of his choice of an athletic naval wife as his favorite golf partner. They reconciled only when Mamie was frightened by a minor automobile accident that drew a crowd; she vomited blood and sank into a coma for several weeks.

Gradually she adjusted to the Philippines. The low cost of living there made the Eisenhowers financially comfortable for the first time in their married life. Mamie found Manila the "partying-est place" in the Far East. She took up golf so that she could play with Ike. Though bad health sapped her energy, by taking siestas and resting when she could, she fulfilled their social obligations. In 1939, with World War II moving from threat to reality, Lieutenant Colonel Eisenhower requested a transfer to the Zone of the Interior.

Back in the United States, they moved from Fort Tacoma, near Seattle, to Fort Sam Houston, to Fort Myer, Virginia, where Eisenhower was assigned to the staff of General George Marshall. Wherever they went, Mamie Eisenhower fulfilled the duties of the traditional army wife, finding places for them to live, redecorating and resettling, and getting up at 6:30 A.M. to cook her husband's breakfast. At Fort Myer she ran a huge house with the assistance only of two orderlies, chaired a group at the Soldiers, Sailors and Marines Club canteen, and served on the committee for the Army Relief Society.

Then in 1942 General Eisenhower was appointed European theater commander and left for England. His wife returned to Washington and moved into the Wardman Tower apartment of Ruth Butcher, wife of an officer on Eisenhower's staff. When this arrangement did not work out, Ruth moved across the hall and the general's wife kept the apartment, resuming her membership in the tight-knit community of army wives. With her women friends she dined and played cards; pooled ration cards; shared potluck suppers and mah-jongg and bridge parties; volunteered for the Red Cross; worked on rummage sales; and served meals to soldiers, sailors, and marines for the American Women's Volunteer Services—but now in the glare of the publicity that came from her husband's high position. Occasionally she attended an official ceremony.

Like other soldiers' wives, Mamie Eisenhower wrote to her husband almost daily; she heard from him regularly, on average three times a week. His letters helped to sustain her through the health problems—among them food allergies—that she was experiencing. He wrote that he wished she were living with him in England: "You cannot imagine how much you added to my efficiency in the hard months in Washington. Even I didn't realize it then; at least not fully—but I do now, and I'm grateful to you."

From other sources, however, she heard unpleasant rumors about her husband. The media hinted at an involvement between him and Kay Summersby, his pretty Irish driver. He tried to reassure his wife, writing, "I love you all the time—don't go bothering your pretty head about WACS—etc etc. You just hold the thought that . . . I'm on the run to you the day the victorious army marches into Berlin!" He spoke of crazy tales "without the slightest foun-

dation in fact." Nonetheless, rumors of an illicit romance continued; later Summersby herself gave substance to them in a book. No one but the principals has ever known the truth of the matter. Mamie kept her head and her marriage, for the most part refusing to believe the rumors, telling herself that it was important for her husband, with his heavy responsibilities, to have someone nearby to listen to him and with whom he could relax. "I know Ike," she told her friends.

He praised her conduct: "I'm prouder of you every time someone brings me news of the way you handle yourself—of the serene way that you (my mother, too, God bless her) brush off the chance to indulge in cheap publicity. You are a thorobred [sic], and, merely incidently, I love the hell out of you." Nevertheless, she was not invulnerable to rumor herself, and there were whispers of a drinking problem. Some say that she never had one, that her symptoms came from Ménière's syndrome, an inner-ear problem. Others allege that in her husband's absence Mamie did drink too much for a while, but that she soon gave up hard liquor. Increasingly conscious of her position in the spotlight, Mamie resolved not to be seen partying in public for the duration of the war, and she refused to accept gifts.

When the Allies' victory in 1945 enabled General Eisenhower to return home, the reunited couple rarely left each other's side, although each had to sacrifice some independence as they readjusted to marriage. The general's high rank now spared them the hardships of the past. Mamie settled them into a new government-owned house, undertook extensive entertaining, and accompanied her husband on most of his scheduled trips.

On October 12, 1948, Ike ended his army career with his inauguration as president of Columbia University. His wife redecorated the president's house and began entertaining with teas for faculty wives and buffet-supper parties for large donors. The limits that the general had set on his presidency, however, kept the Eisenhowers remote from most of campus life and left them time for their army friends.

Transition back into army life was easy when Ike took a leave of absence from Columbia in 1951–52 to command North American Treaty Organization (NATO) forces. Mamie accompanied him to France, where she established quarters at an estate she selected for its "beautiful grounds and great possibilities." Unimpressed by the company she now kept, she wrote to her parents that "the place teems with Princesses and Countesses, but [I] can never remember their names." She traveled about with her husband, who was received by the heads of state and government of each country they visited. At the end of this tour, the general was awarded the Grand Cross of the Order of Malta and his wife the Cross of Merit for her "unselfish service to mankind."

By the time they returned to Columbia, the "Eisenhower for President" movement had gathered momentum. In 1952 the Republican Party nominated the general. His wife was inevitably drawn into the campaign, from the moment the couple appeared together at Convention Hall in Chicago. Though she "dreaded all the hoopla we will need to go through," she accepted the burdens of candidate's wife philosophically, including the revival of the rumors about her drinking and the general's wartime infidelity—though she bitterly resented the charge that he was anti-Semitic.

Mamie showed herself to be a good campaigner, one who could establish rapport with the press and the media. As an army wife she had lived all over the United States, and she used her regional knowledge to advantage. On occasion she helped the candidate refine his speeches, dropping statistics and changing wording that "didn't sound like him." Mamie's freewheeling approach annoyed Ike's managers at times, such as when, without their permission, she agreed to speak to the Denver Black Republican Club after turning down appearances at the exclusive white clubs. She gave up to 10 interviews a day, projecting an image of a woman of common sense. When Hollywood columnist Hedda Hopper asked her if she thought that every American woman should wear her hair in bangs, Mamie-style, Mamie replied, "Certainly not." She explained that she had first adopted her hairstyle in Panama to keep cool and had kept it because it was becoming.

Two campaign songs were composed for her: "Mamie" and "I Want Mamie." Campaign buttons proclaimed "I Like Ike, But I LOVE MAMIE." Columnist James Reston of the *New York Times* thought her worth at least 50 electoral votes. On the campaign train, when Ike would say, "I want you to meet my Mamie," the crowds roared their approval. She shook hands with the hundreds of people who filed through the train every day and met thousands more at receptions, luncheons, and banquets in big cities. She posed readily for photographers, even cooperating in gag shots as long as they were dignified.

At his inauguration on January 20, 1953, President Eisenhower broke precedent by kissing his wife after taking the oath of office and riding back to the White House with her rather than with Vice President Richard Nixon. The new first lady moved easily into the ultimate government-owned house at 1600 Pennsylvania Avenue and thrived there. She had, after all, "kept house in everything but an igloo." She needed no period of adjustment to learn how to run the 132-room mansion with its staff of 80.

She transformed the second-floor private quarters with a pink-and-green color scheme, expanding closets and bringing in the Eisenhowers' own double bed. "I want to be able to lean over and pat Ike on the head before saying good night," she said. For Ike she set up a small painting studio, and she decorated a pretty bedroom for her widowed mother, who lived with them in the White House for five years. Their son John, now married, frequently visited with his wife and four children.

She introduced new rules for the servants, treating them in a more traditional manner than her immediate predecessors, addressing them by their first names, forbidding them to call each other by nicknames, insisting that they go outside the mansion to pass from one wing to another, and eliminating tipping—practices that did not endear her to them. Her compulsive search for perfection in her entertaining caused her to look over their shoulders, making the atmosphere tense. The staff found it strange that this first lady seemed to think of the White House as her own, rather than belonging to the American people, but she was accustomed to the military hierarchy, where rank has its privileges.

Mamie Eisenhower defined her own role as first lady, resisting efforts to make her more visible. The people had elected her husband president, not her, she insisted. She held only one press conference. She told the publisher of the *New York Herald Tribune* that his suggestion that she write a daily column sounded like "a terrible chore and smacks of [Eleanor Roosevelt's] 'My Day' column, of which I have a perfect horror."

She loved clothes, especially pretty, colorful clothes, and, she said, "As a soldier's wife, I learned early in life that pride in personal appearance is not a superficial thing." She changed frequently in the course of the day for the different engagements scheduled for her. True to her lifelong practice, she bargain-hunted and wore her clothes for a long time. The fashion industry, which had dubbed the color of her inaugural ball gown "First Lady Pink," voted her onto the best-dressed list year after year and chattered about "the Mamie Look"—"feminine" ensembles with all accessories matching her dresses. For formal wear she liked a romantic look—diamonds and *décolleté* gowns with wide skirts. Looking youthful mattered to her; she dieted assiduously, frequented a beauty spa, and wanted her grandchildren to call her "Mimi," not "Grandma." Her granddaughter, Susan Eisenhower, remembered the fascination of her dressing table, covered with cosmetics and perfumes.

Because of her health problems, Mamie Eisenhower did a good part of her work at her "command headquarters" in her bedroom, sitting in bed with a writing table over her knees, going over the day's business with her staff, answering mail, and meeting callers. Poor circula-

tion swelled her feet and ankles, and Ménière's syndrome disturbed her balance when she stood. Yet in her husband's first term, according to *Newsweek,* she mustered the strength to shake hands with 100,000 people and launched as many as five charity drives a week.

The first lady and the president divided duties in the White House in much the same way as they had throughout their marriage. She managed the entertainment budget and their own personal accounts frugally and approved all menus, including those for stag affairs. She was to be consulted on proposed activities in the mansion and their scheduling—with the right of veto in case of conflicting events. She visited the oval office only by invitation—four times in eight years. She resented the "interference" of the president's staff and was particularly annoyed when she was kept in the dark about what was going on, but the president did not welcome suggestions about his staff. Mary Jane McCaffree managed Mamie's own 15-person staff, who helped with correspondence and arranged social functions.

As she had all her married life, the first lady entertained extensively in the White House. Her granddaughter, Susan Eisenhower, claims that "Mamie Eisenhower . . . and the General brought more spit and polish, more pomp and circumstance, to their lavish, formal entertaining than any other President and First Lady in my White House existence." They entertained more heads of state than any presidential couple ever had; many of these guests were already their friends.

Beyond these social duties, the first lady discreetly exerted the influence of her position. As an act of good neighborliness, she passed on to those who could help some of the requests that every first lady receives. She welcomed to the White House people from all walks of life. She promoted the American Heart Association, and in quiet ways she worked for the rights of blacks, women, and the unjustly accused. She declared herself in favor of the election of a woman congressional candidate; received and sponsored women's clubs, including the National Council of Negro Women, of which she was an honorary member; reinstated and integrated the White House Easter Egg roll, which had been discontinued during the war; supported inviting Marian Anderson to sing the national anthem at the inaugural; and invited Lucille Ball to the White House while the actress was still on Senator Joseph McCarthy's list of suspected Communists.

However, Mamie Eisenhower took little interest in politics and world affairs. She read about current events, but managing them was up to her husband. She had her realm, he had his. She had never known, and never wanted to know, about military strategy; now she felt no urge to influence the conduct of national or international affairs.

Early in their White House tenure, the Eisenhowers bought a farm in Gettysburg, Pennsylvania, to use as a getaway and later as a retirement home. They enjoyed renovating it, the first home they had ever owned, and moving in the long-stored furniture and family treasures gathered over 38 years of married life and travel. There they settled down when they left the White House on January 20, 1961. While her husband raised cattle and wrote his memoirs, Mamie enjoyed her family and her friends.

In 1966 Ike and Mamie celebrated their golden wedding anniversary. After his death three years later, she went on with her life much as she had been living it, supported by the Secret Service men who ran errands and were company for her. Increasingly, she withdrew from the world, even from her family, and spent more time alone in her room. She worried about living on a fixed income, ample though it was, finding "prices as high as a cat's back." A miniseries on Kay Summersby prompted television reporter Barbara Walters to ask Mamie Eisenhower whether she had ever worried about another woman. "Heavens no," she said. "I wouldn't have stayed with him five minutes if I hadn't had the greatest respect in the world for him, and I never lost my respect." How did she want to be remembered? "As a good

Mamie Eisenhower and son John, going to the hospital to visit Ike *(Library of Congress)*

friend." She died of a stroke on November 1, 1979, and was buried next to her husband at the Eisenhower Center in Abilene, Kansas.

———

As first lady, Mamie Eisenhower functioned as a paradigm of the perfect army wife of the 1950s. She did exactly what she was supposed to do domestically and socially. She looked as she was supposed to look; provided for her husband's comfort at home; impeccably entertained his guests, colleagues, and personal friends; took care of family affairs; and rejoiced in her husband's accomplishments and successes. She was what she wanted to be, what her husband wanted her to be, and what a good portion of the nation wanted her to be.

CHRONOLOGY

1896 *November 14:* Mamie Doud is born in Boone, Iowa

1914–15 Mamie Doud attends Miss Wolcott's finishing school "for ladies of refinement" in Denver

1915 Mamie Doud makes her debut in San Antonio; she meets Dwight David Eisenhower (Ike)

1916 *July 1:* Mamie Doud marries Ike Eisenhower, who is then stationed at Fort Sam Houston, San Antonio, Texas

1917 *September 24:* Son Doud Dwight (Icky) is born

1918 *November:* Mamie's sister Edna Mae (Buster) dies

1921 *January 2:* Son Icky dies

1922 *August 3:* Son John is born

1928 Ike is assigned to Europe; Mamie accompanies him

1929–35 The Eisenhowers return to Washington, D.C.

1935 Ike accompanies MacArthur to the Philippine Islands, where Mamie joins him the next year

1939 The Eisenhowers return to the States.

1942–45 During World War II Mamie Eisenhower remains in Washington while Ike takes command of the European Theater of Operations

1948–50 *February 7:* General Eisenhower retires and assumes the presidency of Columbia University

1951–52 General Eisenhower commands NATO and his wife accompanies him to Europe

1952 Dwight Eisenhower is elected president of the United States

1953 *January 20:* Mamie becomes first lady

1961 *January 20:* The Eisenhowers retire to Gettysburg

1969 *March 8:* Dwight Eisenhower dies and is buried at the Eisenhower Center in Abilene, Kansas

1979 *November 1:* Mamie Eisenhower dies and is buried at the Eisenhower Center in Abilene, Kansas

---

FURTHER READING

Brandon, Dorothy. *Mamie Doud Eisenhower: A Portrait of a First Lady.* New York: Scribner's, 1954.

David, Lester, and Irene David. *Ike and Mamie: The Story of the General and His Lady.* New York: Putnam's, 1981.

Eisenhower, Julie Nixon. *Special People.* New York: Thomas: 1977.

Eisenhower, Susan. *Mrs. Ike, Memories and Reflections on the Life of Mamie Eisenhower.* New York: Farrar, Straus and Giroux, 1996.

Kimball, D.L. *I Remember Mamie.* Fayette, Iowa: Trends and Events, 1981.

JACQUELINE LEE (JACKIE) BOUVIER KENNEDY

(JULY 28, 1929–MAY 19, 1994)

First Lady, January 20, 1961–November 22, 1963

JACQUELINE KENNEDY
(Library of Congress)

Jacqueline Bouvier grew up more influenced by her class than by her time. Insulated by family wealth, she was hardly touched either by the Great Depression or by World War II. Although her immediate family had less money than their relatives, associates, and friends, she grew up in luxury, riding horses, attending private schools, learning social arts and graces, and making a debut. She learned to value money and to believe that women get power through the men they attract. Her two marriages brought her position, influence, and personal wealth, and to the end of her life she relied on men to manage her fortune. However, she was a woman who learned and grew, and she responded to the second American women's movement of the 1960s and 1970s. After the death of her second husband, she began a career of her own, both as a book editor for Doubleday and as a volunteer, particularly for the Municipal Art Society of New York. Feminist and writer Gloria Steinem felt that Jacqueline

271

Kennedy Onassis provided a role model for women wary of losing their femininity, demonstrating that she could live and work on her own without sacrificing her feminine appeal.

—⁂—

Jacqueline Bouvier was born on July 28, 1929, in Southamptom, New York, the elder of two daughters of stockbroker John ("Black Jack") Bouvier and his wife Janet Lee Bouvier. Jacqueline and her sister Lee, three years younger, grew up in a dysfunctional family. Her ethnically prejudiced father (anti-Semitic, anti-Irish, and anti-Italian) prided himself on the descent he claimed from the French aristocracy. He was irresponsible about money, did not fare well in the stock market, and went heavily into debt. Throughout his daughters' early childhood, his persistent womanizing and incipient alcoholism caused trouble in the marriage, and in 1936 husband and wife separated. The girls lived with their mother, Jacqueline yearning for her father's weekend visits, when he treated his daughters to trips to the zoo, through Central Park, or to the stock market, leaving discipline to their mother. Janet Lee Bouvier's marriage to the wealthy Hugh Auchincloss in 1942 stabilized the girls' lives to some extent, though Jacqueline found the new arrangement difficult. Gradually she adjusted, particularly enjoying summers on one of the Auchincloss estates, where she and Lee did farm work.

Jacqueline's life as a poor little rich girl, living in luxury funded by her maternal grandfather or by her stepfather, but without money of her own, made her aware of the power of wealth. She was a highly competitive child, intelligent and boisterous, and she rebelled against rules. Always impeccably dressed, she went to excellent private schools, including Miss Porter's School in Farmington, Connecticut, and had lessons in horseback riding, painting, social dancing, and ballet—all intended to make her a desirable, sought-after woman. She loved to read, listen to music, write poetry and short stories, and sketch and paint. Many of her classmates at Miss Porter's found her remote, secretive, and hard to take, and they nicknamed her "Jacqueline Borgia." Her stepfather paid for her debut, at a tea, the honors of which she shared with her baby half brother, and at a dinner dance shared with another young woman.

Vassar, where she enrolled in 1947, held little appeal for her. Jacqueline took no interest in politics, which were preoccupying many of the young women on campus; she made few friends among them. Instead, she focused on men and dating, but she made the dean's list. After her sophomore year, she talked of dropping out of school to model but settled instead for spending her junior year in Paris at the Sorbonne, happily boarding with a French family, sharing their cold rooms and a dearth of hot water. That year, she liked to say, was the high point of her life—one in which she enjoyed her independence; went to opera, theater, ballet, and museums; frequented the Ritz; and dated a Bohemian young man. Back in the United States, she spent her senior year at George Washington University, graduating in the spring of 1951.

That year she put much effort into a nationwide *Vogue* contest for the Prix de Paris, which included a year's scholarship to the Sorbonne. She succeeded, but her mother and stepfather, fearing that another six months in Paris might expatriate her, persuaded her to refuse the prize, bribing her with a summer trip to Europe with her sister. That fall her stepfather helped her get a job as an inquiring photographer on the *Washington Times Herald,* where she earned her own byline.

About this time, although she was engaged to a New York banker's son, she began to date Massachusetts congressman John F. Kennedy (often known as JFK or "Jack" Kennedy), a notorious womanizer like her father. (She later remarked to a friend, "I don't think there are any men who are faithful to their wives. Men are such a combination of good and evil.") She was 23, Jack some 12 years older. He was handsome, wealthy, and powerful; she listened to him demurely and intently, provided him with lighthearted companionship, translated books for him, ran errands for him, helped him shop, and accompanied him to political dinners. She found his family daunting, but she enchanted his father with her beauty, her social grace, and her independence. Believing that she would help his son fulfill the family's political ambitions, Joseph Kennedy became her adviser and confidante.

Jacqueline Bouvier and John F. Kennedy, by then a senator, were married on September 15, 1953, in a large society wedding in Newport, Rhode Island, with a reception following at one of the Auchincloss estates. Her stepfather gave her away, reportedly because her father was drunk. By arrangement of Joseph Kennedy, the newlyweds honeymooned at the villa of the president of Mexico in Acapulco.

Thereafter, the young couple lived much of the time with his family or hers, though for a period in 1954 they rented a small townhouse in Georgetown. Jacqueline Kennedy—or Jackie, as most people persisted in calling her—decided "to do whatever my husband wanted. He couldn't—and wouldn't—be married to a woman who tried to share the spotlight with him. I thought the best thing I could do was to be a distraction." She entertained, giving small dinners at home and large ones at an Auchincloss estate. With the assistance of gourmet take-out food and her cook, she learned to cope on two hours' notice with 40 luncheon guests. She studied wines; took cooking, golf, and bridge lessons; looked after her husband's diet; organized his wardrobe; helped with his office mail; went to Senate debates when he spoke and read others in the papers; and attended political rallies and social events. Though she did not enjoy women's groups, disliked politicians, and disdained their wives' dowdiness and devotion to their husbands' careers, she joined other Senate wives in their Red Cross work and in fund-raising for cultural institutions. When Jack suffered through a prolonged recovery from a back operation, she entertained him, changed his dressings, and found a publisher for his book *Profiles in Courage*, for which she had done research. With

the other Kennedy women, she campaigned for him. She accompanied him to the Democratic convention in 1956 and wept when he lost the nomination for the vice presidency.

Jackie had difficulty bearing healthy children. Distressed by a miscarriage, a stillbirth, and marital troubles, some of which centered on money, she turned to Joseph Kennedy, who responded to her pleas for more independence from the Kennedy family by finding another Georgetown rental for his son and daughter-in-law. In 1957 they bought a house there, which she decorated. On November 27 of that year, the appearance of a healthy daughter, Caroline, helped to reconcile the couple.

Gradually Jackie added to her still-limited skills as a political wife. She campaigned with her husband for his reelection to the Senate in 1958, joining him in taping a 30-minute television program from their home and winning him votes by speaking to ethnic Americans in their native languages. Politicking did not come easily to her; although she professed to enjoy it, she sometimes showed her boredom and sometimes refused to campaign. She feared and distrusted the press, and crowds frightened her. In time, however, she learned to make connections with women in politics, to exercise her good memory for names and faces—even with minor politicians she scorned—and not to cold-shoulder her husband's critics.

In 1959 and for the first half of 1960, until she became pregnant, she campaigned actively for JFK in his run for the Democratic nomination for president. Dutifully, she visited supermarkets to speak over the public address systems; substituted for the candidate when he had to return to the Senate for a civil rights vote; traveled on his behalf through Wisconsin, accompanied by Ted Kennedy; taped messages in foreign languages for radio and television; granted television interviews; and wrote a newspaper column titled "Campaign Wife." She sometimes wished she could do more in the campaign, but she vacillated—one day, for instance, seeking advice from the politically sophisticated Lady Bird Johnson, wife of JFK's running mate, and the next ignoring her. After the Democratic convention, in the interest of protecting her unborn child, she stayed away from crowds and public appearances, confining her efforts to what she could do at home. She did not endear herself to other politicians when she confessed to voting only for JFK, because, she said, "I didn't want to dilute it by voting for anyone else."

John F. Kennedy was elected president of the United States on November 4, 1960, and John F. Kennedy, Jr., was born prematurely by Caesarean section on November 21. Jacqueline Kennedy veered between looking forward to what she could do as first lady and worrying about the dangers of assassination. After a man arrested with dynamite in his possession said that he had not attacked JFK only because he didn't want to harm her and the children, she fretted, "We're nothing but sitting ducks in a shooting gallery." Still not fully recovered from her Caesarean, she nonetheless set about her new duties. Her visit to inspect the White House, courtesy of Mamie Eisenhower, tired her and left her with the impression of "a hotel that had been decorated by a wholesale furniture store during a January clearance." At home she studied photographs of the mansion's rooms, working with the famed decorator Sister Parish. Joseph Kennedy offered to pay for the new first lady's clothes, provided she chose the American Oleg Cassini as her designer, and she accepted.

Exhausted by the preinaugural celebrations, Jackie left the inaugural parade early to rest in preparation for the festivities that night. She could not rouse herself to entertain the relatives from their assorted families—Bouviers, Auchincosses, Lees, Fitzgeralds, and Kennedys—who swarmed into the state dining room after the parade. That evening her beauty stunned everyone at the two or three inaugural balls she mustered the strength to attend, but fatigue forced her to go home at midnight, leaving the new president to attend the other balls without her.

Like other first ladies, Jackie faced the necessity of doing everything at once as she and

her family moved into the presidential mansion. It was being renovated, and she managed to secure an extra allotment for the purpose from Congress by pointing out that the private quarters had been arranged for the elderly Eisenhowers, rather than for a young family. She met with the staff and, in an effort to protect her family's privacy, insisted that they agree never to write or talk about their experiences with the Kennedys; however, the pledge, extracted under duress, had no legal force. She hired a French chef and a French pastry chef, and at government expense she brought in several Kennedy employees: a personal maid, a secretary, a press secretary for her, a valet, the children's governess, and a masseuse—a move that necessitated the dismissal of other White House staff members. White House usher J. B. West found her publicly "elegant, aloof, dignified and regal," privately "casual, impish and irreverent."

Just as she had insisted on remaining her own woman rather than adopting the lifestyle of her in-laws, so Jackie asserted her right to refuse some of the duties urged on her as first lady. She shifted many of them onto Lady Bird Johnson and some of her Kennedy in-laws. She skipped a luncheon given in her honor by Congressional wives to go to the ballet in New York, and she often missed other obligations in favor of foxhunting or waterskiing. On occasion she embarrassed the administration by refusing to attend White House events held in honor of foreign heads of state or their wives.

Early on she had trouble with the press corps, especially women reporters, whom she called "harpies" and tried to bar from some official events. In turn they criticized her for a myriad of perceived faults: spending too much on clothes, using a government helicopter for trips to the Kennedy's Virginia estate, leaving Washington when her mother-in-law came to town, substituting round tables for U-shaped banquet tables, sending Air Force One to Palm Beach to retrieve forgotten objects, and not doing her job. So regal were her bearing and conduct that they called her the "Cleopatra of the Potomac."

Having always lived amidst wealth, Jackie had developed expensive tastes and expectations, which sometimes exceeded even the Kennedy means. Growing up without a personal fortune, she had learned to scramble to get what she wanted. According to her decorator, Sister Parish, she did not believe that some things had to be paid for. Sometimes she would try to compensate merchants with a donor's tax exemption or a photograph. She negotiated with Tiffany's to borrow diamonds for the inaugural ball in exchange for her promise to buy state gifts there.

Yet in the eyes of the public, Jackie's elegance and glamour more than compensated for such lapses. She impressed them with the sense of history, hard work, and good taste she put into the restoration of the White House, Blair House, and Lafayette Square—the office buildings and historic homes that fronted the White House across Pennsylvania Avenue. She shared the project with them by appealing for funds not only to the wealthy but also, through popular magazines, to the general populace. When she led them through the restored mansion by means of a televised tour her efforts were rewarded with an Emmy and nationwide acclaim. The White House guidebook that she created to help finance the renovations has sold millions of copies and is now updated in every administration. Furthermore, at Jackie's instigation, the White House now has museum status and a permanent curator, and White House property may be removed only to the Smithsonian. Her interest in architecture carried her beyond saving Victorian buildings near the White House, removing unsightly World War II huts from the Mall, and lighting the Jefferson Memorial; it took her into urban planning, particularly revitalizing Pennsylvania Avenue. Indeed, her interest in preservation extended worldwide: "I convinced the president," she later recalled, "to ask Congress to give money to save the tombs at Abu Simbel, which would have been inundated by the building of the Aswan Dam."

Jacqueline Kennedy's beauty, clothes, knowledge of languages, and savoir faire also created favorable impressions abroad. At a luncheon in Vienna honoring her and Nina Khrushchev, wife of the Soviet premier, crowds gathered outside began calling for "Jac-kie." She took the Russian woman's hand and raised both their arms, causing the crowds to switch to "Jac-kie, Ni-na." She served as the president's observer on her journeys, solo or with her sister Lee, to India, Pakistan, Greece, and Italy, earning reams of favorable publicity. This elegant, Spanish-speaking, Roman Catholic mother of two traveled with her husband to Puerto Rico, Venezuela, and Colombia, winning friends for the United States. Communist students in Caracas even waved a sign: "Kennedy—No; Jacqueline—Yes." She made devoted admirers of Charles de Gaulle of France and Nikita Khrushchev of the Soviet Union and strengthened the bonds she had created by continuing a handwritten correspondence with de Gaulle and with Prime Minister Jawaharlal Nehru of India. In France, the enthusiasm of the welcome given her prompted JFK to introduce himself as "the man who accompanied Jacqueline Kennedy to Paris." Coincidentally, these experiences increased her own interest in the problems facing the nation; she read widely about them and observed meetings of the National Security Council.

Americans also appreciated Jackie's leadership in history and the arts. They responded to her flair for the dramatic, as when she persuaded Charles de Gaulle to allow the *Mona Lisa* to be exhibited in the United States, or gave a dinner party for which the guests cruised on the Potomac to Mount Vernon. The White House took on a new tone when she invited the greatest artists of the day to perform there. She sat on the advisory board of the American Symphony Orchestra, which commissioned works by new North- and South-American composers, and chaired the Washington School of the Ballet Foundation, which gave scholarships regardless of race and operated a foreign student exchange. Jackie also sponsored performances and lectures of the Cabinet Artist Series and the Festival of Performing Arts for students, and encouraged new cultural efforts all over the country. She publicized the new Washington Gallery of

Modern Art and worked for the creation of the National Cultural Center, now known as the Kennedy Center. Privately, she collected contemporary art and music, including hot jazz, bossa nova, and Chubby Checker records.

The young president and his wife brought vitality and light-hearted merriment to the White House. Jackie's social secretary, Letitia Baldridge, cherished a memory of the president and first lady: "There are the two of them together, man and wife, laughing, teasing each other, striding through the pages of history with their handsome children in tow. . . . The Kennedys both shared two innate gifts—a sense of style and a sense of history. Both of these gifts live on in the White House," in the beautiful mansion itself and in "their entertaining innovations which have by now become a tradition." Respectful as they were of history, the Kennedys did not hesitate to abandon stuffy convention in favor of a good time for their guests. Whether Jackie was driving a sleighful of children around the White House grounds in one of Washington's rare snows, or she and Jack were conferring to choose imaginative gifts for state visitors, they gave their guests pleasure, and the nation shared their joy.

The death of the Kennedys' infant son, Patrick, born on August 7, 1963, brought them national sympathy. However, presidents and their families are granted little time to mourn, and eyebrows were raised when shortly thereafter Jackie cruised on the yacht of wealthy Greek shipowner Aristotle Onassis, a man with a reputation for womanizing and shady business dealings.

By the time she returned, the president was gearing up for his reelection campaign and urged her to accompany him to Texas. In Dallas, on November 22, 1963, as they rode together in a motorcade, he was shot to death before her eyes. Just hours thereafter she stood, dazed, in Air Force One while Lyndon Baines Johnson was sworn into the presidency. During the flight back to Washington, she sat beside her husband's body.

In the days that followed, Jackie was obsessed by two concerns: locating a home for her children and herself and establishing JFK's reputation in history. The Averill Harrimans resolved the first problem by offering her their Georgetown house for as long as she needed it. For the other, work began with a funeral that dramatically expressed the national grief. Kennedy supporters, devastated by the loss of the leader to whom they were devoted and frustrated by the end of all that they had hoped to achieve, went on to create the Camelot myth. For the "one brief shining moment" of the Kennedy administration, so it went, the United States had enjoyed a period of elegant, glamorous chivalry. As Jacqueline Kennedy wrote in *Look* magazine a year after her husband's death, "So now he is a legend when he would have preferred to be a man. . . . His high noon kept all the freshness of the morning—and he died then, never knowing disillusionment."

Historians have since revised that version of the Kennedy administration, although JFK's closest supporters and many others who shared JFK's vision still look back wistfully at that time. He had appealed to the idealism of the nation, particularly to the young people who joined the Peace Corps in response to his plea, "Ask not what your country can do for you, but what you can do for your country." He and Jackie had roused the country's pride in the American cultural heritage. He had begun to respond to the protests for civil rights for African Americans and for social justice for the impoverished. However, beginning in the mid-1970s, revelations of his personal sexual profligacy, and memories of the failed Bay of Pigs invasion of Cuba and his difficulties with Congress have tarnished the legend.

In her White House bedroom, Jackie left a plaque reading, "In this room lived John Fitzgerald Kennedy with his wife Jacqueline—during the two years, ten months and two days he was President of the United States—January 20, 1961–November 22, 1963." She also left for her successor an 11-page memorandum on her work to renovate the White House, which, President Johnson assured her, would be continued.

At Lady Bird Johnson's request, the former first lady continued to advise on it. However, she declined an appointment as ambassador to France.

After living for a while in Washington, in February 1964, Jackie bought a 15-room cooperative apartment on the upper east side in Manhattan and rented a 10-room summer residence on Long Island; she had also inherited JFK's house in Hyannis Port. As always, her relationship with the Kennedy clan was uneven, particularly in differences over money matters and what they considered her extravagance. She was determined to preserve her independence and her distinctive lifestyle, and she could not go on indefinitely being identified only as JFK's widow. Nonetheless, she continued to propagate the Camelot myth, raising funds for the JFK library and authorizing William Manchester to write a book on the assassination, though later the Kennedys and the author had a falling out over editorial control. She supported JFK's brother, Robert Kennedy, in his bid for election as a senator from New York, and she reacted bitterly after his 1968 assassination: "I hate this country. I despise America and I don't want my children to live here any more. If they're killing Kennedys, my kids are number-one targets."

Increasingly, Jackie moved into international society, consorting with the jet set. Inevitably, at this point and throughout the rest of her life, rumors arose about romances between her and various celebrities. In October 1968 she married Aristotle Onassis, 23 years her senior. Speculations about the motives for the marriage ranged from her search for security and the protection of her privacy to a marriage of convenience in which she gained access to fabulous wealth and he gained the ultimate trophy wife.

The Onassis children disliked her; the Kennedy family disapproved of the marriage; and the union meant long separations from her own children, who attended school in New York. Both spouses traveled extensively; even in the first year, the two spent a third of the time apart, and Ari Onassis publicly continued to see his longtime mistress, opera singer Maria Callas. Difficulties between Jackie and Ari multiplied with the death of his only son in 1973. Reports vary on whether Ari objected to or encouraged Jackie's spending. At any rate, at his death in 1975, legal difficulties over the estate arose between his wife and his daughter. When they were settled, Jackie inherited at least $20 million, as well as an income of $150,000 annually for life.

She moved back to New York City and built a new life for herself there, taking a part-time editorial job, first at Viking and then at Doubleday. Her fame and her access to other celebrities helped her acquire a number of autobiographies that sold well, but she also proved herself talented in editing manuscripts and developing new ideas, especially for coffee-table books. Moreover, she did her homework, doing scholarly research or even taking a course as background for a book she was working on. She sat on the board of the American Ballet Theater and volunteered with the Municipal Art Society, and her reputation attracted public attention to efforts such as the campaign to save Grand Central Station from destruction. As always, she maintained her independence, accepting some charitable and political requests and refusing others; in the main she followed her own deepest interests.

In the midst of the second women's movement, her career and her volunteer work inspired respect, and she helped the movement along with such statements as: "What has been sad for many women of my generation is that they weren't supposed to work if they had families. There they were, with the highest education, and what were they to do when the children were grown—watch the raindrops coming down the windowpane? Leave their fine minds unexercised? Of course women should work if they want to. You have to do something you enjoy. That is the definition of happiness: 'complete use of one's faculties along the lines leading to excellence in a life affording them scope.'"

Jackie put much care and thought into raising her children, who had experienced tragedy at such early ages. After their father's assassination, she put them for a time under the care of the famed child psychologist Erik Eriksson. She invited JFK's friends and associates to talk with them, so that they take a sense of pride in what their father had done and what he had tried to do. As she had in the White House, she strove to procure for them a fair measure of privacy. Caroline, like her mother a high achiever, did well in school, including law school. John F. Kennedy, Jr., burdened with a name, history, and appearance so famous that he attracted crowds everywhere, had a more difficult time growing up. Worried lest he disgrace the family name, his mother disapproved of his ambition to act; she was delighted when he enrolled in law school in 1986. He managed to pass the New York bar only on the third try, with the help of tutelage that Jackie insisted on. In the early 1980s she built a 13-room house with a 6-room adjoining guest house on a large tract of land in Martha's Vineyard—large enough to ensure privacy. There she entertained friends and family, including, eventually, her three grandchildren, offspring of the marriage between her daughter Caroline and Ed Schlossberg, author, artist, and entrepreneur.

Jacqueline Onassis's fortune was managed and greatly increased by a group of several financial experts, chief among them diamond merchant Maurice Tempelsman. Maurice was a charming, daring adventurer who had dealt with dictators, especially in Africa, and also a powerful figure behind-the-scenes in Democratic politics. Master of several languages, collector of Greek and Roman antiques, and a mover in Jewish philanthropies, he attracted her personally. His marriage had long been in trouble, and eventually he and his wife divorced by mutual agreement. Later he shared Jackie's apartment.

All her life Jacqueline Bouvier Kennedy Onassis had taken care to stay fit. She dieted assiduously, rode horseback, did yoga, jogged, and swam; she had face lifts; and she remained a beautiful woman. Yet in early 1994, she was diagnosed with non-Hodgkin's lymphoma. She fought it with chemotherapy, drugs, and radiation, but the disease spread to her brain. When it became apparent that no medical treatment would cure her, she discharged herself from the hospital. She died at home on May 19, 1994. As she had lived, so she died, as her son John

Jacqueline Kennedy holding a silver pitcher presented to the White House on December 5, 1961, by James Hoban Alexander *(John F. Kennedy Library)*

said, "in her own way and on her own terms." He and his sister identified as the major themes of her life her love of words, her emphasis on family, and her desire for adventure. She was buried in Arlington National Cemetery, near John F. Kennedy, their stillborn daughter, and their son Patrick, who had died in infancy.

⸻

During her short tenure as first lady, Jacqueline Bouvier Kennedy won admiration for her style, even as she picked and chose among her duties and pursued her own interests. The nation benefited from her expertise in architecture, historical restoration, and furniture and from her delight in the arts of painting, music, drama, and ballet. Her love of clothes and society, her elegance, and her knowledge of languages provided the country with a first lady who impressed other nations with qualities that many Europeans had supposed Americans to lack. She emphasized the traditional in describing the presidential spouse's first responsibility as caring for the president and their family and in selecting a project in a "woman's area." However, her worldwide travels as first lady and her independence in deciding which duties she would perform set precedents for those who would follow her. In the White House and afterward, she evoked an admiration once again manifested in 2001, when the public flocked to the exhibit *Jacqueline Kennedy: The White House Years* at the Metropolitan Museum of Art in New York City.

CHRONOLOGY

1929   *July 28:* Jacqueline Bouvier (Jackie) is born in Southampton, Long Island

1940   Jacqueline Bouvier's parents are divorced

1942   Jacqueline Bouvier's mother marries Hugh Auchincloss

1944   Jacqueline Bouvier enters Miss Porter's School in Farmington, Connecticut

1947   Jacqueline Bouvier makes debut and enters Vassar

1951   Jacqueline Bouvier graduates from George Washington University; wins but refuses *Vogue*'s Prix de Paris, and takes job as "Inquiring Camera Girl" with the *Washington Times-Herald*

1953   *June 24:* Jacqueline Bouvier and Senator John F. Kennedy announce their engagement

      September 12: Jacqueline Bouvier marries John F. Kennedy

1957   *November 27:* Daughter Caroline is born, after two miscarriages

1960   *November:* John F. Kennedy is elected president of the United States

      November 21: Son John Fitzgerald, Jr., is born

1961   *January 20:* Jacqueline Bouvier Kennedy becomes first lady of the United States

1963   *August 7:* Son Patrick is born, and shortly dies

      November 22: John F. Kennedy is assassinated in Dallas

1968   *October 20:* Jacqueline Bouvier Kennedy marries Greek shipping magnate Aristotle Onassis

1975   Aristotle Onassis dies; Jacqueline Kennedy Onassis begins work as an editor at Viking, then at Doubleday

1994   *May 19:* Jacqueline Kennedy Onassis dies

FURTHER READING

Anthony, Carl Sferrazza. *As We Remember Her: Jacqueline Kennedy Onassis in the Words of Friends and Family.* New York: HarperCollins, 1997.

Baldridge, Letitia. *Of Diamonds and Diplomats.* Boston: Houghton Mifflin, 1968.

Bradford, Sarah. *America's Queen: The Life of Jacqueline Kennedy Onassis.* New York: Viking, 2000.

Curtis, Charlotte. *First Lady.* New York: Pyramid Books, 1962.

Davis, John H. *The Bouviers: From Waterloo to the Kennedys and Beyond.* Washington, D.C.: National Press, 1993.

———. *The Kennedys: Dynasty and Disaster.* New York: McGraw-Hill, 1984.

Hall, Gordon Langley, and Ann Pinchot. *Jacqueline Kennedy: A Woman for the World.* New York: F. Fell, 1964.

Heymann, C. David. *A Woman Named Jackie.* New York: Carol Communications, 1989.

Thayer, Mary Van Rensselaer. *Jacqueline Kennedy: The White House Years.* Boston: Little, Brown, 1967.

CLAUDIA ALTA TAYLOR (LADY BIRD) JOHNSON
(DECEMBER 22, 1912–)
First Lady, November 22, 1963–January 20, 1969

LADY BIRD JOHNSON
(Library of Congress)

ady Bird Johnson created herself. The daughter of a hard-working, self-made father and an advanced mother who advocated women's suffrage and rights for blacks, mentored by an aunt who wanted her to have a career, she grew up in a South that honored graciousness, loyalty, and hospitality. All these values she blended into an extraordinary life in which she remained true to the South but insisted that it must change, and in which she put her husband's needs above hers but built successful careers of her own both in business and in politics. Although the American women's movement of the 1960s did not come along until she was in her mid-50s, she both advocated and exemplified expanding opportunities for women. In environmentalism, too, she set standards for others.

Claudia Alta Taylor was born on December 22, 1912, in Karnack, Texas, the third child and only daughter of affluent storekeeper Thomas Jefferson Taylor, Jr., and Minnie Lee Patillo Taylor. Legend has it that while she was a baby, her black nurse called her "purty as a ladybird," bestowing a nickname she could never escape. Thereafter, despite her best efforts, her family and friends called her "Bird" and the public knew her as "Lady Bird." Her father was a rough-hewn poor boy who had made good and married the wealthy girl of his dreams. Her mother, who died when Bird was five, was an eccentric who held herself aloof, read theologian Emanuel Swedenborg, roamed the back country that surrounded the mansion in which they lived (both on foot and in her chauffeured car), went to operas in Chicago, frequented health spas, advocated votes for women, posted the Taylor property against hunters, and sponsored a Save the Quail Society.

Even before his wife's death, Tom Taylor had dispatched his sons to boarding school; they did not know that their mother had died until a year after the fact. As a single parent, Tom struggled with the problem of how to care for his daughter. At first he took her to his general store with him, bedding her down at night in a room where he also stashed coffins. When summer came, he shipped her off to her mother's relatives in Alabama, where fond aunts and uncles welcomed her—especially her mother's semi-invalid younger sister, Effie. Aunt Effie shared Minnie Taylor's love of reading and opened for her niece the possibility of a career—perhaps, Effie said, as a drama critic.

From then on, Bird spent school years in Texas and summers in Alabama. Her mother's family expanded her world by taking her with them to Battle Creek, Michigan, to stay at the spa of W. K. Kellogg, the health guru of vegetarianism and enemas. The only child in residence, Bird enjoyed the massages and seized the chance for her first airplane ride, paying a woman barnstormer $2.50 to take her up.

At her home in Karnack, her playmates were mostly black youngsters, and sometimes she went to the black church. A tomboy, clad in knickers and kneesocks, Bird spent much of her time alone, reading, or roaming the outdoors, enjoying wildflowers. She attended the local one-room school until it closed. For a time, her father then hired the teacher as her tutor. For two years Bird and Aunt Effie roomed in nearby Jefferson, so that she could attend school there. For high school, Bird moved back into her father's home, called the Brick House. He gave his daughter her first car so that she could drive to school each day in Marshall, the county seat. She enjoyed considerable independence: When she was 14, she and another teenager drove Effie's car from Texas to Alabama and used it to tour that state, visiting relatives.

Bird was shy, and high school was an ordeal for her. Without a mother she was always something of an outsider, and no one had taught her about selecting friends, choosing clothes, or making herself attractive. Nonetheless, she had at least one boyfriend. She soon decided that he would never amount to anything, but his older sister, Eugenia (Gene) Boehringer, became her close friend and mentor. A good student, Bird dreaded the possibility that as valedictorian or salutatorian she might have to give a speech and prayed for smallpox to intervene. As it happened, she graduated third in her class, at the age of 15. Her experiences had made her both independent and self-aware, thoughtful about the choices that she made and the opportunities they might open for her. Seeing that her Aunt Effie's invalidism had shut her off and made her dependent on others, Bird strove to emulate her father's strength, bearing pain stoically all her life.

Her father and aunt, thinking her too young for college, encouraged Bird to board at St. Mary's Episcopal School for Girls, where she converted to the Episcopalian faith. After two years there, on Gene Boehringer's advice she enrolled in the University of Texas at Austin. It was a happy choice for her. She pledged a sorority but gave it up when her father ridiculed the idea. Wanting to be liked for herself and not her appearance, she still dressed dowdily, despite her unlimited charge account at Nieman-Marcus, but she made many friends, both women and men. Gene, who worked for a state governmental official, introduced Bird to people off-campus, and she dated older men as well as college students. To overcome her shyness, she did public relations for women's athletics at the university. After she earned a teaching certificate and a B.A., cum laude, she spent another year studying shorthand and taking a journalism degree. She had armed herself with skills that would not only guarantee her ability to earn her living but also give her a choice of occupations. She continued her education throughout her life, reading widely, preparing herself punctiliously for new undertakings, and learning typing, Spanish, and public speaking, as the need arose.

In late summer 1934, Bird met Lyndon B. Johnson in Gene's office. She thought him "excessively thin but very, very good-looking, with lots of black, wavy hair, and the most outspoken, straightforward, determined manner I had ever encountered." Moreover, she discovered, he had a "mind [that] could follow another mind around and get there before it did." He subjected her to the persuasive treatment he was to make famous as a politician, engaging her in a whirlwind courtship. He asked personal questions and talked volubly about himself, describing his family, telling her how much life insurance he carried, and divulging the salary he earned as secretary to Congressman Richard Kleberg. He took her to visit his parents—a subdued father and an adored and adoring mother. He took her to the enormous King ranch in Texas, to which his boss was heir. He begged her to marry him—the sooner the better. When in a few days he had to return to Washington, he pelted her with telegrams and letters. A few weeks later he was back, demanding that she marry him instantly. Aunt Effie was appalled, but Tom Taylor, confronted with his mirror image in this young man so determined to marry the woman of his choice, commented, "Honey, you've been bringing home a lot of

boys. This one looks like a man." He added that some of his best deals had been quick.

Lady Bird Taylor and Lyndon Baines Johnson were married in an Episcopal church in San Antonio on November 17, 1934, in a ceremony hastily arranged by a friend, with a $2.50 Sears wedding ring purchased at the last minute. The bride, in an effort to satisfy the groom's insistence that she don brighter colors, wore lavender silk, with flowers appliquéd on each shoulder. The newlyweds honeymooned in Mexico, where Bird Johnson tried to sightsee while her husband talked incessantly about Washington and his duties there. In a few days they took the train back to Laredo and then drove to Washington.

For a month they lived in the basement of the Dodge Hotel, after which they took a one-bedroom furnished apartment. No longer the pleading suitor, Lyndon now barked orders and expected service. His wife, who had never cooked or kept house, became, she said, "as busy as a man with one hoe and two rattlesnakes." Bird was to serve him coffee in bed, bring him a newspaper, shine his shoes, fill his cigarette lighter and put it in the right pocket, lay out his clothes, and provide meals for as many as he chose to bring home at whatever hour he chose—sometimes at midnight. He instructed her to learn about the counties that Congressman Kleberg represented and the names of the people there who could get things done. He embarrassed her by criticizing her before their friends, but she made no complaint. Instead, she hired a cleaning lady as soon as she could and took the advice of a congressional wife to learn about the issues of the day, get involved in her husband's career, and find a way to make her life fun. Early on she learned to get along with her mother-in-law, who thought that Lyndon could do no wrong, by treating her as an ally but keeping her distance. Bird enjoyed the people with whom she and Lyndon spent most of their time, a group of liberals who talked about ways to improve the country.

Although she had adjusted to life in Washington, when Lyndon asked Bird in August

1935 how she would like to move to Austin, she was ecstatic. He had been appointed director of the Texas National Youth Administration (NYA), a Great Depression program that put unemployed young people to work to serve the nation. In Texas, the Johnsons decided between them, NYA workers would concentrate on building roadside parks. "Not many things have ever meant so much to us as the NYA," she later said, "brief though it was." In Austin they shared a house with two of Lyndon Johnson's aides and sometimes with Aunt Effie.

The year 1937 saw major changes in the Johnsons' lives, professionally and personally. Lyndon decided to run for Congress, and about the same time he started a long-lasting romantic affair with Alice Glass, the elegant and sophisticated mistress (later wife) of one of his wealthy backers. With remarkable dignity and poise for so young a woman, Bird began to develop techniques for handling her husband's infidelities. She undertook a self-improvement program and made herself essential to his career. When Alice Glass and her friends left her out or ridiculed her, she ignored the slight and concentrated on dieting, dressing to please her husband, and reading widely, particularly history and the classics. She consulted a former Texas state senator to ask about her husband's chances in the campaign for a congressional seat and how much it would cost, then contributed money from her mother's estate to cover the necessary $10,000. She worked behind the scenes on the campaign, right down to election day, which she spent telephoning to get out the vote. They won by a sizable margin. "We sure did *not* know we were going to win," she said. "Looking at it pragmatically, we did not have any right to expect we would win. Lyndon was from the smallest of the ten counties. He was quite young."

In 1941, when Lyndon first tried for a Senate seat, his wife participated in the campaign even more fully. This time they lost, but she remembered the race affectionately: "Oh, the adventures we had. It was in a way the best campaign ever. . . . Perhaps it was the wine of youth—we were never tired. And our troops loved us, and we loved them—it was a *we* campaign." In defeat she cheered her husband, socialized with the wives of his congressional colleagues, and worked harder than ever for his constituents, keeping notes on what they needed and giving them tours when they visited the capital. By then she had become expert in soothing the wounded feelings of people her husband slighted or insulted. "I will not take on Lyndon's animosities or quarrels," she said, "because I don't want him to lose any friends."

Soon after the bombing of Pearl Harbor on December 7, 1941, Lyndon Johnson joined the Navy with the rank of lieutenant commander, at a salary cut of $7,000. In his absence, his wife ran his office, without pay, not only continuing to serve his constituents and probing to learn more about their problems but also helping to organize a petition drive for his reelection, even though he was overseas. She always insisted that the experience gave her an invaluable confidence in her own powers to cope.

By 1942 Bird's hopes for children had been lowered by three miscarriages. "It was," she said, "a big psychological put-down as a woman." Never one to waste time in self-pity, she turned her attention to business. The decision was to some extent another of the many ways she sought to help her husband, the fulfillment of whose political ambitions clearly demanded large sums of money. In addition, at that time his career was being threatened by allegations that he had illegally received contributions and had unethically used his influence to direct government contracts to the advantage of friends and relatives. Carefully and deliberately, and putting to use her knowledge of journalism, in 1943 Bird Johnson risked a considerable part of the money she inherited from her mother and her uncle to buy a radio station—KTBC—in Austin. Over the next few years commuting back and forth between Austin and Washington, she personally supervised the station and turned it from a losing proposition into a moneymaker, the basis for the Johnson family fortune. Eventually she made millions, increasing the station's power and in

1951 procuring the license for what was then the only television station in Austin. Certainly her husband's position helped. His wide acquaintance helped her find staff and sell advertisements, and the couple's known stance as New Dealers got her a favorable hearing before licensing boards. Nonetheless it was her own business, and when the Johnsons disagreed about strategy Bird was capable of reminding Lyndon that it was her own money.

Also around 1943, she bought a two-story brick colonial house in Washington. Lyndon worried that the purchase would raise fears in his constituents that he was ceasing to be a Texan, but ten moves in eight years of marriage had made Bird "tired of living out of a suitcase." She bought not only the Washington house but also a duplex in Austin, on one side of which the Johnsons could live when they were in Texas. She had, she said, "desperately wanted a nest. Psychologically, I think it prepared me to have a family." At any rate, in her fourth pregnancy she carried to term: Lynda Bird Johnson was born on March 19, 1944. Neither her birth nor that of Lucy (later Luci) Baines Johnson on July 7, 1947, turned their mother away from the course that she had chosen. She continued to expand her business, incorporating it in 1947 and transferring some of the shares to her daughters and others to employees; and she continued to put Lyndon Johnson first in the family, catering to his needs and demands before those of the rest.

Her husband's career and happiness and the requirements of her business left Bird with less time than she would have liked for her daughters. Often away, often busy with other duties, she was forced to hand over much of their care to others. Lynda and Luci grew up competing for the attention of both their parents. Their mother taught them to "look at [their father's] job with all the reverence it is due," to support him at every turn, remembering that their actions might harm him, and to learn from his accomplishments. Lyndon's timetable and whims governed what the family did. During grade school the girls lived for half the year in Washington and for the other six

months in Austin. Even when they were with their mother, they might find a notice on her closed door stating: I WANT TO BE ALONE.

In 1948 Bird was determined to do everything she could for her husband's second bid for a Senate seat. By now an experienced political wife, she exercised power in strategy meetings. If she disapproved of what was going on, she walked out; Lyndon invariably summoned her back. She developed her own campaign strategies—for instance, when out driving, she bought only five gallons of gas at a time, so she could buy fuel in more little Texas towns, where she walked up and down Main Street shaking hands and asking people to vote for her husband. He wanted them to do five things, she told voters: "Write a card to all your kinfolks, have a coffee or tea party for your friends, phone ten people and ask each of them to phone ten more, write a letter to the editor of your newspaper, and drive a full car to the polls." Even an auto accident did not daunt her: She sent her companion to the hospital, changed her dress, went on to the scheduled reception, and made her first statewide radio broadcast.

Lyndon's win launched what Bird described as her most intellectually stimulating years. She worked on charitable causes in Ladies of the Senate, an organization of Senate wives formed in World War I to sew for the Red Cross. She attended Senate debates, visited her husband's office several times a week with Texas-shaped cookies, gave his constituents tours, and made sure that the Senate dining room served Texas-shaped hamburgers. She listened to her husband and Sam Rayburn, his mentor, discuss ways to influence close Senate votes. Rayburn, who all but adopted the Johnson family, had been particularly fond of Bird since she was a bride, and she of him. He warned Lyndon against his infidelities to her; she entertained Rayburn at least once a week, learned to prepare his favorite recipes, gave him birthday parties, and went to him for advice.

As always, Bird pampered her husband and he depended on her completely. When he was hospitalized with a heart attack, she stayed in a room next to his, wore beautiful dressing gowns, kept her makeup fresh—and ran his office. He lashed out at her verbally, but he never woke without calling for her.

When Lyndon lost the Democratic nomination for president of the United States to John F. Kennedy in 1960, Bird wept. At first she opposed his accepting the vice-presidential spot, but when he did and Kennedy asked her to carry the women's end of the campaign, she responded loyally and efficiently. Despite the condescending attitude of some of the Kennedys, she organized a series of tea parties with family matriarch Rose Kennedy and two of the Kennedy sisters. She hired Liz Carpenter, co-owner of a Washington news bureau, to help her, listening to Carpenter's advice on what questions reporters might ask and how to field them. To get out the vote and enlist workers, Bird had only to consult the file of friends and political acquaintances she had maintained for years. She traveled 35,000 miles, making 16 solo appearances in 11 states and another 150 appearances with her husband. In Dallas, she experienced what she always described as her worst rejection ever, when young Republican women spit on her and struck her with a sign. For once she lost her temper, but her husband put his hand over her mouth and took her through the crowd.

Lyndon Johnson's vice presidency brought unusual new responsibilities to his wife. Jacqueline Kennedy often asked Bird Johnson to take over portions of the first lady's duties; in the first year the vice president's wife substituted at more than 50 official functions. The Johnsons, finding their Washington house too small for the entertaining they needed to do, bought another house, The Elms, in the capital. When a reporter asked what she did as the wife of the vice president, Lady Bird read her schedule for the day:

"9 a.m.—Spanish lesson, interrupted to make appointment for Lynda with the dentist and for Lucy with a geometry tutor.

"11 a.m.—Opened the National Cathedral Flower Show.

Lady Bird Johnson (*LBJ Library photo by Robert Knudsen*)

"1 p.m.—Attended luncheon for the Heart Fund Drive with 'appropriate remarks' in hand.

"2:30–5 p.m.—Dictated mail, paid bills and signed KTBC checks, with time out to find my last hat in the attic for a church bazaar.

"5 p.m.—Entertained 35 students en route to Chile with the Peace Corps.

"Emergency call set me dispatching Lyndon's tux (with all studs, I hoped) to the Capitol.

"Dressed and joined him at 7:35 in front of the White House for dinner that night."

"Yes, I know, Mrs. Johnson," said the reporter. "But what do you really do?" Her world expanded as they traveled extensively abroad, representing the United States. She loved these new experiences, but, she said, she had enjoyed all the periods of her life.

With the assassination of President Kennedy on November 22, 1963, Lady Bird Johnson was abruptly plunged into a new life as first lady. She stood with her husband in Air Force One as he took the oath as president, not knowing whether or not a conspiracy existed to kill him and other top officials. "I have no statement," she told reporters. "The way I feel, it has all been a dreadful nightmare and somehow we must find strength to go on." She called Rose Kennedy to say, "I'm glad the nation had your son as long as it did." She told Jacqueline Kennedy, "You know we never even wanted to be vice president, and now, dear God, it's come to this." She called her longtime friend Nellie Connally, whose husband lay wounded, and took notes while President Johnson talked with Attorney General Bobby Kennedy.

Ahead of her lay a multitude of tasks: selling The Elms, giving up control of her business, persuading Lynda to transfer to a Washington university, and settling into the White House. But she would not hurry Jacqueline Kennedy out: "I would to God I could serve Mrs. Kennedy's comfort," she said. "I can at least serve her convenience."

Once established in the White House, both the Johnsons confronted so many new duties that they saw less of each other and lost some of the intimacy they had shared, as each of them worked to exhaustion. Bird wanted to be a useful first lady, like Eleanor Roosevelt—and she was. On her desk she placed a sign: *CAN DO.* She did her homework, whether the assignment was a formal dinner or a trip to Appalachia. Guests in the long receiving lines found that she had learned a little something about each of them. Before a trip she studied the area she would visit. She took Spanish lessons. She carried on Jacqueline Kennedy's work, collaborating on a guide to the history of the mansion. She planned and edited her speeches carefully, summoning a speech teacher to rehearse her in their delivery. She knew in detail the legislation her husband was sending to Capitol Hill for

passage. Whenever she thought she had failed, she responded by trying harder. She read the critical mail so that she could tell her husband what was bothering people. The president turned to her for comfort and solace, but also for frank though gently phrased criticism. "I never saw her slice a corner on anything," he told a reporter. "She is the first to tell me about my mistakes, whether they are financial extravagancies or a political boner, and to me that is the test of real character."

As quintessentially a southerner as her husband, but like him wanting a new South, the first lady fully supported the president's determination to push through civil rights legislation in the face of resistance expressing itself in civic unrest and both official and mob violence. "I knew the Civil Rights Act was right and I didn't mind saying so, but I also loved the South and didn't want it used as the whipping boy of the Democratic Party," she said. She made plain her attachment to the South: "I'm mighty glad to be here and see all you folks. You-all may not agree with what I say, but you sure can understand the way I say it." The South must change, she knew, but she hoped that it could retain its customs of "keeping up with your kinfolks, of long Sunday dinners after church, of a special brand of courtesy."

Planning for the 1964 election, in which she encouraged Lyndon Johnson to run, had to start immediately. Knowing the depths of the resentment against him in the South, she volunteered to campaign for him there, asking that she be given the toughest places. Death threats did not deter her. On the campaign train named the Lady Bird Special, she undertook what no first lady had ever tried before. She prepared the way carefully, calling the governor and senators of every state on her route: "Governor, I'm thinking of coming down to your state. I called to ask your advice. . . . I was hoping that you and your wife would join us and ride the Whistlestop through your state."

Putting press secretary Liz Carpenter in charge of arrangements, the first lady and her daughters entrained, along with wives of senators and congressmen and 15 hostesses in blue shirtwaist dresses with *LBJ* embroidered on the pockets. At every stop they ranged themselves in front of the first lady, escorted local politicians and supporters onto the train for picture taking, and distributed souvenirs, including campaign buttons and Bird's recipe for pecan pie. The first lady spoke repeatedly, adding stops along the way. She spoke in the southern drawl natural to her, and she peppered her speeches with the kind of down-home sayings with which she had grown up: "I'll see you Saturday if the Lord be willin' and the creek don't rise." "I find myself in mighty tall cotton." "He's the type who would charge hell with a bucket of water." "He's noisier than a mule in a tin barn." "I look forward to that as much as to a good case of cholera." However, she never waffled on principles: "I never expected for a moment that my husband would do other than all American Presidents have done," she told the crowds, "and this is to make it clear that the Constitution means the same for all the people in all sections and all states. Lyndon has offered to unify this country, to put behind us things of the past. . . . I would like to ask you for your vote for both Johnsons."

Inevitably, in the upheaval that characterized the 1960s, the Lady Bird Special ran into trouble with protests and demonstrations against the administration. Sometimes the first lady quieted the booing crowds with such statements as: "This is a country of many viewpoints. I respect your right to express your own. Now it is my turn to express mine." Once 17-year-old Luci hushed the protestors by saying, "It seems to me that it is easy to holler a lot and make a lot of noise when you're not the one having to handle the problems." Sometimes the Johnson antagonists would not be stilled. Overwhelmingly, however, Bird made friends and won votes with her candor, courage, and sincere love of and respect for the South. She spoke to about half a million people, and experienced politicians believed that she carried the eight states through which she campaigned for her husband. She loved it; she was, she said, right at home, "like Br'er Rabbit in the briar patch."

In the inaugural ceremony on January 20, 1965, Lady Bird Johnson began a new tradition by standing beside her husband and holding the Bible on which he took the oath. Lyndon advised her not to fritter away her time and the influence of her position but to concentrate on Head Start, a program designed to give poor children the stimuli and facts they needed to do well in school, and what he called "beautification," a term she detested, preferring "conservation." By the beginning of the environmental movement of the 1960s, Bird had moved far beyond the love of wildflowers of her girlhood to an understanding of the necessity to protect the planet and of the psychological benefits of traveling and living amid flowers instead of billboards and auto dumps. She defined her project as "our total concern for the physical and human quality of the world we pass on to our children." It was a cause that, as she put it, "made my heart sing." She gave approximately 60 speeches about it and formed a bureau of cabinet and Senate wives to meet requests for speakers on the subject. On a local level she worked to change the appearance of the capital city, both in its public areas, where she and her allies planted 2,000,000 daffodil bulbs, and in its slums, where they built parks, renovated schools, introduced training programs for teenagers, and backed community action for rat control and trash collection. "Beautification," wrote the first lady, "is not only for people, it is by people too." On a national level she worked to make the roadsides lovely and to reforest the country.

Bird encountered strong opposition, both from the billboard industry and from small businessmen fearful that without billboards their businesses would die. Members of her Committee for a More Beautiful Capital divided over whether to work on public places or in poor areas; funding for the latter was hard to come by and even harder to sustain. However, the president pushed through Congress 150 laws to benefit the environment, including one to limit the erection of more billboards—a considerable feat at a time when no environmentalist coalition with political clout existed.

Even more importantly, the first lady stimulated public interest and dialogue over the environment and encouraged citizens all over the country to do what they could to improve their surroundings, from picking up litter to lobbying for better-designed highways. In this cause she traveled thousands of miles through all terrains throughout the United States. As Liz Carpenter wrote:

> We traveled 200,000 miles to plant trees on mountaintops and in ghettos, to open schools in Appalachia, to visit the Head Start projects of a Newark slum, to walk through the fields of bluebonnets in a Texas pasture. From San Simeon perched above the surging Pacific to a mountaineer's shack in North Carolina, from Cape Kennedy to the redwood forests, we traveled by rubber raft, bus, ski lift, surrey, orchard wagon, rail and foot, and in Mrs. Johnson's least favorite vehicle of all, jet plane.

Wherever the first lady went, she spurred discussion of the environment, and tourism in the area soared. "Call it corny if you will," she said, "but I want to boast about America." With her inspired example, the United States was rediscovering itself and learning to treasure its natural riches.

Similarly, she visited numerous sites where Head Start was operating and inspected hundreds of other programs of Lyndon Johnson's Great Society in action. She reported back to the president on how well these programs were working and publicized them nationwide. She invited reporters to travel with her to visit unemployed miners and a textile factory that employed mostly women, where she commented on the necessity for so many women to support their families.

She understood the double burden these working women carried. As devoted a wife as Bird was, she had been ahead of her time in building careers of her own in both business and politics. In an interview conducted by daughter Lynda, she said that her husband was "my lover, my friend, my identity. The need for women to have their individual identity belongs to your generation, not mine." Yet she was her own woman, holding steady to her course despite Lyndon's mercurial moods, preserving her own dignity despite his sexual affairs, running the family business, and becoming an influential political figure. Although never a radical feminist, she learned from the women's movement of the 1960s, and advised young women college graduates to balance their lives between being wives and mothers and holding other jobs. She honored women's achievements in Women Doers lunches and solicited the advice of high-achieving women on the nation's problems. Moreover, she understood that the changes in the pattern of women's lives demanded changes in legislation: "American women are undergoing a great revolution in our lifetime. . . . We must now try to make our laws catch up with what has happened to us as we bounce in and out of the labor market and raise a family."

Impressive as their accomplishments were, Bird and Lyndon Johnson faced increasingly bitter, even vitriolic criticism. The civil rights and women's movements brought cataclysmic change, which frightened many citizens and drove some to violence. The Johnsons' hopes of eliminating poverty in the United States and dealing justly with its black citizens faded as the country divided over the hapless American involvement in Southeast Asia. The military defoliation of Vietnam overshadowed the first lady's achievements in conservation, and funds for beautification dwindled as the costs of war mounted. In Washington and throughout the country, the cries of protestors rang in her ears: "Hey, hey, LBJ, how many kids have you killed today?" She was booed when she spoke at Williams and at Yale.

As a southerner who had been raised with blacks, Bird was dazed by the force with which African Americans expressed their anger at years of oppression. Within the White House itself, at a Women Doers lunch focused on crime prevention, black singer Eartha Kitt denounced her and her adored husband to her face. Bird kept her dignity, replying that the war did not excuse Americans from bettering what they could better, but the cut was deep. She later received 35,000 letters about the incident, and in her replies, salvaging what she could, she incorporated suggestions about what individuals could do to reduce crime. In the face of all discouragements, she kept up her work for conservation not merely to the end of her husband's term but far into the years of private life that followed.

From 1964 on, the first lady had wondered when and whether the president should retire—and so had he. Politics was his very life, but since his youth he had been besieged by serious problems with his health, including two severe heart attacks. The presidency of a nation tearing itself apart imposed stresses that few could withstand, and Bird seriously questioned whether her husband would survive another term. They, their daughters, and their advisers had repeatedly discussed a possible withdrawal. In a speech that the first lady had revised to make it more forceful, Lyndon Johnson finally announced that he would neither seek nor accept the nomination of his party for reelection in 1968. Immediately afterward Lady Bird issued a statement: "We have done a lot; there's a lot left to do in the remaining months; maybe this is the only way to get it done." The decision gave her new energy.

The same could not be said of Lyndon. Much as he enjoyed his young grandson, Luci's son Lyndon Nugent, and much as he loved the ranch, private life did not satisfy him. He began to smoke; he went off the diet the doctors had prescribed for him; and he continued his philandering. He became, in his wife's phrase, "a holy terror," demanding and abusive, crying over trifles, terrified of being alone, depressed one minute and raging the next. He was dying, and they both knew it.

Seemingly serene as ever, Bird turned to Bible study and spiritual meditation. She continued her public duties, accepting a position on the board of regents of the University of Texas, where she met with student demonstrators. When Lyndon died on January 22, 1973, she said, "Well, we expected it, didn't we?" Yet she mourned him deeply, missing him at every turn, and took every opportunity to celebrate his achievements, including work at the Austin library commemorating him. Liz Carpenter said of her that she "was an implementer and translator of her husband and his purposes. She is a WIFE in capital letters." Bird Johnson frequently said that Lyndon was a man who stretched the people around him. He made her more, she felt, than she would have been without him. "Lyndon is the catalyst, and I am the amalgam." "We were a good match. I guess you could sum it up by saying we were better together than apart."

Locally and nationally, she carried on her work in conservation. She served on the board of the *National Geographic*. Retaining a lifetime interest, she gave the ranch to the National Park Service, welcoming the busloads of tourists who visited: "I've had a long, satisfying love affair with G.P.—general public. Lyndon gave me that." She opened and endowed a National Wildflower Research Center and advocated planting wildflowers and native plants along the highways to brighten the roadsides, save money in mowing, and preserve the country's regional distinctiveness. She campaigned for her son-in-law, Charles Robb, in his runs for the governorship and a Senate seat of Virginia, and she continued to run the family businesses.

In 1982, when she was 70, Lady Bird Johnson announced her retirement from public life: "I'm just going to put down a certain amount of my burdens and say no more." She also retired as chair of the board of the LBJ Holding Company. Since then she has lived more quietly, but she remains an icon of the environmental movement—and a great lady.

———ɷ———

Throughout her marriage, Lady Bird Johnson had always placed her husband first, and the last difficult years of his presidency demanded that she devote much of her energy and her political insights to supporting him and helping him reach the decision not to run again. By that time, however, she had already begun to change the face of the American landscape. Her work on the environment went far beyond what her husband labeled "beautification," helping to set off and sustain the movement that has altered the roadsides Americans drive through, the water Americans drink and bathe in, and the air Americans breathe. That achievement and the political skills she displayed in his campaigns, particularly in 1964, expanded the role of first lady. Although *gracious* is the adjective most often applied to her, she is memorable less for her hospitality, warm and abundant though it was, than for her business sense, her principled courage in facing violent opposition, and her imaginative defense and improvement of our surroundings, both local and national.

CHRONOLOGY

1912   *December 22:* Claudia Alta Taylor (Lady Bird) is born in Karnack, Texas

1933   Lady Bird Taylor graduates with honors from the University of Texas at Austin

1934   *June:* Lady Bird Taylor takes a degree in journalism from the University of Texas

       November 17: Lady Bird Taylor marries Lyndon Baines Johnson, then a congressional secretary, at an Episcopal church in San Antonio

1935   *August:* Lyndon Johnson is appointed Texas state director of the National Youth Administration

1937   Lyndon Johnson successfully runs for Congress

1941   Lyndon Johnson loses his first bid for the Senate; Lady Bird Johnson runs his congressional office while he serves as a lieutenant commander in the United States Navy

1943   Lady Bird Johnson buys and begins to run KTBC, a radio station in Austin

1944   *March 19:* Daughter Lynda Bird is born

1947   *July 2:* Daughter Lucy (Luci) Baines is born

1948   Lyndon Johnson is elected to the Senate

1955   *January:* Lyndon Johnson is elected majority leader of the Senate

       July: Lyndon Johnson suffers a massive heart attack

1960   Lyndon Johnson is elected vice president of the United States

1963   *November 22:* After President Kennedy is assassinated, Lyndon Johnson is sworn into the presidency, and Lady Bird Johnson becomes first lady

1964   Lady Bird Johnson's train campaign throughout the South wins many votes for her husband, who is reelected president

1965   *February 5:* Lady Bird Johnson initiates her beautification project

       February 11: The Committee for a More Beautiful Capital first meets

       May: Lady Bird Johnson opens the White House Conference on Natural Beauty

       October 22: Lyndon Johnson signs a bill forbidding a profusion of billboards on highways and requiring that auto junkyards be screened from view

       November 25: Lady Bird Johnson televises a program to persuade Americans to participate in the effort to beautify the country

1966   *August 6:* Daughter Luci marries Patrick Nugent at the National Shrine of the Immaculate Conception

1968   *January 4:* Daughter Lynda Bird marries Captain Charles Robb

1969   *January 20:* Lyndon and Lady Bird Johnson leave the White House and retire to Texas

1973   *January 22:* Lyndon Johnson dies

1982   *December 22:* Lady Bird Johnson announces the donation of land and funds for the National Wildflower Research Center

       Lady Bird Johnson announces her retirement from public life

FURTHER READING

Caro, Robert A. *The Years of Lyndon Johnson: The Path to Power.* New York: Knopf, 1990.

Carpenter, Liz. *Ruffles and Flourishes.* Garden City, N.Y.: Doubleday, 1970.

Gould, Lewis L. *Lady Bird Johnson and the Environment.* Lawrence: University Press of Kansas, 1999.

Gutin, Myra G. *The President's Partner: The First Lady in the Twentieth Century.* New York: Greenwood, 1989.

Johnson, Lady Bird. *A White House Diary.* New York: Holt, Rinehart, and Winston, 1970.

Miller, Merle. *Lyndon: An Oral Biography.* New York: Putnam's, 1980.

Russell, Jan Jarboe. *Lady Bird: A Biography of Mrs. Johnson.* New York: Scribner's, 1999.

THELMA CATHERINE (PAT) RYAN NIXON
(MARCH 16, 1912–JUNE 22, 1993)
First Lady, January 20, 1969–August 8, 1974

PAT NIXON
(Library of Congress)

Until scandal exploded and drove them from the White House, the Nixons' story reads like the American dream, in which through grit and hard work, they won their way from poverty to the White House. Pat Nixon projected the image of a traditional wife and helpmate, and indeed she dutifully sacrificed her own perferences in favor of her husband's career—though not without protest. "I felt that a man had to make up his mind what he wants to do," she said, "then after he made it up, the only thing I could do was to help him." Nonetheless, during the early 1970s, when she was first lady, she reflected the women's movement of that time by advocating for women, especially in countries where women were oppressed.

Thelma Catherine Ryan was born in the copper boomtown of Ely, Nevada, on March 16, 1912, to soldier-of-fortune-turned-miner William Ryan and his immigrant wife Kate Halberstadt Bender Ryan; she was their third child and only daughter. Her "thoroughly Irish" father nicknamed her "Pat" in honor of St. Patrick's Day, the day after her birth, though in her girlhood most people called her Thelma. In 1914 William moved his family to an 11-acre truck farm in Artesia (now Cerritos), California, where Thelma grew up.

As a girl, Pat Nixon said later, she "didn't know what it was not to work hard." The Ryan family lived in a house with neither electricity nor running water. All the children labored in the fields picking fruits and vegetables. "As a youngster," she reminisced, "life was sort of sad, so I had to cheer everybody up. I learned to be that kind of person." She also learned to control her own emotions and to avoid confrontations. Her father, his temper flaring under the influence of too many drinks, picked fights with her mother. Daughter Julie Nixon Eisenhower remembers her mother as once saying: "I detest temper. I detest scenes. I just can't be that way. I saw it with my father. . . . [T]o avoid scenes or unhappiness, I suppose I accommodated to others." She disciplined herself to suppress her feelings.

When Thelma was 14, her mother died of cancer. Three years later silicosis, a miner's disease also known as black lung, killed her father. In his memory his daughter thereafter called herself Pat, or sometimes Patricia. Despite the demands on her time and energy at home, where she kept house for her family, she was a good student, graduating near the top of her high-school class. During the Great Depression, she had to scramble for money, taking what jobs she could find. Nevertheless, she developed ambitions to travel to faraway places as her father had done, to get a college education, to avoid being buried in a small town, and to have a nice family and home. She went on to Fullerton Junior College, earning her way by working as a cleaning woman and then as a

clerk in a local bank. In 1931 Pat interrupted her college education to drive an elderly couple to New York City in their aged Packard, a job for which she was paid bus fare for the trip back home. Intending only a brief visit to New York, she stayed for two years, working first as a stenographer and then, after taking a course in radiology at Columbia University, as an X-ray technician in a Bronx hospital.

Resisting the lures of New York and the fun of dating young doctors and interns, Pat saved her money and in 1933 returned to Los Angeles to finish her college education. She enrolled as a merchandising major at the University of Southern California, working her way by various jobs: dental assistant, department store clerk, telephone operator, and bit player in the movies. She was said to show promise as a movie actor but was uninterested in a film career. In 1937 she graduated with honors and took a job teaching typing and shorthand in the high school in Whittier, California.

Pat Ryan met lawyer Richard Milhous Nixon in January 1938, at the Whittier Community Players, where both were auditioning. For the next two and a half years he courted her; then, on June 21, 1940, they were married in a Quaker ceremony in Riverside, California. Following a honeymoon in Mexico, the newlyweds moved into a small apartment over a garage near his law office in Whittier. Pat continued to teach while Dick built up his law practice.

After the Japanese bombed Pearl Harbor on December 7, 1941, the Nixons moved to Washington, where both worked for the Office of Price Administration (OPA). In June 1942 he resigned to join the Navy. "I would have felt mighty uncomfortable if Dick hadn't done his part," Pat said. "Sure, I was unhappy, but so were thousands of other young wives. Because of Richard's [Quaker] upbringing he did much soul-searching before he made his decision." She joined the hordes of young wives following their husbands from one military base to another, learning to manage short-notice moves, transform small and dingy rooms into something resembling a home, and find a job in a new town. After Dick was posted overseas, she worked as a price analyst for the OPA, first in Washington and later in San Francisco, where she lived in a boardinghouse for 14 months.

In late 1945, shortly before Dick was mustered out of the service, Republican leaders in California invited him to run for the U.S. House of Representatives in the 1946 election, a prospect that appealed to him more than returning to his law practice in Whittier. Even during their courtship, he had talked to Pat about his dream of being president and his vision of her as "destined to be a great lady." Now she deferred to his preference and did not object to taking money from their wartime savings to fund his campaign. She did, however, stipulate that she would not be called upon to make any political speeches and that their home would be kept as a haven where their children could enjoy a normal life—a consideration that weighed heavily on her mind, since she was pregnant with their first child. As it turned out, neither of these conditions survived the turmoil of Richard Nixon's political career.

In 1946, in Dick's first campaign, Pat was his entire full-time office staff, researching his opponent's record, writing and typing campaign literature, mailing pamphlets, stuffing envelopes, and distributing literature from house to house. She never made speeches but consented to stand beside her husband, stiff with tension. When not campaigning, which she hated, she watched and encouraged her husband through his successful runs for reelection to the House of Representatives in 1948 and election to the Senate in 1950. It was not the life she would have chosen. Congressman Nixon, on the other hand, was building a national reputation as an aggressive member of the House Un-American Activities Committee, most notably with his pursuit of Alger Hiss, an official in the State Department, which began in August 1948. Although his wife continued to help out occasionally at her husband's office, she was fully occupied with the duties of a congressman's wife and, her first priority, making a home in their small Washington apartment for them and their children—Tri-

cia, born February 21, 1946, and Julie, born July 5, 1948.

Both undertakings were time-consuming. Like other congressional wives Pat was deluged with invitations, some of them the equivalent of commands to women who did not want to damage their husbands' careers by refusing them. Child care and homemaking on a limited budget demanded most of her time. After the Nixons managed to buy a modest house in the northwest corner of Washington, she made all the curtains, draperies, and slipcovers; cooked; and looked after the house inside and out. Her wardrobe, consisting mostly of tailored clothes, was small, but she put real effort into making her hats, the one thing about the way she dressed that her husband noticed. At home she typed for Dick and took telephone messages for him; at his office she helped the secretarial staff when she could.

Her experience with politics did not make her fonder of such a life—quite the opposite. The more she saw of the political world, the less she liked it. Richard Nixon was never one who inspired public affection, and a good many people not merely opposed his stands but distrusted and despised him. Being Nixon's wife meant stumbling repeatedly over the violent dislike that he often evoked. For Pat, who believed in and loved her husband, attacks on him were painful, and increasingly this ugly side of politics sickened her.

She was traumatized by Nixon's notoriously vicious (and successful) campaign against Helen Gahagan Douglas for a Senate seat from California, his tactics provoking cries of "Foul." So strongly did she react that two years later, in 1952, she tried unsuccessfully to persuade him not to accept the nomination for vice president as running mate to Dwight Eisenhower. For years she had done all that her husband asked. Now she overcame her dislike of arguments and confrontation to express her feelings vigorously. She explained how much she dreaded every aspect of what the nomination entailed—a national campaign, separations from her daughters, constant traveling, and, once the election was over, stressful demands on the vice president's wife. None of her arguments availed, even though she thought she had a commitment from him to leave politics at the end of his Senate term, in 1956—a promise he had made during his 1950 campaign for the Senate. He had even put the agreement in writing, but he kept the paper himself, and it disappeared.

In the end Pat yielded to Dick's determination to run for the vice presidency, saying, "I guess I can make it through another campaign," and again she took up the work she abhorred. When that campaign revealed a secret fund collected for Richard Nixon by wealthy donors, questions were raised about his fitness as a candidate on the Eisenhower ticket, and many wondered aloud whether he should withdraw. Pat felt that he must answer the charges but balked at opening the family's financial records, asking, "Why should we keep taking this?" Her husband countered criticism with a speech in which he talked of his family and their modest way of life. His wife, he said, did not have a fur coat but wore "a good Republican cloth coat." Nor did they improperly accept gifts—but he refused to send back the little dog, Checkers, which had been given to his small daughters. The speech saved his candidacy, and he rode to triumph with Eisenhower.

Despite her dread of the position, Pat performed capably as the wife of the vice president. Her experience as a Senate wife had prepared her to preside over the Ladies of the Senate (renamed during the 1980s the Senate Spouses' Club), a unit of the American Red Cross that has met every Tuesday since World War I. Other Senate wives liked her; Abigail McCarthy, wife of Democratic Senator Eugene McCarthy, described her as "always there, always crisp and correct in her Red Cross uniform," a woman who sometimes showed surprising political astuteness and a good sense of humor. Mamie Eisenhower called her "my Rock of Gibraltar," for Pat frequently substituted for her at official functions.

Pat also proved herself a good ambassador for the United States as President Eisenhower sent the Nixons on numerous official missions. Indeed, Pat Nixon outdid all of her predecessors as vice president's wife in the weeks and miles she traveled representing the United States, acquitting herself well with her poise and pleasant manners. In 1953 they went to Asia, where, with conscious intent, she quietly broke barriers against women. She made the traditional rounds of hospitals, orphanages, and schools, visits where she seemed relaxed and in her element. However, in Japan she gave the first press conference ever held only for women reporters there, and in Kuala Lumpur she accepted an invitation to dine in a club previously for men only. "Everywhere I went," she said, "it helped women."

Pat showed exceptional courage on the South American tour of 1958, where the Nixons were met with hostile and violent demonstrations. In Caracas they sat locked in their limousine while a mob attacked and rocked it, striking it with pipes and large stones. At the Caracas airport, while the Nixons stood at attention for the Venezuelan national anthem, Venezuelans standing above them in the observation gallery spat on them, streaking Pat's face and red suit with expectorated tobacco juice. In Lima, Peru, again under attack, she evoked the praise of journalist Earl Mazo: "That lady showed no fear. She didn't panic, not even remotely. She was utterly calm. She was even calming the reporters, all of whom were scared silly."

On the Nixons' 1959 trip to Moscow, the second lady conducted what *The New York Times* called a "mingle-with-the-Russians" campaign—a newsworthy event in the era of the cold war. Impeccably clothed and coiffed, she tirelessly visited children's hospitals, playing with the children and distributing candy. Yes, she told reporters, she liked meeting the youngsters at a Young Pioneers camp, "but they make me homesick for my little girls." Much as she enjoyed children, however, she did not simply pursue the safe, noncontroversial course of concentrating on them. When no women showed up at the first banquet, she persistently asked Premier Nikita Khrushchev about his wife and the wives of the other Soviet officials; thereafter Mrs. Khrushchev attended. When the vice president asked Khrushchev about solid fuels for Soviet missiles, the premier fended him off by disclaiming expertise on such a technical subject. "I'm surprised that there is a subject that you're not prepared to discuss, Mr. Chairman," said Pat. "I thought that with your one-man government you had to know everything and have everything firmly in your own hands."

Overall as second lady, Pat Nixon compiled an impressive record, becoming a public figure in her own right. As Eisenhower's second term came to an end, she sighed with relief, for, she had written a friend, "I would like to do part-time work rather than all the useless gadding I am expected to do." She had thought the vice presidency an end to her husband's political career, so she was shocked and dismayed by his decision to run for the presidency against John F. Kennedy in the 1960 election—so shocked that, when Dick announced his intention while they were dining in a restaurant with friends, she reportedly left the table in tears. Publicly, however, she put a good face on things, presenting herself as housewife-turned-volunteer for a cause she believed in. Republicans, taking full advantage of the public persona she had established, featured her in their campaign propaganda and on buttons, bumper stickers, and posters. When, by the narrowest of margins, Richard Nixon lost, she wept for him before the television cameras.

For a time that defeat brought her the private life she craved, as the wife of a lawyer in Beverly Hills, California. In 1962, ignoring her pleas and her advice, Dick ran for governor of California; after his loss, he announced to the press, "You won't have Richard Nixon to kick around any longer." The next year he set up a practice in New York City, where she worked part-time as a receptionist and stenographer under the name "Miss Ryan." Reportedly she was overheard to warn her husband, "If you ever run for office again, I'll kill myself."

Nevertheless, the year 1968 saw him again nominated as the Republican candidate for president, and this time he won. Despite her years of experience as second lady, it took Pat a while to adjust to the White House. She disliked the publicity that accompanied the family's every move, yet she knew how to handle herself, and she did her job competently, usually to good press and public approval. She conceived her role as first lady in fairly conventional terms, never "intruding" on the president's work but always ready to do whatever would help him. She chose volunteerism as her "cause," although she never gave it the primacy that other first ladies had given to theirs. "People are my project," she said.

Concern for the American people prompted her to spend up to five hours a day with her correspondence, personally answering as many requests as she could and forwarding others to government departments that could help. She recognized the importance of a letter from the White House to recipients in small towns across America. In Washington she visited day camps for inner-city youngsters, took them on the presidential yacht, and arranged concerts for them.

Quietly, she set about refurbishing the executive mansion's public rooms, which deteriorate quickly under the wear and tear imposed by millions of tourists and guests passing through them annually. A state department antiques curator estimated that when the Nixons moved into the White House, only about a third of the furnishings were genuine antiques; when they left, about 65 or 70 percent were. Pat Nixon and her advisers significantly enhanced the White House art collection and added more than 500 items of American furniture, art, chandeliers, and rugs, many of them paid for by private funds.

Inspired by a conviction that the White House belonged to the American people, she tried to make it more accessible to them. She placed recorded histories of the mansion where tourists could hear them as they waited in line. For working people she instituted evening tours during the holidays, and for the blind, tours in which they might touch objects. She had the mansion lit at night to highlight its architec-

Pat Nixon and husband entertained by dancers in Africa *(Library of Congress)*

tural beauty. On many Sundays the Nixons invited families to ecumenical services held in the executive mansion.

The first lady undertook so heavy a schedule of entertaining that *U.S. News & World Report* called the number of functions held in the White House during the Nixons' first year in office "unprecedented; one would have to go back to Andrew Jackson who opened the mansion indiscriminately to the general public on important occasions." She had a warm way, which showed to advantage especially on those occasions when her guests were ordinary U.S. citizens. Her daughter Julie reports:

a White House reception when Mother received a cherry-tree quilt from the Appalachian Fireside Crafts, a self-help group located in one of the nation's most poverty-stricken areas. The quilt makers were very simple hill

people, in Washington for the first time, and so nervous at the thought of meeting the First Lady that most of them were weeping. When Mother walked into the Diplomatic Reception Room to greet the quilt makers and heard the sobbing, she simply went around the room and wordlessly gave each of her guests a hug.

Pat Nixon also arranged the first wedding ever held in the White House rose garden, where the Nixons' daughter Tricia married Edward Cox on June 12, 1971. Before the Nixons moved into the White House, their daughter Julie had married David Eisenhower, grandson of President Dwight David Eisenhower, on December 22, 1969.

As when she was the wife of the vice president, Pat traveled far and wide, with her husband or alone. As first lady she covered 123,245 miles, visiting 29 countries. When she traveled on her own to Africa, her husband wanted her to talk with the chief executive in each country she visited. In 1970 she broke precedent by accompanying nine tons of privately donated relief supplies to Peru for the victims of a deadly earthquake. President Nixon emphasized the political benefits of her travel when, in planning for his tradition-breaking trip to China in 1972, he told his aide H. R. Haldeman that having the first lady go along "might be a good idea because of the TV coverage she'd get, but if she does, it would have to be understood that she would be the only woman going. Not . . . any other wives." The "people contact," the president felt, was more important than meetings, and her presence would be a way to get "some good people pictures," helping "to convey the human side of the Chinese to the American people." Moreover, it would also spare him from having to go out among the people himself.

Pat was tactful and considerate with the press. Sometimes on her travels, rather than going to a restaurant, she ate in her hotel room to give them a night off. She took their calls even in the late evenings. When they angered the president, she tried to dissuade him from banning them.

When Richard Nixon was reelected president in 1972, reporters were beginning to talk about the emergence of a "new Pat Nixon." H. R. Haldeman had written in his diary on October 21, 1971, of her anger when her husband failed to appoint a woman to the Supreme Court, even after she had made a public statement: "Don't you worry; I'm talking it up. . . . If we can't get a woman on the Supreme Court this time, there'll be a next time." At the 1972 Republican convention, she urged the re-endorsement of the Equal Rights Amendment. An article in the Los Angeles *Times* by Marlene Cimons noted:

Pat Nixon has clearly begun to emerge in her own right. The Pat Nixon who would never discuss controversial issues has had something to say about abortion and women's rights. She

had lobbied for a woman on the Supreme Court. The Pat Nixon who said she would never wear pants in public—her husband disapproved of them—is casually modelling pants in the current issue of a national magazine. In a recent television interview, she wore a pants suit. Clearly there has been a major change in the First Lady.

However, Pat Nixon's days in the White House were growing increasingly stressful. Even in 1969, protests and demonstrations against the Vietnam War and the president's policies were frequent. Finally came the Watergate scandals and the threats of impeachment that eventually forced President Nixon's resignation on August 8, 1974. As always, Pat did what she had to do. She remained smiling and gracious but gradually she retreated from public view. By the end she was almost a recluse, except for official functions. The support of the president's wife, daughters, and sons-in-law as he left the White House evoked more sympathy for him than anything else could. She bore up bravely as her disgraced husband was driven from office, stood by him as he bade a tearful farewell, and walked with him to the plane, from which he gave a defiant victory sign.

Afterward she disappeared into the shadows of their home in San Clemente, California. For her, the "saddest day of my life" was September 8, 1974, the day that her husband was pardoned by President Gerald Ford, since his acceptance of the pardon implied his guilt. She continued to believe that Watergate was partly an international scheme or at least involved double agents. The Nixons' days were darkened by persistent lawsuits, congressional investigations, and Dick's frequent hospitalizations. She found relief in gardening, reading, and music.

In early 1976 the Nixons revisited China. On July 7 of that year, Pat suffered a stroke, after reading part of Bob Woodward and Carl Bernstein's book *The Final Days* [of Richard Nixon's presidency] and learning that her husband was to be disbarred. She told daughter Julie, "Watergate is the only crisis that ever got me down. I guess it did because every day there were more ugly stories and there still are. It is just constant. And I know I will never live to see the vindication."

After her stroke, Pat endured severe physical pain, in large part because of inadequate therapy; exercise finally gave her some relief. In the years during which her husband boldly tried to rehabilitate his reputation, she was seldom to be seen in public. She lived quietly, enjoying her four grandchildren, the rest of her family, and a few close friends. In 1980 the Nixons moved to a New York City apartment to be nearer their close kin and to enable the former president to lead a more active life; the next year they moved again, to Saddle River, New Jersey. Pat's health continued to deteriorate, as she suffered pneumonia, bronchitis, and another stroke. She died in their Saddle River home on June 22, 1993. She is buried at the Richard Nixon Library and Birthplace in Yorba Linda, California.

—⁂—

Reports on the Nixon marriage contradict one another. Close friends and family, especially their younger daughter, Julie Nixon Eisenhower, insist that their relationship was close and intimate, but many observers found that hard to believe. The couple had different ambitions and goals. He wanted public life, she private life. All during their marriage she acceded to his wishes, sometimes under protest. Unlike many another president, he was faithful to his wife physically, but anecdotes abound showing him to have been a husband indifferent to her happiness, mentally cruel, and, according to some accusations, physically abusive.

Richard Nixon often ignored his wife's contributions, as when in 1974, after she had been warmly received in South America, his speech on the relationship between the United States and Latin America made no mention of her visit. At a dinner for representatives of African nations at the Sheraton Park Hotel, he arrived with her on his arm, made his speech, and walked out alone, leaving her standing in embarrassment. He made decisions that changed their lives without consulting her, sometimes without even informing her—as with his determination to run for reelection in 1972. Asked whether he ever tried out important speeches on her, she replied, "He never tries anything out." On airplanes President Nixon sequestered himself with his aides, sending for the first lady only when they landed, so that they could appear together. Guests at the White House talked about the way the couple left the room arm in arm, only to part wordlessly at the elevator. A dinner guest at their New York home after they left the White House reported how Richard Nixon had greeted him with a somewhat mechanical "Glad to see you again," then greeted his wife with exactly the same formula. Even when he made the gracious gesture of dedicating his book *Six Crises* to her, he phrased it unfortunately: "To Pat, she also ran."

Yet publicly Pat Nixon always remained correct and loyal. In one of the efforts to redeem her husband's image, Pat was shown on television saying, "Oh, but you just don't realize how much fun he is! He's just so much fun!"

Pat Nixon's record as first lady for a time was overshadowed by the scandals of her husband's presidency, although it seems doubtful that he consulted her often if at all in the performance of his public duties. Now, however, her work in refurbishing and refurnishing the White House is recognized as outstanding. She also continued and expanded the pioneering diplomatic work of Jacqueline Kennedy in representing the United States in her worldwide travels, with her husband and alone. She was good with people, and Richard Nixon used her appeal to serve both the nation and his own career. In the course of her time in the White House, during some of the most active years of the second American women's movement, she moved toward more independence and toward more open support for opportunities for women.

CHRONOLOGY

1912 *March 16:* Thelma Catherine Ryan is born in Ely, Nevada; nicknamed "Pat" by her father, later becomes known as Patricia

1913 The Ryans move to a truck farm in Artesia (now Cerritos) California

1931 Pat Ryan moves to New York City where she works as a secretary and an X-ray technician

1934 Pat Ryan enrolls at the University of Southern California

1937 Pat Ryan graduates from the University of Southern California with a degree in merchandising and a teaching certificate and begins to teach business at Whittier High School

1940 *June 21:* Pat Ryan marries attorney Richard Nixon

1941 *December:* Richard Nixon accepts a government position in Washington, D.C.

1942 Richard Nixon receives an officer's commission in the U.S. Navy; Pat Nixon works in a government office in San Francisco

1946 *February 21:* Daughter Patricia (Tricia) is born

Richard Nixon is elected to Congress

1948 *July 5:* Daughter Julie is born

1950 Richard Nixon is elected to the Senate

1952 Richard Nixon is elected vice president of the United States

1953–61 Pat Nixon serves as second lady

1960 Richard Nixon, defeated in a run for the presidency, joins a Los Angeles law firm

1962 Richard Nixon, defeated in a run for the governorship of California, joins a New York law firm

1968 Richard Nixon is elected president of the United States

December 22: Daughter Julie marries Dwight David Eisenhower II, grandson of the former president

1969 *January 20:* Pat Nixon becomes first lady

1971 *June 12:* Daughter Tricia marries Edward Cox in the Rose Garden at the White House

1972 Richard Nixon is reelected president

The Nixons go to China.

1974 *August 8:* Richard Nixon resigns the presidency; the Nixons retire to San Clemente, California

1976 *July 7:* Pat Nixon suffers a stroke

1980 The Nixons move to New York City, then to Saddle River, New Jersey

1993 *June 22:* Pat Nixon dies

FURTHER READING

Ambrose, Stephen E. *Nixon.* 2 vols. New York: Simon and Schuster, 1987.

Anthony, Carl Sferrazza. "Pat Nixon's Happy Golden Years," *Good Housekeeping,* January 1991.

David, Lester. *The Lonely Lady of San Clemente: The Story of Pat Nixon.* New York: Thomas Y. Crowell, 1978.

Edmondson, Madeline, and Alder Duer Cohen. *The Women of Watergate.* New York: Stein, 1975.

Eisenhower, Julie Nixon. *Pat Nixon: The Untold Story.* New York: Simon and Schuster, 1986.

Nixon, Richard. *RN: The Memoirs of Richard Nixon.* New York: Grossett and Dunlap, 1978.

"Pat Nixon: Stealth Feminist," *Washington Post,* (Sunday Outlook Section), June 27, 1993.

Small, Melvin. *The Presidency of Richard Nixon.* Lawrence: University Press of Kansas, 1999.

ELIZABETH ANN (BETTY) BLOOMER WARREN FORD

(APRIL 8, 1918–   )
First Lady, August 9, 1974–January 20, 1977

BETTY FORD
(Library of Congress)

Betty Ford was a woman who seized her opportunities, grew, and changed with her times, often in the vanguard of changes herself. Like so many women of her generation, she worked as a young woman, then married and stayed home to raise her children and do volunteer work during the 1950s and 1960s. In this period she kept in touch with public affairs through her husband's career. Women like her—in their 40s and 50s during the women's movement of the 1960s and 1970s—either drew back, appalled, or responded enthusiastically to the changes exploding around them. She chose the latter course, and, taking advantage of the opportunities offered her by her husband's position, courageously and effectively spoke out on such women's issues as abortion, breast cancer, and the Equal Rights Amendment.

301

Her mother said that she "popped out of a bottle of champagne." Elizabeth Ann Bloomer, called Betty, was born April 8, 1918, in Chicago, Illinois, the only girl and youngest child of William Stephenson Bloomer and Hortense Neahr Bloomer. When she was three years old, they moved to a fashionable section of Grand Rapids, Michigan. Her father traveled in industrial supplies; her mother, related to a well-to-do manufacturing family of high social position, participated actively in civic affairs. The family spent their summers at White Fish Lake in Michigan. "My mother was an attractive woman, my father was a good-looking man, and I was a fat little kid," Betty later wrote. She laughed over the story of herself as a baby in rompers with a Dutch boy haircut begging goodies at a nearby hotel from table to table, until her mother hung a sign on her back: "Please do not feed this child." They were a prosperous family, and though in the Great Depression they had to cut back, Betty enjoyed a sunny girlhood, affording plenty of opportunities for fun. It darkened the year she was 16, when her father died from carbon monoxide poisoning while working on his car. He left enough money that her mother did not have to work, although for a time she sold insurance.

From the time she was eight, Betty had taken dancing lessons at the Calla Travis Dance Studio. She preferred modern dance because of the freedom of movement it afforded. As a teenager she taught dances like the Big Apple and the foxtrot to other teenagers in Grand Rapids. She had set her sights on New York, but her mother insisted that she live at home until she was 20.

Eventually they compromised. During the winters Betty modeled, taught dance, joined the Junior League, and dated often. In the summers of 1936 and 1937, she went east to study at the Bennington College School of Dance with such famed dancers as José Limón and Martha Graham. Graham encouraged her to dance professionally, and in 1938 she enrolled in Graham's New York school. The next year she performed occasionally with Graham's auxiliary concert group. A pretty young woman, 5'6" tall and 108 pounds, with light auburn hair and blue-green eyes, she earned a living (with a little financial help from her mother) by modeling for fashion shows through the prestigious John Powers Agency.

Hortense Bloomer still wanted her to come back home, and Betty finally agreed to return for six months. If after that she still wanted to dance, her mother promised she would never say another word against the decision. Back in Grand Rapids in 1941, Betty started her own dance group, choreographed for it, introduced religious dance, taught modern dance for her old teacher Calla Travis, and eventually got a job as assistant to the fashion coordinator of a department store. With her active social life she fashioned a lifestyle in Michigan satisfying enough to displace her dreams of a New York career.

In 1942 Betty married William C. Warren, a furniture dealer. They moved from place to place as he changed jobs. They lived in Toledo, Ohio, where she worked in a department store and taught dance at the university; in Syracuse, New York, where she worked in a frozen-food factory; and in Grand Rapids, where she found more congenial work as executive fashion coordinator for the department store that had formerly employed her. Her husband was little inclined to settle down. She stayed with him for three years of job shifts and two dreary years when his diabetes made him a complete invalid. After he made a miraculous recovery, however, she sued for divorce. She asked for no alimony but kept on at her job, arranging for fashion shows, training models, and coordinating window displays with sales promotions. In her spare time she organized an amateur dance troupe, staged dances that she choreographed, and taught dance to black and handicapped children, among others.

Before long Betty began dating Gerald Ford, a Michigan football hero and young lawyer. After they were engaged, he told her that he was running for the House of Representatives. Although she thought his opponent unbeatable, she plunged into the primary campaign, recruiting her friends and associates to work for him. She knew nothing about politics, she told them, but anyone could lick stamps and stuff envelopes. He won the primary, a victory that almost ensured his election in his heavily Republican district.

Betty and Jerry were married at Grace Episcopal Church on October 15, 1948, the bride in blue satin, wearing a hat and carrying American Beauty roses. Immediately she began to learn the life of a politician's wife, for their honeymoon was studded with rallies, meetings, and speeches.

Upon her husband's election to Congress the next month, they moved to Washington, D.C., where they would live for a quarter of a century. They found a one-bedroom apartment in Georgetown. With a twice-a-week cleaning lady to care for it, Betty had time to pursue her political education as she sat in congressional galleries, visited the Supreme Court, entertained her husband's constituents, helped in his office on weekends, and became active in the bipartisan Congressional Club of cabinet, congressional, and Supreme Court wives.

Soon the Fords began their family: Michael, born in 1950; John, in 1952; Steven, in 1956; and Susan, in 1957. The congressman dedicated his time and energies to serving his constituents and building his career, winning reelection term after term, and in 1965 being elected minority leader of the House. In that capacity he traveled some two-thirds of the time—so much, his wife later said, that occasionally when she woke in the middle of the night she asked him, "What are *you* doing here?" In his absence she did the hard work of a suburban mom. She raised their family almost by herself, for a time in a garden apartment in Park Fairfax, Virginia, and then from 1955 on in their own house in Alexandria. They also maintained a house in Grand Rapids, bought the summer after Michael's birth, so that Congressman Ford could stay in touch with his constituency.

Betty was an attractive woman, compulsively meticulous about her appearance. With the help of a devoted maid, Clara Powell, she did what a good wife and mother of her time and place was supposed to do. She joined the PTA; was a den mother for the Cub Scouts; worked in community projects; taught Sunday School at an Episcopal church for 23 years; drove her children to the orthodontist, oculist, and Little League; and helped them to raise animals—gerbils, rabbits, praying mantises, even an alligator. Because her sons preferred football to other sports, she quickly memorized the route to the hospital emergency room. Now and then, when Jerry could get away, they took the family skiing or, when the children were old enough, to the Republican national conventions.

In 1965 Jerry's election to the position of House minority leader multiplied Betty's political duties. Now she felt a responsibility to urge Republican wives to work harder for charities and be more visible. The position also offered perquisites, like international trips.

Betty kept up with all this despite arthritis, a bout with pancreatitis, and a pinched nerve in her neck that required hospitalization and therapy. She consequently fell into the habit of taking drugs against pain and sleeplessness, and in 1965 she collapsed. Visits to a psychiatrist helped her to gain a new self-confidence and self-respect. She needed these qualities; like many another woman in the era of the feminine mystique, she felt unappreciated. She was proud of her husband, but, she later wrote, "I was beginning to feel sorry for myself. . . . He gets all the headlines and applause, but what about me? On the one hand, I loved being 'the wife of'; on the other hand, I was convinced that the more important Jerry became, the less important I became." It also bothered her that she did not have a college degree.

Still, during those congressional years she learned the ins and outs of official Washington. She took lessons in public speaking and studied Washington protocol. She went to innumerable luncheons. She met Bess Truman, whom she admired, and became friends with Lady

Bird Johnson and Pat Nixon. Mamie Eisenhower invited her to play cards at the White House, and the Fords were entertained occasionally at the Kennedy White House.

Jerry had decided to leave politics after 1974 to practice law, but the 1973 resignation of Vice President Spiro Agnew sharply changed the pattern of the Fords' life. When President Nixon named her husband as his new vice president, Betty Ford found this turn of events an exciting challenge. With the youngest of her children now in late adolescence, she plunged into new activities. She announced that she would choose art and dance as her special projects to support as second lady and redecorate Admiralty House, the new residence of the vice president. She traveled, spoke, and made ceremonial appearances; chaired Heart Sunday for the Washington Heart Association; and presided over the Red Cross Senate Wives Club (renamed during the 1980s the Senate Spouses' Club). On her own initiative she attended the funeral of the murdered Mrs. Martin Luther King, Sr., in 1974. She also began to establish her reputation for frankness when she calmly informed the press, "I take a Valium every day." She did not want to give interviews, but if she had to, she would answer questions honestly. She told television reporter Barbara Walters that she "agreed with the Supreme Court's ruling [in *Roe v. Wade*], that it was time to bring abortion out of the backwoods and put it in the hospitals where it belonged."

Then, eight months into Ford's vice presidency, came the thunderbolt. While Betty was helping arrange son Mike's wedding and preparing to move into Admiralty House, President Nixon resigned, and on August 9, 1974, Gerald Ford became president of the United States. His wife, holding the Bible for him to take the oath of office, felt as if she too were taking it. He paid tribute to her in his inauguration address: "I am indebted to no man and only to one woman—my dear wife." They waved goodbye to the Nixons, waited about 10 days while Julie Nixon Eisenhower and her husband packed up the Nixons' effects, and moved into the White House.

With this abrupt transition, Betty had to plunge at once into her duties as first lady. On August 10, the day after her husband was sworn in, she discovered that King Hussein of Jordan was coming for a state visit, and she had to arrange a state dinner for the 16th. Nonetheless, she at once opened her door and her thinking to the press, who found her, veteran reporter Helen Thomas said, "down to earth and very approachable." She was determined to make her new home "a happy and fun place" and "an open, friendly White House, and not just for Congress, either" to erase the memories of gloom and doom that Richard Nixon had left there. She relished living there and being first lady, and the nation relished it with her. As she wrote of her travels abroad, "I really enjoyed those Presidential trips. I had fun, I was privileged." On occasion she exhibited high spirits—once ending a speech to a conference of dance companies with an impromptu pirouette. On a visit to the Kennedy Center, she joined her friend Pearl Bailey in the University of Michigan fight song, after which they bowed and hugged.

Betty's trademark was her frankness. When reporters asked her whether she knew that her husband frequently tripped and stumbled, she answered, "So what else is new?" She caused "a good deal of whooping and hollering," she said, by commenting that "Jerry and I were *not* going to have separate bedrooms and that we were going to take our own bed with us." In the ruckus few people even heard Gerald Ford's statement that the White House "is the best public housing I've ever seen." Betty's style evolved in part from her own temperament and in part from the Fords' shared conviction that after the Watergate scandals of the previous administration there must be no more cover-ups.

The public manifested approval of that style when, only weeks after the inauguration, Betty was operated on for breast cancer. In the 1970s, cancer was still a taboo word for many people, and breast cancer was seldom mentioned publicly. Her frankness about what was happening to her evoked a flood of gratitude and sent multitudes of women to their doctors for mammograms.

Her husband bore Betty's frankness bravely, his press attaché telling reporters, "The President has long ceased to be perturbed or surprised by his wife's remarks." Had her sons tried marijuana? an interviewer asked her. She did not know, but she supposed she might have tried it herself if she were young. No, of course she would not throw Susan out of the house if she had a premarital affair, though she would not condone it; premarital affairs might help to reduce the divorce rate. In an interview with journalist Myra MacPherson, Betty remarked that she had been asked everything except how often she slept with her husband. If anyone had asked, she said, she would have replied, "As often as possible!"

Betty's role models had always been her grandmother, who worked for a living; her mother, who after her husband's death sold real estate and insurance; and Eleanor Roosevelt, because, she said, "A woman was finally speaking out and expressing herself rather than just expressing the views of her husband. That seemed healthy to me." As first lady, she lobbied hard for women's rights, publicly and privately. She worked for the Equal Rights Amendment, flying from her car a blue satin, lace-trimmed flag with red, white and blue stars. The flag flaunted a pair of bloomers (a pun on her maiden name); above was embroidered *Don't tread on me,* and below the letters *ERA.* In the bicentennial year of 1976, she opened several museum exhibits on the history of American women. She pronounced *Roe* v. *Wade* "a great, great thing" and rejoiced at the appointment of Carla Hill as secretary of housing and urban development. She pillow-talked with her husband about the appointment of more women to governmental posts, especially on the Supreme Court. She also pushed him on the Equal Rights Amendment, telling a reporter that "If he doesn't get it in the office in the day, he gets it in the ribs at night." When he

proclaimed the International Women's Year, she congratulated him, saying, "I am glad to see that you have come a long, long way."

She did not, however, think that all women needed to work outside the home. "In fact," she wrote in her autobiography, "being a good housewife seems to me a much tougher job than going to the office and getting paid for it. . . . But *because* of this, I feel women ought to have equal rights, equal social security, equal opportunities for education, an equal chance to establish credit. . . . I thought motherhood was swell. But I wasn't so sure mothers shouldn't have rights."

As first lady she also helped causes other than women's rights. Her experience as a dancer made her an enthusiastic supporter of the National Endowment for the Arts, and early on she consulted with its head, Nancy Hanks, about how she might promote its programs. Her bout with breast cancer inspired her to publicize the need for mammograms and self-examination and to raise funds for the National Cancer Foundation. Her feeling for retarded, crippled, and handicapped children prompted her labors for the Washington Hospital for Sick Children, where she herself went to volunteer. She worked for the Arthritis Foundation, the Heart Association, Goodwill Industries, and No Greater Love, which helped children of soldiers missing in action. She also worked to stop the abuse of the elderly in nursing homes.

As first lady, Betty developed her own imaginative style of entertaining. She ignored Julia Child's criticism of her for not offering the queen of England a French cuisine, arguing that she wanted to serve American food; she herself, she said, would not want to be fed southern fried chicken in another country. She featured American art at state dinners, sometimes borrowing a Steuben glass crystal collection, sometimes a collection of American-made silver, once a collection of antique Indian baskets, and for the dinner in honor of Prime Minister Sadat of Egypt, who loved the American West, a collection of bronzes by Frederic Remington and Charles M. Russell. She used round

Betty Ford dancing with comedian Marty Allen during a state dinner held in honor of Liberian president and Mrs. William R. Tolbert, Jr., on September 21, 1976 *(Gerald R. Ford Library)*

tables for eight, in part because they allowed her to seat more "women who needed a leg up" at the president's table.

The Fords often talked over the issues with which he was wrestling. In 1975 Jerry said, "She does propagandize me on a number of matters. She obviously has a great deal of influence." When he told her that he was considering a full pardon for Richard Nixon, she agreed, mainly out of feeling for the sufferings of the former president and his family; but, she told her husband, "I'll support whatever you decide."

Betty campaigned hard for him in the 1976 election. With her popularity ratings higher than his, she was an important asset. To her delight, people greeted her with "Hi, Betty," or "Hi, First Momma." Campaign buttons bore the slogans "Keep Betty in the White House" and "Betty's Husband for President." Mischievously, she publicly pinned one of them on the lapel of

Senator Fritz Mondale, the Democratic vice presidential candidate. Betty remembered that Mondale, a very polite man, "looked down and smiled and said thanks and I don't know how long it was before he got a chance to really read what it said and rip it off." Just before the last televised presidential debate, Betty left a note on his opponent's rostrum: "Dear Mr. Carter, may I wish you the best tonight. I'm sure the best man will win. I happen to have a favorite candidate, my husband, President Ford. Best wishes." Gerald Ford's defeat came as a shock, but she rose to the occasion by making the concession speech and facing the aftermath on television, her husband having lost his voice and their children being distraught.

Nonetheless, she left the White House an unhappy woman, depressed, she said, over "Jerry's having lost the election after twenty-eight years of faithful service to the country. I thought the American people had made a big mistake. . . . In a sense, I was out of office too. As First Lady, there had been a lot of demands made of me. I had been equal to most of them, performed well and enjoyed my moment in the sun." She was leaving the city she loved, her children had grown up and left home, and she thought that nobody needed her any longer. "I kept smiling," she later wrote. "I didn't want anyone to know how much it really hurt. All our married life was being left there; I don't know how else to explain it. We were married, we went to Washington, looked for a place to live and found it, our children were born there, Jerry's twenty-eight years of work had been there, and I felt as if the whole thing had just gone down the drain." To ease the sense of disappointment and loss, she resorted to drugs—legal, prescribed medications—and alcohol.

Later she was to say of the White House years that she was so drugged that she was in "a fog that was sometimes euphoric, sometimes depressed." However, a sense of responsibility and a heavy schedule kept her from drinking to excess. The honor of representing the country mattered to her, and she did her duty and more with notable success. Nonetheless, during those years she was under great stress. Twice she went through the agony of having would-be assassins try to kill her husband. The last several months had been given over to intensive campaigning. Pain from her arthritis, from the pinched nerve in her neck, and from muscle spasms dogged her. When she traveled abroad with her husband, pain often forced her to go to bed with hot packs and pills, but she got up in time for the state dinners. Over the years doctors had prescribed pain pills for her, so many that they blocked not only the pain but also reality. Any alcohol she drank compounded their effect.

Fortunately, when they saw her deteriorating in retirement at Palm Springs, California, her loving family intervened, telling Betty that she needed professional treatment. She found it at the naval hospital at Long Beach, California, where she came to recognize her addiction. This time telling the truth to the public cost her suf-

fering, but with remarkable courage she did so, thereby heartening many who were trying to overcome their own addictions. Since then, although she continued to work for other causes and to travel with her husband, she has dedicated much of her time and energy to helping addicts.

In 1982 she founded (and now chairs) the Betty Ford Center for Drug and Alcohol Rehabilitation at Rancho Mirage, California. With the assistance of her friends, she raised the money for it. "I didn't need a cause," she said. "I was already involved in raising money for the American Cancer Society, and the Arthritis Foundation, and mental health and underprivileged children. But the plight of alcoholic women pulled at me." The situation and needs of women addicts differ from those of men, she discovered. Women's smaller size and greater proportion of fatty tissues increase the effects of drugs and alcohol, so that when they enter treatment they are often sicker than their male counterparts. Nine out of ten wives of addicts stay with them; nine out of ten husbands of addicts leave, so many women addicts lack a support system. In therapy groups of both genders, women tend not to talk about themselves but instead to nurture and encourage the men. Moreover, women find it difficult to talk about rape and incest in mixed groups. Betty concluded that women addicts recover better and faster when they are treated only with other women, and her Center focuses on their needs.

The Fords never moved back into their house in Alexandria. Rather, they built a new home in Palm Springs, partly because Betty's arthritis troubled her less in a hot, dry climate and partly because they enjoyed the city. In 1987 Betty Ford underwent a quadruple bypass operation. Once again, she recovered and got on with her life and work, which she continues today.

—⁓—

As first lady, Betty Ford brought a welcome candor to a nation dismayed by the crimes of President Richard Nixon. She impressed the public as valuing honesty above image and being open about herself. She said what she thought rather than what might bring political advantage. She adopted causes—the arts, breast cancer, women's rights, and, later, alcohol and drug addiction—some of them controversial, all of them related to her personal experience. People did not always agree with what she said, but they respected her sincerity, her informality, her sense of fun, and her courage. To some degree she restored the nation's faith in the possibility of hearing a public figure speak the truth.

CHRONOLOGY

1918   *April 8:* Elizabeth Ann Bloomer (Betty) is born in Chicago, Illinois

1921   Betty Bloomer and her family move to Grand Rapids, Michigan

1926   Betty Bloomer begins dancing lessons

1936–37   Betty Bloomer studies dancing at Bennington School of Dance with Martha Graham and other noted dancers

1939   Betty Bloomer joins the Martha Graham auxiliary concert group in New York.

1941   Betty Bloomer returns to Grand Rapids

1942   Betty Bloomer marries William C. Warren

1947   Betty is divorced from William C. Warren

1948   *October 15:* Betty Bloomer marries lawyer Gerald Ford

November: Gerald Ford is elected to the U.S. House of Representatives; he and Betty Ford move to Washington

1950   *March 14:* Son Michael is born

1952   *March 16:* Son John is born

1956   *May 19:* Son Steven is born

1957   *July 6:* Daughter Susan is born

1973   *October 12:* President Richard Nixon appoints Gerald Ford as vice president

1974   *August 9:* President Nixon resigns, Gerald Ford becomes president, and Betty Ford becomes first lady

1977   Betty and Gerald Ford move to Rancho Mirage, California, after he loses his run for a second term.

1978   Betty Ford enters the rehabilitation clinic at Long Beach Naval Hospital for treatment for drug and alcohol addiction

1982   Betty Ford opens the Betty Ford Center for treatment of addiction

1987   Betty Ford undergoes quadruple bypass surgery

FURTHER READING

Cannon, James M. *Time and Chance: Gerald Ford's Appointment with History.* New York: Harper Collins, 1994.

Ford, Betty. *A Glad Awakening.* Garden City, N.Y.: Doubleday, 1987.

———, with Chris Chase. *The Times of My Life.* New York: Harper & Row, 1978.

Kurlyo, Elizabeth. "Cover Mental Illness, Ex-First Ladies Urge," *Atlanta Constitution*, March 8, 1994.

Reeves, Richard. *A Ford, Not a Lincoln.* New York: Harcourt Brace Jovanovich, 1975.

Weidenfeld, Sheila Rabb. *First Lady's Lady: With the Fords at the White House.* New York: Putnam, 1979.

ELEANOR ROSALYNN SMITH CARTER

(AUGUST 18, 1927–   )

First Lady, January 20, 1977–January 20, 1981

ROSALYNN CARTER
(Library of Congress)

Rosalynn Smith Carter was fortunate in having a father who believed that she could do anything. She chose a husband of similar mind, and with him she established a partnership in both their public and their private lives. Both of them as born-again Christians feel themselves obliged to develop their talents to the full and to devote these talents to the service of humanity. Always striving to learn and grow, Rosalynn Carter developed into a woman dedicated to seeing justice done and helping people in the United States and around the world, devoting her time, energies, and influence to these ends.

—⁂—

Rosalynn Smith was born on August 18, 1927, the first of four children of her college-graduate mother, Frances Allethea ("Miss Allie"), and her father, William

Edgar Smith, who ran a garage, farmed, and drove a school bus. In the tiny town of Plains, Georgia, the Smiths centered their family life on church and school. Despite the hard times of the Great Depression, Rosalynn felt prosperous because she had the prettiest clothes in town, which her mother made, and her mechanic father always managed to keep the family car running. With no other girls of her own age nearby, she grew up playing with boys or by herself, reading, doing chores, and learning to sew.

When she was 13, her father's fatal illness put an end to this happy childhood. To support the family her mother took in sewing, clerked in the grocery store, and later got a job in the post office. With young children to raise and her aging parents needing her care, Miss Allie depended on Rosalynn not only for help with the housework and sewing but also as someone to consult on the family budget and child-rearing although she left the youngster time to excel in her schoolwork, play basketball on the school team, and socialize. In her teens Rosalynn formed a friendship with Ruth Carter, with whom she often double-dated.

When she graduated from high school as class valedictorian, Rosalynn fulfilled as best she could her father's wish that she go to college, commuting to a junior college in nearby Americus while continuing to live at home. With the boys who would normally have been her classmates away at war, Rosalynn began to daydream over Ruth Carter's photograph of her older brother Jimmy, then a student at Annapolis. In 1945 Ruth arranged a picnic that began their courtship, much of it later carried on by correspondence between Annapolis and Plains. That Christmas Jimmy proposed, but Rosalynn turned him down on the grounds that at 18 she was not ready to get married. However, at the end of February she accepted him.

They married on July 7, 1946, driving together to the church, where a crowd of friends awaited them. Rosalynn Smith Carter loved being a traditional navy wife. In Norfolk, Virginia, with her husband frequently away at sea, she learned to deal alone with the landlord, the plumber, the electrician, their bills, the cooking, househunting—and a baby, John William (Jack) Carter, born July 3, 1947. She enjoyed the company of other young families coping with similar problems. When Jimmy Carter was in port, they studied art and Spanish together. She loved their next post in Hawaii, where their son James Earl (Chip) Carter III was born on April 12, 1950. The Korean War brought a more difficult assignment in San Diego, where Rosalynn had to endure an unpleasant landlady in inadequate housing in an unsafe area. However, she soon forgot those troubles when they were sent to New London, Connecticut, where son Donnel Jeffrey was born on her birthday in 1952. Finally they arrived in Schenectady, New York, where Jimmy was to work on the nuclear submarine program.

Again a death interrupted Rosalynn's idyll. When Jimmy's father died in 1953, her husband decided that he must abandon his naval career to take over the peanut warehouse business that his father had built. She saw the move as limiting, for their children and for herself, but neither arguments nor tears changed Jimmy's mind. Back in Plains, she kept to herself for several miserable months. Things brightened, however, after her husband asked her to help him in the office and a good crop enabled them to rent a large old house in the country. Together they expanded their warehouse facilities and services to the farmers whose peanuts they processed, played golf, took dancing lessons and a speed reading course, and involved themselves in community service and church work. "As each new project developed," she later wrote in her autobiography, "our minds and our lives seemed to expand with them, and our 'ordinary' lives in Plains became more exciting. We grew together—as full partners."

During the civil rights struggle of the late 1950s and early 1960s, they faced hostility in their hometown. With their experience of black colleagues in the navy and the example of Jimmy's mother Miss Lillian, a registered nurse who had always volunteered in the community and cared for blacks and whites alike, the Carters could no longer accept the segregation with which they had grown up. Jimmy refused to join the racist White Citizens Council and fought on the school board for better facilities for all students, white and black. Defeated and defamed, in 1962 he decided to run for the state senate. While he campaigned, his wife ran the business, tried to call everyone on the voters' list in Sumter County, and went door to door on his behalf. Jimmy's challenge of voting irregularities in this election brought threats on his life and against his business, but he won.

Rosalynn Carter was terrified for the safety of her children and dismayed by what she had learned about political dirt and dishonesty. Nevertheless, she liked feeling that she was contributing to her husband's achievements by running the peanut business during the day and handling his senate correspondence at night. (Everyone helped with the housework.) She wrote:

> I was more a political partner than a political wife, and I never felt put upon. . . . The hard part . . . was learning to cope with the criticisms that seemed to go along with political life. I fluctuated between being very hurt and very mad. . . . Local politics . . . is the worst. At the state or national level, you don't expect everyone to be for you, and you accept the fact that you'll have enemies. But at home you expect everyone to like you, and it hurts to hear untrue, unfair, and unwarranted accusations from people you know personally. . . . I was going to be criticized no matter what I did, so I might as well be criticized for something I wanted to do.

However, it still hurt to watch their children being persecuted for standing up for their father and their own beliefs. Opponents spread rumors that led to a boycott of the Carters' business, but Jimmy and Rosalynn broke up the boycott by exposing the falsity of the rumors.

With more help in the warehouse from Jimmy's only brother William (Billy) Alton Carter and Billy's wife, Rosalynn devoted more time to her husband's 1966 campaign for the governorship of Georgia. Both of them learned a system to help them remember names, and they wrote personal letters to everyone they met. The Carters, their son Jack, and Miss Lillian traveled separately around the state throughout the week, meeting at home to spend Saturday nights together and go to church on Sunday, then starting out again on Sunday afternoons. They drove around the state with posters of Jimmy taped to their borrowed cars. They presented themselves at newspaper offices and radio and television stations, offering to be interviewed. They shook hands all around every new town, passed out brochures, then moved on. And they lost, to archconservative segregationist Lester Maddox.

A month after the election, Jimmy started campaigning for the next run four years later. Benefiting from their experience, he and Rosalynn multiplied and sophisticated their efforts. She kept newspaper files on issues that he needed to talk about, and they widened their group of volunteer supporters. Their neighbors formed a "Peanut Brigade" to advocate for Jimmy around the state. The Carters went everywhere; Rosalynn found herself in a shrimp boat and a hotair balloon, at her first tobacco auction and her first rattlesnake roundup. Despite nauseating stage fright, she gave short speeches. The campaigners were so pinched for money that they always spent the nights with friends and picked up discarded pamphlets to redistribute. But in 1970 they won the governorship.

In the interim, their boys were growing up, living through school integration, and going off to college and the navy. On October 19, 1967, their daughter Amy Lynn was born.

When the family moved into the governor's mansion, Rosalynn made up her mind not to spend all her time managing the household and social events, but also to work on projects of her own. Helped by the information she picked up at a conference for newly elected governors, she quickly learned to manage the constant entertaining and to stretch both her $25,000 entertainment budget and her time. Since the women of the family all wore size 6 or 8, they pooled their formal wardrobes. Jimmy relieved his wife of one duty by telling her, after 25 years of her cooking breakfast for him, that he preferred to have only orange juice. A relative organized volunteer hostesses to act as docents, and Rosalynn studied the governor's mansion and its art and gave tours along with them. She set up an office there and hired a personal social secretary, who also managed the mansion, served as press secretary, and kept track of Amy's schedule. To relieve stress and tension, Rosalynn said, she learned to "give my problems to Jesus."

In these ways she freed time to work on her own projects, mental health programs first among them. She had learned of the needs of the mentally ill and their families from women she had met during the campaigns. At her behest, Jimmy had promised in his campaign to do all he could to help; now he set up the Governor's Commission to Improve Services to the Mentally and Emotionally Handicapped, on which Rosalynn served. Knowing she had a lot to learn, she worked one day a week as a hospital volunteer and toured other state hospitals, reporting to the commission on their needs. She learned from both the lay people and the professionals involved in the care of the mentally ill. During her husband's term as governor, she wrote, "From twenty-three community mental health centers when Jimmy was elected, the number jumped to one hundred thirty-four! And there were twenty-three group homes for the mildly retarded. . . . We were treating 56 percent more mental patients, and the number of resident hospital patients . . . decreased by about 30 percent." They transformed the lives of many children by introducing Special Olympics programs into their mental health centers.

Strong as the partnership between the Carters was, it did not always function smoothly. Rosalynn was startled to hear that her husband, misinterpreting something she had said, had told a Georgia crowd, "I respect your right to oppose the ERA [Equal Rights Amendment], but my mind is made up. I am

for it—but my wife is against it!" His error had arisen from her correct prediction that the legislation could not win in Georgia, but thereafter she wore a big ERA button to show one and all, including booing demonstrators, where she stood. When she and her husband differed, she told the *Ladies Home Journal* in 1979, "I'll listen to his point of view. If he's right, then I agree to do it his way. And if I'm right, then we'll do it my way."

Rosalynn's interest in the women prisoners assigned to work at the governor's mansion led her to work with the Women's Prison Committee of the Commission on the Status of Women. They succeeded in setting up a work-release center for 65 women and got improved quarters for women in the state prison.

Her various activities demanded public speeches, although she disliked giving them and felt that she failed at them. Her husband suggested that she do as he did—jot down a few words to remind her of what she wanted to say, and then just talk. The system worked.

Since 1972, early in his gubernatorial term, Jimmy had been planning to run for the presidency of the United States in 1976. Again the Carters and their supporters went to work, using their tried-and-true tactics, this time nationwide. Rosalynn learned to stop at courthouses to identify the influential people in the community and the most skilled politicians. She insisted on speaking to reporters for either the front page or the news section of a paper, never letting receptionists send her to the society or women's page editors. As she traveled, she looked for large radio antennas and presented herself at the stations for interviews. She stayed in the homes of supporters, where she heard about the problems and issues that concerned local people, and she inspired her hosts to work even harder for the Carter campaign. She mustered up her courage to intrude "on meetings, events, carnivals, any place where people gather," and she forced herself to ask for money. When Rosalynn was not out on the campaign trail, she was telephoning. As she told a reporter, her campaigning was "a labor of love.

Besides I won't have any regrets if he loses because I'm doing everything I can possibly do."

Rosalynn's fortitude while campaigning earned her the nickname of "steel magnolia." After her wig and her wardrobe were stolen, she was forced to wash her clothes and set her hair every night and borrow nightclothes from her hostess. She endured the embarrassment of having her husband confess, in an interview with *Playboy* magazine to "lusting in my heart" for other women; as she told reporters, "Jimmy talks too much, but at least people know he's honest and doesn't mind answering questions." When a reporter asked her on camera whether she had ever committed adultery, she answered, "If I had, I wouldn't tell you!" She told the public not only what her husband as president would do for them but also what she as first lady would do: advocate for the mentally ill, work with the elderly, and get the ERA passed.

The Carters celebrated Jimmy's election by walking from the Capitol to the White House after the swearing-in and by dancing at all seven inaugural balls. Then they settled down to work, Rosalynn establishing her office in the East Wing rather than the living quarters. As first ladies had before her, she soon discovered how expensive it was to live in the White House. In addition to paying for all personal items and incidentals, the Carters had to pay for all the food served in the private living quarters—and they always had a houseful of company. At Camp David they were charged by the meal. When they traveled on Air Force One, they were required to pay full first-class fare plus a dollar for everyone in the family, babies included, except the president. The first lady objected in vain to her husband's ruling that his staff must drive their own cars, arguing that staff members should at least have cars and drivers late at night. She also questioned his decision to turn the White House thermostats down to 65 degrees to set an example for the nation during the oil crisis; she and her staff were so cold that they wore coats, scarves, and gloves in their offices. He would not yield to her arguments that she needed a larger staff—even

though as an activist first lady she not only had to take charge of all White House social functions and handle her mail, which averaged almost 11,000 pieces a month, but also work on her numerous projects. In her "spare" time she always had a stack of photographs, books, paper napkins, programs, and even quilt squares awaiting her autograph. To save time answering requests from children for information, she and her staff and volunteers put together a booklet, "The White House . . . It's Your House Too."

At first the Carters refused all gifts, but when they learned how many people had been hurt when their gifts were returned unopened, they developed a system whereby commercial gifts were politely returned, others were donated to charities, and the rest stored for future display in the Carter Library. The serving of hard liquor on the state floor of the White House was another problem: If they served only wine, they learned, and ended their state dinners before midnight, they might save $1 million. They therefore chose wine and the opportunity to entertain many more people.

They had much to learn about security. The Secret Service taught them just to touch the hands extended to them in a crowd, to minimize the danger of being pulled into the crowd or jerked off a platform. They must, they were told, move quickly through a crowd and never accept anything handed to them—though it wrung Rosalynn's heart to think of refusing a gift carefully made for her.

She quickly settled 10-year-old Amy in public school, taking time to walk her to school every morning. She made few changes in the living quarters, delighted to find that she could fill in the gaps with the furnishings of former presidents that had been stored in a warehouse. She did panel one room with wood from her grandfather's barn, and she had a tree house built for Amy. She also established a White House trust fund to guarantee enough money for future renovations and to buy appropriate furnishings and works of art as they become available. She interested herself especially in acquiring a good permanent collection of American paintings for the mansion.

Because they worked so closely together, the Carters arranged a working lunch every Wednesday. Later, the president's invitation to the first lady to sit in as an observer on cabinet meetings helped her understand his decisions. As much as she could, she adjusted her timetable to his, trying not to schedule anything for herself after 4:30 P.M. so that they could swim, play tennis, or jog, talk for a while on the Truman balcony, dine, and see a movie together. She tried not to work at night— except on the night before she had to give a speech. These arrangements enabled her to act as a sounding board for her husband as he talked about his problems and to report to him what she learned about people's needs as she traveled. When she disagreed with him, she said so. On some issues, she wrote, "I was never able to budge him . . . but neither did he budge me." His insistence on governing his actions by what he thought right rather than on political expediency frustrated her, for, she told him, "The thing you can do to hurt your country most is not get re-elected." She admired his firmness at the same time she deplored it.

Rosalynn immersed herself at once in projects of interest to her—forming a task force to inventory federal programs for the elderly and listing qualified women for possible presidential appointments. Quickly learning how powerful a first lady's influence can be, she exercised it to support such work as that of the Community Foundation of Greater Washington, which makes grants for community betterment. Senatorial wife Betty Bumpers, an old friend, enlisted her help in an immunization program that eliminated measles in the United States.

Above all, she wanted to develop a strategy to help the mentally ill. To this end the President's Commission on Mental Health, with Rosalynn Carter as honorary chairperson, held public hearings for a year and wrote comprehensive statements on research, prevention, and the needs of special populations. On the basis of this study, they formed recommendations for performance contracts to help states care for their mentally ill and for extensive changes in housing programs, Medicare and Medicaid laws, and the National Institute of Mental Health. The first lady also went to Hollywood to urge producers, directors, and stars to portray the mentally ill more sensitively and accurately. Members of the commission then put together a Public Committee on Mental Health to oversee the implementation of their recommendations, while Rosalynn saw to it that their report stayed within the president's line of vision. She invited special interest groups to the White House to encourage them to lobby, and she herself approached members of Congress to educate them on the subject. She testified before the relevant congressional committees and spoke on the subject of mental health all around the world. In September 1980 Congress passed and funded the Mental Health Systems Act.

Rosalynn also informed herself on legislation for the aging and brought together advocacy groups to produce and distribute recommendations on what communities could do to help the elderly. She lobbied for legislation that eliminated mandatory retirement from federal jobs and raised the age of retirement to 70 in the private sector, increased appropriations for programs for the elderly, expanded medical service to rural areas, and reformed Social Security.

Although her hopes for the Equal Rights Amendment were disappointed, at her husband's request Rosalynn worked with his staff and the women's campaign committee on a list of women suited for federal appointments. Consequently, 22 percent of Carter's appointments went to women; the best previous presidential record on this score had been Ford's 12.9 percent.

In June 1977 President Carter broke with precedent by sending his wife as his representative on an official State Department visit to Latin America, despite congressional qualms that as a woman she would not be taken seriously in that culture. Rosalynn prepared carefully, stepping up her Spanish lessons, listening

Rosalynn Carter chairs a meeting in Chicago for the President's Commission on Mental Health *(Courtesy: Jimmy Carter Library)*

to hours of briefings by scholars and officials, studying the administration's foreign policy on Latin America and the Caribbean, and reading extensively. In most places she met a warm welcome from top officials eager to talk with someone so close to the president of the United States, particularly after they learned that she had come prepared to talk about substantive issues. She kept notes on these conversations, not only to remind herself of talking points for further discussion but also to help her prepare detailed reports for the president and the State Department. "Unlike official visitors from the State Department," she remarked, "I could say the unexpected. After having been through the formal meetings, at dinner I would sit on the leader's right and the mood would be very relaxed and informal. . . . Laughingly, I said to

[Admiral Poveda] that evening, having talked all morning about the need to arm his country, 'See what you could do for your people if you just didn't spend all your money on so many weapons. You could educate them all as Costa Rica does. Then you would be a real hero.' I wasn't really teasing, and he knew it."

Such special assignments and work on her own projects did not relieve Rosalynn Carter from the entertaining incumbent on every first lady. In her first 14 months in office, the *Washington Post* reported, she visited 18 nations and 27 U.S. cities, held 259 private meetings and 50 public meetings, made 15 major speeches, held 22 press conferences, gave 32 interviews to individual journalists, had 77 hours of briefings, attended 83 official receptions and social functions, held 26 special-interest and group meetings at the White House, spent more than 300 hours working on mental health, received 152,000 letters and 7,939 invitations, signed 150 photographs a week, and made 16 public appearances around Washington. The Carters' entertainment ranged from the casual to the elegant, from square dances and western movies to classical concerts and ballet, depending on the tastes of their guests. They tried to save the taxpayers money by reducing the numbers of guards and guests and the cost of the food at official dinners; they discarded the pretentiousness of having the menus printed in French. They also arranged to televise a series of Sunday afternoon performances in the East Room by prestigious national artists.

The Carters' most nerve-racking and productive experience as hosts at Camp David and the White House resulted in the momentous Arab-Israeli pact effected between Prime Minister Menachem Begin of Israel and President Anwar Sadat of Egypt in 1978. In 1979, Rosalynn made a trip to Thai refugee camps at the president's request. There she witnessed suffering on a scale that she had never imagined. The consequent publicity immediately increased relief efforts, and upon her return home, she worked through the United Nations and through speeches and media appearances to appeal for even more.

Both the Carters felt that they needed a second term to complete the work they had planned and started. The Iran hostage crisis of 1979, which dragged on into early 1981, defeated their expectations. In the 1980 campaign the president stayed close to the White House, working to resolve the crisis, while the other Carters and their supporters electioneered across the country—but in vain. In 1981 Ronald and Nancy Reagan moved into the White House, bringing with them a conservatism that reversed many of the reforms for which the Carters had worked.

Rosalynn Carter reacted bitterly to her husband's defeat. "I was in such denial," she later said. "It was impossible for me to believe that anybody could have looked at the facts and voted for Reagan." Her sense of unjust rejection by the country for which the Carters had worked so hard was so strong that she ended her 1984 book with these words:

> I would be out there campaigning right now if Jimmy would run again. I miss the world of politics. . . . I'd like people to know that we were right, that what Jimmy Carter was doing was best for our country, and that people made a mistake by not voting for him. But when all is said and done, for me, our loss at the polls is the biggest single reason I'd like to be back in the White House. I don't like to lose.

It took the Carters until the fall of 1981 to realize that there was life after the White House. First they had to deal with their own financial situation. Jimmy had to sell the family business, because he had had to place it in a blind trust during his presidency and it had deteriorated until the Carters were $1 million in debt. They owed another $1.4 million in campaign debts, and they needed another $25 million to build the presidential library. Lucrative book contracts for both of them provided part of the solution. In the years since his presidency, Jimmy has successfully published several books, including volumes of poetry. Rosalynn wrote a best-selling autobiography, *First Lady from Plains,* and a manual for caregivers coauthored by Susan K. Golant entitled *Helping Yourself Help Others.* The Carters' one joint venture in writing, an inspirational book called *Everything to Gain: Making the Most of the Rest of Your Life,* taught them that this was one area in which they did not work well together; there were many days when they would not speak to each other. Nevertheless, the collaboration produced another best-seller.

They turned to their many friends and supporters for help in establishing the Carter Center in Plains. In building his library, the former president was determined not to build simply a memorial to himself. Instead, the Carters created a center for conflict resolution, a private institution founded in 1982, in an impressive building that also houses the Jimmy Carter Library and Museum (now government owned and operated). The center has provided a base for two of their most important undertakings: first, negotiations to settle international disputes and encourage nations to respect human rights; and second, humanitarian projects to improve health around the world, especially in Africa, by wiping out such afflictions as river blindness and guinea worm, and by teaching small farmers new means to achieve subsistence. For these projects they used their influence to raise the money and their fame to publicize the work. As a rule, the Carters have worked closely together in these ventures. Rosalynn has traveled with her husband in his negotiations, sat in on meetings, and taken notes; she jokes that he assigns her the note-taking to keep her quiet. Some negotiations have succeeded, others have not, but their humanitarian programs have made enormous differences in people's lives.

Closer to home, Jimmy and Rosalynn founded the Atlanta Project, a collaborative effort between private and public organizations to fight poverty in that city. They have also worked together on other causes, notably Habitat for Humanity, which undoubtedly owes much of its success to the publicity attracted by their work for it. "My wife has never been more beautiful," said Jimmy Carter, "than when . . . her face is covered with smut from scraping burned ceiling joists and is streaked with sweat from carrying sheets of plywood."

Besides these joint efforts with her husband, Rosalynn Carter works on her own projects. Her travels around the country to call attention to mental health needs have made her that field's spokesperson and advocate. At her alma mater in 1987 she opened the Rosalynn Carter Institute for Human Development. Dedicated to the study of caregiving, the institute holds symposia and sponsors educational programs.

For recreation the Carters jog and play tennis together. With their best friends John and Betty Pope, former members of the Peanut Brigade, they own a getaway in the mountains of northwest Georgia, where both of them enjoy the fishing.

Rosalynn Carter expanded the role of first lady by her involvement in public affairs. Like Eleanor Roosevelt, she testified before Congress. Like Lady Bird Johnson, she campaigned independently for her husband. Like several of her immediate predecessors, she initiated projects of her own, especially in mental health, the rights of the elderly, and vigorous efforts to pass the Equal Rights Amendment. Without precedent, at her husband's invitation she sat in as an observer on cabinet meetings and represented him on a tour of South America in which she discussed substantive matters with the heads of state of seven countries. In the Carters' post-presidential years she has continued to support her causes and to work alongside her husband in worldwide efforts to mediate between nations, reduce disease, improve housing, and protect human rights. Except for Eleanor Roosevelt, Rosalynn Carter has contributed more to humanity since she left the White House than any of her predecessors as first lady.

CHRONOLOGY

1927   *August 18:* Eleanor Rosalynn Smith is born in Plains, Georgia

1940   Rosalynn Smith's father dies

1946   *July 7:* Rosalynn Smith marries Jimmy Carter

1947   *July 3:* Son John William (Jack) is born

1950   *April 12:* Son James Earl (Chip) is born

1952   *August 18:* Son Donnel Jeffrey is born

1962   Jimmy Carter is elected to the Georgia state legislature

1966   Jimmy Carter is defeated in his first bid for the governorship of Georgia

1967   *October 19:* Daughter Amy Lynn is born

1970   Jimmy Carter is elected governor of Georgia

1976   Jimmy Carter is elected president of the United States

1977   *January 20:* Rosalynn Carter becomes first lady

1981   The Carters return to Plains, Georgia

1982   The Carters found the Carter Center for Conflict Resolution to settle disputes and fight disease internationally and the Jimmy Carter Library and Museum

1984   Rosalynn Carter is made an honorary fellow of the American Psychiatric Association

1987   The Carters found Global 2000 to end hunger by teaching small farmers new means to higher productivity

        The Carters coauthor *Everything to Gain: Making the Most of the Rest of Your Life*

        The Rosalynn Carter Institute for Human Development opens

1990   The Carters found the Atlanta Project to marshal the resources of the rich to attack the problems of the poor in Atlanta, Georgia

1995   The Carters' campaign to eliminate guinea worm in Africa has a 97 percent success rate

        The Carters form a partnership with the World Bank and others to combat river blindness

FURTHER READING

Anthony, Carl Sferrazza. *America's Most Influential First Ladies.* Minneapolis: Oliver, 1992.

Brinkley, Douglas. *The Unfinished Presidency: Jimmy Carter's Journey Beyond the White House.* New York: Viking, 1998.

Carter, Jimmy. *Keeping Faith.* New York: Bantam, 1982.

Carter, Rosalynn. *First Lady from Plains.* Boston: Houghton Mifflin, 1984.

———. *Helping Yourself Help Others.* New York: Random House, 1995.

———. "Leave My Husband Alone," *New Republic,* January 30, 1995.

Maddox, Linda, and Edna Langford. *Rosalynn: Friend and First Lady.* Old Tappan, N.J.: Fleming H. Revell, 1980.

Anne Francis (Nancy) Robbins Davis Reagan

(July 6, 1921–   )
First Lady, March 4, 1981–March 4, 1989

Nancy Reagan
(Library of Congress)

Nancy Reagan centered her life and her ambition on her husband and his well-being. The rapt attention with which she listened to his every speech reflected her concern for his health, happiness, and success—as well as the experienced actress's awareness that she was on public view. She supplemented his efforts with her own determination. Actor Jimmy Stewart remarked, "If Ronnie had married Nancy at the time he married Jane Wyman, he would have won an Oscar. She would have *made* him do it." She pleased those conservatives who reacted against the women's movement of the 1960s and who prided themselves on upholding "traditional family values." Her defensiveness at any hint of criticism of her husband was exemplified by her reaction when Reagan's successor, President George Bush, called for "a kinder, gentler" country. "Kinder and gentler," she inquired, "than whom?"

—⁓—

Anne Francis Robbins was born in New York City on July 6, 1921, the daughter of actress Edith Luckett ("Lucky") Robbins and her husband, car salesman Kenneth Robbins, who were separated by 1923 and divorced in 1928. Her mother nicknamed her Nancy. For a short time, after the separation Nancy was a backstage baby; she spent her next five years living with her maternal aunt, Virginia Galbraith, and her husband and daughter in their modest suburban home in Bethesda, Maryland. The Galbraiths welcomed her warmly, but the child still longed to share what she saw as her mother's glamorous life in the theater. In 1929 her mother's marriage to a Chicago brain surgeon, Loyal Davis, introduced Nancy to a more privileged and more stable life. Stepfather and stepdaughter grew close, and her relationship with her birth father had always been tenuous, so when she was 14, Dr. Davis adopted her, and she took his name.

Nancy Davis nevertheless grew up in a theatrical world, for her mother continued to act. The young girl knew and admired many actors: Mary Martin, ZaSu Pitts, Spencer Tracy, Lillian Gish, Walter Huston, Katharine Hepburn, and Nancy's godmother, Alla Nazimova. Nancy herself wanted to be an actress. She concentrated on drama at the Chicago Girls' Latin School and later Smith College, where, she says in her autobiography, "I majored in English and drama— and boys." So absorbing did she find these and her engagement to Frank Birney, that she did not notice Eleanor Roosevelt's visits to the campus nor did she know that Grace Coolidge lived in town. (While Nancy was still at Smith College, Birney was killed as he crossed a railroad track.) During college vacations she apprenticed in summer stock. After her 1943 graduation, with World War II raging, she clerked briefly in a Chicago department store and volunteered as a Cook County nurse's aide.

Nancy seized on ZaSu Pitts's offer of a part in a Broadway show, *Ramshackle Inn*. With her parents' financial help, she pursued her acting career in New York, where Walter Huston and Spencer Tracy looked after her and for one starstruck week she dated Clark Gable. *Ramshackle Inn* closed almost at once, but Nancy then appeared with Mary Martin in *Lute Song*, which won her a mention from critic John Houseman as an "awkward and amateurish virgin," though other reviewers thought her "unusually attractive and talented." Undeterred, she labored on, modeling and appearing on the stage and in television.

In 1949 MGM approached her with an invitation to make a screen test in Hollywood, which Spencer Tracy persuaded George Cukor to direct. Nancy signed a seven-year contract with options at a salary of $250 a week— enough for her to get her own small house, shop for clothes at an expensive boutique, and, some say, hire an astrologer. She liked film acting and had some success in it, making about a dozen pictures, sometimes in starring roles. However, the big breakthrough eluded her. Skeptics have seen her romance with Ronald Reagan as an effort to revive her wavering movie career, but she claims that her real ambition had always been domestic: "I was always interested in falling in love with a nice man and getting married." In any event, what she learned as an actress served her well as a political wife: how to present herself, how to dress, how to pose for photographs, how to make public appearances, how to measure public response, how to maintain an appealing image, and perhaps above all, how to support the star of the show.

Her life began, she says, in 1950, when she met Ronald Reagan, then president of the Screen Actors Guild. She seems to have maneuvered for the meeting, either through MGM executive Dore Schary and his wife or by seeking Ronald's help when she was confused with another Nancy Davis and falsely accused of being a communist sympathizer. Their courtship took a while, in large part because he was traumatized by a recent divorce from actress Jane Wyman. (Ronald Reagan's biographer Edmund Morris discovered "a catty charge by Nancy Reagan that Jane Wyman tricked Ronnie into his first marriage by threatening suicide.") Nancy Davis and Ronald Reagan were married on March 4, 1952, at the Little Brown Church in the Valley in Los Angeles, California, with actor William Holden and his wife as their attendants and only guests.

Their marriage had its problems, although in her autobiography Nancy minimizes her marital difficulties. However, biographer Edmund Morris writes of Ronald as a man whose fantasies often shut him off from reality, suggesting that at times his wife felt frozen out—as when, years later, he failed to console her when her breast cancer was discovered in 1987.

They had trouble with their relationships with his two children by his first marriage, Maureen, born in 1941, and Michael, adopted soon after his 1946 birth, who both felt at times that their stepmother was trying to alienate them from their father. The Reagans also had long-lasting difficulties with their own daughter, Patti, born on October 22, 1952. Ron, born on May 20, 1958, was for many years closer to his parents. In her autobiography Nancy attributes some of these problems to the children's feeling shut out because of the closeness of the bond between their parents. The Reagans' political obligations while the children were growing up evoked resentment within the family, and as parents they found difficulty in adapting to the revolutionary changes in the lifestyles of young people during the 1960s and 1970s. Problems continued after the children were adults: Mike Reagan found it difficult to understand why Nancy had never seen his year-old child.

Nancy has written that during Patti's and Ron's early childhood she did all the things that mothers of the 1950s were supposed to do, spending most of her time being there for the children, chauffeuring them, serving on the school board, and doing the marketing while a housekeeper cooked and cleaned. Although when she married she had resolved against being a working wife, Nancy did make a few films early in their marriage when Ronald's movie career faltered and they needed the money. Soon, however, he got back on his feet financially with a long-lasting television show for General Electric, and she gained the leisure to become friendly with the wives of several corporate executives. She joined the "Colleagues," a group of wealthy women who lunched together and sponsored charity fund-raisers.

Meanwhile, her husband was increasingly involving himself with politics. Even before they married, he had served five terms as president of the Screen Actors Guild and two more as president of the Motion Picture Industry Council, and he had engaged extensively in Democratic politics. Soon after they were married, Democrats had asked him to run for Congress. However, his experience with General Electric gradually moved him to the right. In that job, Nancy Reagan writes, "Essentially he spent eight years campaigning—going out and talking to people, listening to their problems, and developing his own ideas about how to solve them." He eventually changed parties, campaigned for Barry Goldwater for president, and, in 1966, ran as a Republican for the governorship of California.

Nancy was soon actively participating in his campaign, going on her own to places her husband did not have time to visit, answering questions about his opinions, and reporting to him on what she heard. After his election, as the wife of the governor, she had to accustom herself to the scrutiny to which wives of public officials are invariably subjected. She learned to deal with criticism of her husband by holding imaginary conversations in which she triumphed over his critics while she took a bath. For the first time, she experienced the horror of receiving death threats against her husband.

The governor's lady repudiated the historic governor's mansion as a noisy, rundown firetrap.

For a while she stayed in the home the Reagans had bought in Pacific Palisades shortly after they were married, where their eight-year-old son Ron was in school; 14-year-old Patti was attending a boarding school in Arizona. Eventually the Reagans rented a house in suburban Sacramento that wealthy friends had bought to suit their taste, converted the traditional gubernatorial home into a museum, and persuaded the legislature to build a new governor's mansion—an expensive house on a former Maidu Indian burial ground, in which subsequent governors have refused to live. Nancy furnished their rented home with items from a ranch they had recently sold and with others donated at her request. The accusations of a political opponent that she was collecting these items for her personal use so infuriated her that she held her first press conference.

By the mid-1960s, with the women's movement well under way, the American people had come to expect the wives of public officials to have interests beyond their families and their duties as hostesses. When the press asked Nancy Reagan about a project, she found one in the Foster Grandparents Program, originated by former Peace Corps director Sargent Shriver, which paid older people to work with retarded and institutionalized children five half-days a week. While she was the governor's wife, the program expanded into all the state hospitals in California. She spent time in veterans' hospitals, personally calling the wives and mothers of the patients she saw there. She also involved herself with the families of the prisoners-of-war still held in Vietnam and welcomed some of the returning prisoners home.

In 1974, at the end of Ronald's second term as governor, he began to travel the country giving speeches, write a syndicated newspaper column, and do a series of radio commentaries, believing that he could move the country in the direction he thought it ought to go. In 1976 he ran unsuccessfully against President Gerald Ford for the Republican presidential nomination. In this, as in all her husband's campaigns, Nancy Reagan was much involved. She felt that while his staff looked after him as a candidate, it was up to her to look after him as a man, to protect him against exhaustion by calling a halt when he got too tired and by campaigning for him on her own. In the heat of the race, a press-hyped "battle of the wives" developed between her and Betty Ford.

Nancy also saw it as her task to ensure that her husband's staff worked efficiently together to serve him, whether by conciliating quarreling staff members or urging someone's dismissal. Both during campaigns and while her husband held office, she advised him on policy and personnel. Such practices seemed natural to her, a necessary part of looking after her husband's welfare. However, his staff, other government officials, and the press resented what they regarded as interference by someone who had not been elected, who derived her authority only from her husband, and who was responsible to no one except him. They called her "Queen Nancy," the "Iron Butterfly," the "Belle of Rodeo Drive," and "Fancy Nancy."

The 1980 campaign, in which she talked strategy, did interviews, worked on speeches, and appeared independently, put Ronald Reagan into the presidency with a substantial victory. The Reagans sold their Pacific Palisades house and prepared to move into the White House, which she found rundown, dreary, and uninviting. For the first time, she hired a professional staff of her own, a task that she found difficult. Letitia Baldrige, experienced as an aide to several first ladies, helped her, and she learned to rely also on the White House chief usher.

The Reagans thought their reception by the Carters distant and cool, the more so because of the strain caused by the Iranians' refusal to return American hostages until after President Carter had left office. Otherwise, the new president and his wife enjoyed the crowded inaugural day—attending church, the swearing-in ceremony with Nancy Reagan holding the Bible, luncheon at the Capitol, the parade, and the 10 balls, to which she wore a white, beaded, off-the-shoulder Galanos gown reputedly valued at $25,000. All four of their children celebrated with them, as well as Nancy's mother.

The new first lady got off to a bad start. Feeling overwhelmed, she called her friend, silent film star Colleen Moore, who assured her that "You're the star of the whole world. The biggest star of all." "Yes, I know," said the president's wife, "and it scares me to death." Married to the oldest president in the history of the country, she held conservative views, among other things opposing the Equal Rights Amendment, abortion, and gun control. Myra L. Gutin, a scholar of first ladies, remarks that in the early days of Ronald Reagan's presidency his wife "seemed a woman of the 1950s trapped in the 1980s." Writer Joan Didion had earlier described her as "a woman who seems to be playing out some middle-class American woman's daydream circa 1948."

This first lady did not involve herself in the kind of independent activities that her immediate predecessors, Rosalynn Carter and Betty Ford, had worked at. In the public mind, the Reagans were associated with Hollywood glamor. For most of her life, Nancy had mingled with the rich and famous, and she continued to do so in the White House, where she liked to lunch with friends such as Katharine Graham, publisher-owner of the *Washington Post,* and conservative columnist George Will. After the 1981 assassination attempt on the president, Frank Sinatra flew in from California, and supposedly the first lady welcomed him with "Frank! Thank God you're here. There's finally someone I can tell my dirty stories to."

Nancy took heavy fire from the press for the expensive clothes she loved and wore. Much of the nation knew her primarily as the always chic "lady in red." A *Time* magazine story in October 1988 estimated the cost of the clothes she had worn for the past five years as $1 million, not counting the jewelry. She felt that her position required her to look nice, and she had no compunction about borrowing clothes and jewelry, just as, she said, European royalty and heads of state commonly did. The media had a field day, joking that Nancy Reagan was a Christian of the Dior persuasion. In February 1982, warned of the laws forbidding presidents to accept valuable gifts, she announced that she would accept no more presents from designers, jewelers, and other "personal benefactors," but she would continue to accept loans of gowns and return them after use. Toward the end of the Reagan presidency, her press secretary announced, "I'm admitting for her that she basically broke her own promise"—that is, she had sometimes failed to return thousands of dollars worth of clothes "borrowed" from designers Galanos, Adolfo, and Bill Blass.

She evoked more criticism by spending much of the $800,000 she had raised for White House renovations on the private quarters for the president and his family. The public was dismayed when she acquired a $200,000, 220-piece set of china—the gift of a private foundation—just at the time when ketchup was being ruled a vegetable sufficient for school lunches. She attributed at least some of the criticism to jealousy: "Some women," she wrote, "aren't all that crazy about a woman who wears a size four, and who seems to have no trouble staying slim." And again: "What may *really* have bothered some women was my decision to give up my career and devote myself to my husband and our family."

To reverse the first lady's negative image, the Reagans did what came naturally to a pair of actors dependent on their popularity for their livings: They launched a vigorous media campaign. Nancy defused much of the press criticism by speeches mocking herself and a surprise appearance at the Gridiron press dinner in 1982, dressed in rags and spoofing herself in a version of the popular song "Second-hand Rose."

The administration announced that Nancy Reagan would undertake an antidrug program as her personal project. It is hard to judge just how much passion she felt for the program. Her former chief-of-staff, James Rosebush, claims that her visit to the drug-rehabilitation center STRAIGHT, INC. in Orlando, Florida, evoked sobs from her and her staff, including the Secret Service. He also attributes her choice of project to the interest in hospitals that she developed through her adopted father and explains that her concern for the drug problem grew as she learned more about it. She hired experts to organize her campaign, focusing in 1982 on young people in treatment centers, in 1983 on using television to educate a larger audience, in 1984 on soliciting national organizations and service clubs to develop antidrug programs, in 1985 on the international aspects of drug awareness, and in 1986 on the effects of drug use on special groups, like teenage mothers. According to Rosebush, however, she refused to integrate her campaign into any government program and never sought government money to fight drugs.

In her autobiography, Nancy herself says that she devoted a great deal of time in the White House to the antidrug program and that she has continued the effort in the postpresidential years through the Nancy Reagan Foundation. However, she does not demonstrate any previous interest in the problem, she does not write of it at any length, and she manifests less enthusiasm for it than she had for her Foster Grandparents and POW programs when she was governor's lady. No one opposed her choice of project, and it evoked praise from her husband's conservative supporters, though others sometimes questioned its efficacy, especially that of her "Just Say No" slogan. Nancy became the first presidential spouse in office to address the United Nations, speaking on the subject of drugs. She also conferred with the pope and with the first ladies of other countries on the issue. The program helped to bolster her public approval ratings. Nevertheless the Reagan administration did not always give the project full support; in fall 1981, when the first lady was visiting Phoenix House, a leading substance abuse service organization in New York City, that program was losing a quarter of its federal funding because of cuts being made in President Reagan's budget.

What may have stemmed the barrage of criticism of the first lady more than anything else, however, was the near-fatal assassination attempt on the president by John Hinckley on March 30, 1981, only a couple of months after the in-auguration. The nation's sympathies surged to the president and his wife, both of whom met the situation courageously. Nevertheless, it was terrifying for her, particularly as threats on the president's life typically multiply after an assassination attempt. Her terror was aggravated by the so-called 20-year death cycle for American presidents: William Henry Harrison, elected in 1840, died in office; Abraham Lincoln, elected in 1860, was assassinated; James Garfield, elected in 1880, was assassinated; William McKinley, elected in 1900, was assassinated; Warren G. Harding, elected in 1920, died in office; Franklin Delano Roosevelt, elected in 1940, died in office; John Fitzgerald Kennedy, elected in 1960, was assassinated. What, she wondered, lay in store for Ronald Reagan, elected in 1980?

In the aftermath of the shooting, Nancy's weight dropped from 112 to below 100 pounds. She prayed, took counsel with friends, began to question her own opposition to gun control (though she had told reporters that she kept "a tiny little gun" in a drawer near her bed to protect herself)—and, notoriously, consulted an astrologer, whom she paid to tell her which were "good" days for the president and which "bad"; this information she passed on to the president's staff, who sometimes adjusted his schedule accordingly.

The personal lives of first families do not stop when they enter the White House, nor does their position insulate them against grief and illness. Moreover, the Reagans were of an age when loss and physical difficulties commonly strike. While she was living in the White House, both of the first lady's parents died, she had a mastectomy, and her husband underwent operations for cancer of the colon and prostate problems. Throughout all this, Nancy had to put aside her personal worries and physical pain to keep up her schedule as best she could. The demands on her may have slowed her recovery from her operation. She also had to endure reams of publicity about her physical condition and criticism for her choice of a mastectomy over a lumpectomy.

No president's wife in the latter half of the 20th century has escaped the hard work that now comes with the position. Nancy found the first lady's ceremonial role alone almost a full-time occupation. "Every first lady makes her own choices," she wrote, "and mine was to become very involved in planning White House events, right down to the details: the menu, table settings, flowers, and entertainment. I always loved doing this, but it took an enormous amount of time." However, Ronald was no workaholic, and his wife set sharing his leisure as a high priority. Routinely they started their day together, reading the papers and breakfasting in bed from 7:30 until 8:45, when he left for his office. She did her exercises, dressed, and worked in her office, then either went out for lunch or ate alone and telephoned friends in California—in addition, of course, to meeting her many scheduled engagements. In the late afternoon, the president repaired to his study in the private quarters, and in the early evening they dined together. About once a month they hosted a state dinner; they also attended such annual events as the Gridiron press dinner and the dinner of the White House press corps, and occasionally they accepted invitations from friends. Otherwise, they dined with guests in the second-floor family dining room, or alone from trays before a television set. They were usually in bed by 10:00 P.M. and read until they fell asleep. Most weekends they spent at Camp David, or on their California ranch.

All this time together, of course, strengthened the first lady's ability to influence her husband's decisions, and her autobiography clearly reveals that she participated in a great many of them. She wrote:

> Did I ever give Ronnie advice? You bet I did. I'm the one who knows him best, and I was the only person in the White House who had absolutely no agenda of her own—except helping him. And so I make no apologies for telling him what I thought. Just because you're married doesn't mean you have no right to express your opinions. For eight years I was sleeping with the president, and if that doesn't give you special access, I don't know what does!

Nancy and Ronald Reagan at their Rancho del Cielo, March 4, 1982 (Ronald Reagan Library)

Priding herself on being a good judge of character, and thinking her husband far too naive and trusting, Nancy warned him against people who she felt were putting their own interests and reputations above his. Secretary of State Alexander Haig, for instance, she thought too power-hungry, too obsessed with status, and too militaristic: "If Ronnie had given him the green light," she wrote, "Haig would have bombed everybody and everything." The first lady waged a prolonged operation against chief of staff Don Regan that resulted in open warfare. Regan had annoyed her with public statements that denigrated American women, who, he alleged, might hesitate to give up their diamonds, platinum, and gold for economic sanctions against South Africa and would not understand weaponry or events in human rights. "It was bad enough," wrote Nancy Reagan, "that with these . . . comments Don Regan had offended more than half of the American people. But then . . . he went on to insult Ronnie and the whole administration." Nancy encouraged others to tell her husband of their experiences with Regan (like her daughter Maureen, to whom Regan had shouted, "Goddamn it! Who do you think you are? You've been trying to run the West Wing for too long, and you're a pain in the ass.") When the president did not take her advice, she persisted, sitting in on important meetings, bringing up the subject repeatedly, telling him what he did not want to hear and few others dared to tell him. The first lady's participation did not go unnoticed, and on March 2, 1987, William Safire scathingly criticized it in the *New York Times,* calling her "an incipient Edith Wilson, unelected and unaccountable, presuming to control the actions and appointments of the executive branch."

Nancy also advised her husband on matters of policy. She unsuccessfully opposed his going to Bitburg cemetery in Germany, where members of the Nazi SS are buried, though when he persisted she accompanied him on the trip. She encouraged him to tone down his rhetoric toward what he called "the Evil Empire"—the Soviet Union. During the Iran-Contra scandal, for a short time she refused to speak to him. "It would be far better, and more realistic," she thought, "if the president's men included the first lady as part of their team."

On the other hand, Nancy resented the prominence the media gave her relationship with Raisa Gorbachev, wife of the Soviet leader. These two women had little in common and much to differ over. They had chosen far different roles as women, they believed in fundamentally different systems of government, and they had widely differing interests. Apparently they bored and irritated each other, and they could not conceal their mutual dislike from the press. On the other hand, Nancy Reagan's chief of staff, James Rosebush, credited her with assisting in diplomacy: "She has an easy, warm charm, even with Gorbachev. She helped put him at ease and made the meetings much more productive."

Nancy Reagan not only traveled widely with her husband but also appeared for him at many ceremonies at home and diplomatic missions abroad, though on these occasions she never discussed substantive matters and emphasized, her chief of staff wrote, that she represented not him but herself and the American people. She entertained more heads of state than any other first lady. On the occasion of the president's first cancer surgery in 1985, she insisted on going ahead with a barbecue for the Washington diplomatic corps, to convey a sense of confidence and of business as usual.

Shortly before she left the White House, one newspaper commented that Nancy Reagan had "expanded the role of First Lady into a sort of Associate Presidency," helping her husband make major decisions, substituting for him at public events, pursuing causes that made his administration popular, and going in his place to foreign countries. In fact, other first ladies had done all these things, though in considerably different styles. During her husband's second term, Nancy's influence became more obvious; as he grew more hard of hearing, and when he seemed at a loss for words, she could be heard prompting him, or sometimes herself answering a question addressed to him. "Thank God he's got her," said one Reagan intimate. "She's the engine that makes damn sure things get done."

Nancy endured much suffering during her White House years, but for the most part she could rejoice in her husband's popularity. In 1984 he was reelected by a large majority, and the collapse of the Soviet Union during his second term contributed largely to estimates of his success in the office. Ronald Reagan summed up his view of his wife's contribution to his success when he paid tribute to her on July 20, 1985, soon after his colon cancer operation:

There's something I want to say, and I wanted to say it with Nancy at my side, as she is right now, as she always has been. First ladies aren't elected and they don't receive a salary. They've mostly been private persons forced to live public lives. Abigail Adams helped invent America. Dolley Madison helped protect it. Eleanor Roosevelt was FDR's eyes and ears. Nancy Reagan is my everything. When I look back on these days, Nancy, I'll remember your radiance and your strength, your support, and your taking part in the business of this nation. I say for myself, but also on behalf of the nation, thank you, partner, thanks for everything.

The Reagans left the White House for California on January 20, 1989, well-satisfied with what they had achieved there. Nancy Reagan had turned around her own originally negative image, becoming one of the most popular first ladies in recent history, although more recently historians have rated her near the bottom of the scale. Only three other first ladies had lived in the White House as long as she: Julia Grant, Eleanor Roosevelt, and Mamie Eisenhower.

In retirement, Nancy has continued her work with the Nancy Reagan Foundation, which fights drug abuse among children. She has worked on the building of the Reagan Presidential Library and Museum, which was dedicated in November 1991 at a ceremony attended by five other first ladies. She has also served on the board of the Revlon corporation and written her memoirs. The Internal Revenue Service, contending that her practice of accepting free dresses, jewelry, and furs had resulted in taxable income, reportedly presented her with a million-dollar bill for back taxes, interest, and penalties; however, they did not pursue a criminal charge.

The Reagans have bravely faced the onset of Ronald's Alzheimer's disease and his inevitable deterioration. His wife has remained, as always, by his side, protecting him. She has managed his "long goodbye," seeing that he is properly dressed and arranging social get-togethers with friends and other people she knows he would enjoy. During this illness, the Reagans have become reconciled with their children.

Although Nancy Reagan exercised a great deal of influence on personnel and some on policy during the eight years of presidency, she did it in the traditional way, through using her influence on her husband. Her iron will and her single-minded focusing of her energy made that influence remarkable. Powerful as she was, though, not since Mamie Eisenhower, 30 years earlier, had there been so conventional a first lady. Nonetheless, so forceful are the demands of the office of first lady, and to such a degree does it reflect American society, that she represented the American people at home and abroad in ways that would have been unthinkable even to such a first lady as Florence Harding in the early years of the 20th century. Nancy Reagan herself wants to be remembered for her "Just Say No" program against drugs, which she believes successful, and her efforts to make the White House livable and attractive.

CHRONOLOGY

1921   *July 6:* Anne Frances Robbins is born in New York City

1923   At the age of two, after the separation of her parents, Anne Robbins is sent to live with relatives in Maryland

1928   Anne Robbins' parents divorce

1929   When her mother marries Chicago neurosurgeon Loyal Davis, Anne Robbins moves to Chicago

1935   At 14, Anne Robbins is adopted by her stepfather Loyal Davis and takes the name Nancy Davis

1939   Nancy Davis enters Smith College to study drama and spends her summers in stock productions

1943   Nancy Davis graduates from Smith College

1943–52   Nancy Davis acts on Broadway and in the movies

1950   Nancy Davis meets Ronald Reagan

1952   *March 4:* Nancy Davis marries Ronald Reagan

October 22: Daughter Patricia Ann (Patti) is born

1958   *May 20:* Son Ronald Prescott is born

1966   Ronald Reagan is elected governor of California

1980   Ronald Reagan is elected president of the United States

1981   *January 20:* Nancy Reagan becomes first lady

March 30: John Hinckley shoots Ronald Reagan

November: Nancy Reagan kicks off her antidrug campaign

1984   Ronald Reagan is reelected president

1989   The Reagans retire to California

1991   *November 4:* The Ronald Reagan Library opens in Simi Valley, California

1994   *November 5:* Ronald Reagan's Alzheimer's disease is announced

2000:   *September:* Nancy Reagan publishes *I Love You, Ronnie*

FURTHER READING

Hay, Peter. *All the Presidents' Ladies: Anecdotes of the Women Behind the Men in the White House.* New York: Viking, 1988.

Leighton, Frances Spatz. *The Search for the Real Nancy Reagan.* New York: Macmillan, 1987.

Morris, Edmund. *Dutch: A Memoir of Ronald Reagan.* New York: Random House, 1999.

Reagan, Nancy, and Ronald Reagan. *I Love You, Ronnie.* New York: Random House, 2000.

Reagan, Nancy, with William Novak. *My Turn: The Memoirs of Nancy Reagan.* New York: Random House, 1989.

Rosebush, James S. *First Lady, Public Wife: A Behind-the-Scenes History of the Evolving Role of First Ladies in American Political Life.* New York: Madison Books, 1987.

Speakes, Larry, with Robert Pack. *Speaking Out.* New York: Scribner's, 1988.

Wallace, Chris. *First Lady: A Portrait of Nancy Reagan.* New York: St. Martin's Press, 1986.

BARBARA PIERCE BUSH

(JUNE 8, 1925–)
First Lady, January 20, 1989–January 20, 1993

BARBARA BUSH
(Library of Congress)

Barbara Bush grew up to do what her parents had expected her to do. A woman in tune with her class and times, she lived happily, married a man of similar background, had children, and helped her husband in his career. Her father's affluence protected her from the Great Depression, but she grew up quickly in World War II, working at a paid job for the only time in her life (spending a summer in a [defense] factory), dropping out of college to marry a navy officer, and experiencing three days' of anguish not knowing her fiancé's fate after he was shot down in the Pacific. The second American women's movement, erupting when she was in her 40s, caused her briefly to question her value system. "I have to confess," she said in 1989, "that at a certain point in our life when our children were all gone, I went through sort of a—well, sort of a difficult time really because suddenly women's lib had made me feel that my life had been wasted." Her husband reassured her, and in the end she clung to and persuasively defended her own choice of lifestyle. Of women who have no choice but to work outside the home, she said: "Those are the people I'm trying to help with my literacy and education projects and my interest in it. Those are the people, not the people who choose to work, although some of those obviously need help, too, but they don't come under this category of people we're interested in helping."

———⟋⟍⟋———

Barbara Pierce was born in New York City on June 8, 1925, the second daughter and third of four children of Marvin Pierce, a civil and architectural engineer, and his wife Pauline Robinson Pierce. She grew up in Rye, New York. Her beautiful and extravagant mother, a devoted gardener and eventually the conservation chair of the Garden Clubs of America, taught her nothing about housekeeping; the servants took care of such problems. In her privileged childhood, Barbara was plump—according to her own recollections, "a very happy fat child who spent all my life with my mother saying 'Eat up, Martha' to my older sister and 'Not you, Barbara.'" She felt particularly close to her father, loving dogs and reveling in sports as he did. Her formal education began in a Rye public school but was continued at the private Rye Country Day School and at Ashley Hall, in Charleston, South Carolina, which emphasized classical education and good breeding. Additionally, she took lessons in swimming, tennis, and dancing. After graduating from Ashley Hall in 1943, she spent a year and a summer at Smith College in Northampton, Massachusetts.

By then, however, she had met George Herbert Walker Bush, known to family and friends as "Poppy," at a Christmas dance in Greenwich, Connecticut, when she was 16. In 1942 he invited her to his senior prom at Phillips Academy in Andover, Massachusetts; she accepted, and their courtship began. Three years later they were married, on January 6, 1945. The bride had dropped out of college in the fall of 1944 to prepare for the wedding. The groom, instead of going to college, had joined the navy, and he was already a hero who had been shot down in the Pacific theatre of World War II; for three days his fiancée and his family had not known whether he was alive or dead.

After their honeymoon at the Cloisters in Sea Island, Georgia, George's orders sent him around the country while his new squadron was being assembled and trained. His young wife followed him when she could, competing with hordes of others for scarce housing. She later remembered the landlady of the first room they rented laughing at her fumbling attempts at housekeeping: "You should have seen what she did today. She washed all her silk underwear and it shrank." When they were living in Maine, her visiting mother-in-law told her own mother that they were living in a red-light district. "We had a small, one-room efficiency apartment with a kitchen in a closet and a Murphy-in-a-door bed," Barbara reminisced. "It smelled of other people's cooking, and there was really very little to keep me busy all day. So I wandered the streets and read a lot."

V-J Day in August 1945 saved her husband from being sent overseas, and he was soon discharged. The couple moved to New Haven, Connecticut, where George entered Yale University, his tuition and allowance paid by the GI Bill, a program that offered veterans an education and help in buying a home. His wife, rather than return to college, opted to begin their family. While she awaited the arrival of the first baby, she said, she learned to keep house and cook, "played bridge and went to the movies with some of George's more frivolous friends. I did work half a day at the Yale Co-op and audited a course (nicknamed Pots and Pans by the students) given by John Phillips, an authority on American furniture and silver." Like other couples living on the GI Bill and savings from their military pay, they lived in makeshift apartments with shared baths and kitchens and socialized with each other. Their first son, George W. Bush, was born on July 6, 1946.

After he graduated in 1948, George went into the oil business in Texas. For the first time, at such a distance from her family, Barbara felt truly on her own. The next year George's job carried the family to California, where they were living when Barbara's mother died in an automobile accident and where, two months later, daughter Pauline Robinson (Robin) was born. Shortly thereafter, the Bushes returned to Texas, settling in Midland, where George and a neighbor started their own firm, the Bush-Overbey Oil Development Company, which in 1953 merged with another independent company into Zapata Petroleum.

Their second son, John Ellis Bush (Jeb) was born in Midland on February 11, 1953. Barbara has spoken of those years realistically.

> It was a period for me of long days and short years, of diapers, runny noses, earaches, more Little League games than you could believe possible, more tonsils, and those unscheduled races to the hospital emergency room; Sunday school and church, of hours of urging homework, short chubby arms around your neck and sticky kisses and experiencing bumpy moments—not many, but a few, of feeling that I'd never, ever be able to have fun again, and coping with the feeling that George Bush, in his excitement of starting a small company and traveling around the world, was having a lot of fun. . . . There were days I thought I would scream if the children didn't say something intelligent.

Most of the time, though, she loved her life as supermom and volunteer and planned to go on having children. Tragedy struck in fall 1953, when daughter Robin died of leukemia. In 1955 Neil Mallon Bush was born; in 1956, Marvin Pierce Bush; and in 1959, Dorothy (Doro) Bush.

Barbara Bush's life assumed new proportions when her husband entered politics in February 1962 with a bid to chair the Republican Party of Harris County. "I was so naive," she reported. "I had assumed that he had been invited to be chairman. It never occurred to me that he had to run. I can't really remember who the opponent was—maybe I'm purposely forgetting—but it was ugly. Harris County, with 210 precincts, is one of the largest in the country. George, usually with me along, managed to visit all of them. . . . That's when I took up needlepoint, just to keep from looking and feeling bored to death. After all, I had heard George's speech two hundred times! Not only did needlepointing do the trick, it was a good icebreaker." During this race she discovered that she enjoyed campaigning and that her intuitions about people and situations were usually sound. In 1964, when her husband decided to run for the Senate against the incumbent Ralph Yarborough, she entered the campaign with vigor, did her part, and was disappointed when her husband lost.

Two years later George won the new congressional seat that had been awarded to Houston, and the Bush family moved to Washington, D.C. They eventually built a house in a neighborhood that included Supreme Court Justice Potter Stewart and his wife, with whom they developed a strong friendship. In her memoirs, Barbara spoke of her new world as "exciting, overwhelming, intimidating, interesting, exhausting." Briefings for wives new to the District of Columbia left her bemused by customs long considered out-of-date in the rest of the country, like calling cards and long gloves, and by the realization that she would seldom see her husband. However, she sensibly focused on two areas. On the domestic front, she got the children into school and organized the house, the garden, and the family budget. On the political front, she practiced public speaking by developing a slide show on gardens—a technique that became her trademark. She also went to State Department briefings, Republican meetings, congressional wives meetings, luncheons and dinners; avoided embassies because "there were no votes there"; and entertained hosts of visiting Texans. At the 1968 Republican convention in Miami, she found it "very, very exciting" to rub elbows with "all the big GOP names." After George was reelected to the House in 1968, she began reporting on Washington life in a monthly column in Houston newspapers.

After an unsuccessful run for the Senate in 1970, George held a number of posts in the Nixon and Ford administrations: ambassador to the United Nations (1971–73), chairman of the Republican National Committee (1973–74), U.S. envoy to China (1974–75), and director of the Central Intelligence Agency (CIA) (1976–77). As wife of the American ambassador to the United Nations, Barbara Bush reveled in the busy social life: "I was born to the job: I love people and adore eating." Official travel opportunities abounded for Ambassador Bush and his wife.

Her experience as wife of the chairman of the Republican National Committee was another matter. Barbara thought her husband's acceptance of the position a bad career move. Faced with the scandals of Watergate, George had to concentrate on damage control and was forced to be away from home frequently. She kept busy in Washington as best she could: "I had rejoined my International Club; saw a lot of my 90th Congress friends; spent day after day with Andy Stewart [wife of Supreme Court justice Potter Stewart], had twelve to twenty-five people over every Sunday after church for cookouts; carpooled; and worked as a volunteer at the Washington Home, which was a nursing home. And of course I worked for the [Republican] party." She went to the theater, played tennis, and kept in touch with the world by attending meetings of the World Affairs Council.

Exhausted and fed up with Washington, George Bush welcomed President Gerald Ford's 1974 offer of the post of chief of the U.S. Liaison Office in China. Delighted at having her husband to herself, Barbara explored Beijing by bicycle, studied Chinese, and entertained local dignitaries and guests from the United States. Together the couple visited historic places and laughed at their own mishaps with strange customs and language.

When in late 1975 he was asked to return to Washington to head up the CIA, he and his wife were both hesitant. They were having a grand time in China, the CIA was under fire for abusing its power during the 1960s, and Bush's acceptance might embarrass their children, who belonged to the generation wracked by the Vietnam War and the civil rights movement. Barbara wrote: "We talked it over and then decided to call our oldest son, George W., and ask him to feel out his brothers and sister very discreetly. He called back and said, 'Come home.' I often have wondered if George really asked for their opinions or if he just waited a reasonable period of time and called back with his opinion."

The return to Washington was hard on the Bushes. The CIA was the "least favorite" of all the jobs in George's career. As Barbara wrote to a friend: "I shall curl up every time I read or hear a mean word about George, and he tells me that in this new job I'll see and hear one heck of a lot!" In fact, she fell victim to depression. As she put it;

I had a husband whom I adored, the world's greatest children, more friends than I could see—and I was severely depressed. I hid it from everyone, including my closest friends. Everyone but George Bush. He would suggest that I get professional help, and that sent me into deeper gloom. He was working such incredibly long hours at his job, and I swore to myself I would not burden him. Then he would come home, and I would tell him all about it. Night after night George held me weeping in his arms while I tried to explain my feelings. I almost wonder why he didn't leave me. Sometimes the pain was so great, I felt the urge to drive into a tree or an oncoming car. When that happened, I would pull over to the side of the road until I felt okay.

Possibly menopause had created a chemical imbalance. Reared to believe that one's emotional problems are solved by thinking of others and avoiding self-pity, she refused to seek professional help. Even though she discovered that she had Graves' disease, a hyperthyroid condition that caused an 18-pound weight loss and attacked her eyes, she soldiered on. She resumed her volunteer work at a nearby nursing home. She put together a slide show on China "with *no* pictures of George, me, the children, or even C. Fred [their dog]," and traveled around the country giving it to groups of potential supporters. In Washington she kept busy with her International Club, her congressional friends, playing tennis, and entertaining.

When Jimmy Carter defeated Gerald Ford in the presidential election of 1976, George Bush's tenure at the CIA ended. Barbara headed down to Houston to find a house and prepare for a large dinner party there. She had to get the house ready and hire the servants, put in a garden, hire a caterer, buy new garden furniture, and get the pool cleaned. Before the party it poured, washed out the new garden, and delayed the guests. "Just to make it a perfect evening," she reminisced, "the food was cold, not very tasty, and poorly served, and the waiter dropped a steak in the lap of King Hussein of Jordan." In Houston she missed her Washington friends but found it pleasant to be back "home." She traveled a bit, showed her China slides, and raised money for charity. She was also reveling in becoming a grandmother.

In 1980 the Republican Party refused to nominate George Bush for the presidency but made him Ronald Reagan's running mate. The campaign, in which Barbara participated actively, ended in a victory that sent them back to Washington. At her husband's suggestion, she added to the numerous tasks involved in moving that of refurbishing her wardrobe. In New York with Laurie Firestone, her new social secretary, she bought clothes from Bill Blass and Adele Simpson, both of whom she had entertained in China, as well as from other designers.

As second lady, Barbara began the day early with coffee and newspapers in bed, then exercised while she watched the morning news. During their vice-presidential years (1980–88), the Bushes expanded their already wide circle of friends around the world to include many heads of state and other foreign dignitaries. Many of her days, she has written, "were spent out of Washington traveling, including visiting all fifty

states and sixty-five different foreign countries, many of them more than once." Overall, the vice president and his wife traveled an estimated 1.3 million miles, about 54 times around the world. Some of these trips Barbara made alone, as a surrogate for her husband. When Soviet leader Leonid Brezhnev died in 1982, she remembered, "We heard that all the former presidents and secretaries of state wanted to go with George. There was so much pressure being put on the White House and State Department that it was decided 'none of the above'; Barbara Bush would go and then nobody could gripe." At the time she was in Zaire (now Democratic Republic of the Congo), Africa, visiting a literacy program, but she did not mind changing her schedule, for she was thrilled at the opportunity to visit Moscow.

During her eight years as wife of the vice president, Barbara Bush "hosted 1,192 events at the Vice President's House and attended 1,232 other events in Washington." Additionally, her calendar was filled with public appearances in which she visited charities, welcomed Texas students to the capital, met with Republican groups, and accompanied her husband to public dinners and speeches. Every December for the 12 years that her husband was vice president, then president, she was hoisted up in a cherry picker to put the star on top of the national Christmas tree, often taking a grandchild with her. She noticed that "I worked so hard all year long for literacy and got little or no press coverage, and then I would do something frivolous like going up in a cherry picker and my picture is seen around the world. So one year I took Rita and Rex Saurus, two puppets who encourage children to read." In George's 1984 campaign for reelection as vice president, she felt that he was at a disadvantage in having to run against a woman, Geraldine Ferraro. Barbara defended his saying that he had "kicked a little ass," and she called Ferraro something that "rhymes with rich." She later apologized to Ferraro for calling her a "witch" [sic], but the incident damaged her public image as a motherly patrician lady.

Barbara Bush *(The George Bush Library)*

When, after eight years as vice president, George Bush launched his successful campaign for the presidency, Barbara Bush was ready, willing, and able to hit the road on his behalf. She acted as a key campaign adviser, questioning and counseling. Besides working with her husband on speeches and debates and giving interviews on her own, she put on a traveling slide show emphasizing family values and offering personal glimpses of the Bushes in the vice-presidential years. Questioned about her appearance by people who felt that she looked years older than her husband, she announced: "I'm not going to turn into a glamorous princess. I'm not going to worry about it. I have plenty of self-confidence, not in how I look but in how I feel and I feel good about my husband, my children, and my life." Indeed, then and always she presented the picture of a happy and loving grandmother, personifying the Republican emphasis on family values. When rumors surfaced about her husband's supposed infidelities, she was furious. "I hated it for him," she told one interviewer. "I hated it for us. The kids went wild. George told me not to worry, and I didn't worry." To one reporter she quipped, "How can George Bush have an affair? He can't stay up past ten o'clock."

On January 20, 1989, Barbara Bush stepped confidently into her new role as first lady. A veteran of entertaining and politicking, with a host of friends in Washington and all over the country, she liked living in the historic and beautiful executive mansion. "The butlers loved trying to make me guess whose china I was using. Imagine being served a meal on dishes that Abraham Lincoln ate from!" After so many separations necessitated by her husband's work, now he could call and say "Can you pop over to the Oval Office to say hello to so-and-so," or invite her to join him for lunch. For her own work, she made an office out of the small sitting room next to the bedroom she and her husband shared. She thought she had "the best job in America." In the first hundred days, she remembered, "As close as I can count, I hosted . . .: eighteen receptions, sixteen dinners, twenty-four coffees or teas; nineteen lunches; and two breakfasts. I visited nine states and four countries, conducted twenty-four press interviews, and participated in forty-two 'doing and caring' events and forty-one other types of events. We had fifty-one different overnight guests and fed 5,825 people."

Her guests had a good time. Barbara's warmth put them at ease, and she didn't allow protocol to interfere with their pleasure, arranging her dinner tables so that the same people were not always sitting next to each other. Her tennis partner, Ellen Sulzberger Straus, summed it up: "Whatever seems to happen to political wives didn't happen to her. When you live in Washington, you notice that as these people get to the top they get stuffier and stuffier. That just isn't the case with Barbara. She doesn't take herself too seriously. There is no phoniness about her."

The Silver Fox, as her children nicknamed Barbara, had a hard time at first guarding her tongue. Soon after the election, asked whether she favored laws banning the sale of military assault guns, she said yes. "It seemed so clear to me," she explained, "that there was absolutely no need for anyone to have an assault weapon, and frankly I assumed it already was against the law. Apparently it was not. My wonderful brother Jim and my husband were both against gun control," and, she said, so was she because only law-abiding citizens would obey restrictions on gun ownership. Naturally spontaneous and candid, over the years as a political wife she had to learn and relearn to mute her own opinions, especially on such matters as the Equal Rights Amendment and abortion, which she refused to discuss. Even after leaving public life she hedged, saying that abortion is a personal issue to be decided by the doctor and the parents, but that she opposed its use as a contraceptive, that it should be allowed only in the first trimester, and that education is the answer.

Back in 1978, Barbara had recognized the political need to pick a cause of her own and had chosen literacy. "I felt the subject I chose should help the most people possible, but not cost the government money and not be controversial," she later wrote. "A president has enough troubles—he does not need a wife to stir up more controversy for him." She chose literacy, though she then knew nothing about it. "I realized everything I worried about would be better if more people could read, write, and comprehend," she explained. "More people would stay in school and get an education, meaning fewer people would turn to the streets and get involved with crime or drugs, become pregnant, or lose their homes. It seemed that simple. I had found my cause."

As the vice president's wife Barbara worked with the Literacy Volunteers of America and Laubach Literacy Action, raising money by appeals and by assigning to the cause the royalties from her first book, *C. Fred's Story,* about the Bushes' dog. In 1980, as wife of the presi-dent-elect, she established the Barbara Bush Foundation for Family Literacy, which focused on entire families in an effort to break the intergenerational cycle of illiteracy. To this foundation she assigned the royalties from her 1991 *Millie's Book,* about the White House experiences of her husband's springer spaniel. She also raised funds for the foundation through such means as a corporate committee. In her 1990 16-week radio program on ABC, "Mrs. Bush's Storytime," she set an example of reading aloud to children. Tapes of the show were later sold to benefit literacy programs. She visited literacy sites all over the country and annually held "National Literacy Honors" evenings in the White House.

This first lady teased reporters who asked about her political influence, dodging their questions or saying, "Who knows?" As she sometimes admitted in more serious exchanges, the Bushes habitually discussed issues, a practice they continued after moving into the White House, and she served as a sounding board for George's initiatives as president. She usually complied with requests that she pass messages or information to her husband. During the 1991 Gulf War, however, in her efforts to protect him, she discreetly ignored some of them and chose guests carefully to ensure that they would not "hammer him about his conduct of the war." She had a hand in appointments, recommending Dr. Louis H. Sullivan as secretary of Health and Human Services, Jack F. Kemp as secretary of Housing and Urban Development, and William J. Bennett as drug czar. She prodded the president's social conscience, lobbying him to increase funding for AIDS and Head Start and persuading him to sign the National Literacy Act of 1991.

The first lady understood that it was part of her job to campaign not only for her husband but also for his supporters. During the Gulf War, she frequently visited military bases and the families of troops deployed overseas. On a visit to the aircraft carrier USS *Forrestal,* she wrote, she found "4,000 troops lined up on the flight deck. I was led to a mike, introduced and invited to speak. To hold that speech and pray that my dress would not blow up was no mean feat." In Saudi Arabia on Thanksgiving 1990, decked out in a camouflage jacket, khaki pants, white jogging shoes, and pearl earrings, she signed autographs and posed for pictures with soldier after soldier.

A popular first lady, whose appearance and conduct projected a nonthreatening, warm, grandmotherly image, Barbara Bush nonetheless encountered criticism for being an antifeminist "throwback," unrepresentative of and even antipathetic to the working women of the 1990s. She countered by developing a commencement speech that she used several times, advising students to get involved in something larger than themselves, get joy out of life, and cherish human relationships. In 1991, at Wellesley College, she spoke over the protests of students, some of whom wanted a speaker whose fame and position did not derive from her husband. She defused the situation.

> We are in a transitional period right now . . . learning to adjust to the changes and the choices we . . . are facing. . . . Maybe we should adjust faster, maybe slower. But whatever the era . . . whatever the times, one thing will never change: fathers and mothers, if you have children . . . they must come first. Your success as a family . . . our success as a society . . . depends *not* on what happens at the White House, but on what happens inside your house. . . . [W]ho knows? Somewhere out in this audience may even be someone who will one day follow in my footsteps, and preside over the White House as the President's spouse. I wish him well.

Despite such triumphs, however, the growing opposition to her husband's policies and the viciousness of the 1992 reelection campaign took some of the fun out of being first lady. "I did wonder sometimes in the White House if it was worth awakening every day to the abuse that opponents and the press give the President," she wrote. Ever the loyal wife, she saw Congress, top labor leaders, and the press as treating her husband unfairly, and she saw his enemies as hers. "There is a life after politics," she now told herself, according to her autobiography. "My only concerns are for the country and I'd hate for George to lose for his sake. Think how good it would be for our children. They could get on with their lives." By midsummer of 1992 she was counting the days: "I am hiding my head like an ostrich. It hurts too much to see George and the children so lied about. Only three and a half more months to go." Nonetheless, she campaigned all over the country and delivered a major speech at the Republican national convention. When her husband lost the election, Barbara ached for him.

She looked forward, however, to reestablishing a home in Houston and enjoying their family and friends. She worried about "getting acquainted with shopping, cooking, and driving after twelve years of living a grand life" and about handling the mail and engagements of a former first lady without her White House staff. However, her worries proved unnecessary. She received "several very generous offers" for her memoirs, enabling her to pay for a couple of helpers with the proceeds, and reportedly she has commanded $40,000–$60,000 per speech. "But then I worried how to give speeches, write a book, travel with George, build a house, run a house, play golf, be a good friend and a mother, grandmother, and wife all in one lifetime?"

Though she has never liked to cook, Barbara has said, "I can turn out a meal for fifty, but you would never go home afterward and say: 'WOW! What a cook!' But I can light the fire and throw something on it. I can bake a potato and cook vegetables. So while we didn't starve, we did have some pretty lean meals." Other people describe her as much more capable. Lee Atwater, manager of George Bush's 1988 campaign, recalled staying in 1985 in one of the small houses on the Bush compound in Maine, when his shower didn't work. "I went to the house and there was Barbara," he reminisced. "I told her there was no hot water—I figured she'd go tell one of the people. But she grabbed a toolbox, put on one of the Vice President's jackets, and came to the little house. I still thought she was going to call somebody, but she just climbed up on a chair, got her wrench, and started turning until she got the hot water."

The Bushes built a house in Houston, surrounding its courtyard with a six-foot-high brick wall to defeat the tourists driving past and trying to get pictures of the family and their dogs. They also refurbished the compound that George Bush inherited in Kennebunkport, Maine.

In the years since she left the White House, Barbara Bush has worked on literacy, for several charities, and for the George Bush Presidential Library at Texas A&M. She has sat on the board of the Mayo Clinic, spoken frequently, and written her memoirs. Above all, she has devoted herself to the interests of her family—particularly advocating publicly for the political careers of her sons, Jeb, governor of Florida, and George W., governor of Texas. She continues to live, she says, for "faith, family, and friends."

In 2000 both the senior Bushes were prominent in the successful campaign of George W. for the presidency. Barbara Bush has thus become the second woman in history to be both wife and mother of a president.

— *~~~* —

Barbara Pierce Bush ascribes her popularity as first lady, which often outdistanced her husband's, to her age, white hair, and matronly appearance. In that position she emphasized "family values," filling the White House with her children and grandchildren, and stressing the duty to put family first. Skilled, experienced, and active as she was politically, she encouraged people to think of her primarily as a wife, mother, and nice lady. In her judgment, the American public is not yet ready for a political spouse who is "too front and center."

CHRONOLOGY

1925 *June 8:* Barbara Pierce is born in New York City and grows up in Rye, New York

1941 *December:* Barbara Pierce meets George Herbert Walker Bush at a dance

1943 Barbara Pierce graduates from Ashley Hall, Charleston, South Carolina, and enters Smith College

1944 *Fall:* Barbara Pierce drops out of Smith College

1945 *January 6:* Barbara Pierce marries George Bush

1946 *July 6:* Son George Walker is born

1948 George Bush graduates from Yale and the family moves to Texas

1949 *October:* Barbara Bush's mother is killed in an auto accident

December 20: Daughter Pauline Robinson (Robin) is born

1953 *February 11:* Son John Ellis (Jeb) is born

October 11: Daughter Pauline (Robin) dies of leukemia

1955 Son Neil Mallon is born

1956 Son Marvin Pierce is born

1959 Daughter Dorothy (Doro) is born

The Bushes move to Houston

1962 George Bush runs for chairman of the Harris County Republican Party and wins

1964 George Bush loses his bid for the U.S. Senate

1966 George Bush wins a seat in the U.S. House of Representatives and the family moves to Washington

1968 George Bush is reelected to the House of Representatives

1970 George Bush fails to win a Senate seat

1971–73 George Bush serves as the U.S. ambassador to the United Nations and the family moves to New York City

1973– 74 George Bush chairs the Republican National Committee; the family moves back to Washington

1974– 75 George Bush heads the U.S. Liaison Office in Beijing

1976– 77 George Bush serves as director of the Central Intelligence Agency

1980 George Bush makes an unsuccessful bid for the Republican presidential nomination but is elected vice president of the United States

1988 *March:* The Barbara Bush Foundation for Family Literacy is created

November: George Bush is elected president of the United States

1989 *January 20:* Barbara Bush becomes first lady

May: Barbara Bush heads a diplomatic mission to Costa Rica to attend the inauguration of President Rafael Calderon

1993 *January 20:* The Bushes leave the White House and return to Houston

1994 *November:* Son George W. Bush is elected governor of Texas

1998 *November 7:* Son Jeb Bush is elected governor of Florida

2000 *November:* Son George W. Bush is elected president of the United States

2001 *January 20:* The Bushes attend their son's inauguration

FURTHER READING

Bush, Barbara. *Barbara Bush: A Memoir.* New York: Scribner's, 1994.

———. *Millie's Book: As Dictated to Barbara Bush.* New York: Quill, 1992.

Bush, George H. W. *All the Best, George Bush: My Life in Letters and Other Writings.* New York: Touchstone, 2000.

Grimes, Ann. *Running Mates: The Making of a First Lady.* New York, 1990.

Kilian, Pamela. *Barbara Bush: A Biography.* Thorndike, Maine: Thorndike Press, 1992.

Radcliffe, Donnie. *Simply Barbara Bush: A Portrait of America's Candid First Lady.* New York: Warner, 1989.

HILLARY RODHAM CLINTON

(OCTOBER 26, 1947–   )

First Lady, January 20, 1993–January 20, 2001

HILLARY CLINTON
(Office of the First Lady)

Hillary Rodham Clinton is very much a woman of her time. Part of the generation educated during the 1960s and 1970s, she set herself to reform American society from within, taking advantage of the opportunities opened by the women's movement of the 1960s and 1970s. Established in a successful career as a lawyer and as a politician, she worked hard to achieve some of the reforms she had envisioned in her younger days, particularly for children's rights and improvement of the public education system. Her marriage to a male feminist, while troubled because of his extramarital sexual activity, gave her self-confidence and support in her undertakings. In the White House she experienced the full force of a backlash against feminism and harsh criticism from women whose brand of feminism differed from hers. Nonetheless, she owed her success in the 2000 race for a New York seat in the U.S. Senate largely to the support of women voters.

Hillary Rodham was born in Chicago, Illinois, on October 26, 1947, the only daughter and oldest of three children of businessman Hugh Ellsworth Rodham and his wife Dorothy Howell Rodham. When she was three years old, the family moved to Park Ridge, Illinois. Although her parents assumed the traditional roles of breadwinner and housewife, her mother could hit a fast ball and her father could cook. Neither was rigidly bound by gender expectations. Hillary grew up in a supportive family, where her parents encouraged their children to be frugal and hardworking and to do well in school. "It's hard out there [in the working world]," their father taught them. Through the youth ministry of the Methodist Church she attended, Hillary came to recognize the responsibilities of Christians for the welfare of the underprivileged. She shared worship and service projects with black and Hispanic teenagers, discussed civil rights with her peers, went to hear Dr. Martin Luther King, Jr., speak, and debated what war means to a Christian. She organized volunteers to baby-sit the children of migrant laborers while their parents worked.

As an adolescent, Hillary had a good time with neighborhood friends, went to school dances and games, and hung out drinking sodas and talking. Occasionally she dated, but she and her friends usually went places in groups. She earned money working part-time in a child-care center, baby-sitting, clerking in a store, and maintaining the sports equipment in a public park. Her skill in organizing was recognized in her election as vice president of her junior class and her appointment as "senior leader" to help the teachers instruct. Her classmates voted her "Most Likely to Succeed," she won a good citizenship award from the Daughters of the American Revolution, and her high grades earned her membership in the National Honor Society. She was living the life of the stereotypical middlewestern suburban kid of the 1950s and early 1960s.

Yet she was more than a stereotype. Her mother had taught her that character mattered more than clothes; for a while she refused to wear makeup because putting it on wasted time. She was irate when NASA told her that she could not be an astronaut because it did not admit women. She scorned the habit of many girls holding back in school for fear of intimidating boys. She admired Senator Margaret Chase Smith, the first woman elected to both houses of Congress, for standing up against the smear tactics of her Senate colleague Joseph McCarthy.

Raised in child-centered homes by parents who felt lucky to have survived the Great Depression and World War II, Hillary's generation developed both confidence in their own judgment and a sense of entitlement. In college they demanded and got unprecedented privileges, freedom, and power. At Wellesley, where she majored in political science, Hillary led her classmates in protesting against the Vietnam War and for the civil rights movement, boycotting classes, and calling for teach-ins where faculty and students discussed these controversial issues. However, unlike many of her peers, she believed in working from within the system to reform it, not destroy it. For Hillary that meant a career in politics. Later, as first lady, she was to say, "If my husband weren't president, I would be involved in politics, I would be supporting candidates, I would be advocating for issues, just like I did before he was president and I will do again when he is no longer president. And I love it because I think politics, with a small 'p' . . . is how democracies make their decisions."

In the Wellesley Internship Program she spent part of her 1968 summer vacation in Washington doing research and writing for Secretary of Defense Melvin Laird, and the rest of it at the Republican Party convention in Miami, working to nominate Nelson Rockefeller. That winter, however, she supported the presidential candidacy of Democratic senator Eugene McCarthy, who opposed the war in Vietnam. She ended her senior year, during which she served as president of the student government, by delivering a commencement address on the issues of the day as a representative and at the request of her classmates. She shared the platform with Senator Edward Brooke of Massachusetts, and in her speech she charged him with the responsibility of his generation for the sad state of the nation. The magazine *Life* took note.

In fall 1969 Hillary entered Yale Law School because it advertised a philosophy of achieving social and political change by legal means. She turned her appearance into a political and feminist statement, wearing white socks and sandals and the loose pants favored by the Vietcong, with her hair "kind of piled on top of her head," according to a classmate. For the notorious trial of the Black Panthers in New Haven in 1969–70, she organized students to monitor the courtroom under the direction of a faculty member, constitutional scholar Thomas Emerson. She joined protests against the Vietnam War and led a campaign to have tampon dispensers placed in the school's women's rooms. Nevertheless, she always advocated staying within the system, seeking reform rather than revolution, and changing the law school without closing it. In fact, she mediated between the law school administration and the students.

Hillary could be warm with people she liked and trusted, but she could also be sharp and abrasive. Either way, she impressed both students and faculty, and her ambition to be an important political figure did not strike them as improbable. She took a step toward realizing that ambition when the League of Women Voters invited her to a conference of young leaders of the future, at which she met a number of congressional staffers and such Washington figures as attorney Vernon Jordan, then executive director of the United Negro College Fund. In spring 1970 she accepted an invitation to speak at the League's 50th anniversary celebration, where she made more such contacts. Among them was Peter Edelman, who recruited her to work that summer on the project for children, later called the Children's Defense Fund, instituted by his wife, Marian

Wright Edelman. Later Hillary called meeting Marian Edelman, a passionate advocate for children, a turning point in her life. From there Hillary moved on to a staff job with Senator Walter Mondale's subcommittee on the plight of migrant workers' children and their families.

That fall she met and fell in love with fellow law student William Jefferson Clinton (Bill). During his second year in law school and her third, they lived together in a house near the campus. In 1972 Hillary stayed on in New Haven, working at the Yale Child Study Center and doing research for a book by Anna Freud. Under a special program sponsored by Yale's law and medical schools, she reviewed the legal rights of children. After graduating from law school with Bill in 1973, she worked briefly with Marian Edelman, then in January 1974 she joined the legal staff of the committee of the House of Representatives working on the impeachment of President Richard Nixon.

When Nixon resigned that August, Hillary stepped off the fast track, refusing offers from prestigious law firms and the Children's Defense Fund. Instead, ignoring the pleas of her horrified friends, she went to Arkansas to help Bill Clinton with his congressional campaign, accepting a faculty appointment at the University of Arkansas law school. She brought to the campaign her well-honed organizational skills, working on his speeches and shaping his image as a young, idealistic candidate who would effect political change. He told people that she was "far better organized, more in control, more intelligent and more eloquent than I am"—but he was the candidate, not she.

She stayed on, perhaps conflicted over whether or not to marry Bill. His mother did not like Hillary, and her mother did not approve of Bill. Nevertheless, despite his womanizing, Hillary married him on October 11, 1975. She kept her maiden name, a decision that did not sit well with the constituency in Arkansas. Indeed, Hillary herself was a strange phenomenon in that state, where many disliked her, said a Wellesley friend, as "one of those pointy-headed, overeducated Yale types who had come back with Bill to Arkansas to spread the word to the uninitiated." Arkansans were not accustomed to dealing with confident professional women, and she was a northerner to boot.

At the University of Arkansas, a student described her as "a little out of place," but "tough, intelligent, and articulate." She volunteered on such community projects as establishing a rape crisis center and trying to reform the laws governing rape and sexual assault. She also continued to write scholarly articles advocating expanded legal rights for children—arguing, for instance, that if the judge finds a child competent, the child should have legal rights separate from those of the parents. Such arguments have provoked right-wing accusations of destroying families by pitting children against their parents. Beginning in 1976, Hillary served on the board of Edelman's Children's Defense Fund, chairing it from 1986 on, and resigned only during the 1992 presidential campaign.

In 1976, with his wife's help, Bill Clinton was elected state attorney general. They moved to Little Rock, where in 1977 she took a job with the Rose law firm. The next year President Jimmy Carter appointed her to the board of directors of the Legal Services Corporation, a nonprofit organization established by Congress in 1974 to assure equal justice under the law for all. In Arkansas she founded and presided over an organization called Advocates for Children and Families.

In 1978 Hillary acted as chief adviser in her husband's successful campaign for governor. Her ability to look at matters in a straightforward manner counterbalanced his overly optimistic views: "Bill, don't be such a Pollyanna. Some of these people you think are your friends aren't." He was elected despite lively criticism of Hillary for keeping her maiden name, having a career, dressing as she did, and writing articles on children's rights. Personally and professionally, things were going well for her. On February 27, 1980, she gave birth to a daughter, Chelsea, and made full partner at her law firm. Given her increased responsibilities, she had little time to help in her husband's bid for reelection, and he lost.

Upon Bill's defeat, though, Hillary switched her attention back to his career to plan his comeback. Just as she had earlier chosen to leave her promising opportunities in the north to campaign for him in Arkansas, so did she now abandon whatever hopes she may have had for a seat on the federal bench, the presidency of a college, a cabinet slot in a Democratic administration, or a bid for elective office. She remodeled her image, replacing her big glasses with contact lenses and her baggy dresses with tailored suits. She wore makeup and had her hair cut and styled. She even changed her name, now calling herself Hillary Rodham Clinton. Arkansans consequently developed a different view of her; the papers talked about her "major shift in attitude." She campaigned as much and as effectively as the candidate.

The 1982 campaign succeeded, and the Clintons moved back into the governor's mansion. The next year, in a decision that startled many, Bill Clinton appointed his wife chair of the Arkansas Educational Standards Committee, to serve without pay. They worked in tandem: He spoke in big towns and civic clubs, while she worked the back roads, holding hearings before the committee in every corner of the state. She made a good impression, speaking effectively and adeptly handling difficult questions and heckling. When the time came, she lobbied the bill through the legislature. She also lobbied for other bills, like a juvenile justice program, and she learned how to twist legislative arms. In 1983 the Arkansas Press Association named her "Headliner of the Year," a title awarded the person who had made the most good news for the state. "As chairman of the statewide committee on standards in education," the *Arkansas Times* editorialized, "Hillary Rodham Clinton helped educate a whole state, not excluding her husband. If Clinton has shown a new political maturity this fall, it wouldn't be the first time that the key to a man's growing up would prove to be a woman."

Meanwhile, she was developing a national reputation as an advocate for children, working on a nationwide program to help troubled children at school and serving on the William T. Grant Foundation's Commission on Work, Family, and Citizenship. She also acted as a well-paid director on the boards of such corporations as the TCBY yogurt company, Tyson Foods, and Wal-Mart—appointments that sometimes raised questions of conflict of interest, as when Tyson Foods was exempted from some state laws and contributed to the pollution of the state's waterways.

Hillary had adapted remarkably well to Arkansas while at the same time going her own way as a professional woman. She showed herself equally agile at adapting to the state's political cronyism and money manipulation. She was making money—significantly more money than her husband—from her law practice, her seats on corporate boards, and her investments. Her actions during this period have been repeatedly challenged as illegal, unethical, or at the least demonstrative of bad judgment, but her defenders argue that she had little choice, having in a sense "married into the mob." A number of subsequent investigations have resulted in more unease than conviction of her guilt or innocence.

The Clintons' professional success and popularity contrasted with the ugly rumors about the disruption of their marriage caused by Bill's inveterate womanizing, which dated from before their marriage and apparently went on almost without interruption. Rumors also associated her romantically with Vince Foster, a colleague at her law firm. From the start, both Clintons had been planning for Bill to run for the presidency of the United States, but after the exposure of Colorado senator Gary Hart's affair blighted his candidacy in 1984, Bill decided not to run in 1987, because he felt too vulnerable. The decision upset and humiliated his wife, who was further embarrassed when in 1989 new rumors erupted about her husband's dalliance with a woman named Gennifer Flowers.

Inevitably, speculation arose about whether Hillary would sue for divorce. Then and now, whenever she has spoken on the subject, she has favored keeping the marriage going, say-

ing, for instance: "You've got to be willing to stay committed—to someone over the long run. . . ." And: "My strong feelings about divorce and its effect on children have caused me to bite my tongue more than a few times during my own marriage and to think instead about what I could do to be a better wife and partner." On this occasion she took the usual steps of the wronged wife who has decided against divorce: ministerial marital counseling, a diet and another makeover for herself, and accepting renewed promises of reform from her errant partner. Thus the Clintons pulled themselves and their marriage together for the 1992 presidential campaign.

They started out by promising a partnership presidency, a two-for-one bargain in which voters would get two bright, experienced, high-achieving, hardworking executives for the price of one. Almost immediately their polls and focus groups repudiated this baby-boomer power-couple approach in favor of a more traditional image of the first lady—that of gracious lady and adoring wife and mother. Always willing to do whatever it took to achieve her goal, Hillary Rodham Clinton submitted to yet another makeover.

However, opponents accused her of denigrating motherhood when, in an unguarded remark, she said, "I suppose I could have stayed at home and baked cookies." She tried to explain:

> I had understood the question to refer to the ceremonial role of a public official's spouse, and I replied that I had chosen to pursue my law practice while my husband was governor rather than stay home as an official hostess, serving cookies and tea to guests. Now, the fact is, I've made my share of cookies and served hundreds of cups of tea. But I never thought that my cookie-baking or tea-serving abilities made me a good, bad, or indifferent mother, or a good or bad person. So it never occurred to me that my comment would be taken as insulting mothers (I guess including my own!) who choose to stay home with their children full time. Nor did it occur to me that

the next day's headlines would reduce *me* to an anti-cookie—and therefore obviously anti-family—'career woman.'

Later she accurately diagnosed at least part of the problem when she said, "I just never thought about how somebody standing on the sidelines might interpret what I was doing differently than how I intended to do it." On yet another occasion: "I thought that I had some idea of politics at the national level. But I had no idea."

Do what she might, however much she reduced her visibility, however often she cited her long record of concern for children, the public continued to perceive the Clintons as a team and Hillary Rodham Clinton as a competent, even brilliant professional woman—a perception threatening to some, reassuring to others. Erstwhile conservative presidential candidate Pat Buchanan called her "the enemy of everything traditional in American life."

The repeated makeovers and the constant search for an image appealing to a majority of Americans made people uncomfortable. Who was the real Hillary Rodham Clinton? Was she only a conniving woman who would do anything necessary to bring her husband—and not incidentally herself—into a position of great influence and power? What was clear was that she was her husband's most important adviser and strategist throughout the campaign. Professionally and politically they moved in tandem—except when he betrayed her loyalty by lying about his womanizing.

Ironically, when she publicly defended her husband after Gennifer Flowers accused him of having an affair with her, support for Hillary Clinton strengthened in that portion of the public that prefers woman-as-victim to woman-as-achiever. Her defense irritated others, however, especially when she said, "You know, I'm not sitting here as some little woman standing by my man, like Tammy Wynette. I'm sitting here because I love him and I respect him and I honor what he's been through and what we've been through together. And, you know, if that's

not enough for people, then, heck, don't vote for him." Nevertheless, enough people did vote for him to move the Clintons into the White House in January 1993. Like many another first lady, Hillary Clinton rejoiced in seeing more of her husband than in the past: "It's also kind of nice to have your husband live, as it were, above the store. He's actually home for dinner a lot more than he was in our previous life together."

Washington insiders waited breathlessly to see how she would function as White House hostess—but that role was not high on her list of priorities. For one thing, she told the *New Yorker* in 1996, "These years of childrearing go by so fast—I mean, Chelsea's going to be gone. I can go to dinner parties from now to kingdom come when she's in college and when she's grown up." Hillary also had other things about which she cared more than about entertaining: her work for the rights and welfare of children and women, politicking, and damage control in the many scandals and accusations that swirled around the White House all during the Clinton years.

Nonetheless, she did show a sense of obligation to social duty, as when on the Clintons' first day in the White House, a glitch kept many of their supporters from promised entry to the mansion; the first lady could be heard on an open mike saying, "We've just screwed a lot of people." To make up for the error, they opened the doors and stood for hours shaking hands.

She banned smoking in the White House, and fired the French chef in favor of an American specializing in a light cuisine. She also read every book she could find on the history of the mansion and redecorated the private quarters. After a couple of years in the White House, she said that she was doing her best "to fulfill the many different parts of the role" of first lady: "I've enjoyed the entertaining and the chance to contribute something to the White House. I've also enjoyed the chance I've been given to work with my husband on health care and other issues of interest to me."

Despite their determination to protect their daughter against publicity, the Clintons immediately ran into a problem when they enrolled Chelsea in the private Sidwell Friends School. Many questioned why they did not send her to public school and pointedly wondered what they had against public education. The president and first lady tried to explain that the presence of the Secret Service agents assigned to protect their daughter would disrupt a public school, whereas Sidwell was inured to the difficulties they presented. Despite this criticism, the Clintons succeeded in protecting their adolescent daughter's privacy. As Hillary told another presidential daughter, Margaret Truman, "She's a happy teenager, I think. She comes and goes pretty much as she pleases, she has wonderful friends. We've kept the press out of her life. That may be our only achievement so far."

The Clintons set up an office for the first lady in the west wing of the White House, where, the president announced, she would work "on a variety of domestic-policy issues." Hillary organized a multiracial staff of 13, headed by Margaret Ann Williams, the first African American to hold the post. The first lady exercised major influence in political appointments across the executive branch and in the removal of career staffers whom she and Bill thought potentially disloyal. She made important speeches, as when in April 1993 she spoke to an audience at the University of Texas, saying, "We need a new politics of meaning. We need a new ethos of individual responsibility and caring."

A week after his inauguration in 1993, the president named his wife to chair a task force on health-care reform, a high-priority goal for the Clinton administration and a major concern to the American people. Almost everyone agreed that the health-care system needed reform; few agreed on how to achieve it. Much of the medical establishment and many conservative members of Congress were suspicious of anything that smacked of "socialized medicine," but the millions of Americans not covered by health insurance cried out for help. The problem was complicated and demanded complicated solutions, yet any recommendations

that the task force submitted to Congress needed clear understanding and wide support among the populace. It was not forthcoming, the health-care system was not reformed, and much of the blame fell on Hillary Rodham Clinton. Her management of the task force, the secrecy of its deliberations, and the lack of understanding of its recommendations among the public provoked criticism. Certainly the ongoing allegations against the prepresidential conduct of both the Clintons and the right-wing attacks on them clouded the issue.

Whatever the reason for the failure, thenceforth Hillary Clinton's visibility as chief adviser to the president on domestic issues declined publicly, although no one knows what happened in private. Reverberations from the collapse of the health-care reform plan echoed throughout President Clinton's first term, contributing to the Republican domination of the House of Representatives from 1994 onward, which severely limited what he was able to achieve.

From the health-care reform fiasco emerged the D.C. circuit court ruling in *Association of American Physicians and Surgeons v. Hillary Rodham Clinton* (1993) that the first lady was a "de facto federal employee," implying that she was subject to the conflict-of-interest laws that govern federal employees. Whether that judgment will apply to all first ladies or only to those who hold an official appointment remains to be seen. Almost certainly, though, some first lady of the future will hold such an appointment, even though the "Bobby Kennedy law," passed after President John F. Kennedy appointed his brother Bobby as attorney general, now forbids a president to name a family member to a paid government position. Nevertheless, once pioneered, new directions for first ladies—such as that taken by Hillary Clinton—typically become beaten paths.

From its earliest days, the Clinton White House was attacked by accusation after accusation, eventually resulting in the appointment of an independent counsel to investigate the charges—a move that the Clintons originally opposed on the grounds that no previous president had been investigated for actions that preceded his presidency. It was equally unprecedented to look into the affairs of the first lady. Allegations against the president ranged from womanizing to lying to malfeasance in office and eventually resulted in his impeachment in 1998. Although he was acquitted, the trial stripped him of dignity, and the office he filled was besmirched by his acknowledged lies and unbecoming conduct.

Unease about Hillary Clinton's wielding great influence without having been elected underlay the attacks on her. Allegations against her, particularly about her business and political maneuvers in Arkansas with the Rose law firm, resulted in neither clarity nor conviction. After originally taking the position that these issues were nobody's business but hers, she eventually gave a press conference on the allegations of malfeasance against her in her Whitewater Development Company real estate deals and commodity trades, in which she said that inexperience in Washington had caused her to refuse to answer reporters' questions previously. She then promised, "I'm certainly going to try to be more sensitive to what you all need and what we need to give you." Other accusations focused on her 1970s writings on children's legal rights, asserting that she was destroying family values. Throughout her White House days she tended to see scandals and allegations as part of a right-wing conspiracy against the Clintons and their programs. Their struggles to defend themselves resulted in a May 1988 District of Columbia circuit court ruling on the status of the first lady, as Judge Norma Halloway Johnson extended executive privilege specifically to her, among the president's other aides.

These problems, combined with Hillary's obvious sufferings about her husband's infidelities and her efforts to keep him in office, crippled much of her work for the causes she genuinely cares about. However, as the 1996 campaign approached, she shifted attention from her function as presidential adviser to her concern for the "human issues." She undertook to write a syndicated weekly newspaper column

Bill and Hillary Clinton attired for a State dinner
(Office of the First Lady)

of opinion, and in early 1995 she spoke at women's conferences in Copenhagen and New York. That spring Hillary took her daughter with her on a tour of Asia, during which she stressed the importance of education for women. At the United Nations Fourth World Conference on Women that fall, she said: "It is time to break our silence. It is time for us to say here in Beijing, and the world to hear, that it is no longer acceptable to discuss women's rights as separate from human rights." She cited specific abuses, such as forced abortions and sterilization and the denial of political rights and free speech (all common practices in China, the host country). During a tour of South America, she focused on the role of women in developing countries. In 1996 she published her book, *It Takes a Village*, an inquiry into ways to support families and to create a society that will enable children to reach their full potential.

After President Clinton's reelection in 1996, scandal continued to haunt both him and the first lady. Among other problems, Hillary was questioned by a federal criminal grand jury about the reappearance of billing records that had previously gone missing at the Rose law firm. Nonetheless, she continued her work and her speeches on issues important to her.

During this second term Hillary entered the New York race for Daniel Patrick Moynihan's vacated seat in the U.S. Senate inch by inch, creating expectations while postponing a firm announcement. Since early 1999 she had given indications that she intended to enter the race but hesitated to take the definitive step, irritating her friends and foes alike. Finally, in a speech to the United Federation of Teachers on November 24, 1999, in Manhattan, she put an end to speculation about her interest in the race. She announced that she would be in the race, that it was "time to get moving and get started." At about the same time, to establish her residency in the state, she and her husband bought a house in Westchester County for $1.7 million. The formal announcement of her candidacy, however, was postponed until February 6, 2000. Her Republican opponent was at first New York mayor Rudolph Giuliani, and after the mayor's bad health forced his withdrawal, Congressman Rick Lazio.

Hillary had to establish her credentials against a barrage of criticism, much of it coming from out of state. A headline in the *New York Times* made the point: "Giuliani Donors Loathe First Lady From Afar." These donors were motivated more by opposition to Hillary than by support for the Republican candidate. Some of them cited her role in Whitewater and other scandals of her husband's administration; others, quoted in the *New York Times,* thought her "haughty and presumptuous in moving to New York" simply in order to run for office, a "carpetbagger, pure and simple. She is a devious, self-promoting, selfish woman."

Hillary's entry into the race thrust her into the situation of playing two roles simultaneously: first lady and administration defender on the one hand and candidate for political office on the other. Conflicts arose between them, as on her official visit to Palestine in September 1999. On that occasion Sufa Arafat, wife of the Palestine Liberation Organization leader, vigorously criticized Israeli policies while Hillary sat beside her, silently. The Jewish community in New York City found her silence inexplicable; Hillary explained that as the wife of the president she could not express her own feelings. Similarly, when in the late summer of 1999 she endorsed President Clinton's pardon of seven Puerto Rican nationalists, she was criticized for appealing to the Puerto Rican vote in New York, and when she later opposed the pardon, she was criticized for wavering in her convictions.

Nonetheless, according to political experts, she ran a good campaign, and she was elected by a substantial margin. Her candidacy attracted the support of many traditional Democratic demographic groups: women, African Americans, and union members. Exit polls on election day show that 60 percent of women voted for Hillary Clinton.

In victory, Hillary credited her husband for the political advice that he gave her during her campaign. Out-of-stater she might be, but she had impressed New Yorkers all over the state by starting with a "listening tour" that informed her about the issues most important to them. Congressman Lazio's bullying tactics made it easy for thousands of women voters to identify with her. Moreover, they knew that she had devoted herself throughout her life to issues important to them, like education, health care, and the well-being of children. Hillary Clinton impressed the male as well as the female electorate, but it was women who put her over the top.

As of mid-April 2001, Senator Hillary Clinton has created no waves, nor has she retired into back-bench obscurity. She serves on important committees, which in large part represent her own interests: Environment and Public Works; Health, Education, Labor and Pensions; and Budget. She has sponsored 20 bills, none of which has as yet been reported out of committee. In substance, these bills deal with such issues as the financing of new communications technologies, expanding federal assistance to small business, promoting broadband telecommunications services in rural America, and providing for a national teacher corps and principal recruitment. Speculations continue on the possibility of her running for president in 2004, on which she comments only that she intends to serve out her full six-year term as junior senator from New York.

———— ∞ ————

A formidable, independent, and sometimes intimidating force in the White House, Hillary Rodham Clinton was a controversial public figure even before becoming first lady. She began her term as the "partner in power" of the president, but she could not consistently maintain that position after she failed to effect reform of the health-care system. She was attacked for her appearance, her feminism, her stand on children's rights, her disloyalty to friends, and her brusqueness. From the murk of scandal muddying the Clinton presidency, she salvaged her work for the welfare of children, her feminism, and her function as adviser to the president on politics and the affairs of the nation. Most significantly, she broke the tradition that the first lady does not have an independent career by campaigning for and winning a Senate seat during her White House years. Her relative youth could enable her to run for the highest office in the land in 2008.

CHRONOLOGY

1947   *October 26:* Hillary Rodham is born in Chicago, Illinois

1965   Hillary Rodham enters Wellesley College

1969   *Fall:* Hillary Rodham enters Yale Law School

1970   *Summer:* Hillary Rodham works for Edelman's Children's Defense Fund (then called the Washington Research Progression) and for Walter Mondale's subcommittee on the plight of children of migrant workers

Fall: Hillary meets William Jefferson Clinton (Bill)

1972–73   Hillary Rodham works in a Yale special program to review the legal rights of children

1973   *Summer:* Hillary Rodham works on George McGovern's campaign for the presidency and also works as a staff attorney for the Children's Defense Fund in Cambridge, Massachusetts

1974   *January–August:* Hillary Rodham works on the legal staff set up by Congress for the impeachment of Richard Nixon

August: Hillary Rodham goes to Arkansas to work on Bill Clinton's congressional campaign

1975   Hillary Rodham joins the law faculty of the University of Arkansas at Fayette

October 11: Hillary Rodham marries Bill Clinton

1976   Hillary Rodham Clinton works on Jimmy Carter's presidential primary campaign in Indiana and begins serving on the board of Marian Edelman's Children's Defense Fund; Bill Clinton is elected Arkansas attorney general, and the Clintons move to Little Rock

1977   Hillary Rodham Clinton is hired by the Rose law firm; helps found Arkansas Advocates for Children and Families

1978   Bill Clinton is elected governor of Arkansas and appoints Hillary Rodham Clinton chair of the Rural Health Advisory Committee

1980   *February 27:* Daughter Chelsea is born

Hillary Rodham Clinton makes partner at the Rose law firm

1982   Bill Clinton loses reelection for governor; Hillary Rodham Clinton begins work on the next campaign

1984   Bill Clinton is reelected governor of Arkansas, a position that he holds for five two-year terms

1984–92   Hillary Rodham Clinton effects major educational reforms in Arkansas

1992 *November:* Bill Clinton is elected president of the United States

1993 *January 20:* Hillary Rodham Clinton becomes first lady; President Clinton appoints her head of the task force to reform health care, which fails in its mission

1996 *January:* Hillary Rodham Clinton is questioned by a federal criminal grand jury about the reappearance of previously missing billing records in the Rose law firm

Hillary Rodham Clinton publishes *It Takes a Village*

November: Bill Clinton is reelected president

1996– Hillary Rodham Clinton travels widely
1999 abroad and works on such causes as women's and children's rights

1999 *January 7:* Bill Clinton's impeachment trial begins

February 12: Bill Clinton is not convicted in the impeachment trial

2000 *February 6:* Hillary Rodham Clinton formally declares her candidacy for senator from the state of New York

November 7: Hillary Rodham Clinton is elected senator from New York

2001 Hillary Rodham Clinton is appointed to the Senate committees on Budgets; Environment and Public Works; and Health, Education, Labor and Pensions.

FURTHER READING

Boyd, Aaron. *First Lady: The Story of Hillary Rodham Clinton.* Greensboro, N.C.: Morgan Reynolds, 1994.

Clinton, Hillary Rodham. *An Invitation to the White House.* New York: Simon and Schuster, 2000.

———. *It Takes a Village.* New York: Touchstone/Simon & Schuster, 1996.

Dumas, Ernest, ed. *The Clintons of Arkansas: An Introduction by Those Who Know Them Best.* Fayetteville: University of Arkansas Press, 1993.

King, Norman. *Hillary: Her True Story.* New York: Carol, 1993.

Morris, Roger. *Partners in Power.* New York: Henry Holt, 1996.

Noonan, Peggy. *The Case Against Hillary Clinton.* New York: Regan Books, 2000.

Radcliffe, Donnie. *Hillary Rodham Clinton: A First Lady for Our Time.* New York: Warner, 1993.

Spitzer, Robert J. "Clinton's Impeachment Will Have New Consequences for the Presidency," *PS: Political Science and Politics* (September 1999): 542.

Troy, Gil. *Affairs of the State: The Rise and Rejection of the Presidential Couple Since World War II.* New York: Free Press, 1997.

Warner, Judith. *Hillary Rodham Clinton: The Inside Story.* New York: Penguin, 1993.

Wasserman, Carl David. "Firing the First Lady: The Role and Accountability of the Presidential Spouse," *Vanderbilt Law Review* (May 1995).

Woodward, Bob. *Shadow: Five Presidencies and the Legacy of Watergate.* New York: Simon and Shuster, 1999.

LAURA WELCH BUSH
(NOVEMBER 4, 1946–   )
First Lady, January 20, 2001–

LAURA BUSH
(*Office of the First Lady*)

For a decade before Laura Welch Bush was married, she earned her living as an elementary-school teacher and a librarian. Though she avoids controversy and rarely speaks out on issues, she ranks herself as a feminist, supporting equal pay for equal work. She also expresses the hope that some day in the not-too-distant future a woman will serve as president of the United States. For herself, however, she prefers a more conventional course. She said of herself, "I've always done what really traditional women do, and I've been very, very satisfied." She once asked her astonished parents why they had paid for her education as a teacher but had never offered to send her to law school. Her father pulled out his wallet; if she wanted to study law, he said, he would foot the bills. Immediately she backed off, professing her contentment with what she was doing.

Nonetheless, she considers herself a woman of her times: "When I describe myself as traditional," she says, "I mean in the sense that I had jobs that were traditionally women's jobs. But I never felt I was so traditional. . . . For instance, teaching in minority schools, you know, not marrying until my early thirties. I felt I was in many ways very contemporary."

—⁓—

Laura Welch was born on November 4, 1946, in Midland, Texas, the only child of housing developer Harold Welch and his wife, Jenna Hawkins Welch, who worked in civic clubs and kept books for her husband. Laura grew up in Midland, described by her future father-in-law as "Yuppieville, West," the home of many affluent families in the oil business. Harold and Jenna Welch, centered their lives on the First Methodist Church. Although neither of them had completed college, they cherished expectations that their daughter would graduate. Laura fulfilled all their hopes. As her mother has said, "She was just born a nice quiet little kiddo." When she was in second grade, Laura lined up her dolls as her pupils and told her parents that when she grew up she wanted to teach.

As a teen Laura was liked by her peers, although they thought her more reserved and more adult than the rest of them, as well as more given to listening than talking. Nevertheless, she shared their pleasures, riding bikes to the drugstore for cherry cokes, sunning themselves by the pool, and sneaking smokes while hiding in the backseats of cars. (She quit smoking only in the early 1990s.) "In Midland you were very sheltered and watched over," she reminisced, "but you felt totally free. I think there's really something about west Texas—the big sky, no trees, the beautiful sunsets, the stars at night—it's very liberating." Popular with both girls and boys, she never lacked for dates. In 1963 Laura's life was darkened by a tragic automobile accident, in which she drove through a stop sign and hit another vehicle.

Her classmate and friend Michael Douglas who was in the other car was killed. On the accident report, the speed at which she was driving is illegible, and no charges were filed.

In 1964 she entered Southern Methodist University (SMU), then a largely white enclave in Dallas, and pledged Kappa Alpha Theta, which was known for its "smart, good-looking" sorority sisters. She took no interest in the protests of the 1960s—she does not remember a campus visit from Dr. Martin Luther King, Jr.—focusing instead on getting good grades, especially in English; teaching Sunday school; and enjoying the social life. She earned her bachelor's degree in education and immediately put it to use by teaching in the John F. Kennedy elementary school in Houston for two years. At that time she lived with her close friend Jan O'Neill in the singles complex Chateaux Dijon, where, coincidentally, Laura's future husband also resided. They saw nothing of each other, however, as she was living on the "sedate" side of the complex, and he was partying on the other.

Finding that she particularly enjoyed reading to her students, in fall 1971 she enrolled for a master's degree in library science from the University of Texas at Austin, completing it the next spring. She first accepted a position as a children's librarian in the Houston public library system, then moved back to Austin to take a job as librarian in a public elementary school.

From childhood Laura Welch had known of fellow Midland resident George W. Bush, son of George Herbert Walker Bush, president of the United States from 1988 to 1992. Laura's senior by just a few months, George W. Bush had received a bachelor's degree from Yale and an MBA from Harvard, and in 1975 he had gone into the oil business in Midland. Now he was running for a seat in the U.S. Congress. Her friend Jan O'Neill invited Laura and George W. to a barbecue in Midland in the early summer of 1977. O'Neill hoped that their opposite characteristics would complement one another: his messiness against her almost compulsive neatness; her self-effacing manner against his cocky garrulity; his outgoing nature against her reserve; her patience against his impatience; and her devotion to her beloved books, arranged even in her bedroom according to the Dewey decimal system, against his preference for quick summaries.

Although Laura initially hesitated to meet this congressional aspirant, on the grounds that he was too political and she was not interested in politics, she found that he amused her. George was immediately smitten, finding her "gorgeous, good-humored, quick to laugh, down-to-earth, and very smart." From Kennebunkport, Maine, where he was spending the summer in the family enclave, he telephoned her frequently. When she did not answer or said that she was too busy to talk, he flew back to Midland to court her in person. By the time she met his family in October, he had already proposed and she had accepted. Fortunately, the Bush family approved of her. Even the formidable and demanding matriarch of the clan, Dorothy Walker (Mrs. Prescott) Bush, was silenced when she asked Laura Welch what she did and, according to Barbara Bush, Laura replied, "I read, I smoke, and I admire." She herself remembers the incident differently and finds such a reply improbable, but everyone agrees that she was at once accepted into the clan.

Laura Welch and George W. Bush married on November 5, 1977, only a few months after they had met. "We were really ready to get married," Laura later explained. "I'm sure both of us thought, 'Gosh, we may never get married.' And we both really wanted children. Plus, I lived in Austin and he lived in Midland; so if we were going to see each other all the time, we needed to marry."

Immediately she was plunged into George's race for a congressional seat. He had promised her that she would not have to make political speeches—a promise almost immediately broken, giving her one of her favorite lines: "My husband told me I'd never have to make a political speech. So much for political promises." Like her parents, Laura had always

considered herself a Democrat, but she loyally supported her Republican husband's bid for office. Understanding that she was marrying into a nationally prominent Republican family, she decided that she should "submerge [her] own ambitions" for "the greater good" of the Bush clan. She spoke publicly when she had to; practice eventually inured her to the experience and turned her into a competent if not spectacular speaker. In that first congressional campaign, she said, she met "a lot of great people. A lot of our closest friends, we made that year. And that's really what happens in a campaign. That's what you end up with."

After her husband lost the election in 1978, Laura lived happily as a suburban housewife, reading, gardening, and volunteering for the Junior League, while her husband made money in the oil business, although his investors fared less well. For several years the young Bushes' hopes for children seemed futile. In the summer of 1980, however, more than three years into their marriage and just as they were planning to resort to adoption, Laura discovered that she was pregnant with twin girls. The pregnancy was difficult. After she developed the toxic and dangerous condition of preeclampsia in her third trimester, she had to be hospitalized and kept in bed for several weeks. Nonetheless, she remained confident of her ability to carry her daughters to viability. This confidence was justified when the twins were born on November 25, 1981, five weeks before her due date, in an emergency Caesarean delivery necessitated by their mother's threatened kidney failure. By then, however, each baby weighed around five pounds. They were named for their grandmothers, Barbara Pierce and Jenna Welch.

Laura proved herself, according to her friends, a "fiercely devoted mother." Although she continued to read widely, sometimes took classes on such literary topics as William Faulkner and the Greek classics, and enjoyed an active social and volunteer life, she thought of her daughters as her priority. She dedicated herself to them, usually managing to be there when they returned from school even after she had duties as the wife of the governor of Texas. She described staying home with them as "a real luxury."

Throughout her marriage Laura acquired political experience and expertise. Not only did she campaign for her husband in his own bids, first for Congress and then for the governorship of Texas, but she also observed her father-in-law's races for the White House from a ringside seat. These were races in which her husband actively participated, first in 1980, when the senior Bush was elected vice president, and then in 1988, when he was elected president.

With George H. W. Bush in the White House, George W. and Laura Bush returned to Dallas, where they bought a limestone ranch-style home and enrolled their daughters first in a public and then in a private school. Laura did fund-raising and ran balls for charity, while George W. put together a group of investors to buy the Texas Rangers baseball team. According to his wife, his experience as its managing partner fulfilled his primary ambition; it also left him with a profit of several millions when he finally sold out his interest. Both of them were prominent members of the wealthy congregation of the Highland Park United Methodist Church. They were also frequent visitors in the White House and occasionally did errands for President Bush, including diplomatic missions abroad.

In 1994, George W. Bush continued his own political career by defeating the incumbent Ann Richards for the Texas governorship. By then Laura Bush was considered a political asset and a draw at fund-raisers. Even her husband's critics Molly Ivins and Lou Dubose wrote, "Bush was once asked which was the toughest decision he'd ever had to make. . . . He said it was deciding to get married. Laura Bush doesn't look like that tough a choice to us." Texans respected the work she did as wife of the governor. The annual Texas Book Festival, which she created, raised significant funds for the state library system. She personally in-

vited more than 100 Texas authors, including Larry L. King and Larry McMurtry, to participate. Her advocacy of early childhood initiatives helped to procure government funds to support preschool reading programs. She led the statewide First Lady's Family Literacy Initiative for Texas, raising nearly $1 million for community literacy projects; the Barbara Bush Foundation for Family Literacy donated funds to that program. Laura also helped to develop a parenting magazine called *Take Time for Kids* and to initiate a Texas branch of the national Reach Out and Read program, in which doctors and nurses prescribe that parents read to their small children.

Besides all these efforts to improve literacy, Laura raised private funds for breast cancer and a new art museum and lobbied for Head Start funding. She persuaded collectors of 19th- and early 20th-century art to contribute pictures to be displayed in the Austin capitol and promoted the Texas Commission on the Arts' State of the Arts license plate program to raise funds for cultural and arts organizations. She made public appearances for the Rainbow Rooms, which furnish supplies for caseworkers dealing with battered or endangered children, and served on the board of their sponsoring organization, the Community Partners. She also worked on such other boards as the University of Texas Graduate School of Library and Information Science Foundation Advisory Council and the national Reading Is Fundamental Advisory Council.

At the same time she protected her private life both among her friends and within her family. She took adventurous vacations with some of her many women friends, including birdwatching in Belize and river rafting in the Grand Canyon. On occasion she also vacationed with her mother-in-law, Barbara Bush, with whom she shares an interest in literacy and swaps books. For the most part she kept her daughters out of the public eye, letting them grow up as their own young women. She managed time alone with her husband, especially when they drank coffee and read the newspapers together in the mornings, and they shared quiet domestic weekends. Friends and family alike attributed to her a great deal of influence over him. George W. himself credited her with persuading him to stop drinking when he was 40, even though she insisted that he made the decision on his own. They sometimes teased each other publicly; he used to remark that her librarian's conception of oratory amounted to the syllable "Shhhhh!" To get even, she described him as "a gregarious businessman who thought that a bibliography was the biography—the story—of the person who wrote the Bible."

Although Laura said that "I don't give [George] a lot of advice," he reportedly asked her counsel on people and situations, and she provided him with summaries of what newspapers and magazines wrote about him. But, she said, "We don't have a lot of policy discussions where we philosophize." He has been the one to make the decisions about running for office, despite her trepidations about both his gubernatorial and presidential campaigns. "I would never say to George, for something that he really wanted to do, that he couldn't do that," she commented.

George W. Bush conducted his run for the presidency in the year 2000 with the slogan of "compassionate conservatism." In one of the closest races in the history of the nation, he won a majority in the Electoral College, although his opponent, Al Gore, won more votes from the populace. Laura Bush, by then a seasoned campaigner, participated actively in the campaign. Although she confessed to "getting butterflies" about it before the fact, she gave the kickoff speech at the 2000 Republican National Convention, presenting her husband as one who would worthily symbolize the country, "its heart and its values and its leadership in the world." By this time, although her husband continued to describe her political participation as "a huge sacrifice," she was talking about campaigning full time as "an unbelievable life experience."

During the campaign, as earlier, she kept silent on controversial topics like abortion and capital punishment, insisting that "I'm not that knowledgeable about most issues. . . . And just to put in my two cents—I don't think it's really necessary." On occasion she told reporters, "If I differ with my husband, I'm not going to tell you about it—sorry." However, she did diverge from the Republican position when she advocated national financing for the arts. After the election, she departed from her former practice by saying on the *Today* show of January 18, 2001, "I don't think that [*Roe v. Wade,* which affirms a woman's constitutional right to an abortion] should be overturned"—a remark, the *New York Times* commented, that "seemed to contradict the position of her husband, who supports a constitutional amendment to outlaw abortion except in cases of rape, incest, or danger to the life of the pregnant woman."

George W. Bush's inauguration was celebrated with eight inaugural balls and festivities that extended from January 18 until January 20, when the 43rd president took the oath of office, with his hand on the Bible used for his father's swearing-in. On January 18 Laura Bush hosted a televised salute to 18 American authors and with some of them visited public elementary schools in Washington.

Despite the closeness of the election, the future bodes well for the new first lady. She entered the White House respected for the way she kept her balance and remained herself. She has preserved her west Texas drawl and wears her auburn hair in the same "wash-and-go" bob that she has worn for years. Her clothes are designed by the American Michael Faircloth, who describes her style as "cautious and conservative." Her close friends talk about her sincerity, and the effort she puts into preserving relationships with them, and they marvel at her serenity. Jan Bullock, widow of Lieutenant-Governor Bob Bullock, says: "She's constant. She's valiant. She never craters. When I asked her if she was sleeping during the five weeks when the election was up in the air, she said, 'I sleep just fine.'" The Bush in-laws marvel at Laura's ability to calm her husband with a quietly uttered "Bushie, cool it," or "Rein it in, Bubba." Pundits believe that she softens his image and with her intelligence counters the impression that he is not very smart.

She is well-prepared for the position of first lady, having had intimate opportunities to watch her mother-in-law as the president's wife and to weigh the demands of that role. She understands that the first lady of the nation is, in her words, "one of the most visible women in the world. She is a symbol of not only our country, but also of its heart and values," representing a "beautiful land full of caring, hard-working people." Speaking of her own ascension into that role, she told reporters: "I'm reluctant. Absolutely. It's a major life change. I'm not particularly worried about safety. Privacy. I'm very worried about privacy." She cites press respect for Chelsea Clinton's privacy in expressing her hope that reporters will similarly treat the Bush daughters: Jenna, who attends the University of Texas, and Barbara, who is enrolled at Yale. In her work, Laura Bush is aided by an innovation, a first-ever official report on the history and duties of her office, to which former first ladies, public officials, and historians have contributed. (See Further Reading below).

After a quiet first month in the White House, the new first lady launched her education initiative in the library of an inner-city Washington elementary school. There she announced, "One of my goals over the next four years is to encouragee more people to become teachers. I'll do everything I can to highlight initiatives like the DC Teaching Fellows program. We need the best and the brightest in our schools." She followed up on that appearance on February 26 by talking about "The New Teacher Project," a nonprofit group consulting with school districts to create recruiting incentives for better teachers. She also announced that in October 2001 she would volunteer a week of her own time in a classroom during Teach for America Week. She is recruiting others, including her husband, to do likewise. She will also visit military bases to recruit teachers from among the armed forces.

—⁓—

Asked which previous first lady she would most resemble, Barbara Bush or Hillary Clinton, she answered, "I think I'll just be like Laura Bush." However, she has frequently expressed her admiration for her mother-in-law, answering a question about her role models: "Of course my mother-in-law and friend Barbara Bush because of her ferocious love for her children. She loved the president-elect before I did and she loves her grandchildren and I am the mother of two of them. I love her because she is so natural. She is not pretentious and I appreciate that about her." She named Lady Bird Johnson as her second model, "because of her dedication to the preservation of native plants and highway beautification."

She has announced her intention of continuing "sharing [her] love of education and reading with others." She plans to go on implementing her "lifelong commitment to helping children learn to read and succeed," to give them "a fair chance at the best possible future." She does not see lobbying for legislation as a duty of the first lady, but her Texas record as governor's wife suggests that she may make exceptions for a cause dear to her heart.

CHRONOLOGY

1946   *November 4:* Laura Welch is born in Midland, Texas

1968   Laura Welch earns a bachelor's degree in education from Southern Methodist University

1968–   Laura Welch teaches elementary school in
70   Houston

1972   Laura Welch earns a master's degree in library science from the University of Texas at Austin

| 1973– | Laura Welch works as a children's librarian in the Houston public library system | 1987 | The Bushes move to Washington, D.C., so that George W. Bush can work more effectively in his father's campaign for the presidency |
| 74 | | | |

1973–
74   Laura Welch works as a children's librarian in the Houston public library system

1974–
77   Laura Welch works as the school librarian at the mostly Hispanic Dawson Elementary School in Austin

1977   *Summer:* Friends set up a date between Laura Welch and George W. Bush

November 5: Laura Welch marries George W. Bush

1978   George W. Bush loses a race for a seat in the U.S. House of Representatives

George W. Bush's oil business fails, losing $2 million of the investors' money but leaving him with $840,000

1981   *November 25:* Twin girls Barbara Pierce and Jenna Welch are born

1987   The Bushes move to Washington, D.C., so that George W. Bush can work more effectively in his father's campaign for the presidency

1988   The Bushes buy a home in Dallas

1992   George W. Bush arranges to buy the Texas Rangers baseball team with partners

1994   George W. Bush defeats Ann Richards for the governorship of Texas

2000   *November–December:* George W. Bush is elected president of the United States in a close race against Vice President Al Gore

2001   *January 20:* Laura Welch Bush becomes first lady

February 23: Laura Bush launches an education initiative to recruit teachers

---

FURTHER READING

Bruni, Frank. "For Laura Bush, a Direction that She Never Dreamed of," *The New York Times* (July 30, 2000).

Ivins, Molly, and Lou Dubose. *Shrub: The Short But Happy Political Life of George W. Bush.* New York: Random House, 2000.

Minutaglio, Bill. *First Son: George W. Bush and the Bush Family Dynasty.* New York: Random House, 1999.

Mitchell, Elizabeth. *W: Revenge of the Bush Dynasty.* New York: Hyperion, 2000.

Romano, Lois. "Laura Bush Redefines Her Role," *Washington Post* (June 12, 2000).

Watson, Robert P., ed. *The Report to the First Lady.* Huntington, N.Y. Nova Science, 2001.

PRESIDENTIAL SPOUSES WHO DID NOT LIVE TO BE FIRST LADIES

Martha Wayles Skelton Jefferson (October 19/30, 1748–September 6, 1782)

Born the daughter of a wealthy Virginia lawyer and plantation owner, from her infancy Martha Wayles knew death intimately. Her mother died three weeks after she was born. Her father's next wife bore him four daughters before she died; his third wife died less than a year after they married, when Martha was 13. Five years later, in 1766, Martha married Bathurst Skelton, the younger brother of her second stepmother's first husband. In the two years before he died, Martha bore him a son, John, who died in early childhood.

Reportedly Martha, who sang and played the harpsichord, was a pretty woman with hazel eyes and auburn hair, a lovely figure, and graceful, regal posture. The 27-year-old Thomas Jefferson fell in love with her in 1770. On January 1, 1772, they were married at her plantation home, The Forest. On their honeymoon trip to Monticello, a hundred miles distant, they were caught in a snowstorm and had to finish the trip on horseback, arriving cold and wet, late at night, with all the fires out and all the servants in bed. Legend has it that the bridegroom found a bottle of wine hidden behind some books, which cheered the homecoming.

All during their marriage they lived in an unfinished cottage, for Thomas had already begun his efforts to build the perfect home. These were aided by the fortune his wife brought him: When her father died in 1773, he inherited 11,000 acres to add to his own 5,000 and 135 slaves to supplement his own 50 (along with a considerable burden of debt).

Among these 135 slaves were the mulatto Betty Hemings and her offspring, six of whom were Martha's half-siblings, the children of her father—including Sally Hemings, with whom Thomas consorted after Martha's death.

The Jeffersons were deeply in love. He described their years together as a time of "unchecquered happiness," their affections "unabated on both sides." His wife's dislike of his participation in politics often induced him to opt temporarily for a private life with her. They particularly enjoyed making music together, she playing the forte-piano he gave her and he the violin, with an Italian musician to instruct them. He practiced law, but he also managed to practice his music three hours a day. Slowly and inevitably, though, the revolutionary politics of the day took him away from home.

Despite the Jeffersons' joy in each other, their lives were touched with tragedy, as Martha bore in quick succession and with increasing difficulty five daughters and a son. The boy died almost at once, and only three of the girls survived their mother. With each pregnancy, Thomas became more concerned about his wife's health and felt more strongly that he should be at her side. In September 1776 he resigned his seat in the Continental Congress. For the next six years, despite his friends' reproaches, he refused to return to national politics, although he continued to serve in Virginia, both in the legislature and as governor. In late 1781, however, after writing James Monroe that "I think public service and private misery inseparably linked together," Thomas Jefferson left off these activities, at great cost to his reputation. On May 20, 1782, Martha was delivered of yet another baby, and this time she did not recover, remaining dangerously ill.

For the last four months of Martha's life, Thomas was never beyond her call, either sitting by her bedside or writing in the next room. Both husband and wife knew that she was dying. A story handed down among the house slaves alleges that in her last moments she gave him directions about things she wanted done, weeping when she spoke of their children and extracting his promise that they would never have a stepmother. She died on September 6, 1782. He mourned her throughout his life and never again married.

Rachel Donelson Robards Jackson (June 1767–December 22, 1828)

Rachel Donelson was born in June 1767 on the frontier in Pittsylvania County, Virginia, the fourth daughter and 10th of 11 children of affluent surveyor John Donelson and his wife Rachel Stockley Donelson. When she was 12—pretty, black-haired, black-eyed, sparkling, and intrepid—her father took his own and several other families to a new colony, Cumberland (later Nashville) in Tennessee, allegedly because he believed that the marriage of another of his daughters to a laborer in one of his factories had disgraced him. After an arduous four-month journey by water, during which they endured swollen rivers, short rations, Indian attacks, and smallpox, the Donelson family arrived at the new settlement, only to move again shortly thereafter to a farm near Harrodsburg, Kentucky. Worked by the Donelsons' slaves, the farm prospered, but Rachel received only a domestic education and was barely able to read and write.

In 1785 she contracted a disastrous marriage to Captain Lewis Robards, son of a prominent local family. This violent and jealous man, he came to believe that his wife was being wooed by another man and sent her back to her now-widowed mother, who was running a boardinghouse in the Nashville area. Soon re-

penting and admitting that he had been mistaken, Lewis demanded that his wife return to him, and they were briefly reconciled. Again he became jealous, this time of the young lawyer Andrew Jackson, her mother's boarder. The tempestuous Jackson is said to have aggravated the marital difficulties by telling Robards, "If I had such a wife, I would not willingly bring a tear to her beautiful eyes!" The couple again separated, Lewis going to Kentucky and Rachel going first to live with a sister and then fleeing with a trading party to Natchez, Mississippi—with Jackson riding along to help fight off Indians. Meanwhile, in December 1790 Robards presumably procured permission to divorce his wife from the state legislature. Believing that he had done so, Rachel married Andrew Jackson in August 1791; when they learned that Lewis had not actually instituted divorce proceedings until September 1793, they arranged for a second wedding ceremony on January 17, 1794.

A true frontiersman, Andrew Jackson loved horses, gambling, and fighting cocks; he made a living by practicing law and by trading in land, cattle, axes, and cowbells. In 1795 he built the Hermitage on a tract of land he owned, established a store nearby, and lived the life of a cotton planter. Rachel managed the farm, which was run on slave labor. The couple had no children of their own but filled the house with the orphaned children of friends and relatives, among them her nephew Andrew Jackson Donelson and another nephew whom they adopted as a baby and named Andrew Jackson, Jr.

Fun-loving, hospitable "Aunt Rachel," as the children called her, had a fund of good stories of her early days on the Cumberland River, including stories of Daniel Boone and encounters with Indians. She smoked a long reed pipe, which she willingly shared with guests: "Honey, won't you take a smoke?" Although she worried about the swearing and trigger temper of the husband she called "the General," or "Mr. Jackson," she adored him. In 1813 she bemoaned his desire to go to the Northwest but excused it on the grounds that it must be motivated by "the Love of Country the thirst for Honour and patriotism. . . . Shall I see you in twenty Days o God send[.] Showers on Scorching withering grass will not be more reviving."

In the War of 1812 Andrew Jackson distinguished himself by winning the battle of New Orleans. His wife joined him for the victory celebration. Creole society welcomed her, but a local hostess could not help laughing:

> After supper we were treated to a most delicious *pas de deux* by the conqueror and his spouse. To see these two figures, the General, a long, haggard man with limbs like a skeleton, and *Madame la Generale*, a short, round dumpling, bobbing opposite each other like half drunken Indians to the wild melody of 'Possum up de Gum Tree', and endeavoring to make a spring into the air, was very remarkable and far more edifying a spectacle than any European ballet could possibly have furnished.

Soon thereafter Rachel "got religion" and gave up dancing. When in 1821 she joined her husband in Florida, where he had just been appointed governor, she found it a heathen land. Her insistence on Sunday blue laws in this formerly Spanish territory contributed to the Jacksons' unpopularity. The general was frustrated by his inability to appoint his friends to office—a privilege that President James Monroe reserved for himself. Rachel observed that the power of appointment "was in part the reason of his [Jackson's] coming." Both of them were happy to return to Tennessee.

In 1824 Rachel accompanied her husband to Washington, where he served briefly as a senator. His enemies revived the old bigamy scandal, and Rachel found that many of the practices of Washington society conflicted with her fundamentalist principles. Nonetheless, she won many over with her unaffected simplicity and goodness of heart. She wrote a friend at home:

> The extravagance is in dressing and running to parties, but I must say they regard the Sabbath and attend preaching. . . . Oh my dear friend, how shall I get through this bustle.

> There are not less than from fifty to one hundred persons calling in a day. . . . Don't be afraid of my giving way to these vain things. . . . The play actors sent me a letter requesting my countenance to them. No. A ticket to balls and parties. No, not one.

At her husband's urging, however, she attended some of these "devil's doings."

After they returned to Tennessee, Rachel's health deteriorated, and she developed heart trouble. In Andrew Jackson's two presidential campaigns, his opponents viciously attacked her. He tried desperately to keep news of these assaults from her. When he was elected in 1828, she said, "Well, for Mr. Jackson's sake I am glad, for my own part I never wished it. . . . I assure you I would rather be a doorkeeper in the house of my God than to dwell in that palace in Washington." In Nashville for a new wardrobe, so the story goes, she overheard people gossiping about her, reviving the old divorce scandal and talking about the campaign attacks on her. She stayed hidden until they left, because she "supposed they did not know I heard them and would be hurt if they found out I had." Back home, she begged Emily Donelson, her nephew's wife, to take her place in Washington: "I will be no advantage to my husband in the White House and I wish never to go there and disgrace him. You will go and take care of his house for him, and I will stay here and take care of everything until he comes back."

However, on December 17, 1828, she suffered a severe heart attack; five days later she died. Her mourning family dressed her in a white satin dress that she had bought for the White House and buried her in her garden. The inscription on her headstone reads:

> Here lies the remains of Mrs. Rachel Jackson, wife of President Jackson, who died the 22nd of December, 1828, aged 61. Her face was fair, her person pleasing, her temper amiable, her heart kind; she delighted in relieving the wants of her fellow creatures, and cultivated that divine pleasure by the most liberal and unpretending methods; to the poor she was a

benefactor; to the rich an example; to the wretched a comforter; to the prosperous an ornament; her piety went hand in hand with her benevolence, and she thanked her creator for being permitted to do good. A being so gentle and so virtuous, slander might wound but could not dishonor. Even death, when he tore her from the arms of her husband, could but transport her to the bosom of God.

Hannah Hoes Van Buren
(March 8, 1783–February 5, 1819)

Hannah Hoes, of Dutch descent, was born in Kinderhook, New York, on March 8, 1783, to John Dircksen Hoes and his wife Maria Quackenboss Hoes. In this farming community she grew up speaking both Dutch and English and attending the Dutch Reformed Church. She knew Martin Van Buren, who was her first cousin once removed, from childhood; later her brother married one of Martin's sisters.

Hannah and Martin were married on February 21, 1807, at the house of her brother-in-law. Hannah bore their first child, Abraham, in Kinderhook on November 27, 1807. Abraham later graduated from West Point, and his wife, the former Angelica Singleton of South Carolina, served as White House hostess for her father-in-law from 1837 to 1841. The Van Burens' second and third sons were born in Hudson in 1810 and 1812, respectively. Hannah may also have borne a fourth child, who died shortly after birth.

The scanty records on Hannah Van Buren describe her as small, attractive, amiable, sweet-tempered, gentle, shy, and unassuming. As her husband's political career flourished, she withdrew. She suffered from ill health, probably aggravated by tuberculosis. The birth of her last son, Smith Thompson in 1818, worsened her condition. She died in Albany, where the family was then living, on February 5, 1819. She was first buried there, but her body was later moved and interred next to her husband's at Kinderhook.

Ellen Lewis Herndon Arthur
(August 30, 1837–January 12, 1880)

A seventh-generation Virginian from a prominent slaveholding family, Ellen Lewis Herndon was born on August 30, 1837, in Culpepper, Virginia, the only child of explorer and naval officer William Lewis Herndon and his wife, Frances Elizabeth Herndon. Her father died when she was 20, upon which Ellen moved to New York City, where she met the young lawyer Chester A. Arthur. After a long engagement, they were married on October 25, 1859. They subsequently had three children, two of whom survived into adulthood.

During the Civil War, Ellen Arthur's sympathies were with her southern homeland, even though her husband was an officer in the Union army. After the war the Arthurs lived the life of fashionable New Yorkers, as Chester's practice prospered, and Ellen socialized with the wealthy and worked for prestigious charities. A singer known as the "Virginia nightingale," she frequently gave private concerts, often in church and at charitable benefits, and soloed with the Mendelssohn Glee Club, in which her husband also sang.

Doubts have been cast on the happiness of the marriage. Chester Arthur's suspension in 1878 from the office of Collector of the Port of New York during President Rutherford B. Hayes's civil service reform embarrassed her. Her dislike for politics deepened as he grew more absorbed in cultivating Republican connections. Ellen Arthur died from pneumonia in 1880, the year that Chester was elected vice president; according to some reports, just before her death she was planning to file for separation. When Chester was catapulted into the presidency by the assassination of James A. Garfield, his sister Mary Arthur McElroy acted as his official hostess and directed his daughter's education. He gave a memorial window to his wife's memory in a church visible from the White House.

Alice Hathaway Lee Roosevelt (July 29, 1861–February 14, 1884)

The daughter of an old and prominent Boston family, Alice Hathaway Lee was born on July 29, 1861, in Chestnut Hill, Massachusetts, the second of six children of banker George Cabot Lee and his wife Caroline Watts Haskell Lee. Alice was educated fashionably and conventionally. When she was 17, a slender, blue-eyed, curly-haired blonde, she met an exuberant Harvard student named Theodore Roosevelt, who courted her ardently.

They were married on October 27, 1880. For three years they lived happily together, most of the time in the home of Theodore's mother. He began to serve in the New York legislature, and Alice occupied herself by helping her mother-in-law in her charitable activities. In February 1884 she gave birth to her only child, Alice, who grew up to be the famously self-willed and sharp-tongued Alice Roosevelt Longworth, a doyenne of Washington society. Two days later, weakened by childbirth and afflicted with Bright's disease, Alice Hathaway Lee Roosevelt died on February 14, 1884, only hours after the death of her mother-in-law from typhoid fever.

Stricken, Theodore Roosevelt wrote that when Alice died "the light went from my life for ever." Later he added,

> I saw her first on Oct—1878; I wooed her for over a year before I won her; we were betrothed on Jan 25th 1880, and it was announced on Feb 16th; on Oct 27th of the same year we were married; we spent three years of happiness greater and more unalloyed than I have ever known fall to the lot of others; on Feb 12th 1884 her baby was born and on Feb 14th she died in my arms. . . . [M]y mother had died in the same house, on the same day, but a few hours previously. On Feb 16th they were buried together in Greenwood [cemetery in Brooklyn, New York]. . . . For joy or for sorrow my life has now been lived out.

He never again uttered Alice's name.

WHITE HOUSE HOSTESSES

The one American bachelor president and the several widowers who held the office turned to female relatives and to the wives of high-ranking officials to act as White House hostesses. Other presidents have acted similarly when their wives were incapacitated by illness, mourning, or refusing to act. Some scholars call these substitutes "surrogate first ladies," but only rarely did they perform any of the presidential spouse's duties other than acting as hostess (although Betty Taylor Bliss, daughter of Zachary and Margaret Taylor, handled her mother's mail and ran the household). Many other female presidential relatives beyond those listed here helped out from time to time with hostessing, including the daughter and daughter-in-law of Benjamin and Caroline Harrison and Anna Roosevelt Boettiger, daughter of Franklin Delano and Eleanor Roosevelt.

For Thomas Jefferson, widower, 1801–9:

Usually **Dolley Madison,** or sometimes her sister **Anna Payne.**

Occasionally **Martha Jefferson Randolph** (1772–1836), daughter, and **Mary (aka Maria) Jefferson Eppes** (ca. 1779–April 17, 1804), daughter. Both were married to congressmen and, like other congressional wives, usually stayed at home. Both were terrified when they finally accepted one of their father's many invitations to stay with him and act as his hostesses. They immediately sent off a plea for help to Dolley Madison, asking her to buy them appropriate wigs and clothes. Martha Randolph, educated at a Philadelphia boarding school and in France, as well as by private tutors, was reputedly a charming and gracious woman, capable of amusing anecdotal conversation, though she had no interest in public affairs. The beautiful Mary Eppes, convent-educated in France, was a timid woman who clung to home and relatives. (She died at 25, in 1804, while her father was still president.) Their responsibilities to their husbands and children—Martha Randolph's five and Mary Eppes's three—limited their service in the White House to a couple of winter social seasons. Nevertheless, under the guidance of Dolley Madison, who mothered them and their children, both daughters did well in Washington during those two seasons. Their contemporary Margaret Smith wrote: "Mrs. Eppes is beautiful, simplicity and timidity personified when in company, but when alone with you of communicative and winning manners. Mrs. R[andolph] . . . is really one of the most lovely women I have ever met with, her countenance beaming with intelligence, benevolence and sensibility, and her conversation fulfills all her countenance promises. Her manners, so frank and affectionate, that you know her at once, and feel perfectly at your ease with her."

For Andrew Jackson, widower, 1829–37:

Emily Donelson (Mrs. Andrew Jackson Donelson) (1808–36), wife of Rachel Jackson's nephew, who acted as Jackson's secretary. Jackson's deceased wife, Rachel Jackson, had loved Emily Donelson dearly, and the president always called her "my daughter." On his election he invited her to officiate as mistress of ceremonies at the executive mansion; he appointed his daughter-in-law Sarah Yorke Jackson as mistress of his Tennessee estate, The Hermitage. Emily Donelson had been educated, briefly, at rhe Old Academy in Nashville, Tennessee, and brought up in a rural environment that had given her little experience in either politics or social life. Nonetheless, the president deferred to her on all matters of etiquette and sought relaxation in her family circle.

Emily bore four children while living in the White House. She was diminutive and attempted to add to her height, John Tyler wrote, by wearing "three waving ostrich feathers" in her bonnet. Her contemporary, Cora Livingston, described Emily as youthful in appearance, "a beautiful, accomplished and charming woman, with wonderful tact and delightfully magnetic manners." Although her lack of social polish caused occasional comment, her simple, kindly ways made her well-liked, and appreciation was often expressed for the good food and drink she served. Emily was also quick at repartee. When a foreign minister said, "Madam, you dance with the grace of a Parisian. I can hardly realize you were educated in Tennessee," she said, "Count, you forget that grace is a cosmopolite, and like a wildflower, is much oftener found in the woods than in the streets of a city."

The Peggy Eaton incident (see the biography of Sarah Polk) would have tried the powers of the most sophisticated hostess, and it caused difficulty between Emily and President Jackson. John Quincy Adams wrote that in March 1830 the president forced Emily "to visit Mrs. Eaton and to invite her to the christening of her child." Emily then told him that if she were to be obliged to visit Eaton, she would go back to Tennessee. She and her husband carried out her threat, not returning to the White House until 1831, after Eaton's husband had resigned his position as secretary of war. In 1836, her health failing, Emily went home to Tennessee for a rest and died there of consumption.

Sarah Yorke Jackson (Mrs. Andrew Jackson, Jr.) (1805–87), the president's daughter-in-law. Reputedly the most beautiful of three orphaned daughters of a wealthy family, Sarah married Andrew and Rachel Jackson's adopted son An-

drew in 1831. When Emily Donelson died, Sarah took over her duties as White House hostess. At the end of President Jackson's tenure in the White House, she assumed responsibility for running the household at his home, The Hermitage, where all of her children were born.

For Martin Van Buren, widower, 1837–41:

Angelica Singleton Van Buren (Mrs. Abraham Van Buren) (1816–78), daughter-in-law. The matchmaking Dolley Madison, thinking that the White House needed a hostess, introduced the president's son Abraham to Angelica Singleton of South Carolina; they were married in November 1838. Although only 22 when she undertook her duties as White House hostess, this beautiful, graceful woman achieved immediate success and popularity. The *Boston Post* said of her at the 1839 New Year's reception: "She is represented as being of rare accomplishments, very modest, yet perfectly easy and graceful in her manners, and free and vivacious in her conversation. She was universally admired and is said to have borne the fatigue of a three hours' levee with a patience and pleasantry which must be inexhaustible to last one through so severe a trial." However, like all first ladies and White House hostesses, she could not avoid criticism. Detractors of the time said that a Grecian entertainment she put on smacked of royalty, and some historians believe that her refurnishing of the White House and the formality and lack of hard cider at her weekly receptions all contributed to Martin Van Buren's loss in the 1840 presidential election.

For William Henry Harrison, whose wife never reached the White House during his month-long tenure, 1841:

Jane Irwin Harrison (Mrs. William Henry Harrison, Jr.) (dates unknown), the president's widowed daughter-in-law, assisted by her adoptive mother, **Jane Findlay,** and other relatives. She was reportedly possessed of education, refinement, and two sons.

For John Tyler,
husband of an invalid wife and widower for a time after his first wife, Letitia, died in the White House, 1841–45:

Priscilla Cooper Tyler (Mrs. Robert) (June 14, 1816–December 29, 1889) daughter-in-law. Priscilla Cooper was the daughter of a prominent tragedian, with whom she acted from 1835 to 1838 in an effort to salvage his floundering career. On September 12, 1839, she married young lawyer Robert Tyler, eldest son of Senator John Tyler. She campaigned for her father-in-law in 1840 and was thrilled when he won the vice presidency of the United States. Following the unanticipated death of William Henry Harrison, Letitia Tyler, who had shortly before suffered a stroke, asked her daughter-in-law to serve as White House hostess in her stead. It was an admirable choice: her experience as an actress served Priscilla well in this new role, for which she wisely sought the advice of Dolley Madison and Secretary of State Daniel Webster. The counsel she received was not always what she wanted to hear, but she heeded it: "The greatest trouble I anticipate," she wrote, "is paying visits. There was a doubt at first whether I must visit in person or send cards; but I asked Mrs. Madison's advice upon the subject, and she says, return all my visits by all means. . . . So three days in the week I am to spend three hours a day driving from one street to another in this city of magnificent distances." She also heeded her father-in-law, who warned all his family, "You are now occupying a position of deep importance. I desire you to bear in mind three things: Show no favoritism, accept no gifts, receive no seekers after office."

While Congress was in session, Priscilla gave two dinner parties each week, a small one of about 20 for visitors to the capital, and a larger one of about 40 for high-ranking members of the government, the military, and the diplomatic corps. For a time she opened the public rooms every evening during the legislative session until 10:00 P.M., but beginning in early 1842 she limited these informal receptions to two a week. She also gave small private balls, and each month she held a public levee for up to 1,000 guests. In the summer the Marine Band gave a concert on the south lawn once a month. Priscilla also continued the special receptions on New Year's Day and the Fourth of July initiated by the Washingtons. She wrote her sister:

> Here am I . . . actually living, and—what is more—presiding at the White House! I look at myself like a little old woman, and exclaim: Can this be I? I have not had one moment to myself since my arrival, and the most extraordinary thing is that I feel as if I had been used to living here always; and receive the Cabinet, ministers, the diplomatic corps, the heads of the army and navy, etc. etc., with a facility which astonishes me. "Some achieve greatness—some are born to it." I am plainly born to it. I really do possess a degree of modest assurance that surprises me more than it does anyone else. I am complimented on every side; my hidden virtues are coming out. I am considered "charmante" by the Frenchmen, "lovely" by the Americans, and "really quite nice, you know" by the English.

So it went until March 1844. After Letitia Tyler's death, the widower president began courting Julia Gardiner. Priscilla encouraged the love affair and wrote a warm note to Julia praising the president's constant kindness and affection to his family. Priscilla and Robert Tyler then discreetly moved from the White House to Philadelphia, where he resumed practicing law. He fought for the Confederacy in the Civil War, after which the couple settled in Montgomery, Alabama, where he edited a newspaper. Charles Dickens praised Priscilla Cooper Tyler as "a very interesting, graceful and accomplished lady," but the French minister thought her "too sweet to be interesting."

Letitia Tyler Semple (1821–1907), daughter. Letitia Semple served as White House hostess in the interim after the Robert Tylers left the White House until the president remarried. Herself married at 18, Letitia was just 21 when she began her short tenure as hostess while her husband was absent on a naval cruise. After the Civil War, widowed, penniless, and with three nephews and nieces to provide for, Letitia Semple opened the "Eclectic Institute" in Baltimore.

For Zachary Taylor,
husband of an ailing wife, 1849–50:

Mary Elizabeth (Betty) Taylor Bliss (1824–1909), daughter. The Taylors' fifth daughter, Betty, closely resembled her father in appearance. She was reputed to have beauty, good sense, and quiet humor. After being educated at a Philadelphia boarding school, in spring 1840 she toured the East as far south as Kentucky with her parents, and then settled down with them in their small cottage at Baton Rouge. With her mother and sisters Betty participated in the 1847 celebration in New Orleans of her father's victory in the war with Mexico. In December 1848, soon after Zachary Taylor's election to the presidency, she married his aide, Colonel William W. S. Bliss. The young couple moved with her parents into the White House in 1849. At the request of her reclusive mother, Betty assumed many duties as hostess and performed them to general praise, whether at formal dinners or at dances for young people. A guest described Betty Bliss as presiding "with the artlessness of a rustic belle and the grace of a duchess."

When Zachary Taylor died unexpectedly, Betty shared her mother's shock. Immediately after the funeral, which neither mother nor daughters could attend, they moved out of the White House. Margaret Taylor lived with the Bliss family in Mississippi for the rest of her days.

For Millard Fillmore,
husband of a semi-invalid wife, 1850–53:

Mary Abigail (Abby) Fillmore (1832–54), daughter. Frequently separated from her devoted parents because of her father's political career, Abby Fillmore received regular letters from her mother urging self-improvement, correcting her spelling or praising her for good writing, and instructing her not to pay too much attention to clothes and not to waste time. Abby attended boarding school in Lenox, Massachusetts. When she entered the White House at 18, she already spoke five languages. Young as she was, the vivacious girl took over some social duties, while the first lady did what her health permitted. The Fillmores were a close-knit family, and Abby and her mother often made music together, she at the harp and Abigail Fillmore at the piano. With her father and brother, Abby sat by her mother's side as she lay dying in the spring of 1853, just after the Fillmores left the White House. Abby herself died of cholera in July 1854.

For Franklin Pierce,
husband of a melancholic wife, 1853–57:

Mrs. Abby Kent Means (unknown–1857) of Amherst, Massachusetts, aunt of first lady Jane Pierce. Hard though she tried, Abby Means was handicapped in entertaining by the gloom that hung over a White House in mourning for the Pierces' sons. Nonetheless, with the sympathic help of Abby Means and Varina Davis, the first lady gradually assumed some of her duties.

Varina Davis (Mrs. Jefferson Davis) (May 7, 1826–October 16, 1906), wife of President Pierce's secretary of war, later president of the Confederacy. Jane Pierce was grateful for the strong emotional support that Varina gave her and for Varina's assumption of the social leadership of Washington in her stead.

For James Buchanan, bachelor, 1857–61:

Harriet "Hal" Lane (1831–1903), niece. A lively youngster, orphaned in her girlhood, Harriet Lane requested that her favorite uncle, James Buchanan, be named her guardian. She was educated in part at the Visitation Convent in Georgetown. During her uncle's service as secretary of state and later as ambassador to Great Britain, he often took her to official social functions; Queen Victoria ordered that Hal be treated as of the same rank as a U.S. minister. When Buchanan received an honorary degree at Oxford, the students rose en masse to cheer his niece.

At 26 Hal gracefully assumed the duties of White House hostess, a post in which she achieved renown for her blond, violet-eyed beauty, her love of fun, and her social brilliance. Undaunted by the prospect of entertaining even the Prince of Wales, she sparkled through social seasons that dazzled Washingtonians. Despite her own strong loyalty to the Union and the pre–Civil War tensions of her uncle's presidency, which demanded much tact to keep political enemies apart and to avoid controversy at social affairs, Hal enjoyed wide popularity, earning the nickname of "the Democratic Queen." She advocated Indian rights and education.

Though she was wooed by many beaux, it was not until 1866, when she was 35, that she married banker Henry Elliott Johnson, with whom she had five sons, two of whom predeceased her. At Wheatlands, the estate that she inherited from President Buchanan after his death in 1868, she carefully arranged his papers to provide history with an accurate record of his career.

Widowed in 1884, Hal returned to Washington, D.C., where she devoted herself to public service. "She is the most regal of American women," wrote an early biographer. "[H]er presence at the most important and most formal State dinners at the White House is as much a matter of course as is that of the wife of the Vice-President. She has a large house in Washington, and entertains frequently in the season. She has a fine, erect figure, with a haughtily poised head crowned with white hair. For great occasions her toilet is always the same; black velvet and point lace, and her jewels are always pearls and diamonds." In her will, Hal donated her important art collection to the Smithsonian and left money to the Johns Hopkins hospital for a home for invalid children.

For Andrew Johnson, husband of an invalid wife, 1865–69:

Martha Johnson Patterson (October 5, 1828–July 10, 1901), daughter, wife of Judge David T. Patterson, assisted by her widowed sister Mary Johnson Stover (May 8, 1832–April 19, 1883), whose husband had died for the Union. Martha Patterson was much like her father in her ability to reason, her iron will, her love of truth and justice, and her high regard for principle. She was fond of society, well-organized, and efficient in overseeing a $30,000 renovation of the White House. Her charm, tact, and diplomacy kept political frictions out of the drawing room. Martha bought two Jersey cows that grazed on White House ground. She milked them daily and took pride in producing all the butter used in the White House in her dairy, where she introduced the newest equipment. Legend says that President Johnson defeated her efforts to fight rats in the basement kitchen and storerooms by feeding the mice that infested the upstairs with flour and water.

In addition to her duties as housekeeper and hostess, Martha also took care of her mother's correspondence and received petitioners. This "plain woman from Tennessee" was much admired for her lack of pretension and the quaint, friendly tone she established in the White House. William Crook, who served in the White House for five administrations, wrote:

Mrs. Patterson was the real mistress of the establishment. No woman could have acted with greater sense or discretion. She had passed her girlhood days in Washington, had been educated at a school in Georgetown [Mrs. English's Seminary for Young Ladies], and during the Polk administration had been a frequent guest at the White House. . . . She made no pretences of any sort, but was always honest and direct. . . . It is true that the Johnsons did not pretend to be leaders in the social life of Washington, and in their regime there was no joyousness, no special grace, in the White House festivities; there was, however, exactness in the discharge of social duties, and a homely dignity, equally free from ostentation and undue humility. The dinners and public receptions were more numerous than under Johnson's successors, and they were not lacking in brilliancy.

Ulysses S. Grant's widow, Julia Grant, wrote in her memoirs: "Mrs. Patterson was a gentle, charming woman, as was also her sister, Mrs. Stover."

For Chester Arthur, widower, 1881–85:

Mary Arthur McElroy (1842–1917), widowed sister, whose spouse had been a clergyman. An accomplished woman, Mary McElroy had been educated at Mrs. Willard's Female Seminary in Troy, New York. She took over the household when Chester Arthur's wife died; his teenage son, Chester Allan Arthur, was sent away to school, but Mary took care of his eight-year-old girl, Nellie, along with her own two daughters. She was noted for her graciousness in asking many Washington ladies to assist her; at some receptions she had as many as 40 ladies in the receiving line.

The first formal White House function Mary oversaw, the New Year's reception of 1882, was attended by Dr. Mary E. Walker, the first woman commissioned an assistant army surgeon and the first woman to receive the Congressional Medal of Honor. Mary McElroy

did not pay calls, but she did dine out at the homes of intimate friends. An expert hostess, she gave formal dinners that were achievements in gastronomic art and elegant service. She welcomed Nellie Arthur's young friends; had her own afternoons at home, for which the Marine Band played; and gave more private entertainments than had been usual at the White House, for President Arthur had become accustomed to a busy social life in New York City. "If her mannerisms were those of a teacher and independent woman," wrote Senate wife Mrs. John A. Logan, "she was nevertheless cordial, easy, and agreeable. Intellectual people found her attractive, and she was well versed on important questions of the day. . . . As much as she appreciated the dignity of her position, and her brother's advancement to the highest honor in the people's gift, she was too independent to cater to the whims of the frivolous or yield to all the senseless and insatiable demands made upon the lady of the White House."

Known as the "Mistress of the White House," Mary also took charge of the president's summer residence at the Soldiers' Home in Washington, D.C. When she left the White House, wrote William Crook, "The young girls to whom she had been such a fairy godmother of good times escorted her to her train in a delegation and filled the cars with flowers."

For Grover Cleveland, during the part of his term that he was a bachelor, 1885–89:

Rose Elizabeth Cleveland (1846–1918), the President's younger unmarried sister. Rose Cleveland had been liberally educated at her brother's expense. A contemporary columnist described her as "a woman of medium size, with square shoulders and a short neck," with a sallow complexion, "intellectual features," a high forehead, and brown curly hair, who dressed plainly with few ornaments, and who had lectured in public. She graciously sacrificed her own interests to act as hostess, but she was always eager to return to her career as teacher and author. She was therefore delighted at the prospect of her brother's marrying Frances Folsom.

While in the White House, Rose completed her book *George Eliot's Poetry and Other Studies,* which sold through 12 editions, bringing her royalties of $25,000. Her personal integrity softened the public reaction to the discovery that the president might have fathered an illegitimate child. Some of the president's male friends suspected the advocate of temperance of also being "a sharp-tongued young lady with a predisposition to Woman's Rights."

For Benjamin Harrison, husband of an invalid wife, 1889–93:

Mary Harrison McKee (Mrs. James Robert McKee) (1858–1942), daughter. When Benjamin and Caroline Harrison moved into the White House, they took their extended family with them: their son Russell and his wife and daughter; and Mary McKee, her husband, and their two-year-old son and baby daughter. The "Baby McKees" attracted much attention from the press and public. Mary helped her mother with her correspondence, and she and her sister-in-law, **Mrs. Russell Harrison,** helped the first lady in an extensive overhaul of the executive mansion and as hostesses. Mary took over for her invalid mother (who died in the White House) toward the end of her father's term.

For Woodrow Wilson, during the part of his presidency that he was a widower, 1913–21:

Margaret Wilson (1886–1944), oldest daughter. Margaret Wilson suffered from feelings of inadequacy, and a nervous breakdown necessitated her departure from her studies at the Women's College of Baltimore. After she recovered, she took voice lessons in New York. Unlike her two sisters, Margaret never married, but she enjoyed some success as a concert singer. She was generous in contributing her professional services and money to charitable and patriotic causes. In the White House the Wilsons maintained a close-knit and loving family life, in which they included Ellen Wilson's secretaries, Helen Bones and Belle Hagner. The three Wilson daughters enjoyed not only the family amusements of music, art, literature, theater, and billiards, but also parties and dancing. One White House guest described Margaret as "blonde and chill, but refined and intelligent looking." After her mother's death in 1914, she acted as White House hostess. She and Helen Bones (see below) joined in trying to comfort the inconsolable Woodrow Wilson, whom they both idolized. They therefore welcomed Edith Galt, who became his second wife.

Helen Woodrow Bones, cousin. While Ellen Wilson was first lady (1913–1914), Helen Bones, devoted to both Ellen and Woodrow, served as her personal secretary. In that capacity, she helped the first lady not only with her correspondence and accounts but also with love and support. After Ellen's death, Helen continued to live in the White House, serving briefly as hostess. She introduced Woodrow Wilson and Edith Galt, who later married.

Appendix C
First Lady Firsts

Martha Washington (1789–97)

The first first lady

The first woman to appear on U.S. currency (on $1 bills issued in 1889)

Abigail Adams (1797–1801)

The first to live in the White House

The first to have been wife to one president and mother to another

Dolley Madison (1809–17)

The first to preside over an inaugural ball

The only first lady to take snuff in public

The only first lady to be assigned a reserved seat of honor in the U.S. House of Representatives

Louisa Adams (1825–29)

The only first lady born outside the United States

Anna Harrison (1841)

The first to have the equivalent of a modern high school education

The first to be wife of one president and grandmother of another

With the possible exception of Dolley Madison, the first widow of a president to receive a pension; Congress sent her the salary William Henry Harrison would have earned in his first year in office had he lived

The first to become widowed while her husband was in office

At 65, the oldest woman to become first lady

Letitia Tyler (1841–42)

The first to die in the White House

Julia Gardiner Tyler (1844–45)

The first to introduce "Hail to the Chief"

The youngest first lady

The first to employ a press agent

The first to marry a president during his term in office

The first to be born during the 19th century

Sarah Polk (1845–49)

The only first lady to serve as her husband's private secretary in the White House

Abigail Fillmore (1850–53)

The first to hold a job outside of the home after marriage

The founder of the White House library

The first to attend the inauguration of her husband's successor

Eliza Johnson (1865–69)

The first to keep cows on the White House lawn

Julia Dent Grant (1869–77)

The first to employ a housekeeper in the White House

Lucy Hayes (1877–81)

The first to be called "first lady"; however, the title did not become popular until the play *First Lady* by Charles Nirdlinger was produced in 1911

The first to earn a college degree

Lucretia Garfield (1881)

The first to campaign publicly

The first to have her picture on a campaign poster

Frances Cleveland (1886–89, 1893–97)

The first married in the White House

The first (and thus far only) to serve two nonconsecutive terms as first lady

The first to have a baby during her husband's presidential term

The first to have a secretary who was not a family member

Ida McKinley (1897–1901)

The first to be the subject of a campaign biography

Edith Kermit Roosevelt (1901–9)

The first to employ a social secretary

The first to travel outside the United States during her husband's term in office

Helen Taft (1909–13)

The first to publish her autobiography

The only first lady to be the wife of both the president and the chief justice

The first to be buried in Arlington cemetery

The first to furnish a White House bedroom with twin beds

Ellen Wilson (1913–14)

The first to take on a serious special project

Edith Wilson (1915–21)

The first to have Secret Service agents authorized for her protection

Florence Harding (1921–23)

The first to vote for her husband for president

The first to be guarded regularly by the Secret Service; she co-opted one of the men assigned to Warren G. Harding, Harry Barker not only protected her but became her trusted friend and helper, factotum, and escort

The first to admit to being a woman suffragist

The first to hold press conferences for women reporters

The first to have been divorced

Grace Coolidge (1923–29)

The first to graduate from a coeducational university (the University of Vermont)

The first to receive an honorary academic degree (an LL.D. from Boston University)

The first incumbent first lady to vote

The first to smoke cigarettes

Lou Hoover (1921–33)

The first to deliver a radio address

The first with an earned graduate degree (in geology from Stanford University)

Eleanor Roosevelt (1933–45)

The first to attend a congressional hearing

The only former first lady to serve as U.S. delegate to the United Nations

The first to have a commercial radio contract

Bess Truman (1945–53)

The first to reach 97 years of age

The first to install air conditioning in the White House

Jacqueline Kennedy (1961–63)

The first to be born in the 20th century

The only first lady to receive an Emmy award (for her guided tour of the White House)

The first widowed first lady to attend the swearing-in of her husband's successor

Lady Bird Johnson (1963–69)

The first to hold the family Bible while her husband took the inaugural oath

The only first lady to own a radio station

Pat Nixon (1969–74)

The first to represent the United States at the inauguration of a foreign leader

The first to have appeared in movies before she was first lady

Betty Ford (1974–77)

The only first lady to have been a fashion model or a dance instructor

The first to admit that she is a recovering alcoholic

Rosalynn Carter (1977–81)

The first to attend cabinet meetings regularly

Nancy Reagan (1981–89)

The only first lady to have appeared in 10 motion pictures

The first to cohost a morning television show

Hillary Rodham Clinton (1993–2001)

The first to have practiced law

The first to be questioned formally by a special counsel

The first entrusted with the writing of a major legislative proposal

The first to win elective office while a first lady

Laura Welch Bush (2001–)

The first to have earned her living as a school librarian.

First Ladies' Reflections on the Position and on Other First Ladies

Martha Washington

Her years as the presidential spouse, she said, were "lost years."

She found it ironic that she, who "had much rather be at home, should occupy a place with which a great many younger and gayer women would be extremely pleased."

Louisa Adams

To John Adams, her father-in-law: "The woman selected for your wife [Abigail Adams] was so highly gifted in mind, with powers so vast, and such quick and clear perception, altogether so superior to the general run of females, you have perhaps formed a too-enlarged opinion of the capacities of our sex, and having never witnessed their frailties, are not aware of the dangers to which they are exposed, by acquirements above their strength."

Julia Gardiner Tyler

"I don't see or hear that Mrs. Polk is making any sensation in Washington."

Mary Todd Lincoln

Allegedly, to Julia Dent Grant: "I suppose you think you'll get to the White House yourself, don't you?" When Julia Grant replied that she was quite satisfied with her present position, which was more than she had ever expected, Mary Todd Lincoln riposted: "Oh! you had better take it if you can get it. 'Tis very nice."

Julia Dent Grant

In later years, urging that the demands of Washington social life be lessened: "Have no entertainment, dance, dinner, or reception which will extend later than midnight."

Lucretia Garfield

"If the General is elected it will mean four years of almost killing work."

Frances Folsom Cleveland

"I am not saddened by the thought of leaving the White House. One thing, though, would make me very sad—if any change should be made in this beautiful house. It is to me the most beautiful house in the world. . . . It is not only the beauty of the old house that I love, but I have a feel of reverence for its past. . . . Sometimes, when I am alone, and walk through the rooms, and think of the men who have been President and of their wives, the grand old house gives me a feeling of awe."

Edith Roosevelt

"Franklin [Roosevelt] is nine-tenths mush and one-tenth Eleanor."

Ellen Wilson

On her husband's election: "I must make believe very hard now that I am a different kind of woman,—in *some* respects,—not *all*, thank Heaven."

"A person would be a fool who let his head be turned by externals. They simply go with the position."

Edith Wilson

About Jacqueline Kennedy: "I think Mrs. Kennedy will be a great asset to her husband—as she is cultivated and charming."

Florence Harding

Blocking a Congressional bill to buy a residence as a permanent home for the vice president: "I just couldn't have people like those Coolidges living in that beautiful house."

To Mrs. Coolidge, introducing housekeeper Elizabeth Jaffray: "I hope Mrs. Jaffray will like you."

Lou Hoover

When the head cook confessed that she had voted for Alfred Smith and expected to lose her job, Lou Hoover replied, "I am not concerned with your political preferences but with your superlative cooking."

Eleanor Roosevelt

Asked what it was like to be the wife of a public official for more than 30 years: "It's hell."

"People can gradually be brought to understand that an individual, even if she is a President's wife, may have independent views and must be allowed the expression of an opinion. But actual participation in the work of the government we are not yet able to accept."

On Jacqueline Kennedy: "I think back to the days of my husband's Presidency and realize that the problems of that time—first of the depression and then of the war—required a background and understanding of social justice and social needs. That is still needed by the woman in the White House, but much more is required.

"Both the President and his wife can never give way to apprehension even though they are probably more aware than most citizens of the dangers which may surround us. If the country is to be confident, they must be confident. They cannot afford to harbor resentment, or to have enemies where it is possible to turn these enemies into friends. This demands from both the President and his wife a high order of intelligence, of self-discipline and a dedication to the public good. We are extremely fortunate to find these qualifications in the White House at the present time."

To Jacqueline Kennedy: "I know there will be difficulties in store for you in the White House life but perhaps also you will find some compensations. Most things are made easier, though I think on the whole life is rather difficult for both the children and their parents in the 'fish bowl' that lies before you."

Bess Truman

A first lady most needs "good health and a sense of humor."

About Jacqueline Kennedy: "She will find it not too difficult. I think she will be a perfect first lady. Her age is a tremendous asset. . . ."

Mamie Eisenhower

About Jacqueline Kennedy: "Well, she's awfully young. . . . She's planning to redo every room in this house! There certainly are going to be some changes made around here!"

In a note to Pat Nixon, on the eve of President Nixon's resignation: "I only want to say I'm thinking of you today—always you will have my warm affection as will your husband President Nixon."

To Rosalynn Carter: "I stayed busy all the time and loved being in the White House, but I was never expected to do all the things you have to do."

Jacqueline Kennedy

To reporters: "I think the major role of the President's wife is to take care of the President and his children."

"Look, it's a trade-off. There are positives and negatives to every situation in life. You endure the bad things, but you enjoy the good. And what incredible opportunities—the historic figures you meet and come to know, the witness to history you become, the places you would never have been able to see that now you can."

Remarking on her "affinity" for Bess Truman more than any other first lady: "She brought a daughter to the White House at a most difficult age and managed to keep her from being spoiled."

In the White House, at first "I felt like a moth banging on the windowpane."

The title "first lady" sounds "more like a name for a race horse than a title for a person."

In a note she left with a bouquet for Lady Bird Johnson: "I wish you a happy arrival in your new house, Lady Bird. Remember—you will be happy here."

About Hillary Rodham Clinton: "America is getting a bargain with her. She's worth two Helen of Troys."

Lady Bird Johnson

As the wife of the vice president, to Jackie Kennedy: "I do want to express my admiration for all the ways you found to help your husband in that great endeavor of his life. You looked perfectly lovely on television. . . . I have thought many times of your own concern that your condition prevented active participation in the campaign. But, my dear, I want you to

know that for an 'inactive' campaigner, you certainly made a great contribution. . . . It is going to be very nice to have you as First Lady."

After the assassination of John F. Kennedy: "I feel like I am suddenly on stage for a part I never rehearsed."

"One of the things about the White House is that you know from the moment you walk in there that this has a time limitation. . . . And that's one reason why you do as much as you can do, because you know that this will never happen again, and you can drum up the energy from somewhere within you to go more, do more, learn more, for this limited time."

"Life is richer and fuller because I tried harder and did things I never thought I could do and was scared to do. I'm glad for all the things I did and only regret some I did not do."

Replying to an Arab diplomat protesting her support of an Israel Independence Ball: "The easiest course for the wife of a public official would be, of course, never to lend name, head or heart to any endeavor, charitable or commemorative. Alas, letters such as yours make this procedure even more tempting. However, I have, for whatever small value it may be, tried to be accessible and available to as many as possible without distinction as to religion, race or region, and certainly including all states of the Near East. I shall continue to do so."

Pat Nixon

Asked in 1970 whether the wives of public figures should express their own opinions, she responded, "It's a decision they have to make. They should know the facts before they speak out."

Arguing that wives should campaign: "Unless you are willing to work for good government, then you won't have it."

To Betty Ford, as the Nixons left the White House: "Well, Betty, you'll see many of these red carpets, and you'll get so you'll hate 'em."

Betty Ford

"I've been accused of trying to take the play away from [Nancy Reagan]. What play? My feeling was that Nancy didn't want to play. She sat in a glassed-in box, separated from the hurly-burly, throughout the whole convention, except for the time she went upstairs to the television booth to be interviewed. I sat right in the front row of the gallery. 'If they want me, they can come down here,' I said."

"At one time during my husband's administration I made the smart-aleck remark that a First Lady ought to be paid, she had a full-time job, and I'm not sure I wasn't right."

"I believe all citizens—and that includes females—should give two years of service to their country."

"I wanted to be a good First Lady, I was perfectly willing to be educated about the duties of a First Lady, but I didn't believe I had to do every single thing some previous President's wife had done. I figured, Okay, I'll move to the White House, do the best I can, and if they don't like it, they can kick me out, but they can't make me be somebody I'm not."

"While I hope I never get too old to learn and grow, I think it wasn't so much that the White House altered me in any essential way as that I found the resources with which to respond to a series of challenges."

"Being ladylike does not require silence."

Rosalynn Carter

"As the role of American women changes, so, too, does the role of first lady."

Betty Ford "began to make it possible for other spouses not to have to be quite so perfect."

"I had learned when Jimmy was in the state senate that you're going to be criticized no matter what you do. If you stay in the White House and pour tea, you'll be criticized because you don't get out. If you get out a lot, you are trying to do too much. I had learned even before I got to the White House to do what I thought was important, because the criticism is going to come."

Nancy Reagan

"Every first lady makes her own choices, and mine was to become very involved in planning White House events, right down to the details: the menu, table settings, flowers, and entertainment. I always loved doing this, but it took an enormous amount of time."

Mamie Eisenhower was a "very, very strong" woman who "had her opinions" on current events and "power over Ike."

Advice to future first ladies: "First, be yourself. Do what you're interested in. Don't be afraid 'to look after your husband' and speak out 'to either him or his staff.'"

"Once you're in the White House, don't think it's going to be a glamorous, fairy-tale life. It's very hard work with high highs and low lows. Since you're under a microscope, everything is magnified, so just keep your perspective and your patience."

"Nothing can prepare you for living in the White House. . . . And nothing can prepare you for leaving it."

"I think it's an important, legitimate role for a First Lady to look after a President's health and well-being. And if that interferes with other plans, so be it."

"While I loved being first lady, my eight years with that title were the most difficult years of my life. Both of my parents died while Ronnie was president, and my husband and I were both operated on for cancer. Before we had even settled in, Ronnie was shot and almost killed."

Jacqueline Kennedy "was very kind to me when my husband was shot, and we didn't know whether he was going to live. . . . She wrote a very sweet, sensitive note and called me. She couldn't have been nicer at a time when I really needed it."

Barbara Bush

She defined her job as "to offer comfort and security to my husband . . . and . . . try to make a difference by promoting family literacy."

"When a woman President is elected, her husband will be afforded the same luxury that former First Ladies were allowed—to define his own role."

"When there is a male spouse serving in that occupancy, perhaps we can allow him to choose the title he prefers."

"I loved Pat Nixon, who was a sensational, gracious, and thoughtful First Lady. She was personally involved in acquiring some of the White House's most treasured and historic possessions, including original furniture from previous administrations. It was her idea to have the White House lit at night, and she also started the annual Spring and Fall Garden Tours. She worked tirelessly promoting volunteerism, a cause she believed in deeply."

Nancy Reagan was criticized for redecorating the White House "when we all should have been on our knees thanking her. She raised the money privately and not only redecorated but restored the White House, including modernizing the bathrooms and fixing faulty wiring. As her successor, I was eternally grateful to her for that."

When asked her views of Nancy Reagan's use of aides and friends to bring pressure on Ronald Reagan, Barbara Bush was annoyed. 'We do things differently. . . . We have a good marriage. One reason it's good, maybe, is I don't fool around with his office and he doesn't fool around with my household."

"Hillary Clinton from Arkansas . . . gave us a good rundown on her Program H.I.P.Y. [Home Instruction for Pre-School Youths]. This is a program that goes right into the home and works with families. . . . She is a lawyer and very bright and articulate. I noticed that they, the Clintons, were the last to appear for everything. [Shades of things to come?]" *Brackets inserted by Barbara Bush.*

Hillary Rodham Clinton

"We can't stereotype anybody in this experience [that of being first lady]. We should make it possible for everyone, particularly the spouses of presidents, to do what they are comfortable doing. If the next spouse of a president, male or female, says I don't want anything to do with politics, that's not my cup of tea, fine. Why do we have to have a cookie-cutter mold?"

"In the late summer of 1991, my husband received word that both Jackie [Kennedy] and her son had been talking about him and were very interested about whether or not he was actually going to throw his hat in the ring. They were among two of the earliest contributors to his presidential campaign. She was very interested in the positions he took, and found what he had to say to be very much in line with her beliefs. I never got a chance to speak with her until June of 1992, when she invited me to lunch. When I met her in that marvelous apartment with books everywhere, she made me feel like we were old friends. What could have been a short, courtesy lunch turned into a several-hour conversation. She had out a lot of her latest projects and the books that she had edited, and other books that she was interested in. We talked a lot about our mutual interest in writing and kicked around ideas for other books she might do in the future. Mostly, we talked about our children, what it's like to live in the White House. She was convinced that my husband was going to win, and she wanted to give me advice."

"I told [Jacqueline Kennedy] she had a standing invitation to come [to the White House]. It was something she was working herself up to, and [she] gave me every reason to believe that she would visit. She said she had no real desire before Bill became president to come back. She went, however, every year to Virginia to ride, and she laughed about how we would sneak her in, wearing a kerchief and old, baggy riding clothes through a side entrance so nobody would know she was coming in."

Jacqueline Kennedy "gave me good pieces of advice on trying to get the White House to be a home. She was conscious of how, in her own time, it was a real challenge to fulfill her roles and responsibilities in a way that not only bore her own stamp, but also fit who she was. 'You've got to do things that are right for you. Don't model yourself on anybody else. There are certain things other people may have done that are of interest to you, that you should learn about, but you have to be yourself.'"

"Being first lady isn't a job, it's a role."

Laura Welch Bush

"[I will take as a role model] of course my mother-in-law Barbara Bush because of her ferocious love for her children. . . . I love her because she is so natural. She is not pretentious and I appreciate that about her. . . . [As a second model I will take] Lady Bird Johnson, because of her dedication to the preservation of native plants and highway beautification."

The role of the first lady should be "whatever the first lady wants it to be."

BIBLIOGRAPHY

Adams, Abigail. *New Letters of Abigail Adams, 1788–1801,* ed. Stewart Mitchell. Boston: Little, Brown, 1947.

Adams, Abigail, and John Adams. *The Book of Abigail and John: Selected Letters of the Adams Family, 1762–1784,* ed. L. H. Butterfield et al. Cambridge, Mass.: Harvard University Press, 1975.

Adams, John. *The Adams-Jefferson Letters,* ed. Lester J. Cappon. Chapel Hill: University of North Carolina Press, 1959.

Adams, Samuel Hopkins. *Incredible Era: The Life and Times of Warren Gamaliel Harding.* Boston: Houghton Mifflin, 1939.

Akers, Charles W. *Abigail Adams: An American Woman,* ed. Oscar Handlin. Boston: Little, Brown, 1980.

Allen, Anne Beiser. *An Independent Woman: The Life of Lou Henry Hoover.* Westport, Conn.: Greenwood, 2000.

Allgor, Catherine. *Parlor Politics: In Which the Ladies of Washington Help Build a City.* Charlottesville: University Press of Virginia, 2000.

Ambrose, Stephen E. *Nixon.* 2 vols. New York: Simon and Schuster, 1987.

Ammon, Harry. *James Monroe: The Quest for National Identity.* Charlottesville: University Press of Virginia, 1990.

Anderson, Judith Icke. *William Howard Taft: An Intimate History.* New York: Norton, 1981.

Anthony, Carl Sferrazza. *America's First Families: An Inside View of 200 Years of Private Life in the White House.* New York: Touchstone, 2000.

———. *America's Most Influential First Ladies.* Minneapolis: Oliver, 1992.

———. *As We Remember Her: Jacqueline Kennedy Onassis in the Words of Her Friends and Family.* New York: HarperCollins, 1997.

———. *First Ladies: The Saga of the Presidents' Wives and Their Power, 1789–1961.* New York: Morrow, 1990.

———. *Florence Harding: The First Lady, the Jazz Age, and the Death of America's Most Scandalous President.* New York: Morrow, 1998.

———. "Pat Nixon's Happy Golden Years," *Good Housekeeping* (January 1999).

———. "Wythville's First Woman President," *Roanoker Magazine* (October 1990).

Anthony, Katharine. *Dolly Madison: Her Life and Times.* Garden City, N.Y.: Doubleday, 1949.

Armstrong, William H. *Major McKinley: William McKinley and the Civil War.* Kent, Ohio: Kent State University Press, 2000.

Arnett, Ethel Stephens. *Mrs. James Madison, The Incomparable Dolley.* Greensboro, N.C.: Piedmont, 1972.

Baker, Jean H. *Mary Todd Lincoln: A Biography.* New York: Norton, 1987.

Baldridge, Letitia. *Of Diamonds and Diplomats: An Autobiography of a Happy Life.* Boston: Houghton Mifflin, 1968.

Barzman, Sol. *The First Ladies.* New York: Cowles, 1970.

Bassett, Margaret. *American Presidents and their Wives.* Freeport, Maine: Wheelwright, Bond, 1969.

Bauer, K. Jack. *Zachary Taylor: Soldier, Planter, Statesman in the Old South.* Newton, Conn.: American Political Biography, 1993.

Beasley, Maurine H., Holly C. Shulman, and Henry R. Beasley, eds. *The Eleanor Roosevelt Encyclopedia.* Westport, Conn.: Greenwood, 2000.

Belden, Henry S., comp. and ed. *Grand Tour of Ida Saxton-McKinley and Sister Mary Saxton Barber, 1869.* Canton, Ohio: Reserve Printing, 1985.

Boas, Norman F. *Jane M. Pierce. (The Pierce-Aiken Papers).* Stonington, Conn.: Seaport Autographs, 1983.

———. *Jane M. Pierce. (The Pierce-Aiken Papers). Supplement.* Stonington, Conn.: Seaport Autographs, 1989.

Boller, Paul F., Jr. *Presidential Wives: An Anecdotal History,* rev. ed. New York: Oxford, 1998.

Boyd, Aaron. *First Lady: The Story of Hillary Rodham Clinton.* Greensboro, N.C.: Morgan Reynolds, 1994.

Bradford, Sarah. *America's Queen: The Life of Jacqueline Kennedy Onassis.* New York: Viking, 2000.

Brandon, Dorothy. *Mamie Doud Eisenhower: A Portrait of a First Lady*. New York: Scribner's, 1954.

Brendon, Piers. *Ike: His Life and Times*. New York: Harper & Row, 1986.

Brinkley, Douglas. *The Unfinished Presidency: Jimmy Carter's Journey Beyond the White House*. New York: Viking, 1998.

Brock, David. *The Seduction of Hillary Rodham*. New York: Free Press, 1996.

Brodie, Fawn M. *Thomas Jefferson: An Intimate History*. New York: Bantam, 1975.

Brodsky, Alyn. *Grover Cleveland: A Study in Character*. New York: St. Martin's, 2000.

Bumgarner, John. *Sarah Childress Polk: A Biography of the Remarkable First Lady*. New York: McFarland, 1997.

Burner, David. *Herbert Hoover: A Public Life*. New York: Knopf, 1979.

Burns, Paul A. "Profile of the First Lady," *New Yorker* (May 15, 1926): 17–18.

Bush, Barbara. *Barbara Bush: A Memoir*. New York: Scribner's, 1994.

Cannon, James M. *Time and Chance: Gerald Ford's Appointment with History*. New York: HarperCollins, 1994.

Caro, Robert A. *The Years of Lyndon Johnson: The Path to Power*. New York: Knopf, 1990.

Caroli, Betty Boyd. *First Ladies*. New York: Oxford, 1987.

———. *The Roosevelt Women*. New York: Basic Books, 1999.

Carpenter, Frank G. *Carp's Washington*, ed. Frances Carpenter. New York: McGraw-Hill, 1960.

Carpenter, Liz. *Ruffles and Flourishes*. Garden City, N.Y.: Doubleday, 1970.

Carter, Jimmy. *Keeping Faith*. New York: Bantam, 1982.

Carter, Rosalynn. *First Lady from Plains*. Boston: Houghton Mifflin, 1984.

———. *Helping Yourself Help Others*. New York: Random House, 1995.

———. "Leave My Husband Alone," *New Republic*, January 30, 1995.

Chitwood, Perry. *John Tyler: Champion of the Old South*. 1939. Reprint, New York: American Political Biography, 1990.

Citizen of Washington, A. *Etiquette at Washington: Together with the Customs adopted by Polite Society in the Other Cities of the United States*, 3rd ed. Baltimore: Murphy, 1857.

Claxton, Jimmie Lou Sparkman. *88 Years with Sarah Polk*. New York: Vantage, 1972.

Cleaves, Freeman. *Old Tippecanoe: William Henry Harrison and His Time*. Newtown, Conn.: APB Press, 1967.

Clinton, Hillary Rodham. *It Takes a Village*. New York: Touchstone/Simon & Schuster, 1996.

Coleman, Elizabeth Tyler. *Priscilla Cooper Tyler and The American Scene*. Birmingham: University of Alabama Press, 1955.

Colman, Edna M. *White House Gossip: From Andrew Jackson to Calvin Coolidge*. Garden City, N.Y.: Doubleday, Page, 1927.

Cook, Blanche Wiesen, *Eleanor Roosevelt*, Vol. 1, 1884–1933. New York: Viking, 1992.

———. *Eleanor Roosevelt*, Vol. 2, 1933–1938. New York: Viking, 1999.

Coolidge, Grace Goodhue. *Grace Coolidge: An Autobiography*, ed. Lawrence E. Wikander and Robert H. Ferrell. Worland, Wyo.: High Plains, 1992.

Corbett, Katherine, "Louisa Catherine Adams: The Anguished 'Adventures of a Nobody,'" in *Women's Being, Women's Place: Female Identity and Vocation in American History*, ed. Mary Kelley. Boston: G. K. Hall, 1979.

Crook, William Henry. *Memories of the White House: The Home Life of Our Presidents from Lincoln to Roosevelt*, comp. and ed. Henry Rood. Boston: Little, Brown, 1911.

———. *Through Five Administrations*, ed. Margarita Spalding Gerry. New York: Harper, 1910.

Curtis, Charlotte. *First Lady*. New York: Pyramid, 1962.

Cutts, Lucia Beverley, ed. *Memoirs and Letters of Dolley Madison, Wife of James Madison, President of the United States*. Boston: Houghton, Mifflin, 1886.

Daugherty, Harry M. *The Inside Story of the Harding Tragedy*. New York: Churchill, 1932.

David, Lester. *Jacqueline Kennedy Onassis*. New York: Birch Lane Books, 1994.

———. *The Lonely Lady of San Clemente: The Story of Pat Nixon*. New York: Thomas Y. Crowell, 1978.

———, and Irene David. *Ike and Mamie: The Story of the General and His Lady*. New York: Putnam's, 1981.

Davis, John. *The Bouviers: From Waterloo to the Kennedys and Beyond*. Washington, D.C.: National Press, 1993.

———. *The Kennedys: Dynasty and Disaster*. New York: McGraw-Hill, 1984.

Deaver, Michael K. *Behind the Scenes*. New York: Morrow, 1987.

Desmond, Alice C. *Martha Washington, Our First Lady*. New York: Dodd, Mead, 1942.

Diller, Daniel C., and Stephen L. Robertson. *The Presidents, First Ladies, and Vice-Presidents: White House Biographies*. Washington, D.C.: Congressional Quarterly Books, 2000.

Donald, David Herbert. *Lincoln at Home: Two Glimpses of Abraham Lincoln's Family Life*. New York: Simon and Schuster, 2000.

Dumas, Ernest, ed. *The Clintons of Arkansas: An Introduction by Those Who Knew Them Best*. Fayetteville: University of Arkansas Press, 1993.

Dyer, Brainerd. *Zachary Taylor*. 1946. Reprint, New York: Barnes and Noble, 1967 (1946).

Edmondson, Madeline, and Alder Duer Cohen. *The Women of Watergate*. New York: Stein, 1975.

Eisenhower, John. *Strictly Personal*. 1946. Reprint, New York: Doubleday, 1974.

Eisenhower, Julie Nixon. *Pat Nixon: The Untold Story*. New York: Simon and Schuster, 1986.

———. *Special People*. New York: Thomas, 1977.

Eisenhower, Susan. *Mrs. Ike: Memories and Reflections on the Life of Mamie Eisenhower*. New York: Farrar, Straus and Giroux, 1996.

Ferrell, Robert H., ed. *Dear Bess: The Letters from Harry to Bess Truman 1910–1959*. Columbia: University of Missouri Press, 1983.

Fields, Joseph E., comp. *"Worthy Partner": The Papers of Martha Washington*, introd. Ellen McCallister Clark. Westport, Conn.: Greenwood, 1994.

Foraker, Julia. *I Would Live It Again: Memories of a Vivid Life*. New York: Harper, 1932.

Ford, Betty. *A Glad Awakening*. Garden City, N.Y.: Doubleday, 1987.

———, with Chris Chase. *The Times of My Life*. New York: Harper & Row, 1978.

Foreman, Norma Ruth Holly. "The First Lady as a Leader of Public Opinion: A Study of the Role and Press Relations of Lady Bird Johnson." Unpublished doctoral dissertation, University of Texas at Austin, 1971.

Frederick, Pauline. *Ten First Ladies of the World*. New York: Meredith Press, 1967.

Furman, Bess. *Washington By-Line: The Personal History of a Newspaperwoman*. New York: Knopf, 1949.

———. *White House Profile*. Indianapolis: Bobbs Merrill, 1951.

Gara, Larry. *The Presidency of Franklin Pierce*. Lawrence: University Press of Kansas, 1991.

Gardiner, John Lion. *The Gardiners of Gardiners Island*. East Hampton, N.Y.: Star Press, 1927.

Garfield, Lucretia, and James Garfield. *Crete and James: Personal Letters of Lucretia and James Garfield*, ed. John Shaw. East Lansing: Michigan State University Press, 1994.

Garrison, Webb. *White House Ladies: Fascinating Tales and Colorful Curiosities*. Nashville, Tenn.: Rutledge Hill Press, 1996.

Geer, Emily Apt. *First Lady: The Life of Lucy Webb Hayes*. Kent, Ohio: Kent State University Press, 1984.

Gelles, Edith B. *Portia: The World of Abigail Adams*. Bloomington: Indiana University Press, 1992.

Glendon, Mary Anne. *A World Made New: Eleanor Roosevelt and the Universal Declaration of Human Rights*. New York: Random House, 2001.

Goodwin, Doris Kearns. *No Ordinary Time: Franklin and Eleanor*. New York: Simon and Schuster, 1995.

Gould, Lewis L. "First Ladies," *American Scholar* 55 (Autumn 1986): 528–35.

———. "Modern First Ladies and the Presidency." *Presidential Studies Quarterly* 20 (1990): 677–83.

———. *Lady Bird Johnson and the Environment*. Lawrence: University Press of Kansas, 1999.

———, ed. *American First Ladies: Their Lives and Their Legacy*. New York: Garland, 1996.

Grant, Julia Dent. *The Personal Memoirs of Julia Dent Grant*, ed. John Y. Simon. Carbondale: Southern Illinois University Press, 1975.

Grant, Ulysses S. *Personal Memoirs of U.S. Grant*. 2 vol. New York: Charles L. Webster, 1885.

Grayson, Benson Lee. *The Unknown President: The Administration of Millard Fillmore*. Washington, D.C.: University Press of America, 1981.

Grimes, Ann. *Running Mates: The Making of a First Lady.* New York: William Morrow, 1990.

Gutin, Myra G. *The President's Partner: The First Lady in the Twentieth Century.* New York: Greenwood, 1989.

Hagedorn, Hermann. *The Roosevelt Family of Sagamore Hill.* New York: Macmillan, 1954.

Haldeman, H. R., ed. *The Haldeman Diaries: Inside the Nixon White House.* New York: G. P. Putnam's, 1994.

Hall, Gordon Langley, and Ann Pinchot. *Jacqueline Kennedy: A Woman for the World.* New York: F. Fell, 1964.

Hamilton, Holman. *The Three Kentucky Presidents: Lincoln, Taylor, Davis.* Lexington: University Press of Kentucky, 1978.

———. *Zachary Taylor: Soldier of the Republic.* 1941. Reprint, Hamden, Conn.: Archon, 1966.

———. *Zachary Taylor: Soldier in the White House.* 1951. Reprint, Hamden, Conn.: Archon, 1966.

Hartzell, Josiah. *Sketch of the Life of Mrs. William McKinley.* Washington, D.C.: Home Magazine Press, 1896.

Hatch, Alden. *Edith Bolling Wilson, First Lady Extraordinary.* New York: Dodd, Mead, 1961.

———. *Red Carpet for Mamie.* New York: Henry Holt, 1954.

Hay, Peter. *All the Presidents' Ladies: Anecdotes of the Women Behind the Men in the White House.* New York: Viking, 1988.

Healy, Diana Dixon. *America's First Ladies: Private Lives of the Presidential Wives.* New York: Atheneum, 1988.

Hecht, Marie. *John Quincy Adams: A Personal History of an Independent Man* 1972. Reprint, New York: American Political Biography, 1995.

Helm, Edith. *The Captains and the Kings.* New York: Putnam's, 1954.

Helm, Katherine. *The True Story of Mary, Wife of Lincoln.* New York: Harper, 1928.

Heymann, C. David. *A Woman Named Jackie.* New York: Carol Communications, 1989.

Hoff-Wilson, Joan. *Herbert Hoover: Forgotten Progressive.* Boston: Little, Brown, 1975.

Holloway, Laura C. *Ladies of the White House.* Philadelphia: Bradley, 1881.

Hoogenboom, Ari. *Rutherford B. Hayes: Warrior and President.* Lawrence: University Press of Kansas, 1950.

Hoover, Irwin Hood. *Forty-Two Years in the White House.* Boston: Houghton Mifflin, 1934.

Hotchner, A. E. *Choice People: The Greats, Near-Greats, and Ingrates I Have Known.* New York: William Morrow, 1984.

Howar, Barbara. *Laughing All the Way.* New York: Stein & Day, 1973.

Hoyt, Edwin P. *The Nixons: An American Family.* New York: Random House, 1972.

Hunt-Jones, Conover. *Dolley and the "Great Little Madison."* Washington, D.C.: American Institute of Architects Foundation, 1977.

Jaffray, Elizabeth. *Secrets of the White House.* New York: Holt, Rinehart & Winston, 1970.

James, Edward I. et al. *Notable American Women: A Biographical Dictionary.* Cambridge, Mass.: Harvard University Press, 1971.

Jefferson, H. Paul. *An Honest President: The Life and Presidencies of Grover Cleveland.* New York: Aaron, 2000.

Jeffries, Ona Griffin. *In and Out of the White House from Washington to the Eisenhowers.* New York: Wilfred Funk, 1960.

Jensen, Amy LaFollette. *The White House and Its Thirty-Five Families.* New York: McGraw-Hill, 1970.

Johnson, Lady Bird. *A White House Diary.* New York: Holt, Rinehart & Winston, 1970.

Kearns, Doris. *Lyndon Johnson and the American Dream.* New York: Harper and Row, 1976.

Kellerman, Barbara. *All the President's Kin.* New York: Free Press, 1981.

Kelley, Mary, ed. *Women's Being, Women's Place: Female Identity and Vocation in American History.* Boston: G.K. Hall, 1979.

Kelly, C. Brian. *Best Little Stories from the White House.* Charlottesville, Va.: Montpelier, 1992.

Kilian, Pamela. *Barbara Bush: A Biography.* Thorndike, Maine: Thorndike Press, 1992.

Kimball, D.L. *I Remember Mamie.* Fayette, Iowa: Trends and Events, 1981.

King, Norman. *Hillary: Her True Story.* New York: Carol, 1993.

Klapthor, Margaret Brown. *The First Ladies.* Washington, D.C.: White House Historic Association, 1995.

———. *Maryland's Presidential First Ladies: Mrs. Zachary Taylor and Mrs. John Quincy Adams.* Calvert County, Md.: Calvert County Historical Society, 1966.

Klein, Edward. *Just Jackie: Her Private Years.* New York: Ballantine, 1998.

Kurlyo, Elizabeth. "Cover Mental Illness, Ex-First Ladies Urge," *Atlanta Constitution,* March 8, 1994.

Lash, Joseph P. *Eleanor and Franklin.* New York: Norton, 1971.

———. *Eleanor: The Years Alone.* New York: Norton, 1972.

———. *Love, Eleanor: Eleanor Roosevelt and Her Friends.* Garden City, N.Y.: Doubleday, 1982.

Leech, Margaret. *In the Days of McKinley.* New York: Harper and Row, 1959.

———, and Harry J. Brown. *The Garfield Orbit.* New York: Harper and Row, 1978.

Leighton, Frances Spatz. *The Search for the Real Nancy Reagan.* New York: Random House, 1989.

Levin, Phyllis Lee. *Abigail Adams: A Biography.* New York: St. Martin's Press, 1985.

Logan, Mrs. John A. *Thirty Years in Washington, or Life and Scenes in Our National Capital.* Hartford, Conn.: A. D. Worthington, 1901.

Lossing, Benson J. *Mary and Martha: The Mother and Wife of George Washington.* New York: Harper, 1886.

Lyons, Eugene. *Herbert Hoover, A Biography.* Garden City, N.Y.: Doubleday, 1964.

McAdoo, Eleanor Wilson. *The Priceless Gift—The Love Letters of Woodrow Wilson and Ellen Axson Wilson.* New York: McGraw-Hill, 1962.

———, with Margaret Y. Gaffey. *The Woodrow Wilsons.* New York: Macmillan, 1937.

McClure, Alexander. *Recollections of Half a Century.* Salem, Mass.: Salem Press, 1902.

McCullough, David. *Mornings on Horseback.* New York: Simon and Schuster, 1982.

———. *Truman.* New York: Simon and Schuster, 1992.

McLean, Evalyn Walsh. *Father Struck It Rich.* Boston: Little, Brown, 1935.

McLendon, Winzola, and Scottie Smith. *Don't Quote Me! Washington Newswomen and the Power Society.* New York: Dutton, 1970.

McMurty, R. Gerald, and Mark E. Neely, Jr. *The Insanity File: The Case of Mary Todd Lincoln.* Carbondale: Southern Illinois University Press, 1993.

MacPherson, Myra. *The Power Lovers: An Intimate Look at Politics and Marriage.* New York: Putnam, 1975.

Maddox, Linda, and Edna Langford. *Rosalynn: Friend and First Lady.* Old Tappan, N.J.: Fleming H. Revell, 1980.

Martineau, Harriet. *Society in America,* ed. Seymour Martin Lipset 1837. Reprint, Gloucester, Mass.: Peter Smith, 1968.

Means, Marianne. *The Woman in the White House: The Lives, Times and Influence of Twelve Notable First Ladies.* New York: Random House, 1963.

Miller, Merle. *Lyndon: An Oral Biography.* New York: Putnam, 1980.

Milton, Joyce. *The First Partner: Hillary Rodham Clinton.* New York: Morrow, 1999.

Minnigerode, Meade. *Some American Ladies: Seven Informal Biographies.* New York: Putnam, 1926.

Montgomery, Ruth. *Mrs. LBJ.* New York: Holt, Rinehart and Winston, 1964.

Morris, Edmund. *The Rise of Theodore Roosevelt.* New York: Ballantine, 1988.

———. *Dutch: A Memoir of Ronald Reagan.* New York: Random House, 1999.

Morris, Roger. *Partners in Power: The Clintons and Their America.* New York: Henry Holt, 1996.

Morris, Sylvia Jukes. *Edith Kermit Roosevelt: Portrait of a First Lady.* New York: Coward, McCann, 1980.

Nagel, Paul C. *The Adams Women: Abigail and Louisa Adams, Their Sisters and Daughters.* New York: Oxford University Press, 1987.

———. *Descent from Glory: Four Generations of the Adams Family.* Cambridge: Harvard University Press, 1999.

Neal, Steve. *The Eisenhowers.* Lawrence: University Press of Kansas, 1984.

Nelson, Anson and Fanny. *Sarah Childress Polk: Wife of the 11th President of the United States.* 1892 Reprint, Newton, Conn.: American Political Biography, 1994.

Nevins, Allan. *Grover Cleveland: A Study in Courage.* New York: Dodd, Mead, 1934.

———, ed. *Letters of Grover Cleveland.* Boston: Houghton Mifflin, 1933.

Nichols, Roy. *Franklin Pierce: Young Hickory of the Granite Hills.* 1958. Reprint, Newton, Conn.: American Political Biography, 1993.

Nixon, Richard. *RN: The Memoirs of Richard Nixon.* New York: Grossett and Dunlap, 1978.

Noonan, Peggy. *The Case Against Hillary Clinton.* New York: Regan Books, 2000.

Norton, Mary Beth. *Liberty's Daughters: The Revolutionary Experience of American Women, 1750–1800.* Boston: Little, Brown, 1980.

Parks, Lillian Rogers (with Frances Spatz Leighton). *My Thirty Years Backstairs at the White House.* New York: Fleet, 1961.

"Pat Nixon: Stealth Feminist," *Washington Post* (Sunday Outlook Section), June 27, 1993.

Peskin, Allen. *Garfield.* Kent, Ohio: Kent State University Press, 1998.

Peterson, Norma Lois. *The Presidencies of William Henry Harrison and John Tyler.* Lawrence: University Press of Kansas, 1989.

Porter, Horace. *Campaigning with Grant.* New York: Bison, 2000.

Pryor, Helen B. *Lou Henry Hoover, Gallant First Lady.* New York: Dodd, Mead, 1969.

Radcliffe, Donnie. *Hillary Rodham Clinton: A First Lady for Our Time.* New York: Warner, 1993.

———. *Simply Barbara Bush: A Portrait of America's Candid First Lady.* New York: Warner, 1989.

Randall, Ruth Painter. *Mary Lincoln, Biography of a Marriage.* Boston: Little, Brown, 1953.

Raybach, Robert J. *Millard Fillmore: Biography of a President.* 1972. Reprint, Newton, Conn.: American Political Biography, 1992.

Reagan Nancy. *I Love You, Ronnie.* New York: Random House, 2000.

———. *My Turn: The Memoirs of Nancy Reagan,* with William Novak. New York: Random House, 1989.

Reeves, Richard. *A Ford, Not a Lincoln.* New York: Harcourt Brace Jovanovich, 1975.

Riley, Susan. *Political Wives: Lives of the Saints.* Toronto, Ont.: Deneau, 1987.

Romano, Lois. "Laura Bush Refefines Her Role," *Washington Post,* June 12, 2000.

Rosebush, James S. *First Lady, Public Wife: A Behind-the-Scenes History of the Evolving Role of First Ladies in American Political Life.* New York: Madison Books, 1987.

Roosevelt, Eleanor. *On My Own.* New York: Harper, 1958.

———. *This I Remember.* New York: Harper, 1949.

———. *This Is My Story.* New York: Harper, 1937.

Ross, Ishbel. *An American Family, The Tafts, 1678–1964.* Cleveland: World, 1959.

———. *First Lady of the South: The Life of Mrs. Jefferson Davis.* New York: Harper's, 1958.

———. *The General's Wife: The Life of Mrs. Ulysses S. Grant.* New York: Dodd, Mead, 1959.

———. *Grace Coolidge and Her Era: The Story of a President's Wife.* New York: Dodd, Mead, 1962.

———. *Power with Grace: The Life Story of Mrs. Woodrow Wilson.* New York: G. P. Putnam's Sons, 1975.

———. *The President's Wife: Mary Todd Lincoln: A Biography.* New York: G. P. Putnam's Sons, 1973.

Russell, Francis. *The Shadow of Blooming Grove: Warren G. Harding in His Times.* New York: McGraw-Hill, 1968.

Russell, Jan Jarboe. *Lady Bird: A Biography of Mrs. Johnson.* New York: Scribner's, 1999.

Sadler, Christine. *Children in the White House.* New York: G. P. Putnam's Sons, 1967.

Sandak, Cass R. *The Monroes.* New York: Crestwood, 1993.

Sandburg, Carl, and Paul M. Angle. *Mary Lincoln Wife and Widow.* New York: Harcourt, Brace, 1932.

Saunders, Frances Wright. *First Lady Between Two Worlds: Ellen Axson Wilson.* Chapel Hill: University of North Carolina Press, 1985.

Scarry, Robert. J. *Millard Fillmore.* New York: McFarland, 2000.

Schachtman, Tom. *Edith and Woodrow: A Presidential Romance.* New York: G. P. Putnam's Sons, 1981.

Seager, Robert. *And Tyler Too: A Biography of John and Julia Gardiner Tyler.* New York: McGraw-Hill, 1963.

Seale, William. *The President's House: A History.* New York: Harry N. Abrams, 1992.

Sellars, Charles. *James K. Polk: Continentalist, 1843–1846.* Princeton, N.J.: Princeton University Press, 1963.

———. *James K. Polk: Jacksonian 1795–1843.* Princeton, N.J.: Princeton University Press, 1957.

Severn, Sue. "Frances (Clara) Folsom Cleveland," in *American First Ladies,* ed. Lewis Gould. New York: Garland, 1996.

Shaw, John, ed. *Crete and James: Personal Letters of Lucretia and James Garfield.* East Lansing: Michigan State University Press, 1994.

Shepherd, Jack. *Cannibals of the Heart: A Personal Biography of Louisa Catherine and John Quincy Adams.* New York: McGraw Hill, 1980.

Sickerman, Barbara et al., eds. *Notable American Women: The Modern Period.* Cambridge, Mass. Harvard University Press, 1980.

Sievers, Harry J. *Benjamin Harrison.* 3 vols. Indianapolis, Ind.: Bobbs Morrill, 1968.

Singleton, Esther. *The Story of the White House.* New York: McClure's, 1907.

Slayden, Ellen Maury. *Washington Wife: Journal of Ellen Maury Slayden from 1897–1919.* New York: Harper and Row, 1962.

Small, Melvin. *The Presidency of Richard Nixon.* Lawrence: University Press of Kansas, 1999.

Smith, Margaret Bayard. *The First Forty Years of Washington Society in the Family Letters of Margaret Bayard Smith,* ed. Gaillard Hunt. 1906. Reprint, New York: Frederick Ungar, 1965.

Smith, Marie. *The President's Lady: An Intimate Biography of Mrs. Lyndon B. Johnson.* New York: Random House, 1964.

Smith, Richard Norton. *An Uncommon Man: The Triumph of Herbert Hoover.* New York: Simon and Schuster, 1984.

Smyer, Ingrid. *First Ladies in Review.* Charlottesville, Va.: Montpelier, 1992.

Snyder, Charles M. *The Lady and the President: The Letters of Dorothea Dix and Millard Fillmore.* Louisville: University Press of Kentucky, 1975.

Sorenson, Theodore. *Kennedy.* New York: Harper and Row, 1965.

Speakers, Larry, with Robert Pack. *Speaking Out.* New York: Scribner's, 1988.

Spitzer, Robert J. "Clinton's Impeachment Will Have Few Consequences for the Presidency." *PS: Political Science and Politics* (September 1999): 542.

Strakes, George. *Mary Todd Lincoln and the Illuminati.* Bloomington, Ind.: First Books Library, 2000.

Symmes, John Cleves, et al. *The Intimate Letters of John Cleves Symmes and His Family, Including Those of His Daughter Mrs. William Henry Harrison,* ed. Beverly W. Bond, Jr. Cincinnati: Historical and Philosophical Society of Ohio, 1956.

Taft, Helen Herron. *Recollections of Full Years.* New York: Dodd, Mead, 1914.

Thane, Elswyth. *Washington's Lady.* New York: Dodd, Mead, 1960.

Thayer, Mary Van Rensselaer. *Jacqueline Kennedy: The White House Years.* Boston: Little, Brown, 1967.

Thomas, Helen. *Dateline: The White House.* New York: Macmillan, 1975.

———. *Front Row at the White House: My Life and Times.* New York: Scribner, 1999.

Thomas, Lately. *The First President Johnson: The Three Lives of the Seventeenth President of the United States.* New York: Morrow, 1968.

Thompson, Mary V. "The Lowest Ebb of Misery: Death amd Mourning in the Family of George Washington," *Historic Alexandria Quarterly* (Spring 2001).

Trefousse, Hans Louis. *Andrew Johnson: A Biography of the President.* New York: Norton, 1997.

Troy, Gil. *Affairs of State: The Rise and Rejection of the Presidential Couple Since World War II.* New York: Free Press, 1997.

Truman, Margaret. *Bess W. Truman.* New York: Macmillan, 1986.

———. *First Ladies: An Intimate Group Portrait of White House Wives.* New York: Fawcett Columbine, 1995.

Turner, Justin G., and Linda Levitt Turner. *Mary Todd Lincoln: Her Life and Letters.* New York: Knopf, 1972.

Van der Heuvel, Gerry. *Crowns of Thorns and Glory: Mary Todd Lincoln and Varina Davis.* New York: Dutton, 1988.

Waldrup, Carole Chandler. *The Presidents' Wives: The Lives of 44 American Women of Strength.* Jefferson, N.C.: McFarland, 1989.

Wallace, Chris. *First Lady: A Portrait of Nancy Reagan.* New York: St. Martin's Press, 1986.

Warner, Judith. *Hillary Clinton: The Inside Story.* New York: Penguin, 1993.

Wasserman, Carl David. "Firing the First Lady: The Role and Accountability of the Presidential Spouse," *Vanderbilt Law Review* (May 1995).

Watson, Robert P. *The Presidents' Wives: Reassessing the Office of First Lady.* Boulder, Colo.: Lynne Rienner, 2000.

———, ed. *The Report to the First Lady*. Huntington, N.Y.: Nova Science, 2001.

Weaver, Judith L. "Edith Bolling Wilson as First Lady: A Study in the Power of Personality," *Presidential Studies Quarterly* (Winter 1985).

Weidenfeld, Sheila Rabb. *First Lady's Lady: With the Fords at the White House*. New York: Putnam, 1979.

West, J. B., with Mary Kotz. *Upstairs at the White House: My Life with the First Ladies*. New York: Coward McCann, 1973.

Wharton, Anne Hollingsworth. *Martha Washington*. New York: Scribner's, 1897.

Whitcomb, John, and Claire Whitcomb. *Real Life at the White House: Two Hundred Years of Daily Life at America's Most Famous Residence*. New York: Routledge, 2000.

White, William Allen. *A Puritan in Babylon*. New York: Macmillan, 1938.

Whitton, Mary Ormsbee. *First First Ladies, 1789–1865: A Study of the Wives of the Early Presidents*. 1948. Reprint, Freeport, N.Y.: Books for Libraries Press, 1969.

Willets, Gilson. *Inside History of the White House*. New York: Christian Herald, 1908.

Williams, T. Harry, ed. *Hayes: The Diary of a President, 1876–1881*. New York: David McKay, 1964.

Wills, Garry. "The Clinton Scandals." *New York Review of Books* (April 18, 1996).

———. *Reagan's America: Innocents at Home*. Garden City, N.Y.: Doubleday, 1987.

Wilson, Dorothy Clarke. *Queen Dolley: The Life and Times of Dolley Madison*. Garden City, N.Y.: Doubleday, 1987.

Wilson, Edith Bolling. *My Memoir*. Indianapolis: Bobbs Merrill, 1939.

Withey, Lynne. *Dearest Friend*. New York: Free Press, 1981.

Woodward, Bob. *Shadow: Five Presidencies and the Legacy of Watergate*. New York: Simon and Shuster, 1999.

Wooton, James E. *Elizabeth Kortright Monroe*. Charlottesville, Va.: Ash Lawn–Highland, 1987.

N.B.: The National First Ladies' Library at 331 South Market Avenue, Canton, Ohio 44702, 330-452-0876, offers helpful information at its web site: www.firstladies.org.

Entries by Place of Birth

Connecticut
Edith Roosevelt, 1861

Georgia
Ellen Wilson, 1860
Rosalynn Carter, 1927

Illinois
Betty Ford, 1918
Hillary Clinton, 1947

Iowa
Lou Hoover, 1875
Mamie Eisenhower, 1896

Kentucky
Mary Todd Lincoln, 1818

Maryland
Margaret Taylor, 1788

Massachusetts
Abigail Adams, 1744

Missouri
Julia Grant, 1826
Bess Truman, 1885

Nevada
Pat Nixon, 1912

New Hampshire
Jane Pierce, 1806

New Jersey
Anna Symmes Harrison, 1775

New York
Elizabeth Monroe, 1768
Abigail Fillmore, 1798
Julia Tyler, 1820
Frances Cleveland, 1864
Eleanor Roosevelt, 1884
Nancy Reagan, 1921
Barbara Bush, 1925
Jacqueline Kennedy, 1929

North Carolina
Dolley Madison, 1768

Ohio
Lucy Hayes, 1831
Lucretia Garfield, 1832
Caroline Harrison, 1832
Ida McKinley, 1847
Florence Harding, 1860
Helen Taft, 1861

Tennessee
Sarah Polk, 1803
Eliza Johnson, 1810

Texas
Lady Bird Johnson, 1912
Laura Bush, 1946

Vermont
Grace Coolidge, 1879

Virginia

Martha Washington, 1731
Letitia Tyler, 1790
Edith Wilson, 1872

London, England

Louisa Adams, 1775

ENTRIES BY BIRTH DATES

1731
June 2: Martha Washington

1744
November 11: Abigail Adams

1768
May 20: Dolley Madison
June 30: Elizabeth Monroe

1775
February 11: Louisa Adams
June 25: Anna Symmes Harrison

1788
September 28: Margaret Taylor

1790
November 12: Letitia Tyler

1798
March 17: Abigail Fillmore

1803
September 4: Sarah Polk

1806
March 12: Jane Pierce

1810
October 4: Eliza Johnson

1818
December 3: Mary Todd Lincoln

1820
May 4: Julia Gardiner Tyler

1826
January 26: Julia Grant

1831
August 28: Lucy Hayes

1832
April 19: Lucretia Garfield
October 1: Caroline Harrison

1847
June 8: Ida McKinley

1860
May 15: Ellen Wilson
August 15: Florence Harding

1861
June 2: Helen Taft
August 6: Edith Roosevelt

1864
July 21: Frances Cleveland

1872
October 15: Edith Wilson

1875
March 29: Lou Hoover

1879
January 3: Grace Coolidge

1884
October 11: Eleanor Roosevelt

1885
February 13: Bess Truman

1896
November 14: Mamie Eisenhower

1912
March 16: Pat Nixon
December 22: Lady Bird Johnson

1918
April 8: Betty Ford

1921
July 6: Nancy Reagan

1925
June 8: Barbara Bush

1927

August 18: Rosalynn Carter

1929

July 28: Jacqueline Kennedy

1946

November 4: Laura Bush

1947

October 26: Hillary Clinton

Index

Photos and illustrations are indicated by *italic* locators.
Locators for main entries are set in **boldface**.
Locators for material in the appendix are followed by *a*.

K

Kaulani, Princess 144
Keckley, Elizabeth 100, 101, 103
Kellogg, W. K. 281
Kemp, Jack 335
Kennedy, Caroline 273, 278
Kennedy, Jacqueline Lee (Jackie) Bouvier *271,* **271–279,** *278, 372a*
   arts leadership as first lady 275
   and beautification of Washington,
     D.C. 275
   birth 272
   children 273–275
   chronology 279
   and Hillary Clinton 377*a*
   death 278
   education 272
   and Mamie Eisenhower 376*a*
   and Lady Bird Johnson 285, 377*a*
   John F. Kennedy, death of 276
   John F. Kennedy, election to presidency of 273–274
   John F. Kennedy, marriage to 273
   life after White House 276–278
   personal characteristics 271–272,
     278–279
   and Nancy Reagan 379*a*
   and reporters 377*a*
   on role of first lady 377*a*
   and Eleanor Roosevelt 376*a*
   and Bess Truman 376*a,* 377*a*
   and White House 274–275
   and Edith Wilson 376*a*
Kennedy, John F.
   and Hillary Rodham Clinton 345
   and Lady Bird Johnson 285, 286
   and Jackie Kennedy 272–276
   and Pat Nixon 296
   and Eleanor Roosevelt 246
   and Bess Truman 258
   and Edith Wilson 199
Kennedy, John F., Jr., 274, 278
Kennedy, Joseph 273, 274
Kennedy, Patrick 276
Kennedy, Robert F.
   "Bobby Kennedy Law" 345
   and Lady Bird Johnson 285
   and Jackie Kennedy 277
Kennedy, Rose 285
Kennedy, Ted 273
Kennedy Center 276
Kentucky 95
Khrushchev, Nikita
   and Jackie Kennedy 275
   and Pat Nixon 295–296
Khrushchev, Nina
   and Jackie Kennedy 275
   and Pat Nixon 296
King, Larry L. 353

King, Martin Luther, Jr.,
   and Laura Bush 351
   and Hillary Rodham Clinton 340
King, Mrs. Martin Luther, Sr., 304
Kitt, Eartha 289
Kleberg, Richard 282
Kling, Amos 202, 203
Kling, Marshall 202
Korean War 310
KTBC (radio station) 283–284
Kuala Lampur 295

L

Ladies Home Journal 312
Ladies of the Senate
   Lady Bird Johnson and 284
   Pat Nixon and 295
La Farge, John 168
Lafayette Square 275
LaGuardia, Fiorello 243
Laird, Melvin 340
Lane, Harriet
   and James Buchanan 367*a*
   and Frances Cleveland 142
   and Caroline Harrison 151
Lansing, Robert 197–198
Lape, Esther 235
Latin America 314–315
Laubach Literacy Action 335
Lawler, Kathleen 206
Lazio, Rick 347
League of Nations
   Florence Harding and 204
   Eleanor Roosevelt and 235
   Woodrow Wilson and 196, 198,
     199
League of Women Voters
   Hillary Rodham Clinton and 341
   Eleanor Roosevelt and 234–236
Lee, Alice 163
Lee, Caroline Watts Haskell 361*a*
Lee, George Cabot 361*a*
Leech, Margaret 134
Legal Services Corporation 342
LeHand, Missy 235
Levering, Mercy 96
Life magazine 341
Lillie, Lucy C. 141
Limón, José 302
Lincoln, Abraham
   and Julia Grant 116, 117
   and Lucy Hayes 126, 127
   and Eliza Johnson 108
   and Mary Todd Lincoln 96–102
   and Julia Gardiner Tyler 68
Lincoln, Mary Ann Todd *95,* **95–106**
   birth 95
   children 97, 98, 103–104
   chronology 105–106
   death 105
   death of children 101, 104

   education 96
   as first lady 100–102
   and Julia Grant 117, 375*a*
   life after White House 103–105
   Abraham Lincoln, death of 102
   Abraham Lincoln, election to presidency of 99
   Abraham Lincoln, marriage to 97
   personal characteristics 95, 96, 105
   and White House 100
Lincoln, Robert 103–105
Lind, Jenny 86
literacy
   Barbara Bush and 333, 335
   Laura Bush and 353
Literacy Volunteers of America 335
Lodge, Henry Cabot
   adn Edith Wilson 196
   and Florence Harding 208
   and Edith Wilson 198
   and Woodrow Wilson 198
Logan, Mrs. John A.
   and Julia Grant 118
   and Caroline Harrison 152
Longworth, Alice Roosevelt
   and Grace Coolidge 215
   and Florence Harding 208
   and Alice Hathaway Lee Roosevelt
     361*a*
   and Edith Roosevelt 164, 167
   and Eleanor Roosevelt 231, 233
Louisiana 80
Luce, Clare Booth 257
Lute Song 320

M

MacArthur, Arthur 175
MacArthur, Douglas
   and Dwight D. Eisenhower 264,
     265
   and Herbert Hoover 227
MacPherson, Myra 305
Maddox, Lester 311
Madison, Dolley Paine Todd *23,*
   23–34, *371a*
   birth 24
   causes 27
   chronology 33–34
   death 33–34
   as first lady 27–30
   and Thomas Jefferson 363*a*
   life after White House 31–33
   James Madison, death of 31
   James Madison, election to presidency of 27
   James Madison, marriage to 25
   personal characteristics 23, 33
   John Todd, marriage to 24
   and Julia Gardiner Tyler 64
   and White House 27